An Anthology of Syriac Writers from Qatar in the Seventh Century

Gorgias Eastern Christian Studies

39

Gorgias Eastern Christian Studies brings to the scholarly world the underrepresented field of Eastern Christianity. This series consists of monographs, edited collections, texts and translations of the documents of Eastern Christianity, as well as studies of topics relevant to the world of historic Orthodoxy and early Christianity.

An Anthology of Syriac Writers from Qatar in the Seventh Century

Edited by

Mario Kozah

Abdulrahim Abu-Husayn

Saif Shaheen Al-Murikhi

Haya Al Thani

gorgias press

2015

Gorgias Press LLC, 954 River Road, Piscataway, NJ, 08854, USA

www.gorgiaspress.com

2015 ܐ,

ISBN 978-1-4632-0545-4 **ISSN 1539-1507**

Library of Congress Cataloging-in-Publication Data

A Cataloging-in-Publication Record is Available from the Library of Congress

Printed in the United States of America

❖ ܕܒܗܐ ܩܛܪ̈ܝܐ ❖

"To the People of Qatar"

(Isho'yahb III, Patriarch of the Church of the East d. 659.
Letter 18)

TABLE OF CONTENTS

Table of Contents vii
Acknowledgments ix
Preface xi
Abbreviations xv
The *History* of Mar Yawnan 1
Sebastian Brock

Ishoʿyahb III of Adiabene's Letters to the Qataris 43
Mario Kozah

Introduction to the *Book of the Aims of the Psalms* by Aḥūb Qaṭraya 89
Bas ter Haar Romeny (Introduction by Mario Kozah)

Abraham Qaṭraya bar Lipah's *Commentary on the Liturgical Offices* 97
Mario Kozah

Preface to Mar Shemʿūn's *Law Book* by an Anonymous Monk from Beth Qaṭraye 147
Mario Kozah

Dadishoʿ Qaṭraya's *Compendious Commentary* on the *Paradise of the Egyptian Fathers* in Garshuni 155
Mario Kozah, Suleiman Mourad, Abdulrahim Abu-Husayn (Introduction by Mario Kozah)

Introduction to Selections from the Geʿez *Filekseyus* 189
Robert Kitchen

Isaac of Nineveh's *Chapters on Knowledge* 253
Grigory Kessel

Isaac the Syrian: The *Third Part* 281
Mary T. Hansbury

Two Discourses of the *Fifth Part* of Isaac the Syrian's Writings 441
Mary T. Hansbury

The *Fourth Part* of Isaac Qaṭraya's Ascetical Homilies in Garshuni 471
Mario Kozah

Bibliography of Works Cited 693
Ancient Authors and Translations 693
Modern Works 699

Index 705

ACKNOWLEDGMENTS

This book was made possible by NPRP grant NPRP 4-981-6-025 from the Qatar National Research Fund (a member of Qatar Foundation). The statements made herein are solely the responsibility of the authors.

PREFACE

This anthology is the second publication of "The Syriac Writers of Qatar in the Seventh Century" project which was a three year research endeavour funded by the Qatar National Research Fund (QNRF) under its National Priorities Research Program (NPRP 4-981-6-025).

Researchers in the field of Syriac studies have long known of the existence of a number of Syriac monastic and ascetical writers from the seventh century who were born and educated in Beth Qaṭraye (Syriac for "Region of the Qataris") of which Isaac of Nineveh from Qatar is considered to be the most influential and widely translated of all Syriac monastic writers and who continues to exert a strong influence in monastic circles today. Many of the others like Dadishoʿ of Qatar, Gabriel bar Lipah of Qatar, Abraham bar Lipah of Qatar, Gabriel Arya of Qatar, and Aḥūb of Qatar were important Syriac writers on spirituality and commentators or exegetes within the Church of the East tradition. These writers, who all originated from Beth Qaṭraye and were educated there, reveal the presence of an important centre of education that rivalled in its sophistication the other more well-known centres such as the School of Nisibis or the School of Edessa. The Syriac writers of Qatar themselves produced some of the best and most sophisticated writing to be found in all Syriac literature of the seventh century.

The demonym "Qaṭraya" (Syriac for "Qatari/of Qatar") is found added to the names of all of the writers above in the ancient Syriac manuscripts now to be found in the British Library, Paris Bibliotheque Nationale, Vatican Library, University of Birmingham Library, and in a number of locations in the Middle East. In addition, the term Beth Qaṭraye was used by the Syriac speaking communities who lived there to refer to the whole region of what is now Qatar, Bahrain and the adjacent eastern coast of Arabia. The term Beth Qaṭraye along with the place names of specific locations within this region are to be found, for example, in five letters written by Ishoʿyahb III, the Patriarch of the Church of the East from 650–658, to the church authorities, priests, monks, and lay people there.

Unfortunately the Syriac writers of Beth Qaṭraye have not received the scholarly attention that they deserve in the last half century. To this day many of their works remain scattered in manuscripts that are unedited and very rarely fully translated in libraries throughout Europe and the Middle East. Those translations that have been undertaken in English (except for the case of Isaac of Nineveh) are mostly incomplete and fragmentary often as part of articles and without the accompanying Syriac editions. Furthermore, the translations that were completed in the nineteenth century in the Latin language are now inaccessible to the majority of modern readers and, similarly, those few translations to be found in German, Italian, and French are less accessible to the general Arab and Qatari reader.

The aim of this project was to hold, at the end of its second year, an international conference in Doha, Qatar, on the subject of the "Syriac Writers of Qatar in the Seventh Century" involving scholars who are experts in the field of Syriac studies and literature and, in the third year, to publish two books: the first an edited volume of this conference's proceedings entitled *The Syriac Writers of Qatar in the Seventh Century* and this second book entitled *An Anthology of Syriac Writers from Qatar in the Seventh Century*. The present book, then, is an anthology of English translations undertaken by experts in the field of Syriac studies. They cover major works from all the above listed Syriac writers with introductions, annotations, and in some instances also accompanied by edited Syriac texts.

Identifying scholarly communities in the Arabian peninsula that have actively shaped the production of knowledge in the seventh century across the region (including Syria, Persia, and Mesopotamia) will encourage scholars to rethink the ways in which Arabia is constructed and defined. Highlighting the contributions of the Syriac writers from Beth Qaṭraye will thus not only impact the field of Syriac literature but also shape the wider field of Middle Eastern studies. It will align the rich heritage of Arabia (especially the Arabic poetic tradition) with other voices, speaking different languages and producing different knowledge, yet sharing the same or adjacent territory. This will, it is hoped, create crossings in the cultural and historical studies of Syriac and Arabic, pre- and post-Islamic Arabia, Persia, and Byzantium. It will also highlight the Peninsula's role in producing and contributing to intellectual debates of the time, showing a diversity of writings and ideas with wide ranging effects, emerging from and going back and forth between Arabia and the surrounding empires.

The importance of this research lies in its attempt to identify an educational environment and cultural movement that has been hitherto unexplored in any systematic fashion. Identifying Beth Qaṭraye as a vibrant site of cultural production in the seventh century is important because it offers new centres of learning that shift the emphasis from the traditional centres of the time, namely Syria and Mesopotamia. Isaac of Nineveh, for example, who might be mistakenly thought to be from Mesopotamia, given his name, is in fact from Beth Qaṭraye and the product of this vibrant cultural environment.

It is hoped that the new information presented in this anthology will complicate the structure of "centre and periphery" of learning, drawing the Arabian peninsula during the seventh century as a key player in the cultural production beyond its borders. Highlighting the role of Syriac authors from Beth Qaṭraye thus serves to enrich the cultural map of the Middle East at that time. Collecting, translating and discussing the work of the Syriac authors from Beth Qaṭraye is an important part of this process.

Such a historical, archaeological, and literary reality is a true reflection of the spirit of harmony and co-existence found in Beth Qaṭraye in this period and beyond between Christians and Muslims. It reveals the important fact that the Syriac community there was not only surviving but producing the finest and most educated authors of the time many of whom became intellectual, spiritual or religious leaders in the Middle East as whole.

Mario Kozah
Abdulrahim Abu-Husayn
Saif Al-Murikhi
Haya Al-Thani

Abbreviations

AMS	Acta Martyrum et Sanctorum.
ASR	Annali di Scienze Religiose (Milan).
ASE	Annali di Storia dell' Esegesi (Bologna).
CO	Cahiers d'Orientalisme.
ChrOR	Christian Orient (Kottayam).
CPE	Connaissance des Pères de l'Église (Montrouge).
CSCO	Corpus Scriptorum Christianorum Orientalium (Louvain).
DSpir	Dictionnaire de Spiritualité (Paris).
Harp	The Harp: a Review of Syriac and Oriental Studies (Kottayam).
JCSSS	Journal of the Canadian Society for Syriac Studies (Toronto).
JECS	Journal of Early Christian Studies (Baltimore).
JECS	Journal of Eastern Christian Studies (Nijmegen).
JSS	Journal of Semitic Studies (Oxford/Manchester).
JTS	Journal of Theological Studies (Oxford).
LM	Le Muséon (Louvain la Neuve).
MKS	Mémorial Mgr. Gabriel Khouri-Sarkis, ed. F. Graffin (Louvain, 1969).
OCA	Orientalia Christiana Analecta (Rome).
OCP	Orientalia Christiana Periodica (Rome).
OS	L'Orient Syrien (Vernon).
PdO	Parole de l'Orient (Kaslik, Lebanon).
PG	Patrologia Graeca (Migne).
PO	Patrologia Orientalis (Turnhout).
POC	Proche-Orient Chrétien (Jerusalem).
SEERI	St Ephrem Ecumenical Research Institute (Kottayam).
SC	Sources Chrétiennes (Paris).
SympSyr	Symposium Syriacum (OCA).
StPatr	Studia Patristica (Kalamazoo/Leuven/

	Berlin/Oxford).
SVTQ	St. Vladimir's Theological Quarterly (New York).
TS	Theological Studies (Baltimore).
WS	Woodbrooke Studies (Cambridge).
ZAC	Zeitschrift für Antikes Christentum (De Gruyter).
ZNW	Zeitschrift für die neutestamentliche Wissenschaft und die Kunde des alten Christentum (Berlin).

THE *HISTORY* OF MAR YAWNAN

DR SEBASTIAN BROCK
UNIVERSITY OF OXFORD

INTRODUCTION

Yawnan is known as the traditional founder of a famous monastery in the vicinity of Piroz-Shabur/Anbar, on the Euphrates. The main source of information concerning him is the narrative translated below, which locates him in the fourth century, and makes him a disciple of the famous monastic saint, Mar Awgen.[1] The narrative itself cannot date from earlier than about the eighth century, seeing that it knows the *History* of the martyr Mar Qardag which probably dates from the first half of the seventh century, and the *History* of Mar Awgen, of uncertain date, but in any case later than Dadishoʿ Qaṭraya, the earliest author to mention the existence of Awgen. On the other hand, the *History* of Yawnan is earlier than the time of the monastic historian Ishoʿdnah who wrote in the ninth century, who includes him in his "Book of Chastity" (*Ktaba d-nakputa*; on monastic founders) and whose poem on Yawnan is based on information in the *History*. A date of some time in the eighth century would accordingly seem quite likely.

The interest of this *History* of Yawnan for Beth Qaṭraye lies in the fact that it is the only piece of Syriac hagiographical literature whose geographical sphere of interest lies primarily in the region of the Gulf where various remains of monasteries of the

[1] "Mar" (literally "my lord") is an honorific title regularly used, especially for saints and bishops. "Rabban" (also used in the narrative; literally "our master") normally refers to a learned or senior monk.

seventh/eighth centuries CE have in recent years been identified.[2] The purported author of the narrative, Zadoy, abbot of the Monastery of Mar Thomas on "the Black Island" in the region of Beth Qaṭraye, claims to have been a contemporary of the saint, but this is a literary fiction, as is the claim that some of the information comes from a hermit, Philon, said to be living on a neighbouring island. Nevertheless, while the Life cannot be regarded as offering any reliable information about Yawnan in the fourth century, it does provide a very valuable witness to what East Syriac monastic life may have been like in Beth Qaṭraye around the time of the actual author of the narrative. This aspect has been ably exploited recently by Richard Payne, who also tentatively identifies "the Black Island" with Sir Bani Yas, where excavations have brought to light a large monastic complex.[3] His article provides an excellent backdrop for the present text.

The basic aim of the author of the *History* of Mar Yawnan was to provide a link between the monastic life of his own time in the region of Beth Qaṭraye with that of the great monastic founder figures, Pachomius in Egypt and Mar Awgen in Mesopotamia, as well as with the martyr tradition of the late Sasanian period, represented by Mar Qardag. That the East Syriac monastic tradition in Beth Qaṭraye was actually in decline by the time of the author seems to be hinted at in the words of a prophecy made to the alleged author Zadoy by Mar Philon (7:18), "You should be aware that your monastery [of St Thomas, on the Black island] is going to diminish, and that of Abba Yawnan [near Piroz-Shabur/Anbar] will grow".

---

[2] See especially R.A. Carter, "Christianity in the Gulf during the first centuries of Islam", *Arabian Archaeology and Epigraphy* 19 (2008), pp. 71–108.

[3] R. Payne, "Monks, dinars and date palms: hagiographical production and the expansion of monastic institutions in the early Islamic Persian Gulf", *Arabian Archaeology and Epigraphy* 22 (2011), pp. 97–111. For the monastic complex on Sir Bani Yas, see G.R.D. King, "A Nestorian monastic settlement on the island of Sir Bani Yas, Abu Dhabi; a preliminary report", *Bulletin of the School of Oriental and African Studies* 60 (1997), pp. 221–35.

The Syriac text of the *History* of Mar Yawnan is transmitted in a number of late Syriac manuscripts, several of which were used by P. Bedjan in his edition, *Acta Martyrum et Sanctorum* [= *AMS*], I (Leipzig, 1890), pp. 466–525. The variant readings that he gives are only mentioned if they are of real significance (notably, the alternative shorter Introduction). The chapter numbers are already provided in the manuscripts, but the paragraph numbers have been introduced into the translation for convenience of reference.

TRANSLATION

A narrative of the exploits of Rabban Mar Yawnan the anchorite,[4] in brief, by the venerable Christ-loving priest Mar Za'doy, monk and abbot of the monastery of Mar Thomas in the region of Hendu,[5] situated below the region of the Qaṭraye, on the slopes of the Black Island.

Chapter 1. An apologia to the people who asked him to put the history of the saint into writing.

1. Many times, when we were sitting and talking about spiritual matters, my fathers and brothers, I was relating in your presence the stories of the saints and their excellent way of life, their exploits and struggles, and the miracles and signs that Christ performed at their hands, my purpose being to make your love of God all the more fervent, imprinting in your hearts a clear image of their way of life, and fixing in your minds a luminous icon [p. 467] of their virtuous exploits. I did this in my role as head of your brotherhood and your community, seeing that I had been appointed to this role so as to arouse the brethren to the same sort of things. Just as kings on earth frequently act in the same sort of way with their soldiers, arousing their zeal to imitate the warriors who had gone before them, whose exploits had saved the situation, and whose successes,

[4] The term, derived from Greek *anachoretes*, features in the main text at pp. 468, 502; it is first attested in East Syriac writers in the seventh century.

[5] Hendu is here, as often elsewhere, used in a very vague sense, and certainly does not refer to India.

whether in battles with the enemy or in fights with lions, or in hunts for other wild animals, in the same way I too was setting before you the exploits of the saints and their victories. Above all I did this in the case of the holy anchorite, Rabban Mar Yawnan: may his commemoration be for a blessing, and may his prayers be on behalf of us all, amen.

2. At first he settled for thirty years in the wilderness of Piroz Shabur,[6] living an anchorite life, being provided for though divine grace with nourishment by a raven.[7] Later, he came to our community,[8] and I saw him with my own eyes and I enjoyed conversations with him. Out of his own mouth the holy man related to me the story of his departure from the world to this spiritual mode of life. Furthermore, I also saw the sights that Christ performed at his hands.

3. It was in order that I should arouse your love, wanting to imitate and model yourselves on such people that you, my beloved, in your ardent fervour for divine and spiritual matters, urged me, despite my feebleness, to put down in writing the stories that I was setting before you, and in particular that of Abba Mar Yawnan, the anchorite. (You said to me,) "You yourself [p. 468] saw him and enjoyed conversing with him; and you have a clear and accurate knowledge of his history".

4. I was many times held back from doing this, being aware of my deficiencies, my clumsiness and my lack of education, recalling the words spoken by a Sage, "A fool who keeps silent is considered wise".[9] But you pressed your request more and more, pointing out as a way of stirring me into action: "You are already at a great age, and the harvest time is close at hand, with death standing at the

---

[6] Anbar, on the Euphrates. The nearby monastery of Mar Yawnan flourished between the seventh and eleventh century; cf. J.M. Fiey, *Assyrie chrétienne*, III (Beirut, 1968), pp. 237–9.

[7] Cf. 1 Kings 17:4 (Elijah).

[8] That is, the Monastery of Mar Thomas, whose abbot, Mar Zadoy, is the alleged author of the Life.

[9] Proverbs 17:28.

door. Thus we do not know when we will be deprived of your company, and of the record of the story of the exploits of the holy Mar Yawnan the anchorite. Because you have not left it us in writing, it will become erased from memory and forgotten. Look at what a loss that you will be bringing about as a result of this – and not just for other people, but also for yourself: for yourself, because you withheld such a virtuous undertaking, hiding it away just because of a brief and short labour; and for others, because you will have deprived them of the story of a holy man whose exploits were so admirable that they would want to emulate and imitate them".

5. By your telling me "When you don't leave a record in writing of the story of this wonderful man, you will have withheld a virtuous act, and by doing so [p. 469] you will have defied the Lord and giver of virtue: he who causes the sun to rise and who brings rain upon both the good and the bad, on the upright and on the wicked".

6. What did I have to reply to you, my brethren? How should I not stand in fear and trembling when wanting to relate the story of this wondrous man of pious memory, the recollection of whom is sweet, I mean Rabban Mar Yawnan the anchorite? May his prayer be on behalf of the whole world in its entirety, but in particular for our community, amen. How should I not be standing with trembling knees and my hands hanging feebly, when my heart is numbed by all kinds of sin, as I turn over (in my mind) the contemplation of the actions of a man who in his soul is as pure as the sun, and in his body as white as snow? As I contemplate the stirrings of his soul and how his bodily senses act, how can I speak of such a holy man with a tongue that is feeble and weak in the narrow confines of my mouth, and especially with lips that are impure and unclean? For, my brothers, in the case of a person who is about to relate the exploits of the holy saints of the Lord, the Most High, the Holy One, or to portray them in discourses or some narrative form, it is right that first of all he should cleanse his thoughts and purify [p. 470] his mind as far as possible from earthly matters. "Without a pure conscience and imitating the saints, no one is able to attain to the words of the saints and the stories about them". This is what the great star, the patriarch Athanasius, decrees in an excellent manner, and by way of

demonstration he adduces the following:[10] just as if someone wants to see the light of the sun, he continually cleanses his eyes and makes them light, like the object that he wants to see: he cleanses and purifies himself, so that his eye becomes as light as possible, so that it is enabled to see that which is the object of his desire. This ought also to be the case with the person who wishes to relate the story of the exploits of the saints, and to speak of their miracles and signs: first of all let him wash his body clean with a virtuous way of life, and let him illumine his soul with spiritual contemplation, only then let him approach and embark on such a task.

7. But as you have said, the story of this man of God should not be erased from human memory as a result of the length of time and the great many years, in the way that many stories of men clothed in God have often been erased and blotted out because they did not have any memorial in writing. Accordingly, I have yielded to your request, and my intention is to delineate the story [p. 471] of the blessed Rabban Mar Yawnan the anchorite. May his prayers be on behalf of us all, amen.

8. So, having taken refuge in the prayers of this venerable and holy man, and continuing to do so, I now set down his story on the faithful table,[11] trusting in God who, in his grace, is alone able to cause me to attain to the haven that I am looking towards.

[Secondary Preface][12]

History of the way of life of the holy Mar Yawnan, who belongs to the band associated with the blessed Mar Awgen.

---

[10] The source in Athanasius (d.373) remains unidentified.

[11] The sense is unclear; since "table" can also refer to an "altar", perhaps the author intends to say that he is laying his narrative down on the altar as an offering.

[12] This is found in some manuscripts, and is clearly a shorter replacement for the lengthy and rhetorical original preface; for such Prefaces to hagiographical works, see E. Riad, *Studies in the Syriac Preface* (Uppsala, 1988), pp. 111–36 (the present one is briefly mentioned on p. 136).

The grace which created the (two) worlds brought it about in the saints that they should be imitating the mode of life of the angels,[13] being men who have rejected the world and its lusts, and have instead loved what is lasting and enduring; who have rejected error, and travelled in the path of the heavenly King in an upright and diligent fashion on the road filled with blood – for some of them were sacrificed for the sake of the truth of the orthodox confession, while others entered the fiery furnace, others again were crowned with tortures, and yet others were thrown to the beasts; others ended their lives living as strangers, or were scattered among the mountains and islands, or they entered crevices in the earth and found protection, or they completed their days in tiring fasts and night vigils, or they took refuge on peaks and precipices. Others founded and built monasteries and convents, or established schools; some engaged and laboured in the exercise of religious instruction, others became wandering ascetics, and some were seen to be performers of miracles, signs, wonders and mighty deeds, astonishing both angels and human beings – and one of these is this chosen man concerning whose glorious and wonderful mode of life it is our intention to relate, in accordance with what the abbot and Mar Papa related – may their prayers be on our behalf, amen.

[p. 472] Chapter 2. The place of origin of his upright parents; where their family travelled, and what was their profession.

1. As the holy Mar Yawnan related to me, his parents settled in the island of Cyprus. I imagine he said this out of his humility, not wanting to reveal their actual locality of their original city. According to the testimony of trustworthy people who were acquainted with them, their city was Rome the Great,[14] and they were descended from imperial stock and lineage, and were closely related to the victorious emperor Constantine. Because they were already Christians, and by reason of their high imperial stock, they

---

[13] The monastic life as an "angelic life" is based on Luke 20:36; the phrase is found in Syriac writers from the sixth century onwards.

[14] This must be Rome, although Ishoʿdnah takes it to be Constantinople (Cambridge Add. 2042, f.24v).

were afraid to live in the imperial city in view of the pagan emperors who were reigning at that time in Rome; accordingly they departed and came to Cyprus to live there. [p. 473].

2 In secular rank and honour they were formerly senators, but after they had departed from their city and home for Cyprus, they wanted to practice some profession. Because they were philosophers who were also trained in medical writings, they chose to practice the medical profession. This was for three reasons: first, because it is one that imitates God: in that God takes care of human beings, preserving them and protecting them, so too the medical profession is eager to implant good health and drive away sickness by means of remedies and medicines. Secondly, the medical profession is closer to philosophy than the other professions in that the latter takes care of the soul, while the former looks after the body in which the soul exists. Thirdly, because this profession is more honoured and praised among human beings, in that the other ones are only concerned with what is external to the body, while this one is to do specifically with the body itself. Accordingly, after a short while the report of their skill in medicine, and their sagacity, flew all over the territory of Cyprus, and they became wealthy as they grew more and more famous.

[p. 474] Chapter 3. How the departure of the saint from the world and his entry into the monastic life took place, and how he received the ordination of priesthood. Also, how the blessed Mar Awgen met him and brought him along with him to Egypt.

1 We will now tell how Christ chose him and rescued him from the suffocating sea of this world, and how he left his parents and family having fallen in love with spiritual poverty. Once he had reached the full peak of youth and was approximately twenty years old, as he himself told me, and had learnt the Holy Scriptures with proficiency, he entered a holy church one day and heard the sacred lection of the reading of the Gospel being read: in it were the words of our Saviour to his disciples,[15] "He who does not leave father and mother" and the rest, "and take up his cross and follow

[15] Matthew 10:37–8.

me is not worthy of me". That very moment he put into his mind the idea of abandoning the world and everything in it. Once he had made this decision he was eager to put it into practice. He was pondering over to which monastery to go, or where he might find God-fearing people with whom he might live and spend the rest of his days among them. Being in a state of hesitation over this, he committed the matter to God. [p. 475]

2. The saint's parents, observing that he was very clever, intelligent and sharp-witted, they put pressure on him to study medical writings and logic,[16] [*mliluta*], and to be educated in these. When, however, Epiphanius, the bishop of the island of Cyprus,[17] saw that he had abandoned the Holy Scriptures and had begun to study writings on medicine and logic, he summoned the saint's father and told him, "My son, do not labour over Ioannis,[18] because the Lord has already chosen him to be a diligent worker for Himself". His father, however, was greatly put out by this, seeing that the young man was very much suited for the medical profession, and he supposed that the bishop wanted to make him a member of the clergy. Then, one day when the saint was standing in church at the time of the Mysteries, the blessed bishop Epiphanius approached, took him by the hand and brought him to the sanctuary [lit. altar], where he ordained him to the priesthood. After the ordination the bishop said to him, "My son, I wanted to receive a blessing from you before you become a gazelle on the mountains – for you are going to become a "chosen vessel"[19] for Christ and a father of many monks".[20] The blessed man used to keep all these things carefully in his heart, [p. 476] and he would

---

[16] This is probably the sense of *mliluta* here, representing Greek *logike*; Ishoᶜdnah, however, evidently took it to mean rhetoric (f.25r, *ritoriki*).

[17] Famous author (d. 403) several of whose works were translated into Syriac.

[18] Yawnan's earlier name, as explained below (4:3).

[19] Acts 9:15.

[20] Though the term *ihidaye* here could be translated "hermits", its use in this text is rather loose, and in 6:6 it certainly refers to cenobitic monks.

call upon God for assistance so that he might find an escape from these things he was bound up with.

3. While his parents were still endeavouring to have him learn medicine together with logic, the God in whom he had put his trust and to whom he had committed the entire matter, devised a way out for him by getting his parents to send him to the mountains and valleys to learn from sight the medical herbs and plants. When the suitable time for this arrived, they sent him with some people in their profession, the aim being that he should go with them and learn about the medicinal plants, how they grow and the time and season of each of them, what are the uses for their roots and fruits, what their leaves are like, and when they are gathered.

4. When he set out with them from the island of Cyprus, he began to wander in the mountains and heights that he encountered, it was not to learn about the herbs and medicinal plants, but only that he might see the mountains and places that would be suitable for his personal hidden purpose. The men with him began to say to him, "Dear fellow, did your parents send you to look at the mountains and heights, or the medicinal places, the object of [p. 477] our coming here?" The blessed man paid no attention to their words as he pondered in his thoughts, "Blessed is the person who has brought his days to an end in these mountains!"

5. When it was night, he got up at the first watch and stretched out his hands towards heaven in prayer, saying, "O Lord God Almighty, you know what is in the hearts of everyone, you examine the thoughts and search out the innermost feelings,[21] you know my whole intention in departing for these mountains: it is not because I want to learn about medicinal plants and their uses, but to save my soul, and to cause it to escape from the world's stench. Now, O Lord God, do you, in your eternal grace and compassion that is part of your Being, guide your servant to a place of deliverance, for in you has been my trust ever since my childhood, and to you do I look in hope, and in you do I take refuge, so that you may assist me in your grace".

---

[21] Cf. Psalm 7:9, Jeremiah 17:10.

6. Arising from prayer, he sealed himself with the life-giving sign of the cross as he faced the road on which he was about to travel. He then set off in haste, quickening his footsteps and not wearying, for he was afraid lest those fellow companions of his should overtake him and return him to his parents. Having travelled on the road for two complete days without seeing anybody, his soul found rest. In the morning of the third day, as he was walking in the direction of the east, singing psalms and giving praise [p.478] and thanks to God who had held him worthy to escape from the world and its wickedness, he saw a man coming in his direction who called out to him by his name, "Ioannis, Ioannis". The blessed man was perturbed and in great trepidation, thinking it was a deceptive apparition. But again he said to him, "My son, approach me and have no fear, for I am a human being like you, and I am a Christian who worships Christ". The blessed Mar Yawnan was still fearful, wondering how the man had all of a sudden appeared in front of him. Now that man was the holy Mar Awgen,[22] for he had appeared to the blessed man concerning his departure, and so he came to him by the power of the Spirit. Then the blessed Mar Awgen approached the holy Mar Yawnan, embracing him and kissing him. Taking him by the hand, he said, "Welcome, my son, welcome! I have been expecting you for a long time, and now I have come here all because of you".

7. Then he took him with him to Egypt, to the cells where he was living with his spiritual children: at that time there were twenty brothers. The blessed Mar Yawnan remained with Mar Awgen in that locality for fifteen years, following the angelic way of life and excelling in spiritual graces.

---

[22] Traditionally revered as a great fourth-century monastic founder, his name is first recorded in a Syriac source (Dadishoᶜ Qaṭraya) in the late seventh century. His "Life", known in several different forms, was edited by P. Bedjan, *AMS*, III (Leipzig, 1892), pp. 376–480; Yawnan only features there in a list of Awgen's 70 disciples (p. 473).

[p. 479] Chapter 4. Concerning the descent of the blessed man to the eastern regions, and the reason for his change of name.

1. When the brethren had multiplied and reached the number of approximately seventy, the blessed Mar Awgen wished to appoint a leader for them, while he himself would withdraw to a remote region. With this thought in mind, he said to the blessed Mar Yawnan, "Will you come with me to where I am going, my son?" The holy Mar Yawnan said to him, "And where are you going, father?" "For the moment I am going to the monastery of Abba Pachomius, [23] but afterwards, if the Lord wills it, I am ready to go to a far-off region". The blessed Mar Yawnan says to him, "For the moment, go off to the monastery that you mentioned, and when you return and set off to the distant region, I will go with you". Now the blessed Mar Yawnan liked the place where he was, seeing that he had excelled there.

2. When the holy Mar Awgen returned from the monastery of Abba Pachomius, all the brethren came out to meet him, receiving him with hymns and psalms. The blessed man disclosed to them his intention to go down to Beth Parsaye,[24] and how he was making ready to visit the regions of the east. They all exclaimed with one voice, [p. 480] saying to the blessed Mar Awgen, "We will all go there with you, all together". Now the blessed Mar Yawnan and two others of the brethren wanted to remain in that place, but that holy assembly did not permit them; in particular the holy Mar Awgen told them "You too ought to share with us in this great and exalted source of blessing". Then they agreed.

3. Because there were three brothers all named Ioannis, Mar Awgen changed the blessed man's name, calling him Yawnan, saying "So that your name may be distinguished from theirs".

---

[23] This famous Egyptian monastic founder died in 346; the visit of Mar Awgen to the monastery features in his Life, *AMS*, III, p. 386.

[24] Fars.

4. When the fathers set off from there and reached the holy city of Edessa,[25] the blessed Mar Yawnan together with Mar Awgen went in to the holy bishop Mar Miles and greeted him, receiving his blessing.[26] The entire assembly of fathers also greeted him. The blessed Mar Miles was then going off to the western regions, and on seeing Mar Yawnan he felt a great love for him, and wanted Mar Awgen to leave him with him. The blessed Mar Awgen, however, did not agree to this, replying to the holy Mar Miles that "For this great task we have need of him".

5. After they had left Mar Miles and had reached the great city of Nisibis, the arrival of the fathers became known [p. 481] to the citizens as a result of a demoniac being healed by the holy men. That night Mar Awgen together with all the brethren arose and ascended mount Izla, in the vicinity of the village of Mᶜarre.[27] They resided there in a cavern for the length of forty years, assiduous in hymns and psalms.

6. In the time of the victorious emperor Jovian the king of the Persians went up against the border territory, and the city of Nisibis was handed over without any trouble or fighting.[28] When Shabur heard of the exploits and the many wonders that Mar Awgen was performing, he wanted to see him and talk with him,

---

[25] The epithet "holy" probably alludes to the portrait (later, icon) of Christ brought back from Jerusalem to king Abgar "the Black", according to a widespread legend.

[26] No bishop of Edessa (modern Şanliurfa) named Miles is known; the name may have been suggested by that of a famous bishop of Susa (first half of the fourth century).

[27] Izla is the mountain range NE of Nisibis (modern Nuseybin on the Turkish/Syrian border), and Mᶜarre was a large village not far from the famous monastery of Mar Awgen (where monastic life has recently been revived).

See also the Life of Awgen, *AMS* III, p. 389 (where it is said he stayed there for thirty, rather than forty, years).

[28] In the peace treaty of 363, after the emperor Julian's death on campaign within the Persian Empire, his successor Jovian (363–364) had to hand Nisibis over to the Persian shah, Shapur (Shabur) II (309–379).

especially so that he might heal his son who was severely chastised by a demon. He sent to him some Christians from Beth Huzaye who were with him,[29] telling him to come to him with his brethren. The holy man arose at once and came without delay with the king's envoys, together with all the brethren. After they had done obeisance to the king and had greeted him, they were greatly honoured by him, in that they performed great portents and miracles, like the holy apostles, in his presence. This applied especially to the blessed Mar Yawnan: what he performed we intend to set it down in its place.

7. After they had left the presence of Shabur, the blessed Mar Awgen bade the brethren to go in pairs to convert and to baptise, [p. 482], to found monasteries and build convents. The blessed Mar Yawnan approached the holy Mar Awgen and said, "I request of you, father, permit me to go off and live alone, for my soul abhors these Magians and their religion". Then the blessed Mar Awgen remained for a while by himself, praying and asking God to establish his path; afterwards he said to him, "Will you not go with Yawsep to build up monasteries and convents?" "No", he replied, "but I request you to allow me to return to the place where we were previously". "Go off in peace, my son", he said, "and God who was with our holy fathers, preserving them and guiding them all the time of their lives, may he be with you and make you subject to his will, for you are going to become, my son, the head and father for many thousands!"

Chapter 5. How he went to the wilderness of Piroz Shabur, and how long he dwelt, and how he was provisioned.

1. When it was morning he went to the Elder, Mar Awgen, and informed him about his departure. Mar Awgen blessed him and kissed him, saying for the second time, "Christ is going [p. 483] to make you into a great people; therefore be strong and mighty, and may the Lord who was with our holy fathers accompany you and be with you, so as to fulfil his entire will".

---

[29] Similarly in the Life of Awgen, *AMS* III, p. 465.

2. So Mar Yawnan departed from him and began to travel straight on, while praying and saying, "May the Lord guide me according to his will, and do with me in accordance with what is beneficial for my life". Wandering for many days in the bare wilderness, and travelling straight ahead, he reached a town called Piroz Shabur. As he wandered in this wilderness he saw that it was desolate and far removed from human habitation: there was no coming and going, seeing that there was a wet marsh and a large forest there in it, and no one dared to come near because of the large number of lions in the forest. He was circling around the forest for many days praying and supplicating Christ to perform with him whatever was beneficial for him.

3. In the middle of the day, while he was praying, he noticed a little path, very narrow, inside the forest. Wanting to go and see in case Christ had prepared a place for him where he would be protected, he thought that he should not act in haste, in case there might be some deceit of the Evil One who was continually opposing the elect [p. 484] but that he should first of all pray and then enter, for he knew that the evil cunning actions of the Crafty One are made ineffective before the power of prayer. Once he had prayed that whole day and night, up to the time when he had seen that small path, he knew that it was some divine provision. He sealed himself with the sign of the cross and entered the small path. Having travelled along it for a mile or so he discovered a small place in the middle of the forest, higher than all the rest of the ground. This had been prepared either by lions, or with more truth, by divine grace. He prayed in that place and gave praise to God. Filled with immense joy, he dug a small pit there and made a roof over it with the reeds. The holy man's soul was rested with that protection, for he thought, "Who will be able to come to this wilderness? Who can endure the bitter cruelty of the lions?" For when it was evening, they stirred up the wilderness with their howls and roars.

4. Now he was afraid of the holy Mar Awgen's prophecy concerning him, that "You are going to become the head of many thousands of monks". Therefore he was fleeing hither and thither, wishing to save himself from something from which he was not delivered either in his lifetime or in his departure in death!

5. He lived in this place for thirty years – twenty all alone and as an anchorite, without being seen by anyone at all, as he himself said, neither by spiritual brethren nor by ordinary people; and then ten years after the brethren had become aware of him, [p. 485] when they came and resided in the place called Tappa,[30] situated at a distance of about two parasangs[31] from the blessed man's abode.

6. He was provisioned for the entire extent of these thirty years with food that was sent to him by divine grace through a raven: it used to bring him every day half a loaf of beautiful clean bread. This is something which the blessed man hid from us out of his humility, but the holy Abba Philon brought it to light, as we will record in its appropriate place.[32]

Chapter 6. The reason for the holy man's departure from the wilderness of Piroz Shabur, and his arrival at our holy monastery.

1. At the end of the first twenty years, as I mentioned above, the brethren heard about the blessed man, and they came and lived in Tappa, nearby to him. They used to come to him continually, asking him for prayer and for profitable advice for their souls. He would give them advice and strengthen them in faith, hope and love, so that they would overcome the natural passions and demonic struggles; he would also teach them about spiritual conduct, encouraging them with the hope of the good things that are promised to the diligent who conduct themselves well. [p. 486] He did this for the space of twenty years; but after ten brethren had gathered to that holy wilderness, they were putting pressure on the blessed Mar Yawnan to become their head and leader, saying by way of persuasion, "You are the very first to be in this place, and by precedence the headship belongs to you", and "More and more you are appropriate for this, since you are fully enlightened and acquainted with the Holy Scriptures; in your way of life with its

---

[30] Unidentified.

[31] A parasang normally corresponded to 30 Greek stades; since a mile corresponds to 8 stades, the distance here will be about seven and a half miles.

[32] See below, 9:11.

struggles and battles with the demons you are greatly skilled; and you know how to advise and to teach in a superior way". Now when the holy man saw that he would not be left alone, and that they were using strong compulsion in bringing him to this, he was afraid lest he would be drawn along by their urging as a result of his meekness and humility. Accordingly he arose in the night, not telling anyone where he was going apart from a single holy Elder,[33] for whose prayer he asked. He informed him, "I am going to the monastery of Rabban Thomas". For he had heard from the brethren that a monastery named after Rabban Thomas existed: that it had two hundred brethren, and was situated on the slopes of the Black Island.[34]

2. And so he came to this monastery here, firstly, so as to escape from the headship; secondly, so as to see this monastery and the blessed brethren in it; and thirdly, in order for the holy Abba Philon to see him, for the blessed Abba Philon had prayed and besought God that he might see someone from that holy assembly of Mar Awgen.

[p. 487] Chapter 7. The blessed Mar Yawnan's arrival at our monastery, and how he disclosed to me his whole story, as it has been set out above, and about the miracles and signs that Christ performed at his hands here, I being an eye-witness and assistant (or: deacon).

1. Let us turn now to what was spoken and done by the holy Mar Yawnan here amongst us and with us. On the first Sunday of Subbara,[35] when all the brethren were gathered in the church for the Holy Mysteries, all of a sudden an Elder was seen in the sanctuary: he was of noble aspect, full stature, and fair of countenance. No one was able to look upon his face at all, because of the reverence spread over it and the glory. All the brethren

---

[33] Later on, in 9:1, his name is given as Shahdost.

[34] R. Payne, "Monks, dinars and date palms" [see n. 2], p. 103, suggests that this might be identified with Sir Bani Yas where a large monastic complex has been uncovered; for this see King, "A Nestorian monastic settlement on the island of Sir Bani Yas" [see n. 2], pp. 221–35.

[35] Corresponds approximately to western Advent.

supposed that he was a bishop from one of the regions, who had left his see and diocese, and wished to become a "stranger" for the sake of God.[36] But I called one of the brethren and said to him, "Observe this blessed stranger, see with whom he is staying, and where he enters". The brother did as I had bidden him, and after the church service had finished, the blessed man went off in haste; the brother, however, quietly followed him and saw that once he had left the monastery he entered a large ruin,[37] DBWKTY, which was a little distant [p. 488] from the monastery. The brother returned and informed me: "I followed him and he went into a ruined cell". I got up at once, and taking a copy of the Gospels with me, I went off to him, to that cell. When I was still in the courtyard of the cell, the blessed Mar Yawnan came out to me and said, "Don't trouble yourself, my lord abbot, I will come to your cell". I stood there shaking in amazement, firstly, because of the radiance and glory that was spread over his face, and secondly, because astonishment had taken hold of me: how had he been aware of me while he was still in the cell, and I had come from the other side? Then he took me in and we prayed, as is the custom. He then embraced me with both arms, and kissed me lovingly, asking me about the monastery and the brethren. I replied that "they are preserved by your prayers".

2. When we had conversed with one another for a while, the semantron for Ramsha (Vespers) sounded. The blessed man said to me, "Let us arise and serve Ramsha". "Yes, father", I said, and we served Ramsha, continuing on with Subbaʿa (Compline). When we had completed this, the blessed Mar Yawnan sat down facing east, and made me sit beside him. Then all of a sudden along came a raven holding in its beak a double portion of bread. It placed this in an intelligent way in front of the blessed man. When the blessed

---

[36] The term "stranger" can either mean "stranger to the world", someone who has renounced the world (that is, a monk in general), or (as several times below) a monk from somewhere else than the monastery in question.

[37] This is probably the original reading, rather than "cell" in Bedjan's text.

man opened it up he found twelve dates. Then [p. 489] he lifted up his gaze and said to the raven, "When all my teeth are rotten, how is it that you have brought me dates?" The raven flew off at once. The blessed man prayed, broke off half of the bread and set it before himself, while the other half he put in front of me, along with the dates, saying "I can't eat dates because my teeth are rotten". He made the sign of the cross over the food and said to me, "Eat, my lord, eat". But I was in fear and trembling, my eyes having beheld such wonders. And now that raven came back again, holding in its mouth a bunch of grapes. It set these down in front of the holy man, as though it was completely tame. He said to it, "Go in peace", and off it flew at once. I said to the blessed man, "What are these fruits?" He said to me, "Don't you know what these fruits are?" "No", I told him. He said "These are called grapes, and they are the fruit of the vine". Then I told him "I have never seen a vine, nor do I know of grapes except by hearsay, for in this country of ours there is nothing but dates". He took ten grapes from that bunch and gave them to me, saying "Here, then, are fruits from the vine, take and eat".

3. After we had eaten that spiritual food, the Elder said to me, "My lord abbot, do you have a small cell [p. 490] where I can rest for a few days?" I got up and prostrated myself before him. "Yes, my lord and father", I said, "my cell is for you, and I am your servant and attendant". Then the Elder said, "I do not want your cell, but look out for me just a tiny small cell". I went off and prepared a cell in accordance with his desire that very night, and he moved there. Then the blessed man said to me, "I want you to warn the brethren not to knock for me on the door; let no one come to me apart from yourself alone. On Sunday you should knock for me, and that is all". I got up and made a prostration,[38] saying, "Make a rule for your servant, and I will not transgress it, for if possible I won't allow even a sparrow to fly around your

[38] Here the author uses the Greek term *metanoia* (literally "repentance"), but elsewhere (e.g. 7:12) he employs Syriac *tyabuta*, evidently in the same technical monastic sense.

cell". I warned all the brethren, "See that you don't knock at the door of the Elder, the stranger".

4. While I was pondering and considering how I might ask the Elder about his family and lineage, where he used to live, and other such things, I became afraid because of the weightiness and splendour of the man; also, in case he might take offence at this and as a result leave us. One night when I had gone to him and been aroused by conversation with him and acquired a sense of familiarity with him, I made a prostration to the ground [p. 491] in front of him and grasped his feet, begging and beseeching him for a long while. He forced me to get up and said to me, "What is it you want?" I told him, "I want you to tell me, father, from where you come, and how you were instructed in this angelic way of life; and how did you come here?" The Elder pleasantly said to me, "I think that all of you have had your fill of me!" I replied, "Far be it, my lord and father. Even if you were to sit on my head for ten years, you would not be too heavy for me! How can you say such things? But I want to know your true story, so that my soul may be rested". By this means he related to him his whole story, as written down above.

5. As for the signs and miracles that the Lord performed at his hands in this holy monastery, who is able to recount them? For they are so many and surpass counting. But we will tell of a few of them, according to what the listener is able to comprehend.

6. After the Feast of the Nativity one of the brethren went to the town Maron,[39] and stayed in the house of Nu'aym, a true believer.

---

[39] Very probably Mazun (Oman) is meant; in Syriac texts Maron and Mazon are often confused. The precise identity of the town, which clearly played a part in maritime trade, is uncertain; ed-Dur, which had been a functioning port in the first and second centuries CE, subsequently lost its importance; cf. E. Haerink in D. Whitehouse, *Excavations at ed-Dur*, I. *The Glass Vessels* (Leuven, 1998), p. ix. Thus more likely is Sohar, where excavations have suggested that it was probably involved in long distance maritime trade by the end of the Sasanian period: see M. Kevran and F. Hiebert, "Sohar pré-islamique. Note de stratigraphie", in K. Schippmann,

He saw that his son was tormented by a grievous illness. Now Nuʿaym and his household were in a state of great grief, seeing that he had no other son or daughter apart from the sick boy. [p. 492] The brother said to the boy's father, Nuʿaym, "An Elder came to us from the Upper Country, a mighty and godly man. If you bring the boy to him he will heal him without any doubt". Thereupon Nuʿaym said to his family, "Come, let us carry the boy to the holy man whom the brother has told us of; maybe he will be assisted by his prayers". His parents, the members of the household, and a large crowd of their relations, took up the boy and embarked on a boat to go to the monastery. Having travelled by sea for five days and were close to reaching the monastery, for the town of Maron was a six days journey from us, the boy's illness grew serious and he died. Nuʿaym's wife said to him, "If only we had left my son to die at home, and not here amidst the storms of the sea! What can we do with him here? Where are we going to bury him?" But Nuʿaym rebuked his wife sternly, saying "Tomorrow, if the Lord wills it, we will reach the monastery, and the monks will bury him".

7. The following day they arrived at the monastery. It was a Sunday, at the time of Sapra (*or*: in the morning), and we, that is, I together with five experienced Elders of the community, were sitting with the holy man. We heard the sound of much uproar and wailing, and while I was wondering what this lamentation and disturbance was, along came the faithful Nuʿaym with the members of his household to the holy man's cell; they set down the boy in front of him, wailing and crying as they tore their garments. The Elder [p. 493] said to them, "What has happened to you that you are acting like this?" They replied, telling him "This boy fell ill with a serious illness; for a long time he was greatly tormented by the illness. We heard about your holiness and have brought him along to you in order that you may pray and beseech God that he be healed. Yesterday, however, when we were close to the monastery, he died". The blessed man lifted up his gaze towards Nuʿaym, the boy's father, and said, "Why are you weeping and tearing your

---

A. Herling and J-F. Salles (eds), *Golf-Archäologie* (Buch am Erlbach, 1991), pp. 337–43, especially 342–3.

garments like the godless pagans who have no hope? Certainly, my children, death cannot be escaped, whether in childhood or in old age. Give thanks, therefore, to God; go to the community, so that they may sound the semantron, and the brethren be gathered for his funeral rites". When he heard this, the boy's father cried out in a piteous voice, and tore at his hair and beard; he seized the holy man's feet, saying "Have pity on me, O servant of the living God. This boy was my only son and I have no heir apart from him". The holy man could scarcely raise him up from the ground as he groaned heavily. He took the boy in his arms and went into his cell. He remained there for an hour, and then came out holding the boy by his hand, and handed him over to his father. He also gave him a few parsnips[40] [p. 494] that is *gezar* which he had in his cell. The Elder said to Nuʿaym, "My son, take your son, and go in peace. For even though I am a sinner, God has had mercy on you in accordance with your faith". Fear and trembling took hold of us at the sight of the holy man, for together with the miracle we had seen, the holy man's face at that moment resembled the round sun, his countenance being full of radiance and glory. Now the boy was eating without any difficulty the parsnip that the blessed man had given him, seeing that the Elder has told him in a pleasant way, "Eat, my son, eat!"

8. Now the boy was four years old. Because of him Nuʿaym donated to the monastery a boat-(load) that had recently arrived from China.[41] He had bought it, and then we sold it for one thousand three hundred dinars. This miracle was heard about in all the islands around us, and in all the regions of the Qaṭraye. All who heard gave praise to Christ, and they lauded the faith of us Christians.

9. A rich and proud man names Zarqon, from the town of Milon,[42] one of those who bring up pearls from the ocean, heard about the fame of the holy man and the wonders that he performed. He brought along his son, a handsome youth who was

---

[40] The Greek term, *staphulinos*, is used.

[41] *Ṣīn*.

[42] Unidentified, but evidently on the coast.

grievously affected by a demon. When [p. 495] he came to the monastery the brethren told him, "The Elder Mar Yawnan does not come out except on Sundays, only for the liturgy of the Mysteries". So Zarqon remained there, waiting expectantly for the arrival of Sunday. The blessed man left his cell at the time of the Mysteries, while I and the Elders of the community were with him. Then Zarqon came along, fell at the blessed man's feet, saying, "Holy Mar Yawnan, have mercy on me, and on the beauty of this youth, my son, for he is greatly tormented by a demon". Then the blessed Mar Yawnan took him by the hand and raised him up; he drew him aside, and told him, "Remove the concubine from your house, and your son will be healed, for you are a Christian and you ought not to trample on the divine commandments and act like the godless pagans". When the proud Zarqon heard this he groaned bitterly in his heart and was beating his breast as he said, "In very truth, Mar Yawnan, it is because of my sins that my son is being chastised in this way". He then resolved to turn back to the way of truth, and to remove the concubine from his house. Together with the recovery of his son, he also recovered the health of his soul through the prayers of the Elder. And he gave an ample "blessing"[43] to the monastery.

10. One of the brethren came to the blessed man and told him about the battle he had (with demons). Once he had fully healed him through admonition and his prayer, the brother requested him that he might go with him to his cell, so that he might seal it with his prayer and with the sign of the cross. Out of his love of humanity he got up and went with him gladly. On entering the cell he made a prayer, and having fulfilled this act of love, he departed. The brother said to him, "Look at this palm tree, how fine it is and how thick its branches are, but it does not produce any fruit". The holy man struck the palm tree with the staff he had in his hand, and said, "Palm tree, produce fruit for this brother". And in the morning the brother got up and went out into his courtyard, and he saw that the palm tree had seven enormous clusters. In the amazement that took hold of him he came and told me and all the

[43] That is, a donation.

brethren of what had taken place. Once we were all gathered together we went and beheld it. Amazed at what had happened, we gave praise to God who magnifies his holy ones. The brethren then picked those clusters and they were divided up between us, with a few each. The brother had said, "These are the fruits of the Elder's prayer, and they should be divided up among the community of the brethren". Every year, up to today, this palm tree bears seven clusters, and its dates are choice; they are given to the brethren, counting them out, seeing that they are a blessing of the holy Mar Yawnan. [p. 497]

11. One of the brethren had a swelling like a pomegranate in the upper part of his belly, and for a long time he was greatly tormented by it. We thought it certain he would die, but I went to the Elder and informed him about that brother, and he came to visit him. He stretched out his hand and felt him. With a groan he said, "This kind of sickness is incurable". The brother wept bitterly, but the holy man quietened him down. He washed the sacred cross with some water and made him drink it, at the same time anointing the swelling. When Sunday came the brother was so completely healed that it was he who consecrated the life-giving Mysteries for us, while praising God for his healing, and thanking the Elder Mar Yawnan.

12. My nephew, a simple and uneducated man, fell from a date-palm while he was gathering dates; his thigh was completely broken. I went and told the Elder, saying to him, "My sister's son Khosro has fallen from a date-palm and his thigh is completely broken". The Elder said to me, "Bring him immediately to the doctor in the town, and he will bandage him up". I then made a prostration and said to him, "By the power of Christ which dwells in you, you [p. 498] be his healer". The Elder shook his whole head, saying, "My lord abbot, do you want to drive me away from being with you?" At that moment, as he spoke, the brethren brought along Khosro on a couch and placed it in front of the blessed man, while Khosro was crying out amid tears and wailing at the strength of the pain. "Holy Mar Yawnan", he said, "have pity on me by the love of our Lord". The blessed man came down from his cell, weeping; he felt the fracture, and said "This is nothing". He unloosened the belt that was fastened around his hips, and bound up Khosro's thigh, saying to the brethren, "Take him to his

cell". That very night he was healed through the prayers of the holy man.

13. The faithful Nuʿaym, whom we mentioned above, and whose son was restored to life, came to greet the holy man, bringing with him a large glass vessel full of first-class wine that had been sent to him from Fars. He left the wine in the holy man's cell for the sacristan to come and take it. One of the brethren, whose family was from the Upper Region, heard that Nuʿaym had brought some wine to the Elder's cell, and he thought he would go to the holy man and ask for a little. Because he did not have a small vessel in his cell, he took along a large one, like the one [p. 499] Nuʿaym had brought. His idea was that the Elder would give him as much as he wished. He came along to the holy man's cell, saying to himself in his thoughts, "If only the Elder Mar Yawnan would give me the full amount of the wine!" As he knocked on the blessed man's door he felt too ashamed of size of the vessel to bring it in with him, so he left it at the entrance of the cell. He entered and greeted the holy man lovingly. The Elder said to him, "Is there some reason for your coming, my brother?" "It is so that you might pray for me, father", replied the brother. Jokingly the Elder said to him, "Then bring along that vessel which you have brought, so that I may fill it up in accordance with your desire". Ashamed, the brother said, "Forgive me, father; ever since I left our region I have not tasted any wine; it is for this reason that I came to you". He bade him bring in the vessel, and when he had brought it in, the holy man filled it up generously. When the brother had left, the sacristan turned up. The blessed Mar Yawnan said to him, "Come in, my son, and take the vessel of wine which the faithful Nuʿaym has brought for you". At much the same time that brother went to the sacristan for some matter. He came up close to the alabaster jar[44] [*shisha*] and saw that it was full, with nothing gone. He told the sacristan the whole truth about what had happened, and the two of them came and told me. I then went and I saw the two vessels both

---

[44] The Syriac term used here, *shisha*, normally means "marble", but sometimes also "alabaster", though it clearly refers here to the same vessel as the one of glass mentioned earlier.

full. We gave praise to Christ who provides wonders such as these at the hands of his saints. [p. 500] I warned the brethren not to spread the report of this, otherwise the Elder would be upset and depart from living with us.

14. On one occasion the wine ran out on the sacristan, and he wanted to cancel the *Qurbana*[45] that day. The holy man summoned him, and said, "Since you are in need of wine, come and I'll give you some, since I have some with me". The sacristan replied, "In truth, father, I don't have any wine for the libation today". The Elder gave him a jar filled with wine. On that same day I came, and likewise Mar Moshe the head of the community, to receive the life-giving Mysteries. When we had received and had greeted one another, Mar Moshe called to the sacristan and asked him "Where did you get this wine for the libation from, my brother?" He replied, "Forgive me, my lord; today I did not have any wine, and being in straits I did not know what to do. The Elder, Abba Yawnan the Stranger, called for me and he gave me the wine of which you have partaken". Mar Moshe praised God, saying, "Truly this wine is not from earthly grapes, but from water that has been transformed into wine through the holy man's prayer, like the wine at Cana. May our Lord Jesus Christ preserve him and establish him with us in our poverty, so that he may be the fulfiller of our needs". [p. 501]

15. On a Friday, after Sapro the sacristan knocked, saying "Rabban, Rabban, hurry up!" I quickly went out, and he said to me, "The Elder, Mar Yawnan, is calling for you; go to him at once". I hastened my step to the holy man's cell. The Elder said to me, "Send three of the brothers to the east side of the monastery at once, for one of the brethren is in great straits". I hastily sent off five of the brethren, following them myself. The brother who had got up before dawn to bring palm fronds had been met by a Jew, an evil man who, on seeing the brother had hit him out of envy: having struck him with many blows he had knocked him to the ground and was wanting to kill him, (and would have done so) had the brethren not caught him up. He still had a little life in him, and

[45] That is, the Eucharistic "Offering".

carrying him on a couch they brought him to the community, bringing along the Jew as well. The blessed man quickly sent one of the brethren to me, telling me "See that you don't let the brethren do any harm to the Jew, for Christ, whom he has abused, is going to bring about an evil death for him today". I only just managed to rescue him from the hands of the brethren, for they were wanting to take vengeance on him, but I said to them, "No, my sons, not so! But leave your judgement to God". They were arguing with me, saying "Ah, we can't cope with your sense of justice: [p. 502] you are preventing us from getting our own back". For these Qaṭraye are severe when they get very angry. That same night the wretched Jew climbed up a palm tree in order to hide and then escape, but he fell down and all his limbs were broken and he died a bitter death. All who heard about it gave praise to Christ.

16. On the Friday after the Ascension, while I was conversing with him during the night as usual, we called to mind Rabban Philon the anchorite who used to reside on the Black Island. I said to the Elder, "Abba, I've been wanting to see this blessed man". "Come, let us go together, you and I". "When, father?" I said. "Now", he replied. So I got up and went to the community and instructed the steward to take care of the affairs of the community, telling him, "I have a journey of some ten days to make". I took bread and a water skin, and went and told the Elder. We set off together, he going ahead and I following. He turned back to look at me and said, "What is it you are carrying?" "Forgive me, father," I replied, "a little bread and water so that when we are in need of them, we can sustain ourselves with them". He said to me with a groan, "May God forgive us all. There is no need for these". So I left them behind in the monastery, in accordance with his wish. Once we had left [p. 503] the monastery he prayed, as was the custom, and began on the psalm "God has arisen…" [Psalm 82:1]. When we had served some ten *marmyatha*[46] I noticed that we are in the middle of mountains encircling us on either side, and on turning my face this way and that to look, I stumbled and fell. He hastened to come and raise me up, taking me by the hand. "Look

[46] Short sections of the Psalter.

in front of you," he said, "so that you don't fall". I stood there in a daze, not knowing where I am. I said to him, "My lord father, by your prayers, I really don't know where I am". "You are under God's protection, my brother", he said. Since I was in a state of amazement at all this, he took me by the hand and guided me. Smilingly as was his custom with me he said, "I thought you knew the way". "It is true, father, I do know the way, but these mountains now, I don't know where they come from! And here they are just twenty parasangs from us!" As we advanced a little, the Elder began praising, glorifying and thanking Christ. I said to him, "What are you seeing, father?" "I am seeing the light of Philon's soul", he said; "its rays [p. 504] extend even as far as here". It had been revealed to him concerning our arrival, and while we were talking as we descended, with the sea below us, I stood still in fear and wonder. Had he not been holding my hand and guiding me, I would not even have been able to walk.

17. As we approached the coast of the island, I heard a voice saying gently "Climb up and sit on top of us, and cross over to us". With these words there emerged from the sea what looked like a large house: it was a crab! He took me by the hand and the two of us climbed up on it. Then it re-entered the sea, carrying us above the water as it swam on the surface until we reached an island, where Abba Philon met us. There were reeds and thorny thickets on the island, such that a person could not walk amidst them. Rabban Philon likewise climbed up and sat with us on the crab until it reached his cave. We entered the cave and having prayed, as was the custom, we greeted one another and sat down. The crab was standing motionless in the same place until Rabban Philon bade it "Be off to your feeding ground". Mar Yawnan said to Abba Philon, "Abba, this creature is very obedient to you!" Mar Philon replied, "Abba Yawnan, the raven was very obedient to you in the wilderness of Piroz Shabur [p. 505] for thirty years, and it also came with you to the monastery of Rabban Thomas!" Then Mar Yawnan got up and made a sign of contrition to Rabban Philon,

saying, "Forgive me, my lord father, for I thought that only Elisha[47] had been entrusted with mysteries such as these".

18. While they conversed in private with one another, I was standing aside, but I was hearing what they were saying. Rabban Philon was questioning him about the holy congregation surrounding Mar Awgen, and how he had travelled about in the east planting monasteries; and how he had gone off on his own in the wilderness of Piroz Shabur – that fearsome and desolate place, the abode of lions, and in the midst of godless Magians. Then little by little he was urging the blessed Mar Yawnan, "Go back to your original place: the brethren, those "strangers" who are there, are in great sorrow, pain and suffering as a result of your departure from them". He, however, was not inclined to do this. I too made a penitential prostration before Rabban Philon and said, "Forgive me, father, don't tell him to go away from us, for he is very advantageous to our monastery. Because of him the faithful Nuʿaym donated a ship's (cargo) which we sold for one thousand three hundred dinars;[48] with that we bought some land and palm trees for the monastery. We are also going to [p. 506] renovate our sanctuary with the rest of the money". Rabban Philon said to me, "you should be aware, my lord abbot, that your monastery is going to diminish, and that of Abba Yawnan will grow". Abba Philon then said to Mar Yawnan, "You should realize, my brother, that if you do not go, they will send Papa your disciple after you with a letter. But I beg you, do not be grieved at the toil of your journey. Because I had asked our Lord to show me one of the brethren belonging to the holy congregation of Mar Awgen, and now I have seen one, and my soul is at ease!"

19. Rabban Mar Yawnan asked from him some blessing from paradise. Mar Philon said to him, "Give me in return the belt around your waist that belonged to Mar Awgen". The holy Mar Yawnan undid his belt, took it off and gave it to him. Abba Philon took it and reverently held it to his eyes. In turn he brought out of

---

[47] The reference to the prophet Elisha here is puzzling; since Yawnan is the speaker, it is clearly not a slip for Elijah.

[48] See 7:8.

his cave a very small staff; he broke it in half and gave it to the blessed Mar Yawnan, saying, "Bury this in the wilderness where you are, or in the foundations of your sanctuary".

20. When it was morning the two of them went into the interior of the island, [p. 507] not coming back to me until the evening. When they turned up we performed the Consecration with what we had with us, and took (communion). For I had taken with me what was requisite for the liturgy of the Mysteries at the instructions of the holy man. Once we had fulfilled this act of love, and it was already three hours into the night, we arose and made a prayer before saying farewell to one another with a holy kiss. That crab came along and we sat down on its back, in this way crossing the sea we arrived back at the monastery. The blessed Mar Yawnan was continually telling me, "After Mar Awgen I have not seen any human being so perfected in love and in humility as this Mar Philon".

21. After a short while the bishop of the region came to the monastery with a number of his clergy. After he had rested a little, he said to me, "I wish to see Rabban Mar Yawnan and receive a blessing from him". So we went to him and entered. The bishop was greatly delighted to see the blessed man, and his soul found rest in his words. While we were sitting in conversation one of the clergy got up and led up an old priest of the church and made him stand in front of us, saying, "Mar Yawnan, tell this ill-fated old man to return the gold and silver church plate that he has stolen". The holy man looked intently at the cleric for a long time, [p. 508] astonished at his audacity; then he said to him, "Wretched son of Gehenna, along with all the wicked things you are doing, you are stripping and despoiling the sanctuary, and as if this was not enough, you are also tormenting this poor old man!". We then took the cleric aside and said to him, partly cajoling and partly using threats with him, "This Elder Mar Yawnan is a man who has visions; confess, wretch, lest some evil meet you". He confessed straight away that he had stolen the church plate and had baselessly implicated the old priest. At that point the bishop got up, broke his staff and threw off his mitre, saying, "Far be it that I should ever again be a judge for the Christian populace, lest all the judgements I have made be like the one I made against this priest". He made a penitential prostration before the priest, and gave him fifty dinars.

He secluded himself in a cell and did not return again to his diocese.

Chapter 8. Concerning the arrival with us of brother Papa, and concerning the signs and wonders that Christ performed at the hands of the holy man in the wilderness of Piroz Shabur, according to what Papa related to me, and how the holy man returned to his original place.

1. After Nisan (April) a monk, a stranger, came to the monastery [p. 509] and was asking the brethren, "Where does the handsome Elder, Abba Yawnan, reside?" The brethren came and informed me, "A stranger has come and is asking about Abba Yawnan, the Elder". I went out to him and said, "Where are you from, my son?" He told me, "I am from the region of Babylon, and I came here, by providence, because of an Elder called Abba Yawnan". I asked him, "Are you Papa?" "I am", he replied, and I brought him to the holy man who peered over the partition and said to Papa, "Welcome, faithful brother!" Rabban Papa prostrated to the holy man and greeted him. The holy man said to him, "My son, give me the letter". At this the man was somewhat relieved, handing it to him. He took it and said to me, "My lord abbot, take this brother with you and rest him". So I took Papa with me to my cell.

2. After he had taken some rest I went on to ask him about the wilderness where they are living, and about the number of the brethren, how many there are. "We are twenty monks there," he told me, "each of us two miles away from his neighbour, but the blessed brethren gathered together and said 'We ought to build cells close to one another, because the populace around us is growing, and they are building (new) villages and towns.' So we came, all of us together, to Mar Yawnan and told him of the idea that had occurred to us on this matter, and he was greatly delighted. Then the brothers [p. 510] urged him, saying, 'Do you, father, build a cell among us for yourself.' But he replied, 'As for me, my brothers, leave me in the place where I am, so that Christ may come and find me in this den.' Thereupon they collectively made a prolonged penitential prostration, beseeching him to become their head and leader. Being constrained by the urging of the brethren, and feeling the strong pressure of their request, he said, 'Allow me to pray.' That night he departed from us and we did not know where he went until an Elder called Rabban Shahdost

told us. Because he saw how afflicted we were in our search for him in the mountains and in wild and distant places, the blessed Elder told us, 'Don't labour over searching for that holy man, my sons, for he is more than three hundred parasangs distant.' We insistently begged him to inform us where he was. Constrained by our begging him, he told us, 'That night that he left us he told me "I am going to the region of Beth Qaṭraye, to the monastery of Rabban Thomas"' At once they wrote this letter that is with me and sent me off saying, 'We have faith in Christ our hope and source of confidence that on reading this letter he will speedily effect his return to us.' Having prayed over me, they let me go, amid many a grieving tear". [p. 511]

3. "I went into the town of Piroz Shabur, asking and making enquiry whether there might be some people going to the regions of the Qaṭraye. My thoughts weighed heavily on me: what should I do, where should I go? As it were through divine grace I approached a metal-worker who was seated in a street, and with the metal-worker was sitting a merchant from the region of Beth Qaṭraye, selling him pearls. My thoughts urged me to go up and ask him. 'Where are you from, sir,' I said. He replied, 'I am from the region of Beth Qaṭraye, and I am very much wanting to travel there this very night.' I said to him, 'Please do me a favour and take me with you, for I want to go to the monastery of Rabban Thomas.' The man nodded his head in assent with the words, 'Mighty is the god who belongs to the Christians in the monastery of Rabban Thomas.' 'Come with us,' he said, 'since our encampment is close to the monastery of your god Rabban Thomas.' He mounted me on a camel and provided me with plentiful food on the journey here".

4. Then I, Zadoy, made a prostration to him and said, "My lord brother, I would like you to tell me what signs and wonders you have seen from this holy man". He replied, "My lord abbot, it is five years since I was (first) with these Elders, [p. 512] and I have heard them say that a youth from the town of Piroz Shabur was passing through, with his mother, the forest where this holy man was, and a lion leapt out and seized him, dragging him into the forest. The mother of the youth gave a wail and was weeping loudly. Hearing her voice, the blessed man left his hut in haste, and when he saw her wailing and weeping, he asked her, 'What is the

cause of all this lamentation of yours?' She replied, 'It's my son who was with me: a lion leapt out and grabbed him, taking him into the forest. I beg you, go in after him and see if it has killed him or not.' Feeling great suffering as a result of the woman's wails, he made the sign of the cross over himself and quickly entered in after the lion. He saw the youth lacerated and sprawled out in front of the lion. On seeing him his wretched mother began tearing her hair and ripping her clothes as she fell on the corpse of her son. The Elder likewise was weeping with great feeling. He said to the woman, 'Don't be afraid; I have hope in our Lord Jesus Christ that he will return him to life.' They carried him from there, and he brought him to his hut. Having made a prayer over him, he brought him back to life by the power of Christ, and handed him over to his mother. As a result of the woman's [p. 513] proclaiming this in the town of Piroz Shabur and in its villages round about, a large number of Magians congregated to the holy man from all over the place. He employed words of instruction and divine admonition with them, and because of the healings and mighty miracles that he performed in their presence, they turned away from the error by which they were held, and came to the teaching of Salvation, receiving the mark of baptism from the blessed man. He instructed many people from among them".

5. "There was a Marzban[49] there in Piroz Shabur who like us, and even more than us, was distressed at the holy man's departure from us. His son went out with his servants on a hunt, and as they were passing in the vicinity of that forest, he caught sight of the blessed man; mocking and jeering at him, he took an arrow and shot it at him, but at that moment, through divine action, the angel of death struck him and he fell down dead. When his servants came and saw that he had died all of a sudden, and not knowing the cause of his death, they made a great lamentation. When the holy man saw how he had collapsed and heard the servants' lamentations – at the same time being aware of what was about to take place – he left his hut and said to the servants, [p. 514] 'What is all this lamentation?' They told him, 'This man, the son of our

[49] A high-ranking Persian official (governor).

master, got separated a little from us just now, and we don't know what happened to him, and how he died all of a sudden.' The holy man approached the youth and felt him. 'Don't be afraid,' he told them, 'there is still life in him.' He took him by the hand and raised him up. When the youth, and likewise the servants, went and related to the Marzban, his father, all that had taken place, the Marzban set off and came, with his household and his relations, to the holy man. Having admonished them over many matters, he taught them the way of the fear of God, and they believed and all of them were baptized by the blessed man in that holy wilderness".

6. "All this is what I have heard from the fathers; what I myself have seen is the following".

7. "An afflicted stranger used to come to us and bring some water from the Euphrates for the brethren, distributing it amongst us all. As was his custom, he went off one night to fill water in the leather container he had with him, and he was bitten in the foot by a snake. The poor man was greatly tormented with pain, and we were lamenting with him over his distress. We went off and told the holy Mar Yawnan about the case of that stranger, and he came along to see him; he then sealed [p. 515] the place with the sign of the cross and thus healed him. The same night the man took his leather container and set off to bring water as was his custom".

8. "The fathers used to say that when they were travelling by night to the holy man's hut, in order to be assisted by his prayers on occasions when they were faced with certain temptations and vexations caused by demons, they used to see many lions around the hut of the holy Mar Yawnan, but they caused no harm to any of those who went to him".

9. "Again they said, 'When we were sitting with him one night, a lion came to him, having been struck many times with swords by some huntsmen. It started roaring in front of the blessed man by way of complaint. He then got up and took some dust from the ground, sealed it with the sign of the cross, and scattered it over its wounds. It then went off healed'".

10. "I regularly used to go to see my teacher, the holy Abba Barhabdbeshabba, the disciple of Rabban ʿAbdishoʿ who converted the martyr Mar Qardag,[50] and I described the splendid deeds of Rabban Mar Yawnan. After I had related the signs at his hands that I had seen and had heard from the fathers, he said to me, 'The blessed Mar Yohannan,[51] our bishop of pious memory, told me that the brother who entered the flaming fire in the presence of the Shah Shabur [p. 516] at the bidding of the blessed Mar Awgen was this same Rabban Mar Yawnan'".

11. "Since the holy man had not told me this, and I had not heard it either from others, I said to the brother Papa, 'Tell me how this happened'". He said, "When Shabur the Persian Shah came to Nisibis and made peace with the victorious emperor Jovian,[52] through the mediation of Jovian the fierce persecution which Shabur had stirred up against the entire Church of God ceased, and all the Christians went about openly in the faith of Christ. The shah Shabur heard about Mar Awgen and the miracles that were performed at his hands, and he wanted to see him, his purpose being that Mar Awgen might heal his son who was being severely persecuted by a demon.[53] Accordingly he sent some Christians to fetch him, bidding them bring him along with honour. So the blessed Mar Awgen came with the brethren to the court of Shabur. When he saw Mar Awgen as he entered along with the blessed men with him, he beheld a glorious radiance spread over them. He received them with great honour and listened kindly to what they had to say. The accursed Magians, however, were smitten with jealousy and began to stir up an argument with the holy Mar

---

[50] For ʿAbdishoʿ and Qardag, see the *History* of Mar Qardag, *AMS* II, pp. 442–507, with translation in J.T. Walker, *The Legend of Mar Qardagh* (Berkeley, 2006), pp. 19–69; no mention, however, of Barhadbeshabba is to be found there.

[51] Not known from elsewhere; for a different identification, see note 55, below.

[52] See 4:6–7. It was, of course, Shabur and not Jovian, who was "victorious" here!

[53] Cf. Life of Awgen, *AMS* III, pp. 465, 468.

Awgen.[54] When they were badly defeated by him, [p. 517] in order to stop his flow of words, they decided to make accusations against him. The blessed Mar Awgen responded by saying to Shabur, 'My lord the Shah, let your majesty give the order to prepare a vast conflagration in your presence,[55] and then we and the Magians who are disputing with us will enter into its midst, and whichever of us remains in it without getting burnt up, you shall know that the true God is his.' This pleased Shabur and his army. He gave the orders straight away and they brought along wood and made a great conflagration. The holy Mar Awgen said to the Magians, 'You enter first and stand in the midst of these flames; because you are friends of Fire and its worshippers, it will not harm you.' When they did not want even to hear of such a thing, Mar Awgen said to this blessed Mar Yawnan, 'Brother, get up and go up into the flames of this conflagration.'[56] The blessed man, wanting to cause the shah even greater amazement and in order to put the Magians to shame took off his sandals which he was wearing on his feet, put aside his cloak, and leapt into the midst of the fire and sat down there, with the flames going up all around him and above his head. When Shabur saw how he remained there for a considerable time without being harmed at all by the fierce fire, he was greatly astonished and gave thanks to God. He then told those Magians, 'You too, go up and stand with that *Nasraya*[57] in the flames.' When [p. 518] they argued against this, the shah said to them, 'Wretches, see what you are bringing upon yourselves: I am now going to give orders that you be mutilated limb by limb, and that your homes be plundered' which is what he then did with them.[58] The blessed Mar Awgen told this holy man, 'Leave and go off, my son; may the God of

---

[54] Very similar wording in Life of Awgen, *AMS* III, p. 466.

[55] Cf. Life of Awgen, *AMS* III, p. 467.

[56] In the Life of Awgen, *AMS* III, p. 467, the brother is not named; a marginal note in one manuscript, however, identifies him as "Mushe of Telbaqre".

[57] The standard term used for Christians by the Sasanian authorities in the various Persian Martyr Acts.

[58] This punishment, based on Daniel 2:5, 3:29, does not feature in the Life of Awgen.

your father bless you.' Shabur, along with all his nobles and magnates, were astonished when not even the smell of the smoke from the fire was in his hair or on his garment".

12. "This, my lord abbot, is the whole story about him".

13. The next morning the holy man entered the sanctuary and prayed for the brethren and consoled them, departing with Rabban Papa to go to the region of Piroz Shabur. He left us with a mixture of sorrow and joy: sorrow, because we were deprived of his conversation, and joy, because of the hope and encouragement that we had gained through the signs and miracles that we had seen performed at his hands.

Chapter 9. About the arrival of the holy man to the wilderness of Piroz Shabur, and how he was received by the brethren, and what he spoke with them; and about his departure from this life.

1. When the blessed Mar Yawnan reached the wilderness of Piroz Shabur – as we have learnt from some trusty people – those brothers, [p. 519] the "strangers", were filled with immense joy: they all assembled together to go out to meet the holy man. They received him with censers and candles, and with songs of praise and canticles of the Holy Spirit, giving thanks and praise to God, in gratitude for what he had done for them with the arrival of their spiritual father. When they met him they prostrated themselves before him and greeted him, saying, "Why did you leave us, father? Why did you leave your children? Our souls almost expired yearning for you. What mountains of Beth Aramaye[59] were left unsearched? What hills, wildernesses and awesome deserts did we not track out after you? Sorrow never left our hearts and tears never ceased from our eyes, until God had pity on us through the agency of the blessed Elder Mar Shahdost, who saw our distress, affliction, torment and labours, and had pity on us, telling us, 'Do not tire yourselves out: he is not in Beth Aramaye; but by tracking him down you will find him.' We begged him with much

[59] The region to the east of Anbar, and to the north west of Beth Huzaye.

supplication and urging, and eventually he revealed to us that you were in Beth Qaṭraye, in the monastery of Rabban Thomas. Accordingly, without any delay we wrote a letter and sent it at the hands of our dear brother Mar Papa. Out of his virtue and great love he took it upon himself to go all this long [p. 520] journey, doing so gladly. We were begging our Lord that the moment you read our letter, without any delay or putting it off, you would come back to your poor children. And now, father, we are your servants and disciples, obedient to your authority, and subject to your fatherhood".

2. They led him off from where they had met him and conducted him to his hut with songs of praise and the psalms of the Holy Spirit, escorting him and honouring him like a bridegroom on the way to his bridal chamber.

3. When the blessed man entered his cave, he prayed and then came out and spoke to them, "If you keep my words, my brothers, and listen to my feeble self, you should be in a state of joy all your days. As for me, I will be at rest, but if you are wanting something else, I have the possibility of running away from you once again". They replied, "Give the order, father, and all that you order, and are at rest with, we will observe and carry out". The blessed man told them, "I want you to leave me in this hut, without any of you troubling me in any way, trying to make me leave it. In the case of any communal or personal matter, that is, of your community as a whole, and of each one of you individually, you shall come [p. 521] to me and inform me of it, speaking freely, for I will beseech God, being confident in him despite my being feeble, and he, in his grace, will reply to your requests and supplications, effecting with you whatever is of assistance to you and pleasing to his good will". They consented to his counsel and were filled with great joy, conversing with him in spiritual converse the entire day.

4. That Marzban whose son he had revived turned up with his relations and neighbours, a vast crowd. The blessed man rejoiced greatly at them and at their great faith. Then the blessed man dismissed them with a kiss. He told the brethren to be sure to gather together, all of them, every Sunday at the time of the Mysteries in the place specially set aside for this, and to consecrate the Offering, taking delight in the holy and life-giving Mysteries.

The blessed man himself also used to gather with them at the time of the life-giving Mysteries on Sundays and Feasts. The blessed man would continually tell them and us too, when he was here, that everyone who does not neglect the liturgy of the life-giving Mysteries, and who partakes of the holy Body and saving Blood of our Lord Jesus Christ, this person's soul is made pure and luminous, but those who neglect and set aside the liturgy of the Mysteries, and who do not receive the Body and saving Blood that gives life to all, their soul becomes dark and clouded over. [p. 522]

5. After he had remained in that wilderness for some ten years, more or less, and realized that the day of his departure was at hand, he sent for his friend the Marzban, and he came. Now this Marzban used to beg him, after he had raised his son, and both he and his household had been baptized, that the blessed man should make some request of him. Since he was continually begging him in this way, the blessed man told him, "I am intending to request a certain matter of you whereby the memory of me and the memory of you may be preserved for ever". When the Marzban said to him on many occasions "When is the time coming that you will make the request to me about this matter?" the holy man would reply, "It has not yet arrived". But when he came on that final day, the holy man said to him, "Because you put me under compulsion with your asking, I will request of you that matter concerning which I promised you. For this very night I am going to depart from this life. Therefore I request that you build a monastery in this place where I have settled, having in it an altar and chancel, so that the name of God may be perpetually praised there". The Marzban joyfully accepted to do this. [p. 523]

6 When he came the next morning he found the blessed man having taken his rest from this life at the time that the blessed man had told him. He sent at once to Piroz Shabur for a new clay coffin and its cover, and they brought it along for the holy man to be laid in. All the brethren assembled, together with the Marzban and his son and his neighbours, along with a multitude of people who had been brought to the household of Christ through the agency of the holy man. They buried him with great honour, with songs of the Holy Spirit and with canticles. They placed him in his coffin in that holy hut of his, from which he had departed to our Lord.

7. Three days later, the Marzban sent for and gathered a considerable number of workmen and builders from Piroz Shabur and the villages round about. He himself came along there, and gave orders for some of the forest to be cut down and a clearing made in that location, so that there might be ample space for the church and for the community. Once he had built and adorned the church, he instructed the bishop to consecrate it.

8. Every year on the day of his departure – which was the Sunday following New Sunday[60] – the bishop would regularly come with his clergy, along with many of the faithful from all over the place, [p. 524] and they made a great feast, keeping vigil all night with songs of the Holy Spirit, and celebrating the holy Mysteries, taking delight in the Body and life-giving Blood, and all the afflicted who took refuge in his prayers received benefits and healings from the coffin just as in his lifetime he had accorded assistance to everyone who was obedient to what he said.

9. These are the things that Providence provided for the holy man after his departure from us, and his arrival in the wilderness of Piroz Shabur, up to his death. The things done by the Marzban after his death, with the building of the church and its consecration, and the annual feast that was instituted, are what we have received from trustworthy people who have turned up with us. We have noted them down without adding or subtracting anything.

10. This, then, in brief is the history of the godly man of holy memory, whose commemoration is resplendent, namely our glorious and holy father Rabban Mar Yawnan the anchorite: may his memory be a source of blessing, and may his prayers be for the entire world, amen.

11. Taking refuge in his prayers, we supplicate at the same time Christ our Lord, that he hold us, his spiritual children, worthy to aim for his goal and to travel in his footsteps, along with all those who come in faith to his holy hut and take refuge in our Lord and in his prayers; may he grant them joy and happiness at the

---

[60] New Sunday is the Sunday after Easter.

answering [p. 525] of their requests; may he heal their illnesses and restore to health their sicknesses, providing them from the holy shrine the provisions of assistance and salvation; may he prosper them in all worldly prosperity, and protect them from all that causes grief; and from the mouths of us all may we raise up glory to the Father and to his Son Jesus Christ and to the Holy Spirit, now and always and for eternal ages, amen.

INDEX OF NAMES

Abdishoʿ	8:10
Athanasius	1:6
Awgen	3:6–7; 4:1–7; 5:1, 4; 6:2; 7:18–20; 8:11
Babylon	8:1
Barhadbeshabba	8:10
Beth Aramaye	9:1
Beth Parsaye	4:2
Beth Qaṭraye	8:2–3; 9:1
Black Island	6:1; 7:16
Cana	7:14
China	7:8
Cyprus	2:1–2; 3:2, 4
DBWKTY	7:1
Edessa	4:4
Egypt	3:7
Elisha	7:17
Epiphanius	3:2
Euphrates	8:7
Ioannis	3:2, 6; 4:3
Izla	4:5
Jew	7:15
Jovian	4:6; 8:11
Khosro	7:12
Magians	4:7; 8:4, 11
Maron	7:6
Mʿarre	4:5
Marzban	8:5; 9:4–7, 9
Miles	4:4–5
Milon	7:9
Moshe	7:14
Nasraya	8:11

Nisibis 4:5–6; 8:11
Nu'aym 7:6–8, 13, 18
Pachomius 4:1–2
Papa 8:1, 11, 13; 9:1
Persians 4:6
Philon 5:6; 6:2; 7:16–20
Piroz Shabur 1:2; 5:2; 7:17–18; 8:3–5, 13; 9:1, 6–7, 9
Qardag 8:10
Qaṭraye 7:15; 8:3
Rome 2:1
Shabur 4:6–7; 8:10–11
Shahdost 8:2; 9:1
Tappa 5:5; 6:1
Thomas, monastery of 6:1; 7:17; 8:2–3; 9:1
Upper Region 7:13
Yawnan 1:1, 3–4, 6–7; 2:1; 3:6–7; 4:1–4, 6; 5:2; 6:1; 7:1–2, 9–15, 17–21; 8:1–2; 7–8, 10–11; 9:1, 10
Yawsep 4:7
Yohannan, bp. 8:10
Zadoy 8:4
Zarqon 7:9

ISHOʿYAHB III OF ADIABENE'S LETTERS TO THE QATARIS

MARIO KOZAH
AMERICAN UNIVERSITY OF BEIRUT

INTRODUCTION

Ishoʿyahb III of Adiabene (d. 659) was Patriarch of the Church of the East from 649 to 659. He was the son of Bastomag of Kuplana (on the Greater Zab river) in Adiabene, a wealthy and prominent landowner. Ishoʿyahb became a monk in the nearby monastery of Beth ʿAbe, then pursued his education at the School of Nisibis, and was appointed bishop of Nineveh in c. 627. Approximately ten years after this appointment he was raised to metropolitan of Arbela, then in 649 he was elevated to become Catholicos. During his patriarchate Ishoʿyahb III undertook important liturgical reforms and wrote a number of tracts, sermons, and hymns in addition to a *Life of Ishoʿsabran.* It is, however, his extensive collection of 106 letters which are today the subject of greatest scholarly attention since they provide a very valuable glimpse into the life of the Church of the East during a critical period in its history and of the Middle East with the rise of Islam. These letters are divided into three groups in the manuscripts: 52 letters written while he was bishop of Nineveh, 32 letters written during the time he was metropolitan of Arbela, and 22 belong to the time he held the office of Catholicos.

It is during this final period of his life that Ishoʿyahb III wrote five letters (letters 17–21) to the Christian inhabitants, monks and bishops of Beth Qaṭraye. These five letters reveal a great deal of toponymic, historical and ecclesiastical information about the Beth Qaṭraye region where the local church ended up in dispute with the Catholicos. Ishoʿyahb III's letters to its members fully describe the details of this dispute. It would seem that the Syriac community in Beth Qaṭraye were behaving independently of the authorities in Fars and Seleuca-Ctesiphon to his dismay. The Catholicos also complains in these letters about the fact that many members of the church were resorting to non-Christian courts to settle disputes. Expressing his fears for the future of the church in Beth Qaṭraye he refers on a number of occasions to the Christians in neighbouring Mazun (Oman) who had converted to Islam in order to avoid paying the poll-tax. In terms of toponymic information these five letters mention Beth Qaṭraye on numerous occasions in addition to many other place names of specific locations within the Gulf region.

These five letters, published and fully translated here for the first time, thus represent an invaluable primary source for the study of the Church of the East within this region and early Christian interaction with a nascent Islam in the Arabian peninsula.

A NOTE ON THE MANUSCRIPTS

This edition is based on the two extant manuscripts (Vat. sir. 157 and Paris BnF syr. 336) that contain the letters of Ishoʿyahb III. The more important of the two is Vat. sir. 157, an 8° vellum codex containing 123 folios and dated to the tenth century.[1] This was formerly ms. 16 of the Scandar Collection, brought from the East by the Maronite Andrew Scandar (professor of Arabic at Rome's Sapienza) for Pope Innocent XIII (1721–24). The collection is divided into three groups: a. those from the time that Ishoʿyahb was bishop of Nineveh (fol. 1a–46a); b. those written when he was metropolitan of Arbela (fol. 46a–94b); c. those written when he was Catholicos of the Church of the East (fol. 94b–124b).

Paris BnF syr. 336 is a codex containing 181 folios and dated 27 May 1896. The name of the copyist is Peṭros bar Yawsep bar Yuḥanon bar Esṭefanos bar Abraham of Bet Gangi who states in the colophon that he completed this work in the village of Telkef. It is a copy of a manuscript from Alqosh dated 1696.

[1] I am very grateful to Dr. Kristian S. Heal for generously providing me with a copy of this manuscript.

TRANSLATION

Letter 17: To the Bishops of Qatar

It is written in the Gospel that our Lord said to those who at that time were ordained[2] to hear the word: "I have come that they may have life and that they may have it more fully".[3] Indeed he calls life knowing[4] the truth, as he explained when he said: "This then is eternal life: that they may know that you are the only God and the one whom you sent, Jesus Christ".[5] By "that … more fully" he indicates the grace of the Spirit which they would receive, both those who underwent baptism in his name, and those who had imbibed[6] the gift of his honour in this Church of his which is on earth and in that which is in heaven. Indeed, I wrote something similar to this to you a little earlier[7] and invited you to come to me, so that you might receive not only the strength and confirmation[8] from the Church of God like that "life" which was mentioned, but also that you might obtain a yet fuller unhoped for honour, similar to the "that…more fully" which was spoken of by our Lord.

You, however, like those to whom this word was spoken to before,[9] have determined that you yourselves are worthy neither of the exalted honour similar to the "that … more fully", nor of the communion with God, similar to the "life" which was mentioned. You have hindered yourselves from coming to the Church of God and have set off with thoughtless haste[10] towards the leader of your rebellion[11] and you have with unintelligent madness written and sealed the rebellion against God. Furthermore, you have also brought the book of your rebellion to the door of the temporal

---

[2] ܣܡܝܟܝܢ ܗܘܘ
[3] John 10:10.
[4] ܝܕܥܬܐ
[5] John 17:3.
[6] ܡܫܬܠܡܝܢ
[7] ܩܕܝܡ ܩܠܝܠ
[8] ܫܘܡܠܝܐ
[9] ܡܢ ܩܕܝܡ
[10] ܒܣܠܩܬܐ ܕܠܐ ܒܘܝܢ
[11] ܪܫ ܡܪܕܐ ܕܝܠܟܘܢ

rulers,[12] and have already done enough to cut off all hope of a life in the Church.

God's Church, therefore, that is to say, this holy synod, which is gathered at this time in the city of the Catholicos' see, has now done to you what you yourselves had already done to yourselves, namely, removing you from the honour and rank[13] through which you have become renowned. For it is right that those who have cut themselves off from the supreme source[14] of priestly life flowing from heaven, and considered that the mere empty title of priesthood is enough for them, conferring it on one another,[15] should be completely deprived of that empty title, that they may not become the cause of empty error for Christians[16] straying through ignorance.

However, I who have often experienced that the dead can also be recalled to life by God,[17] have delayed the punishment[18] against you a little,[19] until I have sent and visited you through this letter, and if it is that your death has not approached the corruption of ruin[20] from true hope as was said of Lazarus by his sister,[21] the power of our Lord perhaps might call you back, like him, and you might return to life in the Church, just as he (came back to life).[22] But if it is not so, rather there is no hope for you concerning your death from the Church of God, we shall mourn you just as we mourned for your friends the Mazunaye.[23] Therefore, let us know

---

12 ܡܕܒܪ̈ܢܝܬܐ ܕܪܕܝܐ

13 ܐܝܩܪܐ ܘܕܪܓܐ

14 ܪܫ ܢܒܥܐ

15 ܠܚ̈ܕܕܐ

16 ܠܡܫܝܚ̈ܝܐ

17 Hebrews 11:19.

18 ܡܦܣܩ ܕܝܢܐ

19 ܩܠܝܠܐ ܡܟܝܠ

20 ܠܚܒܠܐ ܕܐܒܕܢܐ

21 John 9:39.

22 ܒܩܝܡܬܗ ܕܗܘ

23 ܡܙܘܢ̈ܝܐ. Very probably the inhabitants of Mazun (Oman) is meant; in Syriac texts Maron and Mazon are often confused.

your situation[24] as soon as possible, not just with simple letters, as (you have done) thus far, but with a true demonstration of action and the Lord through his grace will help you to do what is appropriate for your salvation,[25] and be strong.[26]

Letter 18: To the People of Qatar

The love of Christ our Lord, my dear brothers, which is for us the soul of everlasting life in the holy Church and all its earthly wisdom[27] and the bond joining all distant peoples in a spiritual community[28] and the eternal light on the souls of all true believers, urges us, with a communal grief plainly stirred by the fear of God, to turn to you with the love of a spiritual father and to attend to you according to the spiritual law[29] in these things which the spiritual law teaches us to do. Since, even more than rule and custom require, we desire to show the greatest love towards you, we desire to greet you from far away through a letter of salutation, I mean through your bishops,[30] as ecclesiastical law requires. We have made known to them that we are prepared to grant them and you not only our greatest love but also the highest ecclesiastical honour,[31] in this time when you sorely need the excelling power of God's aid for fortifying your faith with a strong wall, with the time requiring this, so that no damage might perhaps occur to the glory of your faith in our Lord which occurred to the distant peoples (who live) beyond you.[32]

However, since in (my) God-fearing mind I had clearly suffered as a man on whom the care[33] of spiritual fatherhood has been laid with the name which means "almighty in the Church of

---

24 ܐܝܟܢܝܘܬܟܘܢ

25 ܠܚܝܝܟܘܢ

26 ܘܗܘܘ ܚܠܝܡܝܢ

27 ܣܘܦܝ̈ܗ̇ ܕܐܬܟܠܐ

28 ܒܐܘܡܬܐ ܪܘܚܢܝܬܐ

29 ܢܡܘܣܐ ܪܘܚܢܐ

30 ܒܐܦܝܣܩܘܦ̈ܝܟܘܢ

31 ܐܝܩܪܐ ܥܕܬܢܐ

32 I.e., the Mazunaye.

33 ܪܥܬܐ

God", I learnt correctly from an evil cause which occurred a little before that this sickness of little faith had occurred in the peoples (living) beyond you and perhaps amongst you as well. I wanted, just like a learned[34] doctor, to carefully cure the natural cause itself of the sickness with the power of our Lord's help, which indeed was (the same as) now.[35] I mean that neither from the ecclesiastical tradition nor from the supreme source of life of the priestly power does the laying on of hands of priesthood come to you legitimately[36] according to ecclesiastical law, but your bishops confer it upon one another mutually, as do the heretics who are outside of the Church, those who apply to themselves the title of the episcopate, but are deprived of the power of the name.[37] And for that reason not even a likeness of the power is found among them, neither in the holy (monastic) way of life[38] which is an image of the life after the resurrection nor in the divine working of miracles, which are usually performed by the saints of our Lord for the healing of the sick and the casting out of evil spirits. For since in the evil fashion of the foul heretics, the bishops of Fars[39] and your own bishops have cut themselves off from the Church of God, they have rendered the faith of Christians among them without example of faith, which makes itself known by the holy (monastic) way of life and the working of divine miracles.

But because there was no faith in the Christians of the kind that it ought to be, in the smallest breath of the southern heat[40] it was pitifully burned up and abandoned for eternal perdition, as long as no family of Christians[41] there offered the customary sacrifices in the blood of witness[42] to God who is over all;[43] and

---

34 ܣܟܘܠܝܐ

35 ܐܝܟܢܘ ܗܫܐ

36 ܢܡܘܣܐܝܬ

37 ܚܝܠܗ ܕܫܡܐ

38 ܕܘܒܪܐ ܕܩܕܝܫܘܬܐ

39 ܐܦܝܣܩܘܦܐ ܦܪܣܝܐ

40 ܫܘܒܐ ܬܝܡܢܝܐ

41 ܫܪܒܐ ܕܟܪܣܛܝܢܐ

42 ܒܕܡܐ ܣܗܕܝܐ

43 ܠܐܠܗܐ ܕܥܠ ܟܠ

only two burnt-out[44] firebrands[45] out of the thousands and tens of thousands of our Lord's, with the empty name of the office of bishop[46] (remaining), who now are the material of a wicked memorial[47] for mourning in the Church of God, in the likeness of the statue of salt into which was turned the wife of Lot, as a memorial of the burning of Sodom.

But if however, the priestly title and honour had flowed from the ecclesiastic and canonical imposition of hands for the Persians and those who obey the Persians, then with the title itself would have flowed as well the priestly power.[48] And if in this said region[49] the faithful people had been sanctified once again by priestly power, the faith in the south of the world[50] would not have perished in this sudden and total end. For either some people would have preserved the profession of their faith unchanged with unyielding firmness, as those who, as I might say, buried it undamaged in the caverns of the earth[51] until such time as the fear had been diminished; or in the blood of holy martyrs, they would have consecrated their faith to the Lord, in a praiseworthy end worthy of the glory of our Lord. For through these outstanding examples was the inheritance of the true faith[52] passed on to us by our spiritual fathers, whose tradition all of us in the holy Church shall keep until the revealing of our Lord from heaven.

But because the bishops of Fars cut themselves off from this tradition, their life has been cut off from the hope of faith, just as at the outset[53] in Mazun.[54] If the Lord had left no remnant in your

---

44 ܐܬܚܡܪܘ

45 Isaiah 7:4: ܬܪܝܢ ܕܘܢܒ̈ܠܐ ܐܘܕ̈ܐ ܡܬܢ̈ܢܐ

46 ܐܦܣܩܘܦܘܬܐ

47 ܥܘܗܕܢܐ ܒܝܫܐ

48 ܚܝܠܐ ܟܗܢܝܐ

49 ܒܦܢܝܬܐ ܗܝ ܕܐܬܐܡܪܬ

50 ܡܢ ܬܝܡܢܗ ܕܥܠܡܐ

51 ܒܡܥܪ̈ܬܗ ܕܐܪܥܐ

52 ܗܝܡܢܘܬܐ ܫܪܝܪܬܐ

53 ܐܝܟ ܫܘܪܝܐ

54 ܡܙܘܢ

region, we would need other tears[55] to assuage the sadness.[56] For desiring to anticipate and remove the peril[57] of the destruction of the faith by the power of spiritual help, I invited the bishops of Fars to a synod of the Church of God for (them) to receive spiritual grace from the treasury of God according to the synodical canon[58] established by our holy fathers in the Holy Spirit. I also summoned your bishops with much love and promise of a higher honour. But they, considering the aid of the Church of God of no value, also reckoning as nothing the honour that arises from the priestly power, nor thinking to pay reverence to Christianity in any way, abandoned the way of life, which (leads) to the Church of God and, on the contrary, hastened along the path of death to the appointed place[59] in Fars, beside the leader of the rebellion,[60] who is against the ecclesiastical laws; and they acted wickedly denying Christianity in a blasphemous book[61] and impious seals, with the result that they defected[62] from communion with the Church of God for eternity. And those are the things which they insanely and foolishly did, more than the devil's own wish. For the devil, their departure[63] from the faith alone was perhaps enough, as to that of the Mazunaye.[64] But the bishops of Fars and of Beth Qaṭraye,[65] eager also about how they could deny Christianity with books of folly and with seals of impiety beyond what the devil wished, wrote, sealed and sent a denial[66] of communion with the Church of God, that is, with Christianity, and presented it sealed, so that the denial of the faith would not only be limited to them, as it was in

55 ܕܡ̈ܥܐ ܐܚܪ̈ܢܝܬܐ

56 ܠܒܘܝܐܐ ܕܚܫܐ

57 ܩܘܕܝܢܘܣ

58 ܢܡܘܣܐ ܣܘܢܘܕܝܩܝܐ

59 ܠܒܝܬ ܘܥܕܐ

60 ܪܫ ܡܪ̈ܕܐ

61 ܒܟܬܒܐ ܡܓܕܦܢܐ

62 ܠܡܬܦܪܩܘ

63 ܫܘܢܝܐ

64 ܡܙ̈ܘܢܝܐ

65 ܒܝܬ ܩܛܪ̈ܝܐ

66 ܟܦܘܪܘܬܐ

the Mazunaye,[67] but also their descendants, if truly they shall have sons who are wicked like them.

But I, unwilling to cut off hope that they might rise up from the death of this wickedness, sent officially two bishops from the Huzaye[68] to those (who live) in Fars and two bishops of the Mayshanoye[69] to your own, with my letters and those of the universal synod; and I instructed them that they should deal with those slayers of their own souls with the struggle of the spirit, until Christ should be formed within them; and, that if they with the hope of resurrection cut off, should have dared to fight against the Church of Christ, they should shake the dust of their feet upon them, as if over the tombs of the lost, and return to us, proclaiming over their tombs their separation from the Church of God in this world[70] and in the world to come. These things we ordered to be done in this way. And those indeed who were sent to the Persians, set off there themselves. But those who were sent to you sent others in their place.[71] But now with what shame and derision[72] and blasphemy from Fars[73] and Beth Qaṭraye[74] they went forth, the priests of God, who had been sent by the Church of God to people who were supposed to be Christians, you have learnt better than we have, if however you were concerned to know.

Since, however, your bishops-in-name were not satisfied with impiety[75] against the Church of God, they presented a public display[76] of their rebellion, which they brought against the supreme authority[77] of the Church of God, to the earthly rulers there and even to the great ruler higher than the rulers of this age; and

---

67 ܡܙܘ̈ܢܝܐ

68 ܗܘ̈ܙܝܐ

69 ܡܝܫ̈ܢܝܐ

70 ܥܠܡܐ

71 ܚܠܦܝܗܘܢ

72 ܒܘܙܚܐ

73 ܒܝܬ ܦܪ̈ܣܝܐ

74 ܒܝܬ ܩܛܪ̈ܝܐ

75 ܪܘܫܥܐ

76 ܡܠܚܘܪ ܒܥܠܡܚܘܝܢܘܬܐ

77 ܪܫܢܘܬܐ

perhaps[78] were despised by the rulers, as befitted their rebellion; and since they themselves do not yet perceive their alienation from the life of God, we are compelled to mourn over them more bitterly than over the Mazunaye;[79] and again by the spiritual law, which requires of us a fatherly concern towards them, we are compelled to protect you from evil communion with those who have acted wickedly and have been cast out of the Church of God, and to join you with us in a unity of soul and a bond of peace, that (you may receive) the inheritance of eternal life through our Lord Jesus Christ, the Ruler of our lives and the Lord of our glory, our God (who is) worshiped.[80]

For this reason, know, beloved brothers, that that punishment which they, the madmen,[81] visited upon themselves in their separation from the Church of God, through an imprudence[82] like that of Judas, has been approved by us all, through a prudence[83] like that of the Apostles and of our Lord himself. For neither was it fitting or possible for us to be more merciful, that is wiser than the holy Apostles or the Lord himself; but rather, by their example, we cast out from the communion of the Church those who like Judas had hung themselves from the communion of the Church of God. And we have confirmed the seal against them, with justice and by the power of the priesthood, (taking from them) the title and honour of the episcopate, whose title they have up till now assumed,[84] and also (withdrawing them) from participation in the sacred mysteries, until we have imposed on them the penance and, recognizing the truth and coming to themselves,[85] they free themselves from the snare of Satan, by which they have been caught to (perform) his will.

78 ܟܒܪ

79 ܡܙܘ̈ܢܝܐ

80 ܐܠܗܢ ܣܓܝܕܐ

81 ܫܢ̈ܝܐ

82 ܠܐ ܒܘܝܢܐ

83 ܒܘܝܢܐ

84 ܡܫܬܡܗܝܢ ܗܘܘ

85 ܢܥܘܪܘܢ ܢܦܫܗܘܢ

Therefore guard, beloved brothers, guard yourselves, holy ones, from communion with those men, so that you may be deemed worthy[86] of the grace of God by whose sacrament you were ordained.[87] If they dare to perform any of the tasks of the priestly ministry after this letter of ours has been read there and they have listened to it, let it be known to you, that what is performed by them is empty of the grace of the Holy Spirit, and that it is committed with temerity and madness, and does not have the power of Christianity. Therefore, guard against the defilement of your faith through the fear of God, and whoever despised the word of our Lord, let wrath from heaven come upon him.

You, however, priests and deacons, fulfill the ecclesiastical ministry[88] with all that is legally just[89] without the communion of those who were called your bishops until a priestly chair is established for you by the Church of God according to the precept and ordinance of the spiritual laws. And you, faithful, in whose hands is placed ancillary authority[90] of the islands[91] and the dwellers of the desert,[92] I mean of Dayrin[93] and Mashmahig[94] and Talon[95] and Hatta[96] and Hagar,[97] strive at this time more than ever to guard your faith and for the legal establishment of the priesthood by which you have been consecrated, more so than for worldly affairs.[98] Make a choice and send to us either those same profane[99] bishops, if you consider them suitable to be trained for

---

86 ܬܫܬܘܘܢ

87 ܪܫܝܡܝܢ ܐܢܬܘܢ

88 ܬܫܡܫܬܐ ܥܕܬܢܝܬܐ

89 ܙܕܩܐ ܢܡܘܣܝܐ

90 ܡܫܠܛܘܬܐ ܡܥܕܪܢܝܬܐ

91 ܓܙܪ̈ܬܐ

92 ܥܡܪ̈ܝ ܡܕܒܪܐ

93 ܕܝܪܝܢ

94 ܡܫܡܗܝܓ

95 ܛܠܘܢ

96 ܚܛܐ

97 ܗܓܪ

98 ܨܒܘ̈ܬܐ ܥܠܡܢ̈ܝܬܐ

99 ܡܛܘ̈ܫܐ

(re)consecration[100] and for the priestly ministry, or others whom you consider more suitable than them for the great work of the lofty service of the Church of God, so that in this way they may be anointed and consecrated and made perfect and sent to you again from the fountainhead[101] of priestly power by the law of Christ.

Watch, and again watch, and watch most greatly, that you may not be seduced in some way by satanic wiles, so that you become the enemy of your lives like those who have strayed. For the enemy of Christians is most cunning and has harmed many people many times. Now indeed the time of his coming is close through the man of sin, the son of perdition;[102] and the book of the Spirit predicted[103] not only the order[104] (of events) signaling his arrival, but also that many shall be led astray, that is, the elect,[105] just as those people of yours have strayed, that is, the bishops-by-name, who, in their madness believing that submission to the Church of God is not a source of spiritual aid for those who are worthy of it, but a harmful and destructive slavery, have renounced it, diabolically, like the demons who rejected slavery to God their creator. They did not know and did not understand, the madmen, that they themselves, as also everyone, were being made slaves, by complete will, of this worldly power that now is master everywhere. Those who are ordered by Christianity to submit to those powers that are ordered by God, only refuse to submit to the authority of Christianity, when they earnestly[106] submit to every authority, excluding Christianity, with body and soul and possessions and in all things, except for submission to Christianity, that is, submission to God, themselves rebelling like the demons. For neither are they, the fools, well-advised[107] concerning the following: that we have been commanded to render to every authority anything owed to it

[100] ܚܘܕܬܐ

[101] ܡܒܘܥܗ ܕܟܠܐ

[102] Reference to 2 Thessalonians 2:3.

[103] ܡܩܕܡ ܐܡܪ̈ reading ܡܩܕܡ ܐܡܪ

[104] ܛܟܣܐ

[105] Reference to Matthew 24:24.

[106] ܚܦܝܛܐܝܬ

[107] ܡܬܒܝܢܝܢ

from us,[108] I mean, the capitation[109] to whom the capitation belongs, the tribute[110] to whom the tribute belongs, fear to whom fear and honour to whom honour belongs. But Christ did not ordain servitude to the law, that is, of each person in his love because he wished that any of our possessions should be given by us to him, but so that he himself might give to us from what is his, namely, the gift of the Spirit, by whom you shall be made strong in order to take up becomingly the adoption of sons[111] and the kingdom of God through priestly power, which flows forth spiritually from our Lord through the successors of the holy Church according to the spiritual tradition,[112] abiding and proceeding unchanged within the Church from age to age,[113] and deprived of his knowledge and power your bishops and those of Fars presented and handed themselves over to the satanic error before the coming of Satan.

Therefore, we warn them that the coming of Satan is already near, and the rebellion which was written about has already arrived, and the man of sin, the son of perdition[114] will shortly reveal himself.[115] And behold I am a mighty preacher for you and an unwavering admonitor, that you should abide firmly in the fear of our Lord and you should be entirely prepared against all error of iniquity that occurs to the perished, who were unwilling to accept the love of truth, by which they might live. Now arise and gird your loins with truth. Put shoes on your feet as preparation for the Gospel of peace.[116] Put on the helmet of salvation. Grasp the sword of the spirit which is the power of God. Take up for yourselves the shield of faith from the treasury of the Lord and from the legal authority, which shares out spiritual gifts justly in

---

108 Reference to Matthew 22:21, Mark 12:14, Luke 11:22.

109 ܟܣܦ ܪܫܐ

110 ܡܕܐܬܐ

111 ܣܝܡܬ ܒܢܝܐ

112 ܫܘܠܐ ܪܘܚܢܐ

113 ܡܢ ܥܠܡ ܘܥܕܡܐ ܠܥܠܡ

114 Reference to 2 Thessalonians 2:3.

115 ܡܬܓܠܐ

116 Reference to Acts 12:7, 8.

which you shall find the power for extinguishing all the flaming arrows of the devil. Behold I am a slave for you and a servant according to the commandment of our Lord,[117] not however a tyrant and a tax-gatherer according to the evil opinion of those who have assumed the title of your bishops and who do not understand that they are only exemplary in their own judgment. Since, through an evil dealing,[118] in the name of the priesthood they are accustomed to tavern keeping,[119] they think that we too hold the authority of the Church of God through evil dealing. And therefore they have both rebelled and acted wickedly with a profane mind foreign to the sublime governance of the ecclesiastical primacy.[120]

If perhaps people from among you should be afflicted by that profane opinion, let them come to us and follow closely our governance. They shall know well our situation[121] and perhaps they will find out, with the Lord helping our weakness, that God is present in the Israel of the spirit and that the spiritual aid from the treasury of the Lord is justly distributed to the whole people of the Lord that is rightly believing. Therefore be strengthened in our Lord and in the strength of his power,[122] my beloved brothers. Guard the concord[123] of the Church of God through the help of God. Receive the priestly grace from the spiritual Holy of Holies which our Lord has fixed in the land of mortals. And become firm in the faith of the truth. Be steadfast in observing the life-giving commands. Make known to us quickly the love of your faith and your firm position in the fear of our Lord, and your situation and your concord with the Church of God, so that when knowing your situation towards our Lord, we may be able to rejoice and give thanks for your sake to our Lord. May he strengthen you and make you zealous so that you may become firm in the love of his faith,

---

[117] Reference to Matthew 20:26–27.

[118] ܒܐܓܘܪܘܬܐ ܒܝܫܬܐ

[119] ܦܠܚܝܢ ܦܘܬܩܘܬܐ

[120] ܪܫܢܘܬܐ ܥܕܬܢܝܬܐ

[121] ܐܡܝܢܘܬܢ

[122] Reference to Ephesians 6:10.

[123] ܫܠܡܘܬܐ

and may excel in the observance of his commands, and that you may do, continually through all the days of your lives, that which is pleasing before him. Amen!

Letter 19: A Second Letter to the People of Qatar[124]

The tale of the evils which have occurred in your region, my beloved brothers, presses us to write to you a second time, since I am very troubled by the fear of other evils which are set to happen[125] in your region. For from the beginning, when I heard that your bishops contrived wickedly, wrote and sealed a document of apostasy[126] from the Church of God, I realized that they were prepared to fall into every evil and would cast down the people of God whose bishops they are called. I anticipated, and I spoke, and I wrote, and I cautioned, but I was not believed and behold now the evil matter is coming to pass with my foreknowledge from the exhortation of the evil chorepiscopi,[127] and if the Lord does not guard the villages of the Qataris,[128] we will mourn once again.

For I heard that Abraham, the (most) excellent, praiseworthy and distinguished of the bishops there, after he gave up hope of the communion of the Church of God, he immediately began to harm God's monks.[129] For the brother monks, who had been consecrated in the monastery[130] of your diocese[131] like a holy offering to God who is above all, who in your region guard an example of heavenly life for the demonstration of Christianity, who were a place of refuge of the oppressed for the region of the Qataris,[132] who were a censer of spiritual incense for the Church of the Qataris for the honour of the glory of our Lord, who indeed

124 ܩܛܪ̈ܝܐ

125 ܕܥܬܝ̈ܕܢ ܠܡܣܬܥܪܘ

126 ܡܣܘܪܘܬܐ

127 ܣܥܘܪ̈ܐ

128 ܩܘܪ̈ܝܐ ܕܩܛܪ̈ܝܐ

129 ܕܝܪ̈ܝܘܗܝ ܕܐܠܗܐ

130 ܥܘܡܪܐ

131 ܬܘܬܒܘܬܐ

132 ܐܬܪܐ ܕܩܛܪ̈ܝܐ

were the secret helpers of the Qatari bishops,[133] through the combat of prayer, for accomplishing their ecclesiastical ministry with the honour of seemliness[134] – these, Abraham, leader of Masmahig,[135] violently disturbed by tyrannical rule. Like a man drunk on impiety, he picked up the holy altar from the sacred place and desecrated it. But because this potent evil was of small value, I mean in his eyes, he continued to do wrong as much as was in his power.[136] He excommunicated and threatened dreadfully all who may have received or helped or given a gift to the monks of our Lord. He cut off as if from himself the hope of Christianity in your region such that the small remainder of God's monks whom he found in your region he shamelessly expelled from your region with unmeasured impudence. And all of you remain quiet.

And here is the wonder. That even if this is love of the monks in your region: that when they are both driven out and harmed and even forced to be displaced from your region you are devoid of grief and feeling and speech and zeal, on account of this nothing prevents you from falling into all evils according to the will of the evil leader, who rules in the town of Masmahig[137] under the name of the episcopacy. Nor is there need for Satan to come to you with the name Antichrist. There has already been done by you whatever Satan wants to be done. If anything is left which has not been done, it is our expectation in Jesus that it will be done just as easily as those things were done. For in as much as that evil servant of satanic works is prospering in this way in your region as he is now, and you not only are not moved by the zeal of God but are perhaps also partakers in the evil, then this evil which is to come upon the world has already come upon the world, that is, upon you before the whole world.

Because of this according to my duty, behold, I address you: take care of your souls and your faith, O Christian people. Open the eyes of your discernment. See the great evil that exists in your

133 ܐܦܝ̈ܣܩܘܦܐ ܩܛܪ̈ܝܐ

134 ܒܐܣܟܡܐ ܕܝܐܐ

135 ܡܫܡܗܝܓ

136 ܠܒܪ ܡܢ ܚܝܠܗ

137 ܒܡܫܡܗܝܓ ܡܕܝܢܬܐ

region. Rouse with fervour the zeal in yourselves against the corruptors of your faith. Open the hands of your love towards the Church of God. Persevere in the truth of the spiritual laws. Never be slack before evil, lest evil conquer you, but be strong in our Lord and in the might of his power, and clothe yourselves in the whole armour of God, so that you can resist the evil one.[138] May the power of our Lord's aid arise in your minds, and may the eyes of your hearts be enlightened, so that you may reach the hope of eternal life with all the monks.[139]

Take the greatest care of and support well the monks of God[140] among you, lest they be moved to depart from your region in this time when you are in the greatest need of the support of the monks of our Lord.[141] Commune with them in spiritual zeal and in the trustworthiness of physical aid, so that you may commune with them according to the word of our Lord in the tents[142] of Light in life immortal and in the good things that do not perish. May then our Lord, the Lord of mercy, render your faith outstanding through zeal for the divine laws, and may he sanctify your lives through a way of living pleasing to his will all the days of your lives, and be strong.

Letter 20: To the Monks[143] of Beth Qaṭraye[144]

O my beloved brothers, our brother the honoured Mar Giurgis,[145] Metropolitan Bishop of Mesene[146] has brought me news of your good countenance on account of the spiritual laws, and I wanted to greet you through this letter of greeting in which I make known to you what you have already begun to do. For you know, O teachers of God, with a just zeal for the truth of God that all his saints from

---

[138] Reference to Ephesians 6:10–11.

[139] ܕܝܪ̈ܝܐ

[140] ܕܝܪ̈ܝܘܗܝ ܕܐܠܗܐ

[141] Allusion to Matthew 24:20.

[142] ܡܛܠ̈ܠܐ

[143] ܝܚܝ̈ܕܝܐ

[144] ܕܒܝܬ ܩܛܪ̈ܝܐ

[145] ܡܪܝ ܓܝܘܪܓܝܣ

[146] ܡܝܫܢ

long ago until now he has elevated and magnified in ecclesiastical glory. Since the types of virtue are many which make people holy both in their body and in their soul, so that they become members of the household[147] of God, yet this (zeal) alone more than all the others is distinctly of God's part[148] and for God. For the other types of virtue gain holiness and familiarity with God only for those who practice them, but the zealous person is the great angel on behalf of truth, who fills the person[149] of God in the struggle against wickedness and iniquity and sin, which are like the demons against God. For the great grace of our good and merciful God has bestowed on us weak human beings this great and wonderful gift, that as spiritual soldiers of the almighty king we might fight against error even to a bloody struggle,[150] when we have the heavenly weapons about which was said: "For the weapons of our combat are not of the flesh, but of the might of God".[151] But what are we to do and how? Perhaps someone may ask. The general of the ranks of spiritual warriors answers and says: "Through Him we bring down fortified citadels,[152] destroying imaginations and every height raising itself against the knowledge of God; and bringing into captivity every intellect to the obedience of Christ, and being ready to exact revenge from those who do not believe,[153] in order that the obedience of those who believe is fulfilled".[154]

For no other virtue does all these (things) except zeal for the truth of God. For from where did Moses[155] the head of the prophets and the most humble begin along the pathway of God except from zeal alone? For he killed the wicked Egyptian and chastised the unjust Israelite. He cast off from himself kingly

---

147 ܒܝ̈ܬܝܐ

148 ܡܢܬܐ

149 ܕܡܠܐ ܦܪܨܘܦܐ

150 ܐܓܘܢܐ ܕܕܡܐ

151 2 Corinthians 10:4.

152 ܚܣ̈ܢܐ ܡܚ̈ܣܢܐ

153 Peshitta 2 Corinthians 10:6 ܘܡܛܝܒܝܢ ܠܡܥܒܕ ܬܒܥܬܐ ܡܢ ܐܝܠܝܢ ܕܠܐ ܡܫܬܡܥܝܢ ܟܕ ܕܬܫܬܡܠܐ ܡܫܬܡܥܢܘܬܟܘܢ ܀

154 2 Corinthians 10:4–6.

155 ܡܘܫܐ

grandeur and walked along the path of prophecy. Again, from where did Samuel[156] begin after Moses, except from a zeal reproving towards the priest of God? From where, again, did Elijah[157] after him begin, except from strong zeal against the king of Israel and from the terrible slaughter of the wicked prophets? And thus all those ancient ones. From where, again, did Peter,[158] head of the apostles, begin in the apostleship, except from the reprobation of the Rabbi priests[159] of Israel and from the death of Anania[160] and Saphira,[161] and from the beating down from top to bottom of Simeon,[162] the deceiver and magician? From where, again, did Paul[163] become worthy of a heavenly calling, take up the power of apostleship from heaven, teach people examples of the kingdom of heaven and plant on earth in the likeness of heavenly things[164] a holy Church among all peoples on earth?[165] Was this not because more than all spiritual people he used a powerful zeal against all those straying in the earth? But because the world of sin was not enough for his zeal for truth, once he also directed the power of his zeal towards the very leaders of the apostles and the pillars of the Church because of their adherence to circumcision.[166] From where, again, did Stephen,[167] the first of the martyrs begin on the way of martyrdom? Was it not from his reproval of the Jews?

Moreover, how did all the successors of the apostles and martyrs establish their martyrdom in the holy Church, and pass it on to us through transformations that are a matter of

---

156 ܫܡܘܐܝܠ

157 ܐܠܝܐ

158 ܦܛܪܘܣ

159 ܪ̈ܒܝ ܟܗ̈ܢܐ = also "usurer priests"?

160 ܚܢܢܝܐ

161 ܫܦܝܪܐ. Acts 4:6; 6:1 ff.

162 ܫܡܥܘܢ

163 ܦܘܠܘܣ

164 ܫܡܝ̈ܢܝܬܐ

165 ܠܟܠܗ ܥܡܡܐ

166 Galatians 2.

167 ܐܣܛܦܢܘܣ

astonishment,[168] unless through a strong zeal for the truth of God? Some, by the blood of martyrs, have been sanctified by deaths of different kinds, and have scorned the lives of this world. And behold they live now for us through the working of divine powers, and among men they are marvelous deities.[169] Others also with exiles of different kinds and sufferings of various sorts have denied the honour[170] of this world: and behold the commemoration of their names exists today in the Church a source of aid for the people of God. For all these, who were martyred in their faith, through nothing other than through zeal for the truth of God took up the honour of this kind from God and became worthy of the gift of eternal life.

Therefore since with this example of spiritual struggles your wisdom was seen in this time of trial, beloved brothers, you manifested a precise likeness through the zeal for truth directed against those who were the opponent of their soul in the region of your dwelling,[171] and cast from themselves the good name and honour of the episcopate which they had as a title. And because they were not able to zealously uphold the truth of God through zeal for the spiritual laws, behold today they are rightly ashamed at your zeal, since the priestly honour from the Church of God has returned to you because of your just zeal for the Church of God. And through you the name and honour of the faith have been protected for the province of your dwelling with a fitting glory.

Because the merciful providence of God which is upon you has led you to all this excellence, such that the glory of your faith is now proclaimed everywhere because of your just zeal for the truth of God, it is just, that behold as has also already been done, for a perpetual prayer and a perpetual blessing to be also made to you from us and from the whole Church of God. May our Lord Jesus Christ, the Lord of glory, our worshiped God and our most merciful King, grant to you according to the abundance of his glory that you may be made strong in power through his spirit and that

---

168 ܒܡܘܬ̈ܢܐ ܕܬܕܡܘܪܬܐ

169 ܐܠܗ̈ܐ ܕܬܕܡܘܪܬܐ

170 ܐܝܩܪܗ ܕܥܠܡܐ

171 ܒܐܬܪܐ ܕܬܘܬܒܘܬܟܘܢ

in your inner person[172] Christ may dwell through faith and in your hearts through love, when your root and your foundation may become strong, that you may be able to understand with all the saints, what the height and the depth and the length and the breadth are like,[173] and that you may grow in the knowledge of the glory of Christ, and be filled with all the fullness of God. "But to Him who is able with power more than all to do for us more than what we ask and conceive according to His power which is at work in us: to Him be glory in His church, in Jesus Christ, in all ages, for ever and ever, amen".[174]

Read carefully the common letter which I wrote to all the clerics[175] and the faithful of your region, before the whole assembly of clerics and faithful, and show them the way of truth and the ecclesiastical law. Similarly too the synodal letter which was written to you and your bishops before, and also the one [written] on account of Simon of Rev Ardashir. For I sent copies with my seal. I also sent a copy of the letter which I wrote before to Simon who is called bishop of Rev Ardashir, so that when you have read it, you may understand that from my good advice to him, and from the exhortation to the worship of God, exhorting him that he should at this time do what aids his soul and all the Church of God. He took the contrary chance[176] to reject Christianity. And he also apostatized, along with himself, your own contemptible bishops. I also sent a copy of the other letter which I wrote to him after this first one, so that you may also because of these know all the more what it is right for you to do. Therefore accomplish everything with diligence, wisdom and fear of our Lord, in the manner that I wrote in the letter to the community of you all. Write and carefully let me know everything you are doing. May our Lord strengthen you and urge you to do what is good before him at all times all the days of your life, and be strong.[177]

---

172 ܕܒܒܪܢܫܟܘܢ ܕܠܓܘ

173 Cf. Ephesians 1:2.

174 Ephesians 3:20–21.

175 ܩܠܪ̈ܝܩܐ

176 ܥܠܬܐ ܗܦܟܐ

177 ܘܗܘܘ ܚܠܝܡܝܢ

Letter 21: Likewise to the Monks of Beth Qaṭraye

It is written in the holy Gospel[178] that the life-giving mouth of our Lord said: that everything surely can happen for him who believes, that is, even those things which by their nature cannot happen. From the contrary side, by a comparative antithesis[179] it is established that also nothing can happen for him who does not believe, from all those things which by their nature can happen. Indeed because the foolish people of the Persians and the Qataris[180] had beforehand wickedly fallen ill under the sickness of unbelief, nothing can happen from them and to them[181] of all those things which happen to the people of God everywhere.

The perfect faith of Christians is confirmed through two proofs:[182] namely, through a holy life and through the divine miracles which are performed through them. And more, then, than through these two, through this: that they gain the life of their faith by the death of their selves. They, then, do these three things wonderfully because they have received beforehand the strength of the Holy Spirit from sacramental baptism. Indeed, the Spirit itself is given rightly and justly from the priestly power which is given to the holy Church of God through the imposition of hands and the apostolic tradition, which flowed canonically into the holy Church of Christ our Lord.

Because the foolish people of the Persians and the Qataris have cut themselves off from this tradition, behold they are completely deprived of all those glorious deeds of Christians, and are mindlessly[183] concerned with denying communion with the holy Church of Christ our Lord, more than the demons. They despise in their sight both the chaste habit[184] and the venerable title, which you are in and by which you are honoured, that is, of monks. They

---

178 Matthew 21:22.

179 ܒܦܘܚܡܐ ܣܘܩܒܠܐ

180 ܕܦܪ̈ܣܝܐ ܘܩܛܪ̈ܝܐ

181 ܡܢܗܘܢ ܘܠܘܬܗܘܢ

182 ܠܬܪ̈ܬܝܢ ܠܡܚ̈ܘܝܬܐ

183 ܣܟܠܐܝܬ

184 ܐܣܟܡܐ ܢܟܦܐ

have expelled you from their country[185] as if strangers from their faith, and have banished you from their communion as if outcasts; neither was their temerity shamed from your habit and your title; nor did the faith, that is your virtue, overcome their madness by the strength of an admirable action, not by your zeal for the truth, nor too by a sign of the help of our Lord which is justly suited to those who believe rightly.

Perhaps someone will ask: Why all these things, if not on account of the weakness of your faith? Perhaps someone will ask. Why is your faith weak, if not because of a weak priesthood from which the power of faith proceeds? Perhaps someone will ask: Why again is your priesthood weak, if not because the priestly power does not flow to you from the tradition of the Church of God through the ecclesiastical canon. But with empty fraud[186] and worldly thinking your worldly bishops give it to each other and receive it from one another, as (if it were a matter) of worldly affairs, to which they are accustomed. How many times furthermore do they buy the title of the episcopate with despicable money, but by no means is the power of the ecclesiastical priesthood with it. And because of this you are in all this feebleness of faith, you and your bishops and your faithful. I called you, and I also made great efforts to give you the gift of the Spirit by which you might be strengthened. And neither did your bishops want to come to receive the gift of God's grace, nor did you and your faithful want to separate and remove yourselves from Dathan[187] and Abiram[188] and Core,[189] your false priests,[190] and draw near to the Church of God. And you who are indeed the elect and holy of the Qatari people,[191] burned a little and quickly grew cold; you swiftly returned to the feebleness of faith of your nature. Some amongst you have already returned to an evil communion, others

---

185 ܐܪܥܗܘܢ

186 ܪܘܚܐ ܣܪܝܩܐ

187 ܕܬܢ

188 ܐܒܝܪܡ

189 ܩܘܪܚ

190 Numbers 16:1, 32, 26:9, Deuteronomy 9:6, Psalms 105:17.

191 ܥܡܐ ܕܩܛܪ̈ܝܐ

amongst you threaten to return. You have written to me about your suffering as if in tears of letters,[192] and you have asked from me a wicked permission that you might have intercourse with the wicked, as if in name Christian. And this request fits very much your feeble faith. But if the bishops of Fars and Beth Qaṭraye had a true priesthood, I would not have forbidden you from communion with them, nor would I have written to them to come to me. For nor are they useful to me in any way to summon them to me, as if I wanted, as they think and say in their folly, to bring them into servitude. For our leadership, that is of the holy Church of Christ our Lord, knows how to give of its own to others from its own[193] and does, but not how to take from others as if its own. Yet the leadership of the Persians and the Qataris, because it does not flow from the Church of God and does not flow by the ecclesiastical canons knows how to take from others and so is accustomed, and not to give from its own to others. And because of this they flee from the servitude of Christ, whom they do not know and do not even desire to know. And, therefore, they flee from his servitude like the demons.

For behold there are more than twenty bishops and two metropolitans in the East, who have undergone and undertake[194] the imposition of hands of the episcopate from the Church of God, and none of them has come to us for many years, nor have we wanted them to come, but far away they justly minister their episcopacy in communion with the Church of God, with the function of their priesthood accepted from us rightly; they write to us, we write to them. If the bishops-in-name of the Persians and the Qataris had been such, we would never have asked them to come to us, nor would we have rejected the things that have been done by them in the name of priesthood; but because they are not such: they are destitute of the power of priesthood and rejected by the Church of God. Foolishly you have asked us to permit you to be in communion with them in priestly works, which are

192 ܒܕܡ̈ܥܐ ܕܐܓܪ̈ܬܐ

193 ܡܢ ܕܝܠܗ ܠܐܚܪ̈ܢܐ ܡܢ ܕܝܠܗ

194 ܩܒܠܘ ܘܡܩܒܠܝܢ

performed by them, because they do not have in them the power of the grace of the Holy Spirit.

For if your bishops and yourselves did not have a discerning mind, from that which you possess, you would have understood, that just as the Christians among you may not be Christians without priests, or the priests among you may not be priests without bishops, so bishops may not be bishops without the metropolitans and so again metropolitans may not be metropolitans without the patriarch; and the patriarch himself, who is the father of rulers, that is, the head of fathers, if he does not come from the episcopate to the patriarchate, some metropolitans determine from the canons that they are to perform the laying of hands on him, and if not so, then his office is without power. Because the Persians and the Qataris do not know these things because they do not have knowledge of the laws of God, they have separated themselves from the Church of God, have been deprived of the grace of God, and have become powerless.

If the Qataris had not been more foolish than the Persians, they would have made bishops for themselves, when it is so easy for bishops to be made; and not have needed to go to the Persians, that they might make them. For the Persians also make bishops for themselves and call them metropolitans. And if when the Persians do this, the Qataris think this is what ought to happen, let them also do this for themselves. And if they say that this should not be done, they should know that what the Persians do in this way is also nothing. And not understanding these things the Qataris are more foolish than the Persians and all the foolish people of the world. If they say, as they truly do say, that they have received this madness from a long custom,[195] let them know that they are not Christians according to the custom of the Church of God, rather according to the custom of madness, and are little different from the Severians[196] and Julianists[197] and Marcionites,[198] who themselves also separated from the Church of God, and according to the

195 ܕܥܝܕܐ ܕܡܢ ܢܘܓܪܐ

196 ܣܘܝܪܝܐ

197 ܘܠܘܠܝܢܝܣܛܐ

198 ܡܪܩܝܘܢܐ

customs of their madness kept the name of Christianity and the episcopate, and not according to the custom of and communion with the Church of God. But if you are so feeble in your faith that you can do nothing useful since you are from him,[199] deliver your life alone from communion with the wicked; run and take refuge in the Church of God; be made perfect rightly in the grace of the Spirit; and rejoice in the life of holiness, that you may find rest for your life.

I have written many letters to Beth Qaṭraye:[200] some to the bishops by name; some to individual persons;[201] and some to Nimparuk bar Dustar,[202] from Hatta;[203] and I sent these to Nimparuk from time to time, since I thought that he would give them all for everyone to read. But, as he himself has now written to me, and he has not shown one of them to anyone, not only those which had been written to him, but not even those which had been written to others. If he did this, he committed a great evil. You, then, ask him for all the letters which I wrote to him and to others, and read them in front of everyone, as there is perhaps one there who has the fear of the Lord and is afraid of the evil staining the Qatari people[204] with impiety towards God; and perhaps there is there one who, reading the letters and understanding, perhaps will groan and be tormented over the madness of the bishops-by-name of Beth Qaṭraye[205] and over the slothfulness and wretchedness of the christians-by-name who are subject to error.[206] But if, even when they read what I wrote, they do not perceive the evil which they are in, for them, perhaps, the sins of the Amorites have already been fulfilled, as is written.[207] And now therefore is the time of final destruction. May the Lord spare his people and in his

---

199 ܕܡܢܗ ܐܢܬܘܢ

200 ܠܒܝܬ ܩܛܪ̈ܝܐ

201 ܦܪ̈ܨܘܦܐ ܝܚܝ̈ܕܝܐ

202 ܢܡܦܪܘܟ ܒܪ ܕܘܣܬܪ

203 ܚܛܐ

204 ܥܡܐ ܕܩܛܪ̈ܝܐ

205 ܒܝܬ ܩܛܪ̈ܝܐ

206 ܛܘܥܝܢ

207 Numbers 21:21, Deuteronomy 2:26, Judges 11:19.

mercy guard his holy Church from every harm until his final revelation. Amen! Be strong! May the Lord help you that you may do his will at all times. Amen!

TEXT

ܝ ❖ ܕܠܘܬ ܐܦܣܩܘܦܐ ܕܩܛܪܝܐ ❖

ܟܬܝܒ ܒܐܘܢܓܠܝܘܢ: ܕܐܡܪ ܡܪܢ ܥܠ ܗܢܘܢ ܕܗܘܝܢ ܫܡܫܝܢ ܗܘܘ ܠܡܫܡܫܢ
ܡܠܟܐ: ܕܐܢܐ ܠܡ ܐܬܝܬ ܕܚܝܐ ܢܗܘܘܢ ܠܗܘܢ. ܘܡܕܡ ܕܝܬܝܪ ܢܗܘܐ ܠܗܘܢ.
ܚܝܐ ܕܝܢ ܗܢܐ ܠܡܬܒܥܬܐ ܕܥܕܪܐ. ܐܝܟ ܕܗܘ ܦܫܩ ܟܕ ܐܡܪ. ܕܗܠܝܢ ܐܢܘܢ ܕܝܢ
ܚܝܐ ܕܠܥܠܡ: ܕܢܕܥܘܢܟ ܕܐܢܬ ܐܢܬ ܐܠܗܐ ܒܠܚܘܕܝܟ. ܘܡܢ ܕܫܕܪܬ ܝܫܘܥ
ܡܫܝܚܐ. ܘܡܕܡ ܕܝܬܝܪ ܕܝܢ ܗܢܐ ܠܡܬܒܥܬܐ ܕܪܘܚܐ ܕܝܗܒܝܢ ܗܘܘ ܠܡܫܡܫܢܘ
ܐܠܗܝܡ ܕܐܦ ܒܥܒܕܝ ܒܥܕܢܐ. ܘܐܦ ܡܫܡܠܝܢ ܠܡܫܡܫܢܘܬܐ[208] ܘܐܡܪܘ: ܒܓܘ
ܒܬܪܗ ܗܘܐ ܕܒܐܪܥܐ ܘܟܘܡܪܐ ܘܟܡܫܚܐ. ܡܛܠ ܓܝܪ ܕܕܥܬ ܠܟܘܢ: ܡܠܟܘܬ ܐܢܐ
ܠܟܘܢ ܩܕܡ ܡܠܟܐ ܘܡܪܘܬܗܘܢ ܠܥܠܬܐ ܟܠܗ. ܐܡܝܢ ܕܠܗ ܒܟܬܒܘ ܡܠܝܠ
ܘܡܘܫܚܬܐ ܠܦܓܪܗ ܡܢ ܒܬܪܗ ܕܐܒܐ: ܒܝܘܡܐ ܚܝܐ ܗܢܘܢ ܕܐܬܐܡܪܘ: ܐܠܐ ܘܐܦ
ܐܡܪܐ ܡܫܠܡܐ ܠܐܚܝܢ ܘܠܐ ܗܟܢ. ܒܝܘܡܐ ܗܘ ܡܕܡ ܕܝܬܝܪ ܕܐܬܐܡܪ ܡܢ ܡܪܢ.
ܐܠܗܝ ܕܝܢ ܐܒܗܬܗܘܢ ܕܗܢܘܢ ܕܟܗܢܘܬܗܘܢ ܐܬܐܡܪܬ ܡܫܠܡܐ ܗܘܐ ܡܢ ܩܕܝܡ: ܒܝ
ܦܘܩܕܢܝ ܟܠ ܢܡܘܣܘܗܝ ܘܠܐ ܗܘܝܢ ܐܢܘܢ[209] ܠܐ ܠܐܡܪܐ ܡܫܠܡܐ ܒܝܘܡܐ
ܗܘ[210] ܡܕܡ ܕܝܬܝܪ. ܘܐܦܠܐ ܠܡܬܦܘܬܐ ܘܐܚܪܢܐ ܒܝܘܡܐ ܗܢܘܢ ܚܝܐ
ܘܐܬܐܡܪܘ[211] ܒܟܠܗܘܢ ܢܡܘܣܘܗܝ ܡܢ ܡܬܬܠܝܢ ܕܟܠܐ ܒܬܪܗ[212] ܘܐܚܪܢܐ:
ܘܐܬܟܠܗܘܢ ܟܠܐ ܙܡܢ[213] ܡܕܪܐ ܕܟܠܗܘܢ ܒܫܘܦܐ ܘܠܐ ܒܟܡܢ. ܘܟܠܗܘܢ
ܘܫܠܡܘܬܗܘܢ ܡܕܒܪܢܘܬܐ ܕܟܡܫܝܚܐ ܐܠܗܐ ܒܡܫܝܚܐ ܘܠܐ ܡܕܡ. ܘܐܦ ܐܢܟܝܠܗܘܢ
ܠܘܬ ܟܠܢܫ ܕܡܕܒܪܢܘܬܗܘܢ ܠܡܬܒܥܐ ܕܡܫܝܚܝܬܐ ܕܪܘܚܐ. ܘܐܬܟܠܡܫܚܠܗܘܢ ܡܢ
ܒܗ ܒܟܠܗ ܦܫܩ ܡܫܪܐ ܕܡܢ ܚܝܐ ܒܬܪܝܐ. ܘܒܝܘܡ ܐܦ ܒܬܪܗ ܘܐܚܪܢܐ.

---

[208] Paris f. 160v. Henceforth P.

[209] P: ܢܡܘܣܘܗܝ.

[210] Vatican f. 113r. Henceforth V.

[211] V: ܘܐܬܐܡܪܘ.

[212] P: ܒܬܪܐ.

[213] P: ܙܡܢ.

ܗܢܘ ܕܝܢ ܣܘܢܗܕܘܣ ܩܕܝܫܬܐ ܗܕܐ ܕܐܬܟܢܫܬ ܒܪܓܠ ܗܘܬ: ܒܡܕܝܢܬ ܒܘܪܫܝܐ
ܡܠܘܟܠܡܣܘܣ: ܒܥܕܬܐ ܟܠܗܘܢ ܡܢ ܒܕܘ ܗܘ ܡܠܐ ܕܐܝܬܝܗܘܢ ܡܕܡܝܗܘܢ ܒܟܕܒܘܬܗܘܢ
ܠܢܦܫܗܘܢ. ܗܢܘ ܕܝܢ ܢܘܟܪܝܘܬܐ ܕܡܢ ܐܡܪܐ ܘܪܓܠ ܕܡܫܠܡܢܘܬܗܝܢ ܐܝܠܝܢ[214]
ܒܗ. ܟܐܒܐ ܗܘ ܓܡܪ. ܕܐܝܟܢ ܕܦܫܩܘ ܢܦܫܗܘܢ ܡܢ ܪܡܫ[215] ܢܟܠܐ ܕܡܢܐ ܒܘܢܝܐ
ܕܪܕܐ ܡܢ ܚܡܝܐ: ܘܫܒܪܘ ܕܫܦܩ ܠܗܘܢ، ܗܘܡܢܐ ܒܟܠܗܘܢ ܗܪܝܟܐ ܕܒܗܘܢܬܐ:
ܗܢܘ ܕܗܢܘ ܡܘܕܝܢ ܠܗ ܠܚܒܪܐ: ܕܢܓܠܘܗܝ ܡܢ ܟܠ ܦܪܘܣ ܐܦ ܡܢܘ
ܕܡܘܡܬܐ ܫܪܝܪܐ. ܕܠܐ ܢܗܘܘܢ ܒܟܠܗ ܛܘܒܢܝܢ ܕܫܪܝܪܘܬܐ: ܠܡܫܡܫܢܐ ܘܠܐ ܚܕܝܢ
ܘܛܒܝܢ. ܒܪܡ ܐܢܐ ܡܛܠ ܕܢܫܡܥ ܙܒܢܝܢ ܣܓܝܐܢ: ܕܡܛܠ ܒܐܝܕܝ ܠܟܠܗ ܐܦ
ܡܢ ܡܕܝܢܬܐ ܠܟܢܫܗ. ܬܗܘܐ ܡܫܡܫ ܒܪܝܐ ܕܒܟܠܗܘܢ ܒܟܠܐ ܡܟܠܐ. ܟܕ ܐܡܝܪ
ܘܐܫܬܘܕܝܗܘܢ ܥܠ ܓܙܪܬܐ ܗܘܐ. ܘܐܝܢܘ ܘܠܐ ܩܪܒ ܠܟܢܫܐ ܕܐܟܪܐ ܡܘܬܒܗܘܢ ܘܡܢ
ܫܒܪܐ ܥܢܝܐ ܒܡܘܬܐ ܗܘ ܘܐܬܬܚܪ ܥܠ ܠܟܪܘ ܡܢ ܚܝܠܗ. ܛܘܒ ܢܦܫܗܘܢ
ܚܝܠܗ ܘܡܢܝ ܐܝܟ ܕܠܗܘܢ. ܘܐܬܦܢܝ ܠܚܝܐ ܕܪ̈ܚܡܐ ܒܡܘܬܗ ܕܗܘ. ܘܗܕܐ ܕܝܢ
ܠܗ ܗܟܢ: ܐܠܐ ܘܠܐ ܫܒܪ ܐܝܠܝܢܘܢ ܠܟܘܢ ܡܘܬܐ ܘܡܢ ܒܢܝܗ ܘܐܟܚܕܐ: ܢܟܝܐ ܣܢܐ
ܐܦ ܠܟܠܗܘܢ: ܐܝܟ ܕܒܡܢ ܥܠ ܦܪ̈ܘܣܚܐ[216] ܡܐܬܝܢܗܘܢ. ܐܘܕܥܘ ܠܝ
ܘܡܫܠܡܢܘܬܗܘܢ ܒܟܝܠܐ. ܠܗ ܠܟܢ̈ܫܐ ܒܠܫܢܗ ܫܡܥܢܐ ܐܝܟ ܕܟܝܢܐ
ܠܗܢܐ. ܐܠܐ ܠܡܫܡܠܝܘܬܐ ܥܢܝܢܐ ܕܟܕܒܐ ܘܡܥܢܐ ܢܒܘܪܗܘܢ ܠܡܟܟ ܡܢܝܡ ܕܦܫ
ܠܒ̈ܢܝܗܘܢ ܒܛܝܒܘܬܗ ܗܘܘ ܡܠܟܝܢ ❖

ܝܚ ❖ ܕܟܠܗ ܡܛ̈ܪܢܐ ❖

ܢܘܟܪܗ ܕܡܫܝܚܐ ܡܢܝ ܐܘ ܐܚ̈ܝ ܡܚܒ̈ܒܐ: ܗܝ ܕܗܘ ܐܝܠܝܢ ܠܝ ܢܦܫܐ ܕܚ̈ܝܐ
ܠܐ ܡܫܘ̈ܚܬܐ ܒܥܕܬܐ ܩܕܝܫܬܐ ܕܒܟܠ[217] ܗܘܦܪ̈ܟܝܐ[218] ܘܐܬܦܫܛ: ܘܚܝܠܐ ܡܣܝܒܪܢܐ
ܕܬܘܒܬܐ ܙܘܥܝܬܐ ܠܟܠ ܒܥܡ̈ܡܐ ܕܚܝܐ: ܘܢܘܗܪܐ ܡܠܘܟܐ ܠܒܝܫܬܐ
ܕܡܬܩܢܝܢ ܫܦܝܪ. ܐܟܙ ܗܘ ܠܝ ܕܟܡܐ ܕܐܦܠܐ ܚܝܐ ܕܡܠܐܟܘܬܐ ܦܪܘܫܘܬܐ
ܒܚܝܠܗ ܘܐܠܗܐ: ܢܛܦܐ ܠܟܠܗܘܢ ܒܡܘܬܐ ܕܐܚܘܬܐ ܕܪܘܚ. ܘܢܫܬܘܕܥܘܢ ܐܝܟ

214 P. f. 161r.

215 P: ܪ̈ܡܫ.

216 ܦܪ̈ܘܣܚܐ = ܦܪܣܢ̈ܓܐ. Cf. Mingana, A., *The Early Spread of Christianity in India*. Manchester, 1926, p. 20.

217 P. f. 161v.

218 V. f. 113v.

ܢܗܘܐ ܪܘܚܐ ܒܐܝܠܝܢ ܕܗܘ ܢܗܘܐ ܪܘܚܐ ܡܫܟܚ[219] ܠܡܫܪ. ܘܟܕ ܙܟܝܢ ܕܝܢ ܕܐܦ ܫܠܡܢ ܡܢ ܛܥܝܐ ܘܒܝܫܐ ܠܢܡܘܣ ܐܘܪܚܗܘܢ ܒܫܘܠܐ ܫܠܡܐ. ܗܘܝܢ ܠܡܠܦܢܘܬܗܘܢ ܡܢ ܪܘܚܐ ܒܠܥܕܪܢܐ ܕܫܡܝܐ. ܗܘ ܕܝܢ ܒܐܦܣܩܘܦܘܬܗܘܢ ܠܗܘܢ. ܐܝܟ ܕܪܘܚܐ ܒܝܬܝܐ ܠܐܒܘܗ ܗܘܐ. ܘܡܘܕܐ ܐܢܐ ܠܗ ܒܟܠܗܘܢ ܫܠܝܛܐ ܚܘܒ ܕܒܠܗܘܢ ܘܒܠܒܗܘܢ: ܐܠܐ ܘܫܠܝܛܐ ܐܡܪܐ ܒܝܬܝܐ: ܕܡܬܚܙܝܢ ܗܘܝܢ ܠܡܫܠܡ ܠܗܘܢ ܘܠܗܘܢ: ܒܪܒܐ ܗܘܐ ܕܒܗ ܫܠܝܛܐ ܡܫܡܫܝܢ ܟܠ ܚܝܐ ܫܠܝܐ ܕܒܘܝܢܗ ܘܐܒܗܐ ܠܡܫܝܚܘ ܘܡܫܝܚܘܬܗܘܢ ܒܡܘܪܐ ܡܫܝܚܐ ܐܝܟ ܕܒܪܒܐ ܠܒܪܐ. ܐܡܝܢܐ ܕܠܐ ܬܘܒ ܢܬܚܙܐ ܠܡܘܒܠܐ ܕܡܫܝܚܘܬܗܘܢ ܕܒܫܪ: ܡܫܬܟܚܐ ܗܘ ܕܚܙܐ ܠܡܨܥܝܐ ܕܪܘܚܐ ܕܠܗ ܫܠܝܛ ܡܢܗܘܢ. ܒܪܡ ܬܒܥ ܟܕ ܚܡܠܝܬܐ ܦܪܘܫܘܬܐ ܒܪܘܚܐ ܕܚܝܠ ܠܠܗܐ: ܐܝܟ ܬܒܥܐ ܕܐܬܬܚܫܒܬ ܠܒܗܘܢ ܙܟܝܬܐ ܕܐܒܗܬܐ ܕܪܘܚ: ܟܡ ܡܘܗܒܬܐ ܕܡܫܟܚܐ ܐܝܬ ܟܠ ܒܒܝܬܗ ܕܐܠܗܐ: ܐܬܒܚܪ ܒܐܝܬܘܗ ܕܡܢ ܟܠܗܝܢ ܒܡܫܬܐ ܕܬܒܥܬܐ ܡܢ ܡܠܟܐ: ܒܪܘܚܐ ܗܘܐ ܕܒܪܘܚܐ ܡܫܝܚܘܬܐ ܬܒܥ ܠܡܨܥܝܐ ܕܠܗ ܫܠܝܛ[220] ܡܢܗܘܢ. ܘܡܛܠ ܐܦ ܠܗܘܢ. ܘܙܟܝܬ ܐܝܟ ܐܚܝܐ ܡܫܘܡܠܝܬܐ ܕܠܗ ܠܟܠܝܬܐ ܒܝܬܝܐ ܕܒܪܘܚܐ ܐܚܝܢ ܡܫܬܠܡܝܬܐ ܒܚܝܐ ܕܒܪܘܚܐ ܕܡܢܝ. ܐܡܝܢܘ ܗܘܐ.[221] ܗܘ ܕܝܢ ܕܠܗ ܡܢ ܡܘܒܠܐ ܒܝܬܝܐ. ܘܠܗ ܡܢ ܪܥܐ[222] ܢܒܝܐ ܕܚܝܐ ܕܚܝܠܐ ܒܗܘܝܐ: ܪܘܙܐ ܠܟܘܢ ܢܗܘܐܬܗ ܗܟܢ ܐܝܟ[223] ܕܒܗܘܢܬܐ ܒܢܗܘܐ ܒܝܬܝܐ. ܐܠܐ ܬܒܥ ܠܡܫܒܪܘ ܡܘܟܝܢ ܠܗ ܐܦܝܣܩܘܦܘܬܗܘܢ ܠܟܝܢܐ. ܐܝܟ ܕܒܥܝܢ ܗܪܗܝܘܬܐ ܕܠܒܪ ܡܢ ܒܝܬܐ. ܗܘܝ[224] ܕܟܕ ܗܘܝܬ ܕܐܦܝܣܩܘܦܘܬܐ ܗܘܝܢ ܠܒܗܘܢ: ܐܠܐ ܡܢ ܚܝܠܗ ܕܡܫܐ ܬܒܥܝܢ ܘܟܕܬܒܘܢ ܐܦܠܐ ܠܡܫܠܡܘ ܕܚܝܠܐ ܡܫܠܚܝܐ ܒܚܝܠܗܘܢ. ܠܐ ܒܝܘܡܬܐ ܕܡܢܝܘܬܐ: ܕܐܡܠܢܗܘܢ ܛܘܦܣܐ ܕܚܝܐ ܕܡܢ ܟܠܙ ܡܫܡܠܝܐ. ܘܠܐ ܒܡܫܘܪܘܬܐ ܕܚܝܐ ܠܠܗܐ: ܕܡܒܝܢ ܡܫܠܡܢܝܢ ܒܐܝܕܝ ܡܢܝܩܘܗܝ ܕܡܪܢ: ܠܡܫܠܡܐ ܕܒܪܗܐ ܘܠܡܫܘܡܠܐ ܕܪܘܚܐ ܒܢܦܫܬܐ. ܟܕ ܬܒܥ ܒܪܘܡܐ ܗܘܐ ܒܡܘܐ ܕܠܗܪܗܝܘܬܐ ܡܫܟܢܐ: ܦܫܝܩܘ ܢܦܫܗܘܢ ܡܢ ܒܝܬܗ ܘܐܠܗܐ ܐܦܝܣܩܘܦܐ ܦܪܝܫܐ ܗܘܝܢ ܕܠܗܘܢ: ܕܠܐ ܠܡܫܠܡܐ ܕܡܫܝܚܘܬܐ ܒܒܪܘܢ ܠܒܝܬܗܘܢ ܠܡܫܝܚܘܬܐ

[219] P: ܡܫܟ ܚ.

[220] P. f. 162r.

[221] V: ܐܡܝܢܘ ܗܘܐ ܬܒܥ ܗܘܐ. ܗܘ ܕܝܢ ܗܘܐ ܕܐܦ ܐܡܝܢܘ ܗܘܐ.

[222] P: ܪܥܐ.

[223] P: ܗܟܢܐ.

[224] V. f. 114r.

ܘܕܬܫܒܚܬܐ. ܗܘ ܕܡܢ ܕܘܒܪ̈ܐ ܕܩܕܝܫܘܬܐ ܘܡܢ ܫܘܘܕܥܘܬܐ ܕܝܬܝܪܐ ܠܟܠܗܝܢ ܡܬܩܝܡܐ. ܘܟܕ ܠܐ ܕܝܢ ܐܬܚܙܝ ܗܘܬ ܠܘܬܢ ܗܝܡܢܘܬܐ ܕܬܫܒܚܬܐ ܐܝܟ ܕܙܕܩ ܕܬܗܘܐ:[225] ܡܢ ܟܠܗܝܢ ܥܕܬܐ ܕܒܟܠ ܡܫܝܚܝܐ ܥܒܝܕܐ ܒܡܕܢܚܐ ܘܡܥܪܒܐ ܠܐܪܒܥܐ ܕܥܠܡܐ. ܟܕ ܠܐ ܐܝܟ ܡܢܟ[226] ܓܢܣܐ ܕܬܫܒܚܬܐ ܕܒܢܝܐ ܘܕܝܠܗ. ܒܝܕܐ ܫܘܒܚܐ ܠܐܠܗܐ ܕܥܠ ܟܠ. ܘܐܝܟ ܕܟܡܐ ܐܘܪ̈ܚܐ ܡܫܝܚ̈ܝܐ ܐܬܦܫܛܘ ܡܢ ܟܠܗܝܢ ܦܢܝ̈ܬܐ ܕܒܡܕܢܚ:[227] ܥܡܡܐ ܣܓܝܐܐ ܕܐܦܣܩܘܦܘܬܐ. ܕܐܝܬܝܗܘܢ ܗܫܐ ܡܟܝܠ ܕܡܘܕܝܐ ܟܝܡܐ ܠܫܡܗ ܟܠܐ ܕܒܪܗ ܘܐܒܘܗ. ܒܝܕ ܗܘܐ ܡܫܝܚܐ[228] ܘܡܫܝܚܐ ܗܘ ܕܗܘܐ ܒܫܠܝܚܘܬܗ ܕܝܠܗ. ܠܒܪܝܬܗ ܕܡܒܪܝܢ[229] ܘܡܚܕܬ. ܐܠܐ ܓܝܪ ܡܢ ܡܫܡܫܢܐ ܕܒܪܝܬܐ ܘܡܫܝܚܐ. ܙܕܩ ܗܘܐ ܠܡܫܝܚܝܐ ܘܠܐܠܗܐ ܕܡܫܡܫܝܢ ܠܡܫܝܚܝܐ ܚܕܐ ܘܐܝܟܢܐ ܟܘܢܐ: ܟܕ ܗܘ ܕܥܡܐ ܙܕܩ ܗܘܐ ܐܦ ܚܝܠܐ ܟܘܢܐ. ܘܐܠܘ ܠܘܬ ܡܢ ܚܝܠܐ ܟܘܢܐ ܡܬܬܩܢ ܗܘܐ ܥܡܐ ܡܘܡܢܐ ܒܥܠܡܐ ܗܘ ܕܐܬܐܡܪ: ܠܗ ܟܘܢܐ ܟܠܗ ܫܘܦܪܐ ܕܡܢ ܡܠܟ:[230] ܐܒܪܐ ܗܘܐ ܗܝܡܢܘܬܐ ܡܢ ܐܒܪܗܡ ܕܒܟܠܐ. ܐܘ ܓܝܪ ܟܘܫܪܐ ܕܟܪܝܣܛܝܢܐ ܢܛܪ ܗܘܘ ܐܢܫܝܢ ܠܐܘܪܚܐ ܕܗܝܡܢܘܬܗܘܢ ܘܠܐ ܢܦܠܬ. ܐܝܟ ܕܒܥܒܕ̈ܘܗܝ[231] ܘܐܘܪܚܐ ܐܝܟ ܕܒܗܢܘܢ: ܡܫܬܘܕܥܝܢ ܗܘܘ ܠܗ ܘܠܐ[232] ܢܦܩ: ܒܝܕ ܠܟܠܐ ܕܒܪܢܫܐ ܕܚܠܬܐ. ܐܘ ܟܕ ܒܝܕ ܕܫܘܒܪܐ ܩܕܝܫܬܐ: ܡܩܒܠܝܢ ܗܘܘ ܗܝܡܢܘܬܗܘܢ ܠܥܠܡܐ. ܒܫܘܠܛܢܐ ܡܫܝܚܐ ܕܗܘܐ ܠܡܬܟܫܦܘ ܕܡܢ. ܟܘܠܗܘܢ ܓܝܪ ܫܘܦܪܐ ܕܡܫܬܘܕܥܬܐ: ܐܬܡܟܟܘ ܟܠܢܝ ܢܘܟܪܝܬܐ ܘܗܝܡܢܘܬܐ ܥܕܪܬܐ ܡܢ ܐܒ̈ܗܬܐ ܪ̈ܘܚܢܐ ܕܗܘܘ ܠܢ. ܗܢܘܢ ܕܒܟܠܗܘܢ ܐܚܝܕܝܢ[233] ܟܠ ܟܪܝܬܐ ܩܕܝܫܬܐ: ܒܝܕ ܠܓܠܝܢܘ ܕܡܪܢ ܕܡܢ ܫܡܝܐ. ܘܟܠ ܕܦܫܛܘ ܕܝܢ ܢܦܫܗܘܢ ܐܦܣܩ̈ܘܦܐ ܦܪ̈ܝܫܐ ܡܢ ܢܘܟܪܝܐ ܗܘܐ: ܐܬܦܫܛܘ ܣܓܝ̈ܐܝܗܘܢ ܡܢ ܫܒܪܐ ܕܗܝܡܢܘܬܐ ܐܝܟ ܫܘܪܝܐ ܕܒܡܕܢܚ.[234] ܘܐܢ ܡܢܐ ܠܐ ܢܬܐܪ ܫܪܝܪܐ ܒܐܬܪܘܗܝ: ܘܥܠܐ ܐܬܪ̈ܘܬܐ ܡܬܒܥܝܢ ܠܢ ܠܫܘܪܝܐ ܕܫܐ. ܟܘܠܐ ܓܝܪ ܡܘܕܝܢܢ ܘܐܒܪܐ ܕܡܢ ܗܝܡܢܘܬܐ.

---

225 P. f. 162v.
226 V: ܟܕ ܠܐ ܠܓܡܪ ܡܢܟ ܐܝܟ.
227 V: ܕܒܡܕܢܚܘܢ.
228 V: ܡܫܝܚܐ.
229 P: ܕܡܒܪܝܐ.
230 P: ܕܡܠܟܐ.
231 V: ܒܥܒܕ̈ܘܗܝ.
232 V. f. 114v.
233 P. f. 163r.
234 ܡܕܢܚ = ܡܕܝܢ. Mingana, A., *The Early Spread.*

ܟܕ ܙܟܝܬ ܐܢܐ ܠܡܥܒܕ ܘܠܡܥܛܐ ܚܝܠܐ ܕܡܕܒܪܢܘܬܐ ܕܪܘܚ: ܡܢܟ ܠܐܦܣܩܘܦܐ ܦܪ̈ܝܫܐ ܠܟܗܢܘܬܐ ܕܐܒܘܗ ܘܐܠܗܐ. ܠܡܫܡܫ ܡܢ ܟܠܗ ܓܘܗ ܕܡܪܢܐ ܒܥܘܕܪܢܐ ܘܣܝܥܐ ܐܝܟ ܢܡܘܣܐ ܩܢܘܢܝܩܝܐ[235] ܕܡܢ ܐܒܗ̈ܬܐ ܩܕ̈ܝܫܐ ܐܬܝܗܒ ܒܪܘܚܐ ܕܩܘܕܫܐ. ܘܡܢܟ ܠܘܬ ܠܐܦܣܩܘܦܐ ܕܟܠܗܘܢ ܒܣܘܥܪܐ ܛܠܝܐ ܘܒܡܕܒܪܢܐ ܘܐܡܪܐ ܡܥܠܝܐ. ܘܗܢܘܢ ܗܠܝܢ: ܟܕ ܠܐ ܠܥܘܕܪܢܐ ܕܡܢ ܐܒܘܗ ܘܐܠܗܐ ܣܢܝܩܝܢ ܠܡܕܡ. ܘܠܐ ܠܘܬ ܠܐܡܪܐ ܕܡܢ ܚܝܠܐ ܟܗܢܝܐ ܣܢܝܩܝܢ ܠܡܕܡ: ܘܐܦܠܐ ܕܝܢ ܠܟܗ ܠܟܪܣܛܝܢܘܬܐ ܣܢܝܩ ܕܗܝܐ ܠܡܬܚܙܝܘ ܕܠܡܕܡ: ܡܢܗ ܐܘܪܚܐ ܕܚܝܐ ܕܟܠܗ ܚܒܐܗ ܘܐܠܗܐ. ܘܙܘܥ ܡܡܘܛܠܬܗ ܠܘܪܚܐ ܕܗܘܬܐ ܠܟܠܗ ܥܕܬܐ ܕܡܫܝܚ ܘܩܕܝܫ ܘܡܫ[236] ܡܪܢܐ ܕܠܘܩܒܠ ܢܡܘܣܐ ܟܢܝܫܐ. ܘܐܪܥܗ ܠܡܘܪܒܝܬܐ ܩ̈ܕܡܝܐ: ܠܡܠܝܚܘܬܗ ܡܢ ܡܘܠܦܢܘܬܐ ܕܐܒܘܗ ܘܐܠܗܐ ܕܠܟܠܟܘܢ. ܘܗܠܝܢ ܠܟܠܗܘܢ ܦܪܘܩܢ ܘܡܢܗ ܘܡܥܕܪܢ. ܡܛܠ ܡܢ ܡܐ ܕܙܒܢܐ ܗܘܐ ܩܛܝܠܐ. ܩܛܝܠܐ ܓܝܪ ܟܒܪ ܩܫܫ ܗܘܐ ܠܗ ܡܘܣܐ ܠܟܠܗܘ ܕܡܢ ܗܡܢܘܬܐ[237] ܐܝܟ ܗܘ ܕܡܪ̈ܘܚܐ. ܐܠܐ ܕܝܢ ܐܦܣܩܘܦܐ[238] ܕܦܪܫ ܘܕܟܝܬ ܡܬܝ̈ܢܐ: ܟܕ ܣܓܝܐܝܢ ܠܐܘܬܗ ܘܐܦ ܡܛܠ ܡܢ ܡܐ ܕܙܒܢܐ ܗܘܐ ܩܛܝܠܐ ܢܦܪܘܢ ܠܟܪܣܛܝܢܘܬܐ ܒܟܠ̈ܝܬܐ ܕܗܝܡܢܘܬܐ ܘܒܝܠ̈ܝܬܐ ܘܪܘܚܢܐ. ܟܠܗܘ ܘܩܛܠܘ ܘܡܕܪܘ ܠܡܘܪܒܝܬܐ ܕܡܢ ܡܘܠܦܢܘܬܐ ܕܟܠ ܚܒܐܗ ܘܐܠܗܐ ܗܘ ܕܝܢ ܕܟܠ ܟܪܣܛܝܢܘܬܐ. ܐܡܝܢܐ ܕܠܗ ܒܗܘܢ ܠܟܠܗܘ ܠܐܢܫ ܠܡܘܪܒܝܬܐ[239] ܕܡܢ ܗܡܢܘܬܐ ܐܝܟ ܗܘ ܕܡܪ̈ܘܚܐ: ܐܠܐ ܘܐܦ ܠܒ̈ܢܝܗܘܢ ܕܡܢ ܠܐܪ̈ܥܗܘܢ. ܐܦ ܐܝܟ ܘܗܘܝܢ ܠܗܘܢ ܒܢ̈ܝܐ ܘܡܪܢܝܢ ܐܒܗ̈ܬܗܘܢ. ܒܪܡ ܐܢܐ ܟܕ ܠܐ ܙܟܝܬ ܠܡܫܡܫ ܠܟܠܗܘܢ ܡܫܪܐ ܕܢܣܝܒܝܢ ܕܡܢ ܡܘܬܐ ܗܢܐ ܕܪܘܚܐ. ܚܕܪܐ ܡܚܕܪܫ[240] ܠܟܠܗܘܢ ܐܦܣܩܘ̈ܦܐ ܕܩ̈ܪܝܐ ܠܟܠ ܗܢܘܢ ܕܒܦܪܫ. ܘܠܟܠܗܘܢ ܐܦܣܩܘ̈ܦܐ ܕܡܫܬ̈ܝܐ ܠܟܠ ܗܢܘܢ ܕܡܠܟܝܢ: ܥܡ ܐ̈ܚܪܢܐ ܕܡܢܝ ܘܕܡܢ ܟܠܗ ܡܘܗܘܒܘܬ. ܘܡܦܝܐ ܐܢܘܢ ܠܡܫܡܠܝܘ ܠܦܘܠܚܢܐ ܕܪܘܚ ܥܡ ܗܢܘܢ ܡܛܠ ܢܦܫܗܘܢ. ܒܝܕܐ ܕܠܬܪܝܢ ܒܗܘܢ ܡܫܡܫܐ. ܘܐܦ ܒܡܫܡܫ ܡܫܪܐ ܕܢܣܝܒܝܢ[241] ܢܣܒܝܢ ܠܡܫܡ ܠܟܠܗܘ ܕܒܝܬ ܘܡܫܡܫܐ. ܢܩܪܘܢ ܠܟܠܗܘܢ ܡܛܠ ܕܚ̈ܫܒܝܗܘܢ ܐܝܟ ܕܡܛܠ ܡܪܢܐ ܘܐܒ̈ܗܬܐ ܘܢܦܫܗܘܢ ܠܟܠܝ. ܟܕ ܡܫܪܝܢ ܟܠܗ ܡܥܪ̈ܝܗܘܢ ܢܦܪܢܘܬܗܘܢ ܕܡܢ

---

235 V: ܩܢܘܢܝܩܝܐ.

236 P: ܪܘܫ.

237 P. f. 163v.

238 V. f. 115r.

239 P: ܕܡܢ ܡܘܠܦܢܘܬܐ ܕܟܠ ܟܪܣܛܝܢܘܬܐ.

240 V: ܡܚܕܪܫ.

241 V: ܕܢܣܝܒܐ.

ܢܝܢܘܐ ܘܐܬܘܪ: ܒܗܝܢ ܟܠܗܝܢ ܘܒܗܘܢ ܕܠܗܝܢ. ܗܟܢ ܓܝܪ ܗܘܝܢ ܚܕ ܦܢܝܢ ܠܡܣܡܟ. ܗܘܘܝ ܡܢ ܕܒܟܠ ܦܪܨܘܦܐ ܐܬܚܙܝܘ: ܗܘܝ ܒܡܘܡܬܗܘܢ ܐܝܟܐ.[242] ܗܘܝ ܕܝܢ ܕܒܐܬܘܗܝ ܐܬܚܙܝܘ: ܠܐܢܫܐ ܚܕܘ ܣܓܝܐܘܬܗܘܢ. ܘܕܒܐܝܢܐ ܕܝܢ ܙܒܢܐ ܘܒܗܝܢܐ ܘܦܘܪܫܢܐ. ܢܦܩܘ ܡܢ ܒܝܬ ܦܪܨܘܦܐ ܘܡܢ ܒܝܬ ܡܕܝܢܬܐ: ܒܗܘܢܐ ܘܐܬܘܪ ܘܐܬܚܙܝܘ ܡܢ ܢܝܢܘܐ ܘܐܬܘܪ: ܟܠܗ ܐܝܟܐ ܕܫܟܝܚܝܢ ܗܘܘ ܕܦܪܨܘܦܐ ܐܠܗܘܗܝ: ܘܐܡܪ ܗܟܢ ܐܠܗܝ ܡܢܟܡ.[243] ܐܢ ܐܝܟ ܘܐܬܟܢܫܘ ܠܟܘܢ ܠܡܣܡܟ. ܘܟܕ ܕܝܢ ܫܡܥܘ ܐܦܝܣܩܘܦܘܗܝ ܕܥܡܐ ܡܢ ܪܘܚܐ ܕܠܘܬܟܠ ܢܝܢܘܐ ܘܐܬܘܪ. ܐܦ ܕܝܢ ܡܬܟܢܫܝܢ ܘܐܡܪ ܘܐܦ ܕܝܢ ܡܬܟܢܫܐ ܪܒܐ ܕܟܠܟܠ ܡܢ ܡܬܟܢܫܐ[244] ܕܒܥܠܡܐ ܗܢܐ. ܡܬܚܙܐ ܠܡܬܚܙܝܢܘܬܐ ܕܦܪܨܘܦܘܗܝ ܕܡܢ ܪܘܚܐ ܕܢܝܢܘܐ ܘܐܬܘܪ ܦܪܨܘܦ. ܘܡܛܠ ܐܬܟܢܫܘ ܡܢ ܡܬܟܢܫܐ ܐܝܟ ܕܫܒܩܐ ܦܪܨܘܦܗܘܢ. ܘܟܕ ܕܝܢ ܒܝܬܟܠ ܦܪܨܘܦܝܢ ܗܘܝ ܒܡܦܪܢܣܘܬܗܘܢ ܕܡܢ ܐܒܗܘܗܝ ܘܐܬܘܪ: ܡܬܐܟܠܝܢ ܕܒܗܝܢ ܒܟܠ ܕܦܪܢܣ ܡܢ ܗܘ ܕܟܠ ܦܪܨܘܦܐ ܢܦܩܝܢ ܠܟܘܢ: ܘܡܬܐܟܠܝܢ ܠܘܬ ܡܢ ܢܦܫܗܘܢ ܪܘܚܐ: ܕܐܬܐ ܠܝ ܐܝܟܢܘܬܐ ܐܒܗܬܐ ܕܟܠܗܘܢ: ܕܐܝܬܝܗܘܢ ܡܢ ܡܬܚܫܒܬܐ ܒܢܝܢܐ ܕܟܠ ܗܘܝ ܕܐܪܥܗ ܘܐܦ ܐܬܟܢܫܘ ܡܢ ܢܝܢܘܐ ܘܐܬܘܪ: ܘܐܬܒܟܝܘ ܒܟܠ ܟܢܘܫܬܐ ܕܪܘܚܐ ܘܒܝܢܬܐ ܕܡܠܟܐ. ܠܡܫܡܫܐ ܐܝܟܐ ܕܟܠܗܘܢ ܒܝܬ ܡܢܝ ܢܦܫܗ ܡܫܝܚܐ: ܪܘܚܐ ܕܝܠܗܘܢ ܘܡܢܐ ܕܐܢܫܝܢ ܐܟܘܬܝ ܫܠܡܐ.[245] ܕܡܢܗ ܘܡܬܚܙܐ ܐܢܫ ܐܚܪܢܐ: ܕܡܫܬܡܥ ܒܪܘܚܐ ܗܘ ܕܐܦܝܣܩ[246] ܡܬܚܙܐ ܠܟܠ ܢܦܫܗܘܢ[247] ܒܡܬܚܙܝܢܘܬܐ ܕܡܢ ܢܝܢܘܐ ܘܐܬܘܪ: ܟܠܐ ܒܗܝܢܐ ܕܪܘܚܐ ܠܗܘܢ ܕܐܫܬܘܐ: ܡܛܠܗܢ ܠܗ ܚܕ ܟܠ: ܒܗܝܢܐ ܕܪܘܚܐ ܠܗܘܢ ܕܡܬܚܙܝܢ ܘܡܠܟܐ ܕܝܘܡܢ. ܐܦܠܐ ܓܝܪ ܪܘܚܐ ܗܘܐ ܘܠܐ ܡܬܚܙܐ ܗܘܐ: ܕܐܝܟ ܢܗܘܐ ܡܢ ܡܬܚܙܝܢܐ ܐܝܟܢܐ ܡܬܟܢܫܐ: ܡܛܠ ܡܢ ܡܬܚܙܝܢܐ ܦܪܨܘܦܐ ܘܡܢܗ ܕܝܘܡܢ. ܐܠܐ ܕܒܗܝܢܐ ܕܠܗܘܢ ܢܦܩܐ ܡܢ ܡܬܐܡܪܢܘܬܐ ܕܒܝܬܐ ܠܗܘܢ ܕܒܗܝܢܐ ܡܬܚܙܐ ܣܓܝ ܢܦܫܗܘܢ[248] ܡܢ ܡܬܐܡܪܢܘܬܐ ܕܢܝܢܘܐ ܘܐܬܘܪ. ܘܡܬܟܢܫܝܢ ܣܓܝܐܐ ܕܟܠܗܘܢ ܒܐܝܟܢܘܬܐ ܘܒܚܝܠܐ ܒܗܝܢܐ: ܡܢ ܫܡܐ ܘܡܢ ܐܪܥܐ ܕܐܦܝܣܩܘܦܘܬܐ: ܕܒܗ ܒܝܬܐ ܠܗܘܢ ܡܬܟܢܫܝܢ ܗܘܘ. ܘܐܦ ܡܢܗ ܕܡܬܐܡܪܢܘܬܐ ܕܐܬܪܐ ܦܪܨܘܦܐ. ܒܝܬܐ ܕܡܛܠ ܠܗܘܢ

---

242 P. f. 164r.

243 V: ܡܢܟܡ ܐܠܗܝ.

244 V. f. 115v.

245 P: ܠܟܘܢ.

246 P. f. 164v.

247 V: ܢܦܫܗܘܢ.

248 V: ܢܦܫܗܘܢ.

ܠܡܘܬܐ: ܘܝܕܥܘܢ ܚܙܘܐ ܘܢܕܘܢ ܢܦܫܗܘܢ. ܘܢܦܪܫܘܢ ܡܢ ܦܓܪܗ ܕܥܠܡܐ ܕܟܠܗ ܐܬܬܙܝܒܘ ܒܪܘܚܗ. ܠܗܘ ܗܘܝܠܬܐ ܐܢܫ ܡܫܟܚܐ. ܠܗܘ ܢܦܫܗܘܢ ܡܫܟܢܐ ܡܢ ܡܘܬܒܬܐ ܕܓܒܪܐ ܗܟܢ. ܐܝܟܢܐ ܕܐܠܗܘܢ ܠܦܘܬܗ ܘܐܟܘܬܐ. ܗܘ ܕܥܠܘܗܝ ܪܚܡܝܢ ܐܢܬܘܢ.[249] ܘܐܢ ܡܕܡ ܡܢ ܒܬܪܐ ܘܠܡܫܡܠܝܘܬܐ ܕܘܚܠܬܐ ܢܦܪܫܘܢ ܠܡܦܩܕ: ܡܢ ܟܠܗ ܕܐܓܪܬܝ[250] ܗܘܐ ܡܬܠܦܢܐ ܐܝܟ ܕܡܫܟܚ ܠܗ: ܗܘܠܝܢ ܚܕܝܢ ܕܓܒܝܢ ܗܘ ܡܢ ܠܡܘܬܐ ܕܪܘܚܐ ܕܩܘܕܫܐ ܗܘ ܗܢܐ ܕܡܫܡܠܐ ܡܢܗܘܢ. ܘܒܡܪܢܝܘܬܐ ܘܒܚܝܘܬܐ ܡܫܡܠܝܢ: ܘܠܐ[251] ܐܝܟ ܚܕܗܘ ܚܝܠܐ ܕܪܘܚܢܝܘܬܐ. ܐܙܕܗܪܘ ܡܕܝܢ ܒܡܠܝܘܬܐ ܕܗܝܡܢܘܬܟܘܢ[252] ܕܢܫܠܡܗ ܘܐܟܘܬܐ. ܘܐܝܟܐ ܕܒܟܠ ܒܠܐ ܡܠܠܗ ܕܡܪܢ: ܙܘܓܐ ܡܢ ܚܡܝܪܐ ܒܝܫܐ ܟܠܗܘܢ. ܘܐܢܬܘܢ ܕܝܢ ܡܫܝܚܐ ܘܡܫܡܫܢܐ: ܡܠܦܘ ܠܡܫܡܠܬܐ[253] ܕܐܝܟܢܐ ܒܟܠܗ ܙܒܢܐ ܢܗܦܟܘܢ. ܟܠܗ ܡܢ ܡܘܬܒܬܐ ܕܗܢܝ ܕܡܫܬܠܡܝܢ ܗܘܘ ܐܦܣܩܘܦܝܗܘܢ. ܕܒܟܠ ܘܢܚܡ ܠܗܘܢ ܡܢ ܚܒܠܗ ܘܐܟܘܬܐ ܒܦܘܪܫܢܐ ܕܘܝܫܐ. ܒܙܘܥܐ ܘܡܫܡܫܢܘܬܐ ܕܢܦܫܬܐ ܪܘܚܢܝܐ. ܘܐܢܬܘܢ ܡܫܬܡܠܝܢ ܐܝܟ ܕܐܚܝܕܗܘܢ ܫܡܥܐ ܡܫܠܡܘܬܐ ܡܕܒܪܢܘܬܐ ܕܓܒܪܐ ܘܡܠܟܐ ܡܒܪܐ: ܗܘ ܕܝܢ ܙܕܝܩܝܢ ܘܡܫܡܫܢܝܢ ܘܠܐܟܘܢ ܘܫܠܝܛܐ ܘܕܘܓܢ: ܐܬܦܩܚܘ ܒܪܚܡܐ ܗܘܐ ܠܡܢ ܡܢ ܕܒܟܠܟܘܢ ܟܠ ܒܘܚܪܢܐ ܕܗܝܡܢܘܬܟܘܢ: ܘܟܠ ܡܘܡܐ ܢܦܫܐ ܕܒܘܗܬܐ ܡܫܬܒܗܠܟܘܢ. ܠܡܢ ܡܢ ܕܟܠ ܫܘܬܦܘܬܐ ܒܟܢܫܐ. ܘܦܪܘܫܐ ܘܡܒܪܗ ܒܥܠܝ. ܐܢ ܒܗܘܢ ܒܗܘܢ ܐܦܣܩܘܦܐ ܡܛܠܬܗ: ܐܢ ܡܫܬܠܡܝܢ ܒܗܘܢ ܕܢܦܫܝܢ ܡܒܙܗ[254] ܟܢܘܫܬܐ ܘܒܡܫܡܠܝܘܬܐ ܕܘܚܠܬܐ: ܘܐܢ ܠܐܢܫܐ ܐܝܟ ܕܐܡܪ ܡܢܗܘܢ ܡܫܬܠܡܝܢ ܒܗܘܢ ܕܢܦܫܝܢ: ܒܟܢܫܐ ܕܥܠ ܘܠܡܫܡܠܝܘܬܐ ܡܫܟܠܬܐ ܕܚܝܠܗ ܘܐܟܘܬܐ. ܘܗܟܢܐ ܢܬܦܣܝܘܢ ܘܢܬܦܪܩܘܢ ܘܢܬܡܠܟܘܢ. ܘܢܬܕܪܫܘܢ ܒܗܘܢ ܡܢ ܙܘܥ[255] ܢܚܠ ܕܚܝܠܐ ܒܘܚܪܢܐ ܒܢܦܫܗ ܘܒܡܫܝܚܐ. ܘܐܙܕܗܪܘ ܘܬܘܒ ܐܙܕܗܪܘ. ܘܝܬܝܪܐܝܬ ܐܙܕܗܪܘ ܕܠܐ ܡܢ ܪ̈ܘܚܐ ܫܓܝܫ̈ܬܐ ܐܬܓܠܝܘ ܒܥܒܕ. ܠܟܘܠ ܫܘܦܪܐ ܠܟܝܢܬܟܘܢ ܒܪܘܚܐ ܕܗܘܝ ܒܗ. ܪܚܡ[256] ܗܘ ܓܝܪ ܒܟܒܪܐ ܕܒܪܫܝܬܐ ܗܟܝܠ. ܘܪܚܡܝܢ ܫܓܝܫܝ ܫܓܝ

249 P: ܪܚܡܝܢܬܘܢ.
250 P: ܐܓܪܬܗܘܢ.
251 V. f. 116r.
252 P. f. 165r.
253 P: ܠܡܫܘܚܬܐ.
254 P: ܡܒܙܗ.
255 P: ܡܒܙܗ.
256 P. f. 165v.

ܠܡܫܝܚܘܬܐ. ܘܗܟܢܐ ܕܝܢ: ܐܦ ܪܒܐ ܗܘ ܕܦܪܢܣܘܬܐ ܡܫܬܡܠܝܢܘܬܗ: ܕܒܚܒܝܒܐ ܕܡܫܝܚܘܬܐ ܒܪܗ ܕܐܠܗܐ. ܘܡܩܕܡ ܐܡܪ ܒܡܠܬܐ ܕܪܘܚܐ. ܠܗ ܒܠܚܘܕ ܫܘܒܚܐ ܡܫܬܘܕܝܢܐ[257] ܘܡܫܬܡܠܝܢܘܬܗ: ܐܠܐ ܘܐܦ ܡܫܝܚܐ ܢܨܚܘܢ. ܗܘ ܕܝܢ ܒܚܝܠܐ. ܐܝܟ ܕܐܦ ܗܠܝܢ ܕܠܗܘܢ ܠܗܘ. ܗܘ ܕܝܢ ܐܦܣܩܘܦܐ ܕܝܠܐ ܕܡܢ[258] ܡܫܪܐ ܒܫܘܬܦܘܬܗܘܢ ܟܠ ܡܘܕܝܐ ܕܒܝܬܗ ܘܐܠܗܐ: ܕܠܗ ܡܫܘܚܬܐ[259] ܗܘ ܕܒܘܪܟܬܐ ܕܪܘܚ ܠܐܝܠܝܢ ܕܡܫܬܘܕܝܢ ܠܗ. ܐܠܐ ܡܘܕܝܐ ܗܘ ܡܫܪܪܐ ܘܡܫܬܟܚܐ: ܒܦܪܘ ܒܗ ܡܠܘܐܝܬ ܒܝܩܪܐ ܕܫܡܝܐ ܕܦܪܝܩ ܒܡܘܕܝܐ ܘܐܠܗܐ ܒܪܘܚܗܘܢ.[260] ܘܠܐ ܢܒܘ ܘܠܐ ܐܫܬܟܚܘ ܡܢܬܐ: ܘܐܦ ܠܡܘܠܟܢܐ ܕܟܝܢܐ ܗܘܐ ܕܗܘܐ ܐܝܟ ܒܟܠܙܒܢ. ܡܫܬܟܚܝܢ ܐܦ ܗܢܘܢ ܐܝܟ ܕܐܦ ܟܠܗܘܢ[261] ܒܪܘܚܐ ܚܕܐ. ܘܗܢܘܢ ܕܐܝܬ ܠܗܘܢ ܦܘܩܕܢܐ ܡܢ ܒܪܫܝܢܘܬܐ: ܠܡܫܬܡܥܘ ܠܡܘܠܟܢܐ ܐܝܟܢ ܕܡܢ ܐܠܗܐ ܦܩܝܕ: ܠܗ ܒܠܚܘܕ ܠܡܘܠܟܢܐ ܕܒܪܫܝܢܘܬܐ ܠܐ ܙܕܩ ܠܡܫܬܡܥܘ. ܘܟܕ ܠܟܠ ܡܘܠܟܢ ܕܒܪ ܡܢ ܒܪܫܝܢܘܬܐ ܡܫܬܡܥܝܢ ܢܫܬܡܥ ܒܫܦܝܪܐ ܘܒܢܦܫܐ ܘܒܡܢܝܢܐ ܘܒܟܠ ܫܘܒܪ: ܒܠܚܘܕ ܡܢ ܡܘܕܝܐ ܕܒܪܫܝܢܘܬܐ. ܗܘ ܕܝܢ ܡܢ ܡܘܕܝܐ ܘܐܠܗܐ ܡܫܪܪܝܢ ܢܦܫܗܘܢ ܐܝܟ ܕܫܡܝܐ. ܘܐܦܠܐ ܓܒܪ ܒܗܠܝܢ ܡܬܠܒܝܢ ܡ̈ܠܝܐ. ܕܟܠ ܡܘܠܟܢ ܡܕܡ ܕܡܬܐܡܪ ܠܗ ܡܢ ܦܩܝܕܝܢ ܠܡܛܠ. ܗܘ ܕܝܢ ܠܡܢ ܕܟܣܦ ܟܣܦ ܪܫܐ:[262] ܘܠܡܢ ܕܡܟܣܐ ܡܟܣܐ. ܘܠܡܢ ܕܕܚܠܬܐ ܕܚܠܬܐ. ܘܠܡܢ ܕܐܝܩܪܐ ܐܝܩܪܐ. ܘܡܘܕܝܐ ܕܝܢ ܢܦܫܐ: ܗܘ[263] ܕܚܕ ܚܕ ܒܫܘܒܚܗ ܕܡܫܝܚܐ ܫܘܐ ܠܗ ܠܡܫܬܡܥܘ: ܠܗ ܕܢܬܠ ܠܗ ܡܕܡ ܡܢ ܕܝܠܝ ܒܝܬ. ܐܠܐ ܕܗܘ ܢܬܠ ܠܝ ܡܢ ܕܝܠܗ. ܗܘ ܕܝܢ ܡܫܘܕܥܘܬܐ ܕܪܘܚܐ: ܕܒܗ ܢܬܝܬܪ ܠܡܐܙܠ ܦܢܝ ܫܡܫܗ ܕܒܝܬܐ ܘܡܫܟܢܘܬܐ ܘܐܠܗܐ: ܒܚܝܠܐ ܕܪܘܚܐ ܕܪܕܐ ܪܘܚܢܝܬܐ ܡܢ ܡܪܝ ܒܡܫܝܚܘܬܐ ܕܒܝܬܐ ܦܪܝܩܘܬܐ ܐܝܟ ܢܘܟܠܐ ܪܘܚܢܐ: ܕܐܝܟ ܙܘܙܐ ܠܐ ܡܫܬܟܚܢܝܬ ܒܗܘ ܒܝܬܐ: ܡܢ ܟܠܗ ܘܒܝܬܐ ܒܟܠܗ. ܗܝܐ ܕܐܦܣܩܘܦܐ ܕܝܠܗܘܢ ܘܦܪܘܫ ܠܟܠܗܝܢ ܡܢ ܢܒܠܗ ܘܡܢ ܚܝܠܗ. ܘܡܫܘܚ ܐܠܗܘܬܗ ܢܦܫܗܘܢ ܠܫܘܒܚ ܡܫܝܚܘܬܐ ܡܢ ܩܕܡ ܡܫܬܡܠܝܢܘܬܗ ܕܫܡܝܐ. ܘܒܪܟܘܢ ܗܐ

[257] V: ܡܫܬܘܕܝܐ.

[258] P: ܘܡܢ.

[259] V: ܡܫܘܚܐ.

[260] V. f. 116v.

[261] P: ܒܟܠܗ.

[262] P. f. 166r.

[263] V: ܗܝ.

ܡܬܝܩܪܝܢ ܠܗܘܢ: ܘܡܪܝܡ ܗܘ ܡܢ ܟܠܗ ܡܬܬܠܝܬܘ[264] ܕܥܠܝܬܐ. ܘܐܬܐ ܠܗ ܡܢ ܟܠܗ ܡܪܘܬܘܬܐ ܗܝ ܕܠܐܠܗ ܠܟܠܗ: ܘܟܕ ܡܟܠܠ ܘܡܫܬܠܠ ܒܪܝܬܐ ܕܫܘܠܛܢܐ ܒܪܗ ܕܐܠܗܐ. ܗܘ ܐܢܐ ܠܟܘܢ ܒܪܐ ܚܕܐ ܘܡܬܝܕܥܐ ܡܫܝܚܐ. ܠܫܘܒܚܐ ܕܐܒܐ ܕܒܫܘܠܛܢܗ ܕܡܪܝ: ܘܠܫܘܡܠܝ ܬܫܒܘܚܬܐ ܕܠܘܬ ܟܠܗ ܫܠܝܚܐ ܕܟܠܗ ܕܗܘܝܐ ܒܐܢܫܐ: ܗܢܘܢ ܕܠܐ ܪܓܘ ܡܛܠܗ ܚܘܒܐ ܕܫܡܝܐ ܕܟܘ ܚܢܢ. ܗܟܢܐ ܗܘܝܬ ܘܡܥܘܠ ܚܝܠܘܗܝ ܒܫܡܝܐ. ܘܫܡܗ ܒܡܠܟܘܬܗ ܠܟܘܢ ܘܐܘܪܚܬܗ[265] ܘܡܠܟܐ. ܘܫܡܥܘ ܫܡܘܥܐ ܕܫܘܪܝܐ. ܘܐܝܟܘ ܫܡܝܐ ܘܪܘܚܐ ܘܐܬܠܘܗܝ ܚܝܠܐ ܕܐܠܗܐ. ܘܫܡܥܘ ܠܟܘܢ[266] ܫܒܪܐ ܕܡܫܝܚܘܬܐ ܡܢ ܟܠܗ ܓܘܗ ܕܡܪܝܐ: ܘܡܢ ܫܘܠܛܢܐ ܢܫܘܫܐ ܕܡܦܪܢܫ ܒܐܬܪܗ ܡܬܦܪܫܬܐ ܪܘܚܢܝܬܐ: ܕܟܘ ܠܐܬܪܗ ܚܝܠܐ ܠܡܥܒܕܘ ܟܠܗܘܢ ܠܐܪܘܗܝ ܡܪܝܐ ܕܫܡܝܐ. ܗܘ ܐܢܐ ܠܟܘܢ ܟܕܐ ܘܡܫܡܫܢܐ ܐܝܟ ܦܘܩܕܢܗ ܕܡܪܝ. ܘܟܠܗ ܕܝܢ ܡܫܡܫܢܐ ܘܠܟܘܠܐ: ܐܝܟ ܡܫܡܫܢܘܬܐ ܒܫܡܝܐ ܕܗܢܘܢ ܕܡܫܬܡܫܝܢ ܗܘܘ ܐܦܝܣܩܘܦܘܢ. ܗܢܘܢ ܕܡܫܬܠܠ ܕܗܢܘܢ ܒܗܘܢ ܠܗܘܢ ܡܫܡܫܝܢ ܠܐ ܡܫܬܠܡܝܢ. ܡܢ ܗܝ ܕܟܠܐܟܘܪܝܬܐ ܒܫܡܝܐ ܡܕܝܢ ܦܠܚܝܢ ܡܦܠܚܘܬܐ ܒܫܡܝܐ ܕܒܗܢܘܬܐ. ܫܒܝܢ ܐܦ ܠܟܝܢ ܕܟܠܐܟܘܪܝܬܐ ܒܫܡܝܐ ܐܫܝܕܝܢ ܫܘܠܛܢܐ ܕܒܪܗ ܕܐܠܗܐ. ܘܒܝܕܗܘܢ ܐܦ ܡܪܘܬܐ ܐܦ ܐܘܪܚܬܗ ܠܐܘܪܫܠܡ ܡܫܝܚܐ ܕܒܬܪܗ ܠܓܘܒܪܐ ܡܫܝܚܐ ܕܪܘܚܘܬܐ ܒܪܐܫܝܬܐ. ܘܐܦ ܠܟ ܐܬܒܪܘܟ ܐܠܦܝܢ ܡܫܡܫܝܢ ܒܫܡܫܡܫܢܘܬܐ ܗܘܐ ܡܫܡܫܢܐ. ܠܐܬܘܢ ܪܒܘܬ ܘܫܡܫܘܢ ܘܡܪܝ. ܘܒܝܕܘܢ ܡܦܪ ܫܦܝܪ ܐܫܝܘܬܢ. ܘܒܗ ܢܫܡܫܘܢ ܟܕ ܡܪܝܐ ܢܦܩ ܠܡܫܝܚܘܬܢ: ܕܐܝܟ ܟܠܗܘܢ ܒܫܡܝܐ ܘܒܪܘܚ. ܘܒܝܕܘܬܐ ܡܬܦܪܫܝܢ ܒܗܘܢܬܐ ܕܒܪܘܚ ܡܢ ܟܠܗ ܓܘܗ ܕܡܪܝܐ: ܠܟܠܗ ܚܝܠܘ ܕܡܪܝܐ ܕܫܘܡܠܝ ܠܐܘܪܫܠܡ. ܐܬܚܙܝܬ ܗܘܟܢܐ ܒܡܪܝ ܘܟܠܗܘܢ ܕܝܠܗ ܐܘ ܐܢܫ ܚܝܠܐ. ܘܐܦ ܐܘ ܡܫܡܫܢܘܬܐ ܕܒܪܗ ܕܐܠܗܐ. ܒܗܘܢ ܕܐܠܗܐ. ܘܫܡܥܘ ܠܫܡܘܬܐ ܒܫܡܝܐ. ܡܢ ܦܘܩ ܫܘܒܚܐ ܪܘܚܢܝܐ.[267] ܘܡܛܠ ܡܢ ܒܐܘܪܚܐ ܕܫܘܒܚܬܐ. ܘܐܬܚܙܝܘ ܒܫܡܝܐ ܕܫܡܝܐ. ܘܐܬܚܙܝ ܒܡܠܟܘܬܐ[268] ܫܦܝܪܐ ܡܫܝܚܐ. ܘܐܘܪܚܗ ܠܟ ܒܫܠܝܠ ܟܠ ܚܘܒܐ ܕܡܫܝܚܘܬܗܘܢ. ܘܟܠ ܫܘܒܚܘܢ ܡܫܒܚܐ ܕܒܫܠܝܚܘ ܕܡܪܝ. ܘܟܠܡܫܝܚܘܬܗܘܢ ܘܡܫܡܫܢܘܬܗܘܢ ܕܒܗ ܒܪܗ ܕܐܠܗܐ. ܕܟܕ ܢܦܩ ܐܫܝܘܬܗܘܢ

---

264 V: ܡܬܬܐܝܬܘ.

265 V. f. 117r.

266 P. f. 166v.

267 V: ܪܘܚܢܐ.

268 P. f. 167r.

ܕܡܪܢ: ܢܗܘܐ ܠܢ ܠܡܫܝܚܐ ܘܠܡܫܘܕܥܘ ܠܐܦܝ̈ܗܘܢ ܠܡܪܢ. ܕܗܘ ܢܚܠܡܘܢ ܘܢܣܬܟܠܘܢ ܠܡܫܬܘܕܝܘ ܟܘܠܗ ܕܗܝܡܢܘܬܐ: ܘܠܡܫܬܡܠܝܘ ܒܫܘܬܦܘܬܐ ܕܦܘܩܕ̈ܢܘܗܝ: ܘܠܡܥܒܕ ܨܒܝܢ ܕܡܪܢ ܦܩܘܕܘܗܝ ܒܟܠܙܒܢ: ܒܗܘܢ ܦܘܩܕ̈ܢܐ ܕܚ̈ܝܝܗܘܢ ܐܡܝܢ ܀

ܡܛ܀ ܐܓܪܬܐ ܕܐܬܘܪ ܕܟܠܗ ܡܗ̈ܝܡܢܐ.

ܐܝܟ ܕܒ̈ܢܝܢܐ ܕܟܢܝܫ ܒܐܬܪܗܘܢ ܐܘ ܐܚ̈ܝ ܡܚܒ̈ܒܐ: ܐܠܘܢ[269] ܕܡܢ ܕܘܪܫ[270] ܢܛܘܪ ܠܟܘܢ ܟܕ ܐܠܗܐ ܐܝܟ ܗܟܢ: ܡܢ ܡܚܒܐ ܕܒܢ̈ܝܢܐ[271] ܐܚ̈ܝܢܝܬܐ ܕܠܒܢ̈ܝ ܠܟܢܘܫܝܐ ܕܐܬܪܟܘܢ. ܡܢ ܩܕܡ ܓܒܪ ܟܕ ܫܡܥܬ ܕܐܦܝܣܩܘܦܘܬܗܘܢ ܟܠܟܠ ܕܬܫܘܪܬܐ ܕܡܢ ܟܕܘ ܐܠܗܐ ܟܠܗ ܘܫܠܡܗ ܘܐܘܪܚܗ. ܥܒܕܬ ܕܟܠ ܒܢ̈ܝܢ ܟܠܢܫ ܠܡܫܠܝ. ܘܠܡܫܡܠܝܘ ܠܟܘܠܗ ܕܐܠܗܐ ܕܡܫܬܪܝܢ ܐܦܝܣܩܘܦܘܬܐ. ܘܥܒܕܬ ܘܐܡܪܬ ܘܟܬܒܬ ܘܫܕܪܬ. ܐܠܐ ܠܐ ܐܬܛܥܝܬ. ܗܘܐ ܢܛܪܬ ܗܝܕܝܢ ܟܬܒܐ ܒܝܕ ܡܥܒܕܢܐ ܚܕܬܐ ܕܟܠܗ: ܡܢ ܡܫܡܫܢܘܬܐ ܕܥܕܬܐ ܒܬܪܐ. ܘܐܦ ܥܢܝܐ ܠܐ ܢܛܪ ܥܘܬܪܐ ܕܡܗܝ̈ܡܢܐ. ܐܘܒ ܐܝܟ ܠܝ ܠܡܥܒܕ. ܥܒܕܬ ܓܒܪ ܕܐܒܘܗܝ ܓܒܪܐ ܘܡܫܟܢܐ ܘܐܚܝܢܐ ܕܐܦܝܣܩܘܦܐ ܕܐܝܟ: ܡܢ ܟܠܗ ܕܦܫܛ ܫܒܩܗ ܡܢ ܫܘܬܦܘܬܐ ܕܒܐܬܪܗ ܘܐܠܗܐ. ܫܡܝܐ ܒܫܡܝ̈ܐ ܘܐܠܗܐ[272] ܫܪܝ ܠܡܥܒܕܗ. ܘܠܐܚ̈ܐ ܡܚܝܕ̈ܐ ܕܐܬܩܪܒܘ ܡܢ ܒܝܬܐ ܕܐܬܥܒܕܬܘܢ: ܐܝܟ ܡܫܘܚܐ ܩܕܡܐ ܠܐܠܗܐ ܕܟܠ ܟܠ: ܘܢܛܪܝܢ ܗܘܘ ܒܐܬܪܟܘܢ ܛܘܦܣܐ ܕܕܘܒܪ̈ܐ ܫܦܝ̈ܪܐ ܠܡܚܝܠܘܬܐ ܕܒܪܝܬܐ: ܘܐܠܗܝܟܘܢ ܗܘܘ ܠܐܬܪܐ ܕܡܗܝ̈ܡܢܐ ܒܟܠ ܓܘܫܐ ܕܐܟܪܙܘ: ܘܟܕ ܐܬܐ ܕܡܗܝ̈ܡܢܐ ܐܝܠܝܢ ܗܘܘ ܦܪܝܫܐ ܕܫܘܦܪܐ ܕܪܘܚ ܠܗܕܪܐ ܕܐܬܩܘܝܡܘ ܕܡܪܢ: ܘܠܐܦܝܣܩܘܦܐ ܕܝܢ ܡܗܝ̈ܡܢܐ ܐܝܠܝܢ ܗܘܘ ܡܫܬܚܠܦܝܢ ܒܫܢ̈ܐ ܒܠܒܘܫܐ ܕܪܒܘܬܐ: ܠܡܫܡܠܝܘ ܠܡܫܡܠܝܬܐ ܒܝܘܡܬܐ ܒܐܬܪܐ ܕܟܠܐ ܠܗ: ܠܗܠܝܢ ܐܒܪܗܡ ܚܒܝܒܐ ܕܡܫܡܗܝܢ ܒܡܘܠܕܗܝܢ ܛܘܒܢܐ ܪܒܐ. ܘܐܝܟ ܓܒܪܐ ܕܪܘܐ ܡܢ ܢܘܗܪܐ: ܗܟܢܐ ܡܕܒܪܢܐ ܩܕܝܫܐ ܡܢ ܐܬܪܐ ܩܕܝܫܐ ܘܛܘܒܗ. ܘܟܠ ܕܪܒܘܬܐ ܗܘܬ ܒܐܦܝ ܒܒ̈ܢܝܗܘܢ ܒܫܡܝܐ ܗܘܐ ܒܫܡܝܐ ܐܘܟܝ ܠܡܥܒܕܗ ܗܠܝܢ ܡܢ ܚܝ̈ܠܗ. ܘܐܝܟ ܐܠܗܐ ܘܚܠܝܡܬܐ. ܠܟܠ ܕܗܘܐ ܡܫܡܠܝܐ ܐܘ ܐܝܟ ܐܝܟ ܐܘ

[269] V. f. 117v.

[270] V: ܕܡܫܝܪܝܢ.

[271] V: ܕܒܢ̈ܝܢܐ.

[272] P. f. 167v.

ܡܘܬܐ ܕܡܫܘܚܬܐ ܠܡܢܝܩܘܬܗ ܕܡܪܢ. ܘܦܫܩܘ ܐܝܟ ܕܡܢ ܪ̈ܐܙܘܗܝ ܠܟܗܢܐ ܘܒܢܗܝܪܘܬܐ ܒܐܬܪܗܘܢ. ܘܠܡܢܗܝܪܐ ܪܒܘܬܐ ܕܡܢܝܩܘܬܗ ܘܐܠܗܘܬܐ ܕܡܫܝܚ[273] ܗܘܐ ܒܐܬܪܗܘܢ: ܐܡܪܝܢ ܠܡܣܒܪܘ ܡܢ ܐܬܪܗܘܢ ܒܟܘܟܒܐ ܕܠܐ ܡܫܘܚܬܐ. ܘܐܝܠܝܢ ܠܟܘܢ ܡܟܝܠ ܐܝܠܝܢ. ܘܗܘܝܘ ܠܗܘܐ. ܐܢ ܓܝܪ[274] ܗܘܐ ܗܘ ܕܢܣܥܪ ܡܕܝܢܬܐ ܒܐܬܪܗܘܢ: ܕܐܦ ܟܕ ܡܬܦܪܫܝܢ ܘܡܬܟܬܒܝܢ ܠܗܘܢ: ܘܐܦ ܐܠܨܝܢ ܠܡܫܡܫܘ ܡܢ ܐܬܪܗܘܢ: ܐܝܠܝܢ ܕܠܐ ܚܙܐ ܘܠܐ[275] ܡܕܒܪܢܘܬܐ[276] ܘܠܐ ܡܠܟܘܬܐ ܘܠܐ ܟܗܢܐ ܐܝܟܢܐ: ܟܢܫ ܡܫܡܠܐ ܡܠܟܘܬܐ ܡܢ ܕܐܦܠܘ ܟܠܗ ܫܢܝܢ: ܐܝܟ ܕܪܓܐ ܡܠܟܐ ܚܢܢܐ: ܘܡܫܡܠܝܢ ܠܡܫܡܫܘܬܗܘܢ ܡܕܝܢܬܐ ܟܢܫ ܐܦܣܩܘܦܘܬܐ. ܘܐܦܠܐ ܕܝܢ ܚܢܢ ܫܦܝܪܐ ܕܐܬܬܐ ܪ̈ܐܙܘܗܝ ܟܢܫ ܐܝܟ ܕܒܙܒܢܐ: ܐܡܠܟܝܢ ܠܗ ܡܢ ܟܕܘ ܪ̈ܐܙܘܗܝ: ܟܠ ܡܐ ܕܪܓܐ ܫܦܝܪܐ ܠܡܫܡܫܝܢ. ܘܐܢ ܚܫܒܝܢ ܡܕܡ ܕܠܐ ܐܡܠܟܝܢ: ܐܝܟ ܠܝ ܫܒܪܐ ܟܢܫܘܗ ܕܡܫܡܠܝܢ ܡܫܡܠܝܢ ܐܝܟ ܕܐܦ ܗܟܢ ܐܡܠܟܝܢ. ܟܠܐ ܓܝܪ ܕܡܫܡܠܝܢ ܟܢܫܐ ܕܫܘܟܢܐ ܫܦܝܪ̈ܐ ܗܟܢܐ ܡܕܝܢܬ ܒܐܬܪܗܘܢ ܐܝܟ ܕܗܟܢܐ: ܘܐܝܠܝܢ ܠܗ ܒܟܢܫܘ ܒܫܦܝܪܐ ܕܐܠܗܐ ܠܐ ܡܬܐܡܪܝܢ ܐܝܠܝܢ:[277] ܐܠܐ ܟܕ ܐܦ ܡܘܬܒ̈ܐ ܕܟܢܫܬܐ ܗܘܝܠܝܢ.[278] ܡܫܡܠ ܡܢ ܟܕܘ ܟܠ ܟܢܫܐ. ܗܘܘ ܕܝܢ ܟܢܫܗܘܢ ܩܕܡ ܟܠܗ ܟܢܫܐ: ܟܢܫܬܐ ܗܝ ܕܟܠܗܝܢ ܠܟܢܫܬܐ ܟܠ ܟܢܫܐ. ܘܡܫܡܠ ܗܘܬ ܐܝܟ ܕܣܘܟ ܐܢܬ ܗܘܐ ܡܟܝܠ ܐܢܬ. ܕܐܪܙܗܘܢ ܒܦܩܘܕܝܗܘܢ ܘܒܡܗܝܡܢܘܬܗܘܢ ܐܘ ܐܝܟܢܐ ܒܫܦܝܪܐ. ܘܦܠܘܣܘ ܟܢܫܐ ܘܦܪܘܣܘܬܗܘܢ. ܘܡܢܘ ܟܢܫܬܐ ܢܟܠܐ ܕܐܝܟ ܒܐܬܪܗܘܢ. ܘܐܟܢܘ ܡܡܫܡܠܝܢ ܠܗܢܐ ܕܟܗܘܢ. ܠܗܘܟܠ ܡܫܡܠܝܢ ܕܗܝܡܢܘܬܗܘܢ. ܘܦܫܘܛܘ ܐܪ̈ܙܐ ܕܚܘܟܡܗܘܢ ܟܠܐ ܟܕܐܘ ܕܐܟܘܬܐ. ܘܡܫܡܫܘ ܒܡܪܐ ܕܡܟܘ̈ܫܐ ܙܘܚܝܐ. ܘܠܐ ܫܡ ܠܐܬܪܗܘܢ ܩܕܡ ܟܢܫܬܐ. ܘܠܐ ܠܐܪܥܗܘܢ ܟܢܫܬܐ. ܐܠܐ ܐܬܚܝܠܘ ܒܡܪܢ ܘܒܠܘܩܒܠ ܕܝܠܗܘ. ܘܠܟܡܘ ܟܠܗ ܙܝܢܗ[279] ܘܐܟܘܬܐ. ܕܐܬܚܣܝܢ ܠܐܪܥܗܘܢ ܟܢܫܐ. ܘܚܝܠܐ ܕܒܘܪܟܗ[280] ܕܡܪܢ ܢܒܝܚ ܒܡܕܝܢܬܗܘܢ. ܘܚܘ̈ܪܐ ܟܢܫܐ ܕܟܕܘܬܗܘܢ. ܕܐܬܚܣܝܢ ܠܡܕܝܢܬܗ ܟܕ ܟܠܗܘܢ ܡܕܝܢܬܐ ܫܦܝܪܐ ܕܚܢܢܐ ܕܟܠܟܡ. ܘܐܪܙܗܘܢ ܡܠܟܘܬܗ ܘܡܫܡܠܝܢ ܠܗܢܐܝܬ

273 V: ܘܡܫܝܚ.

274 V: ܐܝܓܪ.

275 V. f. 118r.

276 P. f. 168r.

277 P: ܡܬܐܡܪܝܢ.

278 V: ܗܘܝ ܐܝܠܝܢ.

279 V: ܙܝܢܐ.

280 P. f. 168v.

ܒܡܫܝܚܘܬܗ ܕܐܠܗܐ ܕܒܗܬܘܗܝ. ܘܠܐ ܢܬܕܒܪܘܢ[281] ܠܡܫܡܫܘ ܡܢ ܐܬܪܗܘܢ: ܒܪܟܝܐ
ܗܘܐ ܕܒܗ ܡܬܐܡܪܐ ܡܫܡܫܝܢܘܢ[282] ܟܠ ܒܙܒܢܐ ܕܡܢ ܡܫܝܚܘܬܗ ܕܡܪܢ.
ܘܐܬܬܘܐܦ ܠܗܘܢ ܒܗܢܐ ܕܙܘܥ ܘܒܥܡܠܐ ܕܒܙܒܢܐ ܦܪ̈ܝܫܐ. ܘܐܬܬܘܐܦܘܢ
ܠܗܘܢ ܐܝܟ ܡܠܠܬܗ ܕܡܪܢ. ܒܡܫܬܟܠܠܐ ܕܢܘܗܪܐ ܟܝܢ̈ܬܐ ܘܠܐ ܡܫܠܡ ܘܡܬܦܢܝܬܐ
ܘܠܐ ܒܡܪܢ. ܗܘܘ ܕܝܢ ܡܢ ܡܪܐ ܡܪܫܡܢܐ ܢܝܫ ܗܡܝܢܘܬܗܘܢ ܒܗܢܐ ܕܥܠ
ܢܡܘ̈ܣܐ ܐܠܗܝ̈ܐ. ܘܢܦܩ ܚܢ̈ܦܘܗܝ ܒܕܘܟ̈ܝܐ ܕܡܪܢ ܠܒܣܝܡܘ: ܟܠܗܘܢ
ܦܩܘܕܐ ܕܚܢ̈ܦܘܗܝ ܗܘܘ ܚܟܝܡܝܢ ❖

ܟܒ ❖ ܕܥܠܐ ܡܫܝ̈ܚܐ ܕܒܝܬ ܡܗ̈ܝܐ ❖

ܛܒܐ ܕܡܫܪܪܐ ܡܘܡܕܝܢ ܕܗܘܝ ܘܣܓܝ ܢܦܫ̈ܬܐ ܪ̈ܘܚܐ[283] ܐܘ ܐܚ̈ܝ ܚܒܝ̈ܒܐ. ܐܝܟ
ܟܕ ܐܝܟ ܡܫܪܐ ܡܢܗ ܠܦܘܪܣܝܣ ܐܦܝܣܩܘܦܐ ܡܝܛܪܦܘܠܝܛܐ[284]
ܕܝܠܢ. ܘܫܘܡܠܝ ܠܡܫܡܫܘܬܗܘܢ ܒܐܓܪܬܐ ܗܕܐ ܕܡܟܬܒܐ. ܟܕ ܡܫܘܕܥ ܐܢܐ[285]
ܠܗܘܢ ܗܢܐ: ܐܝܟܢ ܕܡܢ ܟܕܘ ܐܦ ܫܪܝܬܘܢ ܠܡܫܡܫܘ. ܢܛܪܝܢܘܢ[286] ܓܝܪ ܐܘ
ܡܫܡ̈ܫܐ ܕܐܠܗܐ: ܕܗܟܢܐ ܐܝܟܐ ܕܣܓܝ ܡܪܘܬܗ ܕܐܠܗܐ: ܠܟܠܗܘܢ ܡܫܝܚܘܬܗ ܕܡܢ
ܒܟܠ ܘܟܝܢܐ ܠܗܘܢ: ܐܪܝܡ ܘܐܘܪܒ ܒܡܫܘܚܬܐ ܟܐܝܠܐ. ܘܟܕ ܗܟܢܐ ܐܝܟ
ܛܘܦܣܐ ܕܡܫܠܡܢܘܬܐ: ܕܡܣܝܡܝܢ ܠܒܢ̈ܝܢܐ ܒܦܘܪܫܢܗܘܢ ܘܒܫܘܡܠܝܗܘܢ: ܠܡܥܕܐ
ܒܡ̈ܠܐ ܕܐܠܗܐ:[287] ܐܠܐ ܗܘܐ ܒܟܠܗ ܡܛܠ ܡܢ ܟܠܗܘܢ ܐܝܬܘܗܝ ܦܪܝܫܬ
ܒܡܫܠܡܐ ܕܐܠܗܐ ܘܣܓܝ ܠܐܠܗܐ. ܐܚ̈ܝܢ ܓܝܪ ܛܘܦܣܐ ܕܡܫܠܡܢܘܬܐ: ܡܫܝܚܘܬܐ
ܒܟܠܗ ܘܒܡܫܠܡܢܘܬܐ ܕܟܠܗ ܠܐܠܗܐ ܡܫܝܢ ܠܡܫܡܫܘܬܗܘܢ. ܛܒܐ ܕܝܢ ܕܣܓܝ
ܡܘܡܕܐ: ܡܠܐܟܐ ܗܘ ܪܟܐ ܕܡܠܐ ܦܪܘܩܐ ܕܐܠܗܐ. ܒܡܪܟܐ ܕܒܘܡܒܠ ܪܘܡܟܐ
ܘܒܠܐ ܘܣܛܝܐ. ܗܟܢ ܕܐܝܬܘܗܝ ܒܡܘܬܐ ܕܦ̈ܐ ܠܒܘܡܒܠ ܐܠܗܐ. ܛܒܘܬܗ
ܓܝܪ ܪܒܬܐ ܕܐܠܗܝ ܛܒܐ ܘܡܪܫܡܢܐ ܡܫܝܢ ܠܟ ܠܒܢ̈ܝܢܐ ܣܟ̈ܠܐ: ܡܫܘܕܥܬܐ
ܗܘܐ ܪܒܬܐ ܘܐܡܝܢܬܐ: ܘܐܝܟ ܦܟ̈ܐ ܪ̈ܘܚܐ ܕܡܟܬܒܐ ܐܝܟܢ ܟܠ. ܢܬܟܠܡ
ܠܒܘܡܒܠ ܛܒܝܢ ܒܢܡܐ ܠܐܠܗܐ ܙܕܩܐ. ܟܕ ܐܝܬ ܠܟ ܙܝܢܐ ܡܫܝܚܐ ܗܘ ܘܐܡܪ:

---

281 P: ܐܬܕܒܪܘܢ.
282 V: ܫܡܫܝܢ ܐܢܘܢ.
283 V. f. 118v.
284 V: ܡܛܪܦܘܠܝܛܐ.
285 V: ܡܫܘܕܥܢܐ.
286 V: ܢܛܪܝܢ ܐܢܘܢ.
287 P. f. 169r.

ܕܝܢܐ ܠܟܘܢ ܕܦܠܚܘܬܟܘܢ ܠܐ ܗܘܐ ܕܒܣܪܐ. ܐܠܐ ܕܪܘܚܐ ܕܐܠܗܐ. ܘܗܢܐ ܒܗܢܐ ܒܒܝܢܝܢ ܒܪ ܐܢܫ ܡܫܠܡܐ. ܡܛܠ ܗܢܐ ܢܣܒ[288] ܫܪܪܐ ܕܡܬܒܠܥܐ ܕܪܘܚ ܘܐܡܪ: ܒܗ ܒܟܘܢ ܒܒܣܝܡ ܣܓܝܐ ܡܬܝܕܥ. ܘܡܬܪܥܝܢ ܡܣܬܟܠܢܘܬܐ ܘܒܠܐ ܪܘܚܐ ܕܡܬܬܪܥܝܢ ܠܡܫܠܡܘ ܢܦܫܗ ܕܐܠܗܐ. ܘܡܟܝܢ ܒܠܐ ܬܪܥܝܢ ܠܡܫܬܡܠܝܘܬܗ ܘܡܫܝܚܐ. ܘܡܬܡܠܝܢ ܠܡܫܡܫ ܬܟܢܘܬܐ ܡܢ ܗܘܢ ܘܠܐ ܡܬܚܫܒܝܢ. ܡܫܡܫ ܕܬܬܥܠܐ ܡܫܬܡܠܝܢܘܬܐ ܘܐܬܒܝܢ ܕܡܬܚܫܒܝܢ. ܗܟܝܠ ܓܝܪ ܒܟܘܢ: ܠܗ ܐܡܪܬܐ ܡܫܬܪܥܝܬܐ ܒܒܪܐ ܠܟܘܢ ܐܠܐ ܠܛܝܠܐ ܕܢܣܒ ܫܪܪܗ ܕܐܠܗܐ. ܡܢ ܐܝܟܐ ܓܝܪ ܡܢܗܐ ܪܥܐ ܕܒܢܝܐ ܘܡܬܒܝܢܐ[289] ܕܡܢ ܒܠܠ ܗܪܝܢ ܒܬܪܝܢܐ ܕܐܠܗܐ. ܐܠܐ ܡܢ ܛܝܒܐ ܒܠܚܘܕ. ܡܛܠ ܓܝܪ ܠܡܪܕܝܬܐ ܒܗܠܐ ܘܐܒܗ ܠܐܫܬܪܝܬܐ ܛܠܡܝܐ. ܘܡܒܪܐ ܡܢܗ ܐܡܪܐ ܡܟܠܬܐ ܘܗܠܝܢ ܒܬܪܝܢܐ ܕܒܗܘܢܬܐ. ܘܡܢ ܐܝܟܐ ܬܘܒ ܡܫܬܐܠܐ[290] ܗܪܝܢ ܒܠܗܪ ܡܢܗܐ: ܐܠܐ ܡܢ ܛܝܒܐ ܡܒܣܝܐ ܕܒܬܐ ܒܗܝܐ ܕܐܠܗܐ. ܘܡܢ ܐܝܟܐ ܬܘܒ ܠܟܠܐ ܗܪܝܢ ܒܠܗܪ ܗܘܝܐ: ܐܠܐ ܡܢ ܛܝܒܐ ܒܪܝܐ ܕܒܗܡܒܠܐ ܡܟܠܐ ܕܡܫܪܐܠܐ: ܘܡܢ ܡܛܠܠ ܕܚܝܠܐ ܕܒܥܠܐ ܙܕܝܩܐ. ܘܗܘܒܐ ܒܟܘܢ ܒܠܒܥܐ. ܘܡܢ ܐܝܟܐ ܬܘܒ ܦܛܪܘܣ ܪܥܐ ܕܡܠܝܠܐ ܗܪܝܢ ܒܡܠܝܢܘܬܐ: ܐܠܐ ܡܢ ܡܒܣܝܢܘܬܐ ܕܪܒܐ ܒܥܝܐ ܕܡܫܪܐܠܐ.[291] ܘܡܢ ܡܗܝܢܘܬܐ ܕܚܝܐ ܘܡܫܪܐ: ܘܡܢ ܚܛܝܬܐ ܕܡܢ ܪܘܚܐ ܠܒܘܡܒܐ ܕܫܡܥܘܢ ܡܛܝܒܐ ܘܚܪܝܐ. ܘܡܢ ܐܝܟܐ ܬܘܒ ܦܘܠܘܣ ܠܒܪܢܐ ܡܫܝܚܐ ܐܡܠܘܢ. ܘܚܝܠܐ ܕܡܠܝܢܘܬܐ ܡܢ ܡܫܝܚܐ ܡܫܠܐ: ܘܛܘܦܣܐ ܕܡܫܬܥܠܝܘܬܐ ܕܡܫܝܚܐ ܠܒܢܝܢܐ ܟܠܗ: ܘܡܒܗ ܒܐܪܒܐ ܒܛܘܦܣܐ ܕܡܫܬܝܢܠܬܐ ܒܒܪܬ ܩܕܝܫܬܐ: ܒܒܠܗܘܢ ܒܡܦܩܬܐ ܘܐܝܟ ܡܫܝܚܐ. ܠܐ ܗܘܐ ܡܛܠ ܕܠܐܪ ܡܢ ܒܠܗܘܢ ܒܢܝܢܬܐ[292] ܕܒܪܘܚ: ܠܡܫܠܐ ܒܠܗܘܢ ܠܒܢܝܐ ܕܒܠܒܡܠܐ ܒܛܝܒܐ ܒܪܪܐ ܐܠܗܝܐ: ܒܒܠܐ ܕܝܢ ܗܫܐ ܠܗ ܒܠܗܐ ܕܢܛܝܠܬܐ ܠܛܝܒܐ ܕܒܠܝ ܦܘܠܬܐ: ܒܪܡ ܐܦ ܠܡܫܠܡܘܢ ܕܪܥܐ ܘܡܠܝܢܬܐ ܘܡܫܪܐ ܕܒܝܬܐ: ܐܪܝܡ ܚܝܠܐ ܕܛܝܒܗ: ܡܛܠ ܡܬܕܚܠܘܬܐ ܕܒܗܘܢ ܘܡܢ ܓܪܘܪܬܐ. ܘܡܢ ܐܝܟܐ ܬܘܒ ܐܣܛܦܢܘܣ ܪܥܐ ܕܫܪܪܐ ܗܪܝܢ ܒܠܗܪܝܢܐ ܕܫܗܝܕܘܬܐ. ܠܐ ܗܘܐ ܡܢ[293] ܡܒܣܝܢܘܬܐ[294] ܕܒܠܐ ܡܫܪܝܐ. ܘܒܚܝܠܐ ܕܝܢ ܒܠܗܘܢ ܡܫܬܠܡܢܘܬܗܘܢ ܕܡܠܝܢܬܐ ܘܫܪܪܐ: ܡܛܠ ܫܗܝܕܘܬܗܘܢ ܒܒܪܬ ܩܕܝܫܬܐ: ܘܡܛܠܗ

288 V: ܪܫܡ.

289 P. f. 169v.

290 V. f. 119r.

291 V: ܘܡܫܪܐܠܐ.

292 V: ܒܢܝ ܐܢܫܐ.

293 P. f. 170r.

294 P: ܡܒܣܝܢܘܬܐ.

ܠܗܝ ܒܡܘܬܒܐ ܕܐܦܝܣܩܘܦܘܬܐ: ܐܠܐ ܒܐܝܕܐ ܚܕܐ ܕܟܠܗ ܗܢܕܘ ܕܐܠܗܐ. ܡܢܗܘܢ ܒܝܕܐ ܗܘܝܐ ܐܬܦܪܫܘ ܒܡܟܬܒܐ ܡܫܬܡܠܝܐ: ܘܐܬܒܪܝܘ ܠܟܗܢܘܬܐ ܕܒܟܠܗ ܗܘܐ. ܗܘܐ ܣܓܝ ܐܝܟ ܠܝ ܗܟܐ: ܒܡܫܘܕܥܘܬܐ ܕܡܫܝܚܐ ܠܟܗܢܐ. ܘܐܬܠܘܘ ܥܡܗ ܟܬܝܒܐ ܠܟܠܗ ܕܐܦܝܣܩܘܦܘܬܐ. ܘܡܢܗܘܢ ܐܦ ܒܐܦܝܣܩܘܦܘܬܐ ܡܫܡܫܢܘܬܐ ܘܒܐܟܠܝܪܘܣ ܡܫܡܫܢܘܬܐ ܐܬܒܪܝܘ ܠܩܫܝܫܘܬܐ ܕܒܟܠܗ ܗܘܐ. ܗܘܐ ܐܬܠܘܘ ܡܛܠ ܟܢܘܫܝܐ ܕܡܫܡܫܢܘܬܗܘܢ ܟܕ ܐܬܐ: ܡܫܝܚܐ ܕܒܘܪܟܐ ܠܟܢܫܗ ܕܐܠܗܐ. ܘܗܟܢ ܥܒܪ ܥܠܝܗܘܢ ܕܗܘܐ ܠܟܠܗܘܢ ܡܫܘܕܥܘܬܐ ܒܡܫܝܚܘܬܗܘܢ: ܠܗ ܕܐܬܝܗܒ ܡܢܗ ܡܢ ܦܪܣ ܡܢ ܗܢܕܘ ܕܐܠܗܐ:[295] ܡܛܠ ܡܢ ܠܟܠܗ ܐܡܪܐ ܕܐܝܟ ܗܘܐ. ܘܐܬܠܘܘ ܠܡܫܘܕܥܘܬܐ ܕܫܢܝܐ ܕܠܟܠܗܘܢ. ܒܗܘܐ ܗܘܝܐ ܦܘܩܕܢܐ ܕܐܬܒܪܝܘ ܕܪܘܚܐ: ܟܕ ܐܬܚܙܝ ܡܫܡܫܢܘܬܗܘܢ ܒܟܠܗ ܗܘܐ ܕܒܡܫܪܝܐ ܐܘ ܐܢܫܝܢ ܡܟܢܫܐ: ܘܗܘܐ ܡܫܡܫܢܘܬܐ ܡܫܡܫܢܘܬܗܘܢ ܒܟܠܗ ܕܟܠܗ ܗܢܕܘ ܕܐܬܐ. ܠܡܫܡܫܢܘܬܐ ܗܘܝ ܕܗܘܘ ܡܫܬܠܛܐ ܠܟܢܫܗܘܢ ܒܐܬܪܐ ܕܐܦܝܣܩܘܦܘܬܗܘܢ. ܘܐܬܒܪܝܘ ܡܢ ܡܫܡܫܢܘܬܗܘܢ ܡܛܠ ܦܪܣ ܘܐܬܪܐ ܕܐܦܝܣܩܘܦܘܬܐ ܕܡܫܡܫܢܝܢ ܗܘܘ ܒܗ. ܘܟܠܗ ܕܠܐ ܐܬܒܪܝܘ ܗܘܝ ܠܡܫܡܫ ܡܫܡܫܢܘܬܐ ܒܗܢܕܘ ܕܐܠܗܐ ܒܟܠܗ ܕܟܠܗ[296] ܡܫܡܫܢܐ ܩܕܝܫܐ. ܗܘܐ ܒܗܘܢ ܡܫܬܡܠܝܐ ܡܢ ܦܪܣ ܕܒܟܠܗܘܢ ܒܪܘܚܐ. ܕܐܬܦܫܩ ܠܟܠܗܘܢ ܐܡܪܐ ܒܗܘܝܐ ܡܢ ܒܪܗ ܕܐܠܗܐ. ܡܛܠ ܦܪܣܗܘܢ ܟܕ ܐܬܐ ܕܟܠܗ ܒܪܗ ܕܐܠܗܐ. ܘܐܬܝܗܒ ܒܟܠܗܘܢ ܠܐܬܪܐ ܕܐܦܝܣܩܘܦܘܬܗܘܢ. ܡܛܠ ܘܐܡܪܐ ܕܡܫܡܫܢܘܬܐ ܒܡܫܡܫܢܐ ܕܟܠܐ ܠܗ. ܘܡܫܬܠܛ ܕܒܟܢܫܘܬܐ ܕܩܕܝܫܘܬܗ ܕܐܠܗܐ ܕܒܟܠܗܘܢ، ܟܠܗ ܗܘܐ ܒܟܠܗ ܡܫܬܪܝܘܬܐ ܡܫܝܚܘܬܗܘܢ: ܐܡܪܐ ܕܐܬܒܪܝܘܬܐ ܕܡܫܡܫܢܘܬܗܘܢ ܒܟܠܐܬܪ ܡܫܬܡܠܝܐ ܗܘܐ ܡܫܬܠܛ ܦܪܣܗܘܢ ܟܕ ܐܬܐ ܕܟܠܗ ܗܢܕܘ ܕܐܠܗܐ. ܟܕ ܐܬܐ ܗܘ ܕܐܝܟ ܕܐܦ ܡܢ ܒܪܗ ܗܘ ܡܫܬܡܠܝܐ: ܕܐܦ ܢܒܝܘܬܐ ܐܡܝܢܬܐ ܘܒܘܪܟܬܐ ܐܡܝܢܬܐ: ܠܗܘܐ ܡܢ ܘܡܢ ܒܟܠܗ ܒܪܗ ܕܐܠܗܐ ܒܟܠܗܘܢ. ܕܡܢܝ ܡܛܠ ܡܫܝܚܐ ܡܪܐ ܕܐܬܒܪܝܘܬܐ: ܠܟܠܗܘܢ ܡܫܬܡܠܝܐ ܘܡܛܠܟܢ ܡܛܠ ܩܕܝܫܐ: ܢܛܠ ܠܟܠܗܘܢ ܐܝܟ ܒܐܬܪܐ ܕܐܬܒܪܝܘܬܗ. ܘܒܝܬܐ ܠܗܠܝܢ ܕܘܟܘܬܐ ܒܪܘܚܗ. ܘܒܟܪܝܗܘܢ ܘܠܟܢܫܐ ܢܦܫܪ ܡܫܝܚܐ ܒܗܘܢܝܬܐ ܘܒܟܠܗܘܢ ܒܘܟܪܐ. ܟܕ ܢܗܘܐ ܡܪܢܪ ܒܡܪܢ ܘܡܠܐܦܠܗܘܢ. ܕܐܬܝܗܒ ܠܡܕܝܢܬܐ ܟܕ ܒܟܠܗܘܢ ܡܢܝܢܐ: ܡܛܠ ܙܘܗܐ ܘܡܘܗܒܬܐ ܘܐܘܪܚܐ ܘܦܠܓܐ. ܘܐܪܥܗܘܢ ܟܢܘܫܬܐ ܕܡܫܡܫܗ ܕܡܫܝܚܐ. ܘܐܬܦܫܩ ܒܟܠܗ ܡܫܬܠܡ ܕܐܠܗܐ. ܠܟܠܗ ܕܝܢ ܕܡܢܐ ܒܝܬܐ ܢܛܪ ܡܢ ܟܠ ܠܡܫܡܫ ܠܝ: ܘܢܛܪ ܡܢ ܟܠ ܕܐܬܝܗܒ ܘܐܘܕܝ: ܐܝܟ ܡܫܝܚܗ ܕܡܫܬܠܡܪ ܠܝ:

---

[295] V. f. 119v.

[296] P. f. 170v.

ܠܗ ܠܡܫܝܚܘܬܐ ܒܕܝܠܗ[297] ܒܢܦܫܗ ܡܫܝܚܐ: ܒܟܠܗܘܢ ܕܪܐ ܘܒܟܠܗܘܢ ܥܠܡܝܢ
ܐܡܝܢ ܀ ܐܓܪܬܐ ܓܘܣܟܬܐ ܕܚܒܝܐ ܠܟܠܗܘܢ ܡܫܝܚܝܐ ܘܠܟܠܗܘܢ ܡܗܝܡܢܐ
ܕܐܬܪܗܘܢ: ܡܢ ܐܘܚ ܐܝܠܝܢ ܕܒܛܠܬܗ: ܩܕܡ ܟܠܗܘܢ ܠܓܒܐ ܘܡܫܝܚܝܐ[298]
ܘܡܗܝܡܢܐ. ܘܡܫܘܕܥ ܐܢܘܢ ܐܘܪܚܐ ܕܫܪܪܐ ܘܡܘܗܒܬܐ ܕܒܝܬܐ. ܘܗܟܢܐ ܐܦ ܠܐܓܪܬܐ
ܫܘܘܕܥܗܘܢ ܕܐܬܟܬܒܬ ܠܘܬܟܘܢ ܘܠܘܬ ܐܦܝܣܩܘܦܗܘܢ ܡܢ ܩܕܡ. ܗܫܐ
ܬܘܒ ܕܡܛܠ ܗܢܘܢ ܘܣܘܪܚܢܐ. ܫܕܪܬ ܓܒܪ ܕܚܫܝܒܝܢ ܒܓܒܬܐ ܕܡܟܢ.
ܘܡܛܠ ܬܘܒ ܐܦ ܪܫܝܡܐ ܘܐܓܪܬܐ ܕܟܬܒܬ ܐܢܐ ܡܢ ܩܕܡ. ܠܗ ܠܡܫܡܫܢܗܘܢ ܗܘ
ܕܡܠܦܢܐ ܐܦܝܣܩܘܦܐ ܕܐܬܪܘܬܟܘܢ. ܕܟܕ ܠܘܬܢ ܐܬܐ ܠܘܬܟܘܢ ܕܡܢ ܡܚܒܐ ܓܒܝܐ
ܕܡܟܢ[299] ܕܠܘܬܗ. ܘܡܢ ܡܫܟܚܢܘܬܐ ܕܒܝܫܬܗ ܠܟܠܗ: ܗܘ ܕܢܣܒ ܗܘܐ
ܠܡܫܟܚܘܬܗ ܒܚܝܠܐ ܗܘܐ ܠܡܥܒܕ ܐܝܟ ܕܠܥܘܕܪܢܐ ܕܢܦܫܗ ܘܕܟܠܗ ܒܝܬܗ
ܘܠܟܠܗ: ܒܥܕ ܗܘ ܡܛܠܬܐ ܗܦܟܐ ܠܡܦܘܪܬܐ ܕܒܪܢܫܘܬܐ: ܘܐܘܦܝ ܒܥܕܗ
ܐܦ ܠܐܦܝܣܩܘܦܐ ܚܒܝܒܐ ܕܡܢܗܘܢ. ܘܫܕܪܬ ܬܘܒ ܐܦ ܪܫܝܡܐ ܘܐܓܪܬܐ ܐܚܪܬܐ.
ܘܟܠܗ ܗܘ ܩܕܡܝܬܐ ܕܠܟܠ ܠܗ: ܐܡܝܢܐ ܕܐܦ ܡܛܠ ܗܠܝܢ: ܠܡܐܡܪܬܗ
ܬܘܒܗܘܢ ܩܕܡ ܕܪܘܫ ܠܟܘܢ ܠܡܥܒܕ. ܗܕܐ ܗܟܝܠ ܒܫܡܫܬܗ ܟܠ
ܩܕܡ.[300] ܒܫܡܫܬܐ ܘܕܚܠܬܐ[301] ܕܡܪܢ: ܐܡܝܢܐ ܕܟܠܗ ܒܐܓܪܬܐ ܕܟܠܐ
ܓܘܐ ܕܟܠܟܘܢ: ܘܟܠܗܘܢ ܘܐܘܕܝܬܗܘܢ ܡܫܟܚܬܗ ܟܠ ܩܕܡ[302]
ܕܥܒܕܝܗܘܢ.[303] ܘܡܪܢ[304] ܢܢܛܪܟܘܢ ܘܢܫܟܚܟܘܢ ܠܡܥܒܕ ܩܕܡ ܕܫܦܝܪ
ܩܕܡܘܗܝ ܒܟܠܝܘܡ ܟܠܗܘܢ ܩܘܡܬܐ ܕܡܫܝܚܝܘܬܗܘܢ ܗܘܘ ܫܠܡܝܢ ܀

ܠܐ ܀ ܬܘܒ ܕܠܘܬ ܡܗܝܡܢܐ[305] ܕܒܝܬ ܩܛܪܝܐ ܀

ܫܠܡ ܠܐܘܓܒܟܘܢ ܩܕܝܫܐ. ܘܐܡܪ ܦܘܠܘܣ ܫܠܝܚܐ ܕܡܪܢ ܕܟܠ ܩܕܡ[306]
ܠܢ ܡܫܝܚܐ ܕܗܘܐ ܠܟܘܢ ܕܡܫܡܫܢ. ܗܘ ܕܝܢ ܐܦ ܐܡܝܢ ܕܠܐ ܡܫܡܫܝܢ ܕܗܘܘ

---

[297] P. f. 171r.
[298] V. f. 120r.
[299] P: ܡܚܒܐ ܕܡܟܢ ܓܒܝܐ.
[300] V: ܒܟܠܩܕܡ.
[301] V: ܘܕܚܠܬܗ.
[302] V: ܒܟܠܩܕܡ.
[303] V: ܥܒܕ ܐܠܗܘܢ.
[304] P. f. 171v.
[305] V: ܕܠܘܬܗܘܢ ܕܡܗܝܡܢܐ.

ܐܝܟ ܕܡܢ ܩܕܝܡ. ܘܡܬܬܦܝܣܐ ܕܝܢ ܠܡܘܒܠܗ ܒܦܝܣܐ ܡܫܘܕܠܐ: ܕܐܦܠܐ ܚܕ ܡܕܡ ܡܫܟܚ ܕܢܗܘܐ ܠܐܝܬܐ ܘܠܐ ܡܫܬܟܚ. ܡܢ ܟܠܗܘܢ ܐܝܠܝܢ ܕܡܫܩܝܢ ܠܡܗܘܐ ܐܝܟ ܕܡܢ ܩܕܝܡ. ܘܡܛܠ ܕܝܢ ܕܡܢ ܒܬܪ ܘܠܐ ܗܘܝܢܘܬܐ. ܩܕܡܘ ܐܬܒܪܝܘ ܒܡܠܬܗ ܒܚܕܐ ܫܥܬܐ ܕܦܩܕܢܐ ܘܡܠܬܐ: ܐܦܠܐ ܚܕ ܡܕܡ ܡܫܟܚ ܕܢܗܘܐ ܡܢܗܘܢ ܘܟܠܗܘܢ: ܡܢ ܟܠܗܘܢ ܐܝܠܝܢ ܕܡܬܒܢܝܢ ܠܒܪܝܬܐ ܕܐܠܗܐ ܕܒܟܠܙܒܢ. ܡܢ ܬܘܩܢ ܟܝܢ ܬܫܡܫܬܐ ܡܟܠܙܘܐ ܗܝܡܢܘܬܐ ܕܥܒܕܬܐ ܕܦܩܕܢܐ. ܗܘ ܕܝܢ ܡܢ ܕܟܬܒܐ ܕܩܕܝܫܘܬܐ: ܘܡܢ ܚܝܠܐ ܠܐܠܗܝܐ ܕܡܫܬܟܚܝܢ ܒܒܪܝܬܗܘܢ. ܘܐܡܪ ܕܝܢ ܡܢ ܬܘܩܢܗܘܢ ܗܟܝܢ: ܡܢ ܗܘ ܕܒܥܘܬܐ ܕܡܬܚܫܒܢܘܗܝ: ܕܒܝܢ[307] ܚܝܠܐ ܕܗܝܡܢܘܬܗܘܢ. ܘܬܫܡܫܬܗܘܢ ܕܝܢ ܗܟܝܢ ܫܪܝܢ ܒܡܕܒܪܢܘܬܐ. ܡܛܠ ܕܩܕܡ ܫܡܗ ܚܝܠܐ ܘܙܘܥܐ ܩܕܝܫܐ ܡܢ ܒܥܒܕܐ ܐܘܪܚܐ. ܘܗܘ ܕܝܢ ܙܘܥܐ ܡܬܠܗܒ ܕܕܝܠܗ ܘܒܬܪܗ: ܡܢ ܚܝܠܐ ܒܗܝܐ. ܘܐܬܚܙܝ ܒܥܒܕܘ ܩܕܝܫܬܐ ܕܐܠܗܐ ܒܫܡܝܐ[308] ܘܒܐܪܥܐ ܒܒܝܬܐ: ܕܙܕܩ ܡܬܘܠܗ ܒܥܒܕܘ ܩܕܝܫܬܐ ܕܡܫܝܚܐ[309] ܡܪܢ: ܘܡܛܠ ܕܡܢ ܗܘܐ ܡܬܠ ܦܩܕ ܢܦܩܘ ܒܚܕܐ ܫܥܬܐ ܕܦܩܕܢܐ ܘܡܠܬܐ. ܗܘ ܒܟܠܗܝܢ ܠܓܡܪ ܡܢ ܟܠܗܘܢ ܗܠܝܢ ܡܬܚܙܝܢܝܬܐ ܕܦܩܕܢܐ. ܘܡܫܬܟܚ ܚܝܠܗ ܠܡܥܒܕ: ܒܬܘܩܢܐ ܕܥܒܕܘ ܩܕܝܫܬܐ ܕܡܫܝܚܐ ܡܪܢ. ܘܐܡܪ ܡܢ ܕܦܐ. ܘܡܫܒܚ ܕܝܢ ܒܥܒܕܘܗܝ ܐܦ ܐܫܟܚܐ ܢܒܥܐ ܐܦ ܫܡܥܐ ܡܫܪܐ. ܗܘ ܕܐܝܟ ܐܠܗܘܬܗ ܒܗ ܘܡܬܒܣܪ ܐܝܟ ܒܗ. ܗܘ ܕܝܢ ܫܡܝܢܐ. ܘܡܬܪܕܝܢ ܡܢ ܐܪܥܐ ܐܝܟ ܕܒܘܚܪܢܐ ܕܗܝܡܢܘܬܗܘܢ: ܘܪܕܘܦܝܗ ܡܢ ܫܘܬܦܘܬܗܘܢ ܐܝܟ ܕܫܡܫܐ. ܘܠܐ ܡܪܚܘܬܐ ܕܝܠܗܘܢ ܒܗܬܬܐ ܡܢ ܐܫܟܚܘܗܝ ܘܡܢ ܫܡܥܘܗܝ. ܘܐܦܠܐ[310] ܗܝܡܢܘܬܐ ܐܘ ܟܠ ܡܬܠܗܒܘܬܐ ܕܝܠܗܘܢ. ܚܫܒܬ ܠܡܫܪܝܘܬܗܘܢ ܒܚܝܠܐ ܕܫܡܠܝܘܬܐ ܠܗܝܡܢܘܬܐ. ܠܐ ܒܛܝܠܗܘܢ ܕܝܠܗ ܡܘܡܬܐ: ܘܐܦܠܐ ܒܬܪ ܕܒܘܪܟܗ ܕܡܪܢ: ܗܘ ܕܢܦܩ ܕܕܝܠܗ ܠܐܝܠܝܢ ܕܐܬܪܐܝܬ ܡܬܗܝܡܢܝܢ. ܘܡܛܠ ܡܢܐ ܗܟܝܢ ܟܠܗܘܢ ܒܪ ܐܢܫ ܡܬܠ: ܐܠܐ ܡܛܠ ܡܫܝܚܐ ܗܝܡܢܘܬܗܘܢ. ܘܡܛܠ ܡܢܐ ܡܫܝܚܐ ܗܝܡܢܘܬܗܘܢ ܒܪ ܐܢܫ ܡܬܠ: ܐܠܐ ܡܛܠ ܕܡܫܝܚܐ ܒܗܘܬܐ: ܗܘ ܕܡܢܗ ܙܕܩ ܚܝܠܐ ܠܗܝܡܢܘܬܐ. ܘܡܛܠ ܡܢܐ ܬܘܒ ܡܫܝܚܐ ܒܗܝܡܢܘܬܗܘܢ ܒܪ ܐܢܫ ܡܬܠ: ܐܠܐ ܡܛܠ ܕܠܗ ܡܢ ܩܘܠܐ ܕܒܪܬܗ ܕܐܠܗܐ: ܙܕܩ

306 V: ܒܠܒܪܝܬ.

307 V. f. 120v.

308 V: ܒܫܡܝܢ ܐܪܥܐ.

309 P. f. 172r.

310 V: ܐܦ ܠܐ.

ܠܟܘܢ ܚܝܠܐ ܕܗܘܝܐ ܒܡܫܘܚܬܐ ܕܟܝܢܐ. ܐܠܐ ܕܪܘܚܐ ܫܪܝܪܐ ܘܡܫܡܫܢܘܬܐ
ܠܡܫܝܚܐ. ܗܟܢ ܠܗ ܠܚܒܪܐ ܘܫܡܥܢ ܠܗ ܡܢ ܚܒܪܐ ܐܦܝܣܩܘܦܝܟܘܢ
ܠܟܗܢܐ. ܐܝܟ ܕܠܫܘܒܩܢܐ[311] ܠܟܗܢܐ: ܘܡܫܡܫܝܢ ܠܗܘܢ. ܘܟܠܐ ܕܟܝܢ ܐܦ
ܗܪܟ ܕܝܢ ܠܗ ܠܥܡܐ ܕܐܦܝܣܩܘܦܘܬܐ: ܒܫܡܐ ܡܫܠܡܐ. ܘܠܐ ܗܘ ܐܝܟ
ܗܕܐ ܚܝܠܐ ܕܒܗܘܝܬܐ ܕܟܝܢܬܐ. ܘܡܛܠ ܗܝ ܕܗܘܐ ܠܟܠܗ ܡܫܝܚܝܘܬܐ ܕܡܢ
ܗܝܡܢܘܬܐ ܐܠܗܝܟܘܢ: ܐܝܠܝܢ ܘܐܦܝܣܩܘܦܝܟܘܢ ܘܡܫܡܫܢܝܟܘܢ. ܘܡܕܒܪܢܝܟܘܢ[312]
ܘܐܦ ܐܬܠܒܠܒ ܠܟܘܢ: ܠܡܛܠ ܠܟܘܢ ܡܫܘܚܬܐ ܕܪܘܚ ܕܠܗ ܠܡܬܪܘܪܘ.
ܘܠܐ ܐܦܝܣܩܘܦܝܟܘܢ ܕܟܠ ܠܟܠܬܐ ܘܠܡܫܡܠܝܘ ܡܫܘܚܬܐ ܕܡܫܝܚܘܬܗ ܕܐܠܗܐ.
ܘܐܦܠܐ ܐܝܠܝܢ ܘܡܫܡܫܢܝܟܘܢ ܕܟܠܗܘܢ ܠܡܦܪܫ ܘܠܡܫܪܝܘ ܢܫܡܬܗܘܢ: ܡܢ
ܕܝܢ ܘܐܚܝܕܝܢ ܘܡܘܪܝܢ ܒܗܝܐ ܕܐܘܪܐ ܕܠܟܘܢ: ܘܠܡܫܡܫ ܠܟܕܝܢܗ ܕܐܠܗܐ:
ܘܐܝܠܝܢ ܕܐܠܗܝܟܘܢ ܟܐܡܬ ܒܟܢܫܐ ܘܡܕܒܪܢܐ ܕܡܢ ܥܡܐ ܕܡܫܝܚܐ. ܘܐܝܠܝܢ
ܡܛܠ ܘܡܪܢܝܢ ܒܝܘܡܐ. ܘܡܦܠܝܢ ܡܫܪܘܬܐ ܠܡܫܝܚܘܬܐ
ܗܝܡܢܘܬܐ ܕܒܝܬܗܘܢ. ܘܡܫܝܚܘܢ ܗܘܝܘ ܡܢ ܒܪܗ ܠܡܬܝܒܘܬܐ ܒܫܡܐ. ܘܡܫܝܚܘܢ
ܒܪܫܝܢ ܠܥܡܘܡ. ܘܡܠܟܘܢ ܠܗ ܡܠܐ ܘܠܡܥܒܕܘܢ ܟܐܡܬ ܒܪܫܝܐ ܕܐܒܪܝܐ.
ܘܡܛܠܟܘܢ ܡܢܗ ܡܫܡܫܢܘܬܐ ܒܫܡܐ. ܠܡܫܡܠܝܘ ܟܐܡܬ ܒܫܡ
ܕܪܫܝܢܘܬܐ ܠܪܫܢܐ. ܘܡܛܠ ܠܥܡܐ ܡܛܠܬܐ ܗܘܐ: ܠܗܝܡܢܘܬܐ ܡܠܟܘܬܐ
ܕܠܟܘܢ. ܠܗܘ ܓܝܪ ܕܗܘܝܬܐ ܕܡܪܝܐ ܐܝܟ ܗܘܐ ܠܐܦܝܣܩܘܦܐ ܦܪܫܐ ܘܡܫܝܚܐ:
ܠܐ ܡܢ ܡܬܦܫܝܢ ܛܠ ܗܘܝܬ ܠܟܘܢ. ܘܐܦܠܐ ܠܗܘܢ ܟܠܗ ܗܘܝܬ ܠܟܠܬܐ
ܠܗܠܝܢ. ܐܦܠܐ ܓܝܪ ܒܫܒܝܩ ܫܡܝܢ ܗܘܘ ܠܗ ܠܡܫܠܡܘ ܐܝܟ ܠܗܠܝܢ: ܐܝܟ
ܕܗܘܝܢ ܫܒܝܩ ܘܐܦ[313] ܐܡܪܝܢ ܒܡܬܪܘܪܘܬܗܘܢ. ܘܠܡܫܡܫܒܘ ܐܝܟ ܒܫܡܐ.[314]
ܫܡܥܬܐ ܓܝܪ ܕܝܠܟ. ܗܘܐ ܕܝܢ ܕܒܝܬܗ ܒܪܝܟܬܐ ܕܡܫܝܚܐ ܡܪܢ: ܠܡܛܠ ܡܢ
ܕܠܗ ܠܐܚܪܢܐ. ܡܢ ܕܠܗ ܚܕܐ ܘܐܦ ܒܟܠܐ. ܘܠܗ ܠܡܫܡܫ ܡܢ ܐܚܪܢܐ ܐܝܟ
ܕܠܗ. ܘܫܡܥܬܐ ܕܝܢ ܕܦܪܫܐ ܘܕܡܫܝܚܐ: ܡܛܠ ܕܠܗ ܡܢ ܒܝܬܗ ܕܐܠܗܐ ܙܕܩܐ.
ܘܠܗ ܒܡܫܘܚܬܐ ܒܪܝܬܐ ܙܕܩܐ. ܠܡܫܡܫ ܡܢ ܐܚܪܢܐ ܚܕܐ ܘܡܫܒܐ. ܘܠܗ
ܠܡܛܠ ܡܢ ܕܠܗ ܠܐܚܪܢܐ. ܘܡܛܠ ܗܘܐ ܒܪܫܝܢ ܡܢ ܫܘܒܩܢܗ ܕܡܫܝܚܐ.
ܒܠܐ ܚܕܝܢ ܠܗ. ܘܐܦܠܐ ܕܚܫܘܫܐ ܪܚܡ. ܘܒܓܠܝܢ ܒܪܫܝܢ ܡܢ ܫܘܒܩܢܗ

---

[311] P. f. 172v.
[312] V. f. 121r.
[313] P. f. 173r.
[314] V: ܒܠܐ ܐܢܐ.

ܐܝܟ ܕܬܘܒ. ܗܘ ܓܝܪ ܡܠܦܢ ܡܢ ܟܬܒ̈ܝ ܐܦܝܣܩܘܦܐ ܘܐܦ ܡܝܛܪ̈ܦܘܠܝܛܐ[315] ܐܝܟ ܟܢܘܫܝܐ. ܐܝܠܝܢ ܕܡܢ ܒܝܬܗ ܕܐܬܪܐ ܡܟܠܗ ܘܡܡܟܠܝܢ ܗܫܡܫܝܐ[316] ܘܐܦܝܣܩܘܦܘܬܐ. ܘܠܐ ܐܝܟ ܡܢܗܘܢ ܐܬܬ ܠܟܘܢ ܗܘ ܡܢ ܢܘܟܪܝܐ ܕܫܢܝܐ: ܘܐܦܠܐ ܚܢ ܒܟܝܢ ܐܝܟ ܠܥܠܬܐ. ܐܠܐ ܡܫܡܫܝܢ ܐܦܝܣܩܘܦܘܬܗܘܢ ܕܕܝܠܟ[317] ܟܢܘܫܬܐ ܒܡܐܦܘܬܐ ܕܟܠܗ ܒܝܬܗ ܕܐܬܪܐ. ܟܕ ܡܫܬܡܠܐ ܡܢ ܒܝܬܐ ܕܟܢܘܫܬܗܘܢ ܕܘܟܐ. ܘܡܫܬܠܡܝܢ[318] ܠܟ ܘܡܫܬܠܡܝܢ ܠܟܘܢ. ܘܐܠܘ ܕܐܝܟ ܗܕܐ ܐܝܬܝܗܘܢ ܗܘܘ ܐܦܝܣܩܘܦܐ ܕܥܡܐ ܕܦܪ̈ܨܘܦܐ ܘܡܛܪ̈ܢܐ: ܠܐ ܡܫܬܡܥ ܟܕܝܢ ܗܘܝܢ ܠܟܘܢ ܕܬܐܬܘܢ ܠܟܘܢ. ܘܐܦܠܐ ܡܫܟܚܝܢ ܗܘܝܢ ܠܐܝܟܢ ܕܡܢܗܘܢ ܟܠܗ ܟܗܢܘܬܐ ܡܫܡܠܝܢ ܗܘ̈ܝ. ܘܟܠܐ ܕܝܢ ܐܝܠܝܢ ܗܟܝܠ: ܢܬܬܢܝܚ ܐܝܟ ܟܝܠܐ ܕܟܗܢܘܬܐ. ܘܡܫܟܚܐ ܐܝܟ ܡܢ ܒܝܬܗ ܕܐܬܪܐ.[319] ܘܡܫܬܠܡ ܠܟܠܗܘܢ ܡܢ. ܠܡܦܣܘ ܠܟܘܢ ܘܠܡܠܦܢܘܬܗܘܢ ܒܝܢܬܗܘܢ ܒܡܘܪ̈ܒܐ ܒܕܘܢܐ ܕܡܫܬܡܫܝܢ ܡܢܗܘܢ. ܡܛܠ ܕܟܠܗ ܟܘܢ ܚܝܠܐ ܕܬܚܘܬܐ ܕܪܘܚܐ ܘܡܘܕܥܐ. ܠܗܘ ܓܝܪ ܐܝܟ ܗܘܐ ܡܒܝܠܐ ܘܦܪܘܥܬܐ ܠܐܦܝܣܩܘܦܘܬܗܘܢ ܘܟܠܗܘܢ:[320] ܡܢܗ ܕܗܘ ܡܠܐ ܕܐܚܝܕ ܐܢܘܢ ܡܫܬܡܠܝܢ ܗܘܘܢ. ܕܐܝܟ ܕܠܐ ܡܫܟܚܝܢ ܡܫܡ̈ܫܢܐ ܕܟܠܗܘܢ: ܠܡܗܘܐ ܡܫܡ̈ܫܢܐ ܟܠܒܪ ܩܫܝ̈ܫܐ: ܘܠܐ ܡܫܟܚܝܢ ܩܫܝ̈ܫܐ ܕܟܠܗܘܢ: ܠܡܗܘܐ ܩܫܝ̈ܫܐ ܟܠܒܪ ܐܦܝܣܩܘܦܐ: ܗܟܢܐ ܠܐ ܡܫܟܚܝܢ ܐܦܝܣܩܘ̈ܦܐ ܠܡܗܘܐ ܐܦܝܣܩܘܦܐ. ܟܠܒܪ ܡܢ ܡܝܛܪ̈ܦܘܠܝܛܐ. ܘܗܟܢܐ ܬܘܒ ܠܐ ܡܫܟܚܝܢ ܡܝܛܪ̈ܦܘܠܝܛܐ ܠܡܗܘܐ ܡܝܛܪ̈ܦܘܠܝܛܐ:[321] ܟܠܒܪ ܡܢ ܦܛܪܝܪܟܐ. ܘܐܦ ܗܘ[322] ܦܛܪܝܪܟܐ ܕܐܡܬܠܘܗܝ ܐܚܐ ܕܥܡܝܐ ܐܘܡܢܐ ܕܥܐ ܕܐܬܪ̈ܘܬܐ: ܐܝ ܕܟܠܗ ܡܢ ܐܦܝܣܩܘܦܘܬܐ ܐܬܐ ܠܦܛܪܝܪܟܘܬܐ: ܡܝܛܪ̈ܦܘܠܝܛܐ[323] ܕܝܠܗ ܦܪܝܫܝܢ ܡܢ ܚܘܒܐ ܕܢܫܡܫܘܢ ܗܫܡܫܝܘ. ܘܐܢ ܗܟܢܐ ܠܐ ܗܘܐ: ܕܠܐ ܡܫܬܠܡܝܢ ܟܕܝܘ. ܘܡܛܠ ܕܟܘܠܗܘܢ ܠܐ ܡܫܡܫܝܢ ܦܪ̈ܨܘܦܐ ܘܡܛܪ̈ܢܐ. ܟܕ ܠܟܠܗ ܟܠܗܘܢ ܚܕܐ ܕܢܫܬܡܫܘܢ ܕܐܬܪܐ. ܦܪܫܘ ܢܦܫܗܘܢ ܡܢ ܒܝܬܗ ܕܐܬܪܐ. ܘܐܫܬܪܝܘ ܡܢ ܛܟܣܗ ܕܐܬܪܐ ܘܗܘܘ

315 V: ܡܝܛܪ̈ܦܘܠܝܛܐ.
316 V: ܗܫܡ ܐܝܐ.
317 V.
318 V. f. 121v. P: ܘܡܫܠܡܝܢ.
319 P. f. 173v.
320 V: ܘܟܠܗܘܢ ܡܢܗܘܢ.
321 V: ܡܝܛܪ̈ܦܘܠܝܛܐ.
322 V: ܕܝܢ ܗܘ.
323 V: ܡܝܛܪ̈ܦܘܠܝܛܐ.

ܘܠܐ ܚܝܠܐ. ܐܘ ܠܐ ܡܫܟܚܝܢ ܗܘܘ ܡܗܝ̈ܡܢܐ ܠܡܐܡܪ ܡܢ ܦܪ̈ܝܫܐ: ܗܢܘܢ ܠܗܘܢ ܥܒܝܕܝܢ ܗܘܘ ܐܦܝܣܩܘ̈ܦܐ: ܡܛܠ ܕܗܘܝܐ ܦܝܣ ܠܗܘܘ ܐܦܝܣܩܘ̈ܦܐ. ܘܠܐ ܡܫܟܚܝܢ ܗܘܘ ܠܡܬܐܠܠ ܠܘܬ ܦܪ̈ܝܫܐ ܕܥܒܕܘܢ ܐܢܘܢ. ܘܐܦ[324] ܦܪ̈ܝܫܐ ܓܝܪ:[325] ܗܢܘܢ ܠܗܘܢ ܥܒܝܕܝܢ ܐܦܝܣܩܘ̈ܦܐ: ܘܡܫܡܫܝܢ ܠܗܘܢ ܡܫܡ̈ܫܢܘܬܗ. ܐܘ ܟܕ ܦܪ̈ܝܫܐ ܥܒܝܕܝܢ ܗܘܘ: ܡܫܟܚܝܢ ܠܗ ܡܗܝ̈ܡܢܐ ܕܗܘܘܢܐ ܗܘ: ܢܥܒܕܘܢ ܐܦ ܗܢܘܢ ܠܢܦܫܗܘܢ ܗܘ ܗܘܝܐ. ܐܘ ܐܡܪܝܢ ܕܠܐ ܗܘܐ ܗܘܝܐ[326] ܠܡܥܒܕ.[327] ܢܥܒܕ ܕܐܦܠܐ ܟܕ ܦܪ̈ܝܫܐ ܥܒܝܕܝܢ ܗܘܝܐ. ܗܘܐ ܡܕܡ ܕܥܒܝܕ. ܘܡܛܠ ܕܐܦ ܠܐ ܥܒܝܕܝܢ ܠܐ ܡܫܬܠܡܝܢ ܡܗܝ̈ܡܢܐ. ܡܫܟܚܝܢ ܐܢܘܢ ܡܢ ܦܪ̈ܝܫܐ ܘܡܢ ܟܠܗܘܢ ܡܫܠܐ ܕܟܠܡܐ. ܐܘ ܢܐܡܪܘܢ ܐܝܟ ܕܐܦ ܐܡܪܝܢ. ܕܟܢܫܐ ܕܡܢ ܢܘܟܪ̈ܝܐ ܐܬܟܢܫܘ ܠܗܘܐ ܡܗܝܡܢܬܐ. ܢܥܒܕ ܕܠܗ ܟܢܫܐ ܕܥܒܕܗ ܕܐܠܗܐ ܐܠܡܐܘܢ ܒܦܫܝܛܐ. ܐܠܐ ܟܢܫܐ ܕܡܗܝܡܢܬܐ. ܘܡܫܠܠ ܡܕܡ ܦܢܝܢ ܡܢ ܡܫܘܚܐ ܘܠܟܠܡܫܝܚܝܐ ܘܡܫܝܚܘܬܐ. ܗܟܢ ܕܐܦ ܗܢܘܢ ܡܢ ܥܒܕܗ ܕܐܠܗܐ ܡܕܡܐ. ܘܟܢܫܬܐ ܘܡܗܝܡܢܘܬܗܘܢ ܐܚܝܕܝܢ ܡܫܠܐ ܕܦܫܝܛܘܬܐ ܘܐܦܝܣܩܘܦܘܬܐ. ܘܠܗ ܟܢܫܐ ܘܡܗܝܡܢܘܬܐ ܕܥܡ ܥܒܕܗ ܕܐܠܗܐ. ܘܐܝܠܝܢ ܐܢ ܗܘܝܐ ܡܫܟܚܝܢ ܐܠܗܘܢ ܒܡܫܝܚܘܬܗܘܢ ܐܝܟ ܕܐܦܠܐ ܚܕ ܡܫܘܚܐ ܡܥܒܕ ܐܠܗܘܢ ܠܡܥܒܕ ܕܗܘܘ ܐܠܗܘܢ: ܡܘܪܝܗ ܫܠܝܚܘܗܝ ܠܟܠܗܘܢ ܡܢ ܡܗܝܡܢܘܬܐ ܕܥܡ ܬܫܡܫܬܐ. ܘܗܢܘܢ ܘܐܬܚܙܘ ܥܒܕܗ ܕܐܠܗܐ. ܘܐܡܠܟܘ ܒܡܫܝܚܘܬܐ ܕܪܘܚܐ ܙܘܠܠ. ܘܐܬܟܫܦܘ ܟܢܫܐ ܕܡܗܝܡܢܘܬܐ ܐܡܝܢܐ ܕܐܡܟܢ ܢܗܘܐ ܠܚܝ̈ܠܘܗܝ. ܐܚܪ̈ܢܝܬܐ ܡܫܬܐܠܢ ܟܠܗܝܢ ܠܟܠܗ ܡܗܝ̈ܡܢܐ. ܡܫܟܚܝܢ ܠܐܦܝܣܩܘ̈ܦܐ ܘܟܗ̈ܢܐ: ܘܡܫܟܚܝܢ ܠܘܬ ܦܬܓܡܐ ܡܫܝܚܝܐ.[328] ܘܡܫܟܚܝܢ ܠܘܬ ܢܬܬܒܪܘܢ ܒܪ ܕܡܫܠܡ ܡܢ ܚܝܠ. ܘܡܢܐ ܐܝܟ ܟܕ ܕܐܦ ܠܘܬܗ ܕܢܬܒܪܘܢ. ܟܕ ܡܫܪ ܗܘܐ ܕܠܟܠܗܘܢ ܠܟܠܗܘܢ ܗܘܐ ܕܠܡܫܢܝܢ. ܘܐܝܟ ܕܗܘܐ ܕܝܢ ܟܠܗ ܠܗ ܗܘܝܐ: ܘܠܐ ܚܕܐ ܡܫܟܚܝܢ ܗܘܐ ܠܐܢܫ. ܠܗ ܟܠܗܘܢ ܠܗܘܢ ܕܠܘܬܗ ܐܬܟܠܒ: ܐܠܐ ܘܐܦܠܐ ܠܗܘܢ ܕܠܘܬ ܐܚܪ̈ܢܐ ܐܬܟܠܒ. ܐܘ ܗܘܝܐ ܡܟܝܠ: ܟܢܫܬܐ ܪܒܬܐ ܡܟܝܠ. ܐܠܗܘܢ ܕܝܢ ܟܕ ܡܫܘ ܠܗܘܢ ܠܡܫܒܩܬܐ ܕܥܒܕܐ ܠܗ ܘܠܐܚܪ̈ܢܐ. ܘܡܢܘ ܐܝܟ ܡܕܡ ܟܠܗ. ܕܟܕ ܐܝܬ ܠܗ ܐܢܫ ܕܐܝܬ ܠܗ ܕܢܟܠܝܘܗܝ ܕܡܪܐ:[329] ܘܐܝܬ ܡܢ ܟܢܫܬܐ ܕܡܫܝܚܐ ܠܟܠܐ

324 V: ܐܦ.
325 P. f. 174r.
326 V. f. 122r.
327 V: ܠܡܥܒܕ ܗܘܝܐ.
328 P. f. 174v.
329 V: ܘܐܠܗܐ.

ܕܡܫܝ̈ܚܐ ܒܪܘܫܡܐ ܕܫܘܡܠܝܐ ܠܟܠܗ: ܘܒܪ ܐܝܟ ܐܒܘܟ ܕܒܪ ܩܪܐ ܘܡܫܬܡܥ.
ܡܛܠ ܡܬܐܠܨܝܢ ܘܡܫܬܘܕܥܝܢ ܥܠ ܚܘܒܐ ܘܐܦܝܣܩܘܦܐ ܕܥܡܐ ܕܒܝܬ ܡܫܝ̈ܚܐ.
ܘܟܠ ܙܘܥܐ ܘܟܠ ܕܘܒܪܐ ܕܒܪ̈ܗܡܝܐ ܕܥܡܐ ܕܡܫܬܡܥܝܢ ܠܡܫܝܚܝܢ.
ܘܐܢ[330] ܐܦ ܟܕ ܛܒ ܢܩܪܘܢ ܠܐܠܗܝܢ ܕܡܠܟܘܬܐ: ܠܐ ܢܫܒܩܘܢ ܒܛܝܠܬܐ
ܕܐܬܝܗܘܢ ܒܗ: ܡܫܝܚܐ ܠܗܘܢ ܒܪ ܡܢ ܒܪܗ ܫܘܒܚܗܘܢ ܕܐܦܘܪܐ ܐܝܟ
ܕܠܡܐ. ܘܪܒܐ ܗܘ ܡܫܡܠܐ ܕܐܒܕܐ ܐܝܟܢܐ. ܘܡܪܢܐ ܝܗܒ ܟܠ ܥܡܗ.
ܘܝܗܒ ܚܝܘܗܝ ܠܒܪܬܗ ܡܢ ܫܡܝܐ ܡܢ ܟܠ ܢܦܫܢ. ܒܪܟܐ ܠܡܫܝܚܗ ܐܝܟܢܐ
ܐܡܝܢ. ܘܗܘܐ ܫܠܡܝܢ ܘܡܪܢܐ ܢܒܪܟܝܟ ܠܥܡܟܘܢ ܕܝܠܗ ܒܟܠܙܒܢ ܐܡܝܢ܀

330 V. f. 122v.

INTRODUCTION TO THE *BOOK OF THE AIMS OF THE PSALMS* BY AḤŪB QAṬRAYA

BAS TER HAAR ROMENY
VU UNIVERSITY AMSTERDAM

INTRODUCTION (BY MARIO KOZAH)

Aḥūb Qaṭraya (ܐܚܘܒ ܩܛܪܝܐ),[1] a biblical interpreter frequently cited in later sources, is mentioned in the catalogue of ʿAbdishoʿ bar Brikā as having composed an elucidation (ܦܘܫܩܐ) on the whole of the New Testament (ܘܕܟܠܗ̇ ܚܕܬܐ), the law (ܐܘܪܝܬܐ) and all the prophets (ܘܟܠܗܘܢ ܢܒܝ̈ܐ) in addition to (or except for) an elucidation of the *beth mawtbe* (ܡܘܬ̈ܒܐ ܦܘܫܩ ܒܝܬ). Although none of these works survive Aḥūb is in fact cited in a number of East Syriac biblical commentaries and in particular the East Syriac *Anonymous Commentary* which in its most extended form covers both the Old and New Testaments.

Aḥūb Qaṭraya is also the author of the *Book of the Aims of the Psalms* (ܟܬ̈ܒܐ ܕܢܝܫܝ̈ܗܘܢ ܕܡܙܡܘܪ̈ܐ) which is a short introduction to the Psalter that survives in a number of manuscripts. There is an edition and Latin translation of this introduction by B.

[1] J.S. Assemanus, *Bibliotheca Orientalis Clementino–Vaticana*, III/1, p. 175, incorrectly transcribes his name as Ayyub (ܐܝܘܒ) as first argued by J.B. Chabot, "Aḥôb du Qaṭar", in *Journal Asiatique*, 10:8, 1906, pp. 273–4. This error is confirmed by consulting the manuscripts in which this name features such as BL. Or. 9354, f. 1ᵛ: ܕܡܪܝ ܐܚܘܒ ܩܛܪܝܐ.

Vandenhoff,[2] however, this is based on a single, now lost manuscript. The present translation is based on Vandenhoff's edition.

In the *Book of the Aims of the Psalms* Aḥūb explains the extraordinary usefulness of the book of Psalms, which is "more than all other books excellent and abundant in benefits". According to Aḥūb it is like the head to the body of Scripture. Whereas most books contain prophecy or history or legislation or wisdom, the Psalter contains all of these. It is the most accurate guide to divine knowledge, inspiring us to serve God. Aḥūb then goes on to explain why the Psalms are set to music: this is because music ensures that we will never be satisfied and always want to hear more of it. Finally, Aḥūb praises David, who was "humbler than all other prophets, whereas there is in him request, fasting, prayer, repentance, imploring, worship, love, faith, clemency, hope, goodness, grace, understanding, knowledge, life, healing, and remission of sins". The Fathers encouraged chanting from the Psalter more than from all other books: "first, because Christ is from (David's) seed; second, because he prophesied about (Christ's) divinity and humanity, about the passion, the martyrdom, the resurrection, and the ascension".

TRANSLATION

The book of the aims[3] of the Psalms of the holy David, king, prophet, and heart of the Lord. My Lord, help me!

When I first instruct you, O diligent reader, about the aim of the Psalms (by Aḥūb Qaṭraya), it is necessary to speak before everything else about the utility of this book and about the abundant advantages which those who seek after the study and

---

[2] B. Vandenhoff, *Exegesis Psalmorum imprimis messianicorum apud Syros Nestorianos e codice adhuc inedito illustrata.* Rheine: Altmeppen, 1899, pp. 3–9 of the Syriac part, pp. 17–20 of the Latin part.

[3] I assume this reflects the Greek σκοποί, "causes, objects, occasions, arguments", a typical term in the Antiochene exegetical system, based on Greek pagan grammatical theory. Vandenhoff's "introductions" is incorrect.

examination of the holy words acquire from it. But while all Holy Scriptures which are said and written by the grace of the Spirit are useful to rational people for the acquisition of the fear of God – in accordance with the saying of the Holy Paul: *Every book written in the Spirit of God is useful for teaching*, etc. (2 Tim 3:16) – we find this one more than all other books excellent and abundant in benefits. For all books teach partially and one by one, but this one proclaims in a complete way, because it is in a way clearly in the position of the head to the body of the Holy Scripture: just as each of the parts of the body possesses a particular function towards the need of the whole – vision, so to speak, or hearing and[4] such things – but the head is the home and seat of every function, which consists in the discernment of the senses. Or as one speaks about Paradise, which is abundant in all species of fruits which are tasting sweet and looking pleasant, in comparison for instance to those things which are found here and there partially, thus is the book of Psalms in comparison to other books.

For we find that the word in the Holy Scriptures is divided into four kinds: prophecy, I say, history, legislation, and wisdom, that is, the fear of God.[5] Yet each of these books does not contain just one of these by itself and separated from the others, for even in the books of the prophets there are stories that have happened, and conversely, in the historical books there is also prophecy of things that are to happen, with exhortation, request, and thanksgiving, which are found scattered in all books. With regard then to this book of the Psalms, in it all these are put together, and it is, as it were, composed from limbs and parts of all these. For it both teaches about the Creator and explains about the Ruler, and it brings the adversary of these (notions) to an end, I mean, those who say that this world is a being (in itself) and travels without the bridles of a ruler, and it teaches also about the reward of the diligent and about the punishment of the wicked, and that (man) should refrain from odious things and should approach good ones,

[4] Reading ܥܡ instead of Vandenhoff's ܥܠܡ.

[5] Paraphrasing Proverbs 1:7: *The beginning of wisdom is the fear of the Lord.*

and about the love towards God and the kindness towards human beings. In it there is prophecy of things that are to happen together with stories of events that have already happened, and also (various) kinds of praise and thanksgiving together with admonition on manners and abundant and frequent (indications) of which things we should ask and how we should ask them, etc.

When all divine writings are the image and example of divine knowledge, this one is more accurate than all others. Like an image and statue of a king, which, because of the greater beauty of colours and of complexion of abundance with which it is painted, is more able than all other images and statues to show the onlookers the accurate likeness of a king, thus the likenesses in this (book of Psalms) are (more) accurate and the colours in which the image of divine knowledge is composed are (more) beautiful and admirable. And it is like a guide to the blind and a lamp to one who is in darkness for the approach towards God, while it depicts (and) shows us as in an image the power and grace of God as well as his righteousness and long-suffering; it brings us as it were little by little to the knowledge and servitude of him; it promises us advantages from the service of him; it puts on us its holy words like weapons that have been tried; and it gives us the assurance to win through them all battles. (For these words, when they are recited by saintly people in a way appropriate to them,[6] drive away insolent demons and invite to them holy angels – and indeed, I mean angels who bring even Christ himself, the redeemer of all, to their help and are worthy of the grace of the Holy Spirit –,[7])[8] as it really

---

[6] An important topos, at least since Irenaeus, is the idea that Scripture should be explained and used by people with authority (i.e., standing in Apostolic succession): Gnostics and others were, in this view, appropriating and abusing the Bible. Ahob's caveat in this part of the sentence may echo the same sort of concern.

[7] In this translation it is stressed that good angels are meant; another option, following Vandenhoff, would be to translate: "For these words … drive away insolent demons and invite to them holy angels—but why do I say angels, (as they are words) that bring even Christ himself, the

happened to them and today happens to many people. (For who is not acquainted with the manner of life of saintly people, who while they are on earth apply their minds to heaven, and while they are corporeal become like angels,)[9] the cause of whose meditation on spiritual things is the recital of the Psalms? For as this book of the Psalms is full of all these benefits, our holy fathers, as they were diligent authors of divine (rules), rightly and aptly determined that we should recite only this book more than others, and that without recital of its words no one could approach one of the ecclesiastical ranks or could even be counted among the followers or fellow servants of the Church.

It is necessary however also to say because of what (the author of the Psalms) delivered his prophecy with the pleasant sounds of (all) kinds of music: because the (deeds) of divine providence were mighty and amazing and were to be fulfilled at different times, either among the first people or to all human beings at the end, and all these peoples were to be conscious of them, (divine) Grace rightly made him compose his words in metres on the sounds of (all) sorts of music and different melodies, in order that they, because they sound so sweet, hardly satiate the

---

redeemer of all, to their help and are worthy of the grace of the Holy Spirit?"

[8] The part of the sentence between small brackets is also found in an introduction to the Psalms of Nathniel (or Nathanael) of Shirzor, probably a contemporary of Ahob, which is found in MS Vandenhoff in the fifth position (p. 14 l. 18ff in his edition). In addition to this literal agreement and the one mentioned in the next footnote this introduction contains many ideas also expressed by Ahob. Vandenhoff seems to assume that Nathniel was the more original of the two authors, as he argues that Ahob was the compiler of the collection. However, if Ahob is indeed a late sixth-century author, as is nowadays accepted, he cannot have been the compiler, which also means that the question of the authorship is open again. On Nathniel, see also Anton Baumstark, *Geschichte der syrischen Literatur mit Ausschluß der christlich-palästinensischen Texte* (Bonn: A. Marcus and E. Weber, 1922), pp. 129–30.

[9] This sentence can also be found literally in Nathniel of Shirzor's introduction; see the preceding footnote.

listeners, so that through the great amount of their sweetness they start inducing to the love of his teaching. Just as even today there are to (be) found many who carry in their mouth cheap songs, and although their words are abominable and unacceptable to persons of discernment, their recitation still does not satiate people, because they are composed of sweet sounds. Indeed, just as by the sound, through the sweetness of his words, he awoke at that time the drowsiness of the Hebrews.

Now with regard to the words of the other books, because they have been expressed (here in the Psalms) in metres and because of the words that are joined to them, everyone received them with desire in his memory, just as they are also easily recited everywhere. In order[10] for one of the teachers to establish the basis before (writing) a *Sogita* or *ʿOnita*,[11] he takes material from the Psalms, and with the phrases taken from them he lays down his *ʿOnita* – (words) that because of their sweetness do not even satiate mature people, but as if they have never been said before, we continue to sing the same ones.

(And know that all good things are in (the book of) David.) David was more humble that all other prophets, whereas there is in him request, fasting, prayer, repentance, imploring, worship, love, faith, clemency, hope, goodness, grace, understanding, knowledge, life, healing, and remission of sins. There is in him the garden of Eden, a medicine to all pains, a bandage to all wounds. David, then, is the heart of God and the executor of his will. Therefore the Fathers established the tradition that we chant from it more than from all books of the prophets, because of many reasons: first, because Christ is from his seed; second, because he prophesied about (Christ's) divinity and humanity, about the passion, the

---

[10] Reading ܐܝܟ ܕܣܝܡܐ instead of Vandenhoff's ܐܝܟ ܣܝܡܐ. The text may be corrupt here, as the connection with the preceding sentence is not clarified: one would perhaps expect "just as", but the imperfect ܢܣܒ makes that translation impossible. It is also possible, as Vandenhoff does, to take ܣܝܡܐ as a type of hymn, *Syama*, like *Sogita* or *ʿOnita*. However, it remains unclear what the function of ܩܕܡ "before" would be in that case.

[11] See preceding note.

martyrdom, the resurrection, and the ascension. Praise to him who gives authority to the understanding of the rational, in order that we, when we are cleansed from the impurity of desires through the observance of the commandments, enter the Holy of Holies of his secrets, and gain from there discernment, kindness, and understanding, which (exist) through prayer, in order that we learn that the prophet David found mercy. Amen.

ABRAHAM QAṬRAYA BAR LIPAH'S *COMMENTARY ON THE LITURGICAL OFFICES*

MARIO KOZAH
AMERICAN UNIVERSITY OF BEIRUT

INTRODUCTION

Abraham Qaṭraya bar Lipah was a liturgical commentator of the seventh century from Beth Qaṭraye as his demonym unequivocally indicates. He is the author of a short *Commentary on the Liturgical Offices* in a question and answer format first fully edited and translated into Latin by R.H. Connolly.[1] His name appears in the opening rubric of the Syriac text to be found in the Vatican manuscript Vat. sir. 504:

> The explanation of the liturgy (ܦܘܫܩ ܠܬܫܡܫܬܐ) written by Mar Abraham Qaṭraya bar Lipah (ܡܪܝ ܐܒܪܗܡ ܩܛܪܝܐ ܒܪ ܠܝܦܗ)[2]

In the preface to his translation, both of which are in Latin, Connolly makes the argument that the work belongs to the first part of the seventh century since there is no mention in the *Commentary* of the liturgical reforms undertaken by the patriarch Īshōʿyahb III (649–659). This same argument was later taken up by

[1] R.H. Connolly, *Anonymi auctoris Expositio Officiorum Ecclesiae Georgio Arbelensi vulgo ascripta. II. Accedit Abrahae Bar Lipeh Interpretation Officiorum. CSCO* 72, 76, Scr. Syri 29, 32, 1913–15.

[2] Vat. sir. 504, f. 119r. The same rubric is to be found in another copy of the same *Commentary* in Mingana 566, f. 154r.

S.H. Jammo and used to date the commentary written by Gabriel Qaṭraya bar Lipah.[3] However, Connolly leaves the possibility open that Abraham's *Commentary* is from the early eighth century once again using the content to argue that the author is silent about the recitation of the Lord's Prayer both at the beginning and at the end of the evening office, and indeed about any second recitation of it towards the end of the liturgy. He states that there was no law that the Lord's Prayer should be used in those places in the office until Timothy I required it at the end of the eighth century. This is, however, not a definite indication of date; since there continued to be a variety of practices in this matter amongst the churches even after the law had been promulgated by Timothy. Nevertheless, Connolly continues, if Abraham bar Lipah had lived after Timothy, one might still have expected him to say something about that law.[4]

However, it should be borne in mind that the argument that takes the reforms undertaken by the patriarch Īshōʿyahb III (649–659) as a fixed point for the purpose of dating the content of both Gabriel and Abraham's commentaries may not be entirely convincing given the fact that during the period of Īshōʿyahb III's patriarchate he himself was writing letters to Beth Qaṭraye complaining to the church authorities, priests, monks and lay people there that they had lost all ecclesiastical legitimacy. It would, therefore, seem rather unlikely that the Syriac community in Beth Qaṭraye who were behaving independently of the authorities in Fars and Seleuca-Ctesiphon and in a state of open ecclesiastical rebellion, to the dismay of the patriarch, would at the same time be implementing his liturgical reforms. It is only at a local synod in Dayrīn in 676, approximately twenty years after Īshōʿyahb III's letters to Beth Qaṭraye, that the issue of the acknowledgement of the supreme authority of the patriarch is finally resolved by Īshōʿyahb III's successor Gīwargīs I (c. 659–680). This later date of 676 does not affect the early seventh century dating of Gabriel's commentary given the reference in his commentary to

[3] S.H. Jammo, "Gabriel Qaṭraya et son commentaire sur la liturgie chaldéenne" in *Orientalia Christiana Periodica* 32, 1966, p. 42.

[4] R.H. Connolly, op. cit. See English translation of Connolly's Latin preface below.

Shubḥalmaran, metropolitan of Karka d-Beth Slokh, but allows us to bring forward Abraham's *Commentary* to the second half of the seventh century since what is certain is that his *Commentary* was written after that of Gabriel which is clearly demonstrated by the fact that Memra 5 chapter 2 of Gabriel's commentary is abbreviated in its entirety in Abraham's work. This observation first made by Jammo[5] was later confirmed by Brock[6] in his English translation of this Memra where he italicizes passages taken up by Abraham.

English Translation of Connolly's Preface in Latin

We said something about Abraham Bar Līpheh, or Bar Līph (as his name is equally written) in the preface to the Syriac text. He is often referred to by the anonymous author of the preceding *Description of the Offices*. Only one book is ascribed to him by Ebediesu of Soba, that is the *Interpretation of the Offices*, which we translate into Latin here.

Assemanus [sic.] claims that Abraham Bar Lipheh is the same Abraham that Thomas of Marga calls "the translator" and says was the teacher of Timothy I (the catholicos [d. c. 821]). But that Abraham is not called "Bar Lipheh" by Thomas of Marga; and since the name "Abraham" was common among the Syrians, and especially the Nestorians, there is no reason to think that that reference is to Abraham Bar Lipheh. We now suggest a few things, which could give some indication of how to locate Bar Lipheh's era, although we have found nothing certain in this matter.

1. This *Interpretation of the Offices* has the brevity and simplicity which are associated with the commentaries of the more ancient era. And its allegorical interpretation is not of a

[5] S.H. Jammo, ibid., p. 41: "En effet, R.H. Connolly a publié un commentaire sur la liturgie ayant le meme titre que l'ouvrage que nous étudions et ayant un contenu et souvent un texte semblable".

[6] S. Brock, "Gabriel of Qatar's Commentary on the Liturgy", in *Hugoye* vol. 2, no. 2, July 2003: "In his article of 1966 Jammo ... rightly observes that the published Commentary by Abraham bar Lipeh is nothing but an abbreviation of Gabriel's work".

kind to require a date beyond the seventh century; for the mystical interpretation of the mysteries of the Church developed quite early amongst the Syriacs, and is already found at the end of the fifth century in the sermons of Narsai, the doctor of Nisibis, as also in the *Ecclesiastical Hierarchy* of Pseudo-Dionysius. If Abraham Bar Lipheh's *Interpretation of the Offices* is compared with the anonymous *Description of the Offices* of which we have just produced an edition, both these treatises would appear to be separated by the same distance in time as, according to the Jacobites, lies between the liturgical commentaries of George, Bishop of the Arabs (7th Century) and Moses Bar Kepha (9th Century).

2. Nowhere does Bar Lipheh mention the edicts of Išōʿyabhi I [sic.] (d. c. 660), by which all the ancient offices were reformed and which are continually referred to by the author of the aforementioned *Description* as the norms for the office of the whole Nestorian church. Of the earlier commentators only one is mentioned by Bar Lipheh, and that is Theodore of Mopsuestia, of whom he has this to say: "The Commentator has explained this (the formula 'holy things for the holy'), and we do not dare to speak of it". Theodore is held to have composed the *Book of the Mysteries,* to which Bar Lipheh appears to allude.

3. Bar Lipheh is silent about the recitation of the Lord's Prayer both at the beginning and at the end of the evening office, and indeed about any second recitation of it towards the end of the liturgy. There was no law that the Lord's Prayer should be used at those places in the office until Timothy I required it at the end of the eighth century. This is, however, not a definite indication of date; since the author of the aforementioned *Description* witnesses that there continued to be a variety of practices in this matter amongst the churches even after the law had been promulgated by Timothy. Nevertheless, if Bar Lipheh had lived after Timothy, one might still have expected him to say something about that law.

4. As we are exploring Bar Lipheh's era, there is one particular passage of *The Interpretation* that we should not leave unmentioned, since, at first glance, it appears to offer a definite proof of date; for while explaining the responsary called "the Basilike" he writes thus: "However the fathers decreed the responsary that is called 'Basilike' to honour Constantine, the victorious king, so that there would be a passage of prayer for the king himself as well as for the preservation of the Christian kingdom. But some have said that the fathers established this responsary 'Basilike' in the days of king Basil". Here we must recall that the first Roman king or emperor to carry the name "Basil" died in 886 A.D. Therefore if Bar Lipheh is genuinely referring to this Basil, it is clear that he himself can hardly have been active before the tenth century. But from all that has been said above this seems too late to be accepted as plausible; and we find it impossible to believe that the Syriac Nestorians would admit that any part of their office could trace its origin to those whom they themselves considered heretics, let alone to a Byzantine emperor of the ninth century: nor that the clergy, considered as heretics, who had established the responsary in this Basil's honour, should be called "fathers" by a Nestorian author. However, it is not difficult to find another explanation for this. The anonymous author of *A Description of the Offices* (Tract II, chapter 17) also reports that the responsary was composed in the time of Constantine: he says nothing about Basil. He explains the title "Basilike" as follows: "And the responsary has been called 'of the Royals', that is, of the kings and governors; for that is how the name is translated in the Syriac tongue". Therefore it seems that the theory which Bar Lipheh repeats should be explained thus: The Syriacs, seeing that this responsary was referred to by a Greek title, invented the story about Constantine, as the first Christian emperor; at a later stage some, more elegantly than accurately, create the name "Basilius" for the king in whose honour the responsary was believed to have been established.

We think that we are exercising reasonable caution in dating Abraham Bar Lipheh's *Interpretation* to the seventh or certainly the eighth century.

It is important to note that Bar Lipheh's work on the offices is not contained in its entirety in the codices that we have used. Apart from the descriptions of the offices which we translate into Latin here, it is agreed that Bar Lipheh has also written something about the calendar; for in the foregoing anonymous *Description* (T. I, pages 28, 32, 87) the author disputes a particular interpretation of the "Week of Dedication" which he says was put forward by Bar Lipheh: but no such thing is found in the commentaries that we are editing. Moreover our codices appear to be derived from a copy which contained a version of the work either somewhat abbreviated or defective. It is indeed possible to support that from the descriptions of the night time and early morning offices, which are too brief to be readily considered complete. But neither are all the opinions of Bar Lipheh on the evening and morning office, as reported by the anonymous author of the *Description*, to be found in our text. However, the commentary on the liturgy does seem to be complete; and the sole reference to it quoted by the anonymous author (T. II, p 34) can be read below on page 161.

A Note on the Manuscripts

This edition and translation of Abraham Qaṭraya bar Lipah's *Commentary on the Liturgical Offices* is based on the manuscript Vat. sir. 504 which is a good copy of Alqosh 93 made in 1885 in Alqosh by deacon ʿIsa son of Isaiah and presented to Pope Pius XI. The manuscript Alqosh 93 (last located in the monastery of N.D. des Semences near Alqosh) was completed in 1683 in the monastery of Rabban Hormizd at the time of the patriarch Mar Elia VIII (Jean Maroghin) by a certain priest called Abdisho. This appears to be the oldest extant manuscript containing the *Commentary*. A second copy of this manuscript was also completed in 1885 in N.D. des

Semences by the priest Iaunan from the family Soso of Araden.[7] Another manuscript that includes the *Commentary* is Mingana syr. 566 which is also a copy of Alqosh 93 made by Mingana himself in 1931. Finally, we know of one other manuscript, Alqosh 82, that includes the *Commentary*. This was completed in 1894 at the monastery of N.D. des Semences by a certain novice monk called Paulos Djaʿdan and would appear to also be a copy of Alqosh 93.[8]

It is unclear which copy of Alqosh 93 Connolly uses in his edition and Latin translation of this work. He does not provide a specific reference or folio numbers in his edition. In the Latin preface to his edition he states: "A codex containing the work was quite recently brought into the library at Seert, in the Kurdistan region. The most reverend and learned gentleman, Adai Scher, the Bishop of Seert, kindly copied it out and passed on the copy, at the request of J. B. Chabot, to us for publication. Moreover, since some things were missing from this codex, he took the trouble to transcribe what was necessary (and more) to fill the lacuna, from another codex preserved in the monastery of N.D. des Semences near Alqosh; [this codex could be Alqosh MS 93 or Alqosh Cod. 82]. We label the codices with the numbers I and II".[9] I have found no trace of this codex containing Abraham bar Lipeh's *Commentary* in Addai Scher's catalogue of manuscripts at Seert.[10] However, given that a great deal of variation does exist between Connolly's

---

[7] This is Codex 177 in J.-M. Vosté, ed., *Catalogue de la bibliothèque syro-chaldéenne du Couvent de Notre-Dame des Semences près d'Alqoš (Iraq)*. Rome–Paris, 1929, p. 69.

[8] For a full description of Alqosh 82 and 93 see A. Scher, ed., *Notice sur les manuscrits syriaques conservés dans la bibliothèque du couvent des Chaldéens de Notre-Dame-des-Semences*, extrait du *Journal Asiatique*. Paris, 1906. See also J.-M. Vosté, ed., *Catalogue de la bibliothèque syro-chaldéenne du Couvent de Notre-Dame des Semences près d'Alqoš (Iraq)*. Rome–Paris, 1929.

[9] R. H. Connolly, *Anonymi auctoris Expositio Officiorum Ecclesiae Georgio Arbelensi vulgo ascripta. II. Accedit Abrahae Bar Lipeh Interpretation Officiorum. CSCO* 72, 76, Scr. Syri 29, 32, 1913–15, p. 162.

[10] A. Scher, *Catalogue des manuscrits syriaques et arabes, conservés dans la Bibliothèque épiscopale de Séert (Kurdistan) avec notes bibliographiques*. Mosul, 1905.

edition and Vat. sir. 504 it is clear that Connolly was working with another weaker copy which, by his own admission, contains lacunae.

TRANSLATION

A Part of the Commentary on the Liturgical Offices, Written by Mar Abraham Qaṭraya Bar Lipah.

1. First – The two *marmyatha*,[11] which we serve at the beginning of the evening (office) of weekdays, is on account of the two parts of the human being; so that each particular *marmitha* might be for him a place for an act of thanksgiving on behalf of each part of us. However, on Sunday we serve one *marmitha*, because on that (day) there exists one perfect and undivided will for body and soul, not two, as in this world.

2. **Question** – Why do we begin with the psalms of the Old Testament and not with the New Testament? **Answer:** The Old is the place of a certain foundation for the New Testament in which it clearly teaches about the unity of the divine nature and saves human beings from the multiplicity of gods.

3. **Question** – Why do we change then say the Glory before the *marmyatha* are completed? **Answer:** When, indeed, the Law of Moses had authority, which pronounced a harsh judgment against everyone who sinned, and not allowing at all that repentance should be accepted, John the Proclaimer[12] appeared, he who was given the name of "a voice" by Isaiah, and he preached repentance for the forgiveness of sins.

4. **Question** – What is "Peace be with us"? **Answer:** It is an indication about the reconciliation and peace which God made with us in the coming of Christ.

---

[11] *Marmitha*, pl. *Marmyatha*: a division of the Psalter.

[12] John the Baptist.

5. **Question** – And the drawing of the curtains? **Answer:** It signifies the opening of the gate of repentance, which Christ opened for all sinners.

6. **Question** – The bringing out of the lamps? **Answer:** It signifies the divine epiphany. That great Sun of justice, that was revealed upon the Jordan.

7. **Question** – Also what of our opening the outer curtains at that time, and not the inner curtains? **Answer:** We signify this mystery: that while we are in this world, we walk by faith, not by sight; and "And now we see as in a mirror an image; then, however, face to face";[13] and now indeed "We know a little of much. Afterwards we shall know as we are known".[14]

8. **Question** – The censer of incense which we burn? **Answer:** It signifies the mystery of the knowledge of Christ, which like a sweet scent has made everyone fragrant through the apostles. In the same way, (it is burned) in demonstration of the sweetness of the teaching of Christ. And again: just as the priests were ordered to burn incense in the tabernacle, so too the Church is in harmony with the Old Testament.

9. **Question** – The prayer before the "To you, Lord" (*Lak(h)u Mara*)? **Answer:** It is a teaching about the revelation of Christ.

10. **Question** – The *qanona*[15] "To you, Lord", which is said at this time? **Answer:** That it might be for us a lesson about the coming of Christ, who perfected and completed the Old Testament, and gave the New Testament, and made the two of them one body of the dispensation of God. For just as the nature of the human being consists of two parts, even if the body is inferior to the soul, yet both together are the one person of the human being: so too the Old Testament, (although it) is inferior to the New – yet both are the one body of God's dispensation.

---

[13] 1 Corinthians 13:12.

[14] Variation on 1 Corinthians 13:12.

[15] An appointed chant or hymn, especially a short metrical farcing of a psalm.

11. **Question** – These two *shuraye*,[16] which are arranged? **Answer:** That they might be as a certain act of thanksgiving for these two times of night and day; or that we might be praying through them for our preservation during these two periods. And just as the evening stands in between these two times, so too is arranged between these two *shuraye* that "O Lord, I have called on you" should be said; because in it is (that verse) "The offering of my hands" etc.

12. **Question** – What does the ordering of the proclamation/litany[17] mean for us? **Answer:** Since we Christians are one body in Christ, all of us pray on behalf of the whole congregation of our brethren, according to the commandment of our Lord. Since there are many among us who are busy with the affairs of this world, and are not concerned with prayer, and when they come (to church) do not know what they are to say; and many are concerned about prayer, but do not know how they should pray: because of this this proclamation/litany is ordered, so that the whole congregation may take part in the reply which they make. For there is no one who does not know to answer "Our Lord, have mercy on us". For this reason the whole congregation, women together with the young and all the people, take part in this petition, asking for mercy from God with all the priests, who are praying on behalf of the whole congregation.

13. **Question** – Moreover, what of (the fact that) the deacon says the last proclamation/litany alone and all the people are silent, with everyone praying on their own? **Answer:** This signifies that the priesthood of the Church continually prays for all human beings.

14. **Question** – Moreover, what of (the fact that) after the proclamation/litany the herald (deacon) orders the people to rise from genuflection? **Answer:** This is a demonstration of our rising from the Fall through sin; and is a sign of the acceptance of our prayer.

---

[16] A few verses of the Psalms introducing an anthem or a clause from the Psalter prefixed to a verse of an anthem.

[17] *Koruzutha.*

15. **Question** – Moreover, what of (the fact) that he says: "With the petition" etc. and the people reply: "From you, Lord"? **Answer:** This signifies that from God alone we should hope for all good things and all (sorts of) help.

16. **Question** – Moreover, what (of the fact) that (he says) "Concord and love"? **Answer:** Because without love towards God and love towards (our) neighbour the work of our prayer is vain.

17. **Question** – Moreover, what (of the fact) that he asks for remission and adds and says, "For our souls and for each other" etc.? **Answer:** He teaches that one should not be concerned just for oneself, but (also) for one's companion.

18. **Question** – The reason for this *qanona* "Holy"? (**Answer:**) It was (introduced) in the time of King Theodosius the Younger, who because of his weakness allowed that a corruption of the true faith should enter by the discord of the wretched and shameless Cyril. For since the people had stopped their ears from hearing the teaching of truth, and in their *teshbhata* (praises) had caused the divine nature to suffer, and in everyone was chanted God's capability of suffering, God allowed them to be disciplined by various chastisements; and a dreadful punishment was sent against the mother city. And just as they had roused the holy angels to anger by their *teshbhata* and had shaken heaven with their blasphemies, so too did they (the angels) shake the earth and shifted the strong towers of their walls. And the quaking lasted a space of forty days, and did not cease by night nor by day. And when they did not repent of their iniquities, (God) added for them a tribulation in the midst of this very quaking: from a certain great column built in the middle of the city, on top of which was set a statue of the emperor Theodosius the Great, great stones were torn away, which had been bound with iron and lead and remained in the air for a long time not falling to earth. And since everyone grew terrified because of this, lest they should suddenly fall upon them, all the inhabitants of the city fled into the desert; and in the evening they did not expect that it would dawn on them, and in the morning they did not believe that they would remain alive until the evening. And after they had lost hope of life, since God willed that his chastisement be moderated with wisdom, he sent one of the heavenly powers, who appeared to a certain excellent priest, and

commanded him and said to him: "Enter the city and go to the church and say this *qanona* three times, and the earthquake will cease". However, the priest when he had related the dream to another, the vision appeared to them false. And when the angel appeared to him again and said the same things to him, the priest was hesitant. He appeared to him again on a third night and said to him: "Believe me, man, because I am from those who stand before God. Enter into the city, and do not be afraid, because the Lord is prepared to perform mercies upon you. And when you have entered into the city, behold (whatever) you find me saying, you say too; and the earthquake will cease". Then the priest arose in the morning and, along with certain men, went into the city and entered the church; and the priest saw the angel standing before the altar in the sanctuary, and said in a loud voice: "Holy is God, holy and strong, holy immortal: have mercy on us". Then that priest, and the men who were with him, answered the angel; and when they had said the *qanona* three times the earthquake that had taken place became still. However Anastasius Caesar shamelessly resolved and ordered (the *qanona*) to be changed in all the churches which were under his authority; and in place of "Holy immortal: have mercy on us", on his own authority, he ordered it to be said thus: "Holy immortal, who was crucified for us". Neither was that rebel ashamed, nor did he fear to change that statement passed on to human beings by the holy angel. However the royal city of Constantinople did not consent to change this *qanona*, and neither in Jerusalem nor in the western lands; but they say it as we do.

19. **Question** – And the curtains, through their opening and their closing? **Answer:** It shows the gate of God's mercies, which is not closed in the face of human beings, whenever we ask for mercy from God. For this reason, as soon as the *qanona* "Holy" has been completed, we remove the curtain, because the evening office and also the morning (office) conclude with the *qanona* "Holy".

20. **Question** – And the responsary "The Royal" (*ʿonitha d-basiliqe*)?[18] **Answer:** The fathers arranged it for the honour of Constantine the victorious king, that it might be in place of a prayer

[18] An antiphon at the end of the vespers prayers.

for the king himself, and for the preservation of the kingdom of the Christians. But some have said that the fathers arranged this responsary "The Royal" and a section from the Beatitudes in the days of Basil the king.

21. **Question** – And the morning office? **Answer:** The morning office on weekdays contains the whole course of God's dispensation in this world.

22. Through the first *shuraya*, they indicate to us the praises and shouts of joy of the angels for his creation of light, and about the transgression of our father Adam, and those who perished in the flood.

23. Through the second *shuraya*, they indicate to us the time of blessed Noah and about those who were after him.

24. Through the third *shuraya*, they indicate to us the time of blessed Abraham and his descendants, who grew old in Egypt.

25. Through the fourth *shuraya*, they indicate to us the time of blessed Moses.

26. The second psalm of the fourth *shuraya* teaches us about the time of Joshua bar Nun and the judges.

27. The third psalm of the fourth *shuraya*, reveals to us concerning the time of blessed David and the kings who were after him.

28. The fourth psalm of the fourth *shuraya*: they call to mind for us the time of those who returned from Babylon, and about the Maccabees.

29. The fifth psalm of the fourth *shuraya*: they remind us of the time of blessed John the Baptist.

30. The sixth psalm of the fourth *shuraya*: they affirm for us the epiphany of our Lord and John's testimony about him.

31. And through the "To you, Lord" (*Lak(h)u Mara*) they explain to us the confession of the Apostles concerning Christ.

32. And through the psalm "Have mercy on me, O God", they teach us about the middle age, which is after the Apostles up to the time of the coming of the son of perdition.

33. And through the *teshbohta* they reveal to us concerning the coming of Elijah and about those who will turn to God through him.

34. And through the *qanona* "Holy", they indicate to us concerning the praise and glorifications which the heavenly powers will raise because of the redemption made for human beings out of the accursed Satan's deception.

35. The reason for the ordering of the first session of the night (office) of Sunday is this: since the coming of our Lord from heaven is by night, this ordering is fittingly prescribed for us, that in the very night of Sunday, in which we depict a type of the coming of our Lord, we keep watch with praises (*teshbhata*) and hymns and the reading of the scriptures; in such a way that our bodies may be purified and our souls may be made holy, and our heart may grow warm, and we may eagerly await in our minds the vision of our Lord.

36. Why in the middle of the night (office) do we sound[19] the semantron (*naqosha*) and begin once again to sing praises and chant from the beginning? **Answer:** They hand down that three distinct trumpets will sound on that night;[20] each one of which marks the event for which it sounds. One in fact and the first,[21] is that one about which our Lord said: "In the middle of the night there was a cry"[22] etc., by which (sounding) the sun will be darkened, and the moon will not show its light, and the stars will fall from the sky, and the powers of heaven will be shaken, and the earth will shake and tremble, and the mountains and hills will be made low, and the sea will be stirred up and will cause terrifying sounds to be heard,[23] and the rivers will flood the earth and trees shall be uprooted and buildings will collapse and cities will be overturned, and high walls

[19] Reading ܢܩܫܝܢ rather than ܢܩܫܢ as is given in the text.

[20] I.e., of the resurrection.

[21] What is set out here regarding the trumpets, one finds more or less word for word in *The Book of the Bee* by Solomon of Bosra, chapter 57.

[22] Matthew 25:6.

[23] Luke 21:25.

thrown down, and animals, and cattle, and birds and all things shall be laid waste, apart from human beings, a few in number, who will remain alive, whom the coming of our Lord shall overtake; of whom the apostle says: "We who are left, who live, shall not overtake those who have fallen asleep".[24]

37. The second trumpet is that through which our Lord will rise up in great glory, with a great procession of his holy angels; and at once he will be seen in the power of his divinity, (and) he will cast down Satan and all the demons into the midst of the deep abyss of Sheol.

38. However the third trumpet, which is the last, (is that one) through which the dead will rise up, and will be changed into living, in accordance with the speech of blessed Paul, who said: "Swiftly, like the blink of an eye, at the last trumpet, when it has sounded; and the dead shall rise up without corruption, and we shall be changed".[25] Even though the many sounds of trumpets shall have been heard in that night, of which each one of them is a sign of that which is going to be, according to the speech of the blessed Interpreter.[26] Yet as others also agree, three distinct trumpets shall sound, in which the whole work of the resurrection shall be accomplished and will be brought to fulfillment. And that we in the middle of the night sound the semantron, (through this) we depict a type of the first trumpet, in which the elements will be unbound, and the luminaries will fall, and everything upon the earth will be destroyed. And as it were through this semantron we hear that speech: "Behold the bridegroom is coming, go out to meet him".[27] Moreover, the fact that after these things, in the fourth watch of the night, we again sound the semantron and open the curtains and the gates of the sanctuary: through these we depict images of the second trumpet, in which the firmament will be opened and our

---

[24] Thessalonians 4:15.

[25] 1 Corinthians 15:52.

[26] Theodore of Mopsuestia.

[27] Matthew 25:6.

Lord will rise up from heaven in amazing splendour and great glory, "Then shall lament all the tribes of the earth".[28]

He said this not about the faithful, but about the faithless: for the faithful shall be filled through the vision of the Cross with great joy and praise and exultation, because they know the time has come that they shall be deemed worthy of the vision of Christ; the faithless will weep and wail with lamentations over themselves: and he shall hand over the demons to Gehenna. And then the last trumpet shall sound, in which the dead will rise up and the living shall be changed, as Paul says: "Swiftly, like the blink of an eye"[29] etc. Therefore this is that which our Lord said: "He will send His angels with a great trumpet; and they will gather His elect from the four winds",[30] etc. Moreover our Lord himself makes it known by this, that all human beings, who are in all regions, shall be gathered into one ordained place at the time of the resurrection before our Lord; and in the sight of all he will destroy the Son of Perdition. And then the last trumpet will sound, in which the dead shall rise up and the living will be changed. Thus the church sounds the semantron at the time of the morning (office) so that the sleeping may awake and come from every place, where they are, and shall mingle with the angels of the sanctuary, and stand at the same time before our Lord in the office.

39. **Concerning the service of the Mysteries** – a single *marmitha*, which we serve from the Psalms, signifies that the Lord Jesus Christ Son of God is one, born of Mary the virgin.

40. However, the fact that we begin from the Old Testament is because when Christ was born in flesh, the Old Testament still held power.

41. However, the fact that (this *marmitha* is arranged) out of three psalms is because the name Christ (*mshīḥa*) makes known (the Father) who anointed him, and about the Son who was anointed, and about the Holy Spirit, who fulfilled the role of the oil.

---

[28] Matthew 24:30.

[29] 1 Corinthians 15:52.

[30] Matthew 24:31.

42. Moreover, the fact that we adjoin to each verse (*pethgama*) a *hullala*[31] is an indication of those heavenly powers, which appeared at the birth of our Lord to the shepherds, giving praise.

43. The fact that before the *marmitha* is completed, we change (the chant) with two verses is because of the changes which John the Proclaimer introduced to the Law through baptism.

44. Moreover, the fact that they glorify the Father, the Son and the Holy Spirit is a demonstration of the revealing of the three Persons (*qnome*) which were made known at the baptism of our Lord.

45. The responsary (*ʿonitha*) of the chancels signifies the praises of the angels; or it is a symbol of the (utterance of) praise of John.

46. The coming out of the Cross is a symbol of Jesus' going out into the desert.

47. The ascent of the Cross to the *Bema* is a symbol of Jesus' ascent into Jerusalem.

48. The "To you, Lord" (*Lak(h)u Mara*) is a symbol of the confession of the Apostles.

49. The two lights which accompany the Cross are a symbol of the light of the two Testaments.

50. The fragrance of the incense is a symbol of the happiness which is to come.

51. The "Holy God" is a symbol of the proclamation of sanctification by the angels.

52. The Law and the Prophets which are read, are a symbol of the demonstrations which our Lord brought forth from the Prophets and Moses.

---

[31] A chant or hymn. One of the twenty sections into which the Church of the East divides the Psalms.

53. However, the Acts (of the Apostles) which is read with the Old Testament is a symbol of the demonstration (of the harmony) of the two Testaments.

54. The sitting of the priests on the *Bema* is for a demonstration of what our Lord said: "When the Son of Man comes in glory", etc., "you too will sit" etc.[32]

55. Their rising up from sitting points to the strengthening of the Apostles' minds.

56. The *estatyona*[33] is a symbol of the praise of the people because of John, who preached repentance and prophesied about the Kingdom of the Heaven.

57. The (reading from the) Apostle is a symbol of John's exalted words: "I am not the Christ, but I am a messenger before him".[34]

58. The fact that the deacon reads the Apostle and not the priest is because John was in the order of deacons, not in the order of presbyters and priests of the New Testament.

59. The psalmody (*zummara*) before the Gospel is a symbol of the praise of the crowds and of the children, who were crying out and saying: "Hosanna in the highest" etc.[35]

60. Moreover, the silk vestment which the priest puts on is because he stands in the role of our Lord who was clothed in a robe of glory.

61. The coming forth of the Gospel, and of the Cross with it is a symbol of the humanity of our Lord, which existed in body and soul. The Cross is a symbol of the body which was crucified; the Gospel, a symbol of the soul, in which is reason.

62. Moreover, the procession of the deacons is a symbol of that procession with which the Lord entered Jerusalem.

---

[32] Matthew 19:28.

[33] A Station or doctrinal hymn.

[34] John 3:28.

[35] Matthew 21:9.

63. Moreover, the reading of the Gospel is a demonstration of the response of our Lord to the Scribes and Pharisees.

64. Moreover, the Cross which is fixed on top of the staff is (a symbol of) that which our Lord said, when he declared by what death he was to die: "Just as Moses raised the serpent" etc.[36]

65. Moreover, the lights at that time are a symbol of that which our Lord said: "You are the light of the world"[37] and: "Thus let your light shine out before people"[38] etc.

66. And the fact that there are two lights, not one, is because he did not say this just about the Apostles, but also concerning those who through them were converted.

67. The incense which they burn is a symbol of the sweetness of our Lord's words.

68. The *turgama*[39] is a symbol of that teaching which the Lord spoke before he suffered.

69. The proclamation[40] is a symbol of that (saying): "Stay awake and pray"[41] etc.

70. The prayer of the imposition of hands (*syamida*) which he who fills the role of our Lord prays, is a symbol of that prayer which our Lord prayed over his disciples before he suffered: "Father keep them by your name"[42] etc.

71. Moreover, the Cross and the Gospel upon the *Bema* are a symbol of Jesus' sitting among his disciples.

---

[36] John 3:14.

[37] Matthew 5:14.

[38] Matthew 5:16.

[39] Doubtless a type of homiletic hymn to be performed in place of a homily on the gospel.

[40] Or "litany".

[41] Matthew 26:41.

[42] John 17:11.

72. The taking up of the Cross and Gospel from the Throne of the *Bema* is the arrest of Jesus by the crucifiers and his going out from Jerusalem to the place where he was crucified.

73. The fact that a priest carries the Gospel is a symbol of the attachment of John the Evangelist who accompanied Jesus up to his crucifixion.

74. Moreover, the carrying of the Cross by a deacon, is a symbol of the carrying (of his Cross) by Simon of Cyrene, who was coming from the field.[43]

75. However, the fact that the Cross and the Gospel come down from the *Bema* not in a procession of priests and deacons is because when Jesus was arrested and led away to be crucified, all his disciples abandoned him and fled.

76. Moreover, the raising of the Cross at the threshold[44] of the sanctuary door is a symbol of the crucifixion of Jesus on the wood (of the cross).

77. The separation of the Gospel from the Cross and the setting of it on the other side is a symbol of the separation of the soul of Jesus from his body and its departure to Paradise.

78. The fact that, when they place the Cross and Gospel at the door of the sanctuary, they say: "Whoever has not received baptism", etc., is a symbol which (the Church) depicts that when the soul of Jesus separated from his body and entered into paradise, with the soul of the (Good) Thief accompanying it, there entered after them into Paradise all the souls of the just, from Adam up until that time; however, all the souls of sinners are refused and prohibited from entering.

79. For the type which the Church depicts at this time, is a symbol in which she portrays the crucifixion of Jesus upon the Wood, and the separation of his soul, and its entry into Paradise.

---

[43] Matthew 27:32.

[44] Syriac *prostedha* i.e., prostas.

80. Through the driving out of those, who are not worthy to participate in the living and life-giving body, this signifies that thus the souls of sinners were held back from entering with the souls of the just.

81. From this moment onwards whoever does not receive the mark (*rushma*) of baptism, will not enter that holy place; just as Jesus himself said beforehand: "Whoever is not born of water and the Spirit",[45] etc. Thus everyone who does not sanctify his body and in purity receive the gift of the life-giving Mysteries, his soul will go to the sinners and will not enter Paradise.

82. "Depart, catechumens (*shamoʿe*)", etc. (This is) like the divine sign commanding the angels who are there[46] to guard with care those (souls) who were mentioned (earlier).[47]

83. From this point on, the Church depicts the burial of Christ through the setting of bread and wine upon the altar, for the altar is considered as (taking) the place of the tomb. The veil which is over the bread and wine, is in place of that stone, which was placed above the door of the tomb;[48] and the deacons, who stand on either side are a symbol of the angels who were seen in the tomb, one near his head and one at his feet.[49]

84. The Cross and the Gospel which are placed upon the altar (and the icon of our Lord above them), fulfil the place of the person of our Lord. Accordingly, it is not at all permitted for the Holy Mysteries to be consecrated without the proximity of the Cross and the Gospel and the icon of our Lord.

85. The responsary (*ʿonitha*) of the Mysteries (*raze*), is a symbol of the ineffable songs of praise which the holy angels raised up, and the souls of the just at the time when, with the soul of our Lord,

---

[45] John 3:5.

[46] Sc. at the gate of Paradise.

[47] I.e., as it seems, to keep watch on those who have been excluded from Paradise, so that they do not enter.

[48] Matthew 28:2.

[49] John 20:12.

entered Paradise. Alternatively, it is a symbol of the songs of praise of the angels and human beings at the time of the Passion of our Lord, when they saw that the earth quaked, and the rocks were split, and the sun was darkened, etc.[50]

86. Moreover, the fact that at this time the priests sit on the *Bema* (is because) at the death of Jesus, all the Apostles were sitting in hiding for fear of the Jews.

87. The fact that the priests wash their hands at this time is a symbol of the ablution of their hearts from hatred against the Jews.

88. However, the fact that, when the priests come down from the *Bema*, the deacons come out of the sanctuary and bow down to them, and give way to them, so that they can enter (the sanctuary) before them: this instructs that when the Jews crucified Jesus, the priesthood and the Kingdom was taken away from them; and the Levites left the sanctuary and the house of Simon entered, who do not perform their service with sacrifices of animals, but with the living sacrifice of the Son of God.

89. However, the fact that the deacons bow down to the priest and enter the sanctuary after him, is a demonstration that those who believed in Christ, held the Apostles in great honour, (and) bowed down as if disciples before their masters and respected their words.

90. The fact that, when the priests enter the sanctuary, before everything they say the Creed laid down by our Fathers, indicates that everyone who does not correctly believe in the Holy Trinity and in the Dispensation completed in Christ, is a stranger to the truth and deprived of joy with our Lord.

91. However, the fact that after it (i.e., the Creed) the deacon says: "Pray for the memory", etc. is a demonstration of spiritual love. Thus too we pray for our other fathers and faithful, who are to the Church like sons and daughters, in order to show that the fullness of love is preserved in the Church.

---

[50] Matthew 27:45, 51–2.

92. Up to here the Church depicts through her types the Mystery of the death and burial of Christ.

93. From now on the priest approaches to depict the type of the Resurrection. Just as our Lord Christ, when he handed on these Mysteries, blessed and gave thanks and said: "Do thus in my memory".[51] Thus the Church acts according to his instruction: she appoints one priest to be the one who blesses and gives thanks in the likeness of Christ our Lord. When, through the recital, he indicates that he is speaking the words of our Lord. And after the priest's recital, blessing the bread and the wine, through the grace of the Holy Spirit, which overshadows, they become henceforth the Body and Blood of Christ: not by nature, but by true faith and in efficacy. It is not that Christ has two bodies, one in heaven, and one on earth; rather in the same way that a king and his statue do not make two kings, nor does the humanity taken from us make two sons, rather one Son of God, who has been united to the humanity which is from us. In the same way this Body along with that which is in heaven is the one Body of Christ.

94. The first Peace which the priest gives to the people, is a prayer of the priesthood, where he prays for the people, that there may remain that peace which Christ left behind before he suffered: "My peace I leave to you".[52] And after the people respond to the priest: "May you also have peace with the spirit of priesthood which you have received", then the herald bids the people: "Give the peace to one another in the love of Christ"; that is to say, "Show your peace towards one another in deed; and root out anger from your hearts, that you may become worthy to receive the life-giving Mysteries".[53] For with this peace we fulfil the speech of our Lord: "Forgive, and it shall be forgiven unto you".[54]

95. The reading of the Book of the Living and the Dead is a demonstration that the Mystery of our salvation is carried out on

---

[51] Luke 22:19.

[52] John 14:27.

[53] Matthew 6:14.

[54] Luke 6:37.

behalf of the living and the dead, and together, the dead and the living are in need of what is performed and carried out by us in a mystical fashion.

96. That one priest offers the sacrifice is a symbol of the one High Priest, who was sacrificed for us.

97. Moreover, the priests and deacons who stand in the sanctuary (are) a demonstration that the holy angels are close by when the Mysteries of our salvation are performed.

98. That the herald cries out: "Stand well and be attentive": (this) is an instruction of the priesthood: "Let everyone stand with great attention before God in that dread time, while not putting their back to the choir".[55]

99. The incense which we burn at this time, is a symbol of the aromatic spices with which the body of our Saviour was embalmed.

100. Moreover, the fact that the priest bows three times and recites the sacred words is a symbol of the three days in which the humanity of our Lord was under the authority of death.

101. The fact that he recites the whole section quietly, and at the end raises his voice so that the people can hear, (signifies) that what is being performed is a Mystery, and it is not fitting that all the people should know it; and secondly, so that the words, when heard, should not be learnt by laymen and women and children and that the divine words are treated as common and despised.

102. Moreover, the fact that at the end he raises his voice (is so) that all the people might take part with the priest.

103. Moreover, the fact that the herald cries out "In your minds and in stillness" (is so) that he might teach us that it is not appropriate in this moment, which is full of awe, to say our prayers in an audible voice, but rather in stillness within the heart, nor by any means to dare to recite (out loud).

---

[55] C.f. Romans 14:10.

104. Moreover, the fact that the entire people prostrates together with the priest at the time of the epiclesis (of the Holy Spirit) corresponds to us all supplicating, together with the priest, that the grace of the Holy Spirit may come and perfect and complete the Holy Mysteries. Again in honour of the coming of Grace we kneel and prostrate.

105. Moreover, the fact that, when the priest invokes the Spirit, and she hovers, and he joins the Body to the Blood and the Blood to the Body: is a symbol of the return of the soul of Jesus within his body, and of his resurrection from the dead.

106. Moreover, the fact that after the indwelling of Grace the priest does not make the sign of the cross again over the Mysteries (is) because the Mysteries have (now) been completed by the dissolution of death.

107. Moreover, the fact that at this time we remove the incense from the altar is because corruptibility, which was the reason for the embalming, is dissolved.

108. The fact that the herald cries out: "Let us all with fear". (Through this) the priesthood teaches us concerning the greatness and the exaltedness of the Mystery; and that we should no longer look on the bread and wine according to the order of their nature, but as the Body and Blood of Christ.

109. The fact that at the end of the proclamation we say: "Lord, forgive the sins" etc.: (we say it) because we are in this world of mortality, and it is not possible not to do wrong, as we learn from what has been said: "There is not one who does not sin".[56]

110. After these things we say that prayer which our Lord prayed: "Our Father who is in heaven", because we are depicting the Mystery of the death and the resurrection through which we become children of God, it is good that we now call God "Our Father", just as our Lord said: "You shall not call (anyone) your father on earth", etc.[57]

---

[56] 1 Kings 8:46; c.f. Prov. 22:9, Eccl. 7:20.

[57] Matthew 23:9.

111. Moreover, the Peace, which the priest gives at this time is a symbol of that peace which our Lord gave to the women and to his disciples after his resurrection.

112. Afterwards, the priest says: "What is holy is fitting for the holy, in harmony". We do not presume to speak about this matter which the Interpreter[58] expounded.

113. Moreover, we complete this service by means of thanksgiving, and we say "One holy Father, one holy Son, one Holy Spirit". Through this we make known that the Holy Trinity is not a numerical Trinity in which one is prior to two, and two to three, but (a case of) one, one, one.

114. We make a seal with "Glory to the Father and to the Son and to the Holy Spirit, for eternal ages, amen". Through this we make known that the cause of all our benefits is that adored and glorious Nature, which is confessed (as), Father, Son and Holy Spirit. These things, therefore, we say at this moment in remembrance of what our Lord said to his Apostles: "Go forth, therefore, make disciples of all the nations; (baptize them in the name of the Father, and of the Son and of the Holy Spirit".[59]

115. The fact that we say: "Fearful are You" and the Response (*ʿonaya*), is a symbol of the praises and *hullale* (acclamations) with which all the heavenly hosts give praise for the dispensation which has been effected in Christ.

116. Moreover, that the consecrator is the first to receive (the Sacrament) is a symbol of what (occurred) with Jesus, the High Priest, for the priest stands in his role; for (Christ) who through the sacrifice of his own self first, through the Holy Spirit, received the nourishment of immortality; and then he was capable of giving it to others. And (he should) not, without restraint, presume to receive the Sacrament without anyone else (present), for he stands in the role of the life-giving Spirit. Now the consecrator gives to others as

[58] Theodore of Mopsuestia.

[59] Matthew 28:19.

a demonstration of what will happen as a result of our Lord at the resurrection, who is going to give everyone that future immortality.

117. Moreover, our partaking of the Holy Mysteries is a symbol of that participation that we shall have with him in the Kingdom of the Heaven.

118. The *teshbohta* beginning "Our Lord Jesus, revered Sovereign" is a symbol of that (praise) which will take place in the world to come from all rational beings, for we praise and exalt as heavenly King (the one) "In whom the entire fullness of divinity willed to dwell",[60] and through his mediation we worship the Trinity.

119. The prayer of the signing of the Cross by the priest over the people is in remembrance of that blessing with which our Lord blessed his Apostles at the time in which he was raised up to heaven.

120. Again, the blessing, with which the priest blesses the people as he stands on the threshold of the sanctuary door is a symbol of the inflowing of the grace of the Holy Spirit into the Apostles after our Lord Jesus had ascended to heaven. And with this blessing everything comes to a close.

121. Also the final Peace which we give each other after receiving the life-giving Mysteries is a symbol of that holy union by which we are united there to one another, as limbs, and we are all joined to the Head of the Church and the Firstborn from the dead, our Lord Jesus Christ.[61]

122. The *Commentary on the Liturgical Offices* is finished, glory to God, amen.

123. [Connolly] Where there is no peace towards neighbour, neither is God there. Do not become a disciple of he who praises himself, lest you learn pride in place of humility. When you see two bad men bearing love towards each other, know that each of them

---

[60] Colossians 2:9.

[61] Colossians 1:18.

aids the will of his companion. Hands which do not work are a burden to him who possesses them.

TEXT

[62]ܡܘܬܒܐ[63] ܕܦܘܫܩ ܠܬܫܡ̈ܫܬܐ ܕܥܒܕ ܠܡܪܝ ܐܒܪܗܡ ܩܛܪܝܐ ܒܪ ܠܝܦܗ܀[64]

1 - ܩܕܡܝܬ: ܠܐܘܕܥ ܡܫܡܫܢܘܬܐ ܐܝܟܢ ܕܥܘܗܕܢܐ ܕܪܐܙܐ ܕܡܫܝܚܐ ܡܫܡܫܝܢ ܒܗܕܐ ܠܐܘܕܥ ܡܢܘ̈ܬܗ[65] ܕܟܗܢܐ. ܐܝܟܢܐ ܕܢܗܘܐ ܠܗ ܟܠ ܚܕ ܚܕ ܡܢ ܡܫܡܫܢܘܬܐ. ܘܗܟܢ ܡܘܕܥ ܠܫܘܡܠܝܐ. ܘܚܠܦ ܚܕ ܚܕ ܡܢ ܡܢܘ̈ܬܐ. ܒܚܕܟܡܐ ܕܝܢ ܚܕܐ ܡܫܡܫܢܘܬܐ ܡܫܡܫܝܢ. ܡܛܠ ܕܗܘ ܚܕ ܪܘܚܐ ܒܦܓܪܐ ܘܠܐ ܡܬܦܠܓܐ ܗܘܐ ܠܦܓܪܐ ܘܠܪܫܐ ܘܠܐ ܠܐܘܢ ܐܝܟ ܕܒܟܠܗܘܢ ܗܘܐ.

2 - ܬܘܐܬܐ: ܡܛܠ ܚܕܐ ܡܢ ܪܫܢ̈ܬܐ ܒܚܠܩ̈ܬܐ ܡܫܡܫܝܢ ܘܟܠܗ ܡܢ ܚܕܬܐ܀ ܗܢܐ[66] ܀ ܒܬܫܡܫܬܐ ܘܗܟܢ ܡܠܐܟܘܬܐ ܩܕܡ ܐܠܗܐ ܒܕܡܘܬܐ ܚܕܬܐ ܒܗܘ ܕܟܠ ܚܕܘܬܐ ܚܕܐ ܠܟܘܠܐ ܕܢܣܒܬ ܡܢܗܐ. ܘܡܢ ܗܟܢܐ ܠܟܠܗܘܢ ܠܒܢܝ̈ܢܫܐ ܡܦܪܫܐ܀

3 - ܬܘܐܬܐ ܀[67] ܡܛܠܡܢܐ[68] ܩܕܡ ܕܢܫܠܡܘܢ ܡܫܡܫܢܘܬܐ ܡܫܬܟܚܝܢ ܘܡܢ ܡܬܚܣܢܝܢ܀ ܗܢܐ[69] ܀ ܟܕ ܓܡܪ ܢܡܘܣܐ ܕܡܘܫܐ ܡܫܠܡ ܗܘܐ. ܗܘ ܕܓܡܪ ܘܡܢ ܚܪܬܐ ܚܙܐ ܗܘܐ ܠܟܠ ܟܠ[70] ܘܥܠܡ. ܘܠܐ ܡܫܟܚ ܗܘܐ ܟܠ ܟܠܗ ܕܢܬܩܒܠ ܠܡܘܬܐ. ܐܬܐ ܗܘ ܡܫܝܚ ܒܪܗ. ܗܘ ܕܐܬܝܗܒ[71] ܡܢ ܐܝܟܢܐ ܟܠ.[72] ܘܐܥܒܪ ܠܡܘܬܐ ܒܫܘܒܚܐ ܕܢܨܚܢܐ܀

---

[62] Vat. sir. 504 f.119r (henceforth V).

[63] Connolly (henceforth C): ܡܟܬܒܐ.

[64] C: ܠܡܪܝ ܐܒܪܗܡ ܒܪ ܠܝܦܗ ܩܛܪܝܐ. C states that in his Codex ܩܛܪܝܐ is in fact given.

[65] C: ܡܢܘ̈ܬܐ.

[66] ܗܢܐ missing in C.

[67] V. f. 119v.

[68] C: ܡܛܠ ܡܢܐ.

[69] ܗܢܐ missing in C.

[70] C: ܒܟܠ ܟܠ ܥܡ.

[71] C: ܕܐܬܝܗܒ. C states that in his codex ܕܐܬܝܗܒ is in fact given.

[72] C: ܡܠܐ.

4 - ܬܘܐܠܐ ܀ ܗܘ ܕܡܠܟܐ[73] ܚܕܝ. ܀ ܡܪܝܐ[74] ܀ ܚܠܦ ܠܐܪܟܬܐ ܘܡܠܟܐ ܗܘ ܕܚܕ ܚܕ ܠܟܠ ܒܡܠܬܗ ܘܡܫܝܚܐ ܡܫܘܕܥܐ܀

5 - ܬܘܐܠܐ ܀ ܘܫܒܚܐ ܕܬܘ̈ܐܠܐ ܀ ܡܪܝܐ[75] ܀ ܐܘܪ ܦܨܐ ܠܐܪܟܐ ܕܐܡܟܬܐ. ܗܘ ܕܦܨܐ ܡܫܝܚܐ ܠܟܠܗܘܢ ܚܛܝ̈ܐ܀

6 - ܬܘܐܠܐ ܀ ܡܫܡܥ ܕܠܡܫܡܥ̈ܐ ܀ ܡܪܝܐ[76] ܀ ܐܘܪ ܕܚܝܐ ܠܟܠܗ. ܗܘ ܡܫܡܥ ܩܠ ܕܕܘܫܡܐ ܕܟܠ ܡܫܪܝ ܐܬܩܕܫ܀

7 - ܬܘܐܠܐ ܀ ܐܦ ܗܘ ܕܝܢ ܕܬܘ̈ܐܠܐ ܕܬܝܡܢܐ ܦܠܓܝܢ ܘܬܘ̈ܐܠܐ ܠܓܘܢܝܬܐ ܠܐ ܀ ܡܪܝܐ[77] ܀ ܗܘܐ ܐܘܪܐ ܕܢܘܪܝܢ. ܘܟܕ ܐܠܗܝ ܒܒܠܒܠܐ ܗܘܐ. ܒܬܫܒܘܚܬܐ ܗܘ ܡܫܒܚܝܢ ܘܠܗ[78] ܒܚܝܠܐ. ܘܗܟܢܐ ܐܝܟ ܕܒܫܝܚܘܬܐ ܚܙܝܢ ܒܡܠܐܟܐ. ܗܟܝܠ ܕܝܢ ܐܦܝ̈ ܠܘܡܒܠܐܦ̈ܐ. ܘܗܟܢܐ ܕܝܢ[79] ܡܠܟܐ ܡܢ ܫܡܝܐ ܢܚܬܝܢ. ܒܠܒܘܫ ܢܒܝ[80] ܐܚܝܢܐ ܕܐܬܝܠܕܢ܀

8 - ܬܘܐܠܐ[81] ܀ ܦܪܘܩܐ ܕܒܫܘܩܐ ܘܡܒܠܐܪܝܢ ܀ ܡܪܝܐ[82] ܀ ܡܫܘܕܥ[83] ܐܘܪܐ[84] ܘܝܠܕܗ ܕܡܫܝܚܐ. ܕܐܝܟ ܪܚܝܠ ܒܫܘܩܐ ܒܝܢ ܡܠܟܝ̈ܢܐ ܒܠܝܩ ܦܩܕ ܗܘܐ. ܘܐܘܒ ܠܠܫܘܩܐ ܕܒܫܡܫܘܬܐ ܕܡܠܟܘܬܗ ܕܡܫܝܚܐ. ܘܐܘܒ ܐܝܟ ܕܒܫܘܩܐ ܕܚܠ ܦܩܝܕ ܗܘܘ ܒܢ̈ܝܐ ܕܡܠܟܪܘܗܝ ܒܫܘܩܐ. ܗܟܢܐ ܐܦ ܒܝܬܐ ܡܠܟܐ ܠܒܝܬܐ ܠܠܫܡܝܐ܀

9 - ܬܘܐܠܐ ܀ ܙܒܘܬܐ ܕܩܕܡ ܠܒܘܩܪܐ ܀ ܡܪܝܐ[85] ܀ ܡܫܒܚܘܬܐ ܐܠܗܝܐ ܟܠ ܡܠܟܘܬܗ ܕܡܫܝܚܐ܀

---

[73] ܗܘ ܕ missing in C.
[74] ܡܪܝܐ missing in C.
[75] ܡܪܝܐ missing in C.
[76] ܡܪܝܐ missing in C.
[77] ܡܪܝܐ missing in C.
[78] C: ܘܠܐ.
[79] ܕܝܢ missing in C.
[80] V.f. 120r.
[81] ܬܘܐܠܐ missing in C.
[82] ܡܪܝܐ missing in C.
[83] C: ܡܫܘܕܥ.
[84] ܐܘܪܐ missing in C.
[85] ܡܪܝܐ missing in C.

10 - ܫܘܐܠܐ ܀ ܡܢܘܐ ܕܠܟܘܡܪܐ ܘܡܬܐܡܪ: ܒܡܕܢܚܐ ܗܘܐ ܀ ܦܘܢܝܐ[86] ܀ ܐܝܟ
ܕܗܘܐ ܠܢ[87] ܡܫܟܢܐ ܥܠ ܡܛܠܬܗ ܕܡܫܝܚܐ. ܗ̇ܘ ܕܒܣܪ: ܘܡܫܡܫ
ܒܝܬܐ ܟܗܢܘܬܐ. ܘܐܡܪܢ ܕܝܬܐ ܚܕܐ. ܘܟܕ ܠܐܘܡܝܗܘܢ ܚܕ ܓܘܫܡܐ
ܘܡܕܒܪܢܘܬܗ ܘܐܚܕܐ. ܐܟܢܐ ܓܒܪ ܘܡܢ ܠܐܘܡܝ ܡܢ̈ܘܬܐ ܩܐܡ ܒܗܘ ܘܒܪܢܫܐ. ܐܦ
ܒܪܝܫ ܦܓܪܐ ܡܢ ܢܦܫܐ. ܐܠܐ ܠܐܘܡܝܗܘܢ ܡܢ ܡܢܘܬܐ[88] ܐܝܠܝܗܘܢ ܘܒܪܢܫܐ. ܗܟܢܐ
ܐܦ ܘܟܠܗ ܟܡܫܡܫܢܐ ܒܪܝܫܐ[89] ܡܢ ܚܕܐ. ܐܠܐ ܠܐܘܡܝܗܘܢ ܡܢ ܓܘܫܡܐ
ܐܝܠܝܗܘܢ[90] ܘܡܕܒܪܢܘܬܗ ܘܐܚܕܐ܀

11 - ܫܘܐܠܐ ܀ ܗܟܢ ܠܐܘܢ ܡܘܬܐ ܕܐܬܓܠܝܘ ܀ ܦܘܢܝܐ[91] ܀ ܕܗܘܘ[92] ܐܝܟ
ܡܘܟܠ ܠܡܬܒܠܐ[93] ܡܢܗ. ܘܣܟ ܗܟܢ ܠܐܘܢ ܒܢܝܢ ܘܟܠܗܘܢ ܘܐܣܟܡܐ. ܐܘ
ܕܗܘܐ ܡܬܟܢܫ ܒܗܘܢ ܥܠ ܢܘܬܪ. ܘܒܗܟܢ ܠܐܘܢ ܒܢܝܢ. ܗܟܢܐ ܡܬܟܢܫ
ܗܟܢ (ܠܐܘܢ ܒܢܝܢ. ܘܐܝܟܢܐ ܕܪܫܡܐ ܩܐܡ ܡܬܟܢܫ ܗܟܢ ܠܐܘܢ ܒܢܝܢ. ܗܟܢܐ
ܡܬܟܢܫ ܗܟܢ)[94] ܡܘܬܐ ܐܬܓܠܝܘ.[95] ܘܡܬܐܡܪ ܡܢܐ ܦܪܢܣܐ. ܥܠ ܕܐܝܬ ܒܗ
ܡܘܪܒܐ ܘܐܒܝܕ ܘܡܪܥܐ܀

12 - ܫܘܐܠܐ ܀ ܡܢܐ ܡܫܡܫܢ ܠܢ ܛܘܦܣܐ[96] ܕܒܪܘܪܬܐ ܀ ܦܘܢܝܐ[97] ܀ ܡܛܠ
ܕܐܝܬ ܒܪܘܫܝܐ ܚܕ ܚܕ ܦܓܪ ܒܡܫܝܚܐ. ܘܟܠ ܚܕ ܚܕܐ ܓܘܐ ܕܐܝܬ
ܡܬܟܢܫ. ܐܝܟ ܦܘܠܘܣ ܕܐܡܪ. ܡܛܠ ܕܐܝܬ ܒܗ ܫܘܬܦܘܬܐ ܕܚܕ ܒܡܫܝܚܐ
ܘܒܟܠܗ ܗܘܐ. ܘܠܐ ܡܬܥܪ ܕܒܝܬܐ. ܘܟܠ ܕܐܝܬ ܠܐ ܡܬܢܢ ܡܢܐ ܢܐܡܪܘܢ. ܘܫܘܬܦܘܬܐ
ܡܬܥܪ ܕܒܝܬܐ ܘܠܐ ܡܬܢܢ ܡܢܐ ܢܟܘܢ. ܡܛܠܗܕܐ[98] ܐܬܓܠܝܬ ܒܪܘܪܬܐ ܗܘܐ.
ܕܒܗ ܢܬܚܘܐ ܟܠܗ ܓܘܐ ܟܕ ܚܕܐ ܕܝܢ. ܟܠܗ ܓܒܪ ܐܝܟ ܕܠܐ ܡܕܡ

---

86 ܦܘܢܝܐ missing in C.

87 C gives ܠܗ but states that in his codex ܠܢ is in fact given.

88 C: ܡܢܘܬܐ.

89 C: ܐܦ ܒܪܝܫܐ.

90 C: ܐܝܠܝܗܘܢ ܕܝܢ.

91 ܦܘܢܝܐ missing in C.

92 V. f. 120v.

93 C: ܡܘܟܠܡܬܒܠܐ.

94 The passage in brackets is not to be found in Vat. sir. 504. C suggests that part of the passage is corrupted due to scribal error.

95 C gives ܐܬܓܠܝܘ but states that in his codex ܐܬܓܠܝܘܗ is in fact given.

96 C: ܛܘܒܐ. Vat. sir. 504: ܛܘܦܣܐ.

97 ܦܘܢܝܐ missing in C.

98 C: ܡܛܠ ܗܕܐ.

ܠܟܗܢܐ ܡܢܝ ܐܬܪܫܡܬܘܢ.[99] ܘܡܛܠ ܗܕܐ ܠܟܠܗ ܓܘܐ. ܢܦܩ ܥܡ ܠܟܗ̈ܢܐ ܘܟܗܢܐ ܠܟܠܗ ܡܫܡܠܝܐܝܬ ܒܟܗܢܘܬܐ ܗܘܐ. ܟܕ ܫܠܡ ܬܫ̈ܥܐ ܡܢ ܐܠܗܐ. ܥܡ ܟܠܗܘܢ[100] ܟܗ̈ܢܐ ܗܢܘܢ ܕܣܠܩ ܠܟܠܗ ܓܘܐ ܡܙܠܚܝܢ܀[101]

13 - ܫܘܐܠܐ[102] ܀ ܗܢܐ ܕܝܢ ܕܡܫܡܫܢܐ ܗܘ ܒܟܗܢܘܬܗ[103] ܐܡܪ ܠܗ ܠܒܪܝܘܬܐ ܐܚܪܢܝܬܐ. ܘܟܠܗ ܥܠܡܐ ܗܢܐ. ܟܕ ܡܛܠ ܟܠܗܝ ܡܢܗ ܘܠܗ ܀ ܫܪܝܐ[104] ܀ ܡܫܘܕܥܐ ܘܒܥܘܬܐ[105] ܕܒܢܬܐ ܐܢܫܝܬܐ ܡܙܠܚܐ ܣܠܩ ܠܟܠܗܘܢ ܒܢܝ̈ܢܫܐ܀

14 - ܫܘܐܠܐ ܀[106] ܗܢܐ ܕܝܢ ܕܒܠܒܫ ܒܪܘܪܬܐ ܦܫܛ ܒܪܘܪܐ ܠܟܗܢܐ ܕܢܩܘܡ ܡܢ ܫܡܫ ܒܦܘܪܚܐ ܀ ܫܪܝܐ[107] ܀ ܠܡܘܬܐ ܐܬܠܝܗ ܕܦܘܡ ܡܢ ܡܫܡܠܝܘܬܐ ܕܡܢ ܣܝܡ̈ܬܐ. ܘܐܬܐ ܕܡܫܡܠܝܘܬܐ ܕܪܒܘܬܗ܀

15 - ܫܘܐܠܐ[108] ܀ ܗܢܐ ܕܝܢ ܕܐܡܪ ܒܟܗܢܘܬܐ ܘܡܪܒܐ. ܘܐܝܟ ܟܗܢܐ ܡܢ ܠܒܝܬ ܡܪܝܐ ܀ ܫܪܝܐ[109] ܀ ܗܘܐ ܡܫܘܕܥܐ ܕܡܢ ܠܒܝܬ ܐܠܗܐ ܟܠܗܘܢ ܢܦܫ̈ܬܐ[110] ܠܟܠ ܠܗ̈ܝ ܘܟܠ ܒܘܪ̈ܟܝܢ܀

16 - ܫܘܐܠܐ[111] ܀ ܗܢܐ ܕܝܢ[112] ܕܐܘܪܚܬܐ ܘܫܡܝܐ ܀ ܫܪܝܐ[113] ܀ ܟܠ ܕܟܠܗܝ ܫܡܝܐ ܕܒܪܐ ܐܠܗܐ. ܘܡܫܡܫܢܘܬܐ ܕܒܪܐ ܦܢܝܐ ܦܢܝܢ ܠܡܠܐ ܕܪܒܘܬܗ܀

---

[99] C: ܐܬܪܫܡ ܠܟܘܢ.

[100] ܟܠܗܘܢ missing in C.

[101] Vat. sir. 504: ܡܙܠܚܝܢ.

[102] ܫܘܐܠܐ missing in C.

[103] V.f. 121r.

[104] ܫܪܝܐ missing in C.

[105] C states that his codex at this point reveals lacunae which he has filled in using the transcribed missing text which A. Scher provided him with. C's edition from this point appears to be flawed in comparison with Vat. sir. 504. The reason for this must be related to the fact that he is relying on a corrupt codex with many lacunae and incorrectly using the missing parts which A. Scher transcribed for him.

[106] C: ܫܪܝܐ.

[107] ܫܪܝܐ missing in C.

[108] C has ܫ and states that this abbreviation could be either for ܫܪܝܐ or ܫܘܐܠܐ. C may at this point be using A. Scher's transcribed missing text who is abbreviating ܫܪܝܐ and ܫܘܐܠܐ.

[109] ܫܪܝܐ missing in C.

[110] C: reads ܢܦܫܐ and states that the codex (A. Scher's transcription?) has ܢܦ̈ܫܬܐ.

17 - ܫܘܐܠܐ[114] ܀ ܗܘ̇ ܕܝܢ ܕܫܐܠ ܡܘܟܝܐ. ܘܡܘܟܟ ܘܐܡܪ. ܠܒܢ̈ܝܟܝ
ܘܠܒܢ̈ܬܟܝ ܘܥܢܝܐ ܀ ܥܢܝܢܐ[115] ܀ ܡܠܟܐ ܕܠܗ ܒܠܒܗ ܐܝܟ ܢܘܪܐ ܕܢܦܘܩ ܐܠܐ
ܕܢܚܪܘܢ ܀[116]

18 - ܫܘܐܠܐ[117] ܀ ܠܠܝܐ ܕܡܫܘܚܐ ܗܘܐ ܕܩܝܡܐ. (ܥܢܝܢܐ) ܒܪܡܫܐ ܕܡܠܟܐ
ܠܐܘܪܫܠܡ ܕܠܥܠ. ܗܘ̣ ܕܡܠܟܐ ܪܥܡܐ ܗܘܐ ܠܥܡܐ ܕܢܒܝܐ ܫܒܚܐ ܠܗ ܠܗ ܡܫܝܚܐ
ܕܥܕܬܐ. ܟܕ ܐܫܬܘܕܥܘ ܕܝܘܡܐ[118] ܘܫܘܡܠܝܐ ܡܘܬܒܐ. ܟܕ ܫܡܥ ܗܢܐ
ܐܡܪܗ ܐܘܪ̈ܚܬܗܘܢ ܡܢ ܕܫܡܫܐ ܡܫܡܫܢܘܬܐ ܕܥܕܬܐ. ܘܐܝܟܢ ܠܡܫܡ̈ܫܢܐ ܕܗܘܢ
ܠܠܝܐ ܠܫܡܫܐ. ܘܟܠܡܢ ܡܘܕܝܢܐ ܗܘܐ ܫܘܒܚܐ ܘܐܠܗܐ.[119][120] ܡܛܠ ܐܝܟ
ܠܠܗܐ ܕܡܬܪܘܡ ܒܫܘܪܝܐ ܡܫܬܟܚܬܐ. ܘܐܫܬܪܪ ܒܠܠܝܐ ܕܡܫܝܚܐ ܡܫܡܫ
ܒܪܢܐ ܕܢܦܠ. ܘܐܦ ܕܡܫܡܫܘ ܠܫܠܝܚܐ ܩܕܝܫܐ ܒܡܫܝܚܘܬܗܘܢ. ܘܐܘܪܚܗ
ܠܥܡܐ ܒܣܘܓܦܢܗܘܢ. ܗܘܝܐ ܐܘܪܚܬܗ ܠܐܘܪܚܐ. ܘܐܝܟܢ ܠܡܫܬܒܠܐ ܒܡܫܢܐ
ܕܡܘܬܒܗܘܢ. ܘܡܘܫ ܕܗܘܐ ܡܠܟܐ ܕܐܘܪܚܢ ܥܠܝܗ. ܟܕ ܠܐ ܥܠܐ ܗܘܐ ܠܐ ܠܠܝܐ ܘܠܐ
ܐܝܡܡܐ. ܘܟܕ ܠܐ ܐܬܐ ܡܢ ܫܡܫܬܗܘܢ. ܐܘܫܦ ܠܗܘܢ ܐܘܠܨܢܐ ܒܗ ܒܝܘܡܐ
ܗܘܐ. ܒܫܘܪܐ ܚܕ ܪܥܝܐ ܕܡܝܐ ܗܘܐ ܒܫܘܠܛܢܗ[121] ܕܡܕܝܢܬܐ. ܘܡܢܝܢ ܗܘܐ ܠܟܠܠ
ܡܢܗ[122] ܐܘܪܚܬܐ ܕܡܠܟܐ ܠܐܘܪܫܠܡ ܪܥܝܐ. ܐܫܬܡܥܬ ܡܢܗ ܒܐܝܕܐ ܪܘܪܒܬܐ
ܘܐܫܬ̈ܝܢ ܗܘ̈ܝ ܒܦܪܨܘܦܐ ܘܒܐܒܪܐ. ܘܫܬܡܫܘ ܗܘ̈ܝ ܒܐܬܪ ܕܚܝܐ ܫܡܝܐ. ܟܕ ܠܐ
ܢܦܩܘ ܗܘ̈ܝ ܠܠܐܘܪܚܐ. ܘܟܕ ܒܠܒܗ ܕܠܐ ܗܘܐ ܡܢ ܗܘܐ. ܕܝܢ ܡܢ ܗܟܢܐ ܢܦܩܘ
ܠܠܗܘܢ. ܒܪܗ ܒܠܒܗܘܢ[123] ܒܫܘܪܝܗ ܕܡܫܝܚܐ ܠܥܕܬܐ. ܘܒܪܢܫܐ ܠܐ
ܡܫܡܫ ܗܘܐ ܕܢܓܗܐ ܠܠܗܘܢ. ܘܒܦܪܐ ܠܐ ܡܫܬܡܫܝܢ ܗܘܘ[124] ܕܡܫܡܫ

111 C: ܫ.
112 C: ܕܝܢ ܕܐܡܪ.
113 ܥܢܝܢܐ missing in C.
114 ܫܘܐܠܐ missing in C.
115 ܥܢܝܢܐ missing in C.
116 C: ܕܢܚܪܘܢܝ.
117 C: ܥܢܝܢܐ.
118 V.f. 121v.
119 C: ܕܐܠܗܐ.
120 ܘܟܠܡܢ...ܕܐܠܗܐ missing in C.
121 C: ܒܫܘܠܛܢܐ.
122 C: ܡܢܗ ܕܝܢ.
123 V.f. 122r.
124 ܗܘܘ missing in C.

ܒܢ̈ܝܢܫܐ[125] ܚܕܝܐ ܠܒܪܝܬܐ. ܘܡܢ ܒܬܪ ܕܦܫܩ ܗܟܢܐ ܕܢܚܘܘܢ. ܟܕ ܙܟܐ ܠܐܠܗܐ ܕܒܫܘܒܚܬܐ ܡܫܡܫܝܢ ܡܬܕܘܪܝܢ. ܦܢܐ ܚܕ ܡܢ ܚܝ̈ܠܘܬܐ ܫܡܝ̈ܢܝܐ. ܘܐܬܚܙܝ ܠܐܫܥܝܐ ܢܒܝܐ ܡܠܐܟܐ. ܘܩܪܒܗ ܘܐܡܪ ܠܗ ܕܗܐ ܠܡ ܠܣܦܘܬܟ. ܘܥܠ ܟܕܒܪܐ ܘܐܡܪ ܠܗܘܢ ܡܛܘܠ ܐܠܗܐ ܕܒܢܝ̈ ܘܟܠܐ ܙܘܥܐ. ܗܘ ܕܝܢ ܡܫܝܚܐ ܟܕ ܐܬܓܠܝ ܒܫܡܝܐ ܠܐܝܢܐ ܠܗܘܢܐ ܐܬܚܙܝ ܠܗܘܢ ܚܙܘܐ. ܘܡܢ ܬܘܒ ܐܬܚܙܝ ܠܗ ܡܠܐܟܐ. ܘܗܘܢܢ ܟܕ ܗܘܢ ܐܡܪ ܠܗ. ܘܡܫܡܫܝܢ ܗܘܐ ܡܫܝܚܐ. ܬܘܒ ܐܬܚܙܝ ܠܗ ܒܠܠܐ ܕܬܠܬܐ ܘܐܡܪ ܠܗ. ܗܘܡܢܐ ܐܘ ܓܒܪܐ. ܕܟܕ ܐܢܐ ܡܢ ܚܘܒܝ ܕܡܫܡܫܝܢ ܩܕܡ ܐܠܗܐ. ܗܘܠܐ ܠܡ ܠܡܫܝܚܐ ܘܠܐ ܬܕܚܠ. ܡܛܠ ܕܗܢܐ ܡܛܠ ܕܟܕ ܒܒܥܬܗܘܢ ܕܥܝܐ. ܘܗܘܐ ܕܢܬܓܠܐ ܠܡܫܝܚܐ. ܗܐ ܡܫܡܫ ܐܢܐ ܠܟ ܘܐܡܪ ܐܢܐ.[126] ܐܦ ܐܢܐ ܐܡܪ ܘܗܠܐ ܙܘܥܐ. ܗܟܢ ܡܫܝܚܐ ܡܢ ܟܪܘܒܐ ܘܐܢܫܝܢ ܗܘܘ. ܘܟܠܗ[127] ܠܡܫܝܚܐ. ܘܟܠܗ ܠܟܕܒܪܐ ܘܚܙܐ ܡܫܝܚܐ ܠܡܠܐܟܐ ܟܕ ܩܐܡ ܩܕܡ ܡܕܒܚܐ ܒܗܝܟܠܐ. ܘܟܠܐ ܙܟܐ ܐܡܪ ܗܘܐ. ܩܕܝܫܐ ܐܠܗܐ. ܩܕܝܫܐ ܚܝܠܬܢܐ. ܩܕܝܫܐ ܠܐ ܡܝܘܬܐ. ܐܬܪܚܡ ܥܠܝܢ. ܗܟܢ ܡܫܝܚܐ ܗܘ ܘܐܢܫܐ ܕܒܗܘ ܢܛܘܪܘܢ ܠܡܠܐܟܐ. ܘܡܢ ܐܡܪܝܢܘܢ ܠܫܘܒܚܐ[128] ܬܠܬ ܙܒܢܝ̈ܢ. ܡܛܠ[129] ܠܗ ܙܘܥܐ ܕܗܘܐ. ܐܫܬܘܕܥ[130] ܕܝܢ ܦܫܢ. ܐܪܙܐ ܕܬܠܝܬܝܘܬܐ ܘܦܫܩ ܕܢܬܓܠܐ ܒܬܠܬܐ ܕܒܪܐ ܕܐܝܬܐ ܡܬܓܠܝܢ. ܘܡܛܠ ܩܕܝܫܐ ܠܐ ܡܝܘܬܐ ܐܬܪܚܡ ܥܠܝܢ. ܗܘ ܒܡܬܓܠܝܢ ܦܫܩ ܕܐܬܐܡܪ ܗܟܢܐ. ܩܕܝܫܐ ܠܐ ܡܝܘܬܐ ܕܐܬܬܠܝܬ ܚܠܦܝܢ. ܘܠܐ ܒܗܠ ܗܘ ܡܪܘܪܐ ܐܘ ܕܚܠܐ[131] ܕܢܦܫܩ ܠܫܡܝܐ[132] ܕܡܢ ܡܠܐܟܐ ܩܕܝܫܐ ܐܬܐܡܪ ܠܒܢ̈ܝܢܫܐ. ܦܘܬܬܣܬܘܠܝܣ ܕܝܢ ܡܕܝܢܬܐ ܡܬܩܪܝܐ ܠܐ ܐܬܬܫܝܡܬ ܕܐܬܡܠܝܘܢ ܠܫܘܒܚܐ ܗܢܐ. ܘܠܐ ܐܘܪܫܠܡ. ܘܠܐ ܐܬܪܘܡܬܐ ܡܕܒܪܢܝܬܐ. ܐܠܐ ܐܡܪܢ ܠܗ ܐܟܚܕܐ[133] ܕܝܢ܀

---

125 C: ܒܢ̈ܝܢܫܐ.

126 C: ܘܐܡܪܢܐ.

127 V.f. 122v.

128 ܠܫܘܒܚܐ missing in C.

129 C: ܡܛܠ.

130 C: ܐܫܬܘܕܥ.

131 C: ܕܚܠܐ ܡܢ.

132 C: ܠܫܡܝܐ ܠܗܘܢ.

133 C: ܐܝܟ ܚܕ.

19 - ܫܘܐܠܐ[134] ܀ ܘܐܠܐ ܓܝܪ ܒܥܠܡܝܢ ܘܒܦܘܪܩܢܝܢ ܀ ܦܫܩܐ ܀ ܡܛܠ ܠܐܘܪܚܐ
ܕܢܘܟܪܝܐ ܕܐܠܗܐ ܡܬܒܪܝ.[135] ܗܘ ܕܠܐ ܡܫܬܐܠ[136] ܒܐܦܝ ܒܢܝܢܫܐ ܥܠ ܡܛܠ ܒܗܠܝܢ
ܕܢܘܟܪܝܐ ܡܢ ܐܠܗܐ ܕܝܢ ܡܬܒܥܝܢ. ܡܛܠ ܗܢܐ ܗܘ ܕܐܦܠܐ ܚܘܒܐ ܕܝܢܐ
ܡܬܒܥܝܢ ܒܗܘܢ. ܡܛܠ ܕܠܫܡܫܬܐ[137] ܕܢܘܟܪܝܐ ܘܐܦ ܕܒܪܢܫܐ ܒܫܘܒܐ
ܕܝܢܐ[138] ܡܫܠܡܝܢ ܀

20 - ܫܘܐܠܐ[139] ܀ ܘܒܘܚܢܐ[140] ܕܒܩܝܠܡܐ ܀ ܦܫܩܐ[141] ܀ ܡܛܠ ܐܡܬܪܘ ܕܡܠܟܐ
ܗܝܐ ܡܫܬܡܫܝܢ ܠܒܝܫܐ ܐܚܪܢܐ ܕܣܒܟ ܒܪܟܐ ܘܡܠܗ ܕܡܠܟܐ ܠܗܘܐ.
ܘܡܛܠ ܢܛܪܐ ܕܡܠܟܘܬܐ ܘܕܫܒܝܬܐ. ܘܐܝܟ ܐܡܪܘ ܕܒܘܩܝ ܒܫܠܡܐ ܡܠܟܐ
ܠܫܡܫ ܐܚܪܢܐ ܠܗܘܐ ܒܘܚܢܐ ܕܒܩܝܠܡܐ. ܘܠܫܘܡܠܐ ܕܡܢ ܠܫܡܫܘܗܝ ܀

21 - ܫܘܐܠܐ[142] ܀ ܘܠܫܡܫܬܐ[143] ܕܒܪܢܫܐ ܀ ܦܫܩܐ ܀ ܠܫܡܫܬܐ ܕܡܢ ܕܒܪܢܫܐ[144]
ܕܡܫܬܡܫܐ. ܣܓܝܐ ܒܪܘܚܐ ܡܠܗ ܕܡܬܒܪܝܢܘܬܐ ܕܐܠܗܐ ܕܒܒܠܗܐ ܗܘܐ ܀[145]

22 - ܒܫܘܪܝܐ ܩܕܡܝܐ: ܡܛܠ ܠܫܒܝܚܬܐ ܘܡܫܒܚܘ ܡܠܐܟܐ ܒܒܪܝܬܗ ܕܒܘܗܪܐ.
ܘܡܛܠ ܡܬܒܪܝܢܘܬܗ[146] ܕܐܒܗܝ ܐܕܡ. ܘܕܝܠܗܘܢ ܕܐܒܝ ܠܫܘܡܠܐ[147] ܫܡܥܢ ܠܟ ܀[148]

23 - ܒܫܘܪܝܐ ܕܬܪܝܢ: ܡܛܠ ܕܐܝܟ ܕܠܫܘܡܠܐ ܗܘܐ. ܘܡܛܠ ܗܢܘܢ ܕܒܬܪܗ
ܡܫܘܕܥܝܢ ܠܟ ܀[149]

---

134 C: ܦܫܩܐ.

135 C: ܡܬܒܪܐ.

136 V. f. 123r.

137 ܡܛܠ ܕܠܫܡܫܬܐ missing in C's codex. He notes the lacuna and suggests ܗܢܘܢ ܕܠܫܡܫܬܐ or something similar.

138 C: ܕܝܢܐ ܕܐܠܗܐ.

139 C: ܦܫܩܐ.

140 C: ܒܘܚܢܐ ܕܝܢ.

141 ܦܫܩܐ missing in C.

142 C: ܦܫܩܐ.

143 C: ܠܫܡܫܬܐ ܕܝܢ.

144 ܦܫܩܐ ܀ ܠܫܡܫܬܐ ܕܡܢ ܕܒܪܢܫܐ missing in C.

145 C: ܀ܫ܀.

146 C: ܡܬܒܪܝܢܘܬܗ ܕܝܢ.

147 C: ܘܐܒܝ ܒܠܫܘܡܠܐ.

148 C: ܀ܫ܀.

149 C: ܀ܫ܀.

24 - ܒܥܘܢܝܬܐ ܕܠܝܠܝܐ:[150] ܥܠ ܙܒܢܗ ܕܢܒܝܐ ܐܒܪܗܡ[151] ܘܙܪܥܝܬܗ. ܗܢܘܢ ܕܠܗܘܢ ܒܥܙܪܝ ܘܥܒܪܝ ܠܗ ܀[152]

25 - ܒܥܘܢܝܐ ܕܫܒܚܐ:[153] ܥܠ ܙܒܢܗ ܕܢܒܝܐ ܡܘܫܐ ܡܫܘܕܥܝܢ ܠܗ ܀

26 - ܡܙܡܘܪܐ ܕܠܝܠܝܐ ܘܥܘܢܝܐ ܕܫܒܚܐ:[154] ܥܠ ܙܒܢܗ ܕܝܫܘܥ ܒܪ ܢܘܢ ܘܕܝܢ̈ܐ ܡܠܟ ܠܗ ܀[155]

27 - ܡܙܡܘܪܐ ܕܐܠܠܝܐ ܘܥܘܢܝܐ ܕܫܒܚܐ. ܥܠ ܙܒܢܗ ܕܢܒܝܐ ܕܘܝܕ ܘܡܠܟ̈ܐ ܕܡܢ ܒܬܪܗ ܗܘܘ ܠܗ ܀

28 - ܡܙܡܘܪܐ ܕܫܒܚܐ ܘܥܘܢܝܐ ܕܫܒܚܐ. ܥܠ ܙܒܢܗܘܢ ܕܗܢܘܢ ܕܦܢܘ ܡܢ ܒܒܠ ܘܥܠ ܡܩܕܫܐ ܡܫܘܕܥ ܠܗ ܀

29 - ܡܙܡܘܪܐ ܕܫܒܚܐ[156] ܘܥܘܢܝܐ ܕܫܒܚܐ: ܥܠ ܙܒܢܗ ܕܢܒܝܐ ܝܘܚܢܢ ܡܥܡܕܢܐ ܡܒܕܢܚ ܠܗ ܀

30 - ܡܙܡܘܪܐ ܕܫܠܡܐ ܘܥܘܢܝܐ ܕܫܒܚܐ: ܥܠ ܕܝܫܘܥ ܡܪܢ ܘܥܠ ܣܗܕܘܬܐ ܢܘܚ ܕܫܠܝܚܐ[157] ܡܫܘܕܥ ܠܗ ܀

31 - ܘܠܡܘܬܒܐ: ܥܠ ܬܘܕܝܬܗܘܢ ܕܥܡ̈ܡܐ ܒܥܡܝܐ ܡܫܡܠܝܢ[158] ܠܗ ܀

32 - ܘܒܡܙܡܘܪܐ ܕܢܘܚܡ ܠܢ ܐܠܗܐ:[159] ܥܠ ܙܒܢܐ ܕܫܠܝܚܐ ܕܡܢ ܒܬܪܗܘܢ ܘܡܠܟ̈ܐ. ܒܝܘܡܐ ܠܘܩܒܐ ܘܡܐܬܝܬܗ ܕܒܪ ܐܠܗܐ ܡܫܡܠܝܢ ܠܗ ܀

33 - ܘܠܡܫܡܠܝܘܬܐ ܥܠ ܡܐܬܝܬܗ ܕܐܚܪܝܐ ܘܥܠ ܗܢܘܢ ܕܡܬܦܩܚܝܢ ܠܐܝܩܪܗܘܢ ܡܫܘܕܥ ܠܗ ܀

---

150 C: ܕܠܠܝܐ.

151 V. f. 123v.

152 C: ܀ܗܘ܀.

153 C: lacuna begins.

154 C: lacuna ends.

155 C: ܀ܗܢ܀.

156 C: ܫܒܚܐ.

157 C: ܘܥܠ ܣܗܕܘܬܗ ܕܫܠܝܚܐ.

158 C states that his codex has ܡܫܡܠܝܢ.

159 ܐܠܗܐ missing in C.

34 - ܘܒܥܘܬܐ ܕܩܕܡܐ. ܥܠ[160] ܠܡܫܘܚܬܐ[161] ܘܗܘ̈ܕܠܐ ܕܡܫܡܫ ܫܒܘ̈ܩܐ
ܡܫ̈ܝܚܐ ܚܠܦ ܕܦܘܪܩܢܐ ܕܗܘܐ ܠܒܢܝ̈ܢܫܐ.[162] ܡܢ ܛܥܝܘܬܗ ܕܣܛܢܐ ܠܥܠܡܐ[163]
ܙܒܢ ܠܗ܀

35 - ܒܥܠܬܐ ܕܬܫܒ̈ܚܬܗܘܢ ܘܡܘܕܝܬܐ ܩܕܝܫܐ ܕܟܠܐ ܕܫܒܚܐ. ܗܘܐ ܗܘ. ܡܛܠ
ܕܟܠܢܐ ܗܘܐ ܡܬܐܡܪܐ ܕܡܪܢ ܕܡܢ[164] ܡܫܝܚܐ. ܡܫܪܝ ܐܬܛܟܣ ܠܗ ܛܘܟܣܐ
ܗܢܐ. ܕܒܗ ܒܟܠܢܐ ܕܡܫܒܚܬܐ ܕܒܗ ܪܡܙܝܢ ܛܘܟܣܐ ܕܡܬܐܡܪܐ ܕܡܪܢ. ܢܗܘܐ
ܡܘܕܝܢ ܒܠܡܫܝܚܬܐ ܘܒܡܫܝ̈ܚܬܐ ܘܩܕܝܫܐ ܕܟܠܐ. ܐܝܟܢܐ ܕܡܢ ܕܒܪܘܚܗܘܢ ܦܓܪ̈ܝܢ
ܘܡܩܒܠܝܢ ܢܦܫ̈ܬܗܘܢ. ܘܢܬܐܣ ܠܟܘܢ ܘܢܗܘܐ ܒܪܚܡܝܢ[165] ܒܚܝܠܗ ܕܡܪܢ܀

36 - ܡܛܠ ܡܢܐ ܒܥܕܥܐܕܗ ܕܟܠܐ ܢܩܫܝܢ ܢܩܘܫܐ. ܘܐܘܦ ܡܒܪܟ[166]
ܡܥܒܪܝܢ[167] ܠܥܘܠܠܗ ܘܠܡܬܡܪܡܪܘ܀ ܦܘܫܩܐ܀ ܐܝܟ ܡ̈ܠܝܬܐ ܚܕܝܬܐ
ܡܫܠܡܝܢ ܘܡܥܒܪܝܢ ܒܗܘ ܟܠܐ ܕܟܠ ܚܕܐ ܚܕܐ[168] ܫܘܒܪܐ ܕܡܬܚܫܚܐ[169]
ܡܪܚܡܐ. ܚܕܐ ܡܢ ܘܥܕܥܐܕ̈ܐ. ܗܝ ܕܒܗ ܐܡܪ ܡܪܢ ܕܒܥܕܥܐܕܗ ܕܟܠܐ ܗܘܐ
ܡܛܠܬܐ ܘܡܪܕܐ. ܗܘܐ ܕܒܗ ܫܡܫܐ ܚܫܟ. ܘܣܗܪܐ ܠܐ ܚܘܐ ܢܘܗܪܗ. ܘܟܘܟܒ̈ܐ
ܢܦܠܘ ܡܢ ܫܡܝܐ. ܘܚܝ̈ܠܐ ܕܫܡܝܐ ܢܬܬܙܝܥܘܢ. ܘܐܪܥܐ ܙܝܥܐ ܘܢܝܕܐ.[170] ܘܛܘܪ̈ܐ
ܘܪ̈ܡܬܐ ܢܬܬܙܝܥܘܢ. ܘܝܡܐ[171] ܡܬܥܠܥܠ. ܘܩܠܐ ܕܚܝ̈ܠܐ ܡܫܬܡܥ. ܘܟܘܪ̈ܣܘܬܐ
ܡܬܦܬܚܝܢ ܠܗ ܠܐܪܥܐ. ܘܐܬܪ̈ܘܬܐ ܡܬܚܦܝܢ. ܘܟܪ̈ܟܐ ܢܦܠܝܢ. ܘܡܕܝ̈ܢܬܐ
ܢܬܥܩܪܢ. ܘܥܡ̈ܡܐ ܡܬܬܙܝܥܝܢ. ܘܚܝ̈ܘܬܐ[172] ܘܒܥܝܪܐ ܘܦܪ̈ܚܬܐ
ܘܐܬܥܝܪܘ[173] ܡܬܬܙܝܥܝܢ. ܗܟܢ ܡܢ ܒܢ̈ܝܢܫܐ ܐܝܟܢ ܒܟܢܫܐ. ܐܟܡܐ ܕܩܝܡ

---

[160] V. f. 124r.
[161] C: ܠܡܫ̈ܚܬܐ.
[162] C: ܠܒܢ̈ܝ ܐܢܫܐ.
[163] ܠܥܠܡܐ missing in C.
[164] C: ܡܢ.
[165] C: ܪܚܡܝܢ.
[166] C: ܡܢ ܕܒܪܟ.
[167] C states that his codex has ܡܥܒܪܝܢ.
[168] C: ܚܕ.
[169] C states that his codex has ܕܡܬܚܫܚܐ.
[170] V.f. 124v.
[171] C states that his codex has ܘܝ̈ܡܐ.
[172] C: ܘܥܡ̈ܡܐ ܡܬܬܙܝܥܝܢ ܘܒܥܝܪܐ ܢܥܠܝܢ. ܘܡܕܝ̈ܢܬܐ ܢܬܥܩܪܢ.
[173] C: ܘܐܬܥܝܪܘ ܕܝܢ.

ܒܫܢܝܐ. ܘܡܕܒܪܢܐ ܠܗܘܢ ܡܠܐܟܘܗܝ ܕܡܪܝ. ܗܠܝܢ ܕܒܠܒܗܘܢ ܐܡܪ ܡܫܝܚܐ. ܕܚܝܢ ܐܠܝܢ ܕܡܫܬܚܪܝܢ ܘܚܝܝܢ. ܠܐ ܢܩܕܘܡ ܠܐܠܝܢ ܕܕܡܟܘ܀

37 - ܩܪܝܢܐ ܠܩܕܡܝܬܐ ܐܠܝܫܥ. ܗܢܐ ܕܒܗ ܕܢܚ ܡܪܝ ܒܡܘܗܒܐ ܪܒܐ ܘܒܪܘܚܐ[174] ܫܓܝܐܐ ܕܡܢ ܩܠܝܦܘܗܝ ܡܢܬܐ. ܘܡܫܒܐ ܕܡܫܝܚܐ ܒܚܝܠܐ ܘܐܟܘܬܗ. ܗܫܐ ܠܫܬܩܐ ܘܠܫܠܘܬܐ ܠܟܘܢ ܒܝܘܡ ܗܘܐ ܒܫܡܫܬܐ ܕܫܘܠܐ܀

38 - ܩܪܝܢܐ ܕܝܢ ܠܐܚܪܝܬܐ: ܗܢܐ ܕܗܘܐ ܗܘ ܐܚܪܝܬܐ. ܒܗ ܡܫܡܫ ܡܢܬܐ ܘܡܫܬܡܠܝܢ ܚܝܐ. ܐܝܟ ܕܐܡܪ ܠܗ ܕܛܘܒܐ ܦܘܠܘܣ ܘܐܡܪ. ܕܢܬܡܠܐ ܒܗ ܐܝܟ ܙܒܢ ܚܝܐ ܕܒܢܝܐ ܐܚܪܝܬܐ ܕܝ ܠܐܡܪܐ. ܘܢܦܘܩܘܢ ܡܢܬܐ ܘܠܐ ܚܝܠܐ. ܘܚܝܢ ܢܬܚܙܐ. ܐܦ ܟܠܐ ܫܓܝܐܐ ܕܡܢܬܐ ܡܫܬܡܫܝܢ ܒܗܘ ܟܠܗ. ܘܒܠܒܝ[175] ܚܕ ܡܢܗܘܢ ܐܠܐ ܐܬܦܘܗܝ ܕܗܘ ܡܕܝܢ[176] ܕܗܘܐ. ܐܝܟ ܡܟܬܒܗ ܕܛܘܒܐ ܡܫܡܫܢܐ. ܐܠܐ ܐܝܟ ܕܡܟܬܒܝܢ ܠܗܘܢ ܐܚܪܢܐ. ܠܐܟܐ ܡܢܬܐ ܚܝܒܬܐ ܡܢܬܝܢ. ܗܟܢ ܕܒܗܝܢ ܡܬܥܒܪ ܘܡܫܬܡܠܐ ܒܗ ܒܪܐ ܕܡܫܝܚܐ. ܗܘܐ ܕܝܢ ܕܚܝܢ ܒܟܠܗܘܢ ܕܟܠܗ ܢܦܫܝܢ ܢܦܫܐ. ܛܘܦܣܐ ܕܩܪܝܢܐ ܡܕܡܫܬܐ ܕܙܢܝܢ[177]. ܒܗܢܐ ܕܒܗ ܡܫܬܥܪܝܢ ܐܛܘܦܣܐ. ܘܢܦܠܝܢ ܢܦܫܬܐ. ܘܡܫܬܡܫܠܐ ܟܠܐ ܡܕܝܢ[178] ܕܟܠܐܪܥܐ. ܘܐܝܟ ܗܘ ܕܒܪ ܢܦܫܐ ܗܘܐ. ܫܡܫܝܢ ܒܗܢܐ ܒܪܐ ܡܠܐ ܕܗܘܐ ܡܬܚܐ ܐܠܐ ܦܘܩܐ ܠܐܘܪܚܗ. ܗܢܐ ܕܝܢ ܕܡܢ ܒܬܪ ܗܠܝܢ ܒܡܛܪܬܐ ܪܒܝܥܝܬܐ ܕܟܠܗ. ܠܐܘ ܢܦܫܝܢ ܢܦܫܐ ܘܦܠܚܝܢ ܘܐܠܐ ܠܐܪܥܐ ܕܒܝܬ ܡܘܬܐ. ܒܪ ܗܠܝܢ ܛܘܦܣܐ ܙܢܝܢ ܕܩܪܝܢܐ ܠܘܩܕܡܬܐ. ܗܢܐ ܕܒܗ ܡܬܦܬܚ ܪܫܝܬܐ. ܘܕܢܚ ܡܪܝ ܡܢ ܫܡܝܐ ܒܗܘܪܐ ܠܐܫܝܘܬܐ ܘܡܘܒܠܐ ܪܒܐ. ܗܟܝܠ ܢܬܝܒ ܒܠܒܗܘܢ ܫܬܝܬܝܐ ܕܐܪܥܐ. ܠܗ ܟܠܐ ܡܬܘܬܒܐ ܐܡܪ ܗܘܐ. ܐܠܐ ܟܠܐ ܠܐ ܡܬܘܬܒܐ. ܡܬܘܬܒܐ ܕܝܢ ܒܚܝܘܗ ܕܒܠܒܗ. ܚܕܬܐ ܪܒܝܥܝܬܐ[179] ܡܠܟܘܬܐ. ܘܠܡܫܘܚܬܐ ܘܪܘܙܐ. ܒܗܢܐ ܕܚܕܝܢ ܕܡܛܠ ܠܗ ܙܒܢܐ ܕܢܬܠܘܢ ܒܚܝܘܗ ܕܢܦܫܐ. ܠܐ ܡܬܘܬܒܐ[180] ܚܕܝܢ ܘܐܠܝܢ ܐܘܟܠܬܐ ܟܠܐ ܢܦܫܗܘܢ. ܒܫܠܡܐ[181] ܕܝܢ ܡܫܡܫ ܠܟܠܗܘܢ. ܘܗܕܝܢ ܩܪܝܢܐ ܩܪܝܢܐ ܐܚܪܝܬܐ. ܗܢܐ ܕܒܗ ܡܫܡܫ

174 C: ܒܪܘܚܐ.

175 C: ܕܟܠܐ ܚܕ.

176 V.f. 125r.

177 C: ܢܦܫܐ ܙܢܝܐ.

178 C: ܒܡܕܝܢ.

179 ܪܒܝܥܝܬܐ missing in C.

180 C: ܡܬܘܬܒܐ ܕܝܢ.

181 V.f. 125v.

ܡܫܬܐ ܘܡܬܡܠܟܝܢ ܡܢܗ. ܐܝܟܢܐ ܕܐܡܪ ܦܘܠܘܣ.[182] ܘܡܢܬܠܬܗ ܐܝܟ ܙܕܩ ܚܝܠܐ ܘܡܪܘܬܐ. ܗܘܐ ܗܘ[183] ܗܘܝܘ ܗܘ ܕܐܡܪ ܡܪܢ. ܕܢܚܙܘܢ ܡܠܐܟܘܗܝ ܠܗܘܢ ܢܚܬܘܢ ܘܣܠܩܝܢ. ܘܢܚܙܘܢ ܠܟܠܗܝܢ ܕܠܗ ܡܢ ܐܘܪܚܐ ܕܗܝܐ ܘܡܫܠܡܐ. ܡܛܠ ܕܝܢ ܟܕ ܗܘܐ ܗܘ ܡܪܢ. ܕܟܠܗܘܢ ܟܢܫܝܢ ܕܟܠܗ ܦܝܫ ܐܠܗܘܬܗ ܠܟܝ ܘܡܬܐ ܡܠܟܘܬܐ ܟܢܝܫܐ ܘܡܠܟܘܬܐ ܡܬܒܝܢܐ ܕܡܪܢ. ܘܟܠܗܝܢ ܟܠܗܝ ܢܬܟܢܫܘܢ ܠܟܢ ܐܟܚܕܐ. ܘܢܣܒܘܢ ܡܢܗ ܡܢܗ ܐܝܢܐ ܡܠܬܐ. ܗܘ ܕܟܠܗ ܡܫܬܡܥ ܡܫܬܐ ܘܡܬܡܠܟܝܢ ܡܢܗ. ܗܟܝܠ ܟܕ ܠܐ ܟܕܝܠ ܕܪܘܚܐ ܢܩܝܠ ܢܩܘܠ. ܘܡܬܐܠܨܝܢ[184] ܘܡܠܐ ܘܠܐܠܗ ܡܢ ܟܠ ܒܪ ܕܐܠܗܘܬܗ. ܘܡܬܠܟܠܗ ܟܡ ܟܪܐ ܕܟܘܢܝܐ. ܘܐܝܟ ܩܕܡ ܡܪܢ ܟܡܠܟܘܬܐ ܢܫܡܥ܀

39 - ܥܠ ܠܬܫܡܫܬܐ ܕܐܘܪܐ܀[185] ܚܕܐ ܡܪܡܫܬܐ ܕܡܫܡܫܝܢ ܡܢ ܡܕܡܕܐ: ܡܘܕܐ ܕܚܕܘ[186] ܡܪܢܐ ܢܦܘܩ ܡܫܝܚܐ[187] ܟܪܗ ܕܐܠܗܐ ܕܐܬܝܠܕ ܡܢ ܟܠܗܘܢܐ ܡܪܝܡ܀

40 - ܗܘ ܕܝܢ ܕܡܢ ܟܠܗܘܢܐ ܡܫܪܝܢ: ܥܠ ܕܟܕ ܐܬܝܠܕ ܡܫܝܚܐ ܟܡܫܪ. ܕܟܢܫܠ ܕܐܠܗܐ ܟܠܗܘܢܐ ܗܘܟܠܗܐ ܐܚܝܕܐ[188] ܗܘܐ܀

41 - ܗܘ ܕܝܢ ܕܡܢ ܠܐܠܗܐ ܡܕܡܕܐ: ܥܠ ܕܡܫܐ ܕܡܫܝܚܐ ܡܫܘܕܥ ܥܠ ܕܡܫܝܚܐ. ܘܥܠ ܟܪܐ ܕܐܬܡܫܚ. ܘܥܠ ܙܘܝܦܘܬܐ ܕܡܠܟ ܕܗܘܐ ܡܫܝܚܐ܀[189]

42 - ܗܘ ܕܝܢ ܕܠܟܠ ܦܠܓܘܬܐ ܡܫܡܫܝܢ ܗܘܟܠܐ: ܟܘܕܐ ܗܘ ܗܘ ܕܡܬܟܠܬܐ ܡܫܝܚܐ ܦܢܝ ܕܟܠܒܗ ܕܡܪܢ ܐܬܝܠܕ ܠܟܪܘܬܐ ܕܡܫܡܫܝܢ܀

43 - ܗܘ ܕܡܢ ܩܕܡ ܕܐܬܐܡܪ ܡܪܡܫܬܐ ܟܠܘܩ ܦܠܓܘܬܐ ܡܫܬܟܚܝܢ: ܥܠ ܕܦܘܪܫܢܐ ܐܝܟ ܢܦܩ ܟܪܘܙܐ ܥܠ ܢܗܘܪܐ ܟܕ ܡܫܡܫܝܬܐ܀

44 - ܗܘ ܕܝܢ ܕܡܫܡܫܝܢ ܠܠܐܐ ܘܟܠܟܪܐ ܘܟܪܘܙܐ ܕܗܘܕܐ: ܟܠܗܘܢܐ ܘܡܬܦܠܓܘܬܐ ܕܐܠܗܐ ܦܢܝܬܐ ܕܟܠܡܢܗ ܕܡܪܢ ܐܬܝܠܕ܀[190]

182 C: ܦܘܠܘܣ ܫܠܝܚܐ.

183 C: ܗܘܝܘ.

184 C suggests ܘܡܬܐܠܨܝܢ as the correct reading.

185 C: ܥܠ ܠܬܫܡܫܬܐ: ܕܢܘܗܪܐ܀.

186 C: ܕܚܕ ܗܘ.

187 C: ܡܫܡܫܢܘܬܐ.

188 V.f. 126r.

189 C: ܡܫܝܚܐ.

190 C: ܡܪܢ.

45 - ܒܘܝܢܬܐ ܕܩܪܒܐ: ܐܘܪ ܠܡܒܝܢܘܬܐ ܕܡܠܐܟܐ. ܐܘ ܐܘܪ ܠܡܒܘܝܢܘܬܗ ܕܡܫܝܚ܀

46 - ܡܫܡܫܘܬܗ ܕܪܘܚܐ: ܐܘܪ ܡܫܡܫܘܬܗ ܕܝܫܘܥ ܠܥܒܕܐ܀

47 - ܡܫܡܫܢܘܬܗ ܕܪܘܚܐ ܕܟܠ ܚܝܢ: ܐܘܪ ܡܫܡܫܢܘܬܗ ܕܝܫܘܥ ܠܐܒܪܗܡ܀

48 - ܠܒܘܣܡܐ: ܐܘܪ ܠܬܘܕܝܬܗܘܢ ܕܡܗܝܡܢܐ܀

49 - ܬܘܪ ܢܘܗܪܐ ܕܚܙܘ ܠܗ ܠܪܘܚܐ: ܐܘܪ ܢܘܗܪܐ ܕܬܐܪܬ ܕܬܠܡܝܕܘܗܝ܀

50 - ܒܗܪܐ ܕܫܩܠܐ: ܐܘܪ ܒܥܫܩܐ ܕܫܠܝܢ܀

51 - ܦܪܝܫܐ ܠܠܗܐ: ܐܘܪ ܩܕܝܫܐ ܕܡܠܐܟܐ܀

52 - ܐܘܪܚܬܐ ܘܢܒܝܐ ܕܫܠܝܚܝܢ:[191] ܐܘܪ ܠܐܒܘܗܬܐ ܕܩܝܡܬܐ ܗܘܐ ܡܢܝ ܡܢ ܢܒܝܐ ܘܡܘܫܐ܀[192]

53 - ܦܪܕܝܣ[193] ܕܝܢ ܕܡܠܟܘܬܐ ܥܡ ܠܡܠܟܘܬܐ: ܐܘܪ ܠܐܚܝܘܬܐ ܕܬܪܬܝܗܝܢ ܕܬܠܡܝܕܘܗܝ܀

54 - ܡܘܬܒܐ ܕܝܢ ܕܫܡܝܐ ܕܟܠ ܚܝܢ: ܠܡܫܝܚܘܬܐ ܕܗܘ[194] ܘܐܡܪ ܡܪܢ. ܡܐ ܕܐܬܐ ܒܪܗ ܕܐܢܫܐ ܒܫܘܒܚܐ[195] ܘܡܘܬܒܐ. ܬܬܒܘܢ ܐܦ ܐܢܬܘܢ ܘܡܘܬܒܐ܀

55 - ܦܪܨܘܦܗܘܢ[196] ܕܝܢ ܡܘܬܒܐ: ܟܠ ܚܘܪܪܐ ܕܐܪܒܥܬܗܘܢ[197] ܕܡܗܝܡܢܐ ܡܚܕܐ܀

56 - ܐܣܛܛܘܢܐ:[198] ܐܘܪ ܠܡܒܘܝܢܘܬܐ ܕܒܝܬܐ ܕܫܠܛܐ[199] ܡܫܝܚ. ܗܘ ܕܐܡܒܘܬܐ ܡܒܪ ܗܘܐ. ܘܟܠ ܡܫܒܘܬܐ ܕܥܡܐ ܡܫܝܚܐ ܗܘܐ܀

57 - ܠܡܣܝܐ: ܐܘܪ ܩܕܡܘܗܝ ܡܬܠܬܝܢܬܐ ܕܡܫܝܚ. ܘܠܐ ܠܟܘܢ ܐܝܟ ܡܫܝܚܐ: ܐܠܐ ܠܡܫܝܚܐ ܐܢܐ ܕܡܦܩܘܗܝ܀

---

191 V.f. 126v.

192 C: ܡܢ ܡܘܫܐ ܘܢܒܝܐ.

193 C: ܦܪܕܝܣܐ.

194 C: ܗܘ.

195 C: ܒܫܘܒܚܗ.

196 C: ܦܪܨܘܦܝܗܘܢ.

197 C: ܕܐܪܒܥܬܐ. C states that his codex in fact has ܕܐܪܒܥܐ.

198 V: ܐܣܛܛܘܢܐ̈.

199 C: ܫܠܛܐ.

58 - ܗܢܘ[200] ܕܡܫܡܫܢܐ ܩܪܐ ܠܡܫܝܚܐ[201] ܘܠܗ ܡܫܡܫܐ: ܥܠ ܕܢܘܚ
ܠܟܗܢܐ ܕܡܫܡܫܢ̈ܐ ܐܬܠܘܗܝ ܗܘܐ: ܘܠܗ ܠܟܗܢܐ ܕܡܫܝܚܐ ܘܟܗ̈ܢܐ ܕܝܗܘܕܝܐ
ܚܕܬܐ܀[202]

59 - ܙܘܡܪܐ ܕܩܕܡ ܐܘܢܓܠܝܘܢ: ܐܝܟ ܠܬܫܒܘܚܬܐ ܕܟܢܪ̈ܐ ܘܢܒ̈ܠܐ ܕܩܕܡ ܗܘܘ
ܘܐܡܪܝܢ: ܐܘܟܝܬ ܒܟܢܪ̈ܐ ܘܡܙܡܪ̈ܐ܀

60 - ܠܟܘܠܐ ܕܝܢ ܥܠܘܢܐ ܕܡܫܬܘܬܦ ܟܘܠܐ: ܡܛܠ ܕܠܟܠܗܘܢ[203] ܕܡܪܢ ܩܐܡ.
ܗܘ ܕܡܫܬܘܬܦ ܐܟܚܕܐ ܕܠܬܫܒܘܚܬܐ܀

61 - ܡܫܡܫܐ[204] ܕܐܘܢܓܠܝܘܢ ܘܙܡܝܪܬܐ[205] ܚܕܗܘ: ܐܝܟ ܐܝܩܘܢܗ ܕܡܪܢ. ܘܦܓܪܐ
ܘܢܦܫܐ ܐܠܗܝܬ ܗܘܬ. ܙܡܝܪܬܐ ܐܝܟ ܦܓܪܐ ܕܐܪܥܐ. ܐܘܢܓܠܝܘܢ ܐܝܟ ܢܦܫܐ ܕܒܗ
ܐܝܬ ܡܠܟܘܬܐ܀

62 - ܙܘܚܐ ܕܝܢ ܕܡܫܡܫܢ̈ܐ: ܐܝܟ ܗܘ ܙܘܚܐ ܕܒܗ ܥܠ ܡܪܢ ܠܐܘܪܫܠܡ܀

63 - ܡܢܪܬܐ ܕܝܢ ܕܐܘܢܓܠܝܘܢ: ܠܢܘܗܪܐ ܕܢܘܚ ܦܓܪܗ ܕܡܪܢ. ܕܒܗ ܡܨܛܪ̈ܐ
ܘܩܒ̈ܝܫܬܐ܀

64 - ܙܡܝܪܬܐ ܕܝܢ ܕܡܫܡܫ ܠܥܠ ܡܢ ܣܘܓܐܐ: ܗܢܘ ܕܐܡܪ ܡܪܢ ܟܕ ܡܫܕܪ
ܕܓܠܝܐ ܡܘܬܐ ܠܟܠܗ ܕܥܡܐ. ܐܡܝܢܐ ܠܟܘܢ ܕܐܘܡܐ ܡܘܡܐ ܣܘܡܐ[206] ܘܡܫܪܐ܀

65 - ܢܘܗܪܐ ܕܝܢ ܕܒܗܘ ܫܥܬܐ: ܐܝܟ ܗܘ ܕܐܡܪ ܡܪܢ ܕܐܢܬܘܢ ܐܝܬܝܟܘܢ ܢܘܗܪܗ
ܕܥܠܡܐ. ܘܗܘܝܐ ܢܗܘܪ ܢܘܗܪܟܘܢ ܩܕܡ ܒܢܝ̈ܢܫܐ ܘܡܫܪܐ܀

66 - ܘܗܘ[207] ܕܐܡܪ ܢܘܗܪܐ ܘܠܗ ܚܕ: ܥܠ ܕܠܗ ܠܟܠܗܘܢ ܥܠ ܡܠܟܝ̈ܢܐ
ܐܡܪܗ ܠܥܠܡܐ ܗܘܐ. ܐܠܐ ܐܦ ܥܠ ܗܢܘܢ ܕܐܝܬܝܗܘܢ ܡܬܬܠܡܝܕܝܢ܀

67 - ܒܫܡܐ ܕܡܫܡܫܝܢ:[208] ܐܝܟ ܒܫܡܫܘܬܗܘܢ[209] ܕܩܕ̈ܝܫܐ ܕܡܪܢ܀

---

[200] C: ܗܢܘ ܕܝܢ.
[201] C: ܠܡܫܝܚܐ ܡܪܐ.
[202] C: ܚܪܬܐ ܀.
[203] C: ܕܠܟܠܗܐ.
[204] C: ܡܫܡܫܢܐ ܕܝܢ.
[205] V.f. 127r.
[206] C: ܡܘܡܐ ܒܡܕܒܪܐ.
[207] C: ܗܘ.
[208] C: ܒܫܡܐ ܕܝܢ.
[209] C: ܒܫܡܫܘܬܐ. C states that his codex in fact gives ܒܫܡܫܘܬܗ.

68 - ܛܘܟܣܐ: ܐܘܕ ܗܢ ܡܬܚܫܒܢܐ ܕܐܡܪ ܡܪܝ ܩܕܡ ܕܝܫܘ܀

69 - ܦܘܪܘܩܐ: ܐܘܕ ܗܢ ܕܐܬܬܚܪܪ ܒܗ ܘܢܒܗ ܘܡܪܢܐ܀

70 - ܙܒܘܬܐ ܕܫܡܫܐ ܗܢ ܕܡܫܠܐ ܗܘ ܕܡܫܠܐ ܘܟܠ ܡܢܝ: ܐܘܕ ܗܢ ܙܒܘܬܐ ܕܙܒܢ ܡܢܝ ܟܠܠ ܠܟܘܢܬܗܘܢ ܩܕܡ ܕܝܫܘ. ܐܦܐ ܒܗ[210] ܠܗ ܐܝܟ ܒܡܫܡ ܘܡܢܘܐ܀

71 - ܙܒܢܐ ܕܝܢ ܘܐܘܪܫܠܡ ܕܟܠ ܒܢܡ: ܐܘܕ ܡܘܬܒܗ ܕܡܫܝܚ ܒܝܬ ܠܟܢܘܫܬܗܘܢ܀

72 - ܡܫܬܡܫܢܘܬܗ ܕܙܒܢܐ ܘܐܘܪܫܠܡ ܡܢ ܒܘܪܟܬܐ ܕܒܢܡ: ܡܫܬܐܡܢܘܬܗ ܕܡܫܝܚ ܡܢ ܪܘܩܐ ܘܡܫܡܫܬܗ[211] ܕܡܢ ܐܘܪܫܠܡ ܠܬܪܐ ܕܐܝܘܕ܀

73 - ܗܢ ܕܝܢ ܕܠܐܘܪܫܠܡ ܠܗܢ ܡܫܝܐ: ܐܘܕ ܢܦܫܬܗ ܕܡܫܝܚ ܐܘܪܫܠܡܝܬܐ ܕܟܠܐ ܗܘܐ ܠܡܫܝܚ[212] ܒܝܬܐ ܠܦܓܪܗ܀

74 - ܠܗܘܢܬܗ ܕܝܢ ܕܙܒܢܐ ܕܡܢ ܡܫܡܫܢܐ: ܐܘܕ ܠܗܘܢܬܐ[213] ܕܡܢ ܡܫܝܚ ܡܘܪܝܬܐ[214] ܕܐܬܐ ܗܘܐ ܡܢ ܦܢܝܬܐ܀

75 - ܗܢ ܕܝܢ ܕܟܠܗ ܒܪܘܚܐ ܕܒܝܬܐ ܘܡܫܡܫܢܐ ܢܦܠ ܙܒܢܐ ܘܐܘܪܫܠܡ ܡܢ ܒܢܡ: ܟܠܠ ܕܒܪ ܐܬܐܚܕ ܡܫܝܚ ܘܐܬܕܒܪ ܕܝܘܡܦ: ܒܠܗܘܢ ܠܟܢܘܫܬܗܘܢ ܡܫܡܫܢܘܬܗܘܢ ܘܡܢܝܢܘ܀

76 - ܕܡܫܬܗ ܕܝܢ ܕܙܒܢܐ ܟܠܠ ܦܪܘܫܬܐ ܕܬܘܒܐ ܕܒܝܬ ܡܘܕܝܐ: ܐܘܕ ܕܡܫܬܗ ܕܡܫܝܚ ܕܟܠܠ ܡܢܝܐ܀

77 - ܦܘܪܫܢܗ ܕܐܘܪܫܠܡ ܕܡܢ[215] ܙܒܢܐ ܐܚܪܢܐ. ܘܡܫܬܐܡܢܘܬܗ[216] ܕܒܝܬܐ ܐܚܪܝܐ: ܐܘܕ ܦܘܪܫܢܐ ܕܒܫܡܐ[217] ܕܡܫܝܚ ܡܢ ܦܓܪܗ ܘܡܬܪܒܝܢܘܬܗ ܕܟܢܘܫܬܐ܀

---

210 V.f. 127v.

211 C: ܘܡܫܡܫܬܗ ܕܝܢ.

212 C: ܠܡܫܝܚ.

213 C: ܠܗܘܢܬܐ ܕܡܫܝܚ.

214 C: ܡܘܪܝܬܐ.

215 C: ܡܢ.

216 C: ܘܡܫܬܐܡܢܘܬܗ. C reads this as ܘܡܫܬܡܫܢܘܬܗ.

217 C: ܕܒܫܡܐ ܕܝܢ.

78 - ܗܢܘ[218] ܕܝܢ ܡܫܡܫ ܙܒܢܐ ܘܐܘܓܠܗ ܟܠ ܠܘܚܐ ܕܒܝܬ[219] ܩܘܕܫܐ. ܘܐܡܪܝܢ ܦܫ ܕܠܐ ܡܫܠܐ ܠܗ ܡܫܡܫܢܘܬܐ[220] ܘܡܪܚܐ: ܐܘܪܐ ܕܗܘ ܙܒܢܐ ܕܝܢ ܦܪܫܬ ܢܦܫܗ ܕܡܫܡܫ ܡܢ ܦܓܪܗ[221] ܘܟܠܗ ܠܦܪܕܝܣܐ: ܟܕ ܠܟܠܐ ܠܗ ܢܦܫܗ ܕܝܓܠܐ. ܟܠ[222] ܟܠܗܘܢ ܠܦܪܕܝܣܐ. ܟܠܗܘܢ ܢܦܫܬܐ ܕܙܕܝܩܐ ܕܡܢ ܐܕܡ ܘܥܕܡܐ ܠܗܘ ܙܒܢܐ. ܐܬܟܢܫ[223] ܕܝܢ ܘܐܬܦܪܓܠ[224] ܡܢ ܡܫܟܢܬܐ ܟܠܗܘܢ ܢܦܫܬܐ ܕܚܛܝܐ܀

79 - ܠܦܘܩܕܢܐ ܕܝܢ ܕܙܒܢܐ ܒܬܪܐ ܒܒܬܐ ܗܘܐ. ܕܒܗ ܡܦܩܕܢܐ ܐܘܪ ܙܩܝܦܘܬܗ ܕܡܫܘܚ ܕܟܠ ܡܫܝܚܐ. ܘܦܘܪܩܢܐ[225] ܕܢܦܫܗ ܘܡܫܟܢܬܗ ܕܠܦܪܕܝܣܐ܀

80 - ܟܕ ܟܝܢ ܠܦܘܪܩܢܐ ܕܦܘܡܗ ܕܠܐ ܚܦܝܛ ܘܢܬܬܦܩܘܢ ܕܦܓܪܐ ܚܝܐ ܘܡܚܝܢܐ: ܗܘܐ ܙܩܦܐ ܕܗܘܝܐ ܐܬܟܢܫ[226] ܢܦܫܬܐ ܕܚܛܝܐ ܡܢ ܕܠܡܫܟܢ ܥܡ ܢܦܫܬܐ ܕܙܕܝܩܐ܀

81 - ܟܠ ܦܫ[227] ܕܝܢ ܘܟܠܗ ܠܐ[228] ܡܫܟܚ ܙܘܥܐ ܕܡܫܡܫܢܘܬܐ. ܠܐ ܢܗܘܠ ܠܠܐܘܪܐ ܗܘ ܡܕܝܢܬܐ. ܐܝܟ ܕܗܘ ܡܫܘܚ[229] ܡܕܡ ܐܡܪ:[230] ܕܦܫ[231] ܘܠܐ ܡܬܡܠܟ ܡܢ ܦܬܐ ܘܙܘܥܐ ܘܡܪܚܐ. ܗܘܝܐ ܟܠ ܘܠܐ ܡܫܟܚ ܦܓܪܗ ܘܙܘܬܗ[232] ܢܦܫ ܠܡܫܘܬܦܘܬܐ ܕܐܘܪܐ ܡܫܝܚܐ. ܠܐܪܥܠ ܢܦܫܗ ܠܟܠ ܚܛܝܐ ܘܠܐ ܠܗܘܠ[233] ܠܦܪܕܝܣܐ܀

218 C: ܗܘ.
219 V.f. 128r.
220 ܡܫܡܫܢܘܬܐ missing in C.
221 C: ܦܓܪܐ.
222 V: ܟܠ̈.
223 C: ܐܬܟܢܫܘ.
224 C:ܘܐܬܦܪܓܠܘ.
225 C: ܦܘܪܩܢܐ.
226 C: ܐܬܟܢܫܘ.
227 C: ܒܠܒܕ.
228 C: ܕܠܐ.
229 ܡܫܘܚ missing in C.
230 C: ܘܐܡܪ.
231 C: ܡܢ.
232 C: ܙܘܬܗ.
233 V and C: ܢܗܘܠ.

82 - ܗܢܐ[234] ܕܝܠܗ ܡܥܩ̈ܒܐ ܘܡܙܡܪܐ:[235] ܐܝܟ ܗܘ ܕܙܡܪܐ ܠܐܠܗܐ ܦܩܕ ܒܡܠ̈ܬܐ ܘܐܡܪ ܕܢܬܦܪܢܣ ܢܦܫܢ ܠܐܠܗܢ ܕܐܬܐܡܪ܀[236]

83 - ܡܡܠܠ[237] ܘܒܗܠܠ ܙܡܪܐ ܒܬܪܐ ܡܚܘܪܬܗ ܘܡܫܝܚܐ.[238] ܒܡܬܬܦܫܩܢܘܬܐ ܕܒܫܡܝܐ ܘܒܐܪܥܐ ܕܟܠ ܡܕܒܪܢܐ. ܡܛܠ ܕܡܕܒܪܢܐ ܕܗܘܝܘ ܡܪܐ ܫܡܝܐ. ܘܡܫܬܡܥܐ ܕܟܠ ܡܢ ܒܫܡܝܐ ܘܒܐܪܥܐ. ܕܗܘܝܘ ܬܘܒ ܗܢܐ ܕܡܫܝܚܐ ܗܘܐ ܒܟܠ ܡܢ ܬܪܥܗ ܕܡܪܐ. ܘܡܫܡܫܢ̈ܐ ܕܡܢܫܐ ܡܪܐ ܘܡܪܐ: ܐܘܪ[239] ܡܠ̈ܐܟܐ ܕܐܬܡܢܘ ܒܡܪܐ. ܚܕ ܡܢ ܐܦܪܘܗܝ. ܘܚܕ ܡܢ ܦ̈ܠܚܘܗܝ܀

84 - ܙܟܝܐ[240] ܘܐܘܟܠܘܗܝ ܕܡܬܐܦܫܩܢ ܥܠ ܡܕܒܪܢܐ:[241] ܐܘܪ[242] ܕܗܘܝܘ ܦܘܩܕܢܗ ܕܡܪܢ ܡܫܠܡܢ. ܘܒܟܘܢ ܠܐ ܡܫܡܫ ܥܠ ܟܠܗ ܕܟܠܢ ܡܢ ܡܪܢܘܬܐ ܕܙܟܝܐ ܘܐܘܟܠܘܗܝ ܘܦܘܩܕܢܗ ܕܡܪܢ ܢܬܩܝܡܘܢ ܐܘܪܐ ܡܫܝܚܐ.

85 - ܒܫܡܝܐ ܕܐܘܪܐ: ܐܘܪ ܠܡܫܝܚܘܬܐ ܠܐ ܡܬܡܫܠܡܢܘܬܐ ܕܐܦܫܩ ܡܠ̈ܐܟܐ ܡܫܝܚܐ ܘܢܩܒܠܐ ܕܕܝܢܐ ܒܥܒܕܐ ܕܟܠܗ ܒܗܡ ܢܫܡܗ ܕܡܪܢ ܒܩܘܪܒܢܐ. ܐܘ ܐܘܪ ܠܡܫܝܚܘܬܐ ܕܡܠ̈ܐܟܐ ܘܒܫܝܢܐ ܕܒܟܢ ܫܡܗ ܕܡܪܢ. ܒܝ ܚܝܘ ܠܐܘܪܚܐ ܕܐܬܐܬܝܗܒ[243] ܘܡܩܒܠܐ ܕܐܬܒܪܢܘ. ܘܡܫܡܠܐ ܕܫܡܝ ܘܡܙܡܪܐ܀

86 - ܗܢܐ ܕܝܢ ܕܒܥܒܕܐ ܗܘܐ ܡܫܝܚܐ ܥܠ ܒܗܡ ܬܬܒܝܢ: ܥܠ ܡܬܘܬܐ ܕܡܫܘܚ ܠܒܢܝܐ ܒܟܘܢ[244] ܬܬܒܝܢ ܗܘܘ ܒܬܫܒܚܬܐ ܡܢ ܕܫܠܡܐ ܕܡܘܩܪܐ܀

87 - ܗܢܐ ܕܡܫܝܚܝܢ ܐܝܬܘܗܝ ܒܩܠܐ ܒܥܒܕܐ ܗܘܐ: ܐܘܪ ܚܘܒܐ ܕܠܒܫܘܢ ܡܢ ܐܠܗܐ ܕܟܠ ܡܘܩܪܐ܀

88 - ܗܢܐ ܕܝܢ ܡܠܐ[245] ܕܫܠܡ ܒܩܠܐ ܡܢ ܒܗܡ. ܢܫܡܢ ܡܫܡܫܢ̈ܐ ܡܢ ܒܬܪ ܡܘܕܝܐ ܘܡܫܒܚܝܢ ܠܗܘܢ. ܘܡܘܕܝܢ ܠܗܘܢ ܐܬܪܐ ܠܡܫܟܠ ܦܘܡܗܘܢ: ܗܘܐ

---

234 C: ܗܢܐ ܕܝܢ.

235 V.f. 128v.

236 C: ܕܐܬܐܡܪܘ.

237 C: ܡܫܚܐ.

238 C: ܘܡܫܝܚܐ ܡܪܢܐ ܡܪܢ.

239 C: ܐܘܪ ܕܝܢ.

240 C: ܙܟܝܐ ܕܝܢ.

241 C: ܘܥܠ ܡܫܘܗܝ ܢܘܦܫܗ ܕܡܪܢ.

242 ܐܘܪ missing in C.

243 V.f. 129r.

244 C: ܒܟܘܢ ܒܐܘܪܫܠܡ.

ܡܫܡܫܬܐ ܕܝܢ ܡܣܘ̈ܕܝܐ ܕܡܦܩܘܗܝ ܠܫܡܥܘܗܝ. ܐܬܚܫܒܬ ܡܢܗܘܢ ܒܗܘܢܬܐ ܘܡܠܟܘܬܐ. ܘܕܒܝܫܬ ܠܗܘܢ ܢܦܫܗ ܡܢ ܒܝܫܬ ܩܘܕܫܐ ܘܕܒܝܫܬ ܦܩܕܗܘܢ ܠܗ. ܦܘܡܗ ܕܠܗ ܒܕܒܪܢܐ ܕܡܬܒܥܝܢܬܐ ܥܒܕܝܢ ܠܡܫܡܠܝܘܬܗܘܢ. ܐܠܐ ܒܕܒܝܫܐ ܚܝܐ ܕܒܪܗ ܕܐܒܘܗܝ܀

89 - ܗܢܘ[246] ܕܡܫܡܫܢܐ ܫܦܝܪ ܠܫܡܝܐ. ܘܒܐܘܪܚ ܕܐܠܗܐ ܠܟܠܗ ܩܘܕܫܐ: ܠܡܘܠܟܢܐ ܕܐܝܟܢ ܕܡܫܝܚܐ ܒܫܡܝܐ. ܠܡܠܟܘܬܐ ܕܠܥܠܡ ܙܒܢܐ ܐܝܬܝܗ ܗܘܐ ܐܝܟ ܠܡܫܝܚܐ ܩܕܡ ܙܒܢܘܗܝ ܫܦܝܪ ܗܘܐ. ܘܡܢ ܡܠܟܘܬܗ ܡܫܝܚܐ ܗܘܐ܀

90 - ܗܢܘ[247] ܕܝܢ ܕܝܢ ܕܠܥܠܡ ܒܬܪܐ ܠܟܠܗ ܩܘܕܫܐ ܩܕܡ ܒܠܥܕܝܢ ܒܡܫܝܚܘܬܐ ܕܡܫܝܚܐ[248] ܠܐܒܗ̈ܝܢ ܐܡܪܝܢ: ܡܫܘܕܥܐ ܕܟܠ ܕܠܐ ܡܬܡܫܚ ܠܐܘܪܚܐ ܒܠܚܘܕܝܘܬܐ ܩܕܡܝܬܐ ܘܡܫܒܚܢܘܬܐ ܕܐܬܓܠܝܬ ܒܡܫܝܚܐ: ܢܘܗܪܐ ܗܘ ܠܥܠܡܐ. ܘܓܠܝܐ ܡܢ ܒܫܡܝܐ ܕܒܗ ܡܢܝ.

91 - ܗܢܘ ܕܝܢ ܕܒܐܘܪܚ ܐܡܪ ܡܫܡܫܢܐ ܙܟܘ ܟܠ ܕܒܪܢܫܐ[249] ܘܡܪܟܐ: ܠܡܫܝܚܐ ܕܢܘܟܪ ܙܘܓܐ. ܘܗܟܢܐ ܟܠ ܫܪܟܐ ܕܐܒܗ̈ܬܐ ܘܡܫܝܚܝܬܐ ܡܬܟܢܫܝܢ ܕܐܬܡܠܝܘܗܝ ܠܒܪܬܐ ܐܝܟ ܒܢܝܐ ܘܒܢܬܐ. ܘܚܙܐ ܕܡܫܡܠܝܘ ܕܢܘܟܪܐ[250] ܒܒܪܬܐ ܢܛܪ܀

92 - ܕܡܫܚܐ ܠܡܘܪܟܐ ܙܕܩܐ ܒܪܬܐ ܒܝܬ ܛܘܦܣܗ. ܐܘܪܐ ܕܡܫܝܚܐ ܘܡܫܡܘܪܝܬܐ ܕܡܫܝܚܐ܀

93 - ܡܫܡܫܢܐ ܦܪܫ ܒܗܘܢ ܕܝܘܡ ܛܘܦܣܐ ܕܢܘܟܪܝܐ. ܐܝܟܢܐ ܕܡܢܝ ܡܫܝܚܐ ܒܝܬ ܐܠܗܐ ܠܥܠܡ ܐܘܪܐ. ܒܪܝܟ ܘܐܘܕܝ ܘܐܡܪ: ܕܗܟܢܐ ܗܝܡܢܘ ܒܒܪܝܟ ܠܡܘܪܟܐ. ܗܟܢܐ ܒܟܠܐ ܒܪܬܐ ܐܝܟ ܛܘܦܣܗ. ܦܪܫܐ ܚܝ ܒܗܘܢ ܕܗܘܐ ܡܒܪܟ ܘܡܫܘܐ ܒܡܫܝܚܐ ܕܡܫܝܚܐ ܡܢܝ. ܒܝ ܒܝܬ ܠܚܡܐ ܡܫܘܚ ܕܡܠܟܘܗܝ ܕܡܢܝ ܐܡܪ. ܘܡܢ[251] ܕܠܚܡ ܒܗܘܢ ܘܡܒܪܟ ܠܡܫܝܚܐ ܘܠܡܫܡܫܢܐ: ܒܝܬ ܛܘܦܣܬܐ ܕܙܘܓܐ ܕܩܘܕܫܐ ܕܡܫܝܚܐ. ܗܘܝ ܡܫܡܫܢܐ ܦܪܨܘܦܗ ܘܕܡܘܬܗ ܕܡܫܝܚܐ.[252] ܠܗ ܒܚܝܐ. ܐܠܐ ܒܡܫܝܚܘܬܐ ܫܪܝܪܬܐ ܘܡܫܡܘܪܝܬܐ. ܠܗ ܕܐܘܪܚ ܦܪܨܘܦ ܐܝܟ ܠܗ ܠܡܫܝܚܐ. ܚܝ

245 C: ܕܡܫܐ.

246 C: ܗܢܘ ܕܝܢ.

247 C: ܗܢܘ ܕܝܢ.

248 V.f. 129v. C: ܕܡܫܝܚܐ ܕܝܢ.

249 C: ܙܟܘ ܟܠ ܕܒܪܢܫܐ. V: ܠܐ ܡܫܡܫܐ.

250 C: ܕܢܘܟܪܐ ܙܘܓܐ.

251 C reads ܘܡܫܐ but states that his codex has ܘܡܢ.

252 V.f. 130r.

ܒܥܡܠܐ ܘܥܕ ܒܐܘܪܚܐ. ܐܠܐ ܐܟܪܝܐ ܕܥܠܡܐ ܘܪܓܝܫܘ ܠܐ ܡܬܡܬܚܝܢ ܠܘܬ ܦ̈ܠܚܝܢ. ܘܠܐ ܐܢܫܘܬܐ ܕܐܬܢܣܒܬ ܡܢܢ ܟܝܢܐ[253] ܠܘܬ ܒܢ̈ܝܢ. ܐܠܐ ܐܝܟ ܒܪܐ ܕܐܒܘܗܝ ܕܐܬܝܠܕ ܠܐܢܫܘܬܐ ܕܝܠܢ. ܗܟܢܐ ܦܓܪܐ ܗܢܐ ܟܠܗ ܗܘ ܕܒܥܡܠܐ. ܐܝܟ ܦܓܪܐ ܕܡܫܝܚܐ ܐܬܚܝܗܘܢ܀

94 - ܡܠܟܐ ܩܕܡܝܐ ܕܡܛܐ ܒܗܝܢ ܠܒܝܬܐ: ܙܒܢܬܐ ܗܝ ܕܒܗܘܬܐ ܕܡܪܢܝܐ ܒܠܠ ܒܝܬܐ: ܕܢܦܩ ܒܬܪܗ[254] ܡܠܟܐ ܗܢܐ ܕܒܚܕ ܒܗ ܡܫܝܚܐ ܡܢ ܩܕܡ ܕܢܣܩ.[255] ܡܠܟܐ[256] ܕܠܐ ܡܬܒ ܐܢܐ[257] ܠܟܘܢ. ܘܡܢ ܟܠܗ ܕܡܠܐ ܒܝܬܐ ܠܒܗܝܬܐ: ܕܐܦ ܠܝ ܗܘܐ ܠܟܘܢ ܡܠܟܐ ܒܝܢ ܪܘܚܐ ܕܒܗܘܬܐ ܘܡܠܟܘܬܐ ܀ ܡܛܠ ܦܩܕ ܒܪܘܚܐ ܠܒܝܬܐ. ܕܗܘ ܡܠܟܐ ܐܝܟ ܠܟܝܢ ܒܫܘܒܚܐ ܕܡܫܝܚܐ. ܘܐܡܪ ܕܒܫܘܒܚܐ ܗܘܘ ܡܫܒܚܝܢ ܕܟܠܗ ܐܝܟܢܐ. ܘܡܫܘܪܘ ܡܢ ܠܒܪ̈ܝܬܐ ܐܚܪܢܐ. ܐܝܟܢܐ[258] ܕܐܬܚܠܦܘܢ ܠܥܠܡ ܐܢܫܐ ܡܫܝܚܐ. ܗܟܢܐ ܐܡܪ ܡܠܟܐ[259] ܡܠܟܘܬܗ[260] ܕܡܪܢ ܐܡܪܝܢ. ܕܡܫܘܬܦ ܠܟܘܢ ܘܢܬܠܒܫ ܠܟܘܢ܀

95 - ܩܪܝܢܐ ܕܥܠܡ ܚܝܐ ܘܡܠܟܘܬܐ: ܠܡܠܟܘܬܐ[261] ܕܝܠܟ ܚܝܐ ܘܡܠܟܘܬܐ ܐܬܡܢܪܗ[262] ܐܘܪܚܐ[263] ܕܦܪܘܩܝܢ. ܘܐܚܝܕ ܡܠܟܘܬܐ ܘܚܝܐ ܫܡܝܢ ܟܠܠ ܗܠܝܢ ܕܥܝܢ ܐܘܪܚܗ ܡܠܟ ܡܢܪܗ[264] ܘܡܫܡܠܝܢ܀

96 - ܐܝܟ[265] ܒܗܝܢ ܡܩܪܒ ܩܘܪܒܢܐ: ܐܘܪ ܐܝܟ ܪ̈ܒܘܬܐ[266] ܕܐܬܪܒܝ ܚܠܦܝܢ܀

97 - ܒܗܢܐ ܕܝܢ ܘܡܫܬܡܫܢܐ ܕܡܩܕܫ ܒܚܝܠܗ[267] ܩܘܪܒܐ: ܠܡܠܟܘܬܐ ܗܝ ܕܡܢܝܢ ܡܠܐܟܐ ܩܕܝܫܐ ܟܠ ܕܡܠܟ ܡܢܪܗ ܐܘܪܚܐ[268] ܕܦܪܘܩܝܢ܀

---

253 ܟܝܢܐ missing in C.

254 C: ܒܬܪ.

255 C: ܕܢܣܩ.

256 C: ܡܠܟܐ ܠܟܘܢ.

257 C: ܡܬܒܝܢܐ.

258 C: ܐܝܟܢܐ ܕܝܢ.

259 C: ܡܠܟܐ ܐܡܪ.

260 C: ܠܡܠܟܘܬܗ.

261 V.f. 130v.

262 C: ܐܬܡܢܪ.

263 C reads ܐܘܪܚܐ but states his codex has ܐܘܪ̈ܚܐ.

264 ܡܠܟ ܡܢܪܗ missing in C.

265 C: ܐܝܟ ܕܝܢ.

266 C: ܪ̈ܒܘܬܐ.

267 C: ܚܝܠ.

98 - ܗ̇ܢ ܕܩܒܠ ܒܪܘܪܐ ܕܡܫܡܫ ܡܫܢ ܘܡܘܙܘ[269] ܦܘܩܕܢܐ ܗܘ ܕܡܫܝܚܐ. ܕܡܫܝܚܘܬܐ[270] ܘܟܠܐ ܒܟܠܗ ܢܦܫ ܩܕܡ ܠܐܠܗܐ. ܒܗܘ ܒܚܕܐ ܕܝܠܗ ܒܕܠܐ ܫܡܫܐ[271] ܚܙܘ ܠܡܟܘܪܐ܀[272]

99 - ܒܫܦܝܪܐ[273] ܕܒܗܘܢ ܒܢܝܐ ܡܬܚܙܝܢ: ܐܘܦ ܒܫܦܝܪܐ ܘܗܘܕܝܐ[274] ܕܒܗܘܢ ܐܬܝܠܕ[275] ܦܓܪܗ ܕܦܪܘܩܢ܀

100 - ܗ̇ܢ ܕܝܢ ܕܐܬܟܠܝ ܕܒܢܝܐ ܡܬܚܙܝܢ ܒܗܘܢ ܘܐܢܐ ܡܠܐ ܡܒܝܬܝܐ: ܐܘܦ ܠܐܢܫܐ ܡܩܕܡ ܕܒܗܘܢ ܗܘܐ ܐܝܬܘܗܝ ܕܡܢ ܐܢܫܐ ܡܬܟܠܝܢ ܕܡܬܐ܀

101 - ܗ̇ܢ[276] ܕܟܠܗ ܦܫܝܛܐ ܐܢܐ ܢܣܒܬ. ܘܡܫܘܟܠܐ[277] ܡܕܢܚ ܡܠܗ ܘܡܫܡܫܢ ܠܟܠܐ: ܐܘܪܐ ܗܘ ܕܡܫܡܠܝ. ܘܠܐ ܦܠܐ ܕܟܠܗ[278] ܒܫܠܐ ܢܚܡܘܗܝ܀ ܘܐܬܘܬܐ: ܠܐ ܒܢ ܢܬܩܦܢ ܒܢܝܐ ܡܠܐ ܘܢܬܒܥܘܢ[279] ܡܢ ܒܠܚܘܕܝܐ ܘܡܠܐ ܘܡܟܢܫܐ. ܘܢܬܒܥܘܢ ܘܢܬܬܒܝܢ ܡܠܐ ܠܐܠܗܘܬܐ܀

102 - ܗ̇ܢ ܕܝܢ ܕܡܢܝܢ[280] ܡܠܗ ܒܫܪܪܐ: ܕܒܗܘܢ ܕܒܗܘܢ ܢܬܦܬܚ ܒܟܠ ܡܠܗ܀[281]

103 - ܗ̇ܢ ܕܝܢ ܕܡܢܐ ܒܪܘܪܐ ܒܡܢܝܢܘܬܗܘܢ ܘܡܟܠܐ:[282] ܕܠܟܠ ܕܠܐ ܙܕܩ ܕܒܢܝܐ ܗܘܐ ܕܡܠܐ ܕܝܠܐ. ܕܟܠܐ[283] ܡܫܡܫ ܢܦܩ ܒܫܪ̈ܪܐ. ܐܠܐ ܒܡܟܠܐ ܒܟܠܗ ܠܟܠ. ܘܐܦܠܐ ܠܡܫܡܫܢܘ ܠܡܫܡܠܝܘ ܗܘ܀[284]

---

268 C: ܐܘܪܐ ܕܡܬܟܫܦ.

269 C: ܦܘܩܕܢܐ ܘܡܘܙܘ. V: ܐܘܪܚܐ ܘܐܦ ܗܘ ܕܡܫܠܡ.

270 ܕܡܫܝܚܘܬܐ missing in C.

271 Sic.

272 ܒܠܐ ܫܡܫ ܚܙܘ ܠܡܟܘܪܐ܀ missing in C.

273 C: ܒܫܦܝܪܐ ܕܝܢ.

274 V: ܒܫܦܝܪܐ.

275 C states that his codex has ܐܬܝܠܕ.

276 C: ܗ̇ܢ ܕܝܢ.

277 C: ܒܡܫܘܟܠܐ.

278 V.f. 131r.

279 C: ܢܬܒܥܘܢ.

280 C: ܕܢܒܝܢ. C gives ܕܡܢܝܢ as the possible correct reading.

281 ܡܠܗ missing in C.

282 C: ܒܡܢܝܢܘܬܗܘܢ. ܘܡܟܠܐ. C gives ܒܡܢܝܢܘܬܗܘܢ ܘܡܟܠܐ.

283 C: ܒܟܠܐ.

284 ܘܐܦܠܐ ܠܡܫܡܫܢܘ ܠܡܫܡܠܝܘ ܗܘ missing in C.

104 - ܗܘ ܕܝܢ ܕܒܬܪܗ ܒܥܕܢܐ ܐܚܕܐ ܡܫܒܚܝܢ ܒܗ ܒܩܠܐ ܒܢܝܐ ܕܙܘܡܪܐ: ܐܝܟ ܗܘ ܕܥܕܬܐ ܕܗܘܬ ܒܗ ܡܫܬܡܫܝܢ ܕܐܬܬܐ ܠܡܗܘܬܐ ܕܙܘܥܐ ܕܡܘܬܐ ܘܐܬܚܫܒ ܘܐܬܡܠܠ ܠܕܘܟܬܐ ܡܕܝܢܬܐ. ܠܘܬ ܐܝܟ ܕܠܡܠܟܐ ܕܡܬܐܡܪ ܕܡܠܟܘܬܐ ܒܪܘܚܢ ܘܡܫܒܚܝܢ܀

105 - ܗܘ ܕܝܢ ܕܡܠܐ ܕܫܪܐ ܒܗܘܐ ܒܪܘܚܐ ܘܡܪܥܝܬܐ. ܘܡܫܡܫ[285] ܩܢܘܢܐ ܒܕܡܐ ܘܕܡܐ ܠܩܢܘܢܐ: ܐܘܟ ܡܬܦܪܢܣܝܢܘܬܗ ܕܢܦܫܗ ܕܡܫܘܚ ܕܒܝܬܗ ܩܢܘܢܗ. ܘܡܫܬܡܠܝܬܗ ܕܡܢ ܒܝܬ ܡܢܬܐ܀

106 - ܗܘ ܕܝܢ ܕܒܬܪ ܡܫܝܚܘܬܐ ܕܫܡܝܐ. ܠܐ ܠܘܬ ܪܘܡܐ ܒܗܘܐ ܒܠܐܘܪܐ ܪܒܬܐ: ܒܠܠ ܕܐܬܚܙܝܘ ܐܘܪܐ ܒܡܫܡܠܝܢܘܬܗ[286] ܕܡܫܝܚܐ܀

107 - ܗܘ ܕܝܢ ܕܒܥܕܢܐ ܗܢܐ[287] ܡܪܢܝܢ ܒܩܦܠܐ ܡܢ ܡܕܢܚܐ: ܒܠܠ ܕܐܬܐܪܘܬ ܡܬܢܚܡܘܬܐ ܗܘ ܕܡܬܡܠܝܐ ܗܘܬ ܚܘܬܡܐ܀

108 - ܗܘ ܕܡܠܐ ܒܪܘܙܐ ܒܢ ܒܕܚܠܬܐ:[288] ܒܠܠ ܕܒܗܘܬܗ ܘܡܒܠܒܠܘܬܗ ܕܐܘܪܐ ܡܠܟܐ ܒܢ ܒܗܘܝܐ. ܘܠܐ ܡܒܠܠ ܚܙܘ ܒܠܚܡܐ ܘܡܥܪܐ[289] ܐܝܟ ܕܒܥܠܐ ܕܚܝܘܗܝ. ܐܠܐ ܐܝܟ ܕܒܩܢܘܢܗ ܘܕܡܗ ܕܡܫܝܚܐ܀

109 - ܗܘ ܕܒܡܘܒܠܐ ܕܒܪܘܪܬܐ. ܡܪܢܝܢ ܡܪܝܐ ܚܝܠܐ ܚܬܝܬܐ ܘܡܪܟܐ: ܒܠܠ ܕܒܠܒܐ ܗܘܐ ܕܡܬܘܬܐ ܐܠܗܝ. ܘܠܐ ܡܕܥܐ ܕܠܐ ܢܬܒܠܠ. ܐܝܟ ܕܡܠܟܐ ܒܢ ܗܘ ܕܐܡܪܐ. ܕܒܠܠ ܒܪܝܐ ܕܠܐ ܢܬܠܐ܀

110 - ܒܬܪ ܗܠܝܢ ܐܡܪܝܢ ܫܒܚܬܐ ܗܘ ܕܫܒܚ ܡܪܝ[290] ܐܒܘܢ[291] ܕܒܫܡܝܐ: ܡܛܠ ܒܪ ܕܐܘܪܐ ܕܡܬܐܐ ܘܡܫܡܠܝܬܐ ܫܪܝܢ. ܗܘ ܕܒܗ ܗܘܝܢ ܒܢܝܐ ܕܐܠܗܐ.[292] ܡܫܪܐ ܗܘܐ ܠܐܠܗܐ ܐܒܘܢ ܩܪܝܢ. ܐܝܟܢܐ ܕܐܡܪ ܡܪܝ. ܕܐܠܗܝ ܒܗܘ ܠܐ ܠܐܡܪܘܢ ܠܗܘܢ ܐܒܐ ܒܐܪܥܐ ܘܡܪܟܐ܀

---

285 C: ܡܫܡܫ.

286 C: ܒܡܫܡܠܝܢܘܬܗ.

287 V.f. 131v.

288 C: ܒܕܚܠܬܐ ܘܡܪܟܐ.

289 C: ܘܡܥܪܐ.

290 ܕܫܒܚ ܡܪܝ, missing in C.

291 C: ܕܐܒܘܢ.

292 V: ܠܐܠܗܐ.

111 - ܡܛܠܐ ܕܝܢ ܕܢܦܩ ܒܗܘܢ ܒܗܘܐ ܡܛܠܐ: ܐܝܟ ܗܘ ܡܛܠܐ ܕܢܦܩ ܡܢܝ ܒܢܝ̈ܐ ܘܒܬܠܡܝܕ̈ܘܗܝ[293] ܒܠܚܘܕ[294] ܡܫܬܠܡܐ܀

112 - ܘܡܢ ܒܠܚܘܕ[295] ܐܡܪ ܒܗܘܐ ܗܘܝܐ ܠܡܕܝ̈ܢܬܐ ܐܠܐ[296] ܒܫܠܡܘܬܐ. ܗܘܐ ܕܫܡܥܘ[297] ܡܫܡܫܢܐ. ܘܠܐ[298] ܡܡܪܢܝܢ ܕܒܠܥܘ ܝܬܝܪ.

113 - ܡܫܬܒܠܝܢ ܕܝܢ ܒܬܫܡܫܬܐ[299] ܗܘܐ ܟܕ ܠܘܩܒܠܐ. ܘܐܡܪܝܢ[300] ܚܕ ܐܒܐ ܩܕܝܫܐ. ܚܕ ܒܪܐ ܩܕܝܫܐ. ܚܕ ܪܘܚܐ ܩܕܝܫܐ: ܟܕ ܚܕ ܗܘܐ ܡܘܕܝܢ ܘܠܫܠܝܚܘܬܐ ܩܕܝܫܬܐ ܒܗ ܠܫܠܝܚܘܬܐ ܗܝ ܕܡܫܝܚܐ. ܘܩܕܡ ܚܕ ܒܠܚܘܕ. ܘܠܐܘܡ ܠܟܠܠܐ. ܐܠܐ ܚܕ ܚܕ ܚܕ܀

114 - ܡܫܬܠܡܝܢ[301] ܒܡܘܗܒܐ ܠܐܒܐ ܘܠܒܪܐ ܘܠܪܘܚܐ ܕܩܘܕܫܐ ܠܥܠܡ ܥܠܡܝܢ ܐܡܝܢ. ܡܘܕܝܢ ܟܕ ܗܘܐ: ܕܟܠܬܐ ܕܟܠܗܘܢ ܠܚܢܢ ܐܠܗܘܬܗ ܗܘ ܒܚܝܠ ܗܝܟܢܐ ܘܡܚܝܠܐ[302] ܘܡܫܠܛܢܐ ܐܒܐ ܘܒܪܐ ܘܪܘܚܐ ܕܩܘܕܫܐ. ܗܟܢ ܘܡܫܬܠܡܝܢ ܒܗܘܐ ܡܛܠܐ: ܠܟܗܢܘܬܐ ܘܡܫܠܡܢܗ ܕܡܪܢ ܕܐܡܪ ܠܫܠܝܚ̈ܘܗܝ. ܦܘܩܘ ܗܟܝܠ ܬܠܡܕܘ ܠܟܠܗܘܢ ܥܡ̈ܡܐ ܘܡܪܢܐ܀[303]

115 - ܗܘ̇[304] ܕܐܡܪܝܢ ܕܢܚܬ ܒܒܘܝܐ: ܐܝܟ ܠܡܫܝܚܘܬܐ ܘܗܘܦܟܐ ܕܒܗܘܢ ܡܫܡܫܝܢ ܒܟܗܘܢ ܢܚܬ̈ܐ ܡܫܝܚܐ. ܒܠܚܘܕ ܡܕܒܪܢܘܬܐ ܘܐܫܬܠܡܬ ܒܡܫܡܫܢܐ܀

116 - ܘܡܫܝܚܐ ܕܝܢ ܢܦܩ ܡܫܬܡܠܝ:[305] ܐܝܟ ܗܘ̇ ܕܗܘܐ ܙܕܩ ܡܫܘܚ ܒܟܘܡܪܐ. ܕܟܗܢܐ ܕܦܐܝܢ[306] ܒܟܘܬܗ. ܕܗܘ ܟܕ ܕܚܝܠ ܘܫܘܫܛܗ. ܡܫܬܡܠܝ ܟܕ ܪܘܚܐ

---

[293] V: ܘܠܬܠܡܝܕ̈ܘܗܝ.

[294] C: ܡܢ ܒܠܚܘܕ.

[295] C: ܡܢ ܒܠܚܘܕ.

[296] C: ܕܐܠܐ.

[297] C: ܗܘܐ ܕܫܡܥܘ.

[298] V.f. 132r.

[299] C: ܠܬܫܡܫܬܐ.

[300] C: ܐܡܪܝܢ.

[301] C: ܡܫܬܠܡܝܢ ܕܝܢ.

[302] C: ܘܡܚܝܠܐ.

[303] ܘܡܪܢܐ missing in C. C adds: ܘܐܥܡܕܘ ܐܢܘܢ ܒܫܡ ܐܒܐ ܘܒܪܐ ܘܪܘܚܐ ܕܩܘܕܫܐ.

[304] C: ܗܘ̇ ܕܝܢ.

[305] C: ܗܘܝܐ.

[306] C: ܦܐܝܢ.

ܕܦܘܪܫܐ ܢܦܩ ܠܪܘܫܡܬܐ ܘܠܐ ܡܬܘܠܬܐ: ܘܡܝܬܝ[307] ܦܩܕ ܕܢܬܠܝܗ ܠܐܝܩܪܐ. ܘܟܠܗ ܠܡܫܪܝܘ ܠܡܦܩ ܦܘܪܫܐ ܘܠܐ ܐܝܩܪܐ. ܟܕܟܝ ܐܡܝܪܐ. ܘܡܛܠ ܟܗܢܘܬܐ ܘܙܘܚܐ ܡܢܝܚܐ. ܠܐܝܩܪܐ ܕܝܢ ܗܘ ܡܫܒܚܬܐ ܐܡܪ: ܠܡܘܒܠܬܐ ܗܝ[308] ܕܗܘܝܐ ܡܢ ܡܢܝ ܠܡܫܡܫܢܘܬܐ: ܕܗܘ ܟܠܟܠ[309] ܐܡܪ ܠܐ ܡܬܘܠܬܐ ܗܝ ܕܠܡܝܬܐ܀

117 - ܡܬܐܦܠܢ ܕܝܢ ܕܠܐܘܪܐ ܡܢܬܐ:[310] ܐܘܪ ܡܬܐܦܠܢܘܬܐ ܗܝ ܕܗܘܝܐ ܠܟ ܠܥܠܡ ܠܡܠܟܘܬܐ ܡܬܐ܀

118 - ܠܡܫܡܫܢܘܬܐ ܗܝ[311] ܕܙܡܢ ܡܢܝ ܡܬܘܢ ܡܠܟܐ ܫܠܝܚܐ: ܐܘܪ ܗܝ ܕܗܘܝܐ ܠܡܠܟܐ ܕܟܠܗ ܡܢ ܟܠܗܘܢ ܡܠܟܐ ܐܝܟ ܕܠܡܠܟܐ ܡܫܝܚܐ. ܕܟܘ ܓܒܐ ܟܠܗ ܡܘܟܠܐ ܕܐܬܟܢܫܬܐ ܠܡܫܡܫ ܡܫܡܫܝܢ ܘܡܫܡܫܢܝܢ. ܘܡܫܓܢܘܬܐ ܠܟܠܢܘܬܐ ܦܠܝܚܝܢ܀

119 - ܓܒܐܬܐ ܗܝ ܕܙܡܢ ܓܒܝܐ ܡܘܬܐ[312] ܟܠ ܥܠܡܐ: ܠܟܗܢܘܬܐ ܕܗܝ ܡܘܟܠܬܐ ܕܟܕ ܡܢܝ ܠܡܠܟܘܬܗܘܢ ܟܕܝܬܐ ܕܟܘ ܐܫܬܠܡ ܠܥܠܡܐ܀

120 - ܡܘܟܠܬܐ ܕܝܢ ܬܘܒ ܕܡܟܢܫ ܡܘܬܐ ܠܥܠܡܐ ܟܕ ܦܠܛ ܠܐܣܛܘܟܣܐ ܘܬܘܟܐ ܕܟܠܗ ܦܘܪܫܐ: ܐܘܪ ܡܫܝܚܘܬܐ ܕܡܬܒܪܬܐ ܕܪܘܚܐ ܕܦܘܪܫܐ ܕܟܠ ܡܫܡܫܢܐ ܡܢ ܟܬܪ ܕܫܠܡ ܡܢܝ ܡܬܘܢ[313] ܠܥܠܡܐ. ܘܟܘܠܗ ܡܘܟܠܬܐ ܐܫܬܠܡܬ ܠܥܠܡܝܢ܀[314]

121 - ܐܦ ܓܒܪ ܡܠܟܐ ܐܡܝܢܐ[315] ܕܡܬܚܙܐ ܠܝܕܘܥܐ[316] ܟܬܪ[317] ܡܫܡܫܐ ܕܐܘܪܐ ܡܫܝܚܐ: ܐܘܪ ܚܝܘܬܐ ܗܘ ܦܢܝܬܐ. ܗܝ ܕܟܗ ܡܫܬܚܠܦܝܢ ܬܘܒ ܟܡ ܝܕܘܥܐ ܐܝܟ ܗܘܦܟܐ. ܘܟܠ ܡܬܬܚܠܦܝܢ ܒܙܢܐ ܕܓܒܐ. ܘܟܘܦܪܐ ܕܡܢ ܟܠܗ ܡܢܝܬܐ. ܡܢܝ ܡܬܘܢ ܡܫܝܚܐ܀

122 - ܡܛܠ ܦܘܩܕ ܠܫܡܫܬܐ ܘܠܐܠܗܐ ܗܘ ܐܡܝܢ.

---

[307] V.f. 132v.

[308] C: ܕܗܘ.

[309] C: ܟܠܟܠ.

[310] C: ܡܢܬܐ.

[311] C: ܕܝܢ.

[312] C: ܡܘܬܐ ܕܝܢ ܕܓܒܝܐ ܕܙܘܡܫܐ.

[313] ܡܬܘܢ missing in C.

[314] ܘܟܘܠܗ ܡܘܟܠܬܐ ܐܫܬܠܡܬ ܠܥܠܡܝܢ܀ missing in C.

[315] ܐܡܝܢܐ missing in C.

[316] V.f. 133r.

[317] C: ܟܬܪ ܕܝܢ.

123 - [318]ܐܝܟܐ ܕܚܣܝܐ ܚܝܠܐ ܕܪ̈ܝܫ ܩܪܝܒܐ. ܐܦܠܐ ܠܟܠܗܘܐ ܐܝܟ ܠܐܡܝ ܀ ܠܐ ܠܗܘܐ ܠܥܡܝܪܐ ܕܐܝܠܐ ܕܡܫܡܫ ܢܦܫܗ. ܘܠܐ ܣܠܩ ܡܫܡܫܢܘܬܐ ܪ̈ܘܚܢܝܬܐ ܠܐܠܗܐ ܀ ܡܛܠ ܕܣܝܡܐ ܠܥܠܡܝܢ ܒܢܝܢܫ ܕܢܝܫܝܢ ܣܘܟܠܐ ܠܗܠܐ ܡܢܝܪܐ. ܘܗܝ ܕܟܠ ܚܕ ܡܢܗܘܢ ܠܟܡܝܠܐ ܕܣܒܪܗ ܡܥܒܕ ܀ ܐܬܪܐ ܘܠܐ ܦܠܚܝܢ ܢܘܦܪܐ ܐܠܗܘܬܢ ܠܟܢ ܕܡܠܐ ܠܟܢ ܀

318 Only in Connolly.

PREFACE TO MAR SHEMʿŪN'S *LAW BOOK* BY AN ANONYMOUS MONK FROM BETH QAṬRAYE

MARIO KOZAH
AMERICAN UNIVERSITY OF BEIRUT

INTRODUCTION

A number of Qaṭraye – Syriac Christians from Beth Qaṭraye – are said to have served as translators for important secular and religious authorities in the region between the sixth and eighth centuries. A famous possible example is the Persian translator of king al-Nuʿmān III (579–601), the last Lakhmid king of Ḥīra and vassal of Sassanid Persia, who would almost certainly have been an Arabic speaker. The demand for these skilled translators and the prestigious work that they undertook are a testament to the high level of culture and education they must have received in Beth Qaṭraye providing further evidence that an important centre of learning must have existed there. Their proficiency in the languages of the period including Persian, Arabic, and Syriac is also a reflection of the multicultural intellectual and religious milieu in which they lived.

Another anonymous translator from Beth Qaṭraye, this time a monk, was commissioned by a certain Mar Shemʿūn, referred to in the preface as a teacher and God-loving priest, to translate from Persian into Syriac the *Law Book* of Mar Shemʿūn metropolitan bishop of Rev Ardashir. Although the author of this treatise on family and hereditary law wrote it in Persian it only survives in the Syriac translation which the anonymous monk from Beth Qaṭraye undertook. The *Law Book*, probably originally written and translated in the seventh century, comprises 22 chapters presented in a question and answer format. It begins by establishing the importance of the Fathers as the primary source of Christian law. The Syriac translation of the *Law Book* was an important source for the *Synodicon Orientale* and an authoritative juridical text within the Church of the East canonical tradition.

What is presented here, translated into English for the first time, is the anonymous monk from Beth Qaṭraye's preface to his Syriac translation of the *Law Book* by Mar Shemʿūn metropolitan bishop of Rev Ardashir.[1] This preface is a supremely sophisticated introductory piece of etiquette and diplomacy and a reflection of the translator's refined knowledge and technical mastery of the Syriac language. His repeated articulations of humility and modesty are, paradoxically, expressed in such syntactically complex sentences that they are almost unfathomable to any reader. The effect, it seems, is to demonstrate at the very outset of the commissioned work the translator's linguistic credentials and high scholasticism under the necessary monastic camouflage of self-deprecation.

Such a high level of proficiency in Syriac provides further evidence of the linguistic complexity of Beth Qaṭraye. For in addition to what may be called formal Syriac, the existence of a Qatari Aramaic variant is explicitly referred to in a number of Syriac glosses where the word referring to the language of Beth Qaṭraye is referred to as "Qaṭrayit". This term is used, for example, in the East Syriac *Anonymous Commentary* which includes glosses containing words in Qatari (ܩܛܪܐܝܬ)[2] spoken by Qataris (ܩܛܪܝ̈ܐ) who appear to be distinguished from Arabs (ܛܝܝ̈ܐ) living in the same region who have their own language.[3]

Works such as this translation by educated Qaṭraye reveal that Syriac Christians in Beth Qaṭraye, a diglossic region it seems, used Syriac as their literary and liturgical language but also had

---

[1] The Syriac text is based on Eduard Sachau's edition of the work in E. Sachau, *Syrische Rechtsbücher*, 3. Berlin, 1914.

[2] Abraham Levene, *The Early Syrian Fathers on Genesis from a Syriac Ms. on the Pentateuch in the Mingana Collection*. London, 1951, pp. 37–38.

[3] Ibid., p. 41: ܪܩܒܐ ܐܝܟ ܗܢܘܢ ܕܫܩܠܝܢ ܛܠܝ̈ܐ ܛܝܝ̈ܐ ܘܩܪܝܢ ܠܗܘܢ ܡܫܟ. ܘܩܛܪܝ̈ܐ ܕܝܢ ܫܘܢ: "A water skin (*raqba*) like those which Arab boys carry and which they call *mshak*, and the Qaṭaris call *shūn*".

knowledge of Persian, Arabic, as well as their own Aramaic spoken language. They provide concrete evidence of the rich cultural and linguistic interaction that took place in and around Beth Qaṭraye region which in the seventh century was a centre for both trade and education.

TRANSLATION

Various chapters of common cases in ecclesiastical canons expressed in clear speech by Mar Shemʿūn metropolitan bishop of Rev Ardashir, famous for apostolic teachings, and translated from Persian into Aramaic by one of the monks[4] from the region of Beth Qaṭraye.

Preface to the one who asked him to translate this book from Persian into Syriac.

(Preface by the Anonymous Translator)

Your honourable command has drawn me to take on something that is above my ability to intricately compose, Oh venerable and God-loving priest and teacher Mar Shemʿūn, and you greatly brought me[5] to wonder at your resolve which gently mentions spiritual matters, and with all this esteem you have for me. Moreover, whenever I turned to this matter, knowing that I lack training, I was compelled to excuse myself from completing it, however, I feared lest I may be found to be one who is ungrateful and denies the munificence of your divine love towards me. Your episcopacy, full of great achievements, is decorated like a splendid crown ornamented and adorned with precious stones, and your virtue is glorified by it. It [episcopacy] took refuge in the heavenly way of life of our glorious and elect holy fathers, worthy of good memory, who have honourably attended to the innocent[6] flock that

---

[4] ܐܚ̈ܐ ܐܟܣ̈ܢܝܐ: lit. "brother strangers".

[5] Reading ܐܝܬܝܬܝܢܝ: "you brought me", rather than the probably corrupted ܐܠܠܢܝ.

[6] For the definition of ܡܚܠܠܐ as "innocent" see Sokoloff, M., *A Syriac lexicon: a translation from the Latin: correction, expansion, and update of C.*

was entrusted to them by Christ, the Lord of shepherds, from whom [the fathers], by divine dispensation, the law of nature[7] entered and produced you when you received from them [not only] what belongs to nature, but [also] what belongs to the will, and you were found to be on a part with them, as a zealous and faithful heir, in the likeness[8] of body and soul, in that you have become related to them in a complete and excellent way, with a kinship that belongs both to the senses and the understanding. This is in truth, a profitable inheritance, which is why you now command, with the sceptre of all virtues in the church of God, in which the Lord, the Spirit, has set you, in the grace of His mercy, like a sun in the radiance of His rays. When you gladden those in your presence, as spiritual beings, with the abundance of His [divine] words and with your attractive conversation, you draw those who are far away to admire you through the fame of your great deeds. It is appropriate that [the saying] of the Apostle be addressed to you: "For you are a sweet fragrance for God through Christ".[9] An example of all of these [things] is what you have done for me at this time. For when you wanted to cause to shine out in actions an indication of the genuineness of your perfect love which is poured out towards everyone without stinting, in your particular love you separated me out, singling out my specific abilities from the many persons in the community who are more educated and competent, [and yet] by your singular love you have selected me for carrying out this particular task. For you have urged me to translate many discourses, which you handed to me when I was in your presence, into the Aramaic language, that were composed in the Persian language by persons divinely endowed with excellence and a wealth of apostolic learning. Furthermore, although the request presented itself as very hard for me as one whom you have exhorted to walk along a new and untrodden path, given your benevolent command which is difficult for me, I have nevertheless accepted with

Brockelmann's Lexicon Syriacum. Winona Lake, Ind.: Eisenbrauns, 2009, p. 771.

[7] Course of time?

[8] Reading ܒܕܡܘܬܐ: "in the likeness of".

[9] II Corinthians 2:15.

complete readiness to accomplish this advantageous exhortation of yours through actions.

As a preface I note for you and all those who, with truth-loving will, happen to read these discourses, that you should not blame with displeasure the translator if you do not encounter in the meaning of the words the orderly composition and ornamentation of the pure Aramaic language, but rather to kindly be informed that this has occurred on account of the complexity of the Persian language, which is not ubiquitously amenable to translation into Aramaic. I will endeavour as much as possible to express the meaning of the discourse in an apt manner, without changing the meaning of the words. I seek to interpret according to the sense. Where, then, I was compelled to translate [using] its own style, the disorderly linking of the words is due to the poverty of the language and not the ignorance of the translator.

It is now time, therefore, for me to start the work, while trusting in the prayers and intercessions of my brothers and companions. I call on the heavenly power of that Eternal Teacher to aid my weakness, He who is used to making His power triumph through the weak, that He might extend to me the radiant splendour of meanings from the treasure of His unfathomable wisdom so that this work might be completed by me according to the request of your divinely perfect love.

The beginning of the book:

Preface to the one who requested its composition in writing.

These [questions], concerning the matter of the ecclesiastical canons, that your Beatitude set down for me: why did our Lord not hand down His own benign laws, and for what reason do we not make judgements from the law of Moses…

TEXT

ܬܘܒ ܕܝ̈ܢܐ ܡܦܣ̈ܩܬܐ ܕܥܕ̈ܬܐ ܡܫܝ̈ܚܝܬܐ ܕܕܝܪ̈ܝܐ ܕܒܐܬܪ̈ܐ ܕܐܡܕܝܢ ܒܡܫܠܡܬܐ
ܡܫܝܚܝܬܐ ܠܥܝܕ ܒܘܠܦܢ̈ܐ ܡܟܠܝ̈ܬܐ ܡܪܝ ܫܡܥܘܢ ܐܦܝܣܩܘܦܐ
ܡܝܛܪܦܘܠܝܛܐ ܕܪܝܘܐܪܕܫܝܪ ܘܡܦܩܝܢ ܡܢ ܦܪܣܝܐ ܠܐܪܡܝܐ ܠܚܕ ܡܢ ܐ̈ܚܐ
ܐܦܝܣܩܘ̈ܦܐ ܡܢ ܐܬܪܐ ܕܒܝܬ ܩܛܪ̈ܝܐ. ܡܩܡ ܒܪܘܚܐ ܠܗܘ ܕܟܠ ܡܢܗ

ܘܢܦܫܗܘܢ ܠܒܠܒܠ ܗܘܐ ܡܢ ܦܪܫܐ ܠܡܘܪܫܐ. ܒܪܒܘܬܐ ܪܘܚܐ ܡܢ ܚܕ
ܠܐܪܥܐ ܦܘܩܕܢܗ ܡܫܪܐ ܕܐܬܬܪܝܡܬܗ ܢܦܩܐ ܘܢܦܩ ܐܠܗܐ ܡܢܗ ܥܡܗܘܢ
ܥܡܡܐ ܘܡܠܟܐ ܘܪܘܟܐ ܐܬܐܬ ܠܡܠܟܘܬܗ ܒܪܚܡܝ ܘܐܦ ܒܬܘܚܡܢܬܐ، ܕܗܘܐ
ܠܗ ܡܫܬܪܝܢܘܬܐ ܥܡ ܐܢܫ ܚܕ. ܐܢܐ ܕܝܢ ܦܠܐܫܬܐ ܕܠܗܘܐ ܪܒܘܬܐ، ܟܕ
ܠܐ ܡܬܪܥܝܢܘܬܐ ܕܡܬܠܝ ܡܫܐ ܐܢܐ ܕܐܫܬܐܠ ܡܢ ܫܘܡܠܝܗ ܡܠܟܐ ܐܢܐ. ܡܛܠ
ܐܢܐ ܕܝܢ ܕܝܠܝ ܠܚܘܕܝ ܘܟܠܗ ܥܡ ܡܫܝܚܐ ܢܘܗܪ ܐܠܗܐ ܕܪܐܙܐ ܐܬܓܠܝ.
ܘܒܗܘܬܐ ܟܠܠܐ ܦܐܬܐ ܘܢܗܝܪ ܘܡܪܟܒ ܒܩܐܦܐ ܠܟܠܬܐ، ܡܗܘܕܐ ܒܗ ܢܗܡܬܐ
ܡܠܟܗ ܕܢܛܪܐ، ܘܡܫܡܠܝܐ ܒܗ ܡܬܚܘܝܐ ܠܢܦܫܗ ܒܗܘܪܐ ܡܫܬܐ ܕܡܬܬ
ܒܗܘܪܢܐ ܠܟܠ ܕܢܛܪܐ ܘܒܣܝܪܐ ܐܟܘܬ ܡܕܝܢܐ، ܗܢܘܢ ܕܪܟܗ ܕܗܝܡܢ ܠܡܪܢܝܬܐ
ܡܫܠܡܬܐ ܕܠܗܘܢ ܐܬܓܒܠ ܡܢ ܡܫܝܚܐ ܪܒ ܪ̈ܘܚܐ ܕܢܣܗܘܢ ܒܫܘܪܝܐ
ܡܕܒܪܢܐ ܟܠ ܗܘܡܠܟ ܢܦܫܬܐ ܕܚܝܐ ܒܡܦܪܢܐ ܡܢܝܐ ܡܫܬܪܝܐ، ܒ
ܫܡܠܝ ܡܢܗܘܢ ܗܢܘܢ ܕܚܝܐ ܐܦ ܗܢܝܢ ܕܪܚܡܐ ܘܐܫܬܡܫܬ ܠܗܘܢ ܒܫܠܡܗ
ܢܪܐ ܣܦܝܩܐ ܘܡܗܝܡܢܐ، ܕܕܡܘܬܐ ܕܦܓܪܐ ܘܢܘܪܐ ܒܐܬܓܠܝܬ ܡܫܬܪܝܬ
ܐܘܟܝܬ ܡܫܡܠܝܬ ܒܐܝܩܪܗܘܢ، ܡܫܬܪܚܬܐ ܘܡܫܬܡܠܝܢܘܬܐ. ܗܘܐ
ܕܐܬܚܙܝ ܒܡܪܐ ܢܘܪܐ ܡܬܢܒܝܢܘܬܐ، ܘܒܪܘܚܗ ܗܘ ܡܦܪܓܠܝܬ ܒܦܘܠܚܢܐ
ܘܟܠ ܡܬܠܢ ܒܟܘ ܒܝܬܗ ܕܐܠܗܐ ܘܒܗ ܢܪܚܡ ܡܪܐ ܪܘܚܐ ܒܫܘܒܚܐ
ܕܠܗܘܬܗ، ܒܗܘܬܐ ܫܡܝܐ ܒܪܚܡܐ ܘܒܫܦܝܪܘܬܐ. ܒ ܠܡܪܝܚܘܬܐ ܒܫܡܫܘܬܐ
ܘܡܫܬܪܪ ܐܝܟ ܪ̈ܘܚܐ ܘܡܢܝܚ ܕܚܒܝܒܐ ܡܫܡܫ ܐܝܟ ܠܪ̈ܘܚܢܐ ܕܝܢ ܒܠܗܝܐ
ܕܢܚܝܬܝܢ ܠܐܠܗܐ ܕܒܗ ܢܬܦ ܐܝܟ. ܘܡܫܝܚܐ ܗܘ ܕܐܬܐܡܪ ܠܘܬܗ ܗܘ ܕܚܠܝܐ
ܘܢܘܚܐ ܐܝܟܘܢ ܒܪ ܒܫܝܢܐ ܒܫܡܝܐ ܠܐܠܗܐ. ܘܐܝܬܘܬܐ ܕܗܠܝܢ ܒܠܒܝ
ܐܝܬܘܗܝ ܗܘܐ ܕܪܐܙܐ ܡܫܪܐ ܒܗܘܐ ܙܒܢܐ. ܕܒܪ ܙܒܢܐ ܕܡܘܕܝܬܐ ܕܡܪܘܬܗ ܕܝܫܘܥ
ܒܡܫܪܐ، ܗܘ ܕܠܐ ܚܫܫ ܡܫܚܬ ܠܗܐ ܒܠܒܗ، ܠܐܝܬܘܗܝ ܒܗܘܢ ܒܫܘܒܚܐ،
ܒܡܚܝܕܘܬܐ ܐܢܐ ܕܗܠܝܢ ܕܪ̈ܐܙܐ ܡܢ ܓܘܐ ܕܦܪ̈ܘܫܐ ܡܫܬܐ ܕܢܛܪ ܪܘܚ
ܘܡܕܡܝܢ ܒܦܪܫܘܬܐ ܪ̈ܘܚܢܝܐ ܦܪܫܐܝܬ ܠܡܫܡܫܘ ܕܗܘܐ ܡܫܬܪܝܐ.
ܐܫܬܠܡ ܓܒܪ، ܕܠܡܫܬܐ ܡܫܬܝܐ ܕܟܠܝܐ ܦܪܫܐ ܐܫܬܪܝ ܠܐܢܫܐ ܡܫܬܪܝ
ܬܠܘܬܢܐ ܘܡܠܟܘܬܐ ܒܡܠܟܘܬܐ ܡܫܝܚܐ، ܗܢܘܢ ܕܐܫܬܠܚܘ ܠܗ ܒ
ܒܦܪܫܘܬܝ ܐܝܟ ܗܘܝܐ ܐܣܛܠܝܬܝ ܠܟܠܐ ܐܘܪܚܐ. ܐܢܐ ܕܝܢ ܒ ܠܗܝ
ܐܬܚܫܒܬ ܚܕ ܪܒܘܬܐ ܐܫܟܚ ܕܒܫܠܐ ܚܕܐ ܘܠܐ ܕܪܫܐ ܡܫܠܡܢ ܠܡܪܐ
ܒܪܡ ܒܗܝܡܢ ܚܕ ܦܘܩܕܢ ܕܚܫܐ ܒܒܠܗ ܠܗܘܐ ܡܫܠܡ ܠܡܫܚܬ
ܡܫܬܪܝܐ ܗܘܐ ܕܐܬܓܒܪܘܗܝ ܒܗܘܢ ܒܫܘܒܚܐ. ܡܫܠܡ ܐܢܐ ܒ ܡܫܘܕܥ ܐܢܐ ܠܟܘ
ܘܡܫܬܐܠܢܐ ܕܒܪܚܡܐ ܕܢܚܡ ܡܪܐ ܦܓܪܐ ܒܗܠܝܢ ܡܫܒܚܐ، ܕܐܦ ܡܫܡܫ ܒܗܘܢ
ܟܠܠܐ ܘܠܐ ܡܬܢܝ ܢܚܝܬܘܬܐ ܘܪ̈ܘܚܐ ܕܟܠܝܐ ܡܪܢܝܐ ܕܐܪܥܐ ܠܐ ܢܒܥܐ ܒܚܡܫܐ
ܠܡܫܡܫܐ ܐܠܐ ܢ̈ܐܠܦ ܒܫܘܒܚܐ ܕܡܢ ܟܠܗ ܡܪܢܝܬܗ ܕܟܠܝܐ ܦܪܫܐ ܓܒܝܐ

ܗܕܐ، ܘܠܐ ܢܦܩ ܒܠܒܘܫ ܠܦܘܫܩܐ ܕܠܫܢܐ ܐܪܡܝܐ. ܐܢܐ ܕܝܢ ܒܥܠܐ ܕܡܫܡܫܢ ܐܢܐ ܐܬܥܝܪܬ ܕܐܡܚܐ ܕܠܟܘܢ، ܕܢܬܦܫܩ ܣܦܪܐ ܒܪܝܫܐ ܒܠܐ ܡܫܡܠܝܐ ܢܦܫܐ ܕܡܘܕܥܢ ܕܬܠܐ. ܦܫܩܬ ܐܢܐ ܕܐܦܫܩܘܢ ܙܒܢܝܬܗ. ܐܡܬܐ ܕܝܢ ܕܒܗ ܒܦܓܥܐ ܡܠܟܝܐ ܐܢܐ ܕܐܦܫܩܘܢ ܐܬܐܡܪ ܠܐ ܡܦܫܩܘܬܐ ܕܬܠܐ ܒܪܘܚܩܬܗ ܕܠܫܢܐ ܘܠܐ ܗܘܐ ܟܠܐ ܡܟܠܬܗ ܕܡܚܟܡܬܐ. ܙܒܢܐ ܗܘ ܠܗ ܡܬܚܫܠ ܕܟܕ ܒܠܘܚܐ ܕܠܒܘܬܗܘܢ ܘܡܟܒܫܬܗܘܢ ܕܐܚܝ̈ ܘܒܢܝ̈ ܚܝܝ ܡܫܪܐ ܐܢܐ ܒܗ ܒܟܕܐ. ܐܡܪܐ ܠܐܠܐ ܕܡܣܬܟܠ ܚܝܠܐ ܡܫܝܚܐ ܕܗܘ ܡܠܟܐ ܡܠܘܫܐ، ܗܘ ܕܡܟܝܢ ܡܚܝܢ ܚܝܠܗ ܒܡܣܟܢܐ ܕܢܫܩܘܢ ܠܗ ܡܢ ܠܓܪܐ ܕܡܚܡܠܬܗ ܠܐ ܡܬܕܪܟܢܝܬܐ، ܙܠܓܐ ܒܗܘܪܐ ܕܫܘܟܠܐ ܕܢܛܦܪ ܒܐܝܕܝ ܗܘܐ ܫܘܒܪܐ ܐܝܟ ܠܐܠܗܘ ܕܡܕܡ ܠܦܫܪܐ ܒܐܠܗܘܬܐ. ܫܘܪܐ ܕܡܠܘ ܕܟܠܒܐ، ܡܦܩ ܒܪܘܚܐ ܠܗܐ ܗܘ ܕܒܠܐ ܡܢܗ ܕܢܒܕܘܢ ܒܟܠܬܒܐ. ܗܠܝܢ ܕܡܢܩܘܬܝ ܟܠܠ ܪܓܬܐ ܕܕܝܢܐ ܒܐܝܬܐ ܕܦܫܟ ܠܗ. ܘܡܠܠ ܡܢܐ ܡܢܝ ܠܐ ܐܦܠܛ ܐܝܟ ܒܫܢܝܢ ܢܡܘܣܬܗܘܢ ܘܐܦܐ ܗܘ ܒܟܠܬܐ ܘܠܐ ܗܘܐ ܡܢ ܢܡܘܣܐ ܕܡܘܫܐ ܒܒܝܬ ܕܝܢܐ (ܘܡܫܪܐ)

DADISHOᶜ QAṬRAYA'S *COMPENDIOUS COMMENTARY* ON THE *PARADISE OF THE EGYPTIAN FATHERS* IN GARSHUNI

MARIO KOZAH, SULEIMAN MOURAD,
ABDULRAHIM ABU-HUSAYN

INTRODUCTION (BY MARIO KOZAH)

Dadishoᶜ Qaṭraya is a seventh century Syriac author of monastic and ascetic literature. A Church of the East monk, he was a native of the Qatar region, as his demonym "Qaṭraya" indicates. Dadishoᶜ seems to have become a monk at the otherwise unknown monastery of Rab-kennārē before dwelling for a time at the monastery of Rabban Šābūr and at that of the "Blessed Apostles".[1]

Dadishoᶜ's name and works are to be found recorded at the beginning of the fourteenth century in the catalogue of ᶜAbdishoᶜ bar Brikā who states:[2]

> The renowned Dadishoᶜ (ܕܕܝܫܘܥ ܚܣܝܢܐ), wrote a commentary (lit. commented) on the Paradise of the Occidentals [monks] (ܦܪܕܝܣܐ ܕܡܥܪ̈ܒܝܐ); he elucidated [the book of] Abbā Isaiah; he wrote a book on the [monastic] way of life (ܥܠ ܕܘܒܪܐ); treatises on the sanctification of the cell; consolatory dirges (ܡܐܡܪ̈ܐ ܒܝܐ̈ܢܐ ܕܘܡܠܐ); he also wrote letters and inquiries

[1] A. Scher, "Notice sur la vie et les oeuvres de Dadishoᶜ Qaṭraya", *Journal Asiatique*, 10:7, 1906, pp. 103–111.

[2] As was first established by A. Scher in the above-cited article on Dadishoᶜ Qaṭraya.

(ܐܘܠܨ̈ܢܐ ܘܥܘ̈ܩܬܐ) on quietude in the body and the soul (ܥܠ ܫܠܝܐ ܕܦܓܪܐ ܘܢܦܫܐ).[3]

One very important work of his survives that is catalogued by ʿAbdishoʿ bar Brikā but which remains unedited and with no translation. This is, of course, Dadishoʿ's *Commentary* on ʿNānishoʿ's *Paradise of the Fathers*,[4] which is the Syriac version of the *Paradise of the Egyptian Fathers* translated and compiled in the seventh century. Until recently this *Commentary* was also only to be found surviving in an incomplete form in manuscripts at the British Library, Cambridge University Library and the Paris Bibliothèque Nationale.[5] However, the discovery of the complete text in the Metropolitan Library of the Church of the East in Baghdad has attracted the interest of a number of distinguished scholars and a critical edition and translation of this important text are now underway.[6]

What is, perhaps, less well known is that a Garshuni summary translation of Dadishoʿ's *Commentary* features in a number of manuscripts. Further, the Garshuni *Compendium* does not mark the end of the literary journey of Dadishoʿ's *Commentary* for, in fact, an Ethiopic (Geʿez) translation of the *Compendium* survives in numerous copies and which is yet to be fully edited or translated.[7] The importance of investigating the history of the translation process of Dadishoʿ's *Commentary* from Syriac into Arabic then consequently into Ethiopic is that it will provide a very rare

---

3 J.S. Assemanus, *Bibliotheca Orientalis Clementino-Vaticana*, III/1. Rome, 1725, pp. 98–99.

4 Some excerpts were published and translated by N. Sims-Williams, "Dādišoʿ Qaṭrāyā's Commentary on the *Paradise of the Fathers*", in *Analecta Bollandiana*, 112, 1994, pp. 33–64.

5 Ibid., p. 33.

6 A critical edition of Dadishoʿ's *Commentary* on the *Paradise of the Fathers* is being prepared by D. Phillips. See R. Kitchen, "Dadisho Qatraya's *Commentary on 'Abba Isaiah'*. The *Apophthegmata Patrum* Connection", in *StPatr* 41, 2006, pp. 35–50.

7 See W. Witakowski, "Filekseyus, the Ethiopic version of the Syriac Dadisho Qatraya's Commentary on the Paradise of the Fathers", in *Rocznik Orientalistyczny*, 59, 2006, pp. 281–296.

opportunity to acquire certain important insights into the transmission of knowledge and cultural material from an originally Syriac work into other languages and cultures over the course of many centuries, from the seventh century to the most recent Garshuni and Ethiopic manuscripts of the eighteenth and nineteenth centuries. Only complete editions of the Syriac, Garshuni,[8] and Geʿez versions of Dadishoʿ's *Commentary* on the *Paradise* will bring to light the significance and impact of the work of this great literary survivor from Beth Qaṭraye.

A Note on the Manuscripts

This is an excerpt from the full critical edition and translation of Dadishoʿ Qaṭraya's *Compendious Commentary* on the *Paradise of the Egyptian Fathers* in Garshuni which is currently underway. The edition is based on the oldest extant copy, Mingana Syr. 403, dated 1480 and uses all of the other copies to be found in the Mingana collection (Mingana Syr. 174, Mingana Syr. 370, Mingana Syr. 457). In addition to these, two other manuscripts are used: Berlin Syr. 244 and Vat. ar. 85.

TRANSLATION (BY MARIO KOZAH, SULEIMAN MOURAD, ABDULRAHIM ABU-HUSAYN)

Excerpt beginning in Mingana Syr. 403, f. 9r

The Brothers asked: "When the souls of the righteous depart from their bodies, do they proceed to Paradise or to heaven?"[9]

The Exegete replied: "To Paradise."

They asked: "How did Antony then see the souls of Paul and Ammon ascending to heaven?"

He replied: "Paradise is called heaven because of its elevation from Earth. The apostle [Paul] called Paradise the third heaven.[10]

---

[8] A complete critical edition of the Garshuni Compendium is currently being prepared using the most important extant manuscripts.

[9] The word *heaven* has to be understood in this discussion in its original meaning of sky.

The first [heaven] comprises the celestial spheres, about which God said in the Torah of Moses: 'In the Beginning, God created the heaven and the earth'.[11] The second [heaven] comprises the firmament that God used to split the waters.[12] The third [heaven] comprises Paradise, as called by the apostle Paul. The souls of the righteous rest in Paradise until God brings about the [Last] Judgment, and then they will achieve union with Christ in the Kingdom of Heaven. What proves this is what our Lord said to the thief on his right: 'Today, you will be with me in Paradise'.[13] And his words that when he comes in his glory, he shall place the righteous on his right, praise them and make them inherit his Kingdom."[14]

The Brothers asked: "Why did Antony say to his disciple Paul: 'Depart and seclude yourself so that you learn fighting the devil'?"[15]

The Exegete replied: "Because fighting the devil happens in thoughts. The combatant benefits from the stillness of seclusion. Through this, one also acquires fervent and durable prayer, as well as the purity of the heart. There, the combat is for the glory of God."

The Brothers asked: "Why did Abba Macarios the Alexandrian never spit on the ground for sixty years, from the day he was baptized until he died?"[16]

The Exegete replied: "Because he received the holy sacraments. This is why one should drink the water and eat the bread of benediction after one receives the sacraments. The Fathers used to say to us: 'If one of you has to spit after he receives the sacraments,

---

[10] See Paul's letter 2 Corinthians 12:2.

[11] See Genesis 1:1.

[12] See Genesis 1:6–8.

[13] See Luke 23:43.

[14] See Matthew 25:31–34.

[15] E. A. Wallis Budge, *The Paradise or Garden of the Holy Fathers* […], 2 vols., London, 1907. Vol. II, p. 287.

[16] E. A. Wallis Budge, *The Paradise*, vol. I, p. 124.

but before he drinks or eats, let him swallow it. If he disdains that, let him then wipe it in his garment'."

The Brothers asked: "Why did Elijah build a nunnery, brought to it three hundred nuns and placed himself as their head, but after a few years, he could no longer resist the thoughts of fornication, so he withdrew to the desert? Why did God send to him three angels who relieved him of the yearnings and instructed him to return to the nunnery to lead the sisters and look after them?"[17]

The Exegete replied: "There are three reasons [for this]. The first was due to his [Elijah's] kindness, worthiness, and chastity. For when he realized their number, and that they prefer to live in chastity but could not withdraw to the desert because they would not find someone to look after their needs there, he increased in spiritual love and built for them a nunnery, looked after them and lead them. The second was because God did not ward off from him the stirrings of physical yearnings and demonic struggles [in order] to show people, angels and demons his ability to disregard yearnings, resistance to the devil, love of virtue, and obedience to God. The third was because there is a group who have a corrupt belief and who say inconsiderately: 'This is good and this is bad'. They also allege that their good comes from the good and their evils come from the devil. Others claim that sin became innate in us from our father Adam; they allege that their sins are natural in them. When God willed to undermine these views, he made a group chaste from their birth. He also removed in others the intense conflict with [their] instinctive nature and struggling with demons in order to demonstrate his might and the unity of his divinity."

The Brothers asked: "What did Paphnutius mean when he said: 'the gravity of transgressions by tongue, sense, act and all the body corresponds to the person's arrogance'?"[18]

The Exegete replied: "The transgression through sense is to fail in your thoughts as stated by the blessed Mark: 'Let not your heart

---

[17] E. A. Wallis Budge, *The Paradise*, vol. I, pp. 142–144.

[18] E. A. Wallis Budge, *The Paradise*, vol. I, p. 178.

arrogantly think it knows scriptures lest your mind fall into blasphemy'.[19] The transgression with the tongue is to do what one of the brothers did on account of his arrogance in the Scetis Desert:[20] he cursed Mar Evagrius and the holy Fathers. The transgression through act is to do what the same brother did by committing fornication on account of his arrogance. The transgression with all the body is to do what the same brother did on account of his arrogance, and was caught by thieves who tied him up, placed him on a haystack and set him on fire."

The Brothers asked: "Why was it said that the mind that ceases from the remembrance of God is taken over by the demon of fornication and the demon of wrath? Why did Palladius[21] ask: 'How can the human mind be constantly with God?' and was answered by Diocles: 'Any action or learning that preoccupies the soul for fear of God then its mind is with God'. What did he mean by action and learning?"

The Exegete replied: "Apart from prayer without feebleness and distraction, the learning that is conducted for fear of God is to remember God's promises and read his scriptures. The act undertaken for fear of God is to carry out his commandments and what leads to the fulfillment of his demands. It is as if [Diocles] had said to him: 'If you cannot attach your thought constantly to the remembrance of God, reflection on his divinity, might, wisdom, excellence of his mercy, his love and glory, and if you cannot pray without feebleness and distraction due to disruptions, weakness of the mind, or struggling with demons which is hard to

---

[19] These are in fact the words of the blessed Macarius: see E. A. Wallis Budge, *The Paradise*, vol. II, p. 287.

[20] The Scetis Valley (i.e., valley of the ascetics), also known as Wadi al-Natrun, is located in northwestern Egypt where several monasteries have existed since the third century. The Scetis Desert is the desert around the Scetis Valley, and was a popular retreat for many Christian monks and hermits pursuing solitary life away from their monasteries and Egyptian society.

[21] Palladius of Galatia (born c. 363) is the author of the *Lausiac History*.

carry out – and a virtuous act – then slow down your thought and start slowly by remembering God's promises. Bring yourself to rest, for when your [thought] is rested and a bad idea stirs in it, raise it [your thought] to the remembrance of God. The prayer without feebleness and distraction is achieved similar to those who pray with their body. When they tire of standing and reciting, they rest their bodies by sitting down and they enlighten their minds with reading. When they are rested, they go back to perform the prayer while standing. The mind is with God when it is thinking of God, his commandments and what fulfills his will. But if it thinks of sinful ailments or worldly things that it does not [really] need, then it is with the devil'."

The Brothers asked: "Why do [some] people not have the divine light in their hearts until their hearts have been purified through prolonged [good] works and struggles [with the devil], whereas others receive the light of grace even before they withdraw from the world to the desert, like the light that shone in the heart of Abraham on the seventh day of his marriage and he left his bride and withdrew from the world?"[22]

The Exegete replied: "The Fathers have said that the light has categories; each category [is given] to a person in accordance with his progress in his intention and resolution. Grace is kindled in the person's heart out of love of God, so he hates the glory of this world and comes without any expectation to this work. At the beginning, grace gives him the love of works, facilitates for him adversities, and does not allow the struggles of the demons to exceed his capacity. Only after extensive labor and immense humility is his heart cleansed and he deserves to see Christ in the likeness of light. As he progresses towards encountering our Lord through works and struggles, likewise our Lord comes to encounter him in the form of light until they are united. If he is firmly fixed in the Lord through his love, the Lord is firmly fixed in him through

[22] This is a possible reference to a similar account concerning blessed Ammon. Cf. E. A. Wallis Budge, *The Paradise*, vol. I, p. 377.

His light, as the Lord has said,[23] and the Prophet [David] too: 'My soul thirsts for you, O living God. When shall you come to behold your face?'[24] He also said: 'I walk in your way without transgression, so when shall you come to me?'[25] Some walk fast in straight paths and others walk slowly in corrupt paths. Contemplate the words of the Prophet: 'All your waves and your gales have gone over me',[26] 'you made me cross in water and fire and brought me out to rest'.[27] But the solitaries who deserve [to receive] the light before they withdraw from this world, if they return to live among the brothers, they darken in myriad trials. Through the effort of many works, they earn the purity of the heart and glow with the divine light during prayer, as the Fathers said."

The Brothers asked: "Why did the Apostle Paul say: 'Whoever aspires to the office of bishop aspires to a noble task?'[28] [Why did] the blessed commentator[29] counsel his friend in the book of priesthood and ask him to attain the rank of priesthood? Why did saint Paulinus, Bishop of Antioch,[30] when he realized the many ruptures after fifteen days of assuming his see in the city, pray to God who told him in a vision [to] leave?"

The Exegete replied: "There is nothing more loved and esteemed by our Lord than the purity of the righteous. Because of it, he granted his gifts of priesthood and others. The apostle [Paul] – when he saw that the least in competence in his knowledge and stewardship would seek priestly leadership for the love of leadership and vainglory, but he might be turned down because of

---

[23] See Psalms 89:2: "Forever I will keep my steadfast love for him, and my covenant with him will stand firm."

[24] See Psalms 42:2.

[25] See Psalms 101:2.

[26] See Psalms 42:7.

[27] This is a likely reference to 2 Samuel 22:17–20 or Psalms 66:12.

[28] See Paul's letter 1 Timothy 3:1.

[29] This is a probable reference to Theodore of Mopsuestia (d. 428) known to have written a work on priesthood.

[30] This is a probable reference to Paulinus (d. 388) who was a claimant to the See of Antioch from 362–388.

this, whereas whoever has virtuous knowledge and righteous work avoids leadership due to his modesty and preference for stillness – feared that the teaching of Christianity would be impaired or harmed through the lack of correct instruction and worthy stewardship. He said this thing but did not compel anybody; rather he left it to their desire after he set down the conditions of the episcopacy. It is therefore desirable that whoever seeks a position of leadership – be it spiritual, episcopal, priestly, or an abbotship – does not seek it for leadership's sake and its power. It is also desirable that only he who has moral competence and expertise in the Holy Scriptures seek it. For then, he will be deserving of his trusteeship and successful in his stewardship. He will also have virtues that benefit those who take him as a guide and follow his leadership, such as love, forgiveness, modesty, solace, discernment and knowledge. As for the blessed commentator, he asked his friend to attain the rank of priesthood for five reasons. The first reason was because he had accepted the rank of priesthood. The second reason was because many of those who feared God have chosen him. The third reason was because of his virtuous work. The fourth reason was for his good leadership. The fifth reason was because of his great modesty and conviction, which made him evade taking up leadership. But when he was compelled to assume it, he constantly sought to distance himself from it. As for [Bishop] Paulinus, he was righteous, modest and sought stillness. When he realized that leadership would not win him anything due to constant worries and running affairs, he asked our Lord with tears and in agony to permit him to leave the leadership of priesthood and turn to what he was able to do and in which he could benefit. Our good Lord answered his supplication for two reasons. The first was for his benefit. The second was to deter the insolence of the inept and ignorant from seeking the leadership of priesthood, for they would realize that God's will for humans is that they should be where it is beneficial for them."

The Brothers asked: "The author[31] of the book *The Paradise* said about the blessed Eustathius that his body became dry as a result

[31] This is a reference to Enanisho.

of fasting, prayer and vigil, so much so that the sun could be seen through his ribs."[32]

The Exegete replied: "I have seen a saint who was strong and could walk, but his body was dry as a result of great asceticism, so much so that one thought he had no liver or spleen in his belly. His ribs could be seen under transparent skin. Because of this, Macarius said: 'As fire dries out moisture in wood and burns it, so too the fear of God. If it settles in a person, it dries his flesh and desiccates his bones'.[33] In *The Book of the Perfection of Disciplines* (*Kitāb al-Tadbīr al-Kāmil*),[34] having said that any account fails to relate their perfection, the blessed commentator said about the two solitary biological brothers who lived in Antioch that because of their prolonged asceticism and labor, their bodies weakened and waned so much so that if a person looked at them, he would think he was seeing shadows, not real humans. Also, Palladius said about the brother who lived in Jerusalem that he appeared as a shadow because of the economy of his labors.[35] We must believe what is recounted about the saints from those honest informants, even though they do not live in our own time."

With the assistance of God, the first part is complete.

It is stated in the original copy that the first forty questions are lost.

---

[32] E. A. Wallis Budge, *The Paradise*, vol. I, p. 186.

[33] E. A. Wallis Budge, *The Paradise*, vol. II, p. 224.

[34] *The Book of the Perfection of Disciplines* is a monastic work, extant today in only three other known fragments, written by Theodore of Mopsuestia whose works were translated from Greek into Syriac in Edessa in the first half of the fifth century and who enjoyed a great deal of authority in the Church of the East being quoted extensively by authors such as Dadishoᶜ. See F. Graffin, "Une page retrouvée de Théodore de Mopsueste", pp. 29–34 in *A Tribute to Arthur Vööbus: Studies in Early Christian Literature and Its Environment, Primarily in the Syrian East.* Edited by Fischer, Robert H.. Chicago, Illinois: The Lutheran School of Theology at Chicago, 1977.

[35] E. A. Wallis Budge, *The Paradise*, vol. I, p. 214.

From the second part.

The Brothers asked: "Explain to us the saying of Abba Macarius, the priest: 'I never gave the Eucharist to Mark the mourner. It was an angel who gave him the Eucharist from the altar. I only used to see the angel's hand giving him the Eucharist'."[36]

The Holy Man replied: "At the beginning, in the deserts of Egypt, it was the head of the monastery alone who conducted the mass until his death, as Palladius said: 'There were eight priests running the affairs of the Parnouj Monastery.[37] But as long as the first was alive, none of the others would assume the function of the priesthood or any of the hermits in the caves. One priest only conducted for them the service of the sacraments'.[38] In another place, there was a priest and a deacon serving an entire year. As for the priest Macarius, he conducted the mass alone, and he saw the angel's hand as a link between him and Mark, as one of the seraphs did when it took the burning coal from the altar and placed it in the mouth of the prophet Isaiah.[39] The angel did this because angels do not have authority to conduct the service of the Eucharist and communicate it to people. But because of Mark's great purity and humility, he was made an example for others. His life attested that he had reached in four virtues what no other had attained. Two of them were due to his will and effort: his purity in body and soul and his great humility. Two others were gifts from God: memorizing the Old and New Testaments by heart and knowing their true explanation, and taking the Eucharist from the angel's hand. This is the great Graeco-Egyptian Mark whose knowledge and way of life was not surpassed by any of the solitaries in Egypt. It was he who wrote the book against those who claimed that Melchizedek was the son of God. He is to be differentiated from Mark the Syrian whose original name was Malchus[40] and lived the

---

[36] E. A. Wallis Budge, *The Paradise*, vol. I, p. 197.

[37] Parnouj Monastery was the Coptic name of the large Monastery of Nitria, north of the Scetis Valley and southeast of Alexandria.

[38] E. A. Wallis Budge, *The Paradise*, vol. I, p. 100.

[39] See Isaiah 6:6–7.

[40] E. A. Wallis Budge, *The Paradise*, vol. I, p. 234.

remainder of his life in Syria, nor is he Mark the Less, the disciple of Sylvanus."[41]

The Brothers asked: "The book *The Garden*[42] states that when the priest of the Scetis Mountain went down to the monasteries that were around Alexandria he found the brothers gathered for the fortieth-day anniversary of the death of one and the third-day anniversary of the death of another?"

The Exegete replied: "Saint Antony had said to Eulogius and his leprous companion: 'Do not part company for both your deaths are near'. When the priest arrived to where they were, he found them (the monks) gathered for the fortieth-day anniversary of the death of Eulogius and the third-day anniversary of the leper."[43]

The Brothers asked: "It is written in the life of Abba Moses the Black that for some time he joined his band of companion robbers and did sinful things with them. A good thought came to him. How was the good thought capable of delivering him from bad habits, and from his companions and demons? If this was from the grace of God or from himself, how is it that it did not occur before, but only at that time?"[44]

The Exegete replied: "Every virtue that a human does, as our Lord said, is accomplished with God's help, such as His saying: 'You can do nothing',[45] meaning nothing good. Grace corresponds to exemplariness and aptitude. As when Paul's inclination was to the splendor of truth and he was apt in his effort to spread the truth, thus he was elected. Grace attracts people to virtue through three mediums: thought, education, and reading. Doing good deeds is accomplished through grace and a person's will. Before a person's thought leans towards good or evil, it [grace] neither assists him nor abandons him. Father Abraham, when his thought

---

[41] E. A. Wallis Budge, *The Paradise*, vol. I, p. 278.

[42] *The Paradise of the Desert Fathers* known in its Arabic version as *Bustān al-Ruhbān* or *The Garden of the Monks*.

[43] E. A. Wallis Budge, *The Paradise*, vol. I, p. 196.

[44] E. A. Wallis Budge, *The Paradise*, vol. I, p. 216.

[45] Meaning, "Without me you can do nothing." See John 15:5.

was drawn to sin, his pride rebelled and longed for truth. At that point grace illuminated his thought. Likewise with Abba Moses when his thought leaned [towards the good], grace then assisted him."

The Brothers asked: "Why did the saintly Fathers become accustomed all the time to pursuing virtue, and struggling with yearnings and the devil, yet Abba Isidore the priest said to Abba Moses: 'Do not obstinately dispute with demons for there is a limit even in our works of ascetic life'?"[46]

The Exegete replied: "This was because at the beginning he (Abba Moses) believed that only due to his excessive works and hardships will he gain the upper hand over the demons. When they discovered this, they increased in their struggles with him covertly and overtly. Abba Isidore wished to teach him humility and make him realize that hardships alone are insufficient without the grace of the Holy Spirit that is achieved through baptism and the Eucharist. It is similar to the sick in body. The doctor orders him to take medicine, and also instructs him not to sleep, move around, eat heavy food, and other conditions for taking the medicine. The cure is not achieved though by any of these conditions. Rather, it is achieved through the medicine. Similarly, the sick in spirit is not cured by his works, be it stillness, silence, fasting, vigils, honesty and humility. Rather he is cured and defeats the demons by the grace of the Holy Spirit. Whoever struggles with yearnings and demons must fulfill our Lord's commandments. He should not focus on the success of his work. The wanderer travels between monasteries to benefit [others] or derive benefit in terms of spiritual matters, and the hungry to receive bodily benefit."

The Brothers asked: "Why did the solitary Fathers stretch their hands in prayer and raise them to Heaven?"

The Exegete replied: "This is because the apostle Paul said: 'I desire that in every place men pray, lifting up their hands in purity without rage or bad thoughts'."[47]

---

[46] E. A. Wallis Budge, *The Paradise*, vol. I, p. 217.

[47] See Paul's letter 1 Timothy 2:8.

The Brothers asked: "Is it because of this that the commentator stated that lifting up hands implies lifting up thoughts to Heaven, to the Lord, with love and purity?"

The Exegete replied: "This is not said to the many, but rather only to the solitaries and perfect ones. They do not only lift up their thoughts, but also their eyes and hands. The many are incapable of lifting up their thoughts to God. It is easier for them to lift up their hands and eyes to Heaven. Everyone emulates the prophets and Christ, glory to him, and his apostles and saints. David said: 'I stretch out my hands to you',[48] 'let the lifting up of my hands be as an evening sacrifice',[49] and 'I lifted up my eyes to you, O Lord'.[50] You find Christ too lifting up his hands, eyes and thoughts.[51] Paul said: 'Seek the place above where Christ is seated'.[52] The Fathers lift up their hands and eyes to Heaven to help with lifting up their thoughts to God. Thus did Moses do when he fought the Amalekites.[53] It is also written that Abba Sisoes of Thebais used to stand in prayer and stretch out his hands. His mind would be carried off to our Lord for a long while. But if someone came, he would lower his hands [lest] his mind be carried off. He struggled greatly with this."[54]

The Brothers asked: "Why did the wanderers say to a brother: 'If you wish to become a wanderer like us, sit first in your cell and weep for your sins, then you will become like us'."[55]

The Exegete replied: "This is because whoever distances himself from the world cuts off the activity of yearnings while in solitude and ties his thought to God. He thus attains the rank of wanderers." **He added:** "The phantomlike angel cut open the belly

---

[48] See Psalms 143:6.

[49] See Psalms 141:2.

[50] See Psalms 141:8.

[51] See Luke 24:50, and John 11:41 and 17:1.

[52] See Paul's letter Colossians 3:1.

[53] See Exodus 17:11.

[54] E. A. Wallis Budge, *The Paradise*, vol. II, p. 25.

[55] Cf. E. A. Wallis Budge, *The Paradise*, vol. II, p. 290.

of the wanderer and showed him the pain of his liver, then returned him to his previous condition.[56] Similarly, the angels cut the testicles of Elijah, head of the nunnery, when he fought the desire [of fornication]."[57] **He also added:** "The strength of the demons' struggle with every person is in accordance with their work, labor, effort, way of life, and endurance. When someone asked if he could stay with him in the desert, Abba Apellen replied: 'You cannot endure the trials of the demons'. But when he prevailed upon him he received him and he lived in a cave beside him. The demons came to him at night. At first, they corrupted his thoughts, and finally they wanted to scare him. Apellen came to him and drew around the cave the sign of the cross. Only then could he live in it. Just as not all the apostles were given [the power] to exorcise all the demons, likewise, not all solitaries have the capacity to withstand the struggle with powerful and wicked demons. Only the humble and perfect are capable of this."[58]

The Brothers asked: "Why did the two brothers who lived three years in the Scetis Desert where Abba Macarius was never visit him or anyone else?"

The Exegete replied: "Because the older one was a perfect and humble worker. Had he visited him, he would have revealed his perfection and been glorified. As for the younger one, he was learning from the older one."[59]

The Brothers asked: "The stories concerning the life of Abba Bessarion attest that he lived in desolate places and mountains. One day he came to a monastery, sat at its door and said: 'Thieves robbed me at sea. The storms thundered and waves rose up against me. I have been deprived of the possessions of my house and shorn of my ancestors' wealth and glory'."[60]

---

[56] E. A. Wallis Budge, *The Paradise*, vol. I, p. 237.
[57] E. A. Wallis Budge, *The Paradise*, vol. I, p. 143.
[58] E. A. Wallis Budge, *The Paradise*, vol. II, p. 292.
[59] E. A. Wallis Budge, *The Paradise*, vol. II, p. 292.
[60] E. A. Wallis Budge, *The Paradise*, vol. I, p. 243.

The Exegete replied: "He meant by the sea the life of solitude, by storms the trials, by waves the yearnings, by thieves the demons, and by his ancestors the Father, the Son and the Holy Spirit, the One God, in whose form and likeness we were created, as he said in the Torah,[61] and as our Lord said in the Gospel: 'Be perfect like your heavenly Father, for he is perfect'.[62] By possessions of his house [he meant] the possessions of his soul which it had due to its predisposition and divine grace; its predisposition is what the Creator had planted in it: desire, will, and ability to know the truth and perform pious acts if it chose to. These are the things that the prophet had mentioned that a dignified person squanders out of ignorance of them and runs away with brainless beasts and becomes like them. As for what comes from grace, they are baptism and spiritual gifts. It is written: 'Faith without work is dead',[63] and 'He who does not have, even what he has is taken away from him'.[64] That is, he who has no work that befits faith, then faith is taken away from him in the sense that he would not benefit from it as one who does not have faith at all. As for his ancestors' wealth, [he meant] the virtues that make us resemble our heavenly Father, and make us inherit his kingdom through faith, hope, and love of God and people. Welfare, mercy, patience, purity, magnanimity, humility, knowledge, and spiritual prayer; these possessions are drowned by the seas of worldly desires, and suffocated by the concerns and preoccupations of the world. Vainglory steals them. When the blessed one became mindful that many of the solitaries lack these spiritual possessions, the law of brotherly love stirred in him. He began to weep and bewail them as though he was crying for his own self. As though he was miserable and his possessions had perished and what he had was stolen from his house. He would ask God to make them worthy of the fortune of his love and the possessions of his blessings."

The Brothers asked: "What are the nine virtues of that person?"

---

[61] See Genesis 5:1.

[62] See Matthew 5:48.

[63] See James 2:17 and 26.

[64] See Matthew 25:29.

The Exegete replied: "I believe they are: possessing very little, abstinence, fasting always till the evening, holding vigils, saying the seven hourly prayers day and night, reading the holy books between the prayers, gentleness, humility, and loving people. These virtues are acquired through great labor and enormous struggle. By them one defeats all yearnings. By possessing very little one defeats the love of silver. By abstinence one defeats gluttony. By fasting one defeats desire. By nightly vigils one defeats sleep. By prayers one defeats thoughts. By reading books one defeats foul speech and idle talk. By gentleness one defeats rage and anger. By humility one defeats vainglory and pride. By love of people one defeats hatred, jealousy, enmity and most evils. The tenth virtue, which even he who has the nine virtues is incapable of attaining, is exceeding continuously all bounds in loving our Lord. It is only acquired through inner prayer in the mind without feebleness or distraction, and through constantly exorcising the thoughts of yearnings and the tricks of demons from the first moment they occur in the heart. For this virtue is more perfect than all virtues and the strong and wicked demons often fight the solitaries so that they do not attain it or endure in it. For this reason too, the works that lead to it are the most laborious and difficult of all the virtues. This is why blessed Mark said that due to the opposition of demons to this work that he could not speedily remain in the love of Christ, which is attained by the unity of thought and exceeding all bounds [in loving] God.[65] Saint Evagrius said: 'If you defeat the frivolousness of thoughts and endure in remembrance of God, then you deserve perfection which is in the love of Christ and people, and by which you defeat all yearnings that attach primarily to the love of the self. Whoever possesses this perfection longs to leave this world, depart from this body, and proceed to the Lord who loved him. He will be in Paradise, the home of the pure and abode of the perfect, which is superior to yearnings, demons, struggles and defeats, and the place of repose from the concerns of virtue, until the appearance of Christ, eternally enjoying his glory'."[66]

---

[65] E. A. Wallis Budge, *The Paradise*, vol. II, p. 305.

[66] E. A. Wallis Budge, *The Paradise*, vol. II, pp. 294–295.

The Brothers asked: "Explain to us the way of life of that holy man who had baskets and small stones?"[67]

The Exegete replied: "It is the economy of the mind that leads the solitary to purity of the heart. His labor was that he placed a basket to his right and a basket to his left. Every good thought that occurred to him, he would place a stone in the one to his right, and every foul thought that occurred to him, he would place a stone in the one to his left. This was in addition to his assiduousness in carrying out his duties, prayer and labor. Because of this virtuous work, the demons were envious of him and would stir in his heart many evils. The holy man would refuse to eat if his good thoughts did not surpass the bad ones, and he would suffer in spirit and body. Not only does the soul suffer from the toils of the body due to its unity with it, but also the demons that fight it suffer even more. When Evagrius fought the demon of fornication, he took off his clothes and stood under the sky all night long. He exhausted the demon of fornication to such an extent that he fled from him.[68] The suffering of saints exhausts demons because the angels, by God's command, make them suffer. A demon once intended to separate two biological brothers. When the younger lit a lamp, the demon threw it down with the stand, and extinguished it. The [older] brother smote him [the younger] on his cheek. He [the younger] prostrated before him and said: 'My brother, be patient with me and I will light it'. When God saw the patience of the youth and his humility, he commanded the angel of that youth who tied that demon up in the cell and punished him until the next day. As restitution for one slap that this brother bore calmly from his brother due to the work of the demon, the angel fettered that demon and flogged him all night long."[69]

The Brothers asked: "Why do demons fear the works of solitaries, as the Fathers said: 'If you want that demons fear you, then reject desires'?"

---

[67] E. A. Wallis Budge, *The Paradise*, vol. II, p. 295.

[68] E. A. Wallis Budge, *The Paradise*, vol. II, p. 296.

[69] E. A. Wallis Budge, *The Paradise*, vol. II, p. 296.

The Exegete replied: "For three reasons. The first reason is that our Lord defeated the devil when he rejected the three yearnings that the devil employed to fight him – namely, desire, love of money and vainglory, which unite all types of yearnings – and because he endured the trial in the desert, and [for his] stillness, fasting and prayer. Those who follow his lead destroy the thoughts of sin and the Lord chases demons away from them. For demons do not only fear the cross of Christ, but also making its sign. They are not defeated and do not run away from the works of Christ alone, but also from those who follow his works. The second reason is that if the solitaries succumb to the tricks of demons through sinful thoughts and enjoy them their souls darken due to distance from God. They are saddened, humiliated, weakened and censured. But if they do not succumb to their tricks, cast off thoughts when they occur, and appeal to their Lord to aid them, the demons are disbanded and humiliated, and they depart. Likewise, the blessed Mark said: 'As whoever seeks to fornicate with someone else's wife is struck with fear and runs away when he hears the husband's voice, so too the demon is struck with fear and runs away when he hears us calling upon God'.[70] The third reason is because they attain proximity to God by obedience to God and love of Him. Demons thus keep at a distance from them. For the Lord had said to those who love him: 'I have given you power over all the forces of the enemy; and nothing will harm you'."[71]

The Brothers asked: "Why do demons flee sometimes at the mention of Christ's name and the sign of the cross, but at other times they do not?"

The Exegete replied: "They flee because of what was said earlier. As for why they do not flee at other times, do not fear a name, sign, or prayer but stand firm – they do not only cause fear, but also strike at the solitaries – that is because they have taken from the Lord power for their success. Saint Pachomius was once walking with Theodore at night. The devil appeared to them as an astounding phantom. They prayed for him to be driven away from

---

[70] E. A. Wallis Budge, *The Paradise*, vol. II, p. 300.

[71] See Luke 10:19.

them, but he boldly persisted and said to them: 'Do not exhaust yourselves with prayer in vain, for I was given power to tempt you'.[72] It is necessary that we do not stop making the sign of the cross, calling the name of Christ and praying if demons appear to us. If they leave, it is because of the Lord aiding us. But if they do not, it is because the Lord has released them for our ultimate success."

The Brothers asked: "Three demons came to Evagrius in the likeness of priests and disputed with him,[73] and angels came in the likeness of lay people[74] to the head of the Cells[75] for that [holy man] who had the baskets and stones. They all prostrated before the cross, kissed it and prayed. Was this true or not?"

The Exegete replied: "As for the angels, they prostrated, kissed and prayed in themselves and as forms, just as the souls and bodies of the perfect prostrate, pray and kiss. The demons, however, did so through their deceitful phantasms, because, unlike angels, demons do not have power to take on real forms." **He added:** "At first, youths work for the glory of people. But then grace shows them the eminence of God's glory, so that they reach the point of obedience and love of him alone. Evagrius said: 'If your disciple is defeated, cure him without anger. But if he is victorious, praise him, because praise increases the force of the brave'."

The abridgment of the second part is complete, thanks to God's favor towards me.

From the third part.

The Brothers asked: "The apostle Paul said: 'Love never falls'.[76] But a group reached the heights of the love of God and then fell?"

The Exegete replied: "Their arrogance was the reason for their fall."

---

[72] E. A. Wallis Budge, *The Paradise*, vol. I, p. 304.

[73] E. A. Wallis Budge, *The Paradise*, vol. I, p. 225.

[74] E. A. Wallis Budge, *The Paradise*, vol. I, p. 251.

[75] A location in the inner Nitrian desert.

[76] See Paul's letter 1 Corinthians 13:8.

They asked: "What is arrogance?"

He replied: "That a person considers himself righteous and better than sinners."

They asked: "How can the righteous and virtuous person consider himself a sinner and less than the deficient?"

He replied: "In many ways, such as to think that he cannot love God as God has loved him, nor be humble for God's sake as God has been humble for his sake, nor be humble and love God like the prophets and saints, nor fulfill his obedience and will. For it is written: 'God loved the world', meaning that the Father loved the sinners, 'so much so that he sent his only Son to die for their sake'.[77] The only Son became man and handed himself over to crucifixion and death on their behalf. The Holy Spirit hovers over them as a bird over its chicks and a mother over her children. It is also written that the Lord said: 'Learn from me for I am gentle and humble in heart'.[78] Another way is to think that possibly those he believes to be sinners are more righteous and humble than him, and that in those virtues where he considers himself more perfect than them he is actually less perfect but does not know it. Similarly, the Pharisee who invited our Master to a banquet and said: 'If this man were a true prophet, he would know what kind of woman she is and that she is a sinner'.[79] The Pharisee and others at that time thought that she was a sinner, but our Lord who knows everything and at all times saw that she was righteous. He said: 'Her many sins are forgiven because she has shown great love'.[80] Similarly, [the parable of] the other Pharisee who thought himself more righteous than the tax collector when they prayed, but the Lord said that the tax collector was more righteous than him.[81] Another way is to think concerning the person he believes himself to be more righteous and better than, that it is possible that their states have

[77] See John 3:16.

[78] See Matthew 11:29.

[79] See Luke 7:39.

[80] See Luke 7:47.

[81] See Luke 18:9–13.

been reversed, as in the states of Judas[82] and the thief on the right.[83] If you are righteous and wise, and you love God and are loved by him, remember that brother Solomon who was [righteous] in his youth, but then became in old age ignorant and a lover of pleasures. If you were a prophet, remember how that prophet lapsed and erred when that false prophet prevailed over him and fed him bread, and was then killed by lions.[84] If you were an apostle who exorcises demons and performs miracles, remember how Judas subsequently fell because of his love of silver and was called a demon and a son of perdition.[85] If you saw a murdering bandit, say: 'How would I know. He might be admitted to Paradise before me, like the thief on the right'. If you witness a sinful fornicator, say: 'How would I know. He might in the future love Christ and weep for his sins more than I do'. He who always thinks in this way never falls from the love of our Lord but when he tends towards pride he falls from on high." **The Holy Man also said:** "When the solitary possesses perfect humility, by denigrating himself at all times and in every act, he is released from struggling, whether at the beginning of the struggle, in the middle of it, or at the end of it, as Mark the mourner said. Abba Sisoes said: 'If the solitary attains humility, he attains perfection'."[86] **He added:** "In ranking the solitaries' way of life, they first become weary through bodily labors, then through the struggle with thoughts. After that, they acquire purity of heart. After that they experience the light of their mind, and then through its light they experience the light of Christ through the vision of the spirit. Some can see this light before they withdraw from this world which would be a guide for them to withdraw from the world to the monastery of the solitary. As for ranking the solitary's struggles with the devil, first [it occurs] in thoughts. After defeating bad

---

[82] Meaning his betrayal of Jesus: see for example Luke 22:48.

[83] Meaning the thief who was crucified on the right side of Jesus: see Luke 23:40–43.

[84] See 1 Kings 13:20–25.

[85] Meaning the thirty silver coins that Judas received for betraying Jesus: see Matthew 26:14–15.

[86] E. A. Wallis Budge, *The Paradise*, vol. II, p. 118.

thoughts, [it occurs] in actual vision through fright and then blows. But in some cases, demons might at first fight a solitary through fright and blows. This occurs to those who experience many sins in the world, such as Abba Moses the Black. The demons might boldly fight him visibly through fright and blows for two reasons. One reason is because he did not know at first about the struggle with thoughts, and the other reason is because God's aid had abandoned him. This was in order for the intensity of his repentance, endurance, and effort to transpire."

The Brothers asked: "What does the saying of Abba Apollo mean: 'If the snake's head is crushed, all its body is dead'?"[87]

The Exegete replied: "He meant by 'the snake's head' the first thought of any sin that is stirred in the solitary's heart by the devil. He meant by 'its body' the many thoughts of the solitary that tolerate that deceiving [first] thought and provoke committing a sin."

The Brothers asked: "Why did that brother ask Abba Apollo to pray to God to grant him grace, and when he prayed for him, he was given the gift of humility, denigration [of one's self] and love?"[88]

The Exegete replied: "That brother had committed many efforts for these virtues, but the Lord did not wish to grant them to him without him asking God for them through grace, because if he takes them from God through grace, he would be humbled through them. For this reason our Lord wished that the brothers attain their perfection through the counsel of the Fathers and their prayers for them."

The Brothers asked: "Why was the demon of pride found on the shoulders of Abba Apollo despite his labors, perfection, and God choosing him and sending him to save many?"[89]

---

[87] E. A. Wallis Budge, *The Paradise*, vol. I, p. 342.
[88] E. A. Wallis Budge, *The Paradise*, vol. I, p. 348.
[89] E. A. Wallis Budge, *The Paradise*, vol. I, p. 341.

The Exegete replied: "The Fathers said that after defeating all the demons and yearnings, the struggle with pride and vainglory remains with the perfect ones until death, from God, so that they may persevere in their efforts and perfection. When God said to him: 'Go to the desert near the delta and teach a people so that they may glorify me and do good works'. Abba Apollo said: 'O Lord, free me from pride so that I do not become arrogant with the brothers and lose all the good?' God ordered him to stretch his hand to his neck, throw down what he finds on his shoulder, and bury it in the sand. He found a small Ethiopian screaming 'I am the demon of pride' and buried him in the sand. The Fathers say that the yearning which a person becomes a slave of, a demon sits on the organ through which he commits the act. So you will find the demon of fornication sitting on the testicles of he who is a slave of the yearning of fornication. Whoever is a slave to rage, the demon of rage sits on his heart. Whoever complains and says foul words a demon sits on his tongue. Whoever becomes somnolent while praying a demon sits on his eyes and the thief sits on his right."

The Brothers asked: "Why did the blessed man censure the solitaries who wore silk and grew their hair, even though many have been saved by doing this?"[90]

The Exegete replied: "He did not censure the perfect ones, but only those who lacked the concealed virtues who behaved in this manner vaingloriously."

The Brothers asked: "Why were there many solitaries at the outset of the preaching of Christianity, especially in Egypt, but now there are a few?"

The Exegete replied: "Because the Lord sent his apostles and commanded them to make disciples of people through faith, and teach them the way of perfection. He granted them many great signs to fulfill this. Hence, the full effects of his power were revealed to those who believed and labored. Just as the number of those who believed was in the thousands and more, in all towns and regions, so too those who labored, as is written in the lives of

---

[90] E. A. Wallis Budge, *The Paradise*, vol. I, p. 351.

the monks: Abba Hor led a thousand solitaries,[91] and Isidore a thousand. Abba Ammon led three thousand solitaries, and Pachomius three thousand. Abba Serapion had ten thousand. The bishop of the great city of Bahnasa[92] said that in his see, under his leadership, there were ten thousand solitaries and twenty thousand nuns. Also, at the beginning of the preaching of Christianity, people took the apostles as models because Christ was a solitary and said: 'learn from me',[93] 'whoever does not take up his cross and follow me is not worthy of me',[94] and 'if you wish to be perfect, give all your possessions to the poor and follow me'.[95] The apostle Paul used to say: 'Imitate me, just as I also imitate Christ',[96] 'I wish that all people were like me in purity',[97] and 'It is well for a man not to touch a woman',[98] because he who has a wife endeavors to please her, but he who does not have one endeavors to please God, his Lord. Those who take as models the very most virtuous whom they see who have made a great impact through grace are better than those who imitate by listening to old stories."

The Brothers asked: "Why did some of the saintly Fathers ask God [to reveal to them] the saint they resemble, and he used to send them to lay people inferior to them, such as dispatching Antony to the shoemaker, Macarius to the two women,[99] Paphnutius to the singer thief,[100] and Laban to the shepherd?"

The Exegete replied: "As for their asking God, that is because they have liberty with him, like the liberty John son of Zebedee had with our Lord when he placed his head on his chest and asked him

---

[91] E. A. Wallis Budge, *The Paradise*, vol. I, p. 334.

[92] Coptic: *Pemdje*.

[93] See Matthew 11:29.

[94] See Matthew 10:38.

[95] See Matthew 19:21.

[96] See Paul's letter 1 Corinthians 11:1.

[97] See Paul's letter 1 Corinthians 7:7.

[98] See Paul's letter 1 Corinthians 7:1.

[99] E. A. Wallis Budge, *The Paradise*, vol. II, p. 150.

[100] E. A. Wallis Budge, *The Paradise*, vol. I, p. 358.

about the one who would betray him.[101] They also meant by asking, namely to know which saint they resemble, that their fear be removed, their trust and hope be strengthened and fervor in the love of our Lord increased. As for God sending them to lay people below them in perfection, that is in order to consolidate their humility, and recompense those lay people for the labor of their righteousness and to strengthen their hope, and to make others emulate them when they realize that they would be like the upright solitaries if they exert themselves in good works."

The Brothers asked: "Evagrius used to counsel the brothers not to quench their thirst with water?"[102]

The Exegete replied: "Because our Lord said: 'When the unclean spirit has gone out of a person, it wanders through waterless places seeking rest, but finds none. Then it returns to that person'.[103] The Fathers also used to say: 'Whoever does not minimize his food, especially drinking water, cannot defeat the spirit of fornication or reach perfect chastity'. There is nothing like thirst to dry out the bodily organs, inhibit sexual discharge at night, ejaculation and flow, and calm dirty thoughts during the day. Even he who fasts and minimizes his food will not settle if he drinks too much water, because drinking too much water fills the stomach and the bodily organs with moisture. Thus, the devil finds a way to deceive him through thoughts during the day and dreams at night. Evagrius said: 'If you seek purity, reduce your food and minimize drinking water, then the purity of the heart will shine. Your brain will also shine like a star that you see during your prayer'."[104]

The abridgment of the third part is complete: a section from Hieronymus who wrote down the questions and a section from Palladius because he wrote during the time of

[101] John 13:25.

[102] E. A. Wallis Budge, *The Paradise*, vol. II, p. 316.

[103] See Matthew 12:42–44, and Luke 11:23–25.

[104] E. A. Wallis Budge, *The Paradise*, vol. II, p. 317.

Theodosius the Great.[105] Palladius also wrote during the time of his son Arcadius.[106] Thanks and gratitude to God.

The fourth and last part of the stories of the solitaries written in the book *The Paradise*, from the last part written by Palladius.

The Brothers asked: We begin, with the help of our Lord, to ask in sequence. Why did the saintly Fathers teach us above all else to leave the world and live in a monastery, and then leave communal life and dwell in solitude in a cave?"

The Exegete replied: "Because these are the foundations upon which one builds and from which one proceeds to the high palace of the good. In communal life, they begin by loving people. But in solitude, they become perfect in the love of our Lord. As the Lord and the apostle [Paul] said: 'Love is the fulfilling of the law'.[107] At first, the person leaves the world and ceases to love it because, as it is written, the love of the world is contrary to the love of God.[108] Whoever does not hate his father, mother, wife, children and himself – meaning his sexuality, habits and desires – cannot fulfill the love of God and become a disciple of Christ. True love cannot be accomplished in the world because it is resisted by natural love which is love of sex, habitual love which is love of what is familiar, or egoistic love which is love of the sensual. But after his departure from the world with his heart and entire body, he enters the monastery, the communion of brotherhood, to carry out with them Christ's commandments: fasting, prayer, nightly vigils, reading, and other works by which the brother fulfills the love of brotherhood, such as tending to the sick and serving the saints, welcoming strangers, and being obedient to the holy men and heads. Also, at the beginning of his departure from the world, he cannot struggle, given how numerous the thoughts of the demons are. Thus, in the

---

105 Roman Emperor from 379 to 395.

106 Byzantine Emperor from 395 to 408.

107 See Paul's letter Romans 13:10. See also Luke 10:26–28 and James 2:8.

108 See 1 John 2:15.

community of brotherhood the person is trained in the way, starting with visible struggles and partial weariness. After this training, the grace of solitude in the cell occupies him so that he attains the prospect of fulfilling all the higher commandments by which the perfect love which belongs to God is shaped. This is the utmost goodness and the highest palace of virtue. This mentioned labor involves the remembrance of God, his graces, promises, commandments and punishments, continuous contemplation of him and conversation with him through prayer without feebleness and distraction, abhorrence of yearnings and cutting off foul thoughts from the moment they occur in the heart. Through this labor the solitary acquires the purity of the heart, for Christ to dwell in it, who said: 'I and my Father will come and make our home in it'.[109] At that time, he sees in himself the light of his mind and becomes worthy to witness the light of the Lord of Glory, who is worshipped."

The Brothers asked: "How long does the brother have to stay in the monastery [before] entering in the solitary cell?"

The Exegete replied: "It depends on his form, level, fitness of his body, and vigor of his labor under the authority and knowledge of the learned and experienced holy Fathers. The Holy Synod established that the brothers who possess perfect form, are trained in knowledge and vigorous labors, love fervently, are disciplined through humility, and yet despite all this love the stillness of the cell, it is enough for them to have three years of training in the pure works by which attainable love is shaped. After that, they must enter stillness which is the smelting furnace, where they mold the invisible works through which love in God is perfected. As for those who come to the monastery in their youth and lacking in training, knowledge, vigor and energy of love, it is good for them to stay eight, nine or ten years in the community. Then they will be worthy of stillness in the cell. Blessed Mark said about his subordinates: 'This is what the law means by saying: "Six days shall work be done, but the seventh is rest."'[110] Namely, that it is

[109] See John 14:23.

[110] See Exodus 31:15.

necessary to work in the community for six years, and in the seventh, stillness and rest from pure labor is achieved."

The Brothers asked: "What are the means by which grace calls the brothers to monastic life?"

The Exegete replied: "By several means. Among them is the warning of the conscience, just as Moses the Black's conscience warned him and he repented. Also included among them is recitation, as Antony and Simeon the Stylite who upon hearing the reading of the Gospel in church departed from the world. Included among them too is hearing the words of the sermon, just as Abba Serapion and others who by their teachings brought back many bandits and fornicators. Included among them as well are the fears and struggles brought by the hands of angels, as with Abba Evagrius. And included among them is God's call, just as he called Arsenius."[111]

The Brothers asked: "Why did the book *The Paradise* relate the story of Arsenius at the beginning of the book before the holy men's teachings about departing from the world to the monastery and then the monk's leaving the community to the stillness of the cell?"

The Exegete replied: "Because he was called by God to the monastery and from the monastery to the cell.[112] That is why they began with the story of his life and organized their teachings around it. His story is as follows. In the world he was tormented by many afflictions, so he cried out to God from the pain of the heart, saying: 'O Lord, direct me how to live'. He heard God's voice say to him: 'Arseni, escape from the world, meaning people, and you will live'. When he came to the community, he was borne down by his senses and the distraction of his thoughts. God said to him: 'Escape, live in silence and live in stillness'. Thus, when he abhorred evil and loved good, God became his teacher, first in monastic life and finally in solitary life."

---

[111] E. A. Wallis Budge, *The Paradise*, vol. II, p. 317.

[112] E. A. Wallis Budge, *The Paradise*, vol. II, p. 318.

The Brothers asked: "Explain to us the meaning of the two calls."[113]

The Exegete replied: "The first call is 'escape and you will live'. It means that if you wish to be saved from the death of breaking the commandment, leave your possessions, family and country and live as a stranger in the desert among those who cultivate my commandments, and you will live, as it is written: 'I loved your commandments so make me live by your grace'.[114] As for his saying in the second call 'escape', that is, from the community, and his saying 'live in silence and live in stillness', that is, do not allow many to come in to you, to converse with you and preoccupy you, because seeing and hearing a great deal of talk causes mental distraction. What is meant is silencing the tongue from conversing with people in their presence, and the stillness of the mind from conversing with them in their absence. For one might think about beautiful women and men with the desire of fornication. Accordingly, he would converse with them in his mind with yearning. He might also think about other things and become angry in his heart with some people and accuse them, he might seek through delusional thoughts honor and glorification from others, or think about managing wealth and leadership. For this reason when they asked saint Macarius: 'How must the novice live in the stillness of his cell?' He replied: 'He should not remember any person at all. He will not gain anything if he does not restrain his inner senses from conversing with people and recollect his thoughts in stillness'."[115]

The Brothers inquired: "It is written that a brother said to Arsenius: 'My father, my thoughts disturb me and tell me: "You cannot fast and work, so leave your cell and serve the weak, which is the greatest commandment"'. He said to him: 'Eat, drink, sleep, do no work, and from your cell do not exit'. After sitting for three days, he became weary of idleness, so he took some palm leaves and split them. The following day, he soaked them and started

---

[113] E. A. Wallis Budge, *The Paradise*, vol. II, p. 318.

[114] See Psalms 119:47 and 119:64.

[115] E. A. Wallis Budge, *The Paradise*, vol. II, p. 319.

weaving them. When he became hungry, he said: 'I will eat when I am done'. When he finished, he said: 'I will read a little and then eat without a worry'. In this way, he progressed little by little with God's help until he reached his first rank and acquired power over thoughts.[116] Thus is written in the last part of the teachings of the holy men: 'Stillness in the Cell'. It is also written in the teachings of the holy men: 'Love and Mercy'. A brother asked a holy man saying: '[There were] two brothers, one was living in the stillness of his cell, fasting six days at a time and laboring a great deal, whereas the other served the place [the sick][117] a lot. Whose labor is more acceptable before God?' He answered: 'If that one who fasted would hang by his eyelids he would not equal before God the one who served'."[118]

The Brothers asked: "Do the sayings of the Fathers contradict each other, if not what is the explanation?"

The Exegete replied: "The sayings of the Fathers are not contradictory. Rather, they counsel each person by what they know, through guidance and experience, to be more proper and suitable for him. They agreed to treat as equal he who is in a state of good stillness, the thankful sick, and he who serves with energy and joy. As for the sick, or those in stillness, or in the monastery, if a demon knows this, he becomes envious of them and comes up with tricks to deprive each one of the three from his virtue through the desire of the virtue of the other. He would make stillness desirable and service hard for those who serve the solitaries living in stillness, but they themselves have no ability to live in stillness, thus he makes them lose both virtues. He would make living in stillness hard and service desirable for those living in stillness but have no ability to serve, thus he deprives them of gaining both. In this way, the sick become destitute after fasting, praying, and serving, and become emaciated from patience and thankfulness. They are deprived of the reward of sickness and cannot do good works. He makes each one of the three prefer to move to do the

---

116 E. A. Wallis Budge, *The Paradise*, vol. II, pp. 4–5.

117 Cf. E. A. Wallis Budge, *The Paradise*, vol. II, p. 94.

118 E. A. Wallis Budge, *The Paradise*, vol. II, pp. 93–94.

other's work, not because of its virtue, but rather to seek respite from the labor of his [original] work and accepting the defeat of his effort. Because the Fathers know the causes of sicknesses due to the grace of their guidance and skilled experience, they prescribe for each one the remedy that is proper for him. Abba Arsenius knew that that brother is vigorous in the solitary life of stillness and that the devil fought him with boredom and by cooling his fervor in order to make him leave his cell. [He knew] that if he endured in his cell a short time, boredom would leave him and the fervor of his activity would return, but if he leaves his cell, he would be deprived of his life of stillness and have no ability to endure in the service of the sick, thus he would lose both virtues. He [Arsenius] told him to do what was mentioned above. As for the brother who asked the holy man about the two brothers, he was granted by God the gift of serving the sick and the weak holy men. The devil intended to deprive him of his crown, thus he made the life of stillness [appear] beautiful to him in order to deprive him of what he had and seek what he cannot attain, [knowing] that he could not return to his previous situation. The holy man advised him to do what is more advantageous for him." **He also said:** "Whoever lives in the world cannot see all his sins because his heart is preoccupied with the world and its concerns, even if he shows compassion toward the needy and is a peacemaker between enemies. For the Lord has given blessedness to those too when He said: 'Blessed are the compassionate',[119] and 'the peacemakers'.[120] As for whoever leaves the world, enters the cell after his training in the monastery and devotes himself to [spiritual] battle, he thinks about his sins, sees his deficiencies, and recognizes his yearnings. If he abhors them, drives away his foul thoughts, asks for forgiveness and aid, persists in secret prayer, then his heart would be purified and he would become like an adorned mirror. He would see the light of our Lord Jesus Christ who said: 'Blessed are the pure in heart for they will see God'."[121]

---

[119] See Matthew 5:7.

[120] See Matthew 5:9.

[121] See Matthew 5:8.

The Brothers asked: "What is the meaning of Abba Sisoes' saying to Abba Ammon: 'The freedom of my thoughts is sufficient for me'?"[122]

The Exegete replied: "Abba Sisoes spent his entire life living in a remote desert. After he became old and weak, the Fathers brought him to the monastery of the brothers. They would come to him seeking some profitable counsel and helpful prayer. However, he was not used to making conversation, and his thoughts became unfocused due to his recollection of conversations with the brothers and worrying about matters. Abba Ammon saw that he was sad for having come from the desert and said to him: 'You should not be sad about living among the brothers. Your body has become weak and you cannot labor any more as you did in the desert'. He answered him with dread, saying: 'The freedom of my thoughts in the desert was enough for me. This is not impeded by old age or by sickness such that you think it is easy to attain purity of the mind, which is acquired in the life of stillness and conversation with God, through constant and concentrated prayer, remembrance of Christ and gazing upon him, and through exultation of the soul in loving him and his commandments, desiring his benefits and glory, meditation upon his greatness, and admiration of his humility. These and matters like them are not impeded by old age or weakness. They are, however, destroyed by constant mingling with people and being preoccupied with matters other than them'."[123]

---

[122] E. A. Wallis Budge, *The Paradise*, vol. II, p. 320.
[123] E. A. Wallis Budge, *The Paradise*, vol. II, pp. 320–321.

INTRODUCTION TO SELECTIONS FROM THE GEʿEZ *FILEKSEYUS*

Questions and Answers of the Egyptian Monks Ethiopian Monastic Manuscript Library No. 1387 (ff. 1a–81b)

DR ROBERT KITCHEN

INTRODUCTION

EMML 1387: The Text

What follows is the translation of a selection of logia from a single manuscript, Ethiopian Manuscript Microfilm Library No. 1387 (ff. 1a–81b), Institute of Ethiopian Studies, Addis Ababa, Ethiopia (18th century), and available on microfilm at the Hill Museum & Manuscript Library, St. John's University, Collegeville, Minnesota. The specific Geʿez text is described as *Questions and Answers from the Egyptian Monks by Philoxenos of Mabbug.* Being a lengthy text of great complexity and with a number of manuscripts in various formats, a critical edition is not possible at this time. Therefore, a number of the question and answer units have been selected as representative of the whole work, but certainly not with the intention of being an epitome of the work.

Aware that Philoxenos of Mabbug, the 6th century anti-Chalcedonian bishop and controversialist, was revered in the Ethiopian Church, I traveled to the Hill Museum and Manuscript Library (HMML), St. John's University, Collegeville, Minnesota, and consulted the catalogues of the Ethiopian Manuscript

Microfilm Library (EMML) collection of microfilms. I discovered a number of texts attributed to Filekseyus[1] or Philoxenos, particularly about a dozen long texts with the identifier "Philoxenos of Mabbug." The Syrian Philoxenos must have known the Desert Fathers, but his writings make little or no reference to these classical stories, so I concluded this was just another pseudonymous text.

A seminar conducted by Sebastian Brock introduced me to Dadisho Qaṭraya and his *Commentary on the Paradise of the Fathers*, and referred to the article by Nicholas Sims-Williams.[2] I was astonished to find one of the sample question/answer units addressed not to an anonymous *sābā* or elder, but to Philoxenos. Sims-Williams noted that there were Geʿez translations, so connections between the two versions became clear. Going back to HMML, I saw that the Geʿez manuscripts were indeed translations from the Syriac via Christian Arabic.

After-Life of Dadisho's Commentary: The Book of the Three Monks

On the surface, Dadisho's work appears to be of a secondary level – a commentary directly building upon previous authors' works, including Ananisho, the compiler of the *Paradise of the Fathers*,[3] and

[1] Regarding the Geʿez spelling of Philoxenos, cf. Witold Witakowski, "Filekseyus, the Ethiopic Version of the Syriac Dadisho Qatraya's Commentary on the Paradise of the Fathers" in *Rocznik Orientalistyczny* 49.1 (2006) 281–296. "The ending *-yus*, instead of the supposed *(Fiḥksə)-nus* comes from the error, or rather deficiency, of Arabic writing at this time seldom making use of diacritical points. When deprived of their respective diacritical points, Arabic letters *Ya* and *Nun* look the same, and the Ethiopic translator had no clue as to which was the right pronunciation" (285).

[2] Nicholas Sims-Williams, "Dādišoʿ Qatrāyā's Commentary on the *Paradise of the Fathers*," *Analecta Bollandiana* 112 (1994) 33–64.

[3] Budge, Ernest A. Wallis, *The Paradise or Garden of the Holy Fathers, Being Histories of the Anchorites, Recluses, Monks, Coenobites, and Ascetic Fathers of the Deserts of Egypt between A.D. CCL and A.D. CCCC circiter*. London: Chatto & Windus, 1907.

of course, the various collections of desert father stories and anecdotes included in that work. Nevertheless, this is more than "just a commentary." Following the late 13th century renaissance in Ethiopia, the *Filekseyus* became part of the large *The Book of the Three Monks*, the other two 'monks' being Isaac of Nineveh and John Saba of Dalyatha. This book became the ascetical manual for novice monks for centuries in the Ethiopian Church. Syriac students will immediately notice that all three original authors were from the Church of the East. It has been suggested that Philoxenos was substituted to provide an orthodox miaphysite or anti-Chalcedonian name to a text otherwise very useful.[4] Yet there is no such veil for Isaac of Nineveh (another Beth Qaṭraye author) or for John of Dalyatha, and no one seemed to mind or even mention the issue of confessional tradition. All three texts were written from a monastic setting, and the content addresses the practical theology involved in forming an ascetical discipline of prayer and work in the search for the presence of God while living in a community.

Texts at HMML

This manuscript begins (ff. 1a–81a) with one of the longest versions of the *Filekseyus*, 245 numbered questions by Egyptian monks. The description of the manuscript notes that this text is understood to have been translated initially by Abuna Abba Sälama Matargwem (1348–1388 A.D.) Abuna Sälama was the Coptic patriarch of the Ethiopian Church who unlike some patriarchs took his role seriously, learned Geʿez and translated a number of important works from Arabic into the Ethiopian language. He was given the title "the Interpreter" or "*Matargwem*" to whom most of the monks' questions are directed. He is not to be confused with the other "Blessed Interpreter" or Theodore of Mopsuestia, the Biblical exegete of the Church of the East, who is also referred to as *Matargwem*.

---

[4] Phillips, David, "The Syriac Commentary of Dadishoʿ Qatraya on the Paradise of the Fathers: Towards a Critical Edition," *Bulletin de l'Académie Belge pour l'Etude des Langues Anciennes et Orientales* 1 (2012): 1–23.

The *Filekseyus* of EMML 1387 has copies of varying lengths in the EMML/HMML collections, as well as in the British Library and other libraries.[5] For example, another version of the *Filekseyus* (112a–203b) concludes EMML 1836. This latter *Filekseyus* is divided into 13 divisions, numbers 5–13 are thematically organized, on the model of the Systematic versions of the *Apophthegmata Patrum.*

Oral History and Memory in the Compilation of the Text and Manuscript

The creation of a critical edition for the Filekseyus, for example, will be time-consuming and challenging because of the variations in numbering the question/answer units and among other things, spelling.

Getatchew Haile, the principal cataloguer of the Ethiopian collection at HMML, showed me a large printed volume published in recent years in Addis Ababa of *The Book of the Three Monks* with Amharic commentary. I asked from which manuscripts were these texts transcribed. Dr. Haile shook his head and said, "There were no manuscripts; it was transcribed from memory." The scribe was not utilizing a printed copy, but writing down the questions and answers from memory. This can be readily seen in the spelling of EMML 1387 that operates from a phonetic, not orthographic basis. The scribe is most likely reciting to himself the text and recording it, but Geʿez has a number of pairs of letters with distinct Semitic roots, but over time have lost their phonetic distinction. So the scribe writes what he hears himself reciting and on the same page will often spell the same word in several different ways, yet the words all are pronounced homophonically.

Another piece of evidence for this transcription from memory is the frequent occurrence of a lengthy answer by Dadisho or by an

---

[5] Manuscripts of the *Filekseyus* in HMML are: EMML 15, 17th or 18th century, f. 183r–247v; EMML 418, 18th or early 19th century, f. 3r–80v; EMML 1387, 18th century, f. 1r–81r; EMML 1836, 17th century, f. 112r–203v; EMML 1848, 20th century (1951/52), f. 2r–112r; EMML 2100, 17th century, f. 163r–223r; EMML 2127, 19th–20th century, f. 10r–162v; EMML 2837, 17th or 18th century, f. 4r–81v.

elder/*sābā* in which the Syriac text contains a complex of ideas and recollection of stories from the *Paradise*. The Ethiopic edition omits some of these sections and rearranges the order of the elements of the answer, not always in a manner that flows coherently with the original narrative. This needs further analysis and comparison with the Christian Arabic versions and could be the result of scribal variants, but just as likely it is the Ethiopian scribe transcribing what he remembers and then remembers a story or apophthegm he had forgotten and writes it down out of the original order. Typically, the first and last sentences or statement function as the theme and conclusion for the Ethiopic version of what is a lengthy, anecdote-filled Syriac question/answer unit – pithy propositions easier to remember.

The *Filekseyus* of EMML 1387 follows the Syriac version in order and in structure with two books or parts of uneven length. The first part has 53 question/answer units; the second part has 192 units. Whereas the translator of the *Filekseyus* follows the trajectory of the DQC this is not a full and complete version, although much larger than a translation of the shorter Epitome version of DQC. The DQC in David Philip's critical edition has 399 question/answer units, divided between 108 for the first part and 291 for the second part, so that the editor/translator of *Filekseyus* made a number of choices regarding which units to include or omit, and within a question/answer unit there is a great deal of omission of details, events and names from the Syriac, as well as attempts to summarize and abbreviate the original narrative. A single Geʿez unit's answer sometimes includes the answers of several units of DQC, and a few units in the second part of the *Filekseyus* are taken from the first part of DQC. The translator/editor generally follows the sequence of DQC with a few exceptions, but there is a lengthy section in which *Filekseyus* selects every second question/answer of DQC.

A number of apophthegmata concern a famous abba traveling with another well-known abba in the Syriac version, but in the Geʿez version the second name is often not remembered and reduced to "a companion" at best. Periodically dispersed throughout the DQC is the formulaic question of the monks, "How many people were called Macarius?" The elder responds with a summary description of the various abbas with the same name. One assumes that these trivia questions are intended as mnemonic devices for the novices, but the *Filekseyus* dispenses with all of these questions. If the medium is the message, the editor does not need to have the monks simply memorizing lists of names.

The critical hermeneutical key to understanding the purpose and use of this translation is that seven and more centuries later, the Ethiopian Orthodox Church is not at all interested in the scholarship of the Desert Father legacy of stories and personalities. The intent of the *Filekseyus* is to immerse the novice monk in the spiritual lore of the monastic vocation, and to saturate his mind and spirit with advice and warnings about the pitfalls of aiming to be perfect while remaining nevertheless an imperfect human being. The names of the great Egyptian ascetics, to be sure, are recited as spiritual models and heroes, through both their positive and negative adventures.

Perfection Again

Dadisho/*Filekseyus*' commentary turns out to have something surprising tucked into a corner out in full view, "in between the lines." In the first Logia [DQC 1.2] – a rambling introductory discourse punctuated with a few apophthegmata – an elder declares that there are two levels in the Christian life: the Upright (*kēnē/ḫīrān*) and the Perfect (*gmīrē/feṣūmān*) and discusses and compares the qualities of these two groups. "The perfect way of life is thus the way of life of Elijah and Matthew and Hanna and Mary the sister of Martha. The way of life of Matthew and Elijah is better than the way of life of Abraham and Zacchaeus. And the labour of Hanna and Mary is better than the labour of Sarah and Martha. It is not in the thinking, but in the way of life because Abraham was perfect in his thinking with regard to the friendship of God and humanity and his animals in the world. God loved this person because Christ would come to be from his seed" (1: 1va23–1vb12).

Dadisho and Filekseyus employ the same vocabulary regarding the institution of the Upright and Perfect described in only two earlier Syriac works: the late fourth-century *Book of*

Steps/Liber Graduum[6] and the late fifth/early sixth-century *Discourses* of Philoxenos of Mabbug.[7] Since there were no other known witnesses to its occurrence in later texts or chronicles, the adaptation of the Upright and Perfect to a monastic situation appears to indicate that this ecclesiastical innovation was no longer active in the secular church.

In Logia 3 [DQC 4–5], the definition of the Perfect is given: "As it is written: 'If you wish to become perfect, take up your cross and come after me' which is his boundary – renunciation from place and family and possession and wife and children, and the departure from the world and the endurance of the austerities of solitude." Someone in the world, the Upright, who is married and serves the sick and afflicted, is never equal to those three solitaries mentioned earlier. Christ calls the "virtuous worldly ones" "the sons of the world" and the holy ones or solitaries "the sons of light."

A brief simile in DQC 6 offers an important fact: "just as the worldly faithful ones *bring the solitaries into their houses and receive and comfort [them]*; in the same way also the solitaries bring the faithful ones to the kingdom of heaven and receive them in their tabernacles of light and comfort and give [them] pleasure." This reference to the Upright providing for and assisting the Perfect mirrors the practice in the *Book of Steps* of the Upright serving the physical needs of the Perfect, though the practice is mentioned only a few times. Notably, *Filekseyus* omits this passage, which might indicate that this institution was no longer in favour in such an organized physical manner in the Ethiopian Church. Nevertheless, in *Filekseyus* 239 [DQC 2.280] a clear picture of interdependence between the worldly Christians and the solitaries is outlined. "The worldly ones care for the solitaries with their alms through their possessions, and the solitaries care for the worldly

[6] *The Book of Steps: The Syriac Liber Graduum*, English translation and Introduction by Robert A. Kitchen & Martien F. G. Parmentier (Cistercian Studies 196; Kalamazoo, MI: Cistercian Publications, 2004).

[7] *The Discourses of Philoxenos of Mabbug: A New Translation and Introduction* by Robert A. Kitchen (Cisterican Studies 235; Collegeville, Minnesota: Cistercian/Liturgical Press, 2013).

ones through their prayers for them and their concern for them. The solitaries share physical [concerns] with the earthly ones, and with the spiritual ones the worldly ones share in heavenly [concerns]." Although this irenic statement does not offer specific details, it implies and encourages an ideal mode of relationship to be promoted in the Ethiopian church.

In the *Book of Steps* this service of the inferior to the superior becomes an apparent source of jealousy, rivalry and conflict, even violent reprisals. This theme is rehearsed in several subsequent questions: Are the virtuous worldly ones inferior in virtue and reward to beginning solitaries, even the disturbed and dissolute solitaries sometimes noted by Dadisho? Dadisho/*Filekseyus* reply without hesitation that the virtuous worldly are inferior even to those Perfect of imperfect ascetical fibre. The author of *Book of Steps* is insistent upon a wide gap between Upright and Perfect which can only be bridged by the radical renunciation of possessions and of family life, i.e., celibacy, no matter how good the Upright may have become and how poorly and imperfectly the Perfect have behaved. Philoxenos does not draw such strict boundaries since the Upright are for the most part novice monks who have already renounced the world and family – they are still living mentally in the world and just have not forgotten what they have left behind.

These passages unveil a third chapter of the 'categories/levels/steps' previously only evidenced in the *Book of Steps* and the *Discourses* of Philoxenos, another 150–175 years after Philoxenos, still based in the monastery – Church of the East rather than Miaphysite, but as with *Book of Steps* based in the Persian/Islamic empires – yet apparently in relationship with the worldly Upright. Are there witnesses to its existence in other contemporary texts, perhaps in an unedited or un-translated manuscript? In the interim, a more complete picture needs to be constructed regarding how this institutional paradox of the Virtuous Upright of the world being inferior to the Less Than Perfect of the monastery was allowed to exist and for how long, another piece to the puzzle of early Syriac asceticism.

Questions and Answers

The obvious distinctiveness about these texts of Dadisho and *Filekseyus* is that they are examples of the question/answer genre which Classical and Byzantine scholars call *erotapokriseis*." Recent years have seen a revival in the study of this genre of literature in Late Antiquity, which occurs in Syriac literature as well, Bas ter Haar Romeny being the principal scholar of this phenomenon.[8] Romeny describes a number of the occurrences of this genre, largely in Church of the East circles, and notes that the questions of most of these examples are based upon a text, the Biblical text the most frequent. The DQC and *Filekseyus* are in fact based upon a text, the *Paradise of the Fathers*, itself a compilation of other texts of a similar genre.

Form does lead to function. The *Sitz Im Leben* of these questions and answers appears being located in a monastic setting in which mostly novice monks are seated around an abba and playing with the text that is apparently already very familiar to them. Their questions are at times simple trivia, yet often inquiring about the deeper and sometimes plain meaning of challenging stories and conversations from the *Paradise*. Certainly, the structure of this commentary provides an excellent tool for the monks to memorize and master the various apophthegmata, absorbing eventually the spiritual direction written in the answers, as well as in between the lines.

I wish to pose some unanswerable questions. Was Dadisho's *Commentary* an artificial construct of the author or did it derive out of actual questions and answers put forth by the novice monks in his monastery? That might help explain the selection of passages, deriving from the needs of the monks rather than the didactic instincts of the old man. Certainly, *Filekseyus* was making even more of those decisions and selection. Most likely the truth lies somewhere in between, although ultimately indiscernible.

What I have touched upon is the nature of the questions in these different examples of *erotapokriseis* and their social provenance. Dadisho focuses more emphatically on monastic culture and conundrums than the famous questions and answers of

---

[8] Bas ter Haar Romeny, "Question-and-Answer Collections in Syriac Literature," in *Erotapokriseis: Early Christian question-and-answer literature in context*, edited by Annelie Volgers & Claudio Zamagni (Leuven: Peeters, 2004) 145–163.

Barsanuphius and John,[9] and those of Anastasios of Sinai,[10] both of whom provided practical and spiritual counsel primarily to lay people who came to the monastery seeking advice. On one level, this is a commentary on a set text and the text sets the substance of the questions. But there is a persistent tone throughout this lengthy work that the questions arise out of the needs, concerns and anxieties of the brothers. Dadisho has much to say regarding many of their questions and sometimes even answers the point of their question. In the long run, however, in the original Syriac setting in the monasteries of the Persian Church of the East living amidst the new political and religious reality of Islam, and then among the Arabic-speaking Syrian churches, and finally in the Ethiopian Church, those who read and profited most from Dadisho's answers were the less-experienced monks who found in reading this *Commentary* the kind of questions they needed to ask in order to progress in the monastic and spiritual life, and sometimes the very questions they were burning to ask.

TRANSLATION

Ethiopian Monastic Manuscript Library (EMML) 1387, 18th century, Institute of Ethiopian Studies, Addis Ababa, Ethiopia, microfilmed by Hill Museum & Manuscript Library, St. John's University, Collegeville, Minnesota

(1ra) In the name of Father, and the Son, and the Holy Spirit, One Lord, I will begin by the power of God to set out a book assembled here as a gift of writing. This is the first chapter from the questions which are the account of the Egyptian monastic fathers, which the holy Filekseyus wrote, the Syrian bishop of Mabbug. May his prayers and his blessings be with his servant

---

[9] Barsanuphius and John, *Letters*. Volumes 1–2, transl. John Chryssavgis, (The Fathers of the Church 113/114; Washington, DC: The Catholic University of America Press, 2006/2007).

[10] M. Richard and J. Munitiz (eds.), *Anastasii Sinaïtae: Quaestiones et responsiones* (CCSG 59; Turnhout, Belgium: Brepols 2006; English translation: J. Munitiz (trans.), *Anastasios of Sinai: Questions and Answers* (CCT 7; Turnhout, Belgium: Brepols, 2011).

forever and ever, Amen. [This book is] regarding how the way of life of solitude is superior to the way of the [monastic] community.

[1] [DQC 1.2] *(1ra13–2vb2)*[11] *The brothers said:* Let us start from the beginning of the matter. There were two brothers, the sons of a merchant, and when their father died they divided up their inheritance. There were 5000 dinars for each of them. They lived earnestly in order to please God with perfect righteousness. One of them distributed his inheritance among the Christian churches and the monasteries and the poor and needy people. He was skilled in handiwork for his daily food **(1rb)** and persisted in stillness[12] and prayer and fasting. The other one built a monastery and recruited brothers around him. He received travelers and the destitute and cheerfully offered appropriate relief to all and gave them rest, and in this manner distributed all his wealth.

Some of brothers [thought that] the deeds of one [brother] were better and [others thought] the way of life of the other was better. They asked the blessed Abba Bawmā,[13] "Which of them is better?" He said to them, "Both of them are perfect since one lives in the wilderness like Elijah. And indeed, the second one behaves according to Abraham's way of life." Some of them said, "How are they equal? Which is the first commandment of our Lord that one should fulfill for perfection?" [Remember] what [Jesus] said, "If you desire to become perfect, sell all of your possessions and give to the poor, and follow me."[14] "The second one is this," he responded, saying, "because this is how the other [brother] hears the word of our Lord, 'Who is the wise and faithful manager whom his Lord will place **(1va)** over his house to give them their

---

[11] The first bracketed number is the Geʿez enumeration of Question/Answer units in EMML 1387; the second bracketed number is the [book.section] of the corresponding Question/Answer in the Syriac *Commentary on the Paradise of the Fathers* by Dadisho Qaṭraya (DQC); the third set of numbers in parentheses are the folio numbers of the EMML 1387 Question/Answer.

[12] *ḥedʿāt* – Syr. *šelyā*

[13] Pambo

[14] Mt 19:21

sustenance at its proper time? Blessed is the man whose Lord comes and finds him like this doing what is right. Truly, he will appoint you to administer all his wealth.'"[15] He said, "Be patient a little while until he discerns [something] from God." Some days later they came to him and he said to them, "Have you seen them standing before God in the garden of Eden?"

The Interpreter[16] *said:* In theory they are equal since each one of them intends to please God in as much as he comprehends as he comes to burn with the perfect approval of God and his will. Yet in that way of life, for each one was in the wilderness, they followed the Lord in his excellent way of life. Whoever prescribes the little deeds that distance one from God, his thought does not apply itself to anything that will prevent him from being brought [for judgment] to God.

The Christian way of life consists of two orders, the good[17] way of life and the perfect way of life. **(1vb)** The perfect way of life is thus the way of life of Elijah and Matthew and Hanna and Mary the sister of Martha. The way of life of Matthew and Elijah is superior to the way of life of Abraham and Zacchaeus, while the labour of Hanna and Mary is superior to the labour of Sarah and Martha. It is not in the thinking, but in the way of life because Abraham was perfect in his thinking with regard to the friendship of God and humanity and his animals in the world. God loved this person because Christ would come to be from his seed.

In this same way David the king was humble and righteous, yet the way of life of Elijah was better than his way of life. When a

---

[15] Mt 24:46

[16] The Syriac *Commentary on the Paradise of the Fathers* typically has the brothers' questions answered by a *sābā* or 'old man,' 'elder,' or Philoxenos and in a major manuscript almost always Dadisho Qaṭraya himself. The Geʿez is almost always the Interpreter, '*matargwem*,' referring to Abuna Abba Salama Matargwen (1348–1388), the patriarch who reputedly translated this work and many others from Arabic into Geʿez, a key initiative in the intellectual renaissance of the Ethiopian Church.

[17] Syriac: *kēnē* – 'upright'; cf. *The Book of Steps: The Syriac Liber Graduum*, transl. Robert A. Kitchen & Martien F. G. Parmentier (Kalamazoo, MI: Cistercian Publications, 2004).

brother asked Abba Yestir[18] about the way of life he should institute in himself, he said to him, "It is written that Abraham loved the stranger and God was with him. David was humble and God was with him. Elijah was persevering in stillness and solitude and God was with him. So any deed belonging to God is stronger. God **(2ra)** will be with you and he will not say to you, 'Go back to the world and be married and serve the stranger like Abraham and humble yourself to one who rules over him like David,' but he wants to establish in the monastic life a practice of the labourer who belongs to God, for according to the fathers, the monastic way of life is superior to the three orders of stillness with its struggle and illness with glory. He served him with joyous zeal. Whoever is in stillness is assiduous and humble, and his heart burns for the love of God. Like Elijah he fasts and prays without ceasing and persists in fighting with Satan, which is concealed and uncovered, and he does that for God's sake, and not for people. Whoever is in eternal sickness is similar to David in his appearance, and because of the long suffering spirit of Job he praises God and does not criticize him, nor does he believe the sin which agrees with him. If there is a brother who is not able to remain **(2rb)** in stillness and is never ill, because of that let him minister to his sick brother, or to a tired old man or to his brother who is always in stillness on account of God alone and not on account of the deed. A worldly person will state [his] desire and do what pleases the one whom he serves by his love and with joy, not by rejection and by anger, but he will serve for God's sake and not for the sake of people.

If those three people are like this they will merit equally according to the precedent of the work of the two brothers, for each one of them was perfect in their own way of life – the one who was [engaged] in fasting and the other who was [involved] in service. Because of this Abba Bawma[19] said, "When did either one not fast and pray in accordance with righteousness supposing that he did not attain mercy? As for the ministry of the other, when did

---

[18] Nestir

[19] Pambo

the other not serve him freely? If he were not righteous he would not be equal to the one who is in stillness."

Furthermore, the blessed Antony [said], "Perhaps there is one who sits in his house in stillness for many years, but does not know how to sit in it a single **(2va)** day, for he does not consider himself to be a sinner and powerless and foolish, but justifies himself and reprimands sinners." But in this way, perfect stillness, the excellent way of life according to the spirit of God, is better than the spiritual holy angels.

Another one of our brothers went to [visit] Abba Arsenius, but [Arsenius] did not receive him and did not offer him respite due to his love of stillness and solitude. So he went to Abba Moses, and [Moses] received him gladly and smiled at him. When the other heard from the brothers, he said, "O Lord, why is it one person will flee from people for your sake, and another will receive people on account of you?" So then, see the two ships in the river and Arsenius is in one of them in stillness and the spirit of God is with him; and Abba Moses is in the other one and the holy angels are with him, and they are feeding him honey from a honeycomb. The way of stillness, therefore, is better because it is superior to every kind of human nature and is the excellent way of life **(2vb)** of recluses and exiles and desert monks.

[2] [DQC 1.3] *(2vb2–3rb5) The brothers said*, Why did Abba Bawma say, "When is the one who fasts not equal to the compassion of another, and when is his ministry not [equal] to another who lives righteously, or whether he is not equal to his brother who [dwells] in stillness?"

The Interpreter said, On account of what was written earlier of the righteousness of each one of them concerning his way of life according to his ability, it would not be proper to speak frivolously. Anyone who distances himself from all his wealth and dwells in stillness, yet does not ever fast nor pray without ceasing, he will not be equal to the one who has wealth. For perfect compassion and ministry is one who [dwells] in stillness. If someone is afflicted by illness, he is not able in his illness to become a fast-er and to pray for ever. Indeed, if his brother servant who is in this world has compassion and has a wife and child, he should perform ministry and compassion as long as he is able while he is in that **(3ra)** world. If he has a wife and a child the fathers are not equal to his deed and his reward with his brothers who are in solitary stillness, just as they were not considered equal to the way of life and the reward of Matthew the tax-collector, along with the way of life of Zacchaeus, the judge, and the tax-collectors. The two of them wished to delight God continually with their pure way of life which is the way resulting from his virtuous action. He becomes great and see, his person is stripped of all possession and he establishes [himself] in monastic stillness with fasting and with prayer. However, in the way of life which is not righteous it is because he is seeking the glory of people. See, there is a just way of life, yet his way of life is deficient on account of the weakness of his mind, although not on account of the weariness of his body. In the same way, another arrives with his possession to anchoritism and brings [the other monks] comfort for necessary things, but not because the people grant him power. You see, he does it **(3rb)** for God's sake, not because of his virtue and his love of humanity, but because he does not want to labour in the strenuous [deeds] of stillness.

[3] [DQC 1.4] *(3rb5–5rb20) The brothers said*: We would like to discern for ourselves the reports how one who is in the world is not worthy of equality with the solitaries in the reward. He has a wife and child and wealth, [living] in a virtuous way of life, and gives alms to the poor and rescues the prisoners and frees the slaves. He gives them relief and offers food to those unjustly treated and glorifies the righteous ones and vindicates those among the tired and the strong and does not accept bribes in judgment, nor for the intention of [earning] interest. He takes care of the orphan and goes forward to hire and take care of the prisoner and the sick ones and serves God with all his strength.

The Interpreter said: Take heed of the words of the Lord and the way of the fathers. The Lord named them **(3va)** the saints, the sons of light, and he named a second [group] the worldly ones, the sons of the world, for he said, "The sons of this world are more cunning than the sons of light in this generation."[20] Their virtue is a level road which is rational[21] and the excellence of the sons of light is

[20] Lk 16:8

[21] Lit. "departs from their heads"

difficult to do because it is with their own minds and with the limbs of their bodies. Therefore, they offer themselves as a rational and holy sacrifice according to the commandment of the Apostle.[22] Those who do the commandment of our Lord, in which he said, "If you wish to become perfect, sell all your wealth and give to the poor and take up your cross and follow me,"[23] that is, serve with your mind, not by what is now alien to you and is dead from the lust of this world and its troubles.

Now these angels of the Lord seek him alone where he does not inhibit the followers of the words from worldly labour by the words in which he said, "I am **(3vb)** here, become like me for he has sent me. The Father who has sent me will glorify him."[24] Love the Lord alone. They abandoned other desires on account of the words he spoke, "Whoever loves father and mother or wife, or children more than me is not worthy of me, so then let them renounce their families and their homes."[25] Their desire resisted perfecting his favor on account of his words, in which he said, "Whoever does not hate his father and his mother and his brothers, as well as his sisters and his wife and children and even himself is not able to become my disciple."[26] Therefore, he rejected their souls, and they endured demonic temptation and natural austerity on account of the words, "Whoever wishes to follow me let him hate himself and bear his cross every day and follow me."[27] That is the word the Lord said to those who renounce the world and pursue his glory while enduring a confined dwelling.

He encourages the worldly to draw near to God even up to death. **(4ra)** The Lord even said to them, "Take up for yourselves friends by wicked wealth so that when it is depleted they will receive you in their worldly chapels,"[28] which is how they bring in the worldly outcastes, the worshipers for whom there is not

---

[22] Rom 12:1–2

[23] Mk 10:21; Mt 19:21

[24] Cf. John 17

[25] Mt 10:37

[26] Lk 14:26

[27] Mk 8:34; Lk 9:23

[28] Lk 16:9

anything at all. In the same way, they will bring you into the kingdom of heaven because you have worked with them, and for the sake of the worldly penitent and the poor worshipers. The Lord said, "But you, O my son, are with me all the time and all which is mine is yours and you should rejoice on account of your brother because he was dead and now is alive."[29] He compared the elder son to straying worshipers, those who were with God from their youth up to their perfection and indeed, the kingdom is theirs. As for the younger son he compared him to the conversion to God by the worldly ones and they will have a good portion of the kingdom as **(4rb)** it was determined which is greatly less than ours by the words of the Lord, and for that matter, the remainder of the straying worshipers was so determined. But because he was discerning of the strict way of life since Zacchaeus the chief tax-collector became mature in virtue, and he gave half of his wealth to the poor,[30] but to anyone who consulted diviners he did not give anything instead of [paying back] four-fold with rejoicing and eagerness until the Lord came to his house and established for him what is proper and redeeming. But he was not considered equally righteous with the righteousness and reward of Matthew the tax-collector and did not act like him. However, whoever does renounce something in obedience to scripture, it is because the Lord has called him and he has renounced what he possessed and followed him and lived with him a disciplined life, and has given himself of his own accord.

In this same way, Martha too was worthy on account of the ministry to our Lord as well as his disciple. But Mary was sitting listening to the word of our Lord and did not toil in anything. [Martha] gave up his work for that of the world **(4va)** and she came with [her] whole being to the world. The other one is Christ and when Martha asked the Lord to speak to Mary[31] her sister to help, he said to her, "Because Mary has chosen for herself the good portion, it cannot be taken from her."[32] In as much as Martha did

[29] Lk 15:31–32

[30] Lk 19:1–9

[31] Manuscript reads 'Martha'

[32] Lk 10:42

not understand the disposition of her sister Mary, in this way she was indeed a secular person. But they lived openly in covenant in their flesh and with their wealth.[33] They did not make known the covenant to us solitaries [who are dwelling] in stillness.

According to what is in creation, the soul is better than the flesh in the same way that the hidden spiritual covenant is better than the fleshly covenant. Just as the work of a spiritual messenger is superior to the work of human beings, and the love of God is better than the love of creatures, in the same way the solitaries' works are superior and more numerous than the works of the worldly person. A worldly person's love is a secondary portion on account of their women and children and their possessions and their handicrafts. The seed of their virtue is choked like the word of our Lord **(4vb)** with the thorn of the world – which is its mind and its turmoil – but it leaves behind lusts on every path. He had a single love that on account of his love for the One who is Christ the Creator, however, they will be afraid of many things. Whoever is afraid of these things and what is uniquely alone does not rejoice in anything else.

Since the solitary discerns much more from the teaching of the fathers, look, it was written in the *[Book of] Paradise* regarding a vision of our God to the holy Babnuda.[34] [The vision] said to him, "Go to such and such a town and enter into the house of the chief and teach him the perfect way of life." He went at once and when he entered into his home, he was commanded to reveal to him the way of life. He revealed to him then regarding the commandment of God, and [the chief] said to him, "It has been 30 years since I joined my partner and [only] three times did I know her and had three children by her. Look at these [works] I am ministering **(5ra)** on account of the love of the poor. No one in my city or region refuses hospitality for travelers, so that a poor person does not depart from my house nor travel with his hand being empty. I do not show prejudice for one [involved] in judgment, nor have I despised even one of them. I do not sow my field and harvest until I have assisted the tired with regard to their sowing. There is no

[33] Cf. Lk 10:38–42

[34] Paphnutius

enmity in my region that is not reconciled. So then the holy Babnuda praised the way of life of the chief and kissed him on the head, and said to him, "May God bless [you] from Zion and may you see the beauty of Jerusalem. Indeed, you have done wonderful things and are lacking [only] one thing which is the chief of the ways of life – that is, divine wisdom which a person is not able to acquire unless he renounces himself and the entire world, and bears the cross of our Saviour and follows him at once." He came out [of his house] and followed the holy Babnuda.

The people of his house did not understand and he went [to live] near the blessed one at the monastery and became a solitary and fulfilled his life in **(5rb)** it after a little while. The blessed Babnuda saw his soul with the angels as they were lifting it up into paradise. They were praising God, saying, "Blessed are you whom God has chosen, and is bringing him to dwell in your palace." It was spread around that not even one [person] was living in this world as superlatively as this one, yet he did not become perfect without the way of solitude.

God called the blessed Arsenius, the leading Abba, from heaven, saying, "O Arsenius, flee from people and you will be saved." [God] did not say anything to you about alms and righteousness being established in the world, and you will be kept safe with his powers in this [world], especially from others through one who has wealth and is wise. Therefore, God says, 'O Arsenius, flee from people and be silent.'

[6] [DQC 1.6] *(8ra2–21) The brothers said*: You have built for us from the divine scriptures something exceedingly beautiful, and also from the teaching of the fathers and hearing what is comprehensible and from the analogy of intellect as the worshiping solitaries, the perfect ones and the intermediate ones and the virtuous beginners among the virtuous worldly ones. In as much as one of the solitaries does not turn away from evil he will descend to Gehenna. Whoever performs the virtues of the worldly ones will go to the kingdom of heaven. From now on let us ask concerning the knowledge we are in need of from the questions.

The Interpreter said: By the assistance of our Lord you are the narrators and through the strength of the Lord I will interpret. But all of us shall praise the grace of our Lord who will show you how to seek, and allow me to interpret.

[7] [DQC 1.16] *(8ra21–8va5) The brothers said*: What was said concerning Ammonias, for whenever there was a battle of fornication **(8rb)** he ignited [his] bosom with fire and applied [the iron] to his flesh?

The Interpreter said: Whenever demonic warfare arose against him, he would torment his flesh with affliction to extract whatever might become a sin in order to bring natural movements to an end along with the movements of Satan. When they wished to forcefully elevate him to the episcopacy, he cut off his right ear. He did this to diminish [his] appearance on account of vainglory. This kind of thing happened whenever Satan made him vacillate with fornication, and he would burn his genitals. On account of mental struggle he devoted himself to prayers and fasting and affliction of the soul through humiliation. The destruction of the flesh through austerities is for the service of God and the people, so much so that Abba Evagrius said regarding him, "I have not seen anyone who has surpassed passion[35] more than him."[36]

[This] Ammonias was not the virgin, nor was this Ammonias a bishop, the disciple of Antony, but the one who went with Evagrius to [visit] Abba John of Assiut the prophet the white **(8va)** and asked him concerning the hidden light which is in the mind,[37] and he said, "Because the mind will send forth light by its nature, and will enlighten whatever is beyond its path."

[8] [DQC 1.20/21] *(8va5–8vb8) The brothers said*: When the souls of the righteous depart from their bodies, do they go to Paradise or to heaven?

The Interpreter said: To Paradise.

[The brothers] said, "Why did Antony say that he saw the soul of Paul and the soul of Amoun as they were ascending to heaven? Concerning Paradise he said that because it is above the earth it is named heaven, for you see, the Apostle named Paradise the third heaven.[38] The first one is the foundation which God spoke about

---

[35] i.e. attained passionlessness = Syriac, *lā ḥāšūšūtā*; Greek, *apatheia*.

[36] Evagrius

[37] Lit. "monk's skull cap"

[38] 2 Cor 12:4

in the Law through the tongue of Moses the prophet, "At first God made the heavens and the earth."[39] The second is the firmament by which God made a separation between the waters. The third is Paradise, as Paul the Apostle named it. The souls of the righteous will come to live in Paradise until the Lord comes to reward [them] **(8vb)** and until then they will have communion with Christ in the kingdom of heaven. They will be in his presence on account of the word of our Lord to the thief on his right, "Today you will be with me in Paradise."[40] In the dream when he comes with the Lord into his glory he makes the righteous stand on his right hand and praises them and bequeaths to them his kingdom.

[9] [DQC 1.26] *(8vb8–18) The brothers said*: Why did Antony say to Paul [his] disciple, "Go dwell in solitude so that you might be taught the demonic battles."

The Interpreter said: The demonic war that is in thoughts and visions may occur in solitary stillness. May this person possess prayer which is continually fervent and from it one may possess purity of heart and from that he will see the glory of God.

[10] (DQC 1.27) *(8vb18–9ra9) The brothers said*: "Why is it that Abba Macarius the Alexandrian did not spit for 60 years from the time he was baptized until the time he died?"

The Interpreter said: On account of his reception of the holy mysteries. For this reason it was appropriate **(9ra)** that he would drink water or eat consecrated bread [only] after his reception of the holy mysteries. Look, did not the fathers say to us that when saliva comes up after the Eucharist before one drinks water or eats the consecrated bread, then let him swallow it. But if his soul is great, let him wipe it on a piece of his clothing.

[11] [DQC 1.28] *(9ra9–9va4) The brothers said*: Why did Abba Elijah build a monastery and gather into it 1000 monks and became their spiritual leader? After many years, the battle of fornication held sway over him and he went out into the desert. Three angels were sent to him and removed the passion from him and persuaded him

---

[39] Gen 1:1

[40] Lk 23:43

to go back to the monastery to organize the brothers and take care of the sick for their sake.

The Interpreter said: For three reasons – first, because of his compassion, nature and purity. For when he saw the majority of them earnestly pursuing to live in purity, it was not yet possible for them to go out into **(9rb)** the desert. Since there was no one caring for them amidst the desires of the flesh, he built for them a monastery and cared for them fervently with spiritual love.

The second principle is that God did not hold back from him the impurity of natural passion and the killing of demonic [forces] so that he might show to people, angels and demons the way in which his struggles are on account of prayer for the passions, the transgression of Satan, the loves of his excesses, and obedience to God.

The third [principle] is that the people whose thoughts are corrupt say there are two gods, a good and an evil [one], and they cultivate its evil ones for evil, while others say that sin is in us from Adam our father and they regard their sins as if they were natural in them. When God wished to eliminate this idea, he established a community of righteous people before them and reduced to nothing **(9va)** the strength of creaturely war and demonic conflicts from the people of their community, as his unique divine strength becomes evident.

[12] [DQC 1.29] *(9va4–9vb2) The brothers said*: What did Abba Paphnutius mean when he said that a slip of the tongue, and the thought, mind and entire body is related to the arrogance of this person?

The Interpreter said: The blunder which is proportionate is the collapse in the [inner] mind, as the blessed Mark said, "Do not let your heart be boastful regarding knowledge of the scriptures lest your heart falls into a blasphemous and stumbling spirit by means of the tongue." Just as one of the brothers slipped on account of his pride and his disparagement of Mar Evagrius and the holy fathers in the desert of Sketis, the offenses in the mind are like that second offense on account of pride. He fell into fornication and the offense [went] throughout the entire body. In the same way, he fell again on account of his pride and fell into the hands of brigands and they bound him behind the back and **(9vb)** placed him inside [a pile of] straw and burned him with fire.

[13] [DQC 1.30] *(9vb2–10ra21) The brothers said*: Why was it said that the heart which falls away from the memory of God is handed over to the demon of fornication and the demon of anger? Why did Palladius say, "How is the mind of a human being able to be with God continually?" and Democles responded, saying, "What is the sense or meaning of what happened to his soul for the sake of God?" Look, 'the heart that is with God,' what is the meaning and sense of what he said to him?

The Interpreter said: If prayer without ceasing or wandering were not like this, one will understand through the fear of God and the reading of his scriptures and doing his commandments and perhaps leads to the fulfillment of his wish, if you are persistent regarding the memory of God and his memory in his kingdom and his ability and wisdom and goodness and mercy and glorious love. Just as you pray **(10ra)** without ceasing or wandering on account of the lusts and weakness of heart or demonic war, and whoever increases his conflict and on account of this, poor conduct rushes into your heart at the same time as his memory, and whenever the word of God happens your mind is relieved. When he rests or an evil thought is stirred up in him it elevates him to the memory of God, and through prayer and supplication without ceasing it does not lead him astray. In the same way, those who pray physically, if they are tired from standing up, rest their bodies by sitting and enlightening their minds through reading. When they have rested they will stand in the heights of prayer and when the heart lives in God and in his commandment and the completion of his will, you are with God. When he is [thinking] about the passions of sin [or] worldly [affairs] in which there is no reward, he is with Satan.

[14] [DQC 1.31] *(10ra21–10vb1) The brothers said*: Why is it that until the hearts of worshipers are purified with austerities and labours for a long time the divine light does not enlighten them **(10rb)** in their hearts? But before their departure from the world into the desert the light of grace may shine on some of them, just as it shone in the heart of Abraham [Qidunaya] on the seventh day of his wedding feast, for at once the groom of the wedding feast left and went out from the world into the desert.

The Interpreter said: The fathers said that the light is apportioned to each and every one according to his merit and the knowledge in his mind, for grace bubbles up in the heart of a person through the love of God, and then he is hostile to the glories of this world. He comes without wealth on account of this labour, and grace gives him at first the love of labours and makes smooth for him what is rough, and causes the demonic battle to cease against him that is greater than his strength. After much hard labour and great humility, his heart becomes pure and he is worthy to see Christ in a vision of light. Just as he was nearing to meet our Lord through austerities **(10va)** and struggles, likewise our Lord himself was going out to meet him with light until he finds him. When he was strong in the battle that through his love our Lord dwelt in him with his light, just as our Lord said according to the word of the prophet, "My soul has listened to the divine being; how long until you come and I see your face so that I may travel on the road which is without a blemish." How long until you come to me, yet since some of those linger on the lengthy road and I perceive the voice of the prophet, all of your waves and your tempest passes over me, you make me cross over into the water and fire and allow me to depart in peace. The solitaries who are worthy of the light before their departure from this world become dark when they gather among the brothers due to their hearts mingling. But due to the struggle through many austerities they are worthy of purity of heart and according to the fathers shine with divine light **(10vb)** during the time of prayer.

[15] [DQC 1.32] *(10vb1–11rb20) The brothers said*: Why did the Apostle Paul say, "Whoever desires [to be a] bishop desires a good work"?[41] The Blessed Interpreter[42] informed his friend regarding the book of priesthood and asked him to complete the degree of priesthood. The holy Paul, patriarch of Anṣakiya, after fifteen days of his residence upon his seat over the thrones, saw in the city many distractions. Then he prayed to God our Lord and [God] said to him in a vision, "Go far away."

The Interpreter said: There is nothing more beloved and honourable to our Lord God than purity of heart and because of it the gift of priesthood was given and [all] the other [gifts]. When the

[41] 1 Tim 3:1

[42] Theodore of Mopsuestia

Apostle saw that he did not have wisdom in his knowledge and his way of life even while he is seeking the office of priesthood for the love of rank and vainglory, for this reason he held it back from one who has no excellent knowledge and good works to flee from the status for the sake of his humility and his love for toil. He was afraid **(11ra)** lest he disrupt or harm Christian discipleship due to the absence of righteous teaching and the good way of life. He spoke this word and not one of these words he spoke for the sake of their desire after he related the work of the bishop and the priests or the prestige of the monastery lest he pursue it earnestly on account of its glories. The leaders then were right not to seek without possessing natural wisdom and the knowledge of the Holy Scriptures, and one is just and righteous in his way of life. It had virtues which are valuable in it and it guides him into it and prevails over him in accordance with mercy and order, humility and goodness, advice and knowledge.

The Blessed Interpreter asked his friend to complete the degree of priesthood for five reasons. First, because he had received the degree of priesthood; second, because they had selected him out of many God-fearers; third, on account of his virtuous knowledge; fourth, on account of his good way of life; **(11rb)** and fifth, on account of his great humility and faith, and because he was fleeing from prestige. When they forcibly placed him in [the position] he was persistent in removing himself from it.

Paul, because he was righteous and humble and persistent in stillness, when he saw that he was benefiting from the position due to too much disturbance he was troubled, and prayed to God with tears and passion to reveal to him about [how to] leave behind the prestige of the priesthood and to be [involved] in what he is capable and benefit by it. Our Lord heard his prayer for these two reasons: one of them for his benefit, and the other to withdraw the impudence of the stubborn fool from the desire of priestly prestige in order to show the pleasure of God to a person to be [involved] in what is beneficial for him.

[(16)][43]**[DQC 1.33]** *(11rb20–11vb11) The brothers said: The Book of Paradise* said regarding the blessed Anstasios[44] that he dried out his body through fasting and vigil until **(11va)** the sun appeared through the middle of his ribs.

The Interpreter said: Indeed, I have seen one such holy person who was healthy and still walking, drying out his flesh by a great deal of abstinence until one might imagine that there was nothing in the middle of his stomach and no waste. His rib bones were very visible from under the good skin. Because of this Macarius said, "Just as fire dries out the dampness of the wood, the fear of God will burn like this, and in as much it resides in a person it will dry out his flesh and decay his bones." The Blessed Interpreter [in] the *Book of the Way of Life* spoke about two natural brothers, solitaries who were dwelling in Antioch, following his statement that every word will be inadequate due to of the fact of their perfection, on account of their teaching and the emaciated weakness of their flesh and withering away until a person who sees them will think that he is seeing a ghost, not a human being **(11vb)** who is real.

Palladius said about the brother who was dwelling in Jerusalem that he appeared like a shadow on account of the way of his austerities. So then, these things are worthy for us to believe what was said about the holy ones by righteous narrators, even if they were not in our times.

The first division is finished with the assistance of God and the missing saying from the first [division] of the questions.

[17] [DQC 1.34] *(11vb11–12rb12) From the second division. The brothers said*: Interpret for us the word of Abba Macarius the Elder who said, "Now, I have never offered [the eucharist] to Mark the mourner, except that an angel of the Lord was presenting it to him with his hand from the altar."

The Interpreter said: In ancient times in the desert of Egypt there was one who governed the monastery who alone was consecrating the eucharist until the time of his departure, as Palladius said, that

---

[43] The scribe has omitted the enumeration of this unit, but inserts in rubrics the opening line: "the brothers said."

[44] Syriac: Eustatios

eight priests were governing the monastery of Barnug, but as long as the first one was living there was no functioning as a priest for any of them. There was only one priest and one deacon for the solitaries **(12ra)** who were in the cells of Antioch, ministering the entire year and Macarius the Elder was consecrating [the eucharist] by himself. There appeared the hand of an angel between him and the skin of Mark, just as one of the seraphim did when he took from the altar the fiery coal and put it into the mouth of Isaiah the prophet.[45] An angel was acting in this way because angels do not have the authority to consecrate the eucharist and give it to people. But so that another might imitate him and the fame of his struggles on account of Mark's great purity and humility, he should possess four virtues which occur with him which do not happen to any other on account of his struggles, for his purity in his soul and body and his humility is greater. Two gifts are of God which strengthened the Old and New [Testaments] in his heart; and second, his knowledge of their faithful interpretation and the reception of **(12rb)** the eucharist from the hand of an angel.

This is Mark the Greek [who was dwelling in] Egypt and not the one who in all of Egypt was more knowledgeable than all of the solitaries in knowledge and the [ascetical] way of life. He is the one who wrote a book concerning the answers of discernment which they said regarding Melchizedek as the son of God. He was not that Mark the Syrian who was well-known to the king. He completed his life in Syria and neither was he that Mark the Younger who was the disciple of Sylvanus.

[18] [DQC 1.36/38] *(12rb12–12va22) The brothers said: The Book of Paradise* said concerning the priest of Dabra Natron that when he went down to the monasteries around Alexandria he found the brothers gathered together in forties in one, and three for lepers.

The Interpreter said: In the annals of Abba Moses the Ethiopian it was written that for two days he was walking about with his fellow thieves performing evil acts, and a thought came to him and he was rescued from evil customs and from his companions **(12va)** and from the demons. Did this happen by the grace of God or by

45 Isaiah 6:6–7

himself and why was he not [changed] earlier, but he became then what he was [to be]?

The Interpreter said: Every excellent thing a person does is perfected by the assistance of God. According to the word of our Lord, "Without me you are not able to do anything good."[46] Grace summons a person to excellence for three reasons – by the mind, by instruction, by reading and good deeds – one will then be perfected by grace. A person first desires goodness to incline his thought to a person towards goodness rather than evil. He does not assist it, nor abandon himself from it.

When the mind of Abba Abraham despised the heresy of his fathers and his soul desired the knowledge of righteousness, at that moment grace enlightened his mind. In the same way, when Abba Moses reversed his mind, at once grace aided him.

[20] [DQC 1.39] *(12va22–13ra11) The brothers said*: Why is it that the holy fathers were always prescribing **(12vb)** practicing virtue and battling against the demonic passions? The elder Abba Isidore [went to visit] Abba Moses and said to him, "Do not fight with the demons, for [one should perform] austerities and ways of life in moderation."

The Interpreter said: Abba Moses believed when he began that by his many labours and hardships alone he could prevail over the demons. When [the demons] perceived this softness from him due to his secret and public battles, Abba Isidore wanted to demonstrate humility to him and show that silently through solitude, "A person is not assisted without the grace of the Holy Spirit which you shall possess through baptism and the reception of the holy eucharist. Just as [when] someone's body is sick, a wise person will then prescribe a drink of medicine and orders him to refrain from sleeping and drink and food and anger and anything else medicinal. He does not possess what will heal him by this labour, but he acquires [it] only through medicine. In the same way, whoever becomes sick in his spirit, his spirit will not be cured by his regimen, **(13ra)** [that is] by his labours of fasting and prayer, silence and vigil or from ministry or lamentations and humility, but

---

[46] cf. John 15:5

only through the grace of the Holy Spirit will he defeat Satan and recover [from illness], but this one will fight with the demons. Then he will love to perform the commandments of God and does not see only the path of his practices, but the strength persisting in it by the grace of Christ our Lord. "Are there no wanderers and pilgrims?" he said to one of them.

[21] [DQC 1.41] *(13ra11–16) The brothers said*: Regarding again the distinction among the pilgrims and the wanderers and the exiles. He wanders around in the monasteries in order to receive benefit from [them] and make beneficial spiritual labours, and indeed the wanderers benefit from physical labours.

[22] [DQC 1.42] *(13ra16–23) The brothers said*: Why do the solitary fathers stretch out their hands in prayer and supplicate towards heaven?

The Interpreter said: On account of the word of Paul the Apostle, "I wish that [people] should be praying in every place, lifting up their hands in purity without anger and evil thoughts."[47]

[23] [DQC 1.43] *(13ra23–13va10) The brothers said*: On account of **(13rb)** this the [Blessed] Interpreter said that one should raise his hands to elevate his thoughts towards heaven to the Lord in love and purity.

The Interpreter said: This was not said to many, but it was said to the perfect solitaries, for they were not lifting up only their thoughts, but their eyes and their hands and the majority of them in lifting up their eyes were lifting up thoughts to God, for it is possible for them to lift up hands and eyes to heaven. All of them were similar to the prophets and Christ, to him be glory, to his apostles and to his holy ones. For David said, "I stretched out my hands to you, and I will lift up my hands like alms in the evening."[48] He said, "I lift up my eyes to my God and my ruler." In this same way, Moses the prophet did in the battle of the elders and also Christ when he raised up his hands and lifted up his eyes and his thoughts. Paul also said, "Seek what is above, where the throne

---

[47] 1 Tim 2:8

[48] Ps 141:1–2

of Christ is."[49] The fathers also raised up their hands **(13va)** and their eyes to heaven with the assistance of their thoughts in the presence of God. Look, it is written that Abba Sisoes the Theban was standing in prayer and he stretched out his hands and his heart was brought into the presence of our Lord for a long time. As soon as one of the people came to him, he lay down his hands in order that his heart might also lay down, for this is very tiring work.

[24] [DQC 1.44] *(13va10–19) The brothers said*: Why did one of the desert dwellers say to his brother, "If you are not able to become an anchorite like us, sit in your cell and weep on account of your sin and then you will become like us"?

The Interpreter said: Whoever has become distant from the world and cuts off the desire of passions from himself in solitude, and attaches his mind to God is indeed like an anchorite.

[25] [DQC 1.46] *(13va19–13vb5) The elder said*: An angel who was in the lower world ripped open the stomach of an anchorite and showed him the passion of his heart and restored him, just like what was said regarding the angels [who] tore at the genitalia of Mar Elijah, the abbot of **(13vb)** the monastery, when the desires of fornication were with him there. Then I wish to please my God with his solitary life, but my obedience is afraid of the severity of the conflicts with the demons and such [events] as this.

[26] [DQC 1.47] *(13vb5–14ra1) The brothers said*: Again, every person will be with regard to the demonic struggles against him according to his strength and his struggles and his way of life and his endurance. When Abba Apollo was asked by a monk to dwell with him in the desert, he said to him, "You will not be able to endure the temptations of Satan." When he made him set out with him and reside with him in the next cell to his, the demons went out to him in the night and at first defiled his thoughts and later on wanted to frighten him. Abba Apollo went out to him and set up an enclosure around the cell and sealed it with the sign of the cross. [He made for him] a circle and from then on he was able to dwell in it. Just as all of the apostles did not receive the authority to cast

[49] Colossians 3:1

out all the demons, in the same way not all of the solitaries are able to prevail over the haughty demons [and] the evil powerful ones, but whoever can hold [them] back **(14ra)** is one who has become perfect and humble.

[27] [DQC 1.48] *(14ra1–10) The brothers said*: Why did the brothers who dwelt with Abba Macarius in Sketis for three years not go to see him, nor to the others who were the children of the king?

The Interpreter said: One of them was great of intellect, perfect and meek, and if they had gone to see [Macarius] his perfection and his glory would have been revealed. The younger one was being taught by the one who was greater.

[28] [DQC 1.49] *(14ra10–14va19) The brothers said*: The strivings of Bessarion were famous when he was dwelling in the desert and mountains. One day a certain person came with others to a monastery and he was standing at its door and weeping, saying, "Thieves found me in the sea and tempests rose up against me and waves ascended upon me and I was separated then from the wealth of my house and I was deprived of my fathers and of their pleasures."

The Interpreter said: The sea signifies the way of life of solitude and the tempests point to temptations. The waves [point] to the passions, and the thieves to Satan and his fathers to the Father and the Son and Holy Spirit, **(14rb)** One Lord, who saves by his example and by his imitation. According to what he said in the Law and according to the word of our Lord in the Gospel, "Be perfect like your heavenly Father,"[50] for he is perfect and the wealth of his house is indeed the wealth of his soul which continues by its nature. By divine grace and by nature you are able to create us. It is the desire and the pleasure and the faculty of persistent knowledge and the doing of righteousness and discernment of this thing which the prophet said, because a man who does not destroy it is a human being, in as much as he lives in glory. When he is enraged he is like an animal in which there is no heart and which by grace is baptism and spiritual gifts. Look, it is written that faith without

[50] Mt 5:48

good works is dead,[51] and whoever does not have this [faith] in him, what is being produced from him is not a good work. Faith roused up from him shows that he will not eliminate the profit in him, like someone who does not have faith. The heritage of his fathers are virtues which are **(14va)** similar in it to our famous father. He prepared us to live and established for us his kingdom, such as faith and hope and the love of God and of people: peace and mercy and patience, purity and goodness and humility, knowledge and spiritual prayer. As for this wealth the submersion into the sea, the worldly desire, and the fear of its thoughts, and anxiety for the world and vainglory rises. When the blessed one saw with his heart's eye that many of the solitaries are deprived of this spiritual wealth according to the rule of the love of brothers, then he began to weep and lament for them as he might weep for his own soul. Just as he is poor whose wealth has sunk and whose property is plundered from his house, he prays to God to establish for him what is proper for wealth, its love and its good possessions.

[29] [DQC 1.50] *(14va19–15rb5) The brothers said*: What now are the nine virtues for that person?

The Interpreter said: I consider that the first one is the renunciation of possessions; and the second is maintaining a fast continually until the evening **(14vb)** and a vigil; third are the prayers of the seven hours of the day and night; fourth is the reading of the holy scriptures in between the hours of prayers; fifth is innocence; sixth is humility; seventh is the love of neighbour; eighth is silence. Nine are the virtues which [the holy one] acquires through much toil and great battles, but defeats all the passions.[52]

Through the renunciation of his possessions he defeats the love of money. On account of this he defeats the [lust of] the belly,

---

[51] James 2:14–17

[52] The Filekseyus confuses the enumeration of the nine virtues found in the Syriac. Syriac: renunciation, abstinence, fasting, vigil, Psalms, reading of scriptures, comfort, humility, love of people. Geʿez omits 'abstinence,' and includes 'vigil' in its second virtue. While the seventh Syriac virtue, 'comfort,' is omitted in Filekseyus, the Syriac omits the eighth Geʿez virtue, 'silence.'

with fasting he defeats insolence. Through vigil he defeats sleep and with prayers he defeats [evil] thoughts. Through the reading of the scriptures he defeats the thoughts and evil speech. Through his meekness he defeats indignation and anger. Through his humility he defeats vainglory and arrogance, and through his love of people he defeats hatred and wrath, enmity and much evil. The excellence of the tenth – a rich person lacks these nine – is the fervour which always is through the love of our Lord. But this is what is collected by hidden prayer in the mind without ceasing and without wandering, and by persistently driving out the thoughts of passion and the deceptions of the demons **(15ra)** from the beginning of their movement in the heart, for this is more perfect than all the virtues. The strong evil demons are fighting with many of the solitaries so that they may not attain it and be strong in it. On account of this, the labour which came to it is the most exhausting and the most difficult of the excellent austerities.

For this reason the blessed Mark said, "On account of the enmity of the demons to this labour, he was not able to be quickly perfected in the love of Christ by the gathering of thoughts and the ardor worthy of God." Then whoever is perfect in the love of Christ and of people will defeat all the mind's passions that depend first on the love of oneself. Whoever this perfection rules desires to withdraw from this world and to be cut off from this flesh and to live with the God who loves him in Paradise, the dwelling place of the righteous and the territory of **(15rb)** the perfect which is superior to the passions, demons, difficulties and downfalls. There he will have rest from the cell of excellence until the appearance of Christ who will rejoice in his glory and the joy which never ends.

[30] [DQC 1.51] *(15rb5–15vb3) The brothers said*: Explain to us the labour of this elder, the owner of baskets and pebbles.

The Interpreter said: The way of the mind brings the solitary to purity of heart. As for his labour, he laid one basket on his right and another basket on his left, and every good thought that comes to him he places his pebble into the basket on his right, and every evil thought that comes upon him he places his pebble into the basket on his left – all of this [together] with his fasting in his worship, prayer and labour. As a result of his perseverance in the performance of virtues, the demons were jealous of him, and they perturbed the heart of the man with many evil [thoughts]. He afflicted his soul and his flesh, for not only is the soul disturbed due to the body's toil **(15va)** on account of the condition of one with him, for those demons who were battling [the ascetic] were being greatly wearied.

Mar Evagrius said that when the demon of fornication was fighting with him he stripped off his clothes and stood naked under the sky for the duration of the night during the winter. He wearied the demon of fornication until [the demon] fled from him. The toil of the saints is continually exhausting the demons for the angels torment them by the commandment of God.

Satan wanted to cause a split between two natural brothers. When the younger brother lit a lamp and the demon extinguished it and made his lamp fall down, his brother struck him upon his cheek and forced him to bow down, and [the younger brother] said, "O my brother, be patient with me, and then I will light it." When God saw the patience and humility of the younger, God commanded that younger [brother]'s angel to tie down that demon in the cell and torment him until the next day. Instead of one blow that **(15vb)** one brother endured from his brother through the action of the demon, the angel tied that demon down and beat him the length of the night.

[31][DQC 1.53] *(15vb3–16va18) The brothers said*: Why do the demons fear the labour of the solitaries, according to the word of the fathers, "If you wish to make the demons afraid of you, then reject the desires."

The Interpreter said: On account of three reasons. First, when our Lord rejected three passions – desire, love of wealth and vainglory – which consolidate [all] the deeds of the passions, through which Satan battled him with daring in the desert, and with stillness, fasting and prayer he then defeated Satan. Those who travel in his footsteps destroy the sinful thoughts in order to drive out the demons from them, just as the demons are afraid not only of the cross, but of the signs like it. There is no one who departs and flees from the labours of Christ only, but from the deeds of his followers. Their souls become dark on account of the distance from God through other practices by the solitaries when they accept the enticement of the demons through sinful thoughts and enjoy them. **(16ra)** [The demons] shame and despise and disparage [them] if they do not accept their enticements, but [the solitaries] distance the thoughts from the beginning of their movement and call to their Lord to assist them. Then they destroy the demons and despise and turn away quickly, according to what the blessed Mark said that one should fear and flee whoever wishes to commit adultery with a spouse of his companion. When he hears the clamour of death such as this, the demon is terrified and flees, and when he hears him calling out to God. The third reason regards obedience to God. On account of their love for him he will acquire for them an offering to God, and then the demons will keep them at a distance. Look, says our Lord to his beloved, "See, I have given to you authority over all the enemy hosts, and there is none who will harm you."[53]

[32] [DQC 1.54] *(16ra18–16rb18) The brothers said*: When is it that the demons turn away at the name of Christ and the sign of the cross – and when they do not turn away?

The Interpreter said: They are turned away at first according to the word and their condition which does not turn them away **(16rb)** at [certain] times. They are not afraid of hearing, neither of the signs, nor of prayer, but they are persistent. Look, not only are they not afraid, but they will beat up the solitaries. It is for this reason when [the solitaries] receive from our Lord the authority for their advantage.

For example, while the holy Pachomius was walking with his friend at night, some demons appeared to them in a marvelous disguise and were praying and presenting themselves with audacity and said to them, "Do not labour in vain and do not pray. Look, I have received authority for your temptations." It is necessary that we should not desist from the sign of the cross and the naming of Christ and prayer when the demons appear to us, whether they turn away on account of the assistance of our Lord to us or they tarry providentially from the Lord for our advantage.

[33] [DQC 1.55] *(16rb18–16va11) The brothers said*: Three demons came to visit Mar Evagrius in the likeness of three priests and argued with him; and the angels went about in the likeness of worldly people to visit the abbot of the monastery on account of

---

[53] Lk 10:19

the owner of baskets and pebbles. The [angels] were worshiping the cross and kissing **(16va)** it and praying, was this not the case?

The Interpreter said: The angels were worshiping and kissing and praying with their images, just as the souls of the perfect were worshiping, praying and kissing with their bodies. But the demons were creating lies with their illusions, for demons do not have the authority to create an illusion that is true from the natural elements as do [angels], and if so, they are defeated.

[34] [DQC 1.61] *(16va11–23) The brothers said*: Youth work at first for human glory, and afterwards grace nurtures them by the honour of divine glory so that they might be saved through their obedience and their love by itself. Evagrius said, "If one is defeated, he will be praised because his praise will increase the power of his strength." Whoever diminishes himself is perfected, for he is in the second level. When a brother spoke to the elder, "Now I will pray for those who lead the ascetic life for the sake of human vainglory." The elder then said, "Love him so that this will happen to the perfect one."

[37] [DQC 1.81] *(17vb20–18ra9) The brothers said*: What is the interpretation of the word of Abba Apollo when the head of a snake was crushed and its entire body is dead?

The Interpreter said: **(18ra)** He shows the head of the snake as the first thought which the demons stir up in the heart of the solitary due to a sinful source. He interprets its body as the many thoughts of that solitary monk. This [monk] may slay that first error by which a sinful deed agitates against him, but he will perish from what is generated after it.

[38] [DQC 1.84] *(18ra9–22) The brothers said*: Why did this brother beseech Abba Apollo to pray for him to God so that he might be given grace? When [Apollo] prayed for him humility and poverty and love was given to him.

The Interpreter said: The brother had previously engaged in much struggle for the sake of virtues, but the Lord did not wish to give him [grace] without him seeking from God a humble gift for it and for himself as well. The Lord wished that the brothers might ascend to their perfection with the peace of the fathers' advice and their prayers for them.

[39] [DQC 1.86] *(18ra23–18va12) The brothers said*: Why was the demon of pride found **(18rb)** upon the shoulders of Abba Apollo after his labours and he had become perfect and God had chosen him and sent him for the salvation of many?

The Interpreter said: The fathers said that after the defeat of all the demons and the passions they will be with the perfect ones until their death, but the conflict of pride and vain glory distances them from God so that they may not gain wisdom in their struggles and become perfect. When God spoke to [Apollo], "[Go] to the desert which is far from inhabitants and organize for me a people who will praise me and do good things well," Abba Apollo said to him, "O Lord, remove pride from upon me lest it boast over the brothers and destroy all the good works." God commanded that he stretch out his hand upon his neck and take what is found upon his shoulders and bury it in the sand. He found a young Ethiopian boy and buried him in the sand who was shouting out and saying, "I am the demon of pride."

The fathers **(18va)** said that when a passion is ruling over a person a demon will sit upon his flesh finishing the work over which it has authority. With regard to the passion of fornication, the fathers see the demon of fornication sitting upon his testicles; and whoever submits himself to anger the demon of anger is sitting upon his heart; and whoever submits himself to grumbling and speaks an evil word [the demon] is sitting upon his tongue; and whoever sleeps during prayer [the demon] is sitting upon his eyes; and to the thief [the demon] is sitting upon his right hand.

[40] [DQC 1.88] ***(18va12–18)*** *The brothers said*: Why did the elder find fault with the solitaries who put on irons and [grow] hair and the majority of them made themselves righteous through this labour?

The Interpreter said: He was not finding fault with the perfect, but with those deprived of the hidden virtues who were doing this for the sake of vainglory.

[41] [DQC 1.92] *(18va19–19ra18) The brothers said*: Why was there in the beginning of Christian proclamation many solitaries, and very many were in the country of Egypt, but now they are only a few?

The Interpreter said: **(18vb)** The Lord sent his apostles and commanded them to make faithful disciples. They made a perfect way of life and showed great signs to the perfect. Ten showed themselves to have ability superior to many who believe and work, although those who believed were not inferior. There were not ten thousand in those cities and regions. In the same way, those accomplished according to what is written in the monastic annals that Abba Hor became the abbot over 1000 of the solitaries and Isidore over 1000 and Abba Amoun was over 3000 of the solitaries a long [time] and Abba Pachomius over 3000 and Abba Sarapion had 1000 under his authority and the bishop of the city of Behunos said that he was greater as in his rank he had under his authority 10000 solitaries and 20000 nuns. Again, at the beginning of [Christian] proclamation, the people imitated the preachers. For Christ is authoritative, saying, "Learn from me: whoever does not bear my cross and does not follow me is not **(19ra)** worthy of me.[54] If you wish to become perfect give all of your wealth to the poor and follow me."[55] The Apostle Paul was saying, "Imitate me just as I am imitating Christ, and I wish every person to become like me in purity."[56] He said, "It is better for a man that he does not approach a woman,[57] for whoever has a wife will live in order to please her. This one who does not have a wife will live in order to please God. But those who do not imitate one who shows them their virtues are continuously [caught] in evil. They have grace in the tracks of pride more than those who do not obediently imitate the [good] news for a long time."

[42] [DQC 1.94] *(19ra18–19va3) The brothers said*: Why were some of the saints beseeching God regarding which [saints] they should imitate, and [God] sent them to worldly people who were less educated than them, just as he had sent the holy Antony **(19rb)** to a cobbler and Macarius to two women, and Bamanuda to a tailor and Abba Paphnutius to a shepherd?

The Interpreter said: They sought from God concerning how the explanation was fitting for John son of Zebedee, for on account of

---

[54] Mt 10:38–39, Lk 14:27

[55] Mt 19:21

[56] 1 Cor 4:16

[57] 1 Cor 7:1

our Lord he sat at the table of his guest and asked him what [reward] would he be handing over to him?[58] They wanted to know then on account of this question who they were similar to among the saints according to the level of their reverence and the strength of their trust and their hope and the increase of their ardor due to the love of our Lord. But God sent them to worldly people who were inferior to the perfect in order to strengthen them in humility, and to be profitable to those worldly people as consolation for their righteous labour, and strengthen their hope in order to be beneficial to one another in their imitation of them, in as much as they understood how **(19va)** they were equal to the righteous solitaries, if they contended ascetically for doing what is good.

[43] [DQC 1.98] *(19va3–19vb5) The brothers said*: [Why was] Mar Evagrius directing the brothers not to be satiated with water?

The Interpreter said: Our Lord said that in as much as an impure spirit circulates among people [who are] seeking [water] in places where there is no water, and seeking comfort but cannot find it and then returns to that person, the fathers said that whoever does not reduce eating and drinking too much water will not defeat the spirit of fornication and will not perfect righteousness. There is nothing else that dries up the flesh and prevents one from dreaming and waking and wandering and stills the impure thought during the daytime. Just as one is thirsty if one fasts and reduces drinking, he does not benefit by drinking a great deal of water, filling his stomach and increasing the moistness of his flesh. [It is] then that the demon will find an occasion to seduce him with thoughts during the day and with dreams at night. Mar Evagrius said, "If you wish to be pure, **(19vb)** then reduce [your] eating and it will restrain you from the drinking of water, and at once purity of heart will shine and your mind will shine like a star you will see in your prayer."

[DQC 1.108] The conclusion of the third chapter in the summary of Hieronymus who set down the questions, and the two chapters of Palladius for he wrote during the times of Theodosius the Great.

---

[58] cf. Mk 10:35–40

Palladius wrote during the time of Arcadius his son. To God be praises continually for ever and ever.

The fourth chapter: This is the last [section] of the stories of the solitaries which are written in the *Book of Paradise* from the last chapter in which Palladius wrote down the questions of the brothers.

[54] [DQC 2.15] *(23va19–25ra12) The brothers said*: A brother went to visit Abba Sarmag[59] and said to him, "What should I do, O my father, because I am negligent: I eat and drink and sleep and have perturbed thoughts in confusion **(23vb)** and agitation of soul?" The elder said to him, "Be patient in your cell and whatever you are able, do without disturbance. This small deed that you do in [your cell] is like the great deed that Antony did on his mountain. I believe that if you remain in your cell for the sake of God's name you will find yourself in the place of the famous Antony." How is it that the brother, a beginner and a negligent [monk], eating and drinking and sleeping and taking pleasure in his thoughts, is able to be equal in his reward to the great Antony in lofty good work?

The Interpreter said: God made physical commandments in the days of Moses the prophet for the entire Jewish nation which he showed by speech and by deeds, but not by thought. He wished to give the spiritual commandment which he set down for the Christians through his Only Son, **(24ra)** our Lord Jesus Christ. He said to the believers, "Listen to what was spoken at first to the Jews, 'Do not kill openly, do not commit physical adultery.' But now I say to you, 'Do not be angry, which means, do not kill in your mind. Do not commit adultery, which means, through your vision and in your mind, for he said whoever is angry against his brother for no reason [receives] a judgment of murder. If someone looks at the wife of his brother and desires her, he has already committed adultery with her in his heart."[60]

In the first place he laid down a physical admonition for a physical deed. But afterwards he spoke of a spiritual reward for a spiritual work that exists in the mind and will. The physical deed

---

59 Sarmatus

60 Mt 5:21–28

will pass away, but the spiritual deed does not pass away and it is clear one will become weak in old age on account of physical work. But that is not the case with the spiritual since from the beginning one is not able to inhibit the mind and the will. On account of this some of the fathers said **(24rb)** that one wants to do something and is not able to be equal to one who is able to do it. The righteous one is no longer involved in physical work.

Indeed, one should discern from the work of Martha and Mary her sister because our Lord praised the work of Mary much more than the work of Martha since Martha ministered with her flesh for a physical [act], that is, a meal. But Mary ministered spiritually to the spiritual matters which is listening to the word of our Lord. Righteousness is not in the first place age and [kinds of] ministries.[61]

This is shown regarding how it was [that] Christ loved John more than Peter. He did not prevent the youth of our blessed lady Mary to become blessed among women and much more full of grace than her older [cousin] Elizabeth[62] and more than Hanna the prophetess who fasted and prayed in the temple eighty-four years.[63] But the righteous one does not have more to offer.

The Lord said concerning **(24va)** the woman of two coins that she put in much more than those who were wealthy;[64] and even the tax-collector on account of his humility was more righteous than the Pharisees when they fasted more and gave alms and prayed.[65] Even the sinful woman demonstrated greatly her love through weeping when she was in the house of Simeon the Pharisee. Our Lord praised her and loved her greatly and forgave her many sins.[66] The thief who was on the right blamed himself at the time of his death and pleaded to God to remember him if he should come into the kingdom and be worthy of paradise.[67] But

[61] Lk 10:38–42

[62] Lk 1:26–38

[63] Lk 2:36–38

[64] Mk 12:41–49

[65] Lk 8:9–14

[66] Lk 7:36–50

[67] Lk 23:32–43

[God receives] those who enter into perfection at the eleventh hour to labour in the vineyard. The Lord will give them the wage for the entire day, the full [amount] with those who were afflicted during the weight of the day and the intense heat, that is, from their youth until their old age.[68]

Concerning this work the fathers have performed for the brothers due to their way of life in order to instruct them during the seasons of their temptations **(24vb)** in the good hope that instead they will not acquire melancholy and despondency.[69] He showed the solitaries how to eliminate their willingness for the deeds of the flesh and then at the same time from idleness and from the battle of mind and despondency. On account of this [Abba Sarmatus] affirmed him during the time of his temptation, "If your works are deficient now from the harshness of demonic battles, but your mind is righteous in the toil in your cell, you are not inferior on account of God. Through this you are similar to Antony, and just as your mind is similar to his mind, in the same way your reward will be similar to his reward. Your labour may be small in your testing place with your fortitude in your cell, and your understanding deficient and your strength too weak, and your judgment's single-mindedness may restrain you through asceticism for the sake of Antony's perfect knowledge and his strength and compassion, [yet] **(25ra)** you will be equal with Antony to God in his many deeds. But because of this now your reward will be equal. The expression should not be disconcerting for it is certain. Do not say to your mind lest your heart be diverted by melancholy and despondency." Again he affirmed his statement, "I believe that if your strength is in your cell on account of Christ until your temptation passes away, you will grasp the ardor of his love and the strength of the deeds."

[63] [DQC 2.27] *(28ra4–28va1) The brothers said*: Abḇa Theodore and Abba Luke endured fifty years while their thoughts were being pushed to want to depart from their location. They kept saying, "[Let's wait] until the rainy season," and indeed, when the rainy

---

[68] Mt 20:1–16

[69] Literally, "sadness of idleness and cutting off of hope."

season would come they said, "[Let's wait] until the dry season [summer]." They dwelt like this until the completion of their lives.

The Interpreter said: The devils were fighting with many of the fathers about escaping from hardship and on account of their knowledge from which they had benefited greatly. But some of the fathers were being played with by demonic thoughts like those holy men, and many of them were being harassed by the demons until they departed from their cells and wandered about. Just as in our days there was one[70] who was perfect in the divine way of life and was granted the gift of the expulsion of demons. The battle of exile had control over him **(28rb)** so that he was not seen going very often into his cell, until his disciples built for him a place in the desert. He was escaping from one cell into another cell, but grace protected him from going around in the cities. This happened to him so that he might not be arrogant, as well as the retribution of his transgressions of [his] elder's commandment, for his teacher had said to him, "If you do not dwell in my place after my departure,[71] then wandering will have power over you until the time of your journey."[72] And this is the way it was. When he was ninety years [old] he would ride upon a donkey and his disciples would conduct him to [various] cells to the extent that the fathers were astonished by him, and the brothers took warning from him. In a similar way, Abba Macarius the Great when he kept in mind to observe the desert [fathers] he was fearful of the warfare of wandering and then the struggle of thoughts. For five years he was praying and beseeching God, "Is this from God or from the devil?" And after **(28va)** this he went to [live with] them.

[72] [DQC 2.38] *(30va9–30vb13) The brothers said*: It was said that Abba Babnuda (Paphnutius) declined from drinking wine. He was passing by in the path of some thieves who were drinking. Their leader forceably made him submit to [drinking] a cup of wine. Paphnutius said to him, "I have faith that God will forgive your sins on account of this one cup."

---

[70] Mar Abda (DQC)

[71] i.e., 'death'

[72] i.e., 'death'

The Interpreter said: In many matters the Spirit of God will make [us] aware of our sins whether through thought or sometimes through reading, sometimes through teaching and sometimes merely by seeing the saints. It was like this when the thieves in the wilderness saw the holy Paphnutius. Grace makes the mind aware and then he saw the glory of his soul **(30vb)** which was hidden become visible right upon his face. Then Paphnutius saw spiritually that grace had called the mind of the leader of the ambushers to repentance, and he said, "I believe in God who on account of this cup which is something you gave for the sake of the love of humanity, [God] will forgive your sins which are the works you have done on account of the hatred of people, and then hope has changed his mind from evil to excellence and repentance." He and his companions promised God that they would not return to doing harm to anyone.

[73] [DQC 2.39] *(30vb13–21) The brothers said*: The perfect in their prayer and their interpretations are contrary to what they appear until they neglect their physical food. But without warning, look, their thoughts are snatched up to great things with God. In three days, the flesh's destruction is not recognizable to them.

[88] [DQC 2.61] *(33rb19–33va11) The brothers said*: The clothes of Abba Awr (Or) and his companion[73] were from the skins of sheep. One of them said to the other, "If God would visit us now, what would we do?" They went back **(33va)** to their cells weeping.

The Interpreter said: [What does] their expression 'he will visit us' [mean]?" [Some say] it might be because of death, and [some say] it might be because grace calms the holy ones [who dwell] in the stillness of the cell, revealing to them not only the joy for the righteous, but also Gehenna for the evil. This happened to them along the way, but separately. On account of this when they remembered these things they abandoned their conversation and hurried back to labour weeping.

[91] [DQC 2.66] *(34va5–16) The brothers said*: The brothers went to visit Antony and said to him, "Give us a commandment to keep."

---

[73] Theodore – DQC

He said, "It is written if there is someone who strikes you upon your cheek, offer to him the other one as well."[74] They said, "We are not able to receive a blow upon [our cheeks]." Then he said to his disciple, "Prepare for them a little food since they are ill."

His interpretation of the soul's sickness is that [labours] are necessary for the recovery [of health], just as the flesh's sickness is needy of the preparation of porridge.

[92] [DQC 2.69] *(34va16–34vb19) A broken reed*: When the holy Antony's disciple informed him of the coming of some brothers he said to him, "Are they from Jerusalem or from Egypt? That is, are they famous or worldly ones?" If they tell him they are from Jerusalem he should receive them and converse with them. But if they say they are from Egypt, **(34vb)** he should say, "Entertain them and let them go." When he was talking with those worldly ones and desert dwellers who had found him, he said to his disciple, "Let them taste what they are seeking: a meal for their bodies, not a meal for their souls."

The Interpreter said: The one who is in charge of the monastery should not discourage[75] the brothers who are ailing in their ways of life, nor prevent them too quickly from association with them on account of the slackness of their labour, but be [concerned] for their salvation through prayer and tears and the passion of the heart and humility, and teaching with patience sometimes with advice and at other times with chastisement, according to the commandment of the Apostle to find grace in the presence of God, just as Pachomius did with Sylvanus, and Isidore with one of his sons.

[93] [DQC 2.70] *(34vb19–35ra5) The brothers said*: An elder saw a person carrying a dead [body], and said to him, "Stop carrying a dead [body], and go carry someone who is living."

The Interpreter said: This is the carrying of the Lord because **(35ra)** life is the death of sin. This is like the word of Abba Macarius, "It is necessary for you, O sister, that you should bear

[74] Mt 5:39; Lk 6:29

[75] literally, "to cut off the hope" of the brothers.

the Lord in your heart just as Our Lady Mary bore him in her womb."

[94] [DQC 2.71] *(35ra5–18) The brothers said*: Why are the sinners and righteous tested equally in illnesses and trials?

The Interpreter said: These are the judgments of God in this world as Jeremiah the prophet said. The holy Antony did not find any without him, neither one of the angels nor human beings. But rational beings will perceive it in the perfect world. Look, Solomon the wise was amazed at this until he said, "If a fool is found that comprehends, why then should I become more wise than this dust and wretchedness of heart?"[76]

[95] [DQC 2.73] *(35ra18–35rb11) The brothers said*: Why do some of the people and the majority of them find the opportunities for repentance and some of the people are not given the opportunities for repentance?

The Interpreter said: The understanding of this is difficult, **(35rb)** for our Lord has come to call sinners to repentance, as he said, and indeed [to call] every person to repentance up until the day of his death. It is possible for us to speak what it is since those people were given a long time, yet they did not repent. The understanding of these things as sins and offenses and so on will be internalized for a few because they are not inhibited up to old age and so fall even further away from repentance.

[96] [DQC 2.74] *(35rb11–23) The brothers said*: Only when one begins in the battle of thoughts does his soul come to be purified and enlightened by the light of grace. Mar Evagrius said, "Just as Satan petitioned God on account of Job, in the same way Satan seeks out every soul that is beginning to be enlightened and shine so that grace may be a little too far from it and [the soul] becomes stronger than [grace] so that its steadfastness and the love which is in God may be apparent, and then suddenly many evil things will come upon it."

[117] (DQC 2.109) *(42vb10–19) The brothers said*: When Abba Agathon saw a brother sinning and being led astray, if he judged

---

[76] Cf. Proverbs 14

him in his mind he said to himself, "Why are you blaming your brother and what is the judgment you are laying upon him? Are you investigating about his sins? Now be tolerant with him for God is indeed investigating you on account of your sins and your foolishness, those alone." And then his mind will be broken.

[118] (DQC 2. 111) *(42vb19–43ra11) The brothers said*: Abba Abraham said to Abba Sisoes, "O my father, look, [we] are old. Therefore, [let us] draw a little nearer to people for a little while." [Sisoes] said, "Of course, but let us go to a place where there are no women." Why are **(43ra)** the great elders afraid of women?"

The Interpreter said: For the sake of themselves and their disciples and on account of the wars of youth [who] boast and then fall down.

The disciple of God should distance himself from [women] because all of the solitaries will boast and fall down at the feet of Satan in fornication so that he may humiliate him with the thought of fornication. If one gets too close to one of the women he might fall down with her. Therefore, on account of this, keep far away from women and live together in monasteries.

[119] (DQC 2.112) *(43ra11–43va23) The brothers said*: Abba Poemen said, "How much did the brother believe who considered himself to be a silent [monk], although he was talking [about others] at all hours. Another one was talking every day, but he was a silent one."

The Interpreter said: As for this one who considers himself a silent one while he is [always] talking, he is indeed silent from conversation with the brothers during his labour, and by a word he remembers God once more. If the demons stir up in his heart a brother's memory or insults **(43rb)** or enmity, he fights in accordance to his strength. The brother believes, but does not drive out the angry thought or abuse from his mind through prayer and suffering. Although they welcomed and lived in harmony with him, he was quarreling with his brothers in his heart and harassed them about doing a good deed until they did it. He argues with and reproaches them, and all day long the regimen of the monastery keeps circulating in his mind. He harasses the abbot of the monastery and the servants and does not let go of this thought of the memory of death and the resurrection and judgment and punishment. He does not call out for the assistance of God with prayer and tears and is [not] comforted.

But this [other] person is still talking while he is silent and he is in his labour and does not talk with the fathers without being in desperate distress or for the benefit of the brothers. But the fathers do not allow the perfect to depart from their labour until death. However, as for the solitary who is not worthy to **(43va)** converse in the way of the mind only, except in appearance because after he became perfect in the performance of the commandments through the love of the Lord which renews him, as long as he is in the labour of the divine gifts he will increase in his wealth up to the hour of his death, unless he departs from the cell of his labour as a perfect one and does not desire solitary labour. There is no one who deprives those gifts of renewal of the world in labour, but look he will deprive one who under his control and decrease his perfection. On account of such as this the wise Evagrius said, "One will be better when he does not enter into conflict." The holy John of Thebes said, "If a solitary is perfect in his love and he comes to a vision of Christ it is proper for him to persist in his labour in order to ascend in this vision to the higher levels, which for the perfect is a vision of labour."

[120] (DQC 2.114) *(43va23–43vb19) The brothers said*: **(43vb)** A brother asked an elder, "How is one not able to blame his brother in his heart?" [The elder] responded, "Unless he reflects in his heart as if he is three years in the grave, he is not able." Abba Amoun spoke to Abba Poemen concerning his brother for one year.

The Interpreter said: In three years the flesh will be deprived by death of its stumbling and nothing will be left of the heart and the body's senses or anything in it that would judge his brothers and rebuke them and revile and blame them. When this person asked about rebuking and reviling and blaming without righteousness and without [any] benefit he finds for himself, the elder mentioned three years and this was because he was admonishing his brother to be worthy of the memory of Abba Amoun for one year.

[133] (DQC 2.135) *(47rb14–47va21) The brothers said*: Abba Amoun [while traveling to see] Antony became lost on the road. He stretched out his hands to heaven and prayed, saying, "O Lord, do not destroy your handiwork." A hand appeared to him to show him the road and he came to reach [Antony] safely. Two brothers were going to see him and they became lost on the road. One of them died of thirst; and as for the other one it was revealed to the holy one about him, so he sent some brothers who picked him up **(47va)** and brought him back and he did not die.

The Interpreter said: See, the first saying regarding to this act of God in which a person cannot find [himself] in this world and because of this we know that God establishes for humanity two ways. He establishes for the righteous and the perfect a way of life just for them. He establishes for the rest of the people a universal way of life about which Elijah[77] spoke. "Whoever loves me will keep my word and my Father will love him." For my part, he loves him and we will come to him. This will be because of a great observance.

Abba Amoun, the disciple of Antony, was the abbot of the monastery and a bishop. He was living in the way of solitary perfection and God was establishing a way of life for him. But the brothers were in the lower level in the common ordered community. When one strayed he rescued them for he rescues many of the people.

[134] [DQC 2.136] *(47va21–48ra20) The brothers said:* For two reasons the brotherhood was ruined by the decrease **(47vb)** of their community. One was when a person became perfect in love and humility and was pure from all the passions and was perfect in the love of all the people and then considered everyone pure like him, according to what was written for he was the purest of the pure ones. Yet when a brother came to see him, if he were lackadaisical the holy one considered him negligent and did not care for him.

However, the other [reason] which is not yet finished, his heart was vigilant with tears and repentance in the toil of the cell in which battle and passions live to perceive his sins and be mindful of his passions, yet he did not care for anyone who was lacking his perfect way of life. Again this is the case if a brother came to him he did not push him away. But if he were lackadaisical and negligent he would keep his heart vigilant and remember the sin and would be anxious to maintain his righteousness. Because of this he did not show his own defect to the brothers. Yet this one

[77] DQC: 'Blessed Interpreter' = Theodore of Mopsuestia

whose heart ascended from the suffering of **(48ra)** repentance and sorrow due to his sins does see the defect of one who was coming to see him. He was skeptical and reprimanded him in his mind. But with the other one at those times he was constant in his facial expression regarding what he was seeing from him or what he was hearing on account of a minor failing or the word which he said without heart, but afterwards in his cell he was remembering his defect and rebuked himself in his mind. Moreover, he was possessed [by a spirit] in his heart through his knowledge so that it did great damage to him in his cell. Abba Poemen commands us to remember our sins forever with suffering and groaning so that we do not see the defects of our brothers in order that we may be worthy to be perfect, humble and loving.

[135] (DQC 2.138) *(48ra20–48va23) The brothers said*: The holy Antony said, "I have seen all the snares of Satan that he was laying upon the earth," and he groaned and said, **(48rb)** "Woe to us, who will escape from all of this?" It was said to him, "Humility will escape from all of it." Is this something he saw in a vision or in his heart [imagination]? How does humility escape from all of this?

The Interpreter said: Abba Macarius saw in the desert of Sketis all of the snares of Satan. He saw the likeness of two men: upon the coat of one of them were sewn fruits. The other one was dressed in an old garment covering his whole body and look, in it were many gems and each one of them was in the likeness of a veil tied on at the end with them. [Macarius] saw this with the physical eye. But Antony saw with the eye of the heart the hooks of Satan for the solitaries by which he leads them astray and reviles them and prevents them from traveling on the road of excellence. According to what was written, "Hidden for me on **(48va)** my path are snares and traps. They stretched out their snares on my roads."[78] When the sinner saw that he had spoken, he was amazed at the numerous snares and stakes and thorns into whose holes wild animals had fallen and were ensnared and could not escape. He saw every passion of the body and soul by which the demons were fighting with the solitaries and it was the angels who made it

---

[78] Psalm 140:5

visible to him. They were showing him all [of the snares], each one of them by its name, which ones are the love and lust of the belly and fornication and the love of money and vainglory, and the rest of the passions. When he saw [all of] them he was amazed and wept, saying, "Woe to us. How will we escape from all of this?" [The angels] said to him, "Humility will deliver whoever adheres to it from these deeds." Just as deeds without humility will deteriorate like the flesh, praise without salt is like humility without deeds, one will not be spared just like salt by itself.

[172] *(59rb10–59va20) The brothers said*: "Why did Palladius not record the story of the holy Mar Awkin (Awgin, Eugene) in the *Book of Paradise*?

The Interpreter said: Because he lived in an earlier age, and in the days of king Qwestantinos (Constantine) he came to the region of Persia in the days of king Safor (Shapur) and lived in the vicinity of Nisibin in the mountain(s) Magra and Marden. He worked many wonders in the countries of Rome and Persia.

By his prayer he resuscitated a young man who had been killed by a lion when he was gathering wood in the wilderness. He called him Al'azar (Lazarus) and clothed him in a holy *schema* **(59ra)** and made him a monk, and he became his disciple. At another time he entered into a burning fire, and fell on his face in prayer.

In the country of Persia he exorcized Satan from the daughter of king Safor, and he debated with the magi in the presence of the king and prevailed over them.

As proof of his faith he made a great fire within the king's court, and signed one of his disciples with the sign of the cross and ordered him to stay in the middle of the fire until he summoned him, and the magi were put to shame. Everyone praised God and king Safor gave him authorisation, and he went on to build numerous churches and monasteries in all the regions of Ahwaz (Khuzistan).

One of his disciples wrote his life, a long homily. On account of this, Palladius did [not] mention him again.

[182] [DQC 1.94] *(62va2–12) The brothers said*: Why did God send Antony and some other fathers to worldly men and women, and they saw their excellence and praised them?

The Interpreter said: For the benefit of the fathers and worldly ones because the fathers were perfect in the struggle and austerities and in their desires for humility. The virtuous wealthy worldly ones in the humility of sinners [received] consolation and hope.

[183] *(62va12–62vb4) The brothers said*: Why did they bring them to their community in the desert by the commandment of God and abandon their community in the world?

The Interpreter said: They brought them to their community by the commandment of God because the solitary life is more virtuous than the worldly way of life. They left their community, error constantly being in them, for the benefit of those who imitate them in their austerities, for the people who live in it **(62vb)** are cunning, married with widows, and are considering committing an excessive sin against all the worldly ones.

[184] *(62vb4–21) The brothers said*: The fathers went to a virtuous Christian shepherd and he said to them, "God shows grace to us with everything. From this I divide the few sheep I have into three categories: a portion for love; a portion for the stranger; and a portion for our possessions.

The Interpreter said: The portion for love he shows to one whose relatives pay expenses for the poor, just as Paul the Apostle commanded to send to them.[79]

The portion for the stranger he shows to the poor who are aliens to them, such as the orphans and the elderly and the stranger.

The portion for his needs he will keep for himself and for his wife, that spouse of virtuous virginity.

He makes this clear from the word of Paul the Apostle to the wealthy and the poor to become more virtuous than them for the improvement of their deficiencies.

[227] [DQC 2.260] *(73vb11–74ra21) The brothers said*: Again, the king (emperor) Constantine said, "Praise be to Christ for in my days there were three divine lights – Mar Antony and Mar Alonis and Mar Awgin."

When Alonis came from Syria to where Antony lived, [Antony] said to him, "It is excellent you have come, O morning

---

[79] 2 Cor 9

star, who rises up in the morning just like the morning star increases the light from what is left behind. A star such as Alonis is the perfect light of grace of the solitaries." He wished to show him the glory **(74ra)** of the way of life and its light. He said, "Greetings to you, O pillar of light who supports the world."

He was not that Hilarion who was sent by his parents.

When he was fifteen years old he came to Alexandria in order to be educated in knowledge, discipline and wisdom. When he heard of the reputation of Antony he went to visit him.

He dwelt with him two months and then changed his appearance and became a monk. After two months he went back to his district and in his biography it was written that he contended for our Lord Jesus Christ, a disciple in the country of Egypt for which Antony's reputation made many go visit him. Hilarion was a young man when with pilgrims they brought him to see Antony from Syria. On account of illness he said to them, "Why would you lead an ascetic life with me, my son Hilarion, while they are with you?"

[228] [DQC 2.261] *(74ra21–74rb17) The brothers said*: The brothers asked an elder, "How is it that people work, but do not receive grace **(74rb)** as of old?" He answered, "Because the love of one lures the other upwards. But now love wanes and all the people are drawn downwards."

The Interpreter said: Let us interpret grace as a gift of healing. It expels the demons and is given as of old for their consolation and for the benefit of others. Now because righteousness is not found upon the earth, love fences off the decrease of this gift from many things, as it was written. The saints who are worthy of this grace receive its hidden and spiritual welcome in their souls, and by necessity, its tracks are not seen due to the sins fitting this evil generation.

[229] [DQC 2.262] *(74rb17–74va8) The brothers said*: Abba Jacob said that whoever teaches someone asks him first, "Is a merciful person [equal] with one who persists?"

The Interpreter said: Whoever does not prepare himself does not completely possess the way of teaching, neither by his progress, nor by his righteousness, **(74va)** nor by his works, nor by his tribulations in his old age. He dares to teach something in which an act of grace is not mixed into his teaching and he cannot find the lesson from it. He teaches this without investigating it and without a pretext worthy of the benefit of the listeners, and is therefore foolish.

[230] [DQC 2.266] *(74va8–16) The brothers said*: Sylvanus said, "Do not wish to become a teacher."

The Interpreter said: That one wishes a warning whenever Satan starts heating up about the warfare of fornication, do not mutilate your genitals and do not wish to become a eunuch from the womb of your mother, but be steady in your struggles and be on the lookout and prevail and hope for consolation.

[231] [DQC 2.68] *(74va16–74vb19) The Interpreter said*: When the brothers were dwelling with [other] brothers in order to be taught the way of the mind and the warfare against the passions, the enlightened ones, who by grace were watchful for passions, observed them. Whoever is stirred by the Spirit is not given authority to have in [him] all at once **(74vb)** all the thoughts. When a thought of human passion is stirring up inside them, let them cast the diabolical [thoughts] away from them. However, [the demons] order them to leave some behind in order to tarry with them a little longer. The [demons] advise turmoil, but they are being taught the knowledge of struggle to be beneficial for them and to benefit others, just as Joseph comforted Abba Poemen, "When turmoil is within you bear the passions with them." He advised their endurance and was skilled concerning the struggles. But they were weak and suffering. It was not good for them to ignore the thoughts of passions, but it was better for them to drive them out from the beginning of their agitation through prayer and with anger and hatred.

[232] [DQC 2.269] *(74vb16–75r9) The brothers said*: An elder said that whoever has no tools struggles to work, but there are no tools by which the spiritual worker may find comfort from God in his spirit. There are no physical tools of labour by which he is able then **(75r)** to persevere very long in his cell.

The Interpreter said: The physical natures are fasting and prayer, prostrations, suffering and tears, hourly prayers and the reading of holy scripture in the teaching that then leads up from this and its likeness will be acquired – the light in solitude.

[233] [DQC 2.270] *(75r9–75v19) The brothers said*: An elder said that he had worked at that struggle for 20 years until he could see all of humanity as equal. How, therefore, does a person come to this?

The Interpreter said: Whoever comes to this perfection with prayer and struggles and humility, who like their physical fathers see their children equally with compassion for them and love and the desire for goodness for all of them. He rejoices on account of their happiness and is sad on account of their sadness, for those bigger than them and for those smaller, **(75v)** for the stronger and for the weak, for the beautiful and for the ugly, for the righteous and for the sinners. This again is the work of God with the people that loves them and desires goodness for all of them equally. Even though he is honouring the righteous more than the sinners, he is still concerned for the goodness of the sinners. Moreover, because he said that he seems to summon the sinners, not the righteous, for the heavenly father bestows favor upon the good and the evil, and in the same way the perfect fathers imitate the Lord God in goodness. As they are able they will love equally. In the same way the unbelievers live according to their imitation of Satan.

[233a/234] [DQC 2.272] *(75v19–76r18) The brothers said*: The knowledge of the scriptures has two divisions, the inner one is called spiritual and the external one is called human. The human one is the tool of the teacher **(76r)** in his care on account of his teaching; and the spiritual, the righteous will profit from the spiritual in caring for the righteous and pure austerities from the passions, as the holy Basil and Gregory his brother, and the remarkable Eltawgalos and Girlos and Severus performed righteousness in their compassionate solitary life; [as for] the scriptures they acquired knowledge through its chapters and were watchful of the ruin of pride into which they could fall. But they led an ascetic life up to the point that they became rich on account of human knowledge and were careless concerning the doing of righteousness according to Arius and Nestorius.

[235] [DQC 2.273] *(76r18–76v14) The brothers said*: Why did the fathers become labourers in their upward progress like innocent and meek children?

The Interpreter said: Virtue which resides in **(76v)** the character of people is visible in children on account of their nakedness from evil thought and the love of suffering and demonic conflict. When they were pure from the times of their ascent with the struggles of physical and rational austerities and the assistance of divine grace, again they showed their virtues and become worthy of the kingdom of heaven. According to the word of our Lord, "If you do not turn around and become like children you will not enter the kingdom of heaven."[80]

[236] [DQC 2.274] *(76v15–77rb7) The brothers said*: Why were the worldly ones saying that they were not scandalized by the solitaries when they stumbled or they heard of their offenses?

The Interpreter said: They realized that the fire in the creation of light does not cease without mixing into the light of vapor and being suspended in filthy or beautiful cloth, **(77ra)** for even the earth in which wheat is sown will sprout weeds and thorns with it. Even though the solitaries likewise desire to become like spiritual angels, they are still physical beings because they live in bodies of impurity, infirmity and need. Whenever by desire demonic intentions and conflicts are inserted into them, they will stumble when there are stones in front of them. A second confusion causes their stumbling if one is not in the way of life of God, just as the disciples were driven out from them in order to show their infirmity so that they will not come and be weak in pride and boasting. They considered the virtuous old and making new those whom grace made dwell with such as Aaron and Peter, and indeed, others like them. Even if they demonstrate their weakness and explain the weakness of people **(77rb)** and cause to sin whoever stumbles in imitation of them, Christ will commend their names because not one of them is able to say as he said, "What persists in you on account of sin and Satan? A worldly judge will come to me and he will not find against me nor anyone else."[81]

[237] [DQC 2.275] *(77rb8–77va3) The brothers said*: How is it that they sing a spiritual psalm spiritually without committing an error?

The Interpreter said: They train themselves in their prayer in their cells with great mental concentration and [keep] all their minds

[80] Mt 18:2–5

[81] John 8

from wandering and the intellectual examination of psalms until they do not skip over a single word without the knowledge of its meaning according to what is written. Blessed are the people who know your jubilation, who sing and praise with the mind, but not the intellectual knowledge such as the interpretations of Basil and John Chrysostom and Gregory and those like them, but spiritually like the knowledge of the solitary fathers. They take up **(77va)** all the psalms according to their way of life on account of the passions and excesses and battles with the demons.

[238] [DQC 2.276] *(77va3–78ra2) The brothers said*: A brother said to an elder, "If I am in the city and the time of prayer of our Lord comes and he cries out, 'Who, while he is wealthy, turns back to poverty?'"

The Interpreter said: The pure city is the air [of freedom], which Mark named, through which a brother purifies his heart with labours of struggle and turns to pure prayer, and his heart becomes enlightened, see, with the light of grace. He will grow in the memory of God and spiritual understanding greatly above the norm, [more] perhaps then one who was first in this air [of freedom].

The time of congregational prayer arrived for his father. The fathers [advise] him not to leave this sweet memory and sing the Psalms with the brothers, but command him to persevere in this place until the memory has finished. For the ministry of singing **(77vb)** is a possibility at all times. But he will not be clear of intellect and pure of heart all the time, and not everything that a person desires is he able to have because it is a gift of God. When a person is in prayer and has this benefit he should not then drive out the gift of God and fulfill his own wish, the beginnings which do not come to maturation. As soon as they are in their prayer and through what they have from that memory, they do not then abandon the profit of their prayer, for see, it becomes a memory which they will have through a demonic error. On account of this it is appropriate at the beginning to reveal the way of life of those fathers. The learned ones examine and reveal to them the matter of temptations and how they had them, when it transgresses and when it dominates so that the demons may not lead them astray.

The Interpreter said: Indeed, he is mindful **(78ra)** of the binding of the mind with God.

[239] [DQC 2.280] *(78ra2–78rb23) The brothers said*: Why is it that the solitaries wanted what is necessary from the worldly ones? Look, our Lord made a covenant with them by the saying, "Seek first the kingdom of God and his righteousness, and all of this will be added to you."[82]

The Interpreter said: [It is] for the profit of the worldly ones and for the monks, because for worldly believers alms are their righteousness for the most part, and as for themselves their alms are through what is external from their minds. The solitaries give alms through their heads, that is, the labour of their minds and members, for the sake of love's consummation among them and the benefit of everyone who is different from another, through being able to look after one another. The worldly ones care for the solitaries with their alms through their possessions, and the solitaries **(78rb)** care for the worldly ones through their prayers and concern for them. The solitaries share physical [concerns] with the earthly ones, and with the spiritual ones the worldly share in heavenly [concerns].

On account of this our Lord said, "Acquire for yourself friends by unrighteous wealth [so that] when [the wealth] disappears you will be taken into their worldly shelters."[83] The Apostle said, "May your own abundance be for the need of your brothers."[84] This is what our Lord and his disciples did – and see, we are commanded to become like them. For look, it is written that wealthy women remained while serving with [their] wealth and they had a coffer and whatever was [placed] in it became the alms of the faithful. On account of this the solitary does not despise as he accepts the alms in order to fulfill by it the need and the duty from you. He is able to fulfill by the work of his hands with labour his way of life through the toil of his solitude.

[240] [DQC 2.281] *(78va1–18) The brothers said*: The fathers said, "If due to the weakness of your flesh, if not due to the diseases which are in your bosom or through natural illnesses in your old

[82] Mt 6:33

[83] Lk 16:9

[84] 2 Cor 9:6–12

age, you are not able to perform the austerities of the flesh according to what was written, then perform the austerities of the soul which are the way of the rational mind. If you are not able to fast from food, then fast from an evil thought. If you are not able to pray many psalms of David, then elevate your mind before our Lord by means of secret pure prayers. Be gentle and humble in your sweet heart, forgiving and compassionate and patient, loving to praise. Do not judge in your mind and do not distress anyone with your tongue. Do not let the weakness of the body inhibit this and anything similar to it."

[241] [DQC 2.283] *(78va18–79ra5) The brothers said*: An elder said, "If you see a little one[85] desiring by his own will to ascend to heaven, then grab his foot and pull him back down upon the earth from here because this will be good for him."

The Interpreter said: This is similar **(78vb)** to the word of Abba Isaiah, "Before the senses of passion subside, if one wishes to ascend up to the cross, then the affliction of God will come over him, because he began first by doing what was too high for his rank." Some of the novice brothers were progressing [prematurely] to work beyond their strength and their ranks, and they did not want to be taught or to be commanded the commandment of the fathers. Before they had completed the appropriate time in the community they would dare to enter the [solitary/hermit] cell, as it was written in the *Book of the Paradise* about the brother who when he put on the monastic garb[86] he confined himself [in his cell]. The fathers went to [visit] him and drove him out in disgrace. Other people sought confinement in a hermit's cell even though they would not have any profit in doing so. Others with regard to their labour imitated the fathers in their physical way of life. If all of them do not reveal their thoughts **(79ra)** to the fathers, they will not receive the righteousness appropriate to them, but will condemn themselves by their [own] will because then the demons will take hold of them and mock them.

---

[85] novice

[86] *skema*

[242] *(79ra5–79rb9) The brothers said*: Again, do not pursue a famous person and dwell for that reason in a famous monastery or become a disciple as well to a renowned Abba. But if you desire to dwell in a monastery for the sake of great profit and are capable of sewing in it and becoming a disciple to a famous abba for the sake of wise teaching and profit from excellence and be instructed by his commandments and persevere in his prayer and his beautiful blessing, then die to the world. Just as the Apostle said, "The abolition of thoughts and all worldly cares, and the people will not be what he inhibits and he does not search and covet and does not desire without coming to the perfect love which is on account of God through the Lord, our Lord Jesus Christ."[87] Immediately, he was able **(79vb)** to fulfill the commandment of the Apostle in his saying, "Love God and rejoice in your hope enduring afflictions.[88] Do not think about anything, nor be anxious about anything, but surrender your entire mind to God with every prayer, and with every request before him, to him be praise until for ever and ever. Amen."[89]

[243] [DQC 2.288] *(79rb9–80rb10) The brothers said*: The fathers who were in the desert of Sketis were summoned before Theophilus, the patriarch of Alexandria, to pray and reconsecrate a temple of idolatry. While they were eating they brought before them steak and they ate in innocence. The patriarch picked up a piece of meat and gave it to the elder who was near to him and said to him, "This piece is excellent." They said to him, "But we are eating it up to now as if it were not meat," not refusing to eat anything from them. Why did the patriarch give meat to the fathers to eat, and why were they commanded and ate and why **(79va)** when he said this [saying], "An excellent piece [of meat]," did they not refuse to eat from him?

The Interpreter said: Many corrupt ones dwell in Egypt and in Alexandria whose temptations were giving offense to all of the solitaries. They considered the work of those who renounce [the

---

[87] Cf. 1 Thess 5:23

[88] Rom 12:12

[89] Philippians 4:6–7

world] to be contemptible for they forbade marriage and eating meat. Moreover, the people from the vicinity of the church who were not learned were skeptical about them and reprimanded them on account of the word of Paul in his first letter to Timothy, "The Spirit said this that in later times each one of them will become distant from faith and follow deviant spirits and the teaching of demons and those similar in error."[90] They lead astray and say, "Whoever is hypocritical and their conscience is burning, forbidding marriage and distancing themselves from eating what God has created for nourishment, and giving thanks for those who believe **(79vb)** and know righteousness, for everything which God has created is good and there is not anything worthless when [received] with thanksgiving, for it will be pure by the word of God and by prayers." Many of those who heard this word were scandalized towards the monks.

Then all of the monasteries of the land of Egypt were commanded to eat meat in each year on one day, which was Pentecost. On account of this, Abba Evagrius showed in the previous homily, "O heirs of God, hear the word of God which says, 'Do not say, on the feast day I will drink wine and on the morrow of the feast of Pentecost I will then eat meat.'" The fathers did this in order to wipe away a blemish from themselves.

When those fathers went in to [meet with] the patriarch of Alexandria he commanded that they set meat before them. Just as when the wise ones heard of all of the perverse stumbling blocks **(80ra)** unknown to the Christians, so [when] the monks were eating meat with the patriarch, that perverse blemish and offense to the Christians was taken away. According to the word of the Apostle Paul, "I will become without stumbling blocks to the Jews and the Gentiles and to the Christians for God."[91] So then on account of this, the patriarch ordered them to eat meat and being obedient to him they ate innocently with praises of God and prayer. When he said to one of them, "This piece [of meat] is excellent," which is praise, then they restrained themselves from eating. They said, "We are eating in order to remove from us the

[90] 1 Tim 4:1

[91] 1 Cor 9:19–23

blemish of external things and the offense of inner things within us. We do not desire fatty meat, not even a single piece. We do not fill up daily on dried bread and salt, but we do eat with innocence what is brought to us." But now, there are thoughts to restrain ourselves as we are eating because it is good and praiseworthy. **(80rb)** We do not then refuse to eat, because the Apostle said, "Everything that they bring to you, eat without question on account of freedom."[92] But if he says this [piece] is the sacrifice of an idol, then do not eat it because he speaks to you on account of his freedom. Again, I will not speak on about your freedom. But due to the freedom of whoever speaks to you, say to them, "Why is my freedom being judged by the freedom of others?"

[244] [DQC 2.289] *(80rb10–80vb11) The brothers said*: Why did Paul praise faith, hope and love more than the rest of the virtues?[93] Was he talking about the love of arrogance?

The Interpreter said: All of the virtues should be performed on three levels – in the physical way of life, in the way of the soul, and in the spiritual way of life. These three are connected with faith and love and hope.

Indeed, faith is the faith of righteousness for the sake of God and belief in his words.

Hope for its part is the eternal vision of the mind of **(80va)** the Lord and of the goodness of hope and love. It is the nature of one mind with God and one's desire for all that is his. In the first place then, when a person hears the teachings and reads the scriptures and [receives] the visitation of hidden grace, he confesses the excellence worthy of good for the righteous and the afflicted deserving of evil things. Immediately, he renounces the world and comes out to the monastery and performs the commandments of the Lord among the brothers with a righteous mind. This is the way of faith and is the way of the physical one and the original way of life.

Moreover, when he submerges himself deeply into the practice of the physical [way of life] it becomes for him the

---

[92] 1 Cor 10:27

[93] 1 Cor 13:13

excellent hope of the kingdom of heaven. He enters into the toil of the monastic life in the cell and struggles with the passions and demons in his thoughts, and prays without ceasing and his mind is persistent in speaking about God. The vision for him is indeed the way of hope and it is the joyful **(80vb)** way. The secondary way of life, moreover, is when he purifies his mind from evil thoughts and clears his mind for the struggle and his prayer will be saved from wandering and will enlighten for him the divine light in his prayer in order that his mind may perceive the love of Christ and turn himself towards spiritual prayer. This is the way of love and it is the final way. Indeed, it is superior and greater than both of the former ways of life.

[245] *(80vb11–81ra21)* He said, Now I am completing the desire of your request, a matter without cunning and complete without cleverness concerning three works. One of them, it is not fitting for monks to speak an embellished word, according to the word of Abba Evagrius, for an eloquent word is not appropriate for our way of life. The second too, regarding their entry into the community of solitaries – the words of interpretation which they will learn by heart are revealed in modest speech so that one may not desire another interpretation like one who is wise in their speech and their dwelling. The third, **(81ra)** the discourse of the fathers that wisely establishes the translations does not render it in a foreign language. Palladius did not write in the style of eloquent literature. Indeed, it is necessary that I should follow them in perfect speech for the desire of comfort of the speaker and the hearer, but there is no praise for the translators. I am not like the foreign wise ones with respect to the flesh and the contention which they show and determine. But I am imitating the fathers in love and humility, and therefore, I ask you for the love of our Lord Jesus Christ to pray for me to despise sin so that I may find from our Lord the gift and the strength on account of his will. May I find the delights of the Lord before death and find mercy on the day of judgment that is full of glory, Amen.

Praise be to the Father and the Son and the Holy Spirit, now and for all times and until forever and ever. Amen.

[This is] the completion of the fence [volume] of the translated writings of the *Paradise* which was translated to the end **(81rb)** of the book. It fences off the writing which is lacking in its flow a little bit. He has not had [as much] practice speaking to progress in the Arabic language than [in] the Syriac language according to Aramaic. This was completed by him in the second month in the year 1801, the pure testimony of the preservation of their deeds [is worth] more than the work of the love of gold which is the affliction of the soul.

ISAAC OF NINEVEH'S *CHAPTERS ON KNOWLEDGE*

DR GRIGORY KESSEL
UNIVERSITY OF MARBURG

INTRODUCTION

As is well-known today, the literary heritage of Isaac of Nineveh is preserved in the form of three *Parts* the text of which is almost completely edited. What remains so far unedited is the first half of the Second Part that was not included in the edition of S. Brock. In fact it consists of only three chapters, the third one, *Chapters on Knowledge* (*rīshē d-idaʿtā*), being of disproportionally extensive size. The *Chapters on Knowledge* consist of four sets of "centuries" each divided into a hundred sections of text of varying lengths. Although some consecutive chapters do convey an impression of an implicit connectedness and we may even observe how the author successively unfolds his idea, by and large the chapters constitute independent expressions of Isaac's thought. Notably, according to a personal explanation given by Isaac (I.41) the chapters were composed as his own comments to his text. If indeed so, then their organization into "centuries" must be considered as a later editorial effort, perhaps carried out by the disciples of Isaac.

Be that as it may, the genre of chapters, that is, a collection of monastic maxims that were composed to be reflected and meditated upon, was a very popular genre in the Christian tradition. Known as *Kephalaia* in Greek, the genre is believed to have been introduced by Evagrius Ponticus (d. 399), one of the most influential authors in the field of monastic theology and mysticism. Evagrius' work, the *Kephalaia gnostica*, is not extant in Greek (due to author's condemnation at the Second Council of Constantinople in

553) but survived in a Syriac translation that must have been implemented between the fifth and sixth centuries. The original text is extant in only one Syriac manuscript whereas all the other available texts provide a considerably different version regarded as an adaptation bereft of its original origenistic thoughts and eschatological doctrine.

Not conceived as such, the *Kephalaia gnostica* (*Gnostic chapters*) was received as a mystical treatise relating the mind's ascent to unity with God. This interpretation was further developed by a number of commentators of both traditions, that of the Syrian Orthodox (Dionysius bar Salibi) and that of the Church of the East (Babai the Great). In this manner the text appeared on monks' bookshelves and was highly regarded, especially by learned Syrian monks.

We should not be surprised, therefore, that there appeared a series of treatises all modeling themselves on Evagrius' work. In the course of time the genre of *Gnostic chapters* was apparently seen as one of the possible literary forms for the expression of sublime monastic experience that could not be articulated through discursive and logical genres of writing. Thus we hear about *Gnostic chapters* composed by Shemʿon d-Taybuteh, Aphnimaran, and John bar Penkaye in the seventh century, and John of Dalyatha and Joseph Hazzaya in the eighth, in addition to others. It would be fascinating to compare the extant Syriac texts to see how the genre developed over the course of time. This is, unfortunately, not yet possible as none of them are edited.

To translate Isaac into another language is not a simple task due to the involved nature of his thinking accompanied by a convoluted syntax. A translator is fully aware that their translation is only one of many possible renderings and that it is subject to their understanding of the text without any pretenses concerning its flawlessness.

The present selection of chapters from the *Chapters on Knowledge* is translated based on the manuscript Oxford, Bodleian Library syr. e. 7 and takes into account available translations into French (by the late Fr. A. Louf) and Italian (P. Bettiolo).

TRANSLATION

Ms. Oxford, Bodleian library, syr. e 7

I.1 (f. 20v)
God is truly a Father for the rational beings whom he begot by grace so that they would be heirs of his glory in time to come and in order to reveal them his treasure for the sake of their perpetual delight.

I.3 (f. 20v–21r)
On account of the fact that every word is being said only about what exists it can be classed according to the three orders. It speaks either about what exists, or about what is above it or below it. Whereas about God a word and a thought can think only in one way: beyond that limit a creature cannot move its knowledge but should turn back vested with fear and doubt.

I.9 (f. 21v)
Those who say that the vision of our Savior in this world is of a different nature than through contemplation are the companions of those who say that in the world to come the delight of his kingdom will be [experienced] in a sensed manner and that [there will be] a manipulation of the elements and consolidation of the substances. Both have slipped away from the truth.

I.12 (f. 22r)
A man is being enlightened according to the extent in which his conduct is directed towards God, and he approaches a liberty of the soul according to the extent in which he is attached to knowledge; and according to the extent in which he drew near to the liberty of the mind, he moves from one knowledge to a yet higher knowledge.

I.13 (f. 22r)
The light that is not intelligible comes from natural elements, but in the new world a new light will shine and there will be no need to have recourse to what is perceptible and consists of natural elements. Intelligible light is the mind enlightened by divine knowledge that is boundlessly poured into the [human] nature.

There will be spiritual light in the spiritual world, for darkness [in the new world] does not resemble [the darkness] that is here, and the light [in the world] is not similar to [the light] that is here.

I.14 (f. 22r)
Do not dispute about the truth with the one who does not know the truth and do not conceal the word from the one who desires to know [it].

I.15 (f. 22r–22v)
Let the one who cannot benefit from knowledge benefit from your silence rather than from the word of knowledge. Abase yourself according to his weakness, and talk to him in a language that resembles his in the manner of a bird so that you might catch him for life.

I.19 (f. 22v–23r)
Woe to us because we do not know the desire that our Creator had concerning us nor that grandeur that he will confer to us, whereas our intercourse is with the mundane [world] and its dung. It behoves us to become inebriated with hope [about that], to recall constantly about our [new] great and amazing abode and at any moment to move in our thoughts thither, where our Creator will lodge us at the end. Our abode will be in heaven and we shall become heavenly creatures in the life that has no end and change. That place was pre-established by God for our sake and through Christ the hope of [all] that was sowed in us as it was said also by the blessed Interpreter in a chapter about the firmament: "Now we are in the present state and abide in this land which is between that visible heaven and earth. But in a state that is to come, when we shall become incorruptible and steadfast, we shall abide wholly in heaven, the place of our Lord the Christ who was taken from us and for the sake of us and who is now on heaven and revealed to us our new abode".

I.20 (f. 23r–23v)
Do not think in vain that one can defer protractedly adoration before God, for even a psalmody is not greater than [adoration]. There is no other practice that is greater than [adoration] among all excellent activities (lit. *virtues*) performed by human beings. And for

what do I talk about [other] excellent activities if [adoration] through its constant [presence] near God lowers a virtue itself. [Adoration] is a sign of death to the world and a path to true penitence, according to the word of the Interpreter; it is a humility of a body and mind, termination of bad thoughts, dissolution of desires, preparation of the soul to a complete exodus from the body in mystery, a great eagerness to God's love, and all the good of the present [world] and of [the one] that is to come found in it.
Let not [adoration] be a petty thing in your eyes: if you are able, perform it without rest having renounced everything and yourself, and persevere only in [adoration]. If you give yourself to [adoration] do not talk about your bliss in a mundane language. For I tell you that whatever you encounter in it is ineffable and marvelous [in comparison] to the present [world]. It is truly a perfect exodus from the world and especially from the corrupted way of life. [It is] the end of all toils, pondering over all commandments, and the fulfillment of all virtues.

I.33 (f. 25v)
Impassibility consists not in insensibility to the passions but in rejection of those in inebriety of the mind because of soul's glory.

I.34 (f. 25v)
Do not cease the following prayer in your heart day and night: "Lord, deliver me from darkness of the soul", – because it is the limit of all mind's prayer. A dark soul is the second Sheol, and the enlightened mind is a companion of seraphs.

I.41 (f. 26v)
Those who will come across this book, will notice that all chapters of knowledge are written above the lines and in different places of the book. They should not think that it is done by mistake, for those chapters of knowledge are a certain elucidation of a multitude of things (lit. *words*) [treated] in this book and [should serve] the reader's comprehension and greater pleasure. Although the book was made by us as an aide-mémoire for ourselves from an abundance of contemplation of the Books (as I wrote in the beginning of the book) as well as, partially, from temptations that befell me, we wrote what is treated in those chapters of knowledge above [the lines] in order to explain the meaning of obscure ideas

in the text. In fact, there are some passages that besides an apparent meaning have within them also another meaning.

I.44 (f. 27r)
The one who during his abode in stillness delights in contemplation of the properties of Christ inherits as a pledge [already] here the Kingdom that is to come.

I.47 (f. 27r)
What irrigation means to plants, the very same is a constant silence to the growth of the knowledge.

I.52 (f. 27v)
An intelligible cloud is a mind absorbed in spiritual intellection with astonishment. It suddenly occurs within the soul and holds the mind immovable, whereas all visible things become hidden from it and [the mind loses] a knowledge and perception of the object of its consideration. And the mind stays still like a cloud that surrounds everything and conceals a bodily vision.

I.53 (f. 27v)
A true penitent is a live martyr. Tears prevail over blood because of the effects that they provoke and penitence [prevails] over martyrdom. [Tears and penitence] precede [blood and martyrdom] in coronation. The latter ones will receive the crowns together with others, but the former [will receive the crowns] first. Hence, it seems that a true penitent receives a double crown.

I.60 (f. 28v–29r)
As it is impossible to hear a word without [hearing] the composition of sounds, so it is impossible that the mind deals internally with passions without any matter.

I.62 (f. 29r)
I dare to maintain that the purpose of contemplation of the future world is visible in the existence of the holy angels, when we all will become gods by the grace of our Creator. This is in fact his purpose from the beginning: to bring the creatures endowed with reason to equality, so that there will be no difference between one and another (not due to complexity nor to simplicity) while not

being deprived of the natural body. But then it will be impossible to investigate these things.

I.66 (f. 29v)
Strengthen your mind during service through splendor robed by a flame that is ignited from reading.

I.70 (f. 30r)
When through [the life of] stillness passions in the soul have been weakened and have fallen silent, [then] one can also easily prevail on desires of the body.

I.72 (f. 30v)
The aim of labor of the one who toils rightly must be to render the mind invincible to the passions and to make it healthy and immovable. Whereas the aim of knowledge is to draw the mind near to the gift of divine vision and that is a completion of contemplation.

I.75 (f. 30v)
Meek in thought is the one who while praised deservedly does not find satisfaction in that.

I.85 (f. 32r)
Mortification of the body is to become a stranger to all one's acquaintances, country, family and people (cf. Gen 12: 1); to move to a foreign land, to choose a place of stillness, where the tumults have ceased, and to dwell there alone in poverty and corporal scantiness, keeping from any connection with men, conversations and visible consolations. He should beg God with mourning, tears and compunction of the heart to purify him from communion with sin and to strip off from him the members of the old man, a sinner who is the worldly movements. This mortification gives rise to mortification of the soul.

I.87 (f. 32v–33r)
The mortification of the soul is not to aspire in the heart after the things of this world and its passing comfort, not to indulge in the desires of earthly things with wandering thoughts, but to have always a mind that is longing, while waiting impatiently and

tirelessly, for the hope of what is to come; and that each reflection, converse and motion of his heart wanders, meditates and ponders at any time about that which is going to be to the people in the new life after the resurrection; to an effect that because of the great zeal of motions of his soul towards such things even while asleep the soul's concern is seized and it ponders and wanders in the movements of his dream. Truly, this is a real mortification of the one who died with Christ, that is to say who died the death of Jesus, who is the resurrection of all the worlds. Such mortification cannot be achieved without the operation and assistance of the Spirit's grace. Mortification like that gives rise to mortification of the spirit.

I.89 (f. 33r–33v)
Mortification of the spirit is that the mind is raised to the vision of the divine and ineffable realities through an operation [of the Spirit], and that all thoughts of earthly things become silenced; and while being in the midst of a figure of the future [world, filled] with wonder from intuitions about the realities that are not from the world of the dead he receives through spiritual feelings as a deposit that Kingdom and rises to those dwellings (Jn 14:2) that are not from flesh or from blood. This is [the meaning of] "Let thy Kingdom come before the time" that we are commanded to ask and reflect upon at any time and to long for it incessantly – we are commanded [to do that] by our Savior with diligence.

II.1 (f. 34v)
As the movements of the air show by their changes to have a governor, so the thought with its opposite changes, either to right or to left, reveals that struggles and the assistance of grace adhere constantly to its movements and they lead from one day to another to the apprenticeship of the new.

II.12 (f. 36v)
The fathers say that, at a time when a man begins to separate from the sin that dwells in him and to go away from the dominion of the spirit of this world, what happens to him undergoes the woman whose time of the childbirth has approached; because the sin torments him day and night, so that his soul is almost about to perish, and it brings upon him a myriad of temptations. But when

the air in front of him starts to lighten and he sees hope from afar, then his heart takes courage against the one who opposes him, and he gains a complete victory over sin; every new day the joy calls on him and difficult changes that come upon him pass away easily until gradually he arrives at the haven of mercy, that all the saints, afflicted and troubled for God, waited for after their long labors.

II.16 (f. 37r)
The faith in our Lord is the refuge of the soul in time of temptations and sorrow; confession of his weakness is the refuge of his [ascetic] practice.

II.18 (f. 38r)
Oh! How weak is the power of the ink and the outlines of the letters to demonstrate something with precision in comparison with the knowledge of those who have indeed become worthy of the gift of delight of spiritual realities from the abundant grace of God!

II.23 (f. 39r)
Humility is the virtue of a healthy intellect. As long as it remain in man it does not experience abandonment during any of the temptations [that occur] to test the body or intellect, or during any – either corporal or psychical – sufferings or sorrows.

II.25 (f. 39v)
When vainglory is present in a corporal intellect it passes on to us a passion of lust. When instead it [occurs] in a psychic intellect it nourishes in us pride. The former [comes through] the flatteries of the body, while the latter [comes through] a virtuous behavior or knowledge.

II.31 (f. 40v)
Solitude joins us with the divine intellect and shortly afterwards and without any hindrance brings us near to the clarity of thought.

II.32 (f. 40v)
When the light goes down and the air is stuffy employ zealously the apparent opportunities. I mean, genuflection, extended prayer, and the rest. Because the air will emerge suddenly, and the sun will rise

again, without a notice, and will radiate rays up to the midst of the firmament.

II.33 (f. 40v–41r)
A desert place, because of the great deprivation that reigns there, enables us to acquire the mortification of the heart, grants a child's heart and joins it with God through continuous gazing at him, necessarily, night and day.

II.35 (f. 41r)
The stillness of the mind is the [necessary] condition [to keep] the truth in the soul, because the truth is known without any image. Truth is the limpidity of thought about God that emerges in the mind.

II.37 (f. 41r–41v)
The passion does not rule over the thought that is dead to the world. The death from the world is an expectation of the death. A recollection caused by affection to something moves swiftly and fervently in thought. And when affection fades, the remembrance remains in a man for a long time. And when it occurs then it is cooled and ordinary, and that memory does not trouble us in any way. And this is the death of which I have spoken. When there is no affection in us towards anything, the passion is asleep in us and we are not troubled by its recollection or its sight. However, when we are troubled by its recollection or sight, be aware that it still lives in us because of the affection to it.

II.40 (f. 43r)
Wherever you are, be a solitary in your thought, be single and stranger in the heart and do not get mixed [with the world].

II.46 (f. 45v)
The word of the thief on the right (cf. Lk 23:42) reveals faith and repentance. Those who believe and supplicate like him, no doubt, will not be excluded from sharing with him in the promise that he received. [It even applies to] the murderers or fornicators, provided only that they put an end to their previous modes [of life].

II.48 (f. 46rv)
On account of the resort to sins people receive chastisement while on account of the error of the intellect and pride they suffer a punishment of demons, because both are the causes of blasphemy. The judgment of the former [brings] correction, [the judgment] of the latter [brings] complete perdition.

II.51 (f. 47v)
Holiness is sanctification through prayer and through the power of the operation of the Holy Spirit.

II.52 (f. 47v)
As long as our heart is not sanctified by the Spirit of the Lord we cannot clearly distinguish whether the hidden movements [proceed] from the operation of demons or angels or from nature or from the impact of the Holy Spirit.

II.53 (f. 47v)
As long as our word is not sanctified by the power of the Spirit, it cannot be vigorous over the demons and neither the creatures endowed with reason nor the mute ones submit to it.

II.54 (f. 47v)
The activity of the Holy Spirit is not present in us as long as we are not cleansed from the activity of sin. [Only then] we can become the vessels of holiness for the Lord's descent.

II.58 (f. 49r)
When you fall face down in front of the cross at the [time of] prayer that begins the service, ask from God before you begin the service, while pleading with a sorrowful heart, to give you patience in that [service] so that you can persevere in the repetition of the verses without discouragement, without struggles against disturbance, and say, "Lord, grant me throughout this office the bright motions that gaze at you in the verses that come out of my mouth".

II.68 (f. 52r)
It became all creation to worship the image of the King (cf. Heb 1, 3). To our time no one had seen that angels worshiped a man. The

appellation with the name of an image is proper for the one at whom gaze all creation, visible and invisible, and whom it worships and who is called by the name of God. For it is through him that all creation will draw near to God and in his visible body we saw incomprehensible hidden reality.

II.72 (f. 52v–53r)
When the mind receives the perception of the beauty of its nature, then it grows with the mysterious growth of the angels. Henceforth it becomes worthy of communion with the angels, in the revelations of his mind; because it rose into the primordial state of his created nature [when] it is also able to receive the contemplation of the prototype.

II.76 (f. 53v)
The fathers say that when a man has become worthy to look upon the radiance of his soul during prayer, then he is also worthy [to receive] in his mind the mystery of angelic revelations as well as a revelation of incomprehensible realities. They call the soul's radiance its splendor because when it is purified from any communion with sin at the time of prayer its splendor lights it up like the sun. The same [splendor] radiates the soul during the motions of prayer and during the service and it draws the mind through the operation of the Spirit, with a certain intuition, towards divine and mysterious realities. They call that splendor the primordial creation of the soul. However, sometimes they use the name of radiance and sometimes that of splendor.

II.80 (f. 54v–55r)
Beware not to neglect any of your services, but before going to sleep fatigue your body at service and through many prayers agreements, so that when you sleep the angels may guard all night your body and soul in purity from terrible visions, abominable fantasies and injuries of demons, because your bed and your sleep are sanctified by the hymns to the Spirit and by the work of prayer. It should never happen (unless you are ill) that when you go to bed you do not see how your exhausted body falls on the bed because of great labor in prayers, hymns and frequent psalms during many hours. Do not ever approach our beds without being tired lest the rebellious demons mock at us all night.

II.83 (f. 55v–56r)
The day of a nature endowed with reason [consists in] pondering over a mystery [while trying] to penetrate further into it. And this is [the meaning of]: The righteous will shine like the sun in the kingdom of their Father (Mt 13:43).

II.85 (f. 56v)
Arrange everything [well], so that by all means between the night and morning services to have time for a meditation that is useful for your growth in the divine science in all your days. [Meditation] is also one of the main parts of the practice of vigilance. Do not think that the vigilance [consists] only in the repetition [of the verses] and is limited to what it involves. Although that is the foundation, but the monks' vigilance has numerous forms through which the soul should grow and draw near to the spiritual knowledge.

II.86 (f. 56v–57r)
Balance of sleep is obviously similar to [the balance] of the belly. We make our sleep longer and shorter according to our will, [as] it is placed in our hands. Indeed, if we keep the belly within limits we easily wake up of our own will before the appointed time due to the lightness of the body and thereby [we get] time for both forms of practice.

II.87 (f. 57r)
Do the same thing with respect to the hours of the day and divide them into [different] parts: some for reading, the other for the service, and another for meditation. When this place will be ceded to the raising of the limpidity of the movements, we [as well] come to the completion of the rest. If the mind darkens here, then add a reading appropriate for that time. Indeed, that is an abundant source from which pure water flows to him in a limpid manner.

II.88 (f. 57r)
When the meditation unites to the prayer in its limpidity, then comes to its fulfillment the word of the Lord who said: "Where two or three are gathered in my name, there I am between them" (Mt 18:20). [Those three are:] the soul, the body and the spirit or

the mind, meditation and prayer. And three of those lead to amazement, [whereas only one] cannot reach [even] prayer.

II.89 (f. 57r)
As long as the power of the Spirit is not mixed with the meditation of thought, the amazement at God cannot be intermingled with his movements.

II.90 (f. 57r)
As long as the thought does not become limpid, it does not take part in the operation of the Spirit.

II.91 (f. 57r)
When movements have started to become limpid, then the heart humbles itself and lives as in an abyss. And from that humility it draws near the limpidity.

II.92 (f. 57r–57v)
Love solitude, even if you are weak [to accomplish] everything that it requires. For one prayer offered to God by a man alone is better than a hundred services celebrated in the midst of people. Verily, do not weigh a hundred day labor in agitation and converse when a solitary keeps the fast and celebrates the services [even] with a single sleep when he sleeps alone! Thus pray continuously in your solitude: God, make me worthy of the suffering of mourning in my heart. God, erase from my heart the worldly concerns. This prayer will raise you in the mysteries of Christ, if you do your best to translate it in your conduct.

II.93 (f. 57v)
The pride is present in the work [done] amidst the people; the heart's sorrow is in feebleness that is in the stillness.

II.94 (f. 57v)
Without stillness the heart cannot be humble, and without humiliation of the heart the heart is not ignited by movements; [compared] to those, all labors of a solitary are dust and ash.

II.100 (f. 58v)
God wants to give healing to every man at any time if a sick one implores. His greatness does not despise difficult and abominable diseases, but the worse and more abominable the diseases the greater the concern he reveals if one who is sick implores and converts. His door is not closed and there is no moment [for God] that differs from the other, because whenever somebody invokes him he is ready to help thoughtfully. He does not neglect anybody because of a serious disease but if a sick one invokes him properly he makes worthy of a greater zeal because of the difficulty of his illnesses that tend to death.

II.102 (f. 58v)
The contemplation of judgment and providence of God even for the spiritual beings remains in vagueness as in a cloud [along with] a wonder at their incomprehensibility.

III.1 (f. 59r–59v)
In the past God had no name, and he will not have it in the future.

III.2 (f. 59v)
We are not mortal because we sin but because we are mortal we are necessitated to commit sin. The power of freedom is placed in the middle and can be employed to be of benefit either to life or to death.

III.7 (f. 60r)
The virtue can cause both life and death. Life – to the zealous, and death – to the slothful. Through manifestation of its distinctions you can choose for the benefit out of those two.

III.12 (f. 60v)
The words that prayer sets in motion draw all parts of the soul to God through a sweetness of the soul's love [inspired] by the amazing magnificence of the verses and they watch over the soul to gaze at God fervently and scrutinize him.

III.13 (f. 60v–61r)
When I talk about a wise and perfect prayer I do not mean that it comes from the wisdom of this world, or from education that is

full of foolishness and that puts the soul to shame during prayer before God because of vainglory that stirs in the soul and [such words] that drive away God's aid. Rather I talk about such words of wisdom [recited] during prayer that spring out of the wisdom of God and the luminosity of the soul. Fervent motions in the soul send these out because of the love of the true life that precedes the prayer, warms up the heart and causes the words to be uttered involuntarily – a remembrance urges them to spring forth. Oh how many times do tears spring forth because of the fervor of the heart and God's support! That is what [the Fathers] call pure prayer.

III.16 (f. 62r)
The victim of reconciliation is humility that is offered with invocation to God from a dead heart on account of the faults of which one is guilty before the Life of the Worlds: either those that he committed previously or those that he sins and goes astray every day. [When] his soul awakens and he goes away from those and turns at every moment to repentance keeping in mind God's mercy. God is pleased with this prayer more than with any sacrifice or offer.

III.18 (f. 62v)
As long as man does not humble himself divine support will not draw near him. God's grace is standing constantly at a distance and looks at the man, especially at the hour of prayer. And as soon as the thought of humility starts moving, then [the grace] immediately comes up to him while carrying a boundless assistance.

III.19 (f. 63r)
The help that is given at the hour of prayer is greater than [the help that is provided] at any other moment when man toils. Therefore at that time Satan wages a fierce struggle against a man so that he could not draw near to God in his thoughts.

III.20 (f. 63r)
Every wisdom of this world that is recollected during prayer becomes at that very moment an opponent of the soul that causes it harm. Whereas the wisdom of the Spirit humbles the soul and guards that it contemplates God in awe, and it brings the soul close

to an abyss of humility thanks to the truth that it reveals without a veil.

III.23 (f. 63v)
The saying *Holiness becomes your house* (Ps 93:5) has the same meaning as this: *Holiness is given to the saints*, – because we, the beings endowed with reason, are the house of the Lord. And when we cleanse his house, as befits the Lord, through a withdrawal from everything that is evil, his holiness comes and abides in us, because holiness becomes the saints, in the union of will.

III.24 (f. 63v–64r)
Holiness becomes your house (Ps 93:5) – it is right that the house of God should be filled with holiness and glory. Likewise, it is appropriate for the one who wishes to become the abode of the Holy Spirit that he should purify his soul of all evil so that it might resemble heaven as much as possible. For as heaven is clear of all evil and is the throne of God and the home of the Seraphim and abounding with all spiritual blessings, in a similar manner it is appropriate for the soul that eagerly desires to become the abode of the deity that it ought to cleanse itself from all wicked stirrings and fill itself with every kind of praise. That is when the Lord shall dwell in it and shall fill it with the splendor of his holiness. It will be surrounded on all sides by the spiritual beings, because it is their responsibility to honor the abode of their Lord. At first man purifies himself of evil and fills himself with fine scents, and then the Lord sanctifies him through the Spirit.

III.27 (f. 64v)
Cleanse your mind from corporeal thoughts so that you can enjoy that delight that the language falls short of describing.

III.28 (f. 64v)
The hope for what is to come removes from the mind a remembrance about the mundane things. Continually raise your thought and look at those dwellings where you are to ascend at the end!

III.32 (f. 65r)
It is easy to acquire a soul that remains beyond the notions [formed by] the bodily senses when one abandons hope in the bodily life and rejects its concerns.

III.34 (f. 65r)
Beware lest the weakness of the body hinder you from the life of solitude. Indeed, in the life of stillness with God your delight will double if the body suffers torments. Beware lest you deliver yourself to the two diseases that lead to eternal death: to wit an idleness of the body and the soul that is spoiled through the senses. However, a disease that is accompanied by vigilance cannot cause us any harm.

III.42 (f. 66v)
Pure prayer [can be achieved] when the mind does not wander in what is provoked by the demons in thought or what is aroused by nature or because of a remembrance or an incentive of temperament.

III.44 (f. 66v-67r)
The more a thought is elevated above the love of what is in this world, the more a man will be stilled through the images of the thought at the time of prayer. And when he is completely elevated beyond the love of what is here, the thought no longer remains in prayer, but is raised above pure prayer, because the dawn of grace rises continually in his prayer and lifts [the thought] from time to time through the holy activity.

III.50 (f. 69r)
A prayer that is not followed by fair conduct is [like] an eagle with plucked wings.

III.51 (f. 69r)
There is a pure and spiritual thinking. Pure thinking is when we have thoughts related to what is in the world, but their remembrance is without passion. Spiritual thinking is when it rouses from such recollections to their contemplation. It should not however happen that they remain even in such a pure and impassionate [condition] but with a spiritual eye gaze inside of

them and through perception of their movements inhale a taste of the Spirit. The former may be acquired through labor and vigilance and the latter through exercise and consideration of a spiritual purpose by an active mind.

III.54 (f. 69v)
There is no gnostic [mature monk] void of virtue in his conduct, however you can find many virtuous [monks] who have not acquired knowledge. Therefore let us hasten towards knowledge, because it is that which brings the virtuous conduct of our soul to perfection and it draws our mind to the vision of the wisdom of the divine realities. If our soul is not conversant with knowledge, the practice of virtue cannot remain pure.

III.59 (f. 71v–72r)
According to the demonstrations found in the spiritual books as well as in the teaching of the saints and in their lives, all the revelations that disclose realities or events, such revelations are brought about by holy angels to a man in two ways. The first way is as a dream of someone who is sound asleep, the other [occurs] manifestly through the senses, and [makes use] of visible forms, perceivable vision and voice, as occurred to Jacob, Joshua the son of Nun, Isaiah, Daniel, the twelve prophets and others, the priest Zechariah, and the rest of the saints. Some of them received a revelation manifestly through the audible speech, others while asleep, as in a dream, were relayed and imparted the concealed realities. These are the two ways by which revelations from angels take place disclosing the future and instructing on what is to be done.

III.61 (f. 72r–72v)
The soul of the solitary resembles a water source, to which the ancient fathers likened it as well, because whenever it quiets down from every impulse coming from hearing and sight, the solitary can clearly see God and himself; and he draws from it [the soul] clear and delightful water that is to say sweet thoughts of [its] original condition. However, when he approaches them in confusion that was accepted by the soul then it resembles somebody walking in the night when the sky is covered with clouds so that he cannot see the road and the path in front of him and he easily goes astray to

the deserted and dangerous places. But as soon as he quiets within himself he is like the one on whom blows fresh wind, the sky lightens over his head and lights up in front him; he can see himself and knows where he is and where he should go, and he observes from afar the dwelling of life. […]

III.63 (f. 73r)
It is wrong [to say] that only after one is completely purified, one can perceive the spiritual good things and signs of the New Life. Rather from day to day one can see in his soul the traces of purity to the extent that vanquishes the passions. For as soon as he conquers a passion at once the good that is opposite to it starts to shine; and to the extent that one is purified from the sin so, gradually, in proportion to his purity, he encounters spiritual rest; and to the extent that the mind is freed from the constraints of thoughts concerning the passions, the splendor of knowledge beams in his heart.

III.65 (f. 74r)
My brothers, instances of passion are sweet, but not as much as the fruits of righteousness. Bitter and austere are the instances of justice, my beloved ones, but not as much as the effect of sin.

III.69 (f. 74v)
Revered is the one who in his incomprehensible wisdom placed us at first in the life of learning, the carnal world, and imposed through death a limit to error, the mother of afflictions, and prepared for us a glorious world where life will not be affected by sorrows.

III.71 (f. 75rv)
If God is truly a Father, who engendered all by grace, whereas the rational beings are his children, and this world is as a representation of the school where [God] instructs [our] childhood in knowledge and corrects in proportion to the fault; and if the future world is the heritage for the time of *the fullness of stature* (Eph. 4:13) – then the time will come when these children will become men, and in the world of men, undoubtedly, the Father will change the appearance of instruction into joyfulness, as soon as these children

grow beyond the need to be corrected. *Thy judgments are inscrutable* (Rm 11:33)!

III.73 (f. 75v–76r)
Oh man, how amazing is a meditation on your formation! But even more amazing than that is [a meditation] on the mysteries of your resurrection. Again: it is astounding to investigate a beginning of your formation, but greater and more marvelous is the glory of your resurrection. "My soul is sorrowful, even unto death" [Mt 26:38] but I take heart in the faith, because of the one who died and rose and by his resurrection gave to mankind the consolation of hope.

III.74 (f. 76r)
Do not be sad about your entry into the silence of the tomb, oh mortal man, you who are more beautiful than anything else and corrupted by the abuse of death! Behold, God imposed a limit on your silent humiliation, when [even] your absence is not recognized by anybody. How beautiful is your composition, and how terrible is your corruption! Do not be afflicted by that sorrow, for you are going to be clothed in it again, burning with *Fire and Spirit* [cf. Mt 3:11], and carrying the exact image of your Creator. Do not be troubled by doubts about the strength of such a hope, because Paul comforts you about it: *He shall change our vile body and will fashion it like unto his glorious body* (Phil 3:21).

III.79 (f. 77v)
The natures endowed with intellect infinitely surpassed in knowledge what they comprehended in our Lord Christ (what they had not known before) who came for the sake of their and our liberation and perfection.

III.81 (f. 78r)
After the coming of Christ the intelligible beings acquired an excellent knowledge of the wisdom of God, because they could see how differently he operated the dispensation toward us in order to gather everything in one through the dispensation of Christ. When we receive that, we all will become one. Those who are now zealous in the fear of God, if they persevere in that, will dwell in heaven in abundant felicity together with invisible powers and our

Lord Christ. There, we all will be seen [as] one church with our Lord.

III.82 (f. 78rv)
All that should be perfectly accomplished with regard to the entire creation will not come to God's mind only before its realization, rather it was set and prepared by God for fulfillment from the beginning and before all the generations. However it remained hidden and concealed within him, and was not proclaimed. His mystery was revealed at the end through prophecies and they were implemented in the economy of Christ our Lord. Everything will receive its full accomplishment when our Lord rises from heaven above all and resurrects us from the dust, and to the entire creation alongside us he will grant renewal and deliverance from all sufferings, and he will raise all with him to the heavenly abode.

III.93 (f. 81r)
The kingdom and gehenna are not the reward for good or evil deeds, but the reward of acts of will.

III.95 (f. 81r)
Virtue is not the seed of good practice, but of a good will.

III.98 (f. 81v)
Good and just deeds are different. How often are good deeds performed by a corrupted mind! Whereas justice is a desire that aims at the satisfaction of God's will

III.99 (f. 81v)
One thing is the education [drawn] from books and the knowledge gained from exercise in them, and another is the knowledge of the truth of the books. The former is consolidated through extensive study and laborious learning, the latter arises from the practice of the commandments, and limpid thinking directed to God.

III.100 (f. 81v–82r)
The entire course of the motions of the mind in spiritual movement is limited to three kinds of knowledge that are said to be beyond purity: at the first one becomes educated, at the next one acquires perfection, and at the third one is being crowned. Two of

those belong to the natural course, and one is beyond nature. The first is [called] second natural knowledge, the next is the first natural knowledge, and the one at which is being crowned is the [knowledge] of the honorable Trinity and that is the exact mystery of the Spirit.

IV.1 (f. 82r)
A fulfillment of penitence is the beginning of purity; a fulfillment of purity is the beginning of limpidity. The way of purity is the works of virtue, but to become limpid is a work of revelations.

IV.2 (f. 82r)
Purity is a stripping off of the passions; limpidity is a stripping off of opinions and a transformation of thinking to the exact knowledge of the mysteries.

IV.8 (f. 82v)
A crowning of the pure mind is not a perfection, but its gazing on perfection.

IV.13 (f. 83v)
The spiritual behavior is the amazement before the mysteries which cannot be learned neither from men nor from angels, but it rises in the soul by the Spirit of holiness, through fulfillment of the commandments and through the insights of the divine mysteries that diffuse in the mind.

IV.16 (f. 84v)
There are many people who were instructed by that paucity of sentences that is written in the books of holy men. They embellished their words and started to talk profoundly about them; they believed that they had in reality achieved spiritual behavior. And they did not come to realize and consider that people cannot know this practice through the craft of words, education or teaching. The mysteries of God can not be learned through ink and words, but [only] if they are sown by him in the heart through amazing insights before his grandeur that diffuse at the depths of a pure mind.

IV.18 (f. 84v–85r)
The blessed Paul has written a lot about the spiritual realities, but one cannot perceive from his letters what he had tasted unless he partakes in the Spirit.

IV.24 (f. 86r)
If somebody from among the solitaries without a compelling reason neglects the seven services that were canonically established for the salvation of those who struggle with the demons and should he tell you: "I am freed from submission to the spirit of fornication", – then even if he is an elder in the monastic life (either in [his] practice or thought) you should know for certain and beyond doubt that he deceives you while trying to conceal his shame and to carry off the consciousness of himself in order not to abandon the rest and become submitted to the rule.

IV.27 (f. 66v–67r)
The passions of the body – desire, anger, love of idle talk, and others – are silenced by fasting, regular services and dwelling in stillness. The passions of the soul – that is to say a wandering without knowledge – which are envy, vainglory, pride, and the others, are eliminated through prayer, reading, and [acquired] from that knowledge. Who would like to eliminate the passions of the body or to overcome ignorance of the mind without those [practices] tires himself out. However, with those [practices] even the erroneous idle thoughts that give rise to the darkness of the mind are eliminated.

IV.31 (f. 87r–87v)
Nothing is so dear to God and honored by the angels, abases Satan, frightens demons, shakes sin, brings forth knowledge, attracts mercy, wipes out sins, acquires humility, makes the heart wise, grants consolation, unifies the mind – as a solitary kneeling on the ground who is occupied with constant prayer. This is the haven of repentance for which all penitent thoughts are longing with tears. This is the treasure of stronghold, the washing of the heart, the path of purity, the way of revelations and the ladder of the mind. It makes the mind to resemble God and allows it to receive [God] in his motions through future realities. It atones in a

short time a debt of long negligence. Within its confines it includes different labors that have numerous forms.

There is nothing greater than constancy [in recitation] of the psalms in a chaste manner. But if somebody disregards that even a little, because he is absorbed in desire of that worship, he should not be considered as a wrongdoer, but as one who was raised to a more excellent degree, to a greater work and to the practice which performance makes familiar to God, having received a more internal gift. [...]

IV.45 (f. 91v)
As long as you are still at the first stage you ought to toil above all through long services of the Psalms, abundant recitation and reading of books while accompanying those by a lengthy hunger that cleanses and purges the body through its fervor. That can grant the forgiveness of previous sins through its laborious difficulties more than any other work. It is the power of great penitence and the previous habits that you have adopted through abominable deeds in transgression of the law are abased by hunger.

IV.51 (f. 94r)
The man receives stillness of thoughts insofar as he moves away from dwelling in the world and goes deep into the desert and a wild place and the heart feels remoteness from every human soul. Indeed, my brother, we do not suffer great torment from thoughts in the desert nor do we get tired in a fierce struggle against them. The mere sight of a desert naturally kills the mundane motions of the heart and holds it back from the urge of thoughts.

IV.62 (f. 96r–96v)
If you wish to know your stage, [to know] where you are, and if your soul is on the right path or outside of it, what is your superiority and shortcoming, try your soul in prayer. This, indeed, is the mirror of the soul and the examiner of its defects and beauty. It is there that comes out falsehood and beauties of thought. [Prayer] examines whether [the soul] is negligent or zealous, and if [the soul] labors only in the body or in mind, or in both, if one is separated from the world in his thought, or attached to someone or something. At the time of prayer it is possible to observe clearly what arouses the mind and what motions surge up – divine, natural

or mundane – if it prevails on the passions or suffers defeat. Request a trial for your soul on all those points during prayer more than at any other time. I say this [assuming] that you are a vigilant man who is able to grasp easily what concerns you because of the sagacity of your conduct. At the time of sloth, if one is not blinded by the obvious passions, then even outside of prayer time he can make out his soul; therefore what [was said above] should be observed at the stage of stillness and when it is conducted for a long time, because the paths become narrow there and the doubts may arise whether one is on the right or on the wrong [path].

IV.70 (f. 99v–100r)
We should not be frightened of the duration of the service or of the time span of prayers and their repetition, because what I mentioned earlier arises through the labor of repetition of the words and steadfastness in their prolongation. However, we should hold to those [practices] not for the sake of their fruit, but their root without which no fruit appears and falls in our hands. Every day and every moment we are in search of the fruit to feed us and to take our delight in it, likewise [we ought to value] the root. If we despise and eradicate [the roots] deemed useless, then we will deprive ourselves also of the fruit which may occasionally become visible from their midst. Let nobody break off unchangeable constancy as long as we are clothed with flesh. We should not be anxious: those [things] have an end.

IV.72 (f. 100v–101r)
After God has made you worthy of the gift of stillness so that you could remain alone, you must not disperse yourself in a multitude of books. Limpidity emerges not through considerable learning or through different books, but through a diligence in prayer. What is the use of knowledge of a multitude of books and their commentaries for the recollection of thought and purity in prayer? Truly, every solitary who after having abandoned a mundane way of life [still] reads besides the books about monasticism [at least] one of those, scholarly or mundane, books, first of all, ruins the purpose of the solitary life and afterwards his mind will incline to seek pleasure in those. Even if such books raise you to heaven their reading will not help you unless they teach about the monastic way of life. The books of the New Testament as well as about

monasticism are sufficient for [acquiring] perfect knowledge and limpid thinking. Read [whatever you want] and you will not be injured as soon as you reach at least a little bit of limpidity. Behold, I have given you my testimony about everything.

IV.75 (f. 102r)
The renunciation, stillness and absence of attachment to somebody or something are the intial principals of the solitary life. Its practice [consists in] patience concerning [whatever] may happen, humility and prayer; whereas an entry into hope and joyful delight in God are the fruits. A fulfillment of that is a receipt of the keys to the glorious mysteries of the Spirit. The end of the road is a taste of love and free speech that [is granted] by the one who is beloved. It is obvious that those who do not know the beginning of the way, namely renunciation and stillness, do not possess either humility or prayer. Being deprived of these, they will necessarily be troubled by sins. However the sinner will not have a place not only in the Kingdom, but even in hell will not have a certain place.

IV.79 (f. 104r)
The reason for the existence of the world and the coming of Christ into the world is one: the manifestation of the abundant love of God who made both to take place.

IV.92 (f. 107v–108r)
The first gift that is being granted to the solitary, who [lives] in absolute and vigilant stillness, when he completes the second stage (and that is an intermediate stage of the monastic practice) and his feet are at the threshold of the third stage (which is the spiritual way of life) when the grace of the Spirit overshadows him: first of all, he is given a recollection of thought and afterwards he enters into the great gifts that were described by the fathers.

IV.100 (f. 110r)
Who can glorify you for what you are worthy of, Oh God, Father of all, [who] granted the good things without an entreaty? My Lord, let not your hope cease in our hearts, for it is through it that the remembrance of you is constantly fixed in our thought. And let the one whom for the sake of hope of the entire world you raised to you be a supplier of a thanksgiving on behalf of us. Lord, let

nobody clothed with flesh and bones be left on earth without him, but rather let [everybody] be aroused to his heavenly portion and there the entire world will glorify you looking at its beginning with that new glory that cannot be pronounced by a fleshly tongue. Amen.

ISAAC THE SYRIAN: THE *THIRD PART*

MARY T. HANSBURY

PREFACE

Little is known of Isaac's life. Only two brief references give details.[1]

Both agree that Isaac was a native of Beth Qaṭraye. It is then noted that he became a monk and teacher near his home. Catholicos Giwargis consecrated him as bishop of Nineveh (*ca.* 676). Soon Isaac asked to resign and he lived as a solitary in Beth Huzaye, in the mountains of Khuzistan. He studied Scripture so much that he became blind and had to dictate his writings, which explains certain difficulties of his style. He died at an advanced age and was buried at Rabban Shabur.

This translation of Isaac III is based on one recent manuscript conserved in Tehran, Issayi Collection, ms 5. Of the 133 folios, 111 are by Isaac, or 17 texts. Of these 14 had not previously been known: 1–13, 16. Two others may be found in Is.I: 14 and 15 appearing as 22 and 40. And 17 corresponds to 25 in Is.II. These three chapters have not been included in this translation.[2]

As to the content of Is.III, it seems more concentrated. Concepts already found in Is.I and Is.II are found here. But rather than expansion, there is clarification of important themes already found in Is.I and Is.II. As noted by Chialà, the first theme here is

---

[1] J.B. Chabot, "Le Livre de la chasteté, composé par Jésusdenah, Evêque de Basrah," in *Mélanges d'Archéologie et d'histoire* 16 (1986), 277–78; I.E. Rahmani, *Studia Syriaca* (Lebanon: Charfet Seminary, 1904), p.33.

[2] For a more detailed analysis of the manuscript see S. Chialà *CSCO* 246, VIII–XXIII. And see S. Brock *CSCO* 224, XXXI–XXXII.

prayer and intimacy with God in 1–IV, VIII–IX, and XVI. Whereas God's infinite love for creation is found in V–VI and IX. In VII and X there are texts of prayers. In XII and XIII are letters sent to solitaries in difficulty.

Context

According to Paolo Bettiolo, the major influences on Isaac are Theodore of Mopsuestia, Evagrius and John the Solitary. In addition to the many citations of Theodore, Bettiolo notes how much of Isaac's structure derives from Theodore, including: two worlds, this world and the world to come; the first as pedagogy of the second, and the world as school; angelology; human mortality and salvation history; even Isaac's Christological terminology, though more evangelical in tone than Theodore.[3]

As to Evagrius, Bettiolo sees in addition to the numerous direct quotations of Evagrius, his role as guide in the discernment of experiences of contemplation and as master of pure prayer.

Finally there is the influence of John the Solitary in Isaac, seen in the development of the three stages of the life of the soul as well as a sense of "new world" and all that it implies. And hope is fundamental to John the Solitary's eschatology, a gift from God transcending human initiation, based on the resurrection of Christ and the grace of baptism. It has been said that John the Solitary derives this from Theodore of Mopsuestia.[4]

Sub-text

But perhaps the most striking influence on Isaac, at least in this manuscript, is Scripture. It is reading (*qeryanâ*) which generates continual prayer (IX.12) and of course it is the reading of Scripture which is intended. Reading is for prayer (IX.3). Reading is meditation and prayer (IX.11). Prayer without reading is weak (IX.15). In addition there are very many citations and allusions to Scripture in this manuscript making it seem almost like a sub-text.

---

[3] P. Bettiolo, *Isacco di Ninive, Discorsi Spirituali e altri opusculi* (Bose: Edizioni Qiqajon, 1989), 35–39.

[4] J.-M. Lera, "Theodore de Mopsuestia," *DSpir* XV (1991), 385–400.

Writing about Dadishoᶜ, a contemporary of Isaac who also originated from Beth Qaṭraye and later lived in the same monastery of Rabban Shabur as did Isaac, Bettiolo examines the anthropological dimension of *qeryanâ* and how it leads to purity of heart and to the vision of the spiritual meaning hidden in Scripture and in nature. Bettiolo alludes to Evagrian influence as he sketches this itinerary in Dadishoᶜ, of how one is led by *qeryana* to personal integrity and to the light of the Trinity.[5]

As mentioned there is Evagrian influence in Isaac. And according to Columba Stewart, exegesis was everything for Evagrius. "It was not about finding suitable garnish for his theological speculations or merely an aspect of monastic pedagogy. It was a mode of being, a keying himself into texts recited by heart day in and day out. He wrote that monastic life means 'knocking on the doors of Scripture with the hands of the virtues'." (*Thoughts* 43)[6]

Finally, John the Solitary drew his inspiration entirely from Scripture. I. Hausherr who has written extensively about him says it was a major influence on him and Hausherr had found only one non-Biblical reference in all of John the Solitary's writings: Ignatius of Antioch.[7]

Some recent scholarship has looked at the influence of Evagrius on Isaac in trying to track key concepts like pure prayer.[8] In conclusion, it reflects on how the shift from a Neoplatonic Evagrian approach to what one finds in Isaac might have occurred. I think the shift occurs through Scripture in that while Evagrius is notable for his use of Scripture, Isaac surpasses him.

---

[5] P. Bettiolo, "Esegesi e purezza di cuore. La testimonianza di Dadišo' Qatraya (VII sec.), nestoriano e solitario," *ASE* 3 (11986), 201–13.

[6] C. Stewart, "Imageless Prayer in Evagrius Ponticus," *JECS* 9 (2001), 199–201.

[7] It is quite possible that some references to other authors had been deleted from his work in an effort to sanitize his writings of "heretical influences."

[8] See B. Bitton-Ashkelony, "The Limit of the Mind (ΝΟΥΣ): Pure Prayer according to Evagrius Ponticus and Isaac of Nineveh," *ZAC* 15 (2011), 291–321.

So I have included with the kind agreement of Sabino Chialà, all the citations and allusions to Scripture, for this reason. Also included are many notes from the *CSCO*. These help to offset questions of authorship of Isaac III, since they demonstrate so many connections to Isaac I and Isaac II, as well as giving insight into the text. Only references that I could access personally are included. One could consult the *CSCO* text and profit from many more references.[9]

Great gratitude is also due for the scholarship of Paolo Bettiolo, Sebastian Brock and André Louf† – how helpful this has been.

To conclude with a quote from Isaac:

> We should consider the labor of reading Scripture to be something extremely elevated, whose importance cannot be exaggerated. For it serves as the gate by which the intellect enters into the divine mysteries and takes strength for attaining luminosity in prayer: it bathes with enjoyment as it wanders over the acts of God's dispensation which have taken place for the benefit of humanity – acts which make us stand continually in wonder, and from which meditation too takes strength, this being the first-fruits of this mode of life about which we are talking: from these acts prayer is illumined and strengthened. (Is.II XXI.13)

TRANSLATION

I *Discourse on the solitary life and on the figure of the future realities which are depicted in it by those who hold to it truly; and on the comparison <found> there with the way of life after the resurrection.* p. 287

II *Concerning the order of the body when we are alone, and concerning the modesty of the exterior parts of the body.* p. 296

[9] S. Chialà, *Isacco di Ninive. Terza Collezione CSCO* 246–247 (Louvain: Peeters, 2011).

III	*Of the same Mar Isaac. On prayer: how it binds our mind to God and causes it to cleave to the meditation in it; and how by means of the excellent stirrings which are in it the mind is strong against the love for this world from which <come>the passions.*	p. 299
IV	*Of the same Mar Isaac. Second discourse on prayer: what is the exact prayer which happens according to the perfection of the mind.*	p. 311
V	*Of the same Mar Isaac. On the creation and on God.*	p. 320
VI	*Of the same Mar Isaac. The purpose of exhortation in agreement with the foregoing <account>: concerning the sweetness of divine judgment and the intention of His providence.*	p. 327
VII	*By the same Mar Isaac. Prayer impelled by the insights of the things which were said. For there is in <prayer> a great signification, from time to time at prayer one turns to contemplate it, then again turns back to prayer. And in the noble passion of the mind, one offers amazing stirrings for the sake of all these great things which are ours.*	p. 343
VIII	*Again of the same Mar Isaac. On how the saints are set apart and sanctified by the inhabiting of the Holy Spirit.*	p. 357
IX	*Of the same Mar Isaac. A synthesis of all kinds of labor concerning the part of the mind: what power and action belong to each one of them.*	p. 364
X	*Converse of prayer of the solitaries, composed with metrical speech and according to the limits of insight. Words which seize the heart and restrain from the distraction of earthly things. <Words> composed for the consolation of solitaries with which they converse at night, after the time of the office, that their body might be relieved of sleep.*	p. 374
XI	*Again of the same Mar Isaac. Concerning that: "you*	p. 388

have been raised with Christ," as said by the divine Apostle; and concerning this divine sacrifice which the holy Church accomplishes for the living and the dead for the sake of the hope of what is to come: what is effected by this sacrifice and in a special way for a believing lay person because of the firmness of his hope.

XII *Again, a letter of exhortation by Mar Isaac concerning <how>solitary life can be affected <when lived> in the midst of others, which was sent to a monk who desired to be assured about this. The monk had written him concerning his thoughts, asking if there was in them any blame from God. <Isaac> exhorts to surrender oneself to the afflictions of this life, with a prompt intelligence which examines God's hidden reasons.* p. 399

XIII *Again, a letter on the abodes in which holy men enter by the stirrings existing in the mind, in the journey on the way to the house of God.* p. 413

XVI *Of the same.* p. 422

Chapter I

Discourse on the solitary life and on the figure of the future realities which are depicted in it by those who hold to it truly; and on the comparison <found> there with the way of life after the resurrection.[1]

1. The life of solitaries[2] is higher than this world for their way of life is similar to that of the world to come;[3] namely they do not take wife or husband. Instead of this, face to face, they experience intimacy with God. By means of the true icon of the world beyond, they are always united to God in prayer. For prayer more than any other thing, draws the mind to fellowship with God and makes it shine in its ways.

2. I also think that at the time of prayer our requests are usually granted us by those of former times, so that we might take refuge in the prayers of these excellent ones. Because of their uprightness and their good ways, which especially bring them to mind, also our

---

[1] Way of life after the resurrection (*dubbârâ d-bâtar qyâmtâ*): Is.I 254; Is. II VIII.6; Is.III VI.54. See also John Sol. *Soul* 11, 56, 85–87, 89 and his *Letter on the Mystery of the New Life*, Rignell (1941) 3,10.

[2] Solitary (*îhîdâyâ*) or single one describes a solitary monk as opposed to one living in community. But the term goes beyond celibacy or eremitical life to indicate a unity within the solitary and his unity with God. In the N.T. *îhîdâyâ* is the Only Begotten Jesus Christ (Jn.1:14,18; 3:16,18; 1 Jn.4:9). And Aphrahat says of Christ: "the Only Begotten (*îhîdâyâ*) Who is from the bosom of his Father shall cause all solitaries (*îhîdâyê*) to rejoice," Demonstrations, 6:6. On the term in Aphrahat, see Koltun-Fromm, "Yokes of the Holy-Ones." Koonammakkal, "Ephrem's Ideas on Singleness." And see Griffith, "'Singles' in God's service."

[3] World to come (*'âlmâ da-'tîd*): Heb.2:5; 6:5. See Is.II V.15; XI.13; XIII.2; XXIX.11; XXXVI.1; XXXIX.8,21; XL.14. Found often in Is.I and in the *Keph.* See John Sol. *Soul* 9, 16, 89; see also Evag. Cent. II.26,73; III.65.

prayer is purified from laxity or laziness or the distraction of thoughts, by their zeal[4] for what is excellent.

3. And even God, Lord of all,[5] how many times He condescends to our petitions because of this, so that we might be ever more ardent to imitate what is in them and so as to magnify in our eyes that excellent order which is so honorable for Him.

4. I say this according to the intention of the Scriptures. Because <God> does everything according to the intention ordained by Him, magnifying also His saints in this; as it is written: *I will overshadow this city, I will save it for my own sake and for the sake of my servant David.* [6]

---

[4] Zeal (*tnânâ*): understood in a positive sense in Is.I 392–95. Whereas John the Solitary looks at the negative side, *Soul* 21–22. Is.II has both dimensions: IX.T; XVII.1–4; 9,10; XIX.I; XXI.10; XXXIX.19.

[5] Lord of all (*mârê-kul*): de Halleux cites this as a trace of the early Syriac creed in John Sol., see de Halleux, "Le Milieu Historique," 299–305; see also Connolly, "Early Syriac Creed." Connolly points to *mârê-kul* in Aphrahat and in the *Acts of Thomas* in his attempt to shed light on the Syriac Creed "before it came under the influence of the Nicene and post Nicene definitions." See Aphrahat I.19, II.19; Ephrem, *Hymns on Faith* (21 times), *Homily on Our Lord* VII; *Book of Steps* V,15, IX.1, XXI.7. An alternate translation of *mârê-kul* in Syriac literature is "Lord of the universe." This term as *ribbono shel ʿolam* is often found in the Jewish liturgy and in rabbinic literature. See the *Minor Tractates of the Talmud* 21, 40, 48 50, 98, 548. In *Midrash Tehillim* (a compilation containing material from as early as the 3rd cent. and according to Buber edited in the Talmudic period in Palestine), practically every psalm's commentary includes the invocation. See Buber, *Midrash Tehillim.* See also Braude, *Midrash on Psalms.* In the Jewish Prayer book, in the morning service, "King of the universe (*melekh ha ʿolam*) occurs 27 times. See also 2 Maccabees 7:9.

[6] 2 Kgs.19:34; Is 37:35; cf. 2 Kgs.20:6. On "overshadow" see Brock, "Maggnânûtâ." For a slightly revised version, see Is.II XVI. See also Is.I 390–92. For a helpful survey, see Brock "From Annunciation to Pentecost." And see his "Passover, Annunciation and Epiclesis."

5. These are the ways of converse <with God>.[7] Two of these concern the principles of the labors of the heart in stillness.[8] By these the mind is fortified and purified; it drives away sloth and yearns to remain at all times in converse with what is virtuous.

6. The <mind>, then, proceeds to set on fire the remembrance of the world which rules it but to be inflamed continually with the remembrance of good things. Thus it arrives at the limpidity[9] of the labor of the mind. Of this excellent labor, there are two other principles which remain of the signs from above: the principle toil and the excellent reflection.

7. The first of the principles corresponds to inquiring into created realities and again marveling at the Divine Economy[10] <in

[7] Converse <with God> (*ʿenyânâ d-alâhâ*): Sahdona I 111; Is. *Keph.* II 45; Is.I 548. In 7th cent. East Syrian writers *ʿenyânâ d-ʿam alâhâ* is also found, see Shubhalmaran 1.IV.3. For other forms and examples, see Is.II XXX.1.

[8] Stillness (*šelyâ*): Sahdona (I 107) says that in the life of stillness (*šelyâ*) the "way of life after the resurrection" (*dubbârâ d-bâtar qyâmtâ*) is anticipated.

[9] Limpidity (*šapyûtâ*) or transparency of soul opens one to revelation and entry to the New World. There are two references to it in biblical writings: 4 Esdras 6:32 and Apoc. Baruch 66.1. In the 4th cent. the term occurs several times in Ephrem. In his *Hymns on the Nativity* 3.8, he refers the term to Christ. In the works of John Sol. one finds very frequent usage of *šapyûtâ*, see Lavenant, *Dialogues et Traités*. In the Introd. Lavenant notes a passage in John's writings where Christ is referred to as the model of limpidity. The term also occurs frequently in Isaac (see esp. Is.II VIII.15) as well as in Joseph Hazzaya. See Bunge, "Le 'lieu de la limpidité'."

[10] Divine Economy (*mdabbrânûṯâ*) gr. *oikonomia*: it concerns divine providence for all of humanity from creation to redemption until the New World. It occurs frequently in Isaac II, see Index (*CSCO*). Already in the 5th cent. one sees the concept defined by Philoxenus of Mabbug, concerning episcopal administration but also his vision of God's providential workings for human salvation. See Michelson, "*Practice Leads to Theory.*" Finally, see the analysis by Becker of Divine Pedagogy,

our regard>, for mercy, or for our human nature at the end. On the other hand, the next principle is reflection.

8. Excellent is that one who remains alone with God: this draws him to continual wonder[11] at what is in His nature. His own intelligence is lifted up because from this time it becomes wise concerning spiritual things, having both an excellent knowledge and faith <in the> mysteries. Also concern increases for the new world[12] and care for future things, earnest meditation on these things and continual migration,[13] which is the journey of the mind to these things.

---

including specific remarks about Isaac, see Becker, *Fear of God*, 22–40; 184–88.

[11] Wonder (*tehrâ*): ecstasy begins with astonishment or wonder (*tehrâ*) and may lead to helpless amazement or stupor (*temhâ*). *Tehrâ* sometimes indicates movement and *temhâ* the point of arrival where the spirit is without movement in the fulfillment of desire. The roots of wonder lie deep in Syriac tradition. Isaac quotes Theod. of Mop. that *tehrâ* in God is the "unique science," see Is.I 304. Ephrem is constantly amazed in wonder at the Incarnation and at the Eucharist, but also at the created world as both Scripture and the natural world are revelatory. In John of Dalyatha both *tehrâ* and *temhâ* occur frequently, (see the *Letters*), his use being even more symbolic than that of Ephrem, but they both see wonder as a revelation of the New World. See my " 'Insight without Sight'," and see Louf, "'Temha-stupore."

[12] New world (*ʿalma ḥadtâ*): N.T. Mt.19:28; Odes of Solomon 33:12; Aphrahat, *Demonstrations* 12:2; Theod. of Mop. *WS* V 119; *Book of Steps* X.6, XV.4, IX.40, XXV.3, XXX.3; it occurs frequently in John Sol.: two discourses are dedicated to it. See Jacob of Serug, Bedjan (1906) Hom. 54.612; Bedjan (1902) Hom. 9.815. See also Is.II V.5; VII.2; VIII.4, 5,7; XIV.39; XV.8; XVI.6; XX.6; XXXVIII title. Found frequently in Isaac *Keph.*

[13]Migration (*šunâyâ*): indicates the movement from earthly realities to the life in God. See Is.I 2: "No one is able to come near to God save only he who is far from the world. For I do not call separation the departure (*šunâyâ*) from the body, but from bodily things." In Evagrius there are four types of migration, the last being "with the Trinity," Cent. II.4.

9. Mysteries are revealed, worlds are transfigured in the mind and thoughts are altered within the flesh, <such that> it no longer seems like flesh. The mind changes abodes and is brought from one to another, not of its own will. In its course, however, it remains gathered and united to the Divine Essence; and the intellect[14] at the end of its course, turns to the first cause and origin. Thus the nature of rational beings observes the sublime order of God's love, by consideration of the <Divine Essence>.

10. All of this <occurs for the sake of rational beings even without persuading <God> by good intention. Nor will there be those who are heirs or who are made heirs,[15] for all will be gathered as one and remain quiet to marvel at a love as great as this. They will also be stirred up! For even one's way of life improves with this, since it is more diligent.

11. <Because of> converse <with God> and not working with any of the realities here below, the <solitaries> observe, as with the eyes of the soul,[16] that future way of life. They conform the things of this life to the life beyond. Because of this, indeed, converse ceases there and one is united to the One who is above word and silence. In this also they are careful now, causing the tongue, minister of the word, to cease <speaking>; and commanding with

---

[14] Intellect (*hawnâ*): here "at the end of its course" may refer, according to Brock, to "the ladder of the intellect of which blessed Evagrius spoke, and the being raised up above all ordinary vision…", see Is.II XXXV.7. And see Evag. Cent. IV.43.

[15] Cf. Is.I 201; *Keph.* III 57, indicating that this happens without human mediation but by revelation.

[16] Eyes of the soul (*ʿaynê d-nafšâ*): cf. Eph.1:17, see Is. I 391 for his comment on Ephesians where "eyes of the heart" is used. Both reflect terms of spiritual sensitivity as opposed to bodily perception. Beulay discusses this spiritual awareness which goes beyond knowledge, see his *Lumière*, 64–83. See John Sol. *Soul* 2, 4–6 for his definition of the soul.

authority not to be anxious to speak without necessity, except for stirrings[17] in prayer and the psalms, to help bind the mind.

12. If, indeed, one would persist in these elevated realities, prayer and psalms, and remain according to the order of a life in perfect silence, without trials but being with those things above – previously one was completely incapable of this. Now one may in fact care for the body as a vessel of service for the Creator, purifying it with care, not as a terrestrial reality which serves the earth, but as a vessel of holiness which is ready to be raised to heaven.[18]

13. On account of that kingdom which they will personally delight in beyond, even now in this life they delight <in it> by the earnest desire of their heart. They imagine <it> as in the mysteries, and become transformed in its image by the grace of the Spirit. For even when the reality is remote, with earnest desire one is able to share in it, as it were, mentally. It makes the soul as if insane with joy, freeing it entirely in the mind's flight to make it a sharer[19] with that One who is above all, while nothing at all is mingled with the mind.

14. By stillness of the body and ceasing from this world, solitaries imagine the true stillness and the withdrawal from nature which will occur at the end of the corporeal world. By means of the mind, <the solitaries> are united with the world of the spirit. By means

---

[17] Stirrings (*ẓawʿê*): in pure prayer one's mind can be full of stirrings but in spiritual prayer there is only wonder (*temhâ*). See Is.I 170. On this see: Alfeyev, *Spiritual World*, 218–23.

[18] Isaac seems to suggest that contemplation purifies, making it possible for one to live on earth as a vessel of service in anticipation of the kingdom.

[19] Share (*šautâputâ*): occurs in John Sol. with the sense as found in Theodore of Mopsuestia who chose not to discuss divinization but rather *sharing* in the divine nature through grace. For a listing of the occurrences of *šautâputâ* in Theodore see Abramowski, "Theology of Theodore," 13–17. For some of the Christological aspects of *šautâputâ* in John Sol. and in Philoxenus, see de Halleux, "La Christologie."

of meditation,[20] they are involved in the expanse above. Thus, symbolically they remain continually in the future reality.

15. O our brother, as a weary merchant,[21] more than anything else let us be earnest about the way of life of the mind.[22] If then God and his love, which is above every course of life might only be found by exterior exercises, the philosophers more than us would have attained to His love. Therefore while we forcefully administer the things of the body, let us ask God with suitable zeal for what is necessary, on account of such things.

16. There is nothing which is capable of removing the mind from the world as converse with hope;[23] nothing which unites with God as beseeching His wisdom; nothing which grants the sublimity of love as the discovery of His love for us. There is nothing which

---

[20] Meditation (*hergâ*): Alfeyev gives the definition for Isaac. "Meditation on God presupposes remembrance of the whole economy of God concerning humanity, beginning with the creation of man, including the Incarnation and finishing with the life of the age to come." See *Spiritual World,* 208–16. John of Dalyatha continues this very objective approach to *hergâ.* He dedicates a homily to the *Meditation on the Economy of Our Lord* (Hom.24): meditating on the life of Christ, seeing by thought (*reʿyânâ*) what the disciples saw with the senses. By this meditation one purifies the heart which (like a mirror) reflects the rays of His glory. See Beulay, *L'Enseignement,* 118–22.

[21] Merchant: Isaac encourages being a prudent merchant and avoiding laxity, see Is.I 179, 325, 467, 565. He also speaks of dealing prudently with spiritual merchandise (*têgurtâ*): Is.I 9, 96, 177, 216, 297, 355, 408; Is. II XIV.7.

[22] Way of life of the mind (*dubbârâ d- reʿyânâ*): see Is.I 304, 411; *Keph.* IV 15, 47.

[23] Converse with hope (*ʿenyânâ d-sabrâ*): for some of his reflections on hope, see Is. I 291,454, 511, 543; *Keph.* III 28–29. John Sol.'s vision of hope is evident in Isaac: it is creative and unique in early Syriac literature, based on Scripture and sacramental anthropology; he returns to it constantly in *Soul* 11, 21, 57, 67, 71–73, 89. And see Lavenant, *Dialogues* 47, 48, 51, 52, 163. Lera says John derives *sabrâ* from Theodore of Mopsuestia, see Lera "Theodore de Mopsueste."

lifts the mind in wonder, beyond all which is visible, to abide with Him far off from the worlds, as searching[24] the mysteries of His nature.

17. The nature of the Essence is invisible but can be known by means of His mysteries. That is to say, those mysteries which <God> wills that they be made known. And they are known by means of meditating on the structure of the universe.[25] <This occurs> especially by continual consideration of God's Economy in its various revelations, given indeed to inform the diligent mind which inquires faithfully and searches these things assiduously.

18. This is praiseworthy meditation and pure converse with God. This is what excellent reflection sows in the soul and <the soul> finds there pure wisdom. This is the glorious life of solitaries,

---

[24] Searching (*ʿûqabâ*): here to search is seen in a positive way. Normally the Syriac tradition, for example Ephrem struggling against Arianism, rejects searching and investigating matters of faith, that only wonder (*tehrâ*) and admiration can lead to knowledge of God, i.e. through revelation.

[25] Meditating on the structure of the universe: even if not directly intended by Isaac here, one may see the revelatory aspect of creation mentioned in Rom.1.20. And elsewhere Isaac does say:

> The first book given by God to the rational beings,
> is the nature of created beings. Written things have
> been added only after aberration. (Is.I 61)
> Ephrem said Nature and Scripture are witnesses to God:
> In his book Moses described the creation of the natural world,
> so that both the natural world and His book might testify to the Creator:
> the natural world, through humanity's use of it, the book,
> through his reading of it.
>
> (*Hymns on Paradise* 5.2)

Bou Mansour elaborates on the rich symbolic interplay between the two in Ephrem, see his *Pensée symbolique*, 121–29. See also Brock, "Humanity and the Natural World," and his "World and Sacrament." John Sol. *Soul* 4, has *wisdom of nature* and *wisdom of the Scriptures*. For nature (*kyanâ*) and its revelatory aspects in Jacob of Serug, see Bou Mansour, *Théologie*, 442–47. Evagrius cautions however that God's nature is never seen in creation, only the *mdabbrânûtâ* of his wisdom, Cent.V.51.

dwelling completely alone and choosing a place far from the world: that marvelous place which manifests the mystery of the resurrection, indicating the existence which will be known in heaven and the life with God. Indeed <the solitaries> are mystically dead and mystically alive and they are raised up mystically while the body is on the earth. The Spirit acts by means of the mind and accomplishes all of this.

Chapter II

Concerning the order of the body when we are alone, and concerning the modesty of the exterior parts of the body.

1. For thoughts to be at peace, it is necessary to show great care also for exterior things. External order, indeed, is able to move the thought of the heart in every direction. For it is also a teacher of that one who within <tends> to evil things, even when the realities of the world are distant. Modesty of the body is very useful for excellence of the mind,[1] whereas neglect or even disorderliness of the body can stir up very vicious struggles in the cell.

2. And again, from laxity of the eyes and of the senses, many thoughts are awakened. When they were mortified you were at peace in your affairs. Even now many habits may take root from the ways of the body and prostrations before Him: this increases the prayer of the heart and passion[2] <for God>, humility and meditation of what is excellent.

3. As to ways of converse with excellent realities, these are: to impress one's soul with the beauty of the way of life of the saints, so as to be stirred up by it; to adorn oneself with the virtuous ways of their manner of life so that one might receive in one's person a resemblance of their way of life.

4. That is: patience, joy in afflictions, quietness of ways, perseverance in solitude, modesty of the parts of the body, contempt for bodily desire, incessant solicitude for holiness – while

---

[1] Excellence of the mind (*myattrûtâ d-reʿyânâ*): in Is.III XIII.4, Isaac speaks of three stages of spiritual progress – way of life, fervor and excellence of the mind. See also Is.II XXXIV.3; XXXIX.15. For an overview of various schemata for the development of the spiritual life, including as found in Isaac, see Brock, "Some Paths to Perfection."

[2] Passion (*ḥaššâ*): in Isaac though there are roots in Evagrius, the positive and negative aspects of the term reflect the influence of John Sol. as well. See Brock, "Discerning the Evagrian," 65–6; 70–1.

not reckoning that one has arrived. From this <one learns> to control involuntary zeal in the soul which arises as a manifestation of the pride lying in wait within.

5. Observing such things as the ways mentioned in the stories of all the saints, as in a mirror,[3] one receives a model and effortlessly moves along the way in the remembrance of the patience and the beauty <of the saints>: those whose resemblance truly fills the soul with great joy.

6. Again, by the victories of the saints, the soul <of the solitary> wandering from the world receives consolation in the battles which seize it and obtains contempt of conscience and a humble heart. Adorning oneself with excellent ways, from this time <the solitary is without> doubts or fear[4] and understands only the fatherhood <of God> and his sonship: there is nothing else between him and God.

7. This order of perfection requires the aim of solitary life in stillness and labour alone in the cell. It <requires> a humbled body and a renewed mind; senses weakened and an elevated understanding; enfeebled parts of the body but thoughts shining in their splendor. Also required is a mind which soars and is lifted up to God in contemplation[5] of Him and a mind withdrawn from the world while its thought wanders in God.

---

[3] Cf. 1 Cor.13:12; 2 Cor.3:18. See Brock, "Imagery of the Spiritual Mirror."

[4] On the levels of fear, see Is.I 430: "He who is bodily, fears as an animal fears being slaughtered; he who is rational, fears the judgment of God; he who has become a son is adorned by love and not taught by the rod of fear." See also *Keph.* I 11, 17.

[5] Contemplation (*teʾôryâ*): found frequently in Isaac. See Brock, "Some Uses of the Term *theoria*." See Is.I 17: "Let excellence be reckoned by you as the body, contemplation as the soul. The two form one complete spiritual person, composed of sensible and intelligible parts." And see Is.I 128 where Brock notes (Is.II VII.1) that Isaac provides a definition of *theoria*: *ʿammîqût ḥẓâṯâ napsânâytâ*, "profundity of the soul's vision."

8. Such a one is involved with the flesh but his thought does not dwell with it. And though he is agitated by this, he is completely occupied by the things which abide and which are much greater than him. <His> body is worn and troubled but the heart has exulted with joy, unwittingly, as it is said: *the heart is not lifted up.*[6]

9. O Christ, <You> who enrich all, confirm Your hope in my soul and bring me out of darkness to the knowledge of Your light because I praise You with the praises of the heart, not only with the mouth.

---

[6] Ps.131:1.

Chapter III

Of the same Mar Isaac. On prayer: how it binds our mind to God and causes it to cleave to the meditation in it; and how by means of the excellent stirrings which are in it the mind is strong against the love for this world from which <come> the passions.

1. There is no way of life which is able to withdraw the mind from this world and preserve it from stumbling as meditation about God. This work is difficult but amazing, also easy and sweet. You, my beloved, love to remain in continual meditation[1] on God because it is a door against all corruptible thoughts. Begin with a great number of prayers: continual prayers are a constant meditation on God.

2. That we might be persevering in prayers, this prayer must stir up the heart to increasing meditation about God. Then it makes the mind heavenly, by means of excellent stirrings which are according to divine instruction, through the words of prayer which adhere to the fear of God.

3. By that which our Lord already taught in the commandments which precede prayer, <we are told> how the life of Christians must be and what one ought to ask in prayer.[2] It is known, indeed, that the one who acts according to these ways, has learned by divine instruction and is diligent to present the requests in prayer to God, that they might become realities. One feels that such thoughts at the moment of prayer arise in him because of these ways. Since it must needs be that as we wish our way of life to be, so must be also our prayer.[3]

---

[1] Continual meditation on God (*hergâ ammînâ db-alâhâ*): see Is.II X.16, XVIII.3, XX.27, XXIX.9; *Keph.* I 77, IV 47. For *hergâ ammînâ* on scripture see Is.I 125; 379.

[2] Mt.5:17–6:8.

[3] On how prayer relates to way of life, see Is.I 34: "Prayer accords strictly with behavior." In Is.II XIV.37 commenting on the Our Father, Isaac says: "So our prayer should be inspired by its sense, and we should

4. And lest there be in them anything alien to perfection, those who are brought up according to divine instruction for the life of perfection, have been taught by our Lord not to babble like the pagans, but to present to God wise requests seasoned with heavenly hope.[4] <Our Lord> has shown them the providence of God[5] on their account, and that their mind <ought> not be occupied with worldly and temporal realities. But they must acquire a fine mind for the things which are becoming of those who await familiarity <with God>.[6]

5. Also, not even these realities does God give to them because of their prayer, since He has no need of prayer who at Creation had no need of the supplication of creatures;[7] how then more excellent is Creation than the gifts after it! But <this prayer is necessary> that they might have the fullness of meditation on the invisible realities, and that their mind because of the form of the prayer may be full of these realities, and that they might already perceive what is the hope of things to come.

6. What then of this? That while they remain in this wonderful reflection, discerning each one of the petitions made to God with diligence, rightly henceforward they earnestly desire to proceed in the way of life fit for that good and glory to which they are summoned. And by means of these realities, they remain continually where they are elevated from this world, in familiarity[8]

---

set our lives aright in strict accordance with it…". See similarly Theodore of Mopsuestia, *Homélies* XI 1, 3 and Mark the Monk, *Justified by works* 153.

[4] Cf. Mt.6:7; Col.4:6.

[5] Providence of God (*bṭîlûtâ*): occurs frequently in Isaac. See Is.I 65, 103, 262, 304, 337, 422, 489–90, 498; Is.II VIII.26; XVII. 6, 8; *Keph.* I 51, II 73, 102. See also Evag. Cent.VI. 43, 59, 75. And for divine providence (*bṭîlûtâ alâhâyâ*) see Evag. Muyldermans, "La Foi de Mar Évagre," pp.167–69.

[6] Cf. Mt.6:25–34.

[7] On "…no need of the supplication of creatures…," see Evag. *Letter to Melania*, 56 (Vitestam p.22).

[8] Familiarity (*bayâtyûtâ*): see Is.III IV 19; *Keph.*IV 55; John Sol. *Soul* 86.

and affinity with God and in the study and knowledge of His mysteries.

7. Therefore, if as the blessed Interpreter said, "every prayer whatever it be, is instruction for life,"[9] since for every form of prayer, offered in earnest by an intelligent person according to the order of divine instruction, the mind prepares a certain meaning by which it is released from the flesh. By this reflection it becomes bound to those realities which instruct for life,[10] and that imprint <on the present> the memory of the immortal manner of life and what is beyond life.

8. So the elements in the form of prayer were arranged by our Lord, whose instruction is elevated and very succinct: excellent knowledge about the incorruptible life and of the Spirit. Because of this, every time we pray a thousand insights arise in our mind: from where we are in nature, that is, from the earth; from what we are and by means of whom and with which lineage we are related; with what mysteries we share in; where we are prepared to be led; what manner of life this mystery depicts; in what way, in figure, have we already now learned wisdom regarding the <future> hope. And because by means of the mind, we alone have fellowship and are brought near to the realities of the <future> life and the amazing ways suitable to it, the realities strengthen, indeed, the <mind> according to the mystery here below.

9. Prayer, therefore, according to perfection – of those who as it were have preferred a life such as this, have eagerly desired heaven and have taken on the perfect commandments[11] – commenting, that is: *Do not be preoccupied for your bodies of what we will eat or what we will drink or with what we will be clothed*;[12] and also: *The Father knows that also for you these things are necessary,* before they are made known in

---

[9] See Theod. of Mop. *Homélies* XI 1, as reflected also in Is.II XIV.36.

[10] Cf. Titus 2:12.

[11] Perfect commandments (*paqdânê gmîrê*): *Book of Steps* VII.1, XI.1, XIX.5, XXX.2; see Brock, "Some Paths to Perfection."

[12] Mt.6:31.

confident prayer.[13] And because they have been raised above all earthly realities, in the perfection of the mind, Our Lord gave a commandment: *Seek only the kingdom of God and His righteousness.*[14]

10. Prayer such as this, in the manner of the perfect life and which takes pains to be in accord with the reading <of Scripture>, becomes uprightness of the mind, admonition for excellent ways, freedom regarding realities which elevate, meditation of the Spirit,[15] remembrance of heavenly realities and reflection on hidden realities. Because all of these ways of thinking are enclosed, succinctly, in prayer which instructs concerning the future perfection.

11. So this prayer rightly strengthens the mind of those who dare to conduct themselves on earth, in the perfect way of life of the mystery of future behavior. "Continual prayer clothes the mind with strength," says blessed Basil;[16] that <prayer> which is from the love of this reading of the Gospel. But which mind? It is clear that this concerns those who are eager for heavenly life, who have become strong by the reading of the Gospel. They have despised earth, have longed for heaven and have depicted before their eyes the future perfection.

12. It is clear that from this prayer and meditation of those who engage in it in an excellent way, they obtain encouragement and strength in their minds, because hope inflames their ways of thinking. From here they receive the strength to grasp firmly whatever they possess, and to gladly endure the evils on earth, such as to consider them as nothing at all in comparison with the future good things which were promised them.

---

[13] Mt. 6:32; Mt.6:8.

[14] Mt.6.33.

[15] Meditation of the spirit (*hergâ d-ruḥ*) compare with *hergâ rûḥânâ*, Is.III IX.9.

[16] Based on careful analysis of the research of de Halleux, Brock and Bettiolo, Chialà attributes authorship here to John Sol. See Bettiolo, "Sulla preghiera," pp. 76–77.

13. Soon after, these things will be made ready for them, but even now from time to time, *they become transformed into* <his> *image in the mirror* of their own thought, *by means* of the grace *of the Spirit.*[17] According to the ardent desire of the will, this force suitably clothes the mind, by means of perfect prayer which shows the way to this ascent, beyond the world.

14. Immediately, indeed, at the remembrance of those heavenly realities that are attended to as requests in prayer, the soul which had already despised this world, expands by means of the love of God. And because of this there are struggles against <the soul>, while the mind rests in hope, strengthened by means of the elevated requests which it has learned to make in prayer, persuaded about them by our Lord who said: *Our Father who art in heaven.*[18]

15. O compassion and greatness of the goodness of God, to which He elevates created nature! But it also calls to mind the holiness of that divine Nature[19] of which, by grace, that one who is son has been made worthy. For it has brought him near to such a height of holiness – granting insight – that the Nature, to which belongs the holiness, has given to the creature by grace what does not belong to it by nature.

16. To this <holiness>, it is fitting that the way of life of living beings on earth be in accord, as <God> said to Moses: *You shall be holy, because I am holy.*[20] If holiness is becoming to servants because of the word of God to them, how much more, then, to the sons[21]

---

[17] Cf. 2 Cor. 3:18.

[18] Mt. 6:9.

[19] Divine Nature (*kyânâ alâhâyâ*): see Is.I 570; Is.II VIII.4,6; X.25; XI.35; XIV.42; XVIII.3; XXXVIII, title,4; XXXIX.22; XL,title; *Keph.* I 22; II 19, 44. Brock suggests derivation from Theodore of Mopsuestia *Homélies* I 16–17, V 1, 3–4. See also Vadakkel, *Anaphora of Mar Theodore*, pp. 54, 58, 70. See Evag. *Letter to Melania*, 28 (Casiday; Frankenberg, p.618).

[20] Lv. 19:2.

[21] See the comments of Theodore of Mopsuestia on this distinction between servants and sons – citing Gal. 4:24–25, Eph.2:13, Rom.8:15 – in his "Commentary on the Our Father," *Homélies* XI 7–8.

<for whom> the reflection of prayer makes the mind ascend to insights such as these, and to an elevated meditation such as this. This <occurs> by means of the kinds of requests which conform the force of the verses of <prayer> to divine instruction.

17. So it is for the rest of the verses <of the "Our father">.[22] In them, other insights are in motion, showing us it is good that one of noble birth who is ready to return to the Kingdom, have no corruptible realities of here below. As the mind remains close to <God> it is bound by His love; and it is right that the sons of God consider it shameful that their thinking persist on earth and in what is theirs.

18. For this we ask help in deference to His will, as we ought to do: that His grace which is called Kingdom,[23] be inclined to us and in the apperception of it we forget earth, remaining mysteriously in those <heavenly> realities, by a transmigration which in the mind teaches us about the two <worlds>. From within this, there is the force by which we are transformed, and by means of which we abide in the excellent realities; although being on earth we show the manner of life which is in heaven.

19. May we obtain encouragement as we perceive that we have been given strength and help, a force from heaven which is invisibly near, continually, and it upholds <us>. Unexpectedly, it brings us near to those realities which lift up nature. Though having a weak nature, many opinions, human stirrings and desires remain foreign to us. If it had not been possible – that is, that by means of the force of the Spirit we be transferred at times and we remain in those realities even before there is full growth – our Lord would not have commanded us to ask this of the Father.

20. Because we are still in the flesh, He has taught us to ask today for the thing needed, as now without it, it is not possible <to live>. And though because of what is excellent, temporal realities appear very superfluous, just the same I am persuaded that your nature

---

[22] See Pasquet, "Le Notre Père."

[23] Mt.6:10.

must ask. Ask then, but not for anything more than this.[24] And again about this *give us*,[25] it teaches to put trust in Him, signifying that He is anxious even for our base needs. By means of requests such as these, <God> humbles Himself caring to provide for these things.

21. We learn again from here that He pardons what we ask Him concerning sins. Because He teaches us to present the request for pardon,[26] as one who is persuaded that this is the will of the Father, showing indeed that He loves to pardon. The Father Himself says all these things; and that one ought to grant <to others> what we ask <for ourselves>, so as to receive the same.

22. But as we must fight unexpected temptations, and <even> other than this[27] – stirrings of the flesh whether those afflicting it from without or by a heavenly sign[28] – we need to be preserved in the midst of all these adversities. Then, being necessary that we ask for this, from the same *sedra*[29] we find what may make us wise <about it>.

23. So may we find refuge in the One from whom is salvation for all who breathe in the flesh and for what, beyond the flesh, is impelled by life.[30] Because He governs all and without Him nothing is possible – He whose glory is from His Nature, and His Kingdom is above all, and His power holds all the frontiers – He had willed

---

[24] Theodore of Mopsuestia confirms this, quoting 1 Tim.6:6–8, see *Homélies* XI 14.

[25] Mt.6:11.

[26] Mt.6:12.

[27] Mt.6:13.

[28] Temptations may come from nature, demons and other persons. And some are permitted by God "by a heavenly sign (*remzâ*)": provoked by God – Is.I 298–303, 531; or permitted by Him – Is.I 278–79, 415–16. One is even allowed to pray not to be tempted: Is.I 36–37. And in Is.II XVIII.1: "The soul receives limpidity (*šapyûtâ*) after experiences (consisting) in struggles."

[29] Formula of prayer (*sedra*): here indicates the Our Father.

[30] This is a possible reference to the dead. On the quality of life after death, see Is.III XI.6.

that by <using> the form of prayer with which we attend to these realities that concern Him, the remembrance of Him may be with us always. Because by these realities, we have access to the sublime cloud of thick darkness of the knowledge of Him[31] and His love for humanity.

24. Well said by blessed Mark the Solitary: "The one who prays with insight, endures whatever happens to him."[32] The form of prayer in fact, is such that by various and marvelous insights, it strengthens our mind and prepares it lest it become a receptacle of passions, as Evagrius said. For it happens necessarily, that whoever prays with discernment, prepares that excellent word of prayer, full of insights for the struggle against the flesh. Thus it inflames him with love for future realities; <love> which the knowledge of those realities stirs in the one who prays.

25. When, indeed, on account of this he is ready to resist nature and to separate from what is our own and <to separate> the mind from the flesh, he must ask for great strength to endure those realities which after this are set in motion. But the insights which are from the prayer and the gifts in it, by means of hope, make such difficulty appear as nothing in the eyes of <the one who prays>, even when it is something very hard. When he beheld this, the blessed Evagrius said: "Prayer makes the mind strong and prepares it lest it become a receptacle of passions."[33]

26. Also, indeed, Mark indicated the difficult struggles which are stirred up after the insights of prayer and the intelligence which is in it.[34]

---

[31] Cloud of thick darkness of the knowledge of Him (*ʿarpellâ d-îdaʿteh*): cf. Is.I 193, 217, 517; Is.II V.1; VII.1; IX.11; X.17, 24; *Keph.* I 36, 51, 52; II 73, 102. Though the term occurs in Gregory of Nyssa, see Beulay, *Lumière*, 138–44, Brock suggests that the influence here is more likely Ps. Dionysius, e.g. *Mystical Theology* I.3, II.

[32] Mark the Monk, *On the Spiritual Law* 115.

[33] See Evag. *Praktikos*, 49 (Bamberger); cf. Evag. *Gnostique*, 49 (Guillaumont).

[34] Mark the Monk, *Justified by Works* 81.

27. These insights, while they prepare us by means of the consideration of future realities to be moved outside of the flesh – <while remaining> on earth – they may charge us at the same time to endure the tempests which necessarily are stirred up. Such temptations whether from nature, from demons, or from persons, arise against the one who loves to walk in this way.

28. Evagrius, indeed <said>: "the mind which remains in the sweetness of hope increases the help that comes from prayer"; not only because it is capable of showing how all struggles are as nothing – easy and not difficult – but also because it treats with contempt the flesh which is the cause of the struggle.

29. This is, my beloved, the way of life of prayer; this is our divine meditation in <prayer>; and this is the perfect labor! Whoever wishes to prepare for the divine ascent by means of the mind, seek a solitary habitation abstaining from worldly care: this generates serenity and stillness of the heart. By means of continual rest in God and stillness of thoughts, the mind may observe the whole form of prayer and receive knowledge from it about God by entering the mysteries <contained> in the verses.

30. Prayer, therefore, by means of the meditation <involved>, draws the mind to God at all times. By means of its variety, it strengthens and purifies the mind. By means of the study <included>, it sanctifies it. This meditation is the origin of all meditations, and necessarily ties the mind to God. By this the mind is illumined about hidden realities which are within <the prayer>.

31. From these, one may obtain knowledge of the exalted things of God. Henceforward, indeed, it may be perceived that we are *sons of the Father who is in heaven, heirs of God and fellow heirs with Jesus Christ.*[35] One has the trust to say: *I am ready not only to be imprisoned, but to die for the name of our Lord Jesus Christ*;[36] and: *I am crucified to the world and the world is crucified to me*;[37] and <again>: *Who will separate me*

[35] Cf. Mt.5:45; Rom. 8:17.

[36] Acts 21:13.

[37] Gal. 6:14.

from the love of Christ? Peril, nakedness, poverty, shame, infirmity, death?[38]

32. The holy Nature of Christ is therefore worthy of all praise! By His Economy, He has lifted us up from looking on earthly realities and directs the mind to the divine ascent which is above the world. By means of converse in prayer,[39] He has brought us near to the vision of the heavenly Kingdom and continual meditation of what is in it – to where we prepare to offer to the Father, by means of <Christ>, continual adoration of the Spirit.

33. This <adoration> which cannot be limited, not by the body, not by a place, not by the highest <heavenly> spheres, <occurs> in the mind by its stirrings. It is infinite and uninterrupted *stupor*[40] on account of God. <It happens> in that place without corporeal realities, by that way of life more exalted than the order of prayer. *Wonder* is its minister, and instead of faith providing the wings for prayer, there is the true vision[41] of that in which consists our Kingdom and our glory.

34. Here there is no more need that God reveal Himself, nor need for liturgies or the praise of creatures. Henceforth it is clear to us that, truly for our sake He manifested all these things; and for us He submitted to all of this, and also shows to have need of human praise[42] and of the holiness of spiritual beings.[43]

---

[38] Rom. 8:35 (Peshitta).

[39] Converse of prayer (*ʿenyânâ da-ṣlôtâ*): see Is.II IV.1; V, title; *Keph.* IV 91. See John Sol. *Soul* 1; Philoxenus 319; Shemʿon d-Tabuteh (Mingana) *WS* VII, pages 51–53, 299b, 309ab, 310a.

[40] Stupor (*temhâ*) together with wonder (*tehrâ*): in their relation to prayer and the reading (*qeryânâ*) of Scripture in Isaac, they go beyond normal human perception of God. See Louf, "*Temha-stupore.*" And see my "Insight without Sight." *Keph.* IV 95 includes a definition of *temhâ* by Theodore of Mopsuestia in the context of Gen.15:12 and Gen. 2:21.

[41] True vision (*ḥezwâ šarrîrâ*): Is.I 183; Is.II X.17, XIV.30; John Sol. *Soul* 61; Gregory of Cyprus 102.

[42] On praise due to God, elsewhere in the tradition, praise and thanksgiving are integral to St. Ephrem's thinking. He says the lack of it caused Adam to fall since "he ate fruit and did not give praise." See

35. In the life beyond, indeed, we will receive the whole truth concerning God the creator – not about His Nature but about the order of His majesty, and of His divine glory and His great love for us. There, all the veils and titles and forms of the Economy, will be taken away from before the mind;[44] there, we will no longer receive His gifts in the name of our petition, nor the grace of knowledge in a measured way. In the life beyond, indeed, God will truly show that even in the requests made here below, He does not give what we request because of our petition, but He has made the petition an intermediary. For He has clothed it in the form of words, bringing the mind to wander[45] in the Essence of God and in the knowledge of His care for us.

36. When, then, we receive what the order of prayer at no time could obtain, and for which the mind had not imagined requests – because this had not arisen in the human heart,[46] and so that rational beings might receive what their nature did not know to request – then we perceive that God, in this life and in the life beyond, gives by reason of His love, even making the cause <of the gift> depend on us. And because of His great grace He ascribes His gift to the goodness of our prayer and that of our way of life.

37. O mankind who have received such a Lord! O sweetness and goodness without measure! For when we receive the knowledge of all of this, then we will learn the true fatherhood <of God>, and

---

Memra III.6 in Hansbury, *Hymns of St. Ephrem*. A similar reflection occurs in Ephrem's *Commentary on the Diatessaron* 19.4.

43According to Chialà, intended here is the "Holy, holy, holy" of the seraphim, Is.6.3. See Vergani, "Isaia 6," 179–92 where he examines the rapport between human nature and the uncreated angelic world according to John Sol. And see the *Letter to Hesychius* 66 which instructs to begin personal prayer with the cry of the seraphim: "Holy, holy, holy, Lord almighty, with whose glory both heaven and earth are filled."

44 See *Keph.* III 1; see also Evag. *Letter to Melania*, 22–25 (Casiday; Frankenberg, pp. 616–18): "…names and numbers of rational creation and its Creator will pass away…".

45 Wander (*pehyâ*).

46 1 Cor.2:9.

His love and His goodness everlasting, and that God had no need of the world, nor creation, nor the structure of the future <world>, nor the Kingdom of heaven: He whose Nature are the Kingdom, gladness and light!

38. But it is because of His goodness that He does these things and has brought us into existence! Because of us, He created all these things: as to give us His Kingdom, His glory, His greatness, His magnificence and all the power of His Essence; and to make us beings without end like Him and clothed in light, whose lives are not cut short and whose Kingdom and existence have no end.

39. It is by means of Him that we have been brought near to all this knowledge; although of mortal nature, we are called *sons of the Father who is in heaven*[47] and we have known Him *who is from the beginning*.[48] To Him *be glory through Jesus Christ*, forever and ever. Amen, amen.[49]

---

[47] Cf. Mt.5:45.

[48] Cf. 1 Jn.2:13.

[49] Cf. Rm.16:27.

Chapter IV

Of the same Mar Isaac. Second discourse on prayer: what is the exact prayer which happens according to the perfection of the mind.

1. Authentic prayer[1] is the perception of what is in God. This is that <prayer> in which the mind abides not by means of petitions but by the perfection of love; and one remains in prayer before God not to ask for something or other, but to behold His Essence. So that from those realities which are naturally of the <Essence> one may observe it, at the time of prayer, as by the vision of the eyes, in wonder.

2. There are, indeed, three natural properties which are essentially of that glorious Essence. They <cannot grow> beyond what they are because they are perfect; nor can they be diminished or impoverished by accidental causes.[2] These <properties> are actually known by the mind, which is accustomed to marvel at the stirrings concerning the Essence.

3. As often as the mind seeks to look on what is hidden but falls short of it because of its being concealed <the mind> may, with these <properties> observe as in wonder that Nature which cannot be comprehended naturally, whether by vision, intellect or thought.

4. I say, then, that there are three indications proper to God's Nature: goodness, love and wisdom.[3] By his goodness, indeed, God

---

[1] Authentic prayer (*ṣlôtâ ḥattîttâ*): Is.I 440, 475; *Keph.* IV 69.

[2] God's unchanging Nature: "God's properties are not liable to variations as those of mortals," Is.I 341 (includes a quote from Theodore of Mopsuestia).

[3] On these three indications of the divine Nature – goodness, love and wisdom, see Is.III VII.41: goodness, love and power for good. See also Evag. Cent. II.1: goodness, power and wisdom. And for an extended reflection on love, power and wisdom, see Evag. *Letter to Melania*, 4–12 (Casiday; Frankenberg, p.612).

created the world.[4] He, then, had love for it <even> before He created it,[5] setting it in order in His wisdom, perfecting all things for aid and delight, whether for those present realities or those future ones; so that by these things His true and unswerving love for <creation> might be known.

5. But whoever from these properties continually observes the divine Essence, his prayer becomes unlimited and never ceasing. Because the perfection of love is more exalted than prayer stirred by requests. However, when the mind remains with God without dissipation but by reason of a petition, this <shows> weakness of the mind, that it does not yet perceive divine love.

6. The perfection of love, then, has no need to ask for anything other than the mind's contemplating God, insatiably. When indeed the mind enters into love and divine knowledge, it does not desire to present a petition for something or other, not even for <what is> elevated and very honorable.

7. Beholding the greatness of God from the fervent love[6] of His mysteries – and receiving this perception – is more excellent than to wander in the realities outside of <God> which are not of His Nature. Prayer, then, of petitions and requests is an array of stirrings and prayers for contingencies, while the gift of love in prayer is the silence of the spirit.[7] For when the mind is united to God, it desists from petition and prayer.

---

[4] Repetition here of creation as an act of goodness and love: see Keph. III 70, with quote from Theodore of Mop.; Is.II X.19, XVIII.18, XXXVIII.1–2,5.

[5] On creation as a revelation of His love, see Is.III V.14 and *Keph.* IV 78–79.

[6] Fervent love (*ḥubbâ ḥammîmâ*): Is.II XVIII.5; Sahdona II 52, III 93, IV 52.

[7] Silence of the spirit (*šetqâ d-ruḥâ*): Is. II XV.11; cf. John Sol., Bettiolo, "Sulla preghiera,"5, p. 81.

8. If one desists from prayer by his will while his mind is not attracted, by means of a strong sense of wonder, to one of the divine insights,[8] dissipation will rule him and he will be filled with idle memories. But until one reaches these heights in prayer, it is not right to cease from persistent requests. For by means of constant petition, one may be brought near to those great realities of which we spoke.

9. What, indeed, is greater than the prayer which our Savior committed to His church? And this is entirely of petitions and requests! Is it like this because God has need of these? Or because one by one, we must remind Him of them by name? It is known, indeed, that God has no need of this: "Do for me such and such," as if because of this He would know to give the things He ought to give; or as if He would forget or neglect to give them, when we do not pray for each of the things by name. This opinion is an infantile reflection, not of those who have the intelligence of a <mature> mind, nor who have elevated knowledge about God, Creator of all.

10. Also Macarius, marvelous among the saints, clothed with the Spirit, when he was asked how one ought to pray and why, he said: "It is not necessary to multiply speech, but in prayer to extend one's hand to God and say: 'As You wish and as it pleases You!' He, therefore, knows what helps us."[9]

11. Behold the prayer of the perfect![10] Behold the prayer of those who know God, *as He is*![11] Behold the believer whose faith is strong! As to God's care for His creature, it is truly not because our Lord does not know <about such as this> that He taught explicitly to pray to God: "Give us such and such," but because of our weakness, and to sustain our thought which He gave us to take

---

[8] Divine insights (*sukkâlê alâhâyê*): cf. Is. II IX.11.

[9] *The Sayings of the Desert Fathers,* Macarius the Great #19: Ward, *The Alphabetical Collection.*

[10] Perfect (*gmîrê*): Is.I 250, 271, 495, 568, 578; Is.II VII.3, XIV.27; *Keph.* I 59, II 39, III 46, 89. See *Book of Steps*, XIV; also circulates as Evagrian, see Muyldermans, "Les justes et les parfaits," pp. 143–46.

[11] Cf. 1 John 3:2.

delight in the words of prayer, and for the consolation of our weakness; but above all to direct us to Him.

12. As also those words at the time of the Passion: when because of the disciples, Jesus had made the prayer; and also the request to the Father, announcing to them that it was because of them that He was making <it>,[12] letting be heard with clear sounds those words full of encouragement. But Jesus also made known to the disciples, by the form of the prayer, the mysteries and the knowledge of the hidden realities, while being clear that those were not prayers and that there was no need for such words to the Father by that human nature of our Lord.

13. And this because what He seemed to want to persuade God the Father with words, was <really> according to His will. Since His will was capable of satisfying the prayer immediately for whatever He wished. Therefore, as we have said, they were not prayers which were heard at that time from our Lord, but they were words concerning the mysteries that by means of the Apostles He had wanted to make known to us. As it was the fulfillment of His Economy in that night, it seemed to Him that it was the time in which those <realities> were to be shown to the disciples, being as there was in them a teaching and a prophecy about future realities.

14. From these <words>, then, are hope and encouragement for all the human race, but how much more for those who are preparing to be brought near to faith in Him. And from these <words come> strength and great hope for the disciples. From them, then, are the mysteries of the future realities which in the future world[13] will be made perfect, indeed.

This is for the instruction of the <disciples> and for the whole world which our Lord was showing, while clothing His words with the form of prayer. From these <words> we also know

---

[12] Cf. John 11:42.

[13] Cf. Heb. 2:5; 6:5. Future world (*ʿâlmâ da-ʿtîd*): see *world to come*, Is.III I.1.

about the greatness and the glory which He had with the Father,[14] while He had no need for petition or prayer to God the Father.

15. But all which our Lord attended to and showed is full of instruction. Not even at the time of the Passion was there need for a request, as the blessed Interpreter said in the Commentary on John, concerning what was said by our Lord in that hour by way of prayer. Namely: "The one who encounters this Scripture ought to know that here there is a prophecy concerning future realities to be done for the disciples. These are words spoken in the form of prayer. One ought not examine their forms nor their different varieties and not even the aspect of prayer spoken in it."[15]

16. And a little before this in the *sedra* where he speaks about the whole order of the words of our Savior, giver of life, the <Interpreter> says: "This is clearly the force which the commentary makes known: that <here> there is no request but only the form of a request. <Jesus> says the words of the prayer in the form of a parable; and if anyone wishes to judge it simply, from the outer form as heard, one will find that many of the <words>, it was not even opportune for them to be spoken."[16]

17. Therefore, as how the blessed Interpreter indicates, it is also for us to understand all the instruction of our Lord: from this we may attain to the intention of the admonition and the form of the instruction. With it, <Jesus> makes wise by the transmission of the words of prayer; and in it, it is as if <Jesus> asks the Father, <and so> teaches the mysteries, spiritual knowledge,[17] and concerning hidden realities.

---

[14] Cf. John 17:5.

[15] Theodore of Mopsuestia, C.John VI 17,19 (Vosté p.319).

[16] Theodore of Mopsuestia, C.John VI 16,33 (Vosté p.306).

[17] Spiritual knowledge (*îdaʿtâ ruḥânâytâ*): Is.I 217, 318–20, 377, 473, 522, 526–27; Keph. II 75,77; III 49. See John Sol. *Soul* 64–65; Lavenant, *Dialogues* II, p.16 and XI, p.133. Cf. Evag. *Gnostique*, 47 (Bamberger) and Cent. II. 14,20; III 15.

18. Here in this way, He teaches us to pray for this or that and to ask the Father for these things – as if this knowledge be lacking to our Lord – to show us clearly that there is no need that we remind God in prayer for each one of our necessities, by name; He knows what is in the heart[18] and takes care of everything. But our Savior, to whom belongs the knowledge of everything, because of the loving kindness by which He takes care of all which concerns us, for what is useful for us and for what is for our instruction – He acted in this way to transmit to us the tradition of prayer in a distinct way, and make known the requests by their names.

19. But why like this? So that by continual meditation on these <words>, the mind might ascend from earthly realities and by means of the mysteries which are in the words, attain to the sublimity of hope. Because in them there is <what leads> to the correction of habits and instruction about the realities of the mysteries, of the way of life, of understanding and meditation concerning God and on familiarity with Him which, by means of Christ, we have already obtained. The explanation of these things was shown briefly but sufficiently by us, as I think, in the previous discourse. Whoever accurately accesses the doctrine in these portions, I believe that one will not <miss> the excellent taste reserved in that reading.

20. Now then, of the themes determined for this discourse, it only remains for us to speak about the recollected mind.[19] By insight, we ascend to the origin of the subject and laying open the sense, let us gather it together into one, luminously and briefly.

21. When, therefore, one receives the gift of the Spirit,[20] while being in wonder regarding those realities which are taught by means of insight, the mind consents to be more careful at the time of prayer about requests for anything. Indeed, all one's desire

---

[18] Cf. 1 Kings 8:39; Acts 1:24; 15:8.

[19] Recollected mind (*reʿyânâ knnîšâ*):Is.I 446; Is.II VII.3; XIV.10; XV.5,6,9; XXI.8; *Keph.* IV 49, 56, 63, 72, 92–93. And see John Sol. *Soul* 14; Bettiolo, "Sulla preghiera," p.76.

[20] Cf. Acts 2:38; 10:45.

grows dim by means of revelation and instead of all that, the knowledge of the Spirit[21] fills one with those hidden realities by the revelation of insight.[22] Then one desists from one's will and only is at rest looking on those imperceptible realities.

22. This is his prayer: only to marvel at God, according to the order of the spiritual beings who are in heaven and according to that <order> of the future world.[23] In that this gift of the Spirit,[24] continually shows him ineffable realities by means of insight, and in an inexplicable mystery. The instruction about hidden realities is imprinted on the mind, by means of the force of the Spirit; and like writings on a tablet, insight into profound things is engraved on the heart.[25] But if it happens that one be moved to prayer without these <realities>, only the prayer of praise arises in the heart.

23. God's care for him, indeed, shames him every time he wishes to present a different request from that which says: "As You wish and as it pleases You."[26] If he asks for something of his own will, this would declare him to be wiser than God – He who made him worthy of such a gift! – and not as one whom the Spirit knows and guides.

24. When the soul has become limpid,[27] immediately on encountering some subject about God, in that moment the mind is compelled to silence, a spiritual fervor arises in it and a quiet, amazed love. When, indeed, it is amazed in God, the mind is always recollected and easily withdrawn within itself, without compulsion or care about this on his part.

---

[21] Knowledge of the Spirit (*îdaʿtâ d-ruḥ*): Is.I 30, 221, 337, 475 527; Is.II XII title; XVIII.16; XXXIX.18; *Keph.* II 75, 85.

[22] Revelation of insights (*gelyânâ d-sukkâlê*): revelation by means of understanding, Is.I 162, 352; Is.II VIII.7, 25.

[23] Cf. Heb. 2:5; 6:5.

[24] Cf. Acts 2:38; 10:45.

[25] Cf. 2 Cor. 3:3.

[26] Macarius, see note 9.

[27] On limpidity (*šapyûtâ*): see Is.III I.6.

25. Do you desire to obtain these things, my beloved? Attend to the purification of the soul! Do not be moved because of these realities which quickly are destroyed by passion. But honor your neighbor, more than these realities whose lingering or removal from you happen by chance; they are, indeed, earthly realities!

26. Not to love or hate someone on account of his ways, but to love him for himself, beyond searching <his> ways, as God <does>. Indeed, ways may change but you, before someone of your nature remain immutable, in the image of God. Indeed, *in the washing of regeneration*,[28] He has given you His likeness. Made incorruptible in the mystery, take care to have an incorruptible intelligence, according to the model you have received.

27. You desire to receive the gifts which foreshadow the heavenly home, so as to compel nature towards the resemblance which seems glorious. Now then, I will bring you near to what is the mother of labor in the soul. More than any other thing, be concerned about sweetness: it awakens in you all the excellent realities of the spirit and of the body. It makes you remain continually in peace of thoughts.

28. It is, indeed, a sign of the impassibility[29] of the soul: sweetness is the place of condescension which is the fruit of humility. If one does not descend from the height of one's intelligence, he cannot appear sweet to all who meet him. These admonitions make <for> purity in the soul, setting in motion in it the signs of the immortality which you desire and removing irascibility from it, which is the darkness of the soul.

29. The tendency to anger, then, is from pride. Pay attention to this word: every time that you have humble thoughts within you, not even a trace of anger can come near you. Indeed humility knows how to remain without anger in infirmities, in poverty and in the vexations with neighbors. But there is an anger which is

---

[28] Cf. Titus 3:5.

[29] Impassibility of the soul (*lâ ḥâšôšûṯâ d-napšâ*): Is.I 478. Cf. Is.I 513 (*Keph.* I 33), 243, 367, 494, 520; *Keph.* I 41, IV 34, 87; Evag. *Praktikos*, 2 (Bamberger).

from the stirrings of the temperament, which does not show harshness and immediately becomes calm, indeed it is followed by continual compunction. Whoever does not first acquire these things cannot receive *the gifts of the Spirit.*[30]

30. For Paul, indeed, there is no contradiction at all that we rejoice in the realities of the Spirit, while we journey in what belongs to the flesh.[31]

31. But when not even what is of the intelligence follows the Spirit by eminence of mind or excellent ways worthy of God, then also the soul goes about consenting to what concerns the flesh, even if it is rich in great thoughts from reading and the labor of the body.[32]

32. The grace of the Spirit, then, is not received in the body, but in the heart, and its activity[33] in the interior members of the soul is known by the mind. On that account it is <deep down> within, that we must adorn ourselves,[34] where we who are made poor may receive Christ.

---

[30] Cf.1 Cor.14:1,12 (Peshitta).

[31] Cf. Gal. 5:16–17; Rom. 8:1–12.

[32] Labor of the body (*ʿamlâ d-gûšmâ*): for the distinction between *gûšmâ* and *pagrâ*, see Beulay, *Lumière*, 30–33. For example, Joseph Hazzaya uses *gûšmê* when he speaks of the spiritual bodies of the angels. He also uses it to denote the body after the resurrection. Beulay cites Evag. Cent. I.11 as a possible influence on Isaac.

[33] Activity (*maʿbdânûṯâ*) of the Holy Spirit: Is. I.13, 260; Is. II XIV.12, XVI.3, XVIII.3, XXII.9, XXIII.2, XXXII.4. See *Keph.* I 98, II 14, 51, 54, 90; III 55; IV 85. Brock suggests roots in Macarius 9.

[34] Cf.1 Peter 3:3–4.

Chapter V

Of the same Mar Isaac. On the creation and on God.

1. Even if there was a time when creation did not exist, yet there was never a time when God did not have love for it[1] because even if it did not yet exist there was never a time when it did not exist in His knowledge.[2] Even if because it was not yet created, <God> was not known to <creation>, yet God knew it always, in all its various parts and its natures. He gave it its existence when it pleased Him.

2. One may know the true love of God for creation from this that after He had finished its structure in all its parts, He brought it altogether into one unity: sensible realities and spiritual ones[3] into one bond and He joined it to His divinity and He raised it above all the heavens and set it on an everlasting throne and made it "God" over all.[4]

3. Yet even according to nature, if creation had received a greater position than this, would this have convinced your nature, O man, as a true sign of the abounding love of God for creation?

---

[1] Cf. Is.III IV.4. On the theme of divine love Brock says that "God's boundless love is a central theme throughout Syriac tradition," from Ephrem to Isaac the Syrian, "Spirituality," 84. Others have commented on the insight of Isaac, that the Incarnation did not occur because of sin but only because God loves the world, see Hausherr, "Précurseur de la Théorie Scotiste," 316–20. See also Louf, "Pourquoi Dieu se manifesta," 37–56.

[2] Cf. Is. II V.11; XXXIX.6.

[3] Spiritual realities (*metyad'ânyâta*): found as early as the Clementine Recognitions; earliest Syriac writer, Narsai; Isaac's usage may reflect Evagrius and Ps.Dionysius. See Brock, "Discerning the Evagrian," 63.

[4] On unity of creation, see Isaac *Keph.* III 81; union of the creation with God, *Keph.* II 19 (Is.II V.18); becoming gods *Keph.*I 62; III 70; throne of the divinity Is. II V.17. See also Evag. *Letter to Melania*, 25–27 (Vitestam); Cent. IV.51 (cited by Isaac in *Keph.* III 57).

4. With what petition did creation receive this? And what prayer did it present for itself? And when did this arise in its heart?[5] And what way of life did it offer in exchange for becoming "God"?[6] How is it that our thoughts are distracted with aspects of little importance and we do not draw near to the great riches which we have received; we do not even perceive it. That is to say, we do not meditate night and day on our beauty, already we have become gods! Tell me then, O our beloved, if every choice had been given to us to choose for all of nature what pleases us, even what is more noble: who of us would have chosen for oneself or for nature all that which God has determined to do for us.

5. Now is there yet another place above where creation has ascended? But what position could be greater than that of divinity? And behold: creation has become "God."

6. For we do not come to these details with a request, seeking from them testimony of the reality of the mighty love of God for his creation. But we draw near to its extreme riches and to what binds the greatness of the many aspects of His love into one vision, which impels us to consider it collectively.[7]

7. Where our vision is not dispersed by things when we draw near to partial aspects of His love, as the mind stretches out to certain of the various wonders which were done for us by Him, it is possible, indeed, that from any one of these <realities> we approach, a sign of His fervent love for creation may shine forth.

---

[5] 1 Cor.2:9.

[6] On divinization in the Syriac tradition, see Russell, *Doctrine of Deification*, Appendix I. See also the comments indicating the concept of *theosis* already in Ephrem, seemingly independent of Hellenic influence: "He gave us divinity, we gave Him humanity" (*Hymn on Faith* V.15). See Brock, *Paradise Hymns*, 73–74 and *Luminous Eye*, 148–54. See also Vethanath, "Ephrem's Understanding." And see Buchan, "Paradise as the Landscape of Salvation."

[7] For this synthesis of divine love, see Is.II XXXVIII.2.

8. But let us draw near to the comprehensive reflection where even the division of other <realities> is taken away from our reflection; where our mind is not distracted by a multitude of things when we seek <a comprehensive reflection>. But wonder,[8] which searches thoughts with the very powerful intercession of the mind, generates collectively a unified vision, not dispersed.

9. At the beginning of creation when God created Adam, although not knowing between right hand and left hand,[9] as soon as he was created he desired the condition of divinity.[10] But what Satan sowed in him as evil, that *you will be like gods*,[11] and he firmly believed it in his childishness[12] – God indeed accomplished it. And at the end of days, he was given the diadem[13] of divinity because of the great love of Him who created him. In the case of the fathers who are moved by the Spirit, the divine power[14] which effects these things and reveals the mystery to them, does well to whisper in them, saying:

10. "The union of Christ in the divinity has indicated to us the mystery of the unity of all in Christ."[15] This is the mystery: that all creation *by means of one*,[16] has been brought near to God in a

---

[8] Wonder (*tehrâ*).

[9] Gen.4:11.

[10] As noted by Brock, this is early evidence of *theosis*, through Adam-Christ typology. For Ephrem: "The Most High knew that Adam wanted to become a god, so He sent His Son who put him on in order to grant him his desire." (*Nisibene Hymns* 69:12). See Brock, "Some Paths to Perfection," 93–4.

[11] Gen.3:5.

[12] Childishness (*šabrûtâ*): *Keph.* II 47; III 71; cf. Is.I 525. See also infantile way of thinking (*šabrût tar'îtâ*): Is. I 529; Is. II XXXIX. 2.

[13] Cf. Wisd.5:16.

[14] Divine power (*ḥaylâ alâhâyâ*): Is.I 489, 553; Is.II IX.11; XI.11,13; XXX. I7; XXXV.13; *Keph.* IV 46. See John Sol.: Rignell, *Traktate*, 22; Macarius 47, 80; Ammonius 571–2, etc.

[15] Cf. Evag. Muyldermans, *Admonitio paraenetica*, 7–8.

[16] Cf. Rm.5: 17–19.

mystery. Then it is transmitted to all. Thus all is united in Him as the members in a body;[17] He however is the head of all.[18] This action was performed for all of creation. There will, indeed, be a time when no part will fall short of the whole.[19] For it is not just a matter of this great spiritual intelligence being transmitted only partially, but He will do something greater, once He has made <this> manifest and has indicated it here below.

11. Glory to You, our Creator and our Lord, who by a right contemplation of Your love, have filled me with consolation and joy. You have raised my thinking from the depths of the earth and received it on the throne of Your Essence, to roam in the richness of Your Nature and marvel at the ineffable mysteries of Your love, desisting from the multiplicity of the elements of creation and ascending to the place of its Creator.

12. His invisible aspect inebriates me and His glory makes me marvel. His mysteries stir me and His love stupefies me. He brings me to His mysteries and shows me His riches. When I suppose that my course has concluded, again they pour over me so that they are more glorious than the abodes I have passed through. And when I suppose that I have penetrated within them, I turn back to look at them as they have become a great ocean before me, limitless to cross and pleasant to behold. As I recount this its revelations change, its mysteries increase and its appearances are transformed in the mind.

---

[17] Cf. Rm.12:5; 1 Cor.12:12; Eph.5:30. See Evag. *Letter to Melania*, 616 (Frankenberg); see also *Book of Hierotheos* V.2, p.120. And see Is. III X.92.

[18] Cf. Col.1:18; Eph.1:22–23.

[19] Final recapitulation for all creation: Is.I 127; *Keph.* I 10, 19, 62, 68, 91–92; III 77, 81–82. See Is. II XXXIX with quotes from Theodore of Mopsuestia and Diodore; XL. 4–7; XLI 1.

13. If in what concerns us and our nature, His mysteries which He has performed are to such an extent limitless, who would venture towards those of His Nature? And, again, whence could we cite another nature more powerful in insight than that of the angels without straying from their knowledge? If in this which we have seen and felt,[20] the paths of His Economy by means of wonder[21] are cut off from insight before the movement of the intellect, what then of His invisible realities?

14. O immeasurable love of God for His work[22] <of creation>! Let us look at this mystery with wordless insight so as to know that He has united creation to His Essence, not because He needed to but to draw creation to Him that it might share in His riches, so as to give it what is His and to make known to it the eternal goodness of His Nature. He has conferred on it the magnificence and the glory of His divinity in order that instead of the invisible God, visible creation might be called "God" and in place of what is uncreated and above time, God crowned with the name of the Trinity the creature and what is subject to a beginning. On the work of His creation, in honor of its sacred character, He has set the glorious name which even the mouths of the angels are not pure enough to utter.

15. This is the "emptying" spoken of in divine Scripture: the words *he emptied himself*[23] which Paul spoke of with unspeakable wonder, whose interpretation gives insight into the story of divine love. God loved all of creation to such an extent that creation is called "God," and the name of the majesty of God becomes creation's own.

16. *Great is this mystery*![24] I do not know how I had conceived to swim in this great ocean and who had given me these strong arms

---

[20] Cf.1 Jn.1:1.

[21] Wonder (*tehrâ*).

[22] Work (*ṭuqânê*).

[23] Phil.2:7.

[24] Cf. Eph.5:32.

for swimming with pleasure in the unfathomable abyss without being wearied. But seeing that the ocean is wide and its limit not visible, the more <the arms> are imbued with pleasure and instead of fatigue, joy leaps up from within the heart. And, again, I am not aware of how I was made worthy of this grace of explaining the love of God, ineffable for a created tongue! Even angelic beings are <too> weak to ascend to the height of its contemplation and are <too> lowly to comprehend in their thoughts, all the riches of His love.

17. But because we have not applied ourselves to this height to investigate[25] but so as to take delight in it, this sweet savor will be given to us swiftly because we have taken account of His aid. So we will stop then and remain in silence after He will have shown that for which no limit can be found, <that is> to say, the love of God for His creation. And until the time comes in the other world,[26] when we will find indeed the prototype of His mystery prepared by the revelation of love, we will conclude our discourse here while persevering in this consolation which is like a mirror <of the other>, in the obscure image of our knowledge concerning love, in our faith, until the day of His great and glorious revelation when we will see our riches, with us and close to us in an invisible way.[27]

---

[25] Investigate (*bṣa*) together with "searching" (*ʿûqabâ*) are usually seen in a negative sense, that only delight and wonder lead to knowledge of God. This has its roots in Ephrem's struggle with Arianism in matters of faith.

[26] Other world (*ʿâlmâ ʾḥrinâ*): Theodore of Mopsuestia, C.John (Vosté) p.319; Evag. Cent.V.12; John Sol. *Soul* 7, 18, 23, 24, 55, 56, 69 and his *Letter to Hesychius* 57; Babai *C. Evagrius* 126. See Is.I 257; Is.II, X.19, 28, 30; *Keph.* II 65, III 77. It is also found in Ephrem, *Hymns on Nisibis* 46.17 and Jacob of Serug IV 824, 826 (Bedjan).

[27] Cf. 1 Cor.13:12; 2 Cor.5:7; 1 Jn.3:2.

18. Who is capable of the wonder and the joy at these things that <God> has prepared for us without <our> having asked, in His everlasting love and in His immeasurable mercy. As it is said: *God who is rich in mercy on account of His great love with which He has loved us,* etc.[28] To Him be glory forever and ever. Amen, amen.

---

[28] Eph.2:4:

And why was he stretched out on the Cross for the sake of sinners, handing over his sacred body to suffering on behalf of the world? I myself say that God did all this for no other reason, except to make known to the world the love that he has, his aim being that we, as a result of our increased love resulting from an awareness of this, might be captivated by his love when he provided the occasion of this manifestation of the power of the Kingdom of Heaven – which consists in love – by means of the death of his Son.

(Isaac *Keph.* IV 78, trans. S. Brock)

Chapter VI

Of the same Mar Isaac. The purpose of exhortation in agreement with the foregoing <account>: concerning the sweetness of divine judgment and the intention of His providence.

1. Not to cultivate sufficiently what one ought is more tolerable than that one not examine what one has received, so as to know and confess according as one is able. This is often the weakness of nature and the perversion of the will. But the ocean of the grace of God, who confesses it as is due? Even that one who knows then, is not able to confess <it>: the greatness of the realities which the divine Nature prefigures is immense!

2. The grace and the love of this <Nature> with their abundance are poured forth on the intellect in a deluge of marvelous thoughts and the riches of contemplation. They cover the mind at the time of meditation, and it is silenced before the perception of the knowledge of the realities of God; it also desists from the confession <of faith>. Even the power of wonder which occurs in it, ceases.

3. The perception of one's deficiency regarding the <promised> recompense is equal to not understanding the measure of God's love. Perfect recompense is <in fact> the completion of the work which is God's. The fact alone that we perceive that He loves us, is sufficient in place of the work we ought to do if we are not capable of it. And <our> discovery that we are ignorant of the measure of <His Love> is reckoned by Him as the principle of all knowing. When at times we find ourselves in this <situation>, how our soul is enlightened by it! And who is capable of this joy?!

4. About the realities of God, my beloved – as they are, also as their manifold abundance was given – is written down already in this discourse according to the poverty of our knowledge. That brief discourse, by <its> persuasion regarding the truth, is sufficient to lead the diligent mind to wonder and joy in meditating on <those realities>.

5. Let us remain always in the remembrance of these things, and let us delight in them. Let us gather them continually before the eyes of our intelligence[1] and consider them. We are full of joy, and may our heart be lifted up in God when we have known these things. As it is said: *Let him who boasts, boast in the Lord.*[2] This boast <in> these things of God is amazing. They are, indeed, truly worthy of remembrance, more than our life breath. Let us reckon, then, what is ours as nothing at all.

6. We are justified by what is from God and not by what is ours. We inherit heaven by what is from Him and nor by what is ours.[3] It is said: *Man is not justified before God by his works*;[4] and again: *Let no one boast in works but in the justice which is from faith.*[5] This justice, then, <Paul> says is not *from works but only from faith, that is in Jesus Christ!*[6]

7. This is the interpretation, then, as to how what was said happens, that is, that no one is justified by works.[7] This does not refer only to visible works, that is, the order of the Law. The body, in fact, on its own is not capable of fulfilling all which is commanded <so> as to justify man. By the works of faith one is justified! Listen then to this: if one says he possesses justice according to the Law because of the works of the body, he would be a debtor of all which is commanded by God to be fulfilled. And only then would he be deservedly considered righteous.

8. If then the grace of faith which justifies the conscience does not intervene as mediator, or when works are lacking, or committing a transgression is involved, or one is not able to complete <the works> – the will can take their place. This is not to say that it is impossible to be justified by the Law without need of

---

[1] Nilus, *Discorso di ammonimento* 22, p. 193.

[2] 1 Cor.1:31; 2 Cor.10:17.

[3] On salvation by grace and not by works, see Is.I 315–16; Is.II X.20–21, XI.2. Though works are never excluded, Is.I 302.

[4] Rom.3:20; Gal.2:16.

[5] Cf. Eph.2:9; Rm.4:13.

[6] Cf. Rom.3:22; Gal.2:16.

[7] Cf. Rom.3:20; Gal.2:16.

conversion or pardon; but <the Law> may also declare one deserving of censure.

9. Justice, whether through conversion or conscience, is not given without grace. So that when one is found to be guilty, through conversion suddenly and without works, he stands justified. The Law does not see it this way. In fact, when one has obeyed all <the precepts> but has stumbled in one of them – the one who wished to be justified according to the Law, that is by works and not by grace – not even the precepts which he has done are counted. But for one <precept> he disregarded he will receive punishment, according as the order of the Law has enjoined: "Whoever does not do all which is commanded in this Law will perish, from out of his people."[8]

10. Whoever therefore supposes to be justified in accordance with the Law or by bodily works, what righteousness awaits him? For nature is always deficient, and the penalty of its deficiency after being judged according to the Law is determined by divine punishment. Therefore if one would come to expect to be considered righteous before God, this would be a perilous matter, even to the loss of one's salvation. Because human nature is not able to be without sin and to fulfill all righteousness as God desires since *not even one* has been found who has never fallen.[9] Behold, it is written: "Anyone who does not do all which is commanded will perish."[10] This is the righteousness according to the Law!

11. But if you say: "I am justified by conscience and by the will of the soul and I reveal <my> heart to God," behold you have requested grace! While not having accomplished any work, or having stumbled, or having fallen short because of issues, you are convinced that such a conscience is reckoned as a deed. But if you have no work, you who boast about work, why the boast? It is brought to naught. What joy can there be from our way of life?

---

[8] Dt. 27:26; Gal.3:10; James 2:10.

[9] Cf. Ps. 14:3; Rm.3:12.

[10] Dt.27:26; Gal.3:10; James 2:10.

12. Let every mouth be silenced: the Lord alone has granted victory! One is redeemed by grace and not by works and by faith one is justified, not by one's way of life. In such a way *that one who has not worked, but only believes in the One who justifies sinners*, *the faith* of his conscience *is reckoned* by God *as righteousness.*[11] This is what the Apostle said: *A man is justified by faith and not by works.*[12] But if righteousness were reckoned <on the basis of> work, it is written: "All who do not do everything which is commanded will perish."[13] Behold the righteousness which is from <one's> way of life!

13. This is the righteousness, however, which is from grace when one does a little according to one's strength and fulfills it with one's will, even if the work is not well done. God, on account of His grace, reckons it <as> the fullness of righteousness, ascribing the whole action to him. For myself, even if I am not able to do much, I work according to my strength; certainly I am not able to be without blame or without sin. But O God, for a minimum of work, You give me righteousness!

14. Sometimes I am lacking even this minimum. Not only do I not have a work to give, but many times even that sincere will which I acquired with a good desire, turns aside from You and becomes involved with evil and is separated from You. I am almost emptied of a sincere will towards You. But then when I am empty of works or of will, with only the hint of conversion which You obtained in me, in an instant You give me the fullness of righteousness while the deed is distant – <righteousness> which neither time nor bodily <labor> could yield.

15. But while I remain waiting for all of this, You Yourself receive me, and by means of grace without works, You justify me. You establish me in <my> former high place. And only because of the conversion of <my> will, while I am not capable of anything, You take from me the death of conscience,[14] and You give me

---

[11] Cf. Rm.4:5.

[12] Gal.2:16.

[13] Dt.27:26; Gal.3:10; James 2:10.

[14] Cf. Heb.9:14.

righteousness without fault. Who is righteous <so as> to be able to renounce this grace? And by whom have these things not been received along the path of one's way of life?

16. Who, then, understands this and faithfully discerns is not able to rejoice in works but only in the goodness of God. And the one who truly recognizes that God's goodness is the cause of his joy, does not hold that his joy be only for himself but rejoices for all creatures. His joy comes to be more abundant than the sea, because it is the goodness of the God of the universe affording such joy, and all creation is a partaker in it, even sinners share in this.

17. So then, he is quick to rejoice even for sinners. He says in fact: "They are <not far> from mercy because of the goodness of the Lord of the universe[15] by which righteousness has been given even to me without works." And again he says: "All like me share in this <great> good because God is good: He only requires a little will <then> He gives His grace abundantly and remits sins."

18. This is the grace which strengthens the righteous, preserving <them> by its being near and removing their faults. It is also near to those who have perished, reducing their torments and in their punishment deals with compassion. In the world to come,[16] indeed grace will be the judge, not justice. <God> reduces the length of time of sufferings, and by means of His grace, makes all worthy of His Kingdom.[17] For there is no one <even> among the righteous who is able to conform his way of life to the Kingdom.

19. But if human realities are to be judged and examined according to justice, yet in listening to the word of Scripture one investigates according to exterior knowledge, not entering into the meaning – where is justice here? As it is said, *He is merciful in all his works.*[18] However, even when He chastises here below or in the life

---

[15] A variant of *Lord of all*, see Is.III 1.3.

[16] Cf. Heb.2:5; 6:5.

[17] On Isaac's eschatology, life after death, etc., see Alfeyev, *Spiritual World*, 269–97. See also Beulay, *L'Enseignement*, 488–510; *Lumière*, 157–58.

[18] Ps.145:17 (Peshitta).

beyond, it is not correct to consider this <as> justice, but <rather> fatherly wisdom.

20. Nor do I call "exacting punishment" even those times when God visits one with a severe aspect, either here or in the life beyond, but <rather> "instruction," because they have a good end. On that account, as I said, no one is able to make his way of life resemble that Kingdom and that way of life which is granted <only> by mercy.

21. So then I have explained what was already said, that we inherit heaven by what is His and not by what is ours. And this grace is given every day, not <just> from time to time. If we all receive this grace, let us rejoice in Him who gives it and the greater will be <our> joy! Let us adore and give thanks for it, and an even greater gift will be given.

22. Whoever, then has joy by reason of his way of life, this joy is false, or rather, his joy is wretched. And not only in his joy is he wretched but also in his understanding. Whoever rejoices because he has truly understood that God is good, is consoled with a consolation that does not pass away, and his joy is true joy. <This is> because, as was <just> said his soul has considered and perceived that truly the goodness of God is without measure.

23. Thus human nature is not able to justify itself because daily it remains in need. On account of inclination, because of weakness, because of the body, because of impediments, because of movements, and also what is from outside and is similar to this – God proposed <His> intention to do every stratagem that in every moment one might be reckoned as righteous before Him, as he has heard in <Scripture>.

24. For <God>, one sin does not make a sinner.[19] It is pleasing to Him, that as much as possible, one confute the occasions of <sin>.

---

[19] On compassion for sinners: "Cover the sinner even though you are not harmed by him. Indeed, encourage him for life and the mercy of the Lord will sustain you. Support the weak and distressed with a word as

Yet when one goes astray, <God> does not neglect to extend to him His mercy. When one falls into great <sins, God> covers him; and so that these do not come to the knowledge of anyone, He gives a hand to the one who goes astray. As to the greater <sins>, see how God exposes some in order to alarm the dissolute; while the lesser <sins> He leaves exposed, as a rebuke for the greater ones which are hidden.

25. And while one hides hateful and harmful evils, God indicates one's small omissions so as to shake up mankind with them, though how often they are as nothing in proportion <to greater sins>. By attacking his little faults, He indicates the healing of the greater ones. And for a small <act of> righteousness that one is able to do, God does not neglect to honor him and to crown him with a double portion because of it. Indeed, He turns away from <our> sin as much as is possible[20] but looks mercifully on our <lesser> offenses; and for the least diligence which follows, He remits the offense and the continued carelessness.

26. And so that no one be considered as a sinner before Him, He prepares a scheme. It is said: *The Lord has also removed your debt: you will not die.*[21] And if there would be an offender who takes no care about remorse, He prepares his pardon on account of the presence of the others,[22] since He loves to offer an occasion for pardon. The mediation and intercession of Moses[23] <intervened concerning> Aaron's calf. And for His own sake and because of David, He overshadows[24] the city <of Jerusalem> which was full of idols.[25]

---

far as you are able, that the right hand upholding the universe may sustain you."(Is.I 14). See also Is.I 79, 457.

[20] The discretion shown by God in covering sins is recommended in the *Synodicon Orientale* towards those who have sinned and repented but fear being mocked. The Church must treat them with prudence and mercy, covering their sins. See Canon VI, p. 174–75.

[21] 2 Sam. 12:13.

[22] This suggests the power of intercession, also hinted at in Is.III XI 19, 23.

[23] Cf. Ex.32:1–14.

[24] On *overshadow*, see Is.III I. 4.

27. Where He finds only the mention of conversion, and even if it be in an exterior way, <God> inclines joyfully to pour out pardon. He does this also for the greater faults, even though He knows the heart! One remembers the death of Naboth and the deceptive sackcloth of Ahab, etc.[26]

28. While God does not rejoice at the occasions of sin, where they are, He forgives. Therefore He openly shows His will, which is to be merciful:[27] "I delight in pardon and I do not pardon on account of the occasions but because it pleases my goodness – and I take upon myself to give pardon whether there be occasion <of sin> or where there is rectitude – thanks to that grace which covers everything with a veil." So then, when one is naked grace provides what is necessary.[28]

29. There are two debtors of the same creditor who cry out. One owed five hundred dinars and <the other> fifty: this indicates great sins, and partial ones which contain within them also the little ones. Neither of the two debtors had anything to make restitution, so the creditor remitted <the debts>.[29] Here <God> showed clearly that He loves forgiveness and not the occasions <of sin>.

30. His Economy, however, assumes the <burden> of finding pretexts for those who are negligent and do nothing profitably, but only go back to their <sins>. Even if God were to show clearly all His intelligence in this regard, and yet our inclination were not able for this, and on this account the growth of evil increases from this time – this is no obstacle, any where it happens, for His grace to work openly, that is, the grace which He has shown towards the debtors of the five hundred dinars and the fifty.

31. Not because He loved them more did He care for these; because He does not love the others less than them, since it is not the person He loves but <human> nature. And if it is the nature

---

[25] Cf. 2 Kgs.19:34; 20:6; Is.37:35.

[26] Cf. 1 Kgs.21.

[27] Cf. Evag. *Letter to Melania*, 6 (Casiday; Frankenberg, p. 612).

[28] Cf. Gen.3:7–21.

[29] Cf. Lk.7:41–42.

He loves, all persons are included within the boundary of His love, good and bad.[30] And if, without hesitation, while not hiding faults, He granted forgiveness to these whose great number of sins made them unrighteous, all the more reason He will make worthy those whose <sins> are less.

32. He makes worthy of pardon what is extreme and what is insignificant. Such that those who clearly do not <feel> fit to receive it, receive it equally. For <God>, however, both are equal, as he does not bother with calculations. When he pardons the one who has offended more, He is not vexed nor has difficulty more than when He pardons the one who has sinned less. For He loves human beings and does not love justice deprived of mercy. <He says>: *My thoughts are not your thoughts and my ways are not your ways: I am a merciful God.*

33. I considered all these things and I was amazed at the wisdom of the Lord of the universe! I searched His mercy, whose magnificence surpasses the intelligence of all those endowed with reason. This is therefore His will: to pardon everyone in all occasions <of sin>.

34. While being a sinner for a small fault, at once <God> calls him righteous; and because of the good of one day, He pardons all the iniquity of his life. The one who spent all his days in sins, for one good <deed> God decrees him innocent. If only in his conscience he is sorry, God cancels great faults and instead of good deeds, He accepts from him a feeble will. And for the sins of years, weighty and prolonged, sufficient for him is the repentance of one moment.

35. God reckons this as righteousness, even if the body is not able to abstain from previous faults. As if God says: "Do not sin; then for the sins you have committed I will not lay blame. Only recognize the grace I have done for you!" The publican in the

---

[30] Not only the good and the bad, but even demons: quoting Diodore of Tarsus, Isaac says "...of the demons and their great inclination to evil 'not even their immense wickedness can overcome the measure of God's goodness'." See Is.II XXXIX.13–14, XL.2; *Keph.* IV 87.

temple and the prodigal son testify concerning this: these received a swift pardon though they sinned more than all the others.[31] It is said: *Where sin has increased, there* goodness *has abounded.*[32]

36. Even if it is God who truly gives strength to the will, that it might be able to not consent to sin, and while everything is from Him, yet it pleases Him to call us righteous. As I said, the purpose of this He laid down that by every resource, He might rejoice in everyone as righteous, and <everyone be counted as such>.

37. See how weak our nature is! Even though our good works are few <we take on> the fame of righteousness, but with the least pretext the merciful Lord calls us righteous! Now is there one who doubts these things which I said? Or, indeed, one whose conscience does not witness to these glorious realities of God? Let the remembrance of the thief at the right <of Jesus> be a blessing, as it is known that also he is among the recipients of mercy, freely given.[33]

38. Is there a rational <creature> who is blinded by his will from inquiring into all these things? Or who turns his face from all of this and takes joy in his own way of life? Who is the one endowed with reason who does not search night and day, and does not consider all of these wonders of God and the judgments of His love? That is to say, He does not judge our affairs with justice, but in love subverts right judgment, so that we hateful ones become supposedly well-pleasing.

39. Whoever indeed meditates and studies these things, night and day, and for whom the fount of his joy is to strive to examine these things, and he marvels at God rejoicing while searching the stratagems of His goodness: this one is rich in his poverty! His joy is a joy which <comes> from grace, it is not human. And while not

---

[31] Cf. Lk.18:9–14; 15:11–32.

[32] Rm.5:20. In the citation from Romans, instead of grace (*ṭaybûṯâ*) Isaac has used goodness (*ṭâbtâ*), perhaps intentionally.

[33] Cf. Lk. 3:39–43.

having anything, in faith he possesses everything, because He in whom everything exists, is the cause of his joy.[34]

40. For whoever finds all his joy in this, because of this, all which is his is beautiful. This is his only joy! The one, then, who rejoices in the Nature of God and in the riches which that sublime Nature brings to us – because God Himself is richness and His riches are for us mercy, love and goodness – that one, indeed, whose joy springs up from here, this joy of his renews the universe. Because all which is God's is ours.

41. Besides all which is His, He also added the gift to us of His only-begotten Son, as our Lord said: *For God so loved the world as to give his only-begotten Son, that all who believe in him might not perish.*[35] And also blessed Paul said: *Now God shows his love for us that when we were sinners Christ died for us.*[36] And again: *If while we were enemies God became reconciled with us by the death of his Son, then how much more now, because of his reconciliation,*[37] *will we live by his life!*[38] The one whose joy is in these things, this joy of his is the redemption of creation!

42. May our soul be absorbed continually in this excellent reflection which is the remembrance of God's love for us. Let us sanctify our heart[39] in converse with it because this is eloquent prayer. Let us purify our sins by this reflection! Let us renew our soul at all times by repentance and faith – that is by righteousness without works – which may be understood through compunction and the faith of conscience, when we are mindful of this.

43. One speaks to one's soul and exhorts it with encouragement able to persuade: "If today by means of works I was not saved, tomorrow I will be saved by grace." Let us keep our mind attentive at all times in the hope of God's mercy! Our heart rejoices in His

---

[34] Cf. 2 Cor. 6:10.

[35] John 3:16.

[36] Rom. 5:8.

[37] Chialà here offers a correction to the ms, "reconciliation," based on a reading of the Peshitta text of Romans.

[38] Rom. 5:10.

[39] Cf. James 4:8.

love, because according to the word of blessed Paul, *God loves us very much.*[40]

44. May our mind labor continually in reflection on the Economy of God for us. Let us give ourselves to this reflection because of its great insight and its infinite joy. Its labor is the labor of the angels! By this, rational creatures gradually attain *God's manifold wisdom by means of his Church*, as the Apostle said;[41] and also by means of this meditation we grow strong in the knowledge of God's love.

45. If this reflection delights the angels and increases <their> gladness, how much more then for humans. In this, one must remain continually, not haphazardly, with a strong and genuine insight, so that our soul might be a pure temple for God. For on account of our continual remembrance[42] of Him, He dwells in us continually. Indeed, these remembrances greatly help those who <profess> this divine philosophy <in their way> of life.

46. We turn the gaze of our intelligence continually upon all of this, that is, that the divine intelligence[43] was reconciled with us in perpetuity and from before the ages. This was spoken of sufficiently in this very *memra*, and may we always be filled with amazement and hope by it! Those who persevere in converse with these things and in this meditation, emulate the nature of the angels.

47. In our thought, let us also take up the burden of the way of life of the saints of every generation, as a medicinal indication <for healing>. Let us form in our intelligence the purity of their way of life, their excellent life and their constant toil of separation from this world. Let us imitate, by meditation on their reasonings, the glorious reflection of their intelligence, which is continually lifted up in wonder at these things, beyond all of the things of this life and of the remembrance of corruptible things.

---

[40] Eph. 2:4.

[41] Eph. 3:10.

[42] Continual remembrance (*ʿuhdânâ ammînâ*): Is.III VIII, *passim.*

[43] Divine intelligence (*tarʿîtâ alâhâytâ*): Is.II XIV.4; XV.2; XXXIX.2.

48. They resemble the life of the Spirit, as much as is possible in the way of life here <below>. And while being in the flesh, they are always found above it. Not that they are able to be without food and without what is useful for the necessities of nature – not possible! However when there is also an obstacle to this, they are almost made glad. In their intelligence, they are together with the invisible powers, and in their mind they are found above the world.

49. And with these angelic meditations noted above, they instruct their souls night and day, while the gaze of their mind is always directed towards God. And they await that incorruptible communion with <God>, beyond the world by means of the Spirit, as the holy Ammonas says in one of his letters, when he teaches how one is made worthy of this amazing gift of which the world is not worthy.

50. He says: "Direct your thoughts towards God night and day while asking the Holy Spirit and it will be given to you."[44] Where it says: "Direct your thoughts," he means "mind" instead. Namely: "Weary your mind night and day in meditation on God, because it is necessary that even now you be made worthy of the action of the Holy Spirit." This is the <meaning> of "Ask the Holy Spirit and it will be given to you."

51. While being in these realities, one's intellect is occupied at all times, since by every means it rejects temporal realities; and from here pure ways of life are constantly occurring. From this time, you are made worthy of ineffable communion with God the Father, which happens by means of a revelation in the journey of those who live the migration of the mind,[45] as the fathers say. And in all that concerns you, you show that your way is alien to that of mankind; and while being within a body, in the world, through obedience and <your> manner of thinking, you are <already> lifted up to life, in His Life.[46]

---

[44] Ammonius 586–87.

[45] On *migration*, see Is.III I.8.

[46] Cf. Col. 3:1–3.

52. Not that we have no more need of food, drink and clothes, as I have said <before>; but while it is evident that in all which concerns us we are alien to this world, it is also well-known that all which is ours is opposed to what is <of the world>: in our labor, in our reflection, in our converse, in our word, etc.

53. Some labor to gain possession of this earth but we toil to *inherit the kingdom of heaven.*[47]

54. Some keep vigil and watch at nights to lay up gold and silver, but we watch and weary ourselves by means of our vigil, to taste that way of life after the resurrection.

55. Some adorn themselves for the world and they stumble, but we adorn ourselves for Christ, *the light of the world.*[48]

56. Some become inebriated[49] with wine and so their mind goes astray to their soul's harm. But we become intoxicated with the love of God, and in our intoxication we disregard the corruptible things of this life.

57. Some toil to acquire hurtful knowledge, nothing of which is permitted to go with them in the *future world.*[50] But we weary our soul in the meditation of God.

58. Some say absurd and foul things, and words full of ridicule and debauchery. We, however, speak about the salvation of souls: words about judgment; searching into what will be after the resurrection; a discourse about reconciliation with God; instruction concerning salvation – all these things which fill the soul with compunction. We also speak about the accounts which lead to desire sanctity; about studies which make apparent the hope <that

---

[47] Cf. 1 Cor. 15:50 (Peshitta).

[48] Cf. 1 Peter 3:3–4; Job 33:30.

[49] Inebriated (*rawwîyûtâ*): Is.I 2, 59, 77, 174, 256, 454; Is.II V.21, X.35; *Keph.* I 33, 67, 88; IV 48,82. It occurs in Ephrem, John Sol., Sahdona, Dadisho and Shem'on d-Taybuteh. According to Alfeyev: "*spiritual inebriation* is the single most characteristic mystical theme in the works of Isaac." See Alfeyev, *Spiritual World*, 191, 248–55.

[50] Cf. Heb.2:5; 6:5.

lies> after our death; about the joy of our Lord[51] and exultation in the Holy Spirit;[52] about contempt for a corruptible manner of life; about the remembrance that our joy is in Christ; about thanksgiving for our salvation; about the mystery of life which takes place in our body; about the memorial of the sacrifice of our Savior for us, with tears[53] of joy and of suffering together with lips which are impelled in praise of God.

59. We are diligent in all these <matters> because this <concerns> all of God's mercy to be used towards all mankind. Let it not be for us a pretext for neglect, but rather for diligence in righteousness, lest we be reproved by Him because our ways of life are in contradiction <to His mercy>.

60. As Theodore the Interpreter, marvelous among the saints, said in the <Commentary to the letter> *to the Romans*: "The compassion of God ought not to be an occasion of laxity for those who have received all this mercy, but on the contrary they ought to show great diligence. For we ought to be ashamed to be wrong doers before one who is totally Good. In brief, let us be anxious for all these good things, that our person be adorned so as to arrive properly at the resurrection of the dead, without being summoned to the trial of that decree of judgment reserved for all who in this created world have completely surrendered to evil. But, he says, while the promise of our entrance into rest stands firm, let it not happen that one of us desist from entering."[54]

61. Moreover, not even this is alien to the love of a father: while we act in this world as rational creatures, being diligent about all that concerns us, yet we live this irrationally because we scarcely take cognizance of the life to which we have been led, in which God does not consent to punish for eternity. But when we learn

---

[51] Cf. Phil.4:10.

[52] Cf. Rom.14:17; 1 Titus 1:6.

[53] In Isaac, tears (*demʿē*) accompany purification and rebirth, the eyes are the baptismal font, Is.I 139. See Chialà, *Ascesi eremitica*, 211–13.

[54] Cf. Rom.12:1. See Theodore of Mopsuestia, *Commentary on the letter to the Romans*, PG 66 col. 860.

what would have been due in punishment, with what evils we have been complicit, we will receive in ourselves an experience of what <would have been due in punishment>.

62. How great, indeed, is our ignorance! God, then, proceeds with His work according to His eternal intelligence, as becomes His great love. Regarding this, one may consider His entire will from the beginning, by means of insight into what He has indicated in each of His Economies in every generation. So that henceforward we may be roused from <our> sins and after our departure for the life beyond, we will then be chastened especially by the goading of His love. As is said: *The one who has been forgiven much, loves much.*[55] And then will come to pass that word which is written: *God will be all in all.*[56]

63. To Him be the glory for His wise dispensations which are exalted beyond <all> investigation, forever and ever. Amen.

---

[55] Lk.7:47.

[56] 1 Cor.15:28.

Chapter VII

By the same Mar Isaac. Prayer impelled by the insights of the things which were said. For there is in <prayer> a great signification, from time to time at prayer one turns to contemplate it, then again turns back to prayer. And in the noble passion of the mind, one offers amazing stirrings for the sake of all these great things which are ours.

1. I adore Your majesty, O God, who have created me in Your love and have saved me in Christ from the spiritual darkness which is the ignorance of the soul.[1] You have removed from us the time of error that we may not walk, so to say, in the night in our knowledge of You as in former generations.

2. Glory to You who in <Your> mercy have endured our wickedness; in Your compassion You put right our sinfulness; and in Your kindness You remove our failings. You have given us to believe in You as becomes Your greatness. And You have not paid attention to our faithlessness, which is always before You, because You are a merciful God. And with the dew of Your grace, You always overcome the fire of our sins.

3. What mouth is capable of Your praise? And what tongue is fit to extol You? You have curbed our sins with an increase of Your grace. And instead of the sentence of Your judgment, You have lavished Your treasure also on sinners, because You do not wish *to pronounce judgment on us*[2] but to draw us near to You since we are Your creation. Your grace has surpassed the measure of our understanding: in our stead, the amazing natures of the angels glorify You. <These are> those in whom You have placed a power able to receive the wonderful stirring of Your holiness.[3]

4. Let the angels make You known in our stead, for our nature is too feeble to give you thanks. May the marvelous stirrings of their

[1] Cf. Nilus, *Sulla virtù e sulle passione* 15, p. 285.

[2] Cf. Ps. 143:2.

[3] On angelic mediation, see Is.III VIII.11.

thanksgiving mingle with our praise. They are truly sorry for our being deprived of You,[4] as You have cut us off from mingling with their assemblies concerning the understanding of Your hidden Being. But without our asking, You have given us the great gift of faith by which we may draw near to the mysteries of knowledge – mysteries by which spiritual beings attain gradually to the Shekinah[5] of Your Essence.

5. By means of the mysteries of faith, indeed, those whom You are near to *in faith and not in vision*,[6] remain upright, my Lord, within the cloud of thick darkness of Your glory.[7] This is received by the illumined mind with great understanding. For it is You who bestow this faith as a gift to those endowed with reason, that their stirrings might attempt to believe in that which is not attainable or knowable – that is the Divine Nature which is hidden from all – by the mysteries that You reveal to them in Your love.

6. I am convinced, therefore, that it is not possible to find You anywhere, O eternal God, neither in spiritual beings nor in weak human company, but only from the fountain of Your love. From this <the fountain>, You pour forth at all times on the assemblies which are above and on those below. In fact, according to the measure of each one of the assemblies, You pour out the treasure of Your mercy <granting> them revelations, as much as possible, for the sake of knowledge.

7. The gift of Your grace is a required intermediary, because it lifts our intellect to converse of faith in You. Whereas on account

---

[4] Cf. Lk. 15:10.

[5] Shekinah: Is.I 517; Is.II X.24; XI.5–6, 10, 12, 14, 24. See the Peshitta: 1 Chron. 28:2; 2 Chron. 5:14, 7: 1–2, *passim*; Judges 9:8 (Peshitta 9:11); 2 Macc. 14:35; Sir. 36:15. For its use in rabbinic tradition indicating the presence of God, see Urbach, *The Sages*, ch.3, 37–65. The term appears in Aphrahat, Ephrem, Jacob of Serug, Philoxenus, Sahdona. See Cerbelaud, "Aspects" and Sed, "La Shekhinta."

[6] Cf. 2 Cor. 5:7.

[7] Cf. Ex. 20:21. Cloud of thick darkness of Your glory: (*ʿarpellâ d-šubḥâk*): Is.II X.17, 24.

of the great thick darkness which surrounds <Your> holiness, even the eyes of the Cherubim are confused when looking within the secret place of the thick darkness of Your glory.[8]

8. But if they are sustained, more or less, by Your grace to go up to the top of the mountain of faith; this is the knowledge of the Spirit: that is to say, beams of light which shine upon the intellect from that mighty fire which flashes from the interior place of faith, that <place> which is called the inner sanctuary where one adores the magnificence of the glorious nature of the Essence. That is the <place> where no creature has ever entered or will enter there, except that One who was sanctified to enter[9] *by God's foreknowledge*[10] according to His intelligence, which is good concerning all, to continually make atonement for the sins of His people.

9. For it is by faith one enters a place, further within than the Watchers.[11] It is by means of one of them that at one time the mercy of <God> made <Him> enter and dwell there.[12] And from that time forth <God> gives power to those human intellects who are sanctified to enter by faith, I mean near Him. He is indeed incomprehensible and distant, visible not even for a moment, whether for the eyes of the angels or for ours. By revelation then, the angels were first and nearer than us, until You revealed Yourself for our deliverance.

10. Our true hope, the delight of mankind, our nature's boast, steadfast advocate of our weakness who pardons our sins at all times! Your intercession for pardon for us is mightier, my Lord,

---

[8] Cf. Ex. 20:21.

[9] Cf. Heb. 9:11–12.

[10] Cf. Acts 2:23; 1 Peter 1:2.

[11] The Syriac tradition frequently designates angels as Watchers (Dan. 4:13,17). Watchers figure prominently in pseudepigraphic and later Jewish mystical literature. In Merkabah texts such as 3 Enoch, they are a separate order: "Above all these are four great princes called Watchers…their abode is opposite the throne of Glory…they receive glory from the glory of the Almighty and are praised with the praise." See 3 Enoch 28:1–3.

[12] Cf. Heb. 9:11–12.

than the sacrifice of Israel. If the meat of animals and the ashes of their burnt-offerings undeniably purified and sanctified those for whom they were offered in sacrifice, how much more You purify us at all times, You, sacred oblation offered for the world.[13]

11. You offer and You absolve, You are the priest and You are the one consecrated. You are the sacrifice and You are the one who receives it. If that mute metal leaf[14] which manifests the mystery of Your human nature, gave pardon to those who earnestly entreat, how much more You, glorious image of the divinity! And if Your mysteries pour forth all this richness on those in need, how much more will You, true prototype of the mysteries, pour forth on us Your mercy.

12. For it is You for whom the prophets and the kings have waited according to their generations and the righteous in their descendants.[15] Is it not Your day, O expectation of the Gentiles, for we have received You in our hands and, behold, we rejoice in You! They saw these things in the revelations given them which they marveled at and earnestly desired; whereas we see the interpretation of those mysteries. You poured forth on us the Gihon[16] of Your grace, O our Creator; You have opened Your entire treasury in our generation and we have gained access to it. You have shown us the mysteries of Your Christ. It was by a desire for His Coming that many generations were gripped but they departed from this life without consolation because His days were far removed from their times.

---

[13] Cf. Heb. 9,13–14.

[14] Metal leaf (*ṭassâ*): Ex.25:17, 21–2; Lv.16.2, 13–15 (description of the ark). The Peshitta uses *ḥussâyâ* instead of *ṭassâ*. See Is.II XI.14 for Brock's explanation; see also his trans. of Evag. Cent. IV.52: "the spiritual *ṭassâ* is the true knowledge of the Holy Trinity." And see Narsai, *Homily on the Tabernacle*: "With the term *ṭassâ* (Scripture) tells of the humanity of our Lord, and with the *ḥussâyâ* (it tells of) the Being (*îtûtâ*) who has dwelling in him." As referred to in Is.II XI.15, note 15.

[15] Cf. Mt.13:17; Lk.10:24.

[16] Gen. 2:13; 1Kgs 1:33. Gihon, one of the four rivers of Paradise.

13. *Return, my soul, to your rest*[17] because you have seen the expectation of all the Gentiles. You carried Him upon your hands,[18] in Him you were pardoned of your iniquity and of all your sins. *Bless the Lord, my soul, and all my bones His holy name.*[19] *Praise the Lord, O my soul!*[20] *I will praise the Lord in my life and I will sing to my God as long as I live.*[21] *My heart and my flesh have praised the living God.*[22]

14. I will praise You, Lord, and *my mouth will declare Your righteousness and Your praise all the day.*[23] For You have brought me to the magnificence of Your Lordship. You have associated me with the praise of the angels and have united me with the celebrations of their assemblies. My Lord, You have not deprived us of communion with them which consists in faith, for such is the nature of all spiritual beings: the wings of the Watchers and the mirror of their revelations. Our communion with the angels and our mingling with their assemblies consists in making our will equal with theirs, in the spirit of the faith we have received.

15. This is the praise of spiritual beings, the force of the wondrous revelations concerning the Godhead and the various realities of faith which spring up in their stirrings. For truly, Lord, by them You are experienced *by faith and not by sight.* Your hidden and holy Nature does not fall under the touch or sight of any creature. But by faith, all natures take delight in the rays from Your mercy that flash in their nature.

16. You have brought us near to the mysteries of such glory by means of Your Beloved Son. For You have let us approach the foothills of the mountain of faith – there in the midst of which

---

[17] Ps. 116:7.
[18] Lk. 2:25–32.
[19] Ps. 103:1.
[20] Ps. 146:1.
[21] Ps. 104:33.
[22] Ps. 84:3.
[23] Ps. 71:15.

dwell the nine ranks of the hosts of the spiritual beings,[24] and above which is built Your holy city.[25]

17. Our God, Living and Lifegiving, this is the mountain Your apostle and servant Paul announced to us when he said: *You have come near.* For You have come near to the mountain of Sion[26] – which is faith and knowledge of the Lord – *to the city of the living God, to the heavenly Jerusalem.* This consists in participation in the divine contemplation[27] *with the assemblies of the archangels.*[28] For the mind which shares in the revelation with them is in ascent on the ladder of faith to Sion, the mountain of God.

18. <To bring> an end to our evils, You have brought us to this, O God Just Judge,[29] who is not always angry but turns and refrains from looking at our sins.[30] You did not spare Your Beloved Son, but You gave Him up for us all[31] that His death might justify us. You have made known to us in Christ hidden aspects of Your eternal wisdom and You have brought us to the knowledge of faith in You.[32]

19. Do not abandon me, my Lord, depriving me of this mercy which is upon me! For You have called me without my asking, and brought me in Your eternal love to Your glorious kingdom.[33] Let me not be deprived of meditation on this love. Send Your power, my Lord, to assist me and rescue me from the sea of temporal life.

---

[24] On the nine choirs of angels alluded to here, see Is.I 187. See also Ps. Dionysius, *Celestial Hierarchy* VI–X, 200c–273c.

[25] Heb.12:22.

[26] Ascent to Sion: Evag. Cent.V.6; VI. 49.

[27] Divine contemplation (*te'ôryâ alâhâytâ*): Is.I 23, 31, 161, 198, 571; Is.II XIX.5; *Keph.* IV 48. Brock lists occurrences in Ps.Dionysius, Sergius, Babai, Gregory of Cyprus – and notes its absence in Evagrius.

[28] Heb. 12:22.

[29] Ps. 9:5.

[30] Ps. 85: 3–7.

[31] Rom. 8:32.

[32] Rom. 16: 25–26.

[33] 1 Titus 2:12.

O Sea of help, continue to help me and do not abandon me to the abyss of evils.

20. Guide of Life, direct my mind to You: open before my thoughts the door of reflection on You. O Renewer of all,[34] You have gladdened me with Your knowledge. Stir up in my heart a genuine hope in You. O Ocean of compassion, rescue me from the anxiety of wandering away from[35] You. Bring me within the burning fire of Your faith. Give me to drink the wine of perception of your hope. Make me worthy of that fervor of heart that once the drop of hope in You has fallen upon it, it burns without being consumed.[36]

21. Who has received this thought and can endure its vehemence? Who has experienced it and again remembers himself? What body or thought can even endure the fragrance of faith in You? Christ the culminator of truth, make Your truth shine *in our hearts*.[37] O Power who have shown forth in the saints, by Your love I have *overcome the world*[38] and its pleasures. O Power who have put on our body, make the insights of Your truth shine in my darkened soul. O Ocean that has sustained the world, draw me out of the stormy sea.

22. My Lord, You know that I am sad because my sins are always before You:[39] hidden tears spring up when I see the weakness of my soul. But when I seek to heal my sins through sighs, desires rush in with them to change in ruin my pain of heart and to turn my thought away from intercession and my meditation regarding You.

23. You are a capable healer for the torments of my heart. Strengthen my heart against the passions which are in it, for You

---

[34] Cf. Rev. 21:5.

[35] Wandering away from (*pehyâ*): here seen in a negative sense but may also be understood positively as "pondering," see Is.II XVIII.3.

[36] Cf. Ex. 3:2.

[37] Cf. 2 Peter 1:19; 2 Cor.4:6.

[38] Cf. 1 Jn. 5:4.

[39] Cf. Ps. 51:5.

know that it is not in me to overcome in this struggle. It is Your might which conquers but which ascribes the victory to me. Conquer in me, as You know how, and reckon the victory to me according to Your wisdom! For those who have conquered in this goal, it is their victory.

24. Let my heart's compunction be a witness before You, that the tumult of the flesh is stronger than my will.

25. While everyday I weep about what has come to pass, there is no moment when I do not incur the same faults, renewing those things for which I seek conversion. O Conqueror, who grants victory to the guilty whose own nature can never grant victory, give me that power which overcomes nature. While its own defeat is within nature, it is said to conquer by grace, yet it knows no victory by it own nature

26. Another power weaves a crown for him:[40] that One who has wisely formed his wretchedness so as to reveal His goodness, knows his tendency to change. Such that everyday, he must be justified by forgiveness of his faults which God grants and does not hinder. <This occurs> to show in him the goodness of His nature, that the weakness of human nature might be a herald of His sweetness and a witness of His mercy.[41]

27. Meditation on the perception of You conquers in me the difficulty of the struggle. Sweet converse with Your hope leads me captive from consent with the flesh. May this sweetness of the knowledge of You separate me from the way of nature. Make me worthy, my Lord, of true insights concerning Your will with regard to us. Make me worthy of that meditation which, in the process, transfigures thoughts so as to see within the other world without resembling it.

28. The power which teaches me to seek these things, plants in me a taste for the love of these things. For You have drawn me to

---

[40] Cf. 2 Tm. 4:8.

[41] Cf. 2 Cor. 12:9.

You by what <You have sown> in my senses: accomplish in me, within my spirit, to know its meaning by experience.

29. Since You have associated me in the mystery of Your glorious divinity, strengthen me in this hope by the assurance of faith. Because, my Lord, by means of Your Beloved Son You have drawn me to this understanding, instruct me in a hidden way that I might think about Your majesty. Give me a sound mind that it may flourish continually by means of a clear reflection regarding You.

30. Remove from me an ignorant mind which thinks silliness; stir up in me how to think rightly about Your splendor, so that I do not begin to give praise concerning Your divine judgments in a human manner subject to passions about the ways of Your intelligence, Savior of our souls! Prepare in me the paths of Your wisdom and open to me the door to meditation on Your glorious will, for I do not know, my Lord, how to enter there.

31. O Christ, door of the mysteries,[42] make me a sharer in the apperception of Your mysteries. By You, my Lord, I enter to the Father and I receive insights of the grace of Your Holy Spirit. O Christ, key of the mysteries and end of the mysteries: by You, my Lord, the door is opened for us to the mysteries which from of old were hidden in Your Father.

32. Make me worthy to receive You within me, that by You I may open the mysteries past and future and enter there. O Lord, You make me worthy of the sweetness of hope in You. Whoever tastes this cup will persevere in controlling himself and return again to his true self. This cup, indeed, becomes sweet in the heart of those who receive it, like the juice of the grape.

33. You who make all things new,[43] renew me by the apperception of hope in You. Joy of creation, make me worthy of that joy which arises beyond the flesh and is received in the silence

---

[42] See Is.I 544: "The cross is the gate of the mysteries; here takes place the entrance of the mind unto the knowledge of the heavenly mysteries."

[43] Cf. Rev.21:5.

of the soul.[44] Bury within my members the fire of Your love. Place on my heart the bonds of wonder at You. Bind my stirrings in the silence of the knowledge of You because knowledge of You consists in silence. Make me worthy to behold You with opened eyes which are more interior than the eyes of the body.[45]

34. Create new eyes in me, You who created new eyes for the blind man.[46] Close my exterior ears and open hidden ears, which hear the silence and the sounds of the Spirit, that by Your Spirit I might proclaim the word of silence[47] which arises in the heart but is not written, which moves in the intellect but is not spoken – though spoken by the lips of the Spirit and is heard by incorporeal hearing. O Ocean of pardon, begin to wash nature's uncleanness from me and make me fit for Your sanctuary.

35. My Lord, You have not formed me like a clay vessel that when broken cannot be restored and when encrusted is not able to take on its former polish when new. But in Your wisdom, You have created me in the form of elements of gold and silver that when tarnished, in the refining sorrow of compunction, again imitates the color of the sun and shining is brought to its former condition by means of the crucible of repentance. You are the craftsman who polishing our nature makes it new. I have soiled the beauty of baptism and I am sullied, but in You I receive a more excellent beauty. In You is the beauty of creation: You have brought it back again to that beauty from which it was altered in paradise.[48]

---

[44] Silence of the soul (*šetqâ d-napšâ*): in John Sol., Bettiolo, "Sulla preghiera," 5, p.81. And see Is.III IV.7.

[45] See interior eye (*ʿaynâ gawwâytâ*) Is.II XXXV.4; Keph. IV 67, cf. And see Is.III I.11.

[46] John 9. See Christ as Creator in Ephrem. For Ephrem, "God is the source of healing and he sent His Son into the world to heal humanity and fulfill what was lacking in nature. The fulfilling and healing of the world is considered by Ephrem as a second creation." See Shemunkasho, *Healing in the Theology*, 381–387; 407–21.

[47] Word of silence (*melta d- šetqâ*): cf. John Sol. *Letter to Hesychius* 1.

[48] Cf. Gen. 3.

36. New Sun, light Your lamp in my obscure mind! O Christ who removes nature's lament, give me hidden lamentation and tears within the eyes from a discerning mind: tears whose moisture does not exude from the body but from the fervor of hidden repentance. This fervor leads to true inner joy and to the consolation which silences the mouth and holds out to the heart an unusual nourishment. It establishes it as a true witness within the body, testifying at all times to the guarantee of forgiveness[49] of one's sins that one has received by mercy.

37. My sins are many, my Lord, but Your compassion is greater than my sins. My wicked deeds increase in number but they are incomparable to Your mercy. Your love is greater than my sins. I look, my Lord, at my sins and I am speechless at how willful I have been. Observing Your deeds towards me, wonder seizes me, how I have been rewarded by You in a way opposite to what I have merited.

38. Your gift has brought me to the knowledge of You and not to Your chastisement. In Your mercy, You have watered me with Your sweetness, without the help of ascetic labor. You have clothed me with a fragile nature which each day is a witness to Your grace. Your wisdom shows us, by means of our weakness, Your love towards us. You have placed in us an inclination to be a witness of Your Nature which is more patient than our faults and sins.

39. My Lord, has Your patience no other way than to inflict us with more pain than expected? We never consider that the goodness which is in Your Nature might be a bad thing. If a stirring like this dare enter in us, it would be by ignorance that it springs up. My Lord, untroubled You put up with us and without constraint You bear our sins.

40. It is easy for You to bear our iniquity as it was simple for You to bring forth our creation out of nothing. For us, my Lord, both of these are difficult since we are not able to bear even a small sin which we happen to see. And according to our judgment, my Lord,

[49] Cf. 2 Cor. 1:21–22; 5:5; Eph. 1:13–14.

we judge even the great ocean of Your love which with its waves exceeds the measure of all our iniquity. We suppose, according to our human intelligence, that You, our Creator, are afflicted when You bear with us. Our suffering is a mirror to see what is in us, and by the passions we consent to, we weigh, my Lord, Your richness.

41. Grant us understanding, my Lord, that we may look on You as You are and not as we are, and we might think about You as becomes You, Giver of all our gifts! This is Your great opulence in our favor: true knowledge which is stirred up in us concerning Your concealment. Because my Lord, Your goodness and Your love and the power for good which is in Your nature, are the reasons that You carry the burden of our sins. And on this account, while not even expecting his conversion, You grant time to the sinner.

42. My Lord, may we not proceed with our insights in an exterior approach to Scripture which only denounces occasions of sin. But make us worthy of Your truth which is within Scripture. Grant us to search unceasingly in wonder, the reason for which You endure sinners. Not when wanting to know something You do not know, do You give time while waiting for it to happen, or not. For this would be shameful, my Lord, to think this about Your prevenient intelligence which with its knowledge precedes all the stirrings of our nature, even before our formation.[50] This only befits servants who do not know what will be in the future.

43. While this is true, it is right that we reflect on Your holy Nature. It is because of Your goodness and Your limitless mercy that You tolerate the sinner, even that one whom You know will not convert. You endure this not like one who does not know, awaiting possible good deeds, but because of Your compassion; as One who knows all, everything is manifest to You. Infinite, our Creator, is Your love for humanity!

44. Your goodness, my Lord, which You pour out on everything, may it not be for me a pretext for evil, that because of Your

---

[50] Nature (*ṭuqânân*): cf. Is.II XXXIX.6. God foreknew our structure before our creation, cf. Ps.138.

sweetness I might do evil. Hold me with the reins of Your mercy, that I might be able to stand up against the stirrings which assail me and against the accidents[51] which happen to me. Send me Your holy guardian angel and heal the infirmity of my thoughts,[52] for <being> mortal I am filled <with infirmity>. Keep my steps from the snares the enemy has hidden for me,[53] to lead to the way of wickedness of a sinner.

45. Most of all, my God, keep me from all stupidity of the intellect which reasons with erroneous opinions, filled with madness and worthy of weeping. Before Your majesty it thinks about Your Essence with an abominable opinion. Grant me, my Lord, the humility which knows the measure of nature and the misery of its weakness. Grant me a mind of right knowledge, proper to rational beings.

46. Guide of the living, reveal to me my thoughts and show me the paths of converse with You. My Lord, create for me, within me, the spiritual light[54] which is the knowledge of Christ. May I find Your truth in it, and think right thoughts about Your divinity and about the matters of my soul. My Lord, let me not be tried by my adversary and become derided by the demons, for those who are tempted by pride are delivered up to them.

47. But under the protection of humility which created me, I grow strong in the knowledge of You, by the help which is from Your grace. I adore the great Light of creation, Jesus Christ,[55] which has shone forth in its time according to the ineffable intelligence of God, Creator of all. Intelligence which thought, before all moments and times to send forth the magnificence of creation and its joy –

---

[51] Accidents (*gdêšê*): occur to spur one on, or to test, train or reward. See Is.I 175, 496, 503. More commonly the tradition speaks of "variations" (*šuhlâpê*): afflictions, adversities, sufferings.

[52] Cf. with the angel of providence in Is.I 433 who in times of trial "provides thoughts of righteousness."

[53] Cf.Ps.142:4.

[54] Spiritual light (*nuhrâ d-ruḥânâ*), see *Keph.* I 13.

[55] Cf. Gen. 1:16; Jn. 8:12.

only-begotten Light[56] from the nature of that intelligence – completing His work *in the consummation of this world*[57] and it rises in our hearts.[58] At the time pleasing to His will, the Light has brought us near to His great intelligence.

48. This Light has brought me back to the *house of my Father*[59] and has shown me that He also prepares for me an inheritance of glory beyond the confines of the worlds. Because of this He has created me, that the principle of Good and His creative action might be made visible, which brings all into existence. Blessed be this magnificence forever and ever. Amen

---

[56] Only-begotten Light: occurs in Ephrem, *Hymns on the Crucifixion* VIII.12.

[57] Cf. Gal. 4:4.

[58] Cf. 2 Pt. 1:19; 2 Cor. 4:6.

[59] Cf. Lk. 15:17.

Chapter VIII

Again of the same Mar Isaac. On how the saints are set apart and sanctified by the inhabiting of the Holy Spirit.

1. The temple of God is a *house of prayer.*[1] The soul, then, is a house of prayer in which the memory[2] of God is celebrated continually. If all the saints are sanctified by the Spirit to be temples of the adorable Trinity:[3] the Holy Spirit sanctifies them by means of the constant remembrance[4] of His divinity. Constant prayer,[5] then, is the continual remembrance of God. Therefore, by means of continual prayer, the saints are sanctified, becoming a dwelling for the action of the Holy Spirit.[6] As one of the saints said: "Be mindful of God always and your intelligence will be a heaven." [7]

2. Therefore, if our soul becomes a second heaven by continual prayer, in heaven no good thing is lacking, nor does any evil come there, nor temptation, nor passions of the body or of the soul, nor remembrance of evil things, nor any of the afflictions of the body, nor the darkness or vexations of the soul. If, however, all of these temptations do come to us, it is because we go astray and are far from the remembrance of God. Hence we err, falling into all kinds

---

[1] Cf. Is. 56:7; Mt. 21:13.

[2] Memory (*dukrânâ*).

[3] Cf. 1 Cor. 3:16.

[4] Constant remembrance (*ʿudhânâ ammînâ*): Is.I 35, 253, 258, 321, 508; Is.II VIII.15; XXIX.7; XXX.4,13.

[5] Constant prayer (*ṣlôtâ ammîntâ*): Is. I 304, 441– 42, 544; *Keph.*II 97. Cf. *ammînûtâ da-ṣlôtâ*): Is.I 15, 107, 259, 557; Is.II XIV.41–42 (including references to Evagrius, Theodore of Mopsuestia, Macarius, Babai, Sahdona, Dadisho, Shem'on d-Taybuteh); *Keph.*IV 34.

[6] Activity of the Holy Spirit (*maʿbdânûtâ d-ruḥâ d-qudšâ*): here Isaac specifically links the action of the Holy Spirit to prayer and remembrance of God. When the Spirit takes its dwelling place in a person, one does not cease to pray because the Spirit will constantly pray in him. See esp. Is.I 259. And see Is.I 70, 353; Is.II V.33; Is.III VI.45. Cf. Is.III IV.32.

[7] Also cited anonymously by Sahdona II, 8,59. Cf. Nilus, *Perle* 2, p. 10 and see Joseph Hazzaya, *Lettres*, 138, "firmament of the heart."

of evil. Prayer, then, is the definition of the remembrance of God, removing the occasions of error which cause all the evils we suffer.

3. So then, let us persevere in prayer which is the luminous form of the remembrance of our Lord God: all temptations will be removed from us which are sent providentially for this – to set in us the remembrance of God by means of persistent intercession and the crucifixion of the intellect.[8] These torturers – which are the temptations – constrain us necessarily to make <prayer>. As a holy one has said: "Pray continually that the spirit of error may flee from you."[9]

4. When we apply ourselves to <prayer> and make space in ourselves for the remembrance of the Lord by means of our continual prayer to Him, temptations flee and passions cease. Even Satan is driven far away; adversities find no place in us and afflictions grow weak. All evil things give way, somehow, to the remembrance of God which is in us; shouting, they flee from before their Lord.[10]

5. The angels celebrate in that house where the holy altar is set for the continual mystery of their Lord. The continual remembrance of God is in fact an altar which is established in the heart,[11] from it all the mysteries ascend to the sanctuary of the Lord;[12] one finds there not one of the contrary events we have set forth. They are, indeed, fearful before the splendor of the divine light which burns in the midst of the mysteries. And as it were, naturally, all adversities are conquered where God is named.

---

[8] Crucifixion of the intellect (*zqîfûtâ d-hawnâ*): Is.I, 15–16, 223, 232; Is.II XXX.6. See Abba Isaiah *Ascetical Discourses* XXVI.4. See also de Andia, "Hèsychia et contemplation," 28–34.

[9] Budge, *Paradise* II, 439.

[10] Cf. Mk.9:26.

[11] Cf. Heb.8:2.

[12] On the heart as altar see Is.I 167; on the altar of prayer and prayer being sacrificed, Is.II XIV.20, XXI.4. See *Book of Steps* XII.1–4 and John Sol. *Soul* 88. See also Evag. Muyldermans, *Parénèse*, 27; Macarius 344 and Sahdona III 24. See Brock, "Spirituality of the Heart."

6. But sometimes, even when we are diligent about <prayer>, some of these realities are allowed to remain and show their impudence to vex us, because we have not begun in a right way this continual remembrance of the Lord. And so because of our failure, they even have the opportunity to assail us. <Whereas> the annoyance of the adversaries is not able to approach the house of the king when he is there.[13]

7. The divinity, however, dwells in human beings not with its Nature. For its Nature is infinite, and not limited or contained in a place. Heaven and earth, indeed, are full of it yet there is no place sufficient for it.[14] It is in every place yet remote from every place, because of the immensity and sublimity of its Nature. It is said that God dwells in a place by the will and by the action of His power, as it is written: *I will dwell in them and I will walk among them*;[15] that is: "I will manifest in them the power of my action." As it is also written that <God> overshadows[16] the temple in Jerusalem or the tent which was erected by Moses.

8. When the house of <God> was built and completed by Solomon, it is said that *his* Shekinah[17] *overshadowed it and the house was filled with his glory*;[18] it is also said that *the priests went out from the holy place, from before the* Shekinah *of the Lord, because they were not able to serve in that the whole house was filled with the cloud of the glory of the Lord.*[19] This was the sign that God was well pleased by it and dwelt in it. It is like this for the soul which has been built upon virtue, when at the time of prayer it perceives this cloud which overshadows the intellect at prayer.

9. This happens in a concealed way, and the one who prays is not able to complete the recitation of his prayer. Therefore, one

---

[13] Cf. Mt.12:29.

[14] 1Kgs. 8:27. Cf. Theodore of Mopsuestia, *Homélies* V 4.

[15] Lv. 26:11–12.

[16] Overshadows (*aggen*), see Is.III I.4.

[17] Shekinah, see Is.III VII.4.

[18] Cf. 2 Chron. 7:1–2 (Peshitta).

[19] 2 Chron. 5:13–14.

becomes tranquil and is speechless in stupor before the glory of the Lord, which is revealed by an intuition of the intellect. This is a sign that the Lord is well pleased in him and has overshadowed him! This is like what Ezekiel saw when it was shown to him in a vision concerning the building of the temple. After the house was finished, which had been constructed in his presence – it was shown to him as in a divine revelation[20] – then also he saw the divine *Shekinah* which overshadowed the temple, and it was filled by it.[21]

10. In the vision which he saw, there was like a divine operation imprinted in his soul. By means of this previous marvelous vision, what he saw became visible to him before it had come to be. And while being physically in Babylonia, he had seen the revelation in Jerusalem,[22] which was distant by a journey of more or less <three to four miles>. Thus it was shown to him how to go up to the temple while the *Shekinah* of God overshadows it, as he says: *He conducted me to the door which looks to the east.*[23] This one then, who was showing him all these things in a revelation, was an angel who said: *Put in your heart all which I show you because I have come as a proof to you.*[24]

11. By means of these visions, two things are made known to us: all of the visions which happen to the saints were done for them by the mediation of angels,[25] and they are instructed by the angels until one has approached the revelations of the divine vision;[26] the second thing is that angelic revelations precede the divine revelation and the service which is performed for them by the activity of the Holy Spirit, as is here made known. Therefore

---

[20] Divine revelation (*gelyânâ alâhâyâ*): Is.I 161, 371, 391, 545, 549; Is.II XVI.5; Theodore of Mopsuestia *WS* VI 239; John Sol. *Soul* 61. It also occurs in Narsai, Dadisho and Sahdona.

[21] Cf. Ez. 43:5.

[22] Cf. Ez. 40:1–2.

[23] Ez. 43:1.

[24] Ez. 40:4 (Peshitta).

[25] On mediation of the angels in Isaac, see Hansbury, "Insight without Sight," 68–70.

[26] Divine vision (*ḥzâṯâ alâhâyâ*): Is.I 161; *Keph.* I 72.

<Ezekiel> says: *He conducted me to the gate which faces the east and behold the glory of the God of Israel came from the way of the east, and his voice was like the sound of many waters.*[27]

12. Also that revelation which <God> shows him is according to the order of the life beyond. It says in fact: *The earth has shone with his glory*; and, *I fell on my face and the glory of the Lord entered the temple.*[28] Again in another place it says: *The inner court was filled with the cloud and the glory of the Lord went up above the cherubim and the house was filled with the cloud.*[29] Also: *The inner court was filled with the splendor of the glory of the Lord*;[30] and other similar things which the Scriptures make known concerning the working order of the *Shekinah*, whose power overshadows the place set apart for the Name of His holiness, and in which His memory is sanctified at all times. Thus the <Scriptures> manifest the action of His glory by means of a clear vision, so as to instruct.

13. As to how it is said that <God> abides or dwells, it is not in His Nature but in His glory and in His energy that He abides, in the place set apart for His holiness – whether this be in a building made by hand and in things not endowed with reason called vessels of His sanctuary, or in the rational temples which are the souls. It is the power and energy <of God> that sanctifies and sets apart from the other souls that soul in which the Lord is sanctified, by means of the remembrance of Him: by the manifestation of a revelation and the knowledge of the mysteries revealed in it, and not by an inhabiting of the divine Nature <in us>.

14. Let us earnestly desire this good and continually sanctify the parts of our body, together with our soul, in the praise of God. Let us sanctify ourselves by the continual remembrance of Him which we call to mind by means of prayer. We become holy temples by prayer,[31] to receive within ourselves the adorable action of the

[27] Ez. 43:1–2.

[28] Ez. 43: 2–4.

[29] Ez. 10: 3–4.

[30] Ez. 10:4.

[31] Cf. 1 Cor. 3:16–17.

Spirit. As the Apostle says: *Everything is purified and sanctified by the word of God and by prayer!*[32] By means of the remembrance of God which is called to mind there and the Name of the Lord which is invoked over him,[33] one is sanctified and renounces all defilement and every alien power.

15. Surely, *In every place where you remember my name, I will come to you and I will bless you.*[34] Let us continually remember God and our mouth will be blessed, as one of the saints once said to some seculars: "Stand and greet the solitaries that you might be blessed! Because their mouths are holy since they continually speak with God."[35]

16. You see how the mouth which always speaks with God is made worthy of holiness and the heart is sanctified in which the Name of the Lord is blessed continually! Bless God continually in your heart that you might be blessed, and do not cease blessing Him. Sanctify your soul and all your limbs with His blessings, saying: *Bless the Lord, O my soul; and all my bones, his holy name*;[36] also: *I exalt you, my Lord and King*, etc.[37]

17. Speak His praise with your mouth and never be sated of His glory, in order that His magnificence and His excellency might fill your soul. May God always be exalted in your heart, and may you never be sated of His magnificence and His blessings, not even of that splendor which the prophet saw dwelling over Jerusalem – so also your soul will be filled with it. He said in fact: *The earth has shone with his glory.* It also has been said: "Always remember God and your intelligence will be a heaven."[38]

---

[32] 1 Tim. 4:4–5.

[33] Cf. James 2:7.

[34] Ex. 20:24 (Peshitta).

[35] Budge, *Paradise* II, 634, p.148.

[36] Ps. 103:1.

[37] Ps. 145:1.

[38] Nilus, *Perle* 2, p.10.

18. Let us ardently desire this magnificence, to be temples of God[39] by means of continual remembrance of Him in prayers and praises. As the holy bishop Basil said: "Pure prayer is what causes the continual remembrance of God in the soul. Thus we will be temples for God in that He dwells in us by the continual remembrance with which we call Him to mind."[40] Those who are a *house of prayer*[41] are made worthy of this heavenly glory. And the temple in which the continual memory of the Lord thus dwells, gives light such that the rays from it shine forth and show clearly even from a far.

19. The continual remembrance of God is the mystery of the *future world*:[42] there we receive fully all the grace of the Spirit.[43] And there the remembrance of God will no more depart from us because we will be wholly His temple. The saints on earth ardently desire that mystery of the future joy, by means of constant absorption in prayer. Of these realities we are made worthy, by the grace and the mercy of *Christ our hope*,[44] *together with all of His saints*,[45] forever and ever! Amen.

---

[39] Cf. 1 Cor. 3:16–17.

[40] Basil of Cesarea, *Lettere* II, 4. See Is.I 353 where Isaac cites the same passage of Basil. See also Brock, "Traduzioni siriache," 175–76.

[41] Cf. Is. 56:1; Mt. 21:13.

[42] Cf. Heb. 2:5; 6:5.

[43] Cf. Mt. 13:17.

[44] Cf. 1 Tim. 1:1.

[45] Cf. 1 Titus 3:13.

Chapter IX

Of the same Mar Isaac. A synthesis of all kinds of labor concerning the part of the mind: what power and action belong to each one of them.

1. Prayer is the place of the soul where the fulfillment of the bodily way of life occurs. The way of life is from the working of the body: fasting, the office, alms, labors, chastity, service to the sick, silence, weeping, obedience, renunciation, mercy, with the rest of what is similar; and there are yet many other realities such as these.

2. These ways are the limit for <bodily> activity. Prayer, however, is the contemplation of the soul,[1] which is above the body and visible things and the understanding of what is in them, which are more profound than what can be examined but are intelligible, though not being of the earth. When solicitude for prayer is not joined to these ways <of life>, they remain in the order of bodily labor. And even if they are beautiful things, found in the parts of the soul, this labor is only for visible things.

3. That which the power of prayer is to the way of life, reading is for prayer. Every prayer, then, which is not sustained by the light of the Scriptures is offered with bodily understanding.[2] And even if one makes supplication for good things and noble stirrings arise from it, so as to lean towards the hidden realities that by means of the mind one cannot know, and what one asks for <with> desire be acceptable to God – this is of a lower degree than the knowledge <from Scripture>.

---

[1] Contemplation of the soul (*teʾôryâ d-napšâ*): Evag. Cent. II.15; V.41.

[2] On the importance of Scripture in the life of prayer: Is.I 52–53, 124–5, 135. Is. II XXI.13; XXIX.5–11. *Keph.* I 66–67; IV 63. See John Sol. *Letter to Hesychius* 24: "Pay attention to the reading of the words of Scripture, in order to learn from them how to be with God…In this way you will be illumined in prayer as a result of your reading." And see Sahdona II 8, 51.

4. Indeed, this is because while meditating on glorious things and seeming to be occupied with amazing realities, <such a one> is <really> far from God. And so he is not able to attain to the beautiful things for which he hopes, but walks keeping his own counsel and reflects on his own will: the admonition, then, which is from the true knowledge of the light of the Scriptures does not <affect> him.

5. The way of life is the body, prayer is the soul but the vision of the mind is of the spiritual order.[3] Vision of the mind,[4] I call revelation of hidden things, and the understanding of incorporeal things, and that certain understanding which is <given> by the Spirit. These realities receive power from reading regarding knowledge – its deepening and progression from insight to what follows which is more amazing and more luminous. As to prayer, which is excellent intercession of the soul and salutary petitions offered up, it is said: "It is good that these things (intercession and petitions) be provided by the soul and remain with it."

6. Meditation, then, consists only in the reflection on what is in God, while marveling only at what is of <God>, seeking out only Him and His majesty, and that the mind be occupied only with Him without a reflection on what is beyond, nor a remembrance of beautiful and excellent things concerning the body or corporeal things. The <mind ought> only be occupied with meditation on the Essence while not associating this with a reflection on <other> realities, or the thought that something might happen to me from you or from another place. This meditation has indeed scorned all which is of <human> nature – whether excellent realities or what might be alarming – by means of the memory[5] of God alone, which is sanctified in the mind.

7. How many times in prayer, meditation such as this is brought forth. And from here, there is the entrance of the mind near the

---

[3] On the stages of the life of the soul – corporeal, psychical, spiritual – in John Sol., see Hansbury, *On the Soul*, Introd. xi–xiii.

[4] Vision of the mind (*ḥzâṯâ d-ʿreyânâ*): Is.I 49; Is.II XIV.2.

[5] Memory (*dukrânâ*).

ineffable height, while the spirit by grace is sustained in the realities of prayer. Moreover, when <the spirit> is sustained by meditation and by reading, no one is able to discuss towards which marvelous stirrings it is lifted by intercession, and to what desire it leans and in what delight the mind remains. The reading of a portion <of Scripture> brings to perfection this work of meditation, and it is <the reading> which assists with marvelous realities, so as to last. See to the order of reading because it is useful for this labor.

8. One who is wise, then, who wishes to grow strong in spiritual realities, let him read the lesson according to the understanding which the meditation generates. Not just any reading is suitable for growth in the Spirit, but only that which tells about divine realities. This enriches the mind regarding spiritual mysteries, and instructs about the hope which is above the body. It transfers the thought from earth to the world above, so as to raise it to that way of life of immortality.

9. The <reading> moves the senses of the soul to look into the hidden mystery of divine wisdom. It brings one to the understanding of its incomprehensibility and the truth about its nature. It makes one marvel at the hidden Essence and direct one's thoughts to the mysteries of the future hope.[6] It brings forth the riches of His love, revealed to all and ready, indeed, to be spread abroad. These realities are the root of spiritual meditation, to which reading, by means of insight, continually lifts the mind making it wander[7] about and delight in the divine virtues which are above all, and in the hope for humanity preserved near God. Giving a glimpse, God shows the properties of His nature which are in Him for us and for the two worlds, whether the creation of spiritual beings or all of those who are in need in the world of mortal humanity.

---

[6] Future hope (*sabrâ da-ʿtîd*): Is.I 418, 430, 438, 508; *Keph.* I 38, 84; II 17. Cf. Is. II XXIX.11. John Sol. returns often to the theme of hope, see *Soul* 71,73; Rignell, *Briefe* 21, 29, 35, 51, 101.

[7] Wander (*pehyâ*): here wander is intended in a positive sense, may also be understood negatively.

10. When, then, this labor <of meditation> grows strong and is consolidated in the soul, at that time there is not much need for reading. Not that one may be entirely without it but there is not much need for extensive reading. Which is to say that a continual meditation on the Scriptures is not necessary, although Scripture ought not to leave one's hands. In that, even when one is occupied with a small matter in these things, by means of the power that one draws out of a few verses, one is captivated with the Lord in contemplation.

11. Even if the reading is such as this, it is meditation and it is prayer. It is meditation in that it is not just part of the tongue, but its only intention is to bring the mind to discernment. And it is prayer in that by the memory[8] of God, it always captivates and fills within and without, with the desire and the meditation of heavenly realities. Then the <reading> moves completely with prayer which concurs with these impulses because an effortless exaltation stirs through the mind in the hidden part of the intellect. This is the prayer which occurs without the body, which we call incorporeal, in that it is not moved by sensible realities and is not visible by the body.

12. From this reading, limitless prayer is generated, whose meditation arises secretly in the mind and continually fills the intellect with God,[9] and as I said, it always captivates and attracts the mind with the realities of the Lord. This order of prayer is sublime, more than all ways of life, in that it is <prayer> which gives life to them with the life which is in God. <Prayer> is <the means of ascent> which lifts up to heaven as far as the order of revelation, in the place of a ladder.[10] This is its work, lifting up to whatever high place requested.

13. When, however, one has ascended to that place, then prayer will have another use there: at once the use for which it *went up on*

---

[8] Memory (*dukrânâ*).

[9] The intellect as a dwelling of the Trinity, see Evag. Cent. III.71.

[10] Cf. Gen. 28:12, ladder of Jacob. On prayer as a ladder (*sebeltâ*), see Evag. Cent. IV.43.

the roof[11] has arisen for it, and until it descends again to earth, its function of ladder is no longer needed. But if prayer is a figure of a raised ladder which lifts up to heaven, by which the intellect ascends continually – prayer satisfies the purpose of a ladder for the intellect – therefore as long as we are on earth, we always need this ladder which is prayer, by which we ascend at all times to God, so as to be made worthy by it of the heavenly light.

14. Meditation also strengthens, refines and grants victory to the prayer of the heart. It shows the intellect the way of heavenly and mysterious realities, for it is moved towards them at the time of prayer. Then this prayer rises up like a ladder and makes the intellect ascend.

15. Prayer, however, of itself, without meditation and reading is <too> weak and obscure to make the intellect ascend and come together with the heavenly realities. But because in place of the offering and the sacrifice which those of former times were offering, an excellent grace was given to us by God: we sacrifice the stirrings of our intelligence instead of dumb objects[12] – that is, thanksgiving and praise – by means of prayer which is the *acceptable sacrifice*![13] That is what we offer to Him as Lord, cause of our salvation[14] and guardian.

16. Even if <such a sacrifice> is dark and obscure, we do not neglect to offer <it>. And even if we are not ravished by a revelation, but by one of these causes considered as excellent, let us

---

[11] Cf. Acts 10:9: Isaac on Peter's ascent in the context of revelation, see Is.I 154–61; cf. 172–73. On Acts 10:11, see Evag. Cent. IV, 46. Theodore of Mopsuestia comments on the ascent of Peter and its relation to revelation, see Nahum 1.1 in his *Commentary on the Twelve Prophets*, 249–50. Isaac, like Theodore, uses Peter's ascent to show how a life of prayer leads the soul to revelations of hidden mysteries, as the prophets were led to the knowledge of things beyond description, see Is.I 156 where he quotes Theodore. See Hansbury, "Insight without Sight," 63–67.

[12] Cf. Heb. 10:1–18.

[13] Cf. Phil. 4:18; Ps. 50:23; Heb. 13:15.

[14] Cf. Heb. 5:9.

fall prostrate continuously with diligence.[15] Let us offer in sacrifice stirrings of incorporeal sacrifices, owed to the Creator of all. Let us not neglect to pour out thanksgiving for what we are indebted, while laying our faces on the ground. This is the function which prayer performs for humanity.

17. As long as we remain on the earth, the function of prayer is for those who exist here below and continually seek to ascend to the house-tops.[16] Prayer is the way of nature and it is the ascent to that place which is above nature, that is heaven. Without it, there is no ascent to that place. In heaven, then, it has no other function. Prayer, therefore, is the queen of the ways of life: because from earthly realities, it makes heavenly ones and in corporeal realities, it sets in motion the state of being fully alive.

18. Its order, however, is inferior to that of revelation. When, then, prayer has come near to this place <of revelation>, it has no space, nor care, nor memory, so that it must again ascend above where the soul had ascended. This is called the height of incorporeal realities and knowledge of the mysteries of the Spirit. When, indeed, the intellect is clothed with the Spirit, from that time it possesses the stirrings of the cherubim, the knowledge of the Spirit, the reflection of the Spirit and the vision of the Spirit; it remains completely in God, in the delight which is above nature. And it is brought from insight to insight; and from this towards the vision of contemplation.

19. Contemplation is said to be sublime or imperfect by what leads it from insight to insight, according to the sense of the things which are moved in them. These realities are of the order of the revelation of the mysteries. Of all which is accomplished in the soul, this is the most sublime. It is the way of the Spirit[17] and not a

---

[15] On kneeling and prostration during prayer, see Is.I 341–43. And see Chialà, "L'importance du corps dans la prière," also Hunt, "Praying with the Body."

[16] Cf. Acts 10:9.

[17] Way of the Spirit (*dubbârâ d-ruḥ*): best understood here in the context of John the Solitary's tripartite division; see *Soul* 12, 17, 24, 60, 64,

stirring of the soul. Yet without prayer, <such realities> do not come to pass; and <prayer> without these does not shine and is not strengthened, since to pray is of the soul.

20. The one, however, who is directed towards hidden realities, remains in the Spirit and in the revelation of the intellect[18] which <is from> God. By revelation, then, I do not intend realities visible to the eyes or audible to the ears, and not even something which can be perceived on earth while among others. What place is there for sensible realities in a spiritual revelation and in the stirrings of the intellect which are enlightened by the Spirit, as the fathers say who were lifted up from earth and from the flesh?[19]

21. These realities which are conceived through vision, or hearing or in the presence of the senses, by angelic action, are useful for this world and for the way of life beyond because they increase the growth of the fear of God in souls. They are similar to those <realities> realized by means of the visible revelation entrusted to the Economy through Moses, by means of that angel to whom the Economy of that people was entrusted and the glorious things shown in their midst.

22. These are similar to what had already been realized regarding Moses, as Scripture has said: Moses was tending the flock of Jethro, his father-in-law, and conducted the flock to the desert, and he came to the mountain of God, to Horeb. The angel of the Lord appeared to Him in a flame of fire from within a bush; and <Moses> saw that the bush was not consumed.[20] Clearly it may be seen, that even if the vision be attributed to the presence of God, and the speech and the amazing realities be realized in a supernatural way, according to the Economy, nevertheless the

---

66–67. See Is.I 303, 368, 376. Is.II VII.2; X.2; XX.2,5,6,10. *Keph.* I 28, 36, 37; III 14, 46; IV 12,13, 15–16, 47, 92. Chialà notes an Evagrian influence.

[18] Revelation of the intellect (*gelyânâ d-hawnâ*): Is.I 161; Is.II XV.7; *Keph.* I 80.

[19] Cf. 2 Cor. 12:2–3.

[20] Ex. 3:1–2.

action happened by means of an angel who was showing to <Moses> that he was the leader of the people.

23. As also the blessed Paul said: *If then the word spoken by means of the angel was confirmed, etc.*[21] And as also Stephen said: *God sent them this Moses, chief and savior, by means of that angel who appeared to him in the bush. It is he who led them out, working signs, in the land of Egypt, at the Red Sea, and in the desert for forty years,*[22] thus clearly indicating that it was an angel who revealed himself to Moses in the bush, that one to whom was entrusted all this Economy and all these dreadful things done there.

24. The angel, indeed, appeared in various ways, with mighty and great visions, and performed all these things in the name of God, as is said in the book of Exodus: *Behold, I send my angel before you to guard you in your way and to bring you into the land which I have prepared. Pay attention to him and listen to his voice. Do not strive against him lest he not forgive your debts, because my name is in him.*[23]

25. Clearly Scripture has shown that all these things were spoken there by the command of God. And whether that great revelation on the top of Mount Sinai, or all those which were spoken of in the Law to Moses, they are as from God Himself. And the words of the Law which were celebrated by them are an angelic revelation, as God said: *My name is in him.*[24] Because in the name of God the angel was visible, spoke, visited, admonished and affirmed the Law, leading <the people> whether in the cloud or in the fire, in dark night, or in the vision of smoke and thick darkness,[25] and in all these realities which were made visible. Thus <the angel> guided the divine flock by means of visions and revelations of every kind, signs and portents, by voices and words, dreadful and mighty.

---

[21] Heb. 2:2.

[22] Acts 7:35–36.

[23] Ex. 23:20–21.

[24] Ex. 23:21

[25] Cf. Ex. 13:21–22; 19:18; 20:21.

26. Therefore, blessed Paul says: *If the word spoken by means of the angel was confirmed*,[26] to show that it was not God revealing Himself in the visions and images but an angel. This is not of God! The revelations of God, then, which are without images are invisible and ineffable; and the revelations of the Holy Spirit are in silence. They are delights <in> the stillness of nature, and not visions.

27. As <God> is elusive and invisible, thus also are His revelations. There were none before the coming of our Lord as a man; as also, then, the way of life of the world to come[27] was not known, nor yet had the fullness of the grace of the Spirit been given until after the descent of the Paraclete on the Apostles.[28] At that time the revelations of hidden realities and the future mysteries which are not like what is of this world, began to be given and made known to each one of the saints. From this time, then, the angel was showing all of these wonderful realities by God's command.

28. God was not transformed into images. God forbid! As our Lord said to the Jews: *You have never heard his voice, nor have you seen his form.*[29] And because this is from an angel, the word spoken through him was confirmed by means of the tablets with the writing, and with the voice on the mountain, lest the sons of Israel transgress <the word>.[30] The Apostle said: *Anyone who has heard it and transgressed it, has received a just retribution; how can we escape if we neglect these realities <of> salvation which have begun to be spoken by our Lord.*[31]

29. Thus <the Apostle> showed that these present revelations are not similar to those previous ones; there, indeed, an angel was showing them but here it is God Himself, Word by human means.[32] It is said: *The distributions of the Holy Spirit are conceded*

---

[26] Heb. 2:2.

[27] Cf. Heb. 2:5; 6:5.

[28] Cf. Acts 2.

[29] John 5:37.

[30] Cf. Dt. 5:22.

[31] Cf. Heb. 2:2–3 (Peshitta).

[32] Cf. Jn. 1:14.

according to His will,[33] that is to say, that the revelations now are by means of the action of the Holy Spirit, while the previous ones were an angelic action. Those previous ones were useful for the way of life of this world because they led <only> to the knowledge of the fear of God and not to the knowledge of revealed realities.

30. The revelations, however, which are made known by the Holy Spirit, lead to the knowledge of the future world.[34] This is as Moses said to the people. When that great and dreadful revelation appeared on the top of the mountain, it was before the eyes of all the people, with flashes of thunder, fire, hurricane, clamor of horns sounding and proclaiming an amazing sound full of terror. But the people greatly feared those dreadful realities, and could not endure the awful vision and the intensity of the sounds of the angelic horns which became terrible. Moses was encouraging them and made known the reason for the revelation and its terrible might, saying to them: *Take heart because God has come close to you, so that the fear of Him be in you and you do not sin.*[35]

31. With all of this <Moses> made known that the visible and perceptible revelations are of use in the way of life here below, for the growth of faith and the fear of God. As for what is of the mystical part and which is in the mind – that is, the understanding of incorporeal realities and the delight of silence – it is for the of use for the perfect.[36] In this, we speak of the highest place of prayer, to which one is raised up by means of prayer. In this a mirror[37] of the new world[38] is received, making us taste by means of the Spirit that life beyond, which we shall receive.[39] Only the Spirit is able to make known this His mystery; He who by His power is prepared to give that greatest way of life which is beyond words. To Him be glory forever and ever. Amen.

---

[33] Heb. 2:4.

[34] Cf. Heb. 2:5; 6:5.

[35] Ex. 20:20–21; cf. 19:16.

[36] Cf. 1 Cor. 2:6; Phil. 3:15.

[37] Cf. 1 Cor. 13:12.

[38] Cf. Mt. 19:28 (Peshitta).

[39] Cf. 1 Cor. 2:10–11.

Chapter X

Converse of prayer[1] *of the solitaries, composed with metrical speech and according to the limits of insight. Words which seize the heart and restrain from the distraction of earthly things. <Words> composed for the consolation of solitaries with which they converse at night, after the time of the office, that their body might be relieved of sleep.*[2]

1 At night when all sounds are still,
also the stirrings of the soul and all sorts <of things>,
our soul, with its stirrings, shines in You,
O Jesus, light of the just.[3]
2 At the time when darkness abounds
over all like a garment,
Your grace, my Lord, shines for us
Instead of the perceptible light.
3 The light of the material[4] sun
delights the eyes of our body:
Your light, which surpasses the sun in its greatness,
shines within our darkness.
4 In the night which calms all the efforts
of the world wearied by affairs,
receive our soul, astonished by You,
in that stillness which is greater than silence.
5 At the time which gives rest to the weary,
by means of sleep which makes everything sweet,
in You, my Lord, our thoughts become drunken,

---

[1] See Chialà's Introd. to Is.III (CSCO) for questions of authorship of this chapter, Isaac or Ephrem, etc. Chialà concludes that the chapter probably is not by Isaac, but perhaps was intentionally included here by him. Concerning authorship, see also Bou Mansour, "La distinction," 7.

[2] Compare with Preface to the chapter of prayers: Is.II, V.

[3] Cf. Ps. 112:4.

[4] Material (from the gr. στοίχείον): Is.I 50, 304–05, 460, 471, 478; *Keph.* I 9,13; II 59; IV 89.

in You, delight of the saints!
6 In the hour when all sleepers break forth
for corruptible deceptions,
awaken, our Lord, in our souls
that knowledge which does not go astray.
7 At the moment when each one
puts clothing on his limbs,
clothe with joy, our Lord,
our inner person.[5]
8 By day, when all are called
to earthly work,
make us worthy, our Lord, to take delight
in our way of life which is in heaven.
9 When each one removes
his night garment,
remove, our Lord, from our heart
the remembrance of the passing world.
10 In early morning, when sailors
begin <to work> in the world,
in Your harbor,[6] my Lord, our souls
are at rest from all stirrings.
11 At the hour when all begin
distressful worldly work,
make us worthy, our Lord, to be enfolded
in that consolation which does not pass away.
12 In the hour when darkness comes to an end
and each one begins work,
grant us, our Lord, to delight

---

[5] Cf. Rom. 7:22 (Peshitta); 2 Cor. 4:16; Eph. 1:13–14. Inner person (*barnâšâ gawwâyâ*): Is.I 125, 244, 483, 562, 575–76; Is.II V.31, VIII.I, 2,16, XIII title, XXXI.1; *Keph.* IV 60. It occurs occasionally in Evag. Cent. VI.39 and frequently in Macarius, e.g. 9, 12, 66. See John Sol. *Soul* 7, 8, 23, 39, 41, 91; *Letter to Hesychius* 28. See Ammonius 637. Cf. Aphrahat *Dem.* 6:1 and Ephrem, *Hymns against Heresies* 32:12.

[6] Your harbor (*lmênâk*): Is.I 105, 217, 317, 325–26, 346. 408. Is.II V.14, VII. 2–3, XVII.12, XVIII.19. *Keph.* I 80; II 12, 79, 96; IV 31,93. Cf. Macarius 49; Shubhalmaran 45v, 1 XII,7

in the stirrings of that future world.[7]
13 Origin of the luminary course,
head of mortal labor,
place, my Lord, the foundations in our mind
of that day that does not end.
14 A new sun shines for us
in the hour of darkest night,
in which is prefigured that understanding
kept for us <until> the resurrection.
15 Grant us, our Lord, to imitate
that vigilance of the resurrection,
that by night and by day, my Lord,
our mind may be attentive to You.
16 Make us worthy to see in ourselves
that life which will be <after> the resurrection,
lest there be anything which separates
our mind from delighting in You.
17 Of that day which does not begin
with the stirrings of the course of the luminaries,
inscribe, my Lord, its mystery in our person
by our persevering with You.
18 Everyday we have embraced You in Your mysteries,
and within our bodies we have received You;
make us worthy to perceive in ourselves
our hope in the resurrection.
19 Be, my Lord, wings for my thought
to fly in the air,
so as with <these> wings to be present
at our true abode.
20 You have hidden Your treasure within our body,[8]
by means of the grace which dwells
at the elevated table of Your mysteries:
grant us to see our being made new.
21 Because, my Lord, we have buried You in ourselves,

---

[7] Cf. Heb. 2:5; 6:5. Future world (*ʿâlmâ da-ʿtîd*): see "world to come," Is.III I.1.

[8] Cf. Mt. 13:44.

<having eaten> at Your spiritual table,
may we feel, our Lord, in that deed,
the future renewal!

22 May we see the beauty of ourselves
by means of Your spiritual beauty,
that which within mortal nature
stirs immortal signs.

23 Your crucifixion, our Savior,
was the boundary of the bodily world:
grant us to crucify our mind
in the mystery of Your spiritual world.

24 Your resurrection Jesus, is the greatness
of our spiritual person:[9]
may the vision of Your mysteries be for us
a mirror to understand it.

25 Your Economy, our Savior,
is the mystery of the spiritual world:[10]
grant us, our Lord, to proceed in it
according to our spiritual person.

26 Our wretched body pulls us
to swim in the dark world:
make us worthy, our Lord, of that converse <with You>
which breaks through the thick darkness.

27 May our mind, my Lord, not be void
of spiritual reflection on You,
nor in our limbs grow cool
the warmth of Your delight.

28 The mortality which is in our body,
behold, it belches forth its foulness:
may the great joy of Your spiritual love
cleanse the trace of it from our hearts.

29 As in a prison,
the hateful things in our members hold us captive:

---

[9] Cf. 1 Cor. 2:15. Spiritual person (*barnâšâ ruḥânâ*): Is.I 245, 332. Cf. Is.II XXI.14; *Keph.* III 92; John Sol. *Soul* 12, 14, 16.

[10] Spiritual world (*ʿâlmâ ruḥânâ*): Is.I 454; *Keph.* I 13. See John Sol. *Dialogues* II, p.19.

may their odor fade from our body,
by the intoxication which <comes> from Your gift.

30 Our body is for us like the sea
which always submerges our boat:
bring near, our Lord, <our> ship
to Your divine harbor.

31 At the time when we are separate
from others and their converse,
be our gain, our Lord,
and in You may our sadness be made glad.

32 By trusting in Your grace
we go out to be alone:
may we see clearly, our Lord,
the power of Your aid at work.

33 Pour forth Your peace on our hearts
and Your calm on our stirrings,
so that the night which is beyond all darkness
may be for us as the day.

34 At that time in which we are left destitute,
because night has hemmed us within its darkness
and we are separate from everyone,
in You, my Lord may our consolation grow.

35 In that place which is void of all
and there is no voice in it which encourages,
fortify our mind, our Lord,
within the bulwark of Your grace.

36 Rouse us up, our Lord, from our sloth
with that knowledge which does not go astray,
lest our mind be submerged
by the deep sleep of desires.

37 Our Lord, make us worthy by Your grace,
together with the wise virgins,
that being prepared with works <like> theirs,[11]
our way of life be vigilant.

---

[11] Mt. 25:1–13. See Jacob of Serug, "A Homily on the Ten Virgins Described in our Saviour's Gospel," Bedjan, *Homiliae Selectae* II, 375–401; trans. in *The True Vine*.

38 So that we may not dwell within darkness,
while our minds are obscure,
<rather> may we see a reflection of Your grace,
in our prayer, at all times!
39 The day of Your knowledge, my Lord,
follows the night of our mind:
in Your sun, chief of lights,[12]
may we renew the way of life of our chastity.
40 Grant us to keep vigil in our prayer,
together with the just at night,
so that our lamps be lit
towards the sun of Your revelation.[13]
41 At night the just are inebriated
with the love of God;
at night-time, provide
consolation to our weakness.
42 Grant that our mind might labor
in the memory of Your holy manifestation,
while our souls shine
in the fervor of Your love.
43 In this hour, the saints
labored at prayers;
make us worthy, our Lord, to share
in that consolation of their vigils.
44 Grant us to feel in our self
and to receive in our way of life, the fragrance
of that consolation which they shared in,
during the journey of their minds.
45 O Christ, who watch for us
in prayer with <Your> Father,[14]
grant us to feel a pledge
of pardon[15] for our iniquity, during our prayer.
46 O Christ, who sweat at prayer

---

[12] Cf. James 1:17.

[13] Cf. Mt. 25:1–13.

[14] Cf. Mt. 26:39.

[15] Cf. 2 Cor. 1:21–22; 5:5; Eph. 1:13–14.

for us, during the night,[16]
make us worthy that our mind may perceive
Your suffering for our salvation.
47 O Christ, who have poured out <Your> gift
on the saints at prayer[17]
gladden, our Lord, our intelligence
by means of the perceptions of Your grace.
48 O God, to whom are
the days and the nights,[18]
make us glad, our Lord, by means of hope in You,
when the night is dark.
49 In the converse of prayer with You,
we draw near while bowing down:
<breathe> on our mind and gladden it
that by our prayer, it may communicate with You.
50 Enlighten the stirrings of our intelligence
so that we may observe with wonder,
and our thought be enfolded in You
for the whole length of our prayer.
51 At the dawn of Your coming
our mind receives Your manifestation,
and its power of reason anticipates
that incorporeal way of life.
52 Grant us, our Lord,
to hasten to our holy city,
and like Moses from the top of the mountain,
may we <foresee> it by means of Your revelation.[19]
53 Even if the body afflicts
and by means of its miseries brings us low,
may Your grace my Lord,
overcome in us the law within our flesh.[20]
54 Our Lord, with my mind

---

[16] Cf. Lk. 22:41–44.

[17] Cf. Acts 2:1–2.

[18] Cf. Ps. 74:16

[19] Cf. Dt. 34:1–4.

[20] Cf. Rom. 7:23.

I love Your spiritual law,[21]
but *a law* which is placed *in my members*[22]
leads me captive from being occupied with it.
55 <it is> as if the soul were led captive
by hateful works,
or as if it were pulled away
by compulsion from spiritual converse.
56 But <the soul> does not wish
to be enslaved in the tent of the body's passions,
and it calls for help while groaning,
and its misery is indescribable.
57 Like the widow who, wronged,
passionately cries for help to God;
she, whom in that Gospel is promised
satisfaction, <according as she desires>.
58 *Avenge me* – she says in prayer –
from my body which is *my adversary.*[23]
And that sweet judge
gives a reward for her compunction.
59 As we are swimming in the ocean
of our bodily stirrings at all times,
wash, our Lord, our mind
from the stains of hateful things.
60 To You we call from out of the waves,
O our wise Mariner:
cause to blow on us a serene breeze,
but if we sink, draw us out.[24]
61 In the middle of the night I rose up, my Lord,
to announce You with great passion
and to offer You a sacrifice of praise,[25]
to You, *just judge.*[26]

---

[21] Cf. Rom. 7:14.

[22] Cf. Rom. 7:23.

[23] Lk. 18:3. Cf. Is.I, 107. See also Nilus, *Sulla virtù e sulle passioni* 17, p. 286.

[24] Cf. Mt. 14:24–31.

[25] Cf. Heb. 13:15.

62 Because You have not forgotten our dereliction
and our humiliation at all times,
<just> how eager our mind is
for what is excellent, is manifest to You.
63 Even if our weaknesses prevail
a thousand, thousand <times> all day <long>
and we immerse ourselves in their hateful things,
we do not desist from converse with You.
64 Our Savior, who have come to wash
the impurity of the sinful world,
grant us compunction at all times
that we might cleanse the impurity of our thoughts.
65 Sanctify our hearts, my Lord,
and fill <them> with the Spirit of Your glory,
and by means of the holy remembrance of You
may they receive the Spirit of joy.
66 Create in us, my Lord, *a new heart*,
infuse in us *a new spirit*,[27]
that by the renewal of our mind
we may put on the garment of the Kingdom.[28]
67 By the mysteries of Your Spirit, we are renewed,
and by Your grace, we are sanctified,
while we continually forget everything,
by means of the converse with You.
68 And that holy hope of ours
we always feel in our prayer,
when we are led by it continually
<far> from the corporeal world.
69 The mortal world is <too> weak
to receive all of Your gift:
from Your abundance overflows
fullness on its weakness.
70 My Lord, our souls are thirsty for this hope,
as we are afflicted:

---

[26] Cf. Ps. 9:5.
[27] Ez. 11:19.
[28] Cf. Mt. 22:1–14.

gladden our souls, our Lord,
that we may see Your favor in our substance.
71 In this world we are separate
from humanity and its converse,
be for us a guide, our Savior,
and a companion at all times.
72 In this time that we are deprived
from <being> with the world and its business,
be consolation for us, our Lord,
and may we not be deprived of Your love.
73 Because our heart is full of adversities
and we are always sad
make us worthy, our Lord, of Your consolation
which is beyond all adversities.
74 Our souls are full of weeping
and it is always bitter for us:
gladden, my Lord, our sadness
and refresh our burning heart.
75 Troubles encircle us
and suffering, night and day:
secretly refresh, our Lord,
our burning hearts.
76 There is no hope for us anywhere
which consoles our sadness:
Savior of all, may Your finger touch
the hidden sorrow which is in our heart.[29]
77 Because incessant battles pursue us
night and day,
and they have cut off our hope in You:
be our commander in the struggle!
78 Weeping and tears in secret
are shed upon our mind,
because we are always fearful
lest we deprived of Your hope.
79 Encourage, our Lord, our souls
with Your hidden voice which <comes> from the stillness,[30]

---

[29] Cf. Lk. 16:24.

when You teach us, by means of the Spirit,
the hidden aim of our struggle.
80 May our mind not be lacking
in Your encouragement, our Savior,
lest it be drowned in the sea
by the waves which cut off hope.
81 For that true hope
You show us, our Lord, from afar,
so that by seeing it we might be strengthened
and defy all miseries.
82 We are inexperienced in the struggle
to resist at the times of battles:
make wise in You our childishness,
<even> in this <our> spiritual maturity.
83 From converse with You we have become wise,
and we receive help from Your Spirit
which always instructs us
about the path which ascends to heaven.
84 Anoint, my Lord, our heart with Your Spirit,
that we might be priests in secret,
and fulfill the priestly ministry for You with our stirrings,
in the Holy of Holies of the knowledge of You.
85 May the coercion of Your grace prevail
upon our intellect, through the stirrings of our meditation,
and may we be led, by means of Your gift,
to the dwelling of the incorporeal beings.
86 In that house of rest of the saints,
and the elevated place of the pilgrims,
let us come together in the faith,
assisted by the power of Your grace.
87 By means of Your revelation may we become wise
about the way which leads to our city;
sustain our journey to it,
<far> from the world of struggles.
88 O Jesus, whose majesty descended
to raise up the lowly that they might be exalted,

---

[30] Stillness (*šelyâ*).

increase Your gift with us
that we may attain to Your love.
89 Grant us a holy mind
that we might receive Your likeness in our deeds,
and depict the true model
of Your humility in our person.
90 Grant us to perceive mystically
the taste of Your sweet love,
and may our mind fly to You,
by means of its savor at all times.
91 Moisten our arid soul
that it may bear fruits of praise,
and may it be a holy temple
for the dwelling-place of Your glorious realities.
92 Make our members, our Lord,
partners with You, head of the whole body,[31]
lest one of us be alienated
from communion with Your gladness.
93 O true Son of our race,
who goes to receive the Kingdom,[32]
do not renounce Your kindred
when You rise upon the clouds.[33]
94 Our souls are thirsty for Your manifestation
and the revelation of Your great dignity:
grant us confidence, from this time,
in the *pledge*[34] of our communion <with You>.
95 Even if we are wretched
and our race is dust,
raise up our soul according to our greatness,
because we have become God's kin.[35]
96 What mercy not able to be measured!
What sea of total compassion!

---

[31] Cf. Rom. 12:5; 1 Cor. 12:12; Eph. 1:22–23; 5:30; Col. 1:18.
[32] Cf. Lk. 19:12–15.
[33] Cf. Mt. 24:30; Mk. 13:26.
[34] Cf. 2 Cor. 1:21–22; 5:5; Eph. 1:13–14.
[35] Cf. Acts 17:29.

What grace without limit!
What love, greater than the world!
97 Our vision of Your love is imperfect
because we encompass its riches with our understanding!
O the depth of Your grace, our Creator,
for creatures!
98 It is not for the good of a few:
the Son of our human race was the Son of the King,
but He went to prepare
a Kingdom for all our nature.
99 Even if I be despised or mocked
ten thousand times for this,
never, my Lord, will I deny
the greatness of our hope in You.
100 My folly is greater than the word,
and the sea is not able to wash it away!
I said this and I say it <again>
Your love is greater than my debts!
101 The waves of the sea are less
than the number of my sins,
but if we weigh <them> against Your love,
they vanish as nothing.
102 I am a dwelling-place for all evils
and the mountains are slighter than my iniquity,
yet with Your love,
I do not fear to call myself just.
103 To You thanksgiving from all of us,
the *remnant*[36] of our wretched human race;
and to You from our race is due
loving adoration at all times.
104 The benefits transmitted
to us by Your hands are ineffable:
we adore the foot stool of Your feet,[37]
with weeping and joyful suffering.
105 Because our mouth is <too> weak to praise You,

---

[36] Cf. Rom. 9:27–29.

[37] Cf. Ps. 110:1.

may Your mercy recompense us
which has shone forth over our mortality,
and has taken up and embraced our foulness.
106 For Your love which is joined to our nature,
is not ashamed that we call ourselves <Your> members,[38]
and has attached our filth to <Your> body,
glory <to this love> from all creatures!

107 These <words> my beloved are full of spiritual meditation for the mind, and they are converse in the Spirit with our Lord! Let us make some place in our soul for these things that, by means of our quiet rest, the mind might discern and enter into converse with our Lord. For all of you, it is clear that converse with the world is contrary to converse with God. Therefore your wisdom must make this separation and honor the part which is good.[39] Indeed, if there are one or two persons who seek this mystery of spiritual converse, and they meet together with one another once a week, while quietly engaged in this divine converse – the gain, when they are enlightened, is even greater than the advantage which they receive from their solitude. This is because they help one another by means of the light they receive from one another, but without a mediator. This becomes perfect stillness, if accidental things <do not occur> which might dislodge them from their goal, and <that they> keep themselves also from worldly words.[40]

---

[38] Cf. Heb. 5:30.

[39] Cf. Lk. 10:42.

[40] According to Chialà, this paragraph is probably an addition made by Isaac, cf. Is.II V.31–33.

Chapter XI

Again of the same Mar Isaac. Concerning that: "you have been raised with Christ,"[1] *as said by the divine Apostle; and concerning this divine sacrifice which the holy Church accomplishes for the living and the dead for the sake of the hope of what is to come: what is effected by this sacrifice and in a special way for a believing lay person because of the firmness of his hope.*

1. "How indeed is our resurrection and our renewal[2] visible in us which the Apostle Paul proclaims frequently?"[3] Those who are enlightened know about our resurrection. That is to say, we are resurrected but in the faith; and we are renewed in a mystery. The resurrection and the renewal of which the Apostle speaks do not happen to our body, for behold, our <human> race is still afflicted with mortality and corruptibility, and living beings are troubled by the flesh capable of suffering in this world. How can one say that these are resurrected and renewed, for behold the miseries of mortality are lifted up against them at all times?

2. But we ought to look beyond the flesh with the insight of divine Scripture. We have risen by a virtuous way of life; we have risen by faith in the future realities; we have risen in the knowledge concerning the divine Nature, in the perception of His Essence, in the glory of His greatness, in the height of His Nature, in the hope for the good things kept for us, in the knowledge of the mysteries of the *new world*,[4] in faith in the marvelous transformation[5] which is prepared for creation.

---

[1] Col. 3:1; cf. Eph. 2:6; Col. 2:12.

[2] Renewal (*ḥuddâtâ*): renewal of the universe, of all (*kul*), of the inner person. See Is.I 127, 256, 374, 471; Is.II V.1, 6,7; VIII.16; X.19; *Keph.* I 90; II 19; III 21,82; IV 46, 59, 61,78. John Sol. *Dialogues* X, pp.122, 125 and *passim; Letters*, p.3 (Rignell, *Briefe*); Evag. Cent. III. 48,51; Nilus, *Discorso di ammonimento* 41, p. 202; Theodore of Mopsuestia, *Homélies* VI 12.

[3] Cf. Col. 3:1; Eph. 2:6; Col. 2:12; and on "renewal," cf. Rom. 12:2; Eph. 4:23; Tt. 3:5.

[4] Cf. Mt. 19:28 (Peshitta).

3. Rightly then does the Apostle proclaim to us a true resurrection in Christ, as a reality in which we already exist. That is to say, we have risen by the renewal of the mind.[6] In the former generations, there was no remembrance of God; indeed remembrance of Him was completely dead. As to the intermediate generations, even while knowing Him, they knew Him in a limited way.

4. We, indeed, have been renewed in our mind[7] by a new knowledge that was not revealed to them. For we have known this Being who has neither beginning nor end. And again, they had a childish way of thinking about God: that He is hard, vindictive; that He requites and is just when He requites, irascible, wrathful; that He remembers *the debts of the fathers in the children of the children.*[8]

5. But we possess a greater sense of God and we have an elevated knowledge of Him. Indeed, we know Him as one who pardons, who is good, who is humble. Even for one good thing <done>, if only in thought or compunction, He pardons the sins of many years. And the sins of others He does not remember, lest they be associated <with ours>. But even those who have died in their sins and passed over already, He rends asunder the greater part of their sins[9] by means of His mercy.

6. There is also the offering which is the best of all for our atonement – swift for the living and for those in the afterlife – which in His wisdom he has prepared for all. The oblation offered

---

[5] Transformation (*šuḥlâpâ*): found frequently in Isaac, Is.I 4, 12, 25, 127. Is. II VIII.7, 15; XXII.7–8; XXXVIII.2. *Keph.* IV 57.

[6] Renewal of the mind (*ḥuddâtâ d-madʿâ*): see Is.I 469; *Keph.*IV 54. On resurrection as a progression in knowledge, see Evag. Cent.V. 22, 25.

[7] Cf. Eph. 4:23.

[8] Cf. Ex. 34:7. Elsewhere Isaac criticizes this infantile way of thinking (*šabrût tarʿîtâ*) as not recognizing "His kindness, goodness and compassion." And that one "should not understand everything (literally) as it is written, but rather that we should see, (concealed) inside the bodily exterior of the narratives, the hidden providence and external knowledge which guides all…" – an aspect of Isaac's exegesis. See Is.II XXXIX.2, 19.

[9] Cf. 1 Peter 4:8.

up in the Church witnesses to it – the mystery of the body and the blood of the Lord – which is offered in the hope of forgiveness of the deceased, the sinful race of those already departed. But if the dead may no longer be helped by anything, what profit to offer for them the mystery of the body of our Lord, according to the tradition which is held by all the Church: oblation for the departed in the hope of atonement?[10]

7. Now does it seem to you that this tradition is empty or an ignoble thought? Or indeed is it a tradition according to an interpretation: that in the mystery celebrated for the departed, there is the hope of the forgiveness of sins? Or is it profitable only for the righteous? But then what would be the advantage to sinners for whom the oblation is offered, and with it the prayer and petition of the priest at the altar, in which with the sacrifice of our Lord, he also remembers the dead one concerning this hope?

8. Certainly, sinners are assisted by the oblation and it reduces their burden. Whenever it is offered on account of the quantity of sins, they are greatly assisted. Besides, there are those whose fault is not that they have sinned but have shared in ungodliness and have apostatized; or they have blasphemed even while sharing in the <mysteries> of salvation. I think that it is to separate these from participation that the expression is heard, according to church custom at the moment of the mysteries: "And for all the children of the Church who are worthy to receive this oblation before you."[11]

9. This expression does not separate sinners, but those who are not worthy to be counted with the sons of the Church, because of the wickedness they have committed concerning the mysteries of

---

[10] Cf. 2 Macc. 12:43–45. See the homily of Jacob of Serug, "On the Memory of the Dead and on the Eucharist," Bedjan, *Homiliae selectae* VI, 535–550. For trans. see Connolly, *Downside Review*. Full title: "On the commemoration of the departed and on the loaf brought for the Eucharist, and that the departed profit from the offerings and the alms that are done in their behalf."

[11] See Vadakkel, *Anaphora of Mar Theodore*, *Qanona* p.79.

the Church; like the heretics and heresiarchs, who among other things, also consider as ordinary the holy mysteries of the Church.[12] But the expression does not point to those who have sinned, as if it were not possible for them to share in the aid that comes from the mysteries of the Church.

10. <There are> those who have not apostatized or separated themselves from the Church, but in all their lives have believed in the Church and its mysteries and have kept stainless their profession of faith and their baptism. Yet because of their weakness, in some manner they are guilty of sin. But even though they do not have the fullness of hope, as <do> the excellent righteous for their part, when they draw near to the divine Nature in their intellect, they are not separated from the communion of hope in Christ, and the aid of the Church <is> fully in their spirits.

11. This is like what the Apostle said: *Whoever eats the bread of the Lord and drinks of his cup, while not being worthy, eats and drinks his own condemnation, because he has not discerned the body of the Lord.*[13] In fact, "unworthy" and "worthy" here do not depend on bad or good deeds, the Apostle says, but on mental discernment. And on the occasion of writing these things, the Apostle shows clearly in the same letter the way of thinking he laid down: let no one suppose that only the righteous are permitted to have part in the holy mysteries, or those who are blameless or who remain sincerely repentant.

12. But if it were not so, one must completely cease partaking of the mysteries in the city, since in these places it is difficult to find one occupied about conversion or <even> concerned about things such as these. Those who understand the words of Scripture <implied here> wrongly, relying on their own opinion, do harm not only to themselves but many <others> are led astray by them, since there are many who follow because of the ignorance

[12] Chialà suggests that Isaac refers here to Messalians which elsewhere he names: Is.I 171, 495; Is.II XIV. 22, 47; *Keph.* IV 31,34. See Hagman, "Isaac of Nineveh and the Messalians."

[13] 1 Cor. 11:27–29.

concerning this apostolic word. But we learn his doctrine from the order of the text.

13. Blessed Paul wrote this discourse to the Corinthians on the holy day of Sunday, when they were gathered in church; that the rich who were among them shared equally with the poor, in the holy mysteries according to the order held to by the Church. But after this, each was sitting down and eating and taking delight in what each had prepared at home. The poor, then, would sit while hungry and looking at the rich who were drinking and enjoying themselves.

14. Blessed Paul heard about this and he wrote to them that while they shared in the nourishment of the mysteries together, as to bodily nourishment, however on their own they judged that the poor are not worthy to share with them. This shows that the ordinary table for them was more important than the table of the mysteries. Paul made known to them that: "If the mystery is considered by you as an ordinary reality such that it does not even seem to be like the ordinary table, well then it is to your condemnation that you eat the bread and drink the chalice of the table of the Lord."[14]

15. Also the blessed Interpreter, in his commentary where he explains the thinking of the Apostle, brings forward and also affirms the things which we have said above. And after having shown its cause, he explains the meaning of Paul's discourse saying: "This is clearly what the Apostle wishes to make known: it is right that the mysteries be offered with a perfect mind and not slackly as if it were ordinary bread;"[15] and at the very end of his discourse, the blessed Interpreter says: "Whoever has perfect faith regarding the mysteries of Christ – for which the Apostle lays out his discourse – I think he is never deprived of the expected good things."[16]

---

[14] Cf. 1 Cor. 11:17–34.

[15] Theodore of Mopsuestia on I Cor. 11: 27–29 not found but see Isho'dad of Merv: Vol. IV, Bk. XVII. p.36.

[16] Cf. Theodore of Mopsuestia 1 Cor. 11:33–34 in PG (Migne) 66, col. 889.

16. You see, O mankind, that the Apostle does not condemn nor declare alien to the blessing expected from the mysteries, those who by their way of life are not worthy, but rather those who are not worthy of the mysteries because of the corruption of their mind. There is great harm for an unprepared mind to rely on its own insight into the word of holy Scripture. Therefore we do not give heed to an imperfect human way of thinking, but I said and I say again and I don't deny: there is help for deceased sinners from the sacrifice of our Lord on their behalf!

17. And if only for the righteous is remembrance to be made, why does the priest also bring to God, in prayer before the altar, the memory of all sinners of Adam's race? I, indeed, do not deny these holy and acceptable sayings, full of redemption, which the priest repeats with great passion near the offerings while inclined before the altar.[17] I am not in error on account of them, nor am I a transgressor.

18. Nor do I regard it burdensome to put the *sedra* in this place, that everyone might know the power which is in the mysteries of the body of Christ; so as to send the help of grace even to the dead, that the bright lights of its strength might descend even to Sheol. Let it be known to those who are ignorant, that not one of the mysteries set by the holy Church, was set and confirmed unadvisedly or by chance.

19. But all of these <mysteries> are full of hope, and great discernment is hidden in them for those who fulfill them. How great is the power of faith and how exalted the knowledge of Christians and what intelligence they have of God! We believe in

---

[17] Inclined (*ghîn*) before the altar: in the *Anaphora of Mar Theodore* there are four *gehanta* cycles each including a specific *gehanta* or prayer recited while inclined. The third *gehanta* concentrates on the Economy of Christ and concludes: "...we are gathered together, even we, your humble, weak and miserable servants, that by the permission of your grace we may celebrate this great, respectful, holy and divine mystery wherein is realized the great salvation for the whole race of mankind." See Vadakkel, *Anaphora,* text 56, p. 87.

fact that the power of the mysteries of the Economy of the Only-Begotten is able to give absolution even to the dead, and even in Sheol to help those who believed in it during their lives. From this, those who concerning the resurrection hold that such hope is also for their deceased, have received instruction and with great faith make petition for this and ask absolution also for the dead.

20. And as if it were already indeed a reality placed in his hands, the priest with undivided faith presents the offering, and makes petition to God in the remembrance of the sacrifice of Christ for the pardon of sinners, living and deceased, so that they might be purified: the living by receiving <the sacrifice> and the dead by the remembrance on their account. For the priest says without hesitation: "Thus, our Lord and our God, accept from us according to your grace, this sacrifice of praise which is the reasonable fruit of our lips."

21. Why? He says: "That before you there might be a memorial of the righteous of former <times>, of the holy prophets, of the blessed apostles, of the martyrs, of the confessors, etc."; furthermore: "and of all the sons of the holy Church who have departed from this world in the true faith."[18] You see how he describes the word faith: he does not speak of those who departed without sins and who have passed from this world in righteousness. Rather he says: "Those who in their faith have departed from this world and cleave to your grace, my Lord, pardon all their sins and transgressions which in this world, in a mortal body and in a mutable soul, they have committed and acted foolishly before you."[19]

22. You see that the priest is not ashamed to speak about the sins of the departed and ask pardon of God. You heard how he presents to God this powerful request, without hesitation at a forceful moment, while not doubting that God holds this in reverence. Have you learned what hope is placed in the Church of Christ? Have you understood the way God has taught mankind,

---

[18] Fourth *gehanta*, Vadakkel, *Anaphora,* text 70–71, p. 90.

[19] Fourth *gehanta*, Vadakkel, *Anaphora,* text 77, p. 91.

and how He has put in them the faith concerning His will, which is set in prayer and offered before Him in the Church? Why do you consider this prayer as bold? Are you lacking in faith? Or are you indeed an adversary of God's will?

23. That there is some means which God offers, the Holy Spirit has taught by placing in the Church, through intercession, the great power of Christianity and God's gladness for our earthly nature. All the will of God is externally revealed, in a symbolic way,[20] by means of His holy Church. But the haughty and the ignorant do not want to believe in the mystery of His good will for our race.

24. Let it not be that we doubt, my beloved, concerning these verses full of holy things about God. Being in accord with the will of God, they are placed with the thanksgiving for the mysteries set by the Church, and with the holy divine things. As such, God the Lord of all is especially pleased, and because of this, <the verses> are placed with the mystical words of the sacrifices of revelation. Let it not be that we deny the word or the meaning concerning the power of this perfect and divine prayer, which is full of hope for all mankind.

25. I have not written these things so that relying <on them> you become remiss but in order for you to grow strong in your hope. Thus may your mind grow <continuously> in God and the future ways increase in your soul, while earthly things be despised in your eyes. May your mind be filled with wonder at God,[21] and the fire of His love shine in your soul while it proceeds in meditation on the insights of His mysteries, towards the place which is above the world.

26. However it is not right because of fear of being slack to hide or to diminish understanding of the mysteries of our worship, or to deny the power of the confession of the marvelous Economy on our account. Nor should fear make us cease from marveling at God, nor from giving glory with incomparable joy. If someone

---

[20] In a symbolic way: from *remzâ*; cf. Is.II IX.6, XXXIII.2.

[21] Wonder at God (*tehrâ db-alâhâ*): Is.I 304–05, 376, 492; Is.II XX.10–11, XXI.7; *Keph.* I 36, II 55, 89, IV 47.

believes that being without faith and knowledge is able to be more helpful, let him earnestly take pains with this for his <own> soul.

27. But we are saved by faith! And by it we are moved and regenerated to immortal and *true life*,[22] while we marvel at God's mercy, how He has arranged everything for our benefit, by that salutary wisdom towards our sinful race. He it is who has openly revealed the accomplishment of all the good of His will, eternal and mysterious, by means of the Economy of Christ, our Lord. He appointed for us an incorruptible advocate: the body and blood of our Savior; He who is not guilty of any one of the sins of creatures.

28. Let it not be <thought> that I am defending sin! However, I lift up the power of the advocate of sinners who is in heaven![23] And I make manifest the great hope within the liturgy for Him which the Church fulfills, more excellent than the word or the power of creatures. The knowledge of our <human> race is not able now to possess or draw near to the whole truth about its hope.

29. And not without inquiry, I endeavor to show the effect of sin while I myself marvel at God's wisdom. I am amazed at this Economy of Christ and at the power of His mysteries, while with this insight, I approach <in> amazement[24] and I turn to silence. How <the Economy> is full of salvation for mankind![25] Because of this Economy, a *multitude of sins* is pardoned[26] by means of the sacrifice of the body of Jesus[27] offered for them. And not only, but because of the sacrifice, the judgment concerning them will be merciful. Not even one ten-thousand of what <punishment> they are worthy of will be required.

30. Perhaps those whose sins are very few and of slight quality, <God> does not hold them accountable. Even for those whose sins are of a great number, He diminishes the torments from the

---

[22] Cf. 1 Tim. 6:19.

[23] 1 Jn 2:1.

[24] Amazement (*temhâ*).

[25] Cf. 1 Tm. 2:4.

[26] Cf. 1 Pt. 4:8.

[27] Cf. Heb. 10:10.

balance sheet for a reason centrally placed by the will of the Creator. He loves to show mercy by means of that One whom *God has predetermined for atonement by faith in his blood.*[28] But few are worthy of this faith and of the understanding of the mysteries, in the hope of the body and blood of Jesus.

31. This is therefore the true resurrection which <occurs> by knowledge, by an assured faith and the renewal of the mind. Those who were baptized in Christ[29] have received it in the hope of the *future world.*[30] The blessed Paul says: *<Christ> raised us up and made us ascend and sit with him in heaven.* Whoever has entered the thick darkness[31] of the knowledge of faith and has known the power of its mysteries, is always in heaven in his intellect, and sits with Christ by means of the continual appearance of His marvelous Economy.

32. This Economy in all its parts is often in the mysteries which are full of hope, to signify that our belief in the *knowledge of truth*[32] is a gift of God. Those who are pleasing to God believe because of Him and not by the power of nature or the will and human discipline.

33. Who is able to receive the fountain of His mysteries? That one before whom is opened an entrance to its intuitions, which like a fountain springs up and flows for the delight of his soul, and which always finds new things in the treasure of his mind![33] This is what

---

[28] Cf. Rom. 3:25.

[29] Cf. Rom. 6:3; Gal. 3:27.

[30] Cf. Heb. 2:5; 6:5; hope of the future world (*sabrâ d-ʿâlmâ da-tîd*): Is.I 41, *Keph.* IV 78. In John Sol. *Soul* see *sabrâ da-ʿtîdâtâ*, 21 and *sabrâ da-ʿtîd*, 73. All who have written about John Sol. have noted the importance he places on hope; hope in the world to come for him is based on the resurrection of Christ and the grace of baptism.

[31] Cf. Ex.20:21.

[32] Cf. 1Tim. 2:4; 2 Tim. 3:7; Heb. 10:26. Knowledge of truth (*îdaʿtâ da-šrârâ*): Is.I 430, 494. Is.II VIII.1; IX title, 2, 4; X.15,16; XIII.1; XIV.33, 34; XXV title; XXXV.5; XXXVII.3, 4. It is common in Evag., see Cent. I.14, 52, 89; II.10, 19. See also Theodore of Mopsuestia, Vadakkel, *Anaphora*, text 70, p. 89.

[33] Cf. Mt. 13:52.

was said by our Savior: *The one who believes in me, as the Scriptures said, streams of living waters will flow from within him.*[34] To Him be glory for ever and ever. Amen.

34. The end of the *memra* on the holy mysteries of our Savior, composed by blessed Mar Isaac, solitary and orthodox,[35] who was bishop of the city of Nineveh.

---

[34] John 7:38.

[35] According to Chialà it may have been a copyist who mentions Isaac's orthodoxy, or one of his disciples, given the insistence in this chapter on prayer for the dead and how God pardons the sins of the deceased in His mercy and the possible polemical interpretation of this. But elsewhere Isaac gives a similar assurance of his own orthodoxy, see Is.I 127; Is.II XXXIX.7.

Chapter XII

Again, a letter of exhortation by Mar Isaac concerning <how> solitary life can be affected <when lived> in the midst of others, which was sent to a monk who desired to be assured about this. The monk had written him concerning his thoughts, asking if there was in them any blame from God. <Isaac> exhorts to surrender oneself to the afflictions of this life, with a prompt intelligence which examines God's hidden reasons.

1. I believe, O our brother, that for consolation and for your encouragement, as well as to give confidence to your mind in this suffering which has seized you, this alone is sufficient which is manifest and clear to all: that since antiquity and from before the many initial generations, there is this way of solitary life and of the migration from human company, for the peace of mind of whoever chooses it. This continues and is handed down in every generation by whoever wishes to give rest to the mind, whatever be the reason which summons and sets in motion one's exodus <from the world>.

2. Whether it be the adversities and evils which happen to humans in every generation, or an excellent request or good desire which is stirred within them by means of undivided faith – what is said by our Lord, the Christ, arises in their mind about what is impossible for humans but possible for God.[1] Because, indeed, it is certain for them, without a doubt, that by complete separation from the world and migration to God, they may receive liberation from all adversities and find the excellent desire which is in their souls.

3. We also may see from the description of their accounts, how different and dissimilar was the exodus of each one of them. And the object of their thinking was not the same for all those holy ones in their migration from human habitation. Even the cause of exodus was not the same for all of them. Because of this, each one

[1] Mt. 19:26.

may find a model and a mirror among the things which occurred in the past in those who were called to this way of life.[2]

4. If the cause of migration be from sadness or adversities, or from joy, or from zeal, or love, or fear, or passion and compunction, or from afflictions brought on by others, etc.; or if migration occurs through a sense of righteousness or for repentance on account of sins. All of these things one may find in those who have gone before us.

5. For various causes, indeed, persons have abandoned human contact and have followed after God. They have surrendered their souls to death. They have been made worthy of the mercy and providence of God and have been received by grace.

6. Some have <followed after God> because of the distress of persecution for the faith, or fear of human wickedness, as the blessed Paul, first of the solitaries, who entrusted his soul to God and despising himself went out without clothing.[3] Some have acted out of fervor for God or by zealous thoughts, like the blessed Onesima. She went out with even less clothing, she did not take even a cloak for her body, but she went out stripped and barefoot.[4] Many others have been seen <to live> in this way, as the accounts about them demonstrate.

7. Again there are those who, weary of the world, because of the treachery and deceit they found in those who dwell there, have left it and moved on, such as those two brothers, sons of a governor, whom Serapion saw in the desert. When they were asked by him the reason for coming to this harsh place and for enduring for a long time near bitter waters, they said that their father had left them great riches when he died of which many friends and loved ones profited. But when the riches were spent, they all changed and became enemies instead of friends.

---

[2] Cf. Nilus, *Discorso sulle osservanze* 3, p. 78.

[3] Paul the Hermit, his life by Jerome may be found in Budge, *Paradise* I, 197–203. See also Is.I 560; Is.II XIV.21.

[4] Hermit in Egypt, recorded in a Syriac *Vita* edited by Bedjan, *AMS* V, 405–421.

8. They added: "While seeing the deceitfulness and cunning of the world and that love there was not true nor desire for God enduring, only serving the times, and friendship there changed with the circumstances – in fact only one in a thousand, loves because of God – we have chosen to go out and to be with God: He who stands by His love for His friends and His love does not change."[5]

9. There are others who because of fear of falling, and the deceit of Satan's ways by means of a woman, have abandoned being near habitation and have gone out to a remote desert, so as not to lose the purity of their bodies. For example, holy Martinianus, having separated from the snare of a woman, burned his feet and departed to an island in the midst of the ocean where there was stillness and no humans at all.[6]

10. There is also <the story of> blessed Carpus, whom holy Serapion saw on the top of a mountain, in a remote desert with a little fenced celery garden. He was deceived by Satan by means of the wife of the governor, his friend, who frequently went up to his cell to see him. But one day, at the working of Satan, she gazed at him lustfully, etc. With these occasions, and again for other things with which Satan defiled his thought by an obscene vision in his imagination because of being near habitation, and lest something unpleasant happen to him, he left that place and moved to another. There he lacked most material necessities, befitting a meager existence, as the little celery garden indicates.[7]

11. Some have risen up from a life of ruin but because of great fear of future judgment, or on account of having repented <only> a few days before dying, they have gone forth with little hope of salvation. They thought it not even right to be shown salvation and they held themselves in contempt. Such was the case of that solitary who fell into sin with a virgin for six months, but his affliction was transformed by an angel.[8]

---

[5] Concerns Serapion, Bedjan, *AMS* V, 320–21. See also Is.I 554.

[6] On Martinianus, see Budge, *Paradise* II, 300–02. And see Is.I 554.

[7] Chialà links Carpus with Polycarp in Bedjan, *AMS* V, 322–27.

[8] Cf. Is.I 553.

12. Or like the bishop who had apostatized and went out to the desert in repentance. These went out without any bodily provisions, thinking to be close to death.

13. Or like James the *gyrovague*[9] who fell into sin. He committed adultery, also killed and even threw the body into the river. But after all these things, he went out strengthened by a divine sign and dwelt in a tomb for ten years. Indeed, like Adam,[10] with a broken heart he went into that cave which became a tomb. All which happened to him is revealed in his account that also clearly informs how his nourishment was vegetarian, like for animals, twice a week.

14. There are other causes such as these, for which many saints separated themselves from mankind and went to deserts and mountains without any provisions. And they gathered together in mountain caves, and in ravines or even in gorges of terrifying depth, without planning or being solicitous for life.[11] But they dwelt there and let go of their lives, in expectation of certain death.

15. If you wish, also you may become like one of these: follow the path in imitation and keep the cause of your exodus in your mind. If they acted in fervor or by a sense of righteousness; or if by suffering or compunction, or in repentance for sins; or if they were afraid and fled, mortified, lest the purity of their bodies be defiled: may one of these be your consolation, whichever is according to your intention. Take it for consolation at your death and for the afflictions which happen then, because in your way of life you are not alone among your kind.

16. I said these things to satisfy your mind. How for various reasons, many have despised life and delivered themselves to death, while taking on the thought <of death>, and choosing a dwelling place fit for his. Not only were they not accused by God on this account, but they were also made worthy of His great providence.

---

[9] James the *gyrovague,* information on his life available but unedited, see Is.III XII.13 (*CSCO*).

[10] Adam, used in an adverbial way perhaps to indicate human weakness, or in this case, nudity as alluded to in Is.III XII.6.

[11] Cf. Heb. 11:38.

17. Remember that youth in a certain city, who had committed many sins and a great number of grievous evil deeds. He was mentioned by blessed John in his account or by its compiler: "This one, at a sign from God concerning his sins, repented and moved to a cemetery." Clearly, he was without provisions or whatever might be necessary, but was not preoccupied by such things. He remained like this for a whole week and persevered with weeping and lamentation for his sins, without any remembrance or concern for food. In addition, he received harsh torments from the demons for three nights, one after another, without any care or thought at all whether or not he would live, nor was he afraid of death.[12]

18. If you so desire, you may become like him in this. Do not let Satan cast you down in anxiety or care, as to whether or not you will die. Behold, these icons of all the types are before you: may you be a willing martyr like one of them.[13]

19. Nevertheless, this is assured: the word is true that whoever takes on the afflictions of repentance preparing his soul <to suffer> for what is excellent, and because of the fear of God introduces his soul to pains and temptations – this one is not able to be abandoned by the providence of God.

20. In faith, keep going forward on the way of virtue, hoping always in God's salvation, lest you be reproached like that people whose heart is blind. Because of their lack of faith, they were reproached by the Prophet, namely: *They did not believe in God nor hope in His salvation.*[14] Although seeing His wonders daily and His cares for them, in their mind they were utterly without hope in Him. Despairing of divine providence is clearly Satan's way of mastering the mind.

---

[12] This concerns John of Lycopolis (John of the Thebaid), late 4th cent. The episode is found in Budge, *Paradise* I, 327–28. See also Is.I 152, 568.

[13] On ascetical life as a martyrdom, see Is.I 31, 209, 242, 436, 456–57; *Keph.* I 53.

[14] Ps. 78:22.

21. As also blessed Theodore says in his Commentary on Matthew: "Satan takes care to persuade all mankind that God is not concerned about them. Because he knows, indeed, that as long as we truly know this, that is to say, concerning God's providence for us, we will love Him and we will do what is right according to His commandments. We will, then, have no anxiety in all adversities, and we will be anxious only for virtue. This is the thought – he says – of which <Satan> takes pains to deprive us.[15]

22. Thus, said <Theodore>, Satan also did with Adam. While God, indeed, managed everything for his benefit, <Satan> said: *God knows that the day in which you eat of it, your eyes will be opened and you will be like God, knowing good and evil.*[16] When in this way, he made Adam think that God not only helps but also advises in a contrary way, he was able easily <to do> his work to dissuade from keeping the commandment.[17]

23. But you, therefore, do not be with God in a Jewish way of thinking, like that people, nor childishly like Adam. But let faith

---

[15] On the work of Satan to destroy trust, see the words of Is.II VII.21, worth quoting:

> For someone to entrust himself to God means that, from that point onwards, he will no longer be swallowed up in anguish or fear over anything, (or) be tormented again by a thought such as when he imagines that he has no one to look after him. Once a person has fallen away in his mind from this confidence, he starts falling into myriads of temptations in his thoughts, just as the blessed Interpreter says in the Volume on Matthew the Evangelist: Satan's entire concern is this, to persuade a person that God has no concern for him. For he knows (very well) that as long as we recognize this (concern) clearly, and (an awareness of it) is fixed in us, our souls will abide in complete peace, and we will furthermore, acquire love towards (God) and a concern for all the things that please Him; it is this thought that (Satan) endeavors to snatch away from us.

[16] Gen. 3:5.

[17] This Commentary of Theodore of Mopsuestia has not been conserved. Chialà suggests a possible reference to Mt. 4.1–11, cf. Is.I 418; and see again Is.II VIII.21.

adhere to you, which on the way of virtue, generates hope in every temptation and affliction. In this way you will not be without strength, fearful and trembling in your mind, on the way of repentance and in the afflictions and adversities on account of virtue.

24. Whoever's faith is weak concerning God's care for him, will always be wretched and fearful in his mind. And this drives away from him the great riches of virtue.

25. It is right and fitting, remembering one's sins, to consider oneself not worthy of God's providence. But one must also, on the other hand, remember the mercy of God so as to be comforted. True confidence in God, then, makes one's thinking vigorous and not feeble in every affliction which occurs, and makes one strong so as to endure everything. Faith in the providence of God is the light of the mind, which rises in a person, by grace.

26. Encouragement accompanies temptations endured on the way of virtue, by reason of the confidence that God is near and treats kindly those who love Him, according to the word of the Apostle.[18] Also according to the word of the Prophet: *His salvation is* always *near to those who fear Him.*[19]

27. For even if before, you lived very much as an adversary,[20] now you adhere with your will to the afflictions of repentance. You are one who does righteousness because the grace of God accompanies you everywhere. It allows you to be severely afflicted, while not abandoning you as you receive proof of its aid, so that you might suffer affliction for the fear of God, and prove yourself, in the endurance of evils for its sake. In your mind there is a place for confidence now, not seeming to have walked wholly at rest without having experienced misfortunes in God's presence, according to your previous faults.

---

[18] Cf. Rom. 8:28.

[19] Ps. 85:10.

[20] Cf. Rom. 5:10; Tt. 3:3.

28. The sinner who has sinned and is defiled in his body, but afterwards is numbered with the company of penitents, is not afflicted in his will on account of the fear of God. This is not possible until that moment he becomes a companion of God, and has acquired confidence of heart and the trust that his former sins have been forgiven.

29. Whoever knows to be a sinner, and in his heart suffers the dread of his sins, does not fear afflictions and death. On the contrary, he rejoices that in the afflictions of repentance he may arrive at death, in that when the suffering of compunction subdues his heart, truly he reckons it as audacity to be alive. He agrees to die in the misfortunes he brings on himself in repentance for his sins. He considers it a sin, indeed, that one not have in his heart a sense of sorrow for his sins, for these thoughts would cast him down <again>.[21]

30. The holy fathers, while living in sublime righteousness, were taking upon themselves prolonged fasts and intercession, for four or five, even seven days. And suffering severe pain because of hunger, they wore down their bodies while they were in barren places. Also after their fast, they <ate> very little and not to satiety, even this was poor quality and very wretched. How many times they had no bread for food, but <only> steeped pot herbs and fruit of the trees. So it is written about many of the saints for whom this was their nourishment, in that they could not endure bread nor any cooked food after having fasted all their lives. With these torments, they tortured and wore down their bodies every day. They considered it as a sacrifice pleasing to God, to be dead to all these things. How much more, then, are these things becoming for a sinner!

---

[21] This striking paragraph speaks of the importance of knowledge of one's sins. Elsewhere (Is.I 463), he says: "Better is he that has been deemed worthy of seeing himself, than he that has been deemed worthy of seeing the angels."

31. One who is just, however, afflicts himself rejoicing to die like this as an *acceptable sacrifice* to God.[22] Many of these were often found dead in their <cells>. And there are those who were found lying in their caves in distant and lonely places. No one was aware of them at the time of their illness, nor was <anyone> near them at their death, because of their remoteness and their being alone. Some were found while kneeling at prayer, as their souls were leaving their bodies.

32. And others, how many times they exhausted themselves in the snow in rugged places for many days. Others were tormented by thirst, yet they praised God while rejoicing. But if such as these, *of whom the world is not worthy*,[23] lived with these afflictions and because of them have gone out from the world, how right for the sinner to consider his soul and what profit to his soul from his life <offered> to God!

33. Remember your sins at all times so as to keep watch over yourself, because remembering them you may gladly endure the afflictions and adversities which happen to you in your zeal for those things which grieve your heart. Remember how great and numerous your sins are. Do not mention your righteousness, to your ruin, lest you be found twice guilty. In the first place, that you forget your debt to God for your great and numerous sins which He forgives you; and for His grace towards you, without doing away with you, when you did these great faults. Even after all this, He draws you near to Him through His compassion.

34. The other aspect of guilt is that if you think you are righteous, you might become slack in virtuous labors and shrink back from the afflictions you ought to endure because of them, as long as you are alive. You will fall into murmuring and pusillanimity. Even if lifted up, you will fall to the judgment reserved for Satan[24] for having forgotten your former things, so hateful and disgraceful.

---

[22] Cf. Phil. 4:18.

[23] Heb. 11:38.

[24] Cf. Is. 14:12–15.

35. Whoever forgets the measure of his sins, forgets the measure of God's grace towards him. He forgets how much he owes God in labor and recompense, on account of what he has <done> against Him *and His might.*[25] Whoever truly remembers his faults and his sins, considers as insignificant all the troubles and afflictions which he encounters, whether by choice or by necessities. And after becoming humble, he endures them with thanksgiving.

36. Appease your thoughts by remembering the *just judgment of God*,[26] and suddenly consolation will come to you in secret. You will have rest from all your adversities. If evil surrounds you, do not forsake what is good, and you will be victorious!

37. If you are weary, afflicted and tormented in the way of virtue, remember those who were afflicted, weary and prostrate under all kinds of violent torments, not of their will, but because of the world. Praise God who has made you worthy to be exhausted voluntarily because of the fear of Him and the life of repentance, by love of virtue and out of terror for sin, according to the choice of your will.

38. And if your thinking is afflicted by this, remember the holy martyrs who voluntarily endured all kinds of torments for love of faith, such that there was nothing else in their mind. They endured all this joyfully, even though they were able to turn aside from it, if they had sought to live at rest without love for God. And these were not only men, but women and children who naturally have a bond with this world and with the body, and what is peculiar to it.[27] Yet, they also were touched by all the torments which you have in mind.

39. If you speak about hunger or thirst or the suffering <involved>, also the persecutors torment the martyrs with these things. And if you speak about lying on scorching hot ground, the force of which inflames the body, also they have endured this.

---

[25] Cf. Ps. 78:4; Eph. 6:10.

[26] 2 Macc. 9:18; Rm. 2:5; 2 Thess. 1:5.

[27] Cf. Sahdona I 3, 64.

40. About one of the holy martyrs it is written, that after many torments, they brought a skin and laid it in the sun on very warm days, until it was hot. Then they bound the blessed one and placed him on that skin in the sun. Besides, during the night he was continually lying on dry and hot ground, <as part> of their torments.

41. So if you say you suffer from cold or frost or ice, <know that> many of these <holy martyrs>, without clothing, were tormented by very stormy weather in cold regions.

42. If separation from loved ones and friends concerns you, or being cut off in remote places from acquaintances: all of these things the martyrs suffered. There were also the straits of confinement, or prison for a long time while being deprived of any acquaintance, friend or comforter – such as this they suffered; without speaking of torments, or wounds, or mutilation of limbs and death on a cross. Some were strangled and were suspended in the sun head downwards, on the walls, on the doors and on trees. They were harassed and died a miserable death. Some were stoned <to death>. For some, their soul departed from the hard suffering because of the mutilation of their limbs which overpowered them, and they died.

43. They did not weaken in thought nor in word, <persevering> in these afflictions until the end of their lives. It is written that the greater part of these things were received and endured by your women and girls, having a nature that loves the world and is tied to love of the body with its pleasures. Yet they endured bravely and were valiant, giving proof of their soul's virtue when they were compelled to endure for the love of God, as even one of the authors writes in the account of their lives.[28]

---

[28] Chialà suggests various examples of women who were martyred in Persia: martyrdom of Martha, of Tarbo, of Thekla, of Anahid; and the martyrs of Karka d-Beth Slokh; as well as others. These accounts may be found in Brock – Ashbrook Harvey, *Holy Women*, 63–99.

44. At this time, the author wrote, wicked pagans inflicted injuries on those of the Covenant,[29] even many women were seized: some from the Pact, some from lay-life; some of them were free-born, but even some servants; some rich and some poor. The fragility of their nature did not prevent them from excelling in the struggle on account of the fear of God. But like strong men, valiantly <the women> endured the persecutions: those bitter sufferings which came upon them, wounds from violent persons, scourging by strong arms, being strangled in prisons, the severe pain of heavy chains, hunger and thirst, heat and cold, weariness and sadness, anxieties and adversities.

45. They considered these <persecutions> as comforts and joys, proclaiming their faith with a loud voice in the eyes of all: "One is for us and we suffer for Him, as He suffers for our salvation."[30] Then the pagans who surrounded them, like destroying devils, slew them mercilessly with all kinds of sufferings. Some after being tortured were exposed to intense heat and they died. Some were beaten with swords, their limbs destroyed and they died.

46. It happened to some to be stuck with a spear in their sides, and they died. For others, a sword passed through them from their belly to their loins, and they died. Yet others had their eyes plucked out, and they died; others were battered with stones, and they died. Others had their noses and lips destroyed and by breaking their teeth, blood flowed inside their mouths, and they died. There were those who had children by natural partnership and because they had also raised them in the true faith, the persecutors angrily slaughtered them before their eyes, and mercilessly poured the blood of their children into their mouths, killing them at the end.[31]

---

[29] Covenant / Pact: refers to an early Syriac form of religious life, "sons and daughters of the Covenant." See Brock, "Early Syrian Asceticism"; Nedungatt, "Covenanters."

[30] Cf. the martyr Maḥya in Brock – Harvey, *Holy Women*, 109–11.

[31] The fate of martyrs at Najran, see Brock – Harvey, *Holy Women*, 114.

47. The love of the world did not weaken their intelligence, nor love for children, nor remembrance of their loved ones and their friends. Not desire for their riches or their houses, neither allurements nor threats, weakened their will. Yet others, saws passed through the middle of their bodies; they were divided in two parts and lifted up on the two sides of the road where the king's army passed between them, etc.[32] What things the fragile nature of women endured and resisted! But you, weary solitary, your mind is weakened by fear of hunger and thirst; by even the <thought> of lying on dry ground; by heat and cold; by the fear of demons.

48. Such things happened to <these women and men>, yet they laughed much and were not weakened. While just the <thought of these things terrifies this <solitary>, and for very little labor he glorifies himself not remembering the members of the Church, both women and men – how they acted very mightily and were received at all times near Christ. But this <solitary> is weak from an affliction of his own choosing. And while occupied with his labors and freely having left <the world>, he becomes weak in his intelligence, and at the remembrance of death is fearful of offering <his> blood to God.

49. Those who were tied to the world and the pleasures of the body, when it was required <of them>, they renounced the world and left the body in order not to deny God nor be guilty, even in word. Yet the one who is supposed to have left the world already, and was considered as dead to the body, is afraid of hunger and the adversities which afflict the body, for <fear> of dying.

50. The heavens are amazed at how much the love of this life has ruled us, on account of the love of the pleasures that have laid hold of us. Consider, then, our brother, the things which I have written you, examine them in the crucible of your mind. See if there is assurance in them, giving rest to your mind on account of a word of righteousness. But if, indeed, you are frightened by these afflictions and you turn back to remain in what defiles life, you will

---

[32] Cf. the martyrdom of Tarbo, her sister and her servant: see Brock – Harvey, *Holy Women*, 73–76.

be like those who have feared afflictions and renounced true life, on account of temporal life.

51. Therefore, one of the saints says: "All the afflictions and troubles which happen to you on this way of virtue, reckon them as jailers, leading you with the commands of cruel kings and harsh rulers. Endure and ask help, remembering the crowns reserved[33] for the blessed martyrs, and you will share their inheritance."

The letter of Mar Isaac is finished.

[33] Cf. 2 Tm. 4:8.

Chapter XIII

Again, a letter on the abodes in which holy men enter by the stirrings existing in the mind, in the journey on the way to the house of God.

1. Together with what I wrote you before, now I want to make this known to you, our venerable brother: from where is the joy of the saints generated, how far is it transmitted, into which dwelling place does it go into when it leaves them and by what is it substituted. This you must know our beloved: everywhere that there is joy in God,[1] it is from fervor and in every place, fervor is the cause of joy; because where there is no fervor, nor is there joy. However the place of joy is inferior to the place of perfection.[2] The place of perfection is in fact knowledge, while joy is not from knowledge but from fervor, as I said.

2. Fervor, then, is between an excellent way of life and excellence of the mind. Beneath excellence of the way of life, there is neither fervor nor joy; even above an excellent mind there is, therefore, neither fervor nor joy. In fact, beneath an excellent way of life coldness[3] prevails. But above excellence of the mind is the place of stillness of the mysteries.[4] Truly great, indeed, is the joy in God, yet it is inferior to the stirrings and impulses in the Spirit.

---

[1] Joy in God (*ḥadûtâ db-alâhâ*): Is.I 368, 431; Is.II VIII.11, XX.15.

[2] In the *Letters* of John of Dalyatha two Letters are included, which are probably by Joseph Hazzaya. In Letter 48 the author refers to the three places (*atrâwâtê*): Purity *dakyûtâ*; Limpidity *šapyûtâ*; Perfection *gmîrûtâ* (not spiritual perfection, more like a fullness / *šumlâyâ* of the mystical life). These places are connected to the three levels (*taksê*) inherited from John the Solitary. The level of the body leads to Purity; the level of the soul to Limpidity; the level of the spirit to Perfection. See Beulay, *Lumière*, 97–124; Harb, "Doctrine Spirituel," 225–60; and Hansbury, *Letters*.

[3] Coldness: lack of fervor, in Evag. Cent. VI. 25 it indicates demonic action. See also *Letter to Melania*, p.12 (Vitestam).

[4] Place of stillness of the mysteries (*atrâ…šelyâ d-râzê*): place (*atrâ*) and place of (*atrâ d-*) occur in John Sol. and in East Syrian writers such as John of Dalyatha, in his *Letters* and very often in his *Homélies*. These

3. So then, from when a person begins <to do> excellent deeds before God, fervor begins to stir in him, even joy. And one proceeds in this way of joy until arriving at excellence of the mind which is the light of the mind and the revelation of hidden things. And when one has come near to this place, the stirring of joy[5] begins to lessen and be tranquil in him, because from this time he comes near to a certain calm.

4. And when he enters here, then fervor has possession and continual joy, though he is lifted above the order of joy, because he feels what is better than joy. If one is brought down from excellent deeds, this joy grows cold. But even when by excellent deeds, gradually he is brought near to excellence of the mind, also here joy ceases. And do not marvel that I said that when he draws near to the excellence of the mind, fervor begins to have possession and the mind is at peace from being diffused with joy.[6]

---

occurrences of *atrâ* may be due to an Evagrian influence. Evagrius saw the purified mind as the "place of God" from Exodus 24.10–11 (LXX). Shifting from Sinai to the human mind, he also speaks of "the place of prayer," internalizing the "place of God" within the person. See Columba Stewart, "Imageless Prayer," 173–204. Golitzin analyzes another perspective: the occurrence of *atrâ* in Aphrahat, also giving its linguistic history including *maqom* in the Hebrew Bible as the place of divine manifestation and as a "stand-in for God himself." In the Hekhalot literature *maqom* is used as a divine name. See Golitzin, "The Place of the Presence of God," 1–31. On *atrâ* see also his "The Image and Glory of God," esp. 338, 352–59. On *maqom* in Jewish sources see Urbach, *The Sages*, ch. IV.

[5] Stirring of joy (*zawʿâ d-ḥadûtâ*): Is.II IX.8 (plur.); *Keph.*III 30.

[6] There are many references in Is.I which help to understand the complexity of joy (*ḥadûtâ*). It is a sign of grace (58). It may come without a cause (177, 471). Joy in God is stronger than earthly life (431). Healing occurs through spiritual joy (484). Joy which no tongue can express (486). And in (550) Isaac allows that one give up occasionally even the recitation of the Psalms because of the power of joy, seeming to be what he allows for divine interruptions in prayer. Finally joy may be unspeakable, leading to inebriation in God / *rawwîyûtâ db-alâhâ* (555).

5. There is, indeed, among these divine gifts something more excellent than joy, that is to say, astonishment of thoughts. Together with the mind beginning to abound in hidden things, it begins to have astonishment of thoughts; and as the mind grows in this way it is strengthened until it arrives at what blessed Paul said when he recounted the ravishing of his mind: *Whether in the body or whether without the body, I do not know.*[7]

6. For one may not immediately nor suddenly draw near to this perfection directly, nor to this fulfillment; but at the beginning the soul is illumined[8] in the mysteries which are beneath this <fullness>. This amazement of thoughts begins to show itself in the mind from when the mind begins to be illumined[9] and to grow in hidden realities. So this partial amazement grows in it, and it proceeds to that perfection of the mind of Paul which is called by the Interpreter, and by the solitary fathers, an "authentic revelation of God."[10]

7. Here is the summit of the revelations about God; before this, however, is the mystery. To these particular realities, the force of the mind draws near by virtue of the Spirit, in that from time to time grace dwells in it. Its way of life is strengthened by the Spirit and every time it attains a certain calm, it remains above the stirrings of joy. But because it is not possible to always remain in these realities, in that such a constant and uninterrupted gift is reserved for the future world,[11] one who is of God is never completely deprived of joy and fervor, but every time he enters that place, he is raised up from the realities of nature.

8. When one goes out from there and returns to the realities of nature – which are reflection, thoughts, work, prayer and the rest – he is in these realities and also in fervor and in joy. They are,

---

[7] 2 Cor. 12:2–3.

[8] Illumination of the soul (*nahhîrûtâ d-napšâ*) Is.I 485; *Keph*. III 13.

[9] Illumination of the mind (*nahhîrûtâ d-re*ʿ*yânâ*) Is.I 448; Is.II VI.2,4.

[10] Authentic revelation (*gelyânâ ḥattîttâ*): possibly attributable to Theodore of Mopsuestia.

[11] Cf. Heb. 2:5; 6:5.

indeed, the abodes which he passes through and in which he stays: in each one according to the measure of his way of life;[12] sometimes in the abodes of nature, other times in the abodes which are above nature. Thus he is free, by means of the Economy of the grace of the Spirit, from all which is of nature or of the will.

9. There are three places conceivable by the mind, according to the word of the fathers, which the intellect passes through in its transformation: nature; <what is> outside of nature, <what is> above nature.[13]

10. When, therefore, the <intellect> proceeds in the realities of nature, that is to say, in work and in excellent deeds, as I said above, it exists in joy and in fervor; also battles, gloom, temptations and the passions which assail, because all of these are part of nature. When, however, <the intellect> penetrates what is outside of nature, through negligence in a virtuous way of life and giving in to passions and sin, it remains in coldness and hopelessness. These, then, follow from negligence of good works and giving in to passions. And as the thoughts grow cold and <there is> hopelessness, there is neither fervor nor joy there.

11. When, however, the <intellect> penetrates what is above nature, by means of the excellence of those realities on which the soul rests, the mind is lifted from the passions and the battles, likewise from labor, by means of that sublime recollection in God which sees by wonder which is elevated above all stirrings. This

---

[12] Measure of his way of life (*mšuḥtâ d-dubbârê*): Is.I 19, 492; Is.II XX.5, XXI.17; Evag. *Gnostique,* 40 (Guillaumont).

[13] In his 3rd homily, Isaac comments at length on what is natural to the soul (an understanding of all created things), what is outside of its nature (passions / *ḥaššê*) and what is above its nature (an impulse from divine contemplation). Khalifé-Hachem sees a dependence in this of Isaac on John Sol. The text may be found in Hansbury, *Ascetical Life*, 43–61. For an analysis of the text, see Khalifé-Hachem, "L'âme et les passions." See also his "La prière pure." And see Hansbury, *On the Soul,* Introd.

takes place in freedom from all the things of this life and in limpidity of the intelligence,[14] which is more exalted than the world.

12. All of these realities are within the light of the mind.[15] The <intellect>, indeed, begins to arrive at this light of the mind from when it begins the conflict against the passions and has begun to subdue them. And as it subdues and silences them, so it abounds in the light of the mind and is enlightened about hidden realities. From that time, after the victory over the passions, the light of the mind begins; and as the passions are subdued, rest appears in the mind. From here, then, it abounds in the vision of hidden things, and continually draws near to the wonder of thoughts.

13. The order of joy, therefore, is yet a childish measure compared with these divine realities. How, indeed, is joy <only> near the order of perfection? Because even if it is great to rejoice in God – if one rejoices for a good cause and not for stupid thoughts – however the perfection of the mind is greater than everything <else>.

14. This <is something> one may learn even from the realities of nature: joy in the young is more vigorous, because for some small thing their temperament is fervent and at once they rejoice; but as easily they change back to what is opposite. As, however, youth advances to the measure of manhood, above all it takes on tranquility and modest stirrings. Thus also in the realities of the house of God: every time that one advances in the knowledge of God and perceives God in tranquility, his thoughts are gathered and he sees the greatness of God, as in amazement, in ineffable silence and in reverence.

15. Then modesty descends on him to the point that he does not even dare to raise his thought to <God>, nor observe the throne of His glory. As the revelation of the Prophet teaches us about the seraphim at the time of the Trisagion, how they covered their faces with their wings so as not to observe freely the brightness of the

---

[14] Limpidity of the intelligence (*šapyûtâ d-tarʿîtâ*): Is.I 526; *Keph.* II 38, IV 33.

[15] Light of the mind (*nuhrâ d-reʿyânâ*): Is.I 482; *Keph.* IV 57–58, 69.

glory of God.[16] So it is for those who have arrived at the knowledge which is the perception of what is in God, which looks on in amazement at something higher than human intelligence, as also the holy John the Solitary of Apamea says.

16. For he says: "The soul is reduced to silence when it is lifted up from the stirrings of the passions, has seen the hidden things and its knowledge has remained in the realities of the Spirit." He says again: "That which is unspeakable, it perceives when it dwells in silence."[17] The order of joy, then, is yet the measure of infancy, in comparison with the delight in which is the movement in the Spirit <which dwells> near God, through the knowledge of His nature. That is to say, this concerns His wisdom and the rest of the riches of His mysteries which from time to time appear suddenly in the mind, when speech ceases from the natural course of its stirrings, in the haven of rest, which is the knowledge of Him.

17. By knowledge I do not intend a rational motion or what is of the cognitive part, but that perception which assuages the rational power with a certain pleasure of wonder and it brings to the sweetness of stillness, <away> from the course of all thought. And by this mystery, we are prepared to be in the kingdom of heaven, if our way of life is worthy. This is the taste of the future perfection mystically foretold in this life, and also in a mystic way about the joy which is the taste of the *pledge* of the Kingdom;[18] for those who are not <yet> capable to hear about the order of perfection, from the taste of this pledge they may understand about things which are above their measure.

18. Therefore, from when the mind begins to be enlightened, after it has settled and rested a little from the battle, the tumult of the passions, and the distraction of empty intentions which disturb its vision – this wonder of thoughts begins to appear upon it, by means of the intelligible light of the mind.

---

[16] Cf. Is. 6:2.

[17] Cf. John Sol.: Rignell, *Briefe*, 118–19

[18] Cf. 2 Cor. 1:21–22; 5:5; Eph. 1:13–14.

19. Many times a day, wonderful stirrings arise in it, and the mind is gathered within itself and stays tranquil and the person sits silent and astonished. This occurs sometimes at moments of prayer or sometimes at the office. How pleasant, then, is this silence and this calm! Who knows this, except those who have been overshadowed![19] But this gathering together of the mind, when the light of the mind begins, lasts an hour, then again the mind returns to its order, until other similar <occasions> arise in it.

20. There <is possibility> of delay in this, according to the measure of the mind. The mind, then does not reach these realities whenever it wishes, or as often as it asks, omitting the recitation of the psalms. For sometimes when one begins the office, because of the wonderful stirrings which appear in the mind, the tongue is stopped and reduced to silence; and the verse is interrupted and does not proceed, because the mind is reduced to stillness and has stopped.

21. At this time, the Psalms are no longer allowed because the attention of his mind is removed from the Psalms to those hidden things which arise from within. These are not usual thoughts but are wonderful and ineffable.[20] If one, then, of his own will ceases the office and prayer, while not <yet> perceiving these realities, he is filled with bad thoughts, and empty distraction dominates him.

22. This gathering together of the mind and the vision of the intellect is fruit of great separation from others, from prudence <concerning> thoughts and the fight against passions. And as I said, every time that this gathering together of the mind and the marvelous stirrings occurs, at the beginning there is a brief moment; then the mind returns to what is its own, until other stirrings happen again.

23. So when the solitary has arrived at this order, and this sweetness is mingled with his hidden work with God, then he is

---

[19] *Overshadowed*, see Is.III I.4.

[20] On interruptions in prayer, see Is.I 53, 490; Is.II IV.4–5, VI.3, XXXII.2, XXXV.1, 4–5; *Keph.* II 78, IV 25. See Is.III XVI. And see Beulay, *L'Enseignement*, 215–39.

uplifted a little from listlessness. His soul is not afflicted by the stillness or the long separation from others, nor by the afflictions or the infirmities of the body, as at one time. In that the delight of his mind and the consolation of his heart remove these adversities far from him. Until the solitary receives hidden consolation, the burden of listlessness in him does not diminish.

24. But when by this he is a little refreshed, then the difficult way of the solitary life becomes easy in his eyes. Now this which I have already said, I repeat, as a reminder especially for those who long for these realities: that these delights and apperceptions happen when grace rests upon the mind and it takes on the power of the Spirit.

25. This force, indeed, is of the Spirit[21] and is not a force <gained through> exercise or simple thoughts that a solitary possesses, by correcting the passions which are in him,[22] or abandoning the world and staying in stillness <away> from others.

---

[21] Variant of ms A: 'of the Spirit'. The ms of Teheran has "hidden."

[22] Elsewhere (Is.I 25) Isaac says: "All existing passions are given for the support of each of the natures to which they belong naturally and for whose growth they were given by God (for support and growth of body and soul)." This approach to the passions is transformative rather than a work of extirpation not unlike the approach in John Sol. where the Evagrian *apatheia* never occurs. In fact regarding this positive approach Beulay comments concerning John of Dalyatha who was also influenced by John Sol. Beulay notes that he had only found one usage of the term *lâ-ḥâšôšûtâ* for impassibility in all the writings of John of Dalyatha. For East Syrian writers, impassibility is not necessarily a complete absence of all sensation of the passions, rather they are altered in their root and redirected: not simply a denial of human beauty or intimacy but exchanging them for an even greater reality. See the recently edited text of John Sol.: "We have forsaken beauty on account of His beauty and pleasure for His pleasure and the sweetness of all our restful desires for His sweetness." See Maroki, "Quatre lettres inédites," 3.2. On the passions in John Sol. see Hansbury, *Soul*, Introd. For the comments on John of Dalyatha see Beulay, *L'Enseignement*, 285–86; *Lumière*, 21–3.

26. May the Lord grant you this, that it not only be from simple reading that you know these things, but that in the experience of your person you may know, feel and taste these things, by means of the grace of the holy Spirit which rests upon your intellect. Amen.

Chapter XVI

Of the same.

1. There is pure prayer and there is spiritual prayer.[1] The second is greater than the first as the light of the sun than its rays.

2. Pure prayer[2] is exalted beyond the distraction of thoughts and earthly reflection by means of the reflection on <celestial> good things and the remembrance of the future world.[3] <Pure prayer> has in it a petition for fine things and it is free from the confusion of transient things.

3. Spiritual prayer[4] is what is stirred in the intellect by the action of the Holy Spirit, with an impulse of perception which is superior to the understanding of creatures. There is no place in it for requests, not even for what is excellent, nor the desire of things promised, nor for the Kingdom of heaven. But by the action of the Holy Spirit, nature goes out from what is its own, outside of the will, and the soul remains only in that amazing divine glory, in the order of those holy hosts in ineffable praises: the hosts which Paul indicates further concerning them.[5]

---

[1] See Is.I 164–75 for a systematic discussion of prayer. The chapter is actually part of Isaac III as ch.14. Included are fathers on prayer: Theodore of Mopsuestia, Ps.Dionysius and Evagrius. See also Khalifé-Hachem, "Prière Pure."

[2] Pure prayer (*ṣlôtâ dakyûtâ*): Is.I 165, 167, 168, 175, 354, 447, 453. Is.II IV.5; VI.7; XV title 2, 3, 7; XXXII.4. *Keph.* I 63, 97; III 11, 13, 14, 41–43, 46; IV 35, 63, 65, 66. See also Aphrahat I, 4; IV 1, 4, 18,19. Evag. *Thoughts* 16; Mark the Monk, *Justified by Works* 162–63, p.182; Sahdona, II 8, 44.

[3] Cf. Heb. 3:5; 6:5.

[4] Spiritual prayer (*ṣlôtâ ruḥânâytâ*): Is.I 168, 170, 175 519; Evag. *On Prayer* 28 (Bamberger). See John Sol. *Soul* 90; Bettiolo, "Sulla preghiera," 2, p. 79.

[5] Cf. Eph. 1:21; Col. 1:16.

4. In the first prayer, then, there is labor and it is under the power of the will. Its stirrings are set because it is the soul which prays together with the body and the mind.

5. In the second, neither the soul nor the mind pray, not even the bodily senses. <The prayer> is not even under the power of the will. But while all is quiet, the Spirit accomplishes its own will, when even there is no prayer, only rather silence. This is the incorporeal liturgy which is performed by the saints, in the likeness of the heavenly realities, on earth as in heaven.[6]

6. When the soul sees what is in the mind, by means of the contemplation of what is in these <realities>, the eyes shed tears from the sweetness of their vision.[7] How many times thoughts assail the soul, but when it is in the Godhead <there is only> wonder and not one of these <thoughts>.

---

[6] See the *Book of Steps* XII on the three liturgies in heaven, on earth and in the heart. And see Is.III VIII.5; X.84.

[7] On tears at an advanced stage, see Is.I 49, 93, 125–26, 144–46. Tears and weeping occur frequently in Is.II, see the Indexes (*CSCO* 225). John Sol. dedicates three pages to a discussion of tears, *Soul* 16–18. Beulay looks at tears of repentance, and tears of joy and wonder, comparing John of Dalyatha and John Sol. and how tears come during the stage of Limpidity, see Beulay, *L'Enseignement*, 201–05. See *Book of Steps* XVIII, 18: "On the Tears of Prayer." Tears are mentioned throughout the *Ascetic Discourses* of Abba Isaiah. See also G. Panicker, "Prayer with Tears." And see Harb, "Doctrine Spirituelle," 251–54.

BIBLICAL REFERENCES

Genesis
1.16: VII, 47
2.13: VII, 12
2.21: III, 33
3: VII, 35
3.5: V, 9; XII. 22.
3.7-21: VI, 28
15.12: III, 33
28.12: IX, 12,13

Exodus
3.1-2: IX, 22
3.2: VII, 20
13.21-22: IX, 25
19.16: IX, 30
19.18: IX, 25
20.20-21: IX, 30
20.21: III, 23; VII. 5,7; IX, 25; XI, 31
20.24: VIII, 15
22.26: VI, 32
23.20-21: IX, 24
23.21: IX, 25
25.17: VII, 11
25.21-22: VII, 11
32.1-14: VI, 26
34.7: XI, 4
39.3: VII, 11
40.34: VIII, 7

Leviticus
16.2: VII, 11
16.13-15: VII, 11
19.2: III, 16
26.11-12: VIII, 7

Numbers
16.38-39: VII, 11

Deuteronomy
5.22: IX, 28
27.26: VI, 9, 10, 12
34.1-4: X, 52

2 Samuel
2.13: VI, 26

1 Kings
1.33: VII, 12
8.27: VIII, 7
8.39: IV, 18
21: VI, 27

2 Kings
19.34: I, 4; VI, 26
20.6: I, 4; VI, 26

1 Chronicles
28.2: VII, 4

2 Chronicles
5.13: VIII, 7
5.13-14: VIII, 8
5.14: VII, 4
7.1-2: VIII, 4, 8
24.14: I, 12

Judith
9.8 (Peshitta 9.11): VII, 4

2 Maccabees
9.18: XII, 36
12.43-45: XI, 6
14.35: VII, 4

Job
33.30: VI, 55

Psalms
9.5: VII, 18; X, 61
14.3: VI, 10

SOME KEY CONCEPTS

In order of appearance:

Chapter I

way of life after the resurrection: title
solitary: 1
world to come: 1
zeal: 2
Lord of all: 3
overshadow: 4
converse with God: 5
stillness: 5
limpidity: 6
Divine Economy: 7
wonder (*tehrâ*): 8
New World: 8
migration: 8
intellect (*hawnâ*): 9
eyes of the soul: 11
stirrings: 11
meditation: 14
converse with hope: 16
searching / investigation: 16

Chapter II

excellency of the mind: 1
passion: 2
mirror: 5
contemplation: 7

Chapter III

continual meditation on God: 1
providence of God: 4
divine Nature: 15
cloud of thick darkness: 23
converse of prayer: 32
stupor (*temhâ*): 33
true vision: 33

Chapter IV

authentic prayer: 1
fervent love: 6
silence of the spirit: 7
divine insights: 8
future world: 14
spiritual knowledge: 17
recollected mind: 20
knowledge of the Spirit: 21
revelation of insights: 21
impassibility of the soul: 28
labor of the body: 32
action of the Holy Spirit: 32

Chapter V

spiritual realities: 2
divinization: 4
divine love: 6
divine power: 9
other world: 17

Chapter VI

salvation by grace: 6
eschatology: 18
compassion for sinners: 24
continual remembrance: 45
divine intelligence: 46
inebriation: 56
tears: 58

Chapter VII

Shekinah: 4
cloud of thick darkness: 5
divine contemplation: 17
silence of the soul: 33
interior eye: 33
word of silence: 34
accidents (*gdêšê*): 44
spiritual light: 46

Chapter VIII

constant prayer: 1
activity of the Holy Spirit: 1
crucifixion of the intellect: 3
heart as altar: 5
divine revelation: 9
mediation of the angels: 11
divine vision: 11

Chapter IX

contemplation of the soul: 2
reading: 3, 5, 7, 9, 10, 11, 12, 15
vision of the mind: 5
future hope: 9
way of the spirit: 19
revelation of the intellect: 20

Chapter X

inner person: 7
harbor: 10
future world: 12
spiritual person: 24
spiritual world: 25

Chapter XI

renewal: 1
transformation: 2
renewal of the mind: 3
Messalians: 9
wonder at God: 25
hope of the future world: 31

Chapter XII

ascetical life as martyrdom: 18
Covenant: 44

Chapter XIII

joy in God: 1
place of stillness:2
stirring of joy: 3
illumination of the soul: 6
illumination of the mind: 6
authentic revelation: 6
measure of his way of life: 8
limpidity of the intelligence: 11
light of the mind: 15

Chapter XVI

pure prayer: 2
spiritual prayer: 3
tears: 6

ABBREVIATIONS

AMS	Acta Martyrum et Sanctorum.
ASR	Annali di Scienze Religiose (Milan).
ASE	Annali di Storia dell' Esegesi (Bologna).
CO	Cahiers d'Orientalisme.
ChrOR	Christian Orient (Kottayam).
CPE	Connaissance des Pères de l'Église (Montrouge).
CSCO	Corpus Scriptorum Christianorum Orientalium (Louvain).
DSpir	Dictionnaire de Spiritualité (Paris).
Harp	The Harp: a Review of Syriac and Oriental Studies (Kottayam).
JCSSS	Journal of the Canadian Society for Syriac Studies (Toronto).
JECS	Journal of Early Christian Studies (Baltimore).
JECS	Journal of Eastern Christian Studies (Nijmegen).
JSS	Journal of Semitic Studies (Oxford/Manchester).
JTS	Journal of Theological Studies (Oxford).
LM	Le Muséon (Louvain la Neuve).
MKS	Mémorial Mgr. Gabriel Khouri-Sarkis, ed. F. Graffin (Louvain,1969).
OCA	Orientalia Christiana Analecta (Rome).
OCP	Orientalia Christiana Periodica (Rome).
OS	L'Orient Syrien (Vernon).
PdO	Parole de l'Orient (Kaslik, Lebanon).
PG	Patrologia Graeca (Migne).
PO	Patrologia Orientalis (Turnhout).
POC	Proche-Orient Chrétien (Jerusalem).
SEERI	St Ephrem Ecumenical Research Institute (Kottayam).
SC	Sources Chrétiennes (Paris).
SympSyr	Symposium Syriacum (OCA).
StPatr	Studia Patristica (Kalamazoo/Leuven/Berlin/Oxford).
SVTQ	St. Vladimir's Theological Quarterly (New York).
TS	Theological Studies (Baltimore).
WS	Woodbrooke Studies (Cambridge).
ZAC	Zeitschrift für Antikes Christentum (De Gruyter).
ZNW	Zeitschrift für die neutestamentliche Wissenschaft und die Kunde des alten Christentum (Berlin).

BIBLIOGRAPHY OF WORKS CITED

Ancient Authors and Translations

Abba Isaiah

R. Draguet, *Les Cinqs recensions de l'Asceticon syriaque d'Abba Isaïe*, CSCO SS 120-23 (Louvain, 1968); cited by Discourse and section number.

Acts of the Martyrs

P. Bedjan (ed.), *Acta Martyrum et Sanctorum* I-VII, (Paris – Leipzig, 1890-97).

Acts of Thomas

W. Wright, *The Apocryphal Acts of the Apostles*, Vol.1 *Syriac Texts* (London, 1871); cited by page.

Ammonius

M. Kmosko, *Ammonii Eremitae Epistolae* (PO 10, 6; 1914).

Aphrahat

A. Lehto (tr.), *The Demonstrations of Aphrahat the Persian Sage* (Piscataway: Gorgias Press 2010).

K. Valavalonickal, *Aphrahat, Demonstrations*, I-II (Moran Etho 23-24; Kottayam, 2005).

Babai

Babai the Great, *Commentary on Evagrius' Centuries* in W. Frankenberg, *Evagrius Ponticus* (AKGWG, 1912), 8-471.

Basil

M. Forlin Patrucco (ed.), *Basilio di Cesarea. Le lettere I* (Turin, 1983).

Book of Steps

R. Kitchen and M.Parmentier, *The Book of Steps: The Syriac Liber Graduum* (Kalamazoo: Cistercian Publications, 2004).

M. Kmosko, *Liber Graduum*, *Patrologia Syriaca* 3 (1926).

Dadisho Qaṭraya

R. Draguet, *Commentaire du livre d'Abba Isaie (logoi I-XV) par Dadisho Qatraya (VII e s.)*, CSCO *SS* 144-5 (Louvain, 1972); cited by Discourse and section number.

Ephrem

E. Beck, CSCO *SS*: *Hymns on Faith* 73-4; *Hymns against Heresies* 76-7;

Hymns on Paradise 78-9; *Hymns on Nisibis* 92-3, 102-3; *Hymns on Unleavened Bread* 108-109.

S. Brock (tr.), *The Paradise Hymns* (New York: St. Vladimir's Seminary Press, 1990).

M. Hansbury (tr.), *The Hymns of St.Ephrem the Syrian* (Oxford: SLG Press, 2006).

L. Leloir (ed.), *Commentaire de l'Évangile Concordant, Texte syriaque*, Chester Beatty Monographs 8 (Dublin, 1963; french trans., SC 121 Paris 1966).

J.B. Morris (tr.), *Selected Works of St.Ephrem the Syrian* (Piscataway: Gorgias Press, 2008).

E. Mathews and J.P. Amar (tr.), *St. Ephrem the Syrian Selected Prose Works* (Washington: CUA Press, 1994): *The Homily of Our Lord.*

C. Mc Carthy, *St. Ephrem's Commentary on Tatian's Diatessaron* (*JSS* Supplement 2, 1993).

Evagrius

J-E. Bamberger (tr.), *Evagrius Ponticus The Pratikos Chapters on Prayer* ((Kalamazoo MI: Cistercian Publications, 1981).

A. M. Casiday (tr.) *Evagrius Ponticus*, The Early Church Fathers (London: Routledge, 2006): *The great letter* (Letter to Melania); *On Thoughts*; *Notes on Ecclesiastes.*

W. Frankenberg, *Evagrius Ponticus*, Berlin 1912.

P. Gehin (ed.), *Évagre le Pontique. Scholie aux Proverbes* SC 340 (Paris, 1987).

A. Guillaumont and C. Guillaumont, *Le Gnostique* SC 356, 1989.

A. Guillaumont (ed.), *Les six Centuries des "Kephalia Gnostica" d'Évagre le Pontique* (PO 28, I; 1958); cited by Century and number.

W. Harmless and R. Fitzgerald (tr.), "The Sapphire Light of the Mind: The Skemmata of Evagrius Ponticus," *TS* 62 (2001), 498-529.

J. Muyldermans (ed.), *Evagriana Syriaca* (Louvain, 1952). *Admonitio paraenetica*; *Paraenesis*; *La foi de Mar Évagre*; *Les justes et les parfaits.*

M. Parmentier, *Evagrius of Pontus* "Letter to Melania," Bijdragen 46 (1985) 2-38; repr. E. Ferguson, *Forms of Devotion* (New York: Garland, 1999).

G. Vitestam (ed.), *Seconde partie du traité qui passe sous le nom de "La grande lettre d'Évagre le Pontique a Melania l'ancienne" publiée et traduite d'après le manuscrit du British Museum Add. 17192*, Lund 1963.

Gregory of Cyprus

I. Hausherr (ed.), "Gregorii Monachi Cyprii De Theoria," OCA 110, 1937.

Hierotheos

F.S. Marsh, *The Book of the Holy Hierotheos* (London/Oxford, 1927).

Holy Women

S. Brock – S. Ashbrook Harvey (tr.), *Holy Women of the Syrian Orient* (Berkeley: Univ. of California Press, 1987).

Isho'dad of Merv

M. Gibson (ed.), *The Commentaries of Isho'dad of Merv on the New Testament*, The Acts & Epistles in Syriac and English Vol.IV (Cambridge: University Press, 1913).

Isaac the Syrian

P. Bedjan (ed.), *Mar Isaacus Ninivita, de Perfectione Religiosa* (Paris/Leipzig, 1909).

P. Bettiolo (tr.), *Isacco di Nineve. Discorsi Spirituali* (Magnano, IT: Edizioni Qiqajon, 1985; 2nd ed., 1990). (Kephalia gnostica/ *Keph.*)

S. Brock (ed.), *Isaac of Nineveh 'The Second Part' Chapters IV – XVI*, CSCO SS 224-25 (Louvain: 1995). (Part II)

S. Chialà (ed.), *Isacco di Ninive.Terza Collezione*, CSCO SS 246-47 (Louvain: 2011). (Part III)

M. Hansbury (tr.), *Isaac of Nineveh, On Ascetical Life* (New York: St.Vladimir's Seminary Press, 1989).

A. Louf, *Isaac le Syrien, Oeuvres Spirituelles – III* , Spiritualité Orientale 88 (Bellefontaine, 2009).

D. Miller (tr.) *The Ascetical Homilies of Saint Isaac the Syrian* (Boston, 1984).

A. J. Wensinck (tr.), *Mystic Treatises by Isaac of Nineveh* (Amsterdam, 1923; repr. Wiesbaden, 1969). (Part I)

Jacob of Serug

P. Bedjan (ed.), *Homiliae Selectae Mar-Jacobi Sarugensis* I-V

(Paris/Leipzig, 1905-10).

H. Connolly (tr.), "A Homily of Mar Jacob of Serugh on the Memorial of the Departed and on the Eucharistic Loaf," Bedjan, *Homiliae Selectae*, V 615-27; trans. in *The Downside Review* 29 NS 10 (2010), 260-70.

A. Golitzin (tr.), *On that Chariot that Ezekiel the Prophet Saw* (forthcoming, Gorgias Press).

"A Homily on the Ten Virgins Described in our Saviour's Gospel," Bedjan, *Homiliae Selectae*, II 375-401; trans. in *The True Vine* 4 (1992), 39-62.

John of Dalyatha

R. Beulay, o.c.d. (ed.) *La Collection des Lettres de Jean de Dalyatha* PO 180 (Belgium: Brepols, 1978).

B. Colless (ed.), *The Mysticism of John Saba*. Syriac text and English trans. of the *Discourses*, reprint of Ph.D. thesis submitted in 1969 to the University of Melbourne.

M.Hansbury (tr.), *The Letters of John of Dalyatha* (Piscataway: Gorgias Press, 2008).

N. Khayyat (ed.), *Jean de Dalyatha, Les Homélies I-XV* Sources Syriaques (Lebanon: CERO/UPA, 2007).

John the Solitary

P. Bettiolo, "Sulla Preghiera: Filosseno o Giovanni?," *LM* 94 (1981), 74-89.

S.P. Brock (ed.), "John the Solitary, On Prayer," *JTS* ns 30 (1979), 84-101.

_____(ed.), "Letter to Hesychius" in *The Syriac Fathers on Prayer and the Spiritual Life* (Kalamazoo: Cistercian Publications, 1987), 78-100.

M. Hansbury (tr.), *John the Solitary on the Soul* (Piscataway: Gorgias Press, 2013).

R. Lavenant (tr.), *Jean d'Apamée, Dialogues et Traités,* SC 311 (Paris: Éditions du Cerf, 1984).

S. Maroki (ed.), "Jean le Solitaire 'Quatre lettres inédites' Textes syriaques et traduction française," *PdO* 35 (2010), 477-506.

D. Miller (tr.), Mar John the Solitary, "An Epistle on Stillness" in *The Ascetical Homilies of Saint Isaac the Syrian* (Boston, 1984).

L. Rignell (ed.), *Briefe von Johannes dem Einsiedler* (Lund, 1941); cited by page.

_____ (ed.), *Drei Traktate von Johannes dem Einsiedler* (Lund, 1960); cited by page.

W. Strothmann (ed.), *Johannes von Apamea Sechs Gesprache mit Thomasios, der Briefwechsel zwischen Thomasios und Johannes und drei an Thomasios gerichtete Abhandlungen* Patristiche Texte und Studien 11 (Berlin: Walter de Gruyter, 1972).

Joseph Hazzaya

P. Harb, F.Graffin (ed.), *Joseph Hazzaya, Lettre sur les trois étapes de la vie monastique,* PO 45, 2 (Brepols, 1992).

Macarius

W. Strothmann, *Die syrische Uberlieferung der Schriften des Makarios,* Teil 1, Syrischer Text (GOFS 21, 1981).

Mark the Monk

T. Vivian and A. Casiday (tr.), *Counsels on the Spiritual Life* (Mark the Monk) 2 vols. (Crestwood, NY: St.Vladimir's Press, 2009): *On Baptism*; *Concerning Those Who Imagine That They Are Justified by Works*; *On the Spiritual Law.*

Narsai

J. Frishman (ed.), *The Ways and Means of the Divine Economy.* An Edition, Translation and Study of Six Biblical Homilies by Narsai (Diss. Leiden, 1992): V, *Homily on the Tabernacle.*

Nilus

P. Bettiolo (ed.), *Gli scritti siriaci di Nilo il Solitario* (Louvain-la-Neuve, 1983): *Discorso di ammonimento*; *Discorso sulle osservanze*; *Lettera per gli uomini virtuosi*; *Perle*; *Sulla virtû e sull'uscita da mondo*; *Sulla virtû e sulle passioni.*

Odes of Solomon

J.H. Charlesworth (tr.), *The Odes of Solomon* (California, 1977).

J.A. Emerton (tr.), *The Odes of Solomon* in *The Apocryphal Old Testament* ed. H.F.D. Sparks (Oxford, 1984).

Paradise of the Fathers

E.A.W. Budge (tr.), *Paradise of the Holy Fathers,* 2 vols. (London: 1907; repr. Blanco, Texas: New Sarov Press, 1994).

Philoxenus

E.A.W. Budge, *The Discourses of Philoxenus* I (London 1894); cited by page.

Pseudo-Dionysius

Colm Luibheid (tr.), *Pseudo-Dionysius, the Complete Works* (New York: Paulist Press, 1987).

Rabbinics

P. Alexander (tr.), *3 (Hebrew Apocalypse of) Enoch* in The Old Testament Pseudepigrapha ed. J.H. Charlesworth, 2 vols. (New York: Doubleday, 1983), vol.1.

W. Braude (tr.), *The Midrash on Psalms,* 2 vols. (New Haven: Yale Univ. Press, 1959).

S. Buber (ed.), *Midrasch Tehillim,* 2 vols. (Trier, 1892-93).

A. Cohen (ed.), *Minor Tractates of the Talmud,* 2 vols. (London: Soncino Press, 1965).

I. Epstein (ed.), *The Babylonian Talmud* (London: Soncino Press 1935-52)

Sahdona

A. de Halleux (ed.), *Martyrius (Sahdona). Oeurvres spirituelles*, CSCO SS 86-7, 90-91, 110-113 (Louvain, 1960-65); cited by text volume and page.

Sergius of Resh'aina

P. Sherwood, "Mimro de Serge de Reshayna sur la vie spirituelle," *OS* 5 (1960), 433-59; 6 (1961), 95-115, 121-56; cited by section number.

Shem'on d-Taybuteh

P. Bettiolo (tr.), *Simone di taibuteh. Violenza e Grazia. la coltura del cuore* (Rome, 1993).

A. Mingana, *Early Christian Mystics* (WS VII,1934) 282-320; cited by page and column.

Shubhalmaran

D. Lane (tr.), *Šubḥalmaran The Book of Gifts*, CSCO SS 236-37 (Louvain, 2004).

Synodicon Orientale

J.B. Chabot (ed.), *Synodicon orientale ou recueil des synodes nestoriens*

(Paris, 1902).

Theodore of Mopsuestia

R. Greer, *Theodore of Mopsuestia. Commentaries on the minor Epistles of Paul* (Atlanta, Ga: Society of Biblical Literature, 2010).

R. Hill (tr.), *Theodore of Mopsuestia: Commentary on the Twelve Prophets* (Washington: CUA Press, 2004).

F. McLeod (tr.) *Theodore of Mopsuestia,* The Early Church Fathers (London: Routledge, 2009).

J.-P. Migne, *Patrologia Graeca* (1856-66) Vol. 66.

A. Mingana, *Commentary of Theodore of Mopsuestia on the Nicene Creed WS* V (Cambridge, 1932); cited by page.

______ *Commentary of Theodore of Mopsuestia on the Lord's Prayer and on the Sacraments of Baptism and the Eucharist WS* VI (Cambridge, 1933); cited by page.

H.B. Swete, *Theodori Episcopi Mopsuesteni in Epistolas B. Pauli Commentarii* 2 vols. (Cambridge, 1880 and 1882).

R. Tonneau and R. Devreese, *Les Homélies Catéchétiques de Théodore de Mopsueste* (Rome, 1949).

J. Vadakkal (ed.), *The East Syrian Anaphora of Mar Theodore of Mopsuestia. Critical Edition, English Translation and Study,* (Kottayam: Vadavathoor, 1989).

J-M Vosté, *Theodori Mopsuesteni Commentarius in Evangelium Iohannis Apostoli,* CSCO SS 62-3 (Louvain, 1940); cited by page of text volume.

Modern Works

L. Abramowski, "The Theolgy of Theodore of Mopsuestia," *Formula and Context: Studies in Early Christian Thought* (Variorum, 1992), 1-36.

H. Alfeyev, *The Spiritual World of Isaac the Syrian* (Kalamazoo: Cistercian Publications, 2000).

I. de Andia, "Hesychia et contemplation chez Isaac le Syrien," in *Collectanea Cisterciensia* 53 (1991), 20-48.

I.A. Barsoum, *The Scattered Pearls* A History of Syriac Literature and Sciences, 2nd rev.ed. tr. Matti Moosa (Piscataway: Gorgias Press, 2003).

A. Becker, "The Dynamic Reception of Theodore of Mopsuestia in the Sixth Century," in *Greek Literature in Late Antiquity*, ed. S.F. Johnson (Aldershot, Hampshire: Ashgate, 2006), 29-47.

_____ *Fear of God and the Beginnng of Wisdom* (Philadelphia PA: University of Penna. Press, 2006).

P. Bettiolo, " 'Avec la charité comme but': Dieu et création dans la méditation d'Isaac de Ninive," in *Irénikon* 3 (1990), 323-45.

_____ "Esegesi e purezza di cuore. La testimonianza di Dadišo' Qatraya (VII sec.), nestoriano e solitario," ASE 3 (1986), 201-13.

_____"Lineamenti di Patrologia Siriaca" in *Complementi interdisciplinari di patrologia*, ed. A. Quacquarelli (Rome: Citta Nuova, 1989), 503-603.

_____ "Povertà e conoscenza. Appunti sulle Centurie gnostiche della tradizione evagriana in Siria," *PdO* XV (1989), 107-25.

_____ " ' Prigioneri dello Spirito'. Libertà creaturale ed *eschaton* in Isacco di Ninive e nelle sue fonti," *ASR* 4 (1999), 343-63.

R. Beulay, *L'Enseignement Spirituel de Jean de Dalyatha* (Paris: Beauchesne, 1990).

______. *La Lumière sans forme. Introduction a l'étude de la mystique chrétienne syro-orientale* (Belgium: Éditions de Chevetogne, 1987).

B. Bitton-Ashkelony, "The Limit of the Mind (ΝΟΥΣ): Pure prayer according to Evagrius Ponticus and Isaac of Nineveh ," *ZAC* 15 (2011), 291-321.

G. G. Blum, *Mysticism in the Syriac Tradition* (Kerala: SEERI, vol.7).

T. Bou Mansour, "La distinction des écrits des Isaac d'Antioche," in *JECS* 57 (2005), 1-46.

_____ *La pensée symbolique de saint Ephrem le Syrien* (Lebanon: Kaslik, 1988).

_____ *La Théologie de Jacques de Saroug*, 2 vols. (Lebanon: Kaslik, 1993).

B. Bradley, "Jean le Solitaire," *DSpir* VIII (1974), 764-772.

S.P. Brock, "Dieu Amour et Amour de Dieu chez Jacques de Serug," Actes du Colloque VIII, *Patrimoine Syriaque* (Lebanon: CERO, 2003), 175-182.

_____ "Discerning the Evagrian in the Writings of Isaac of

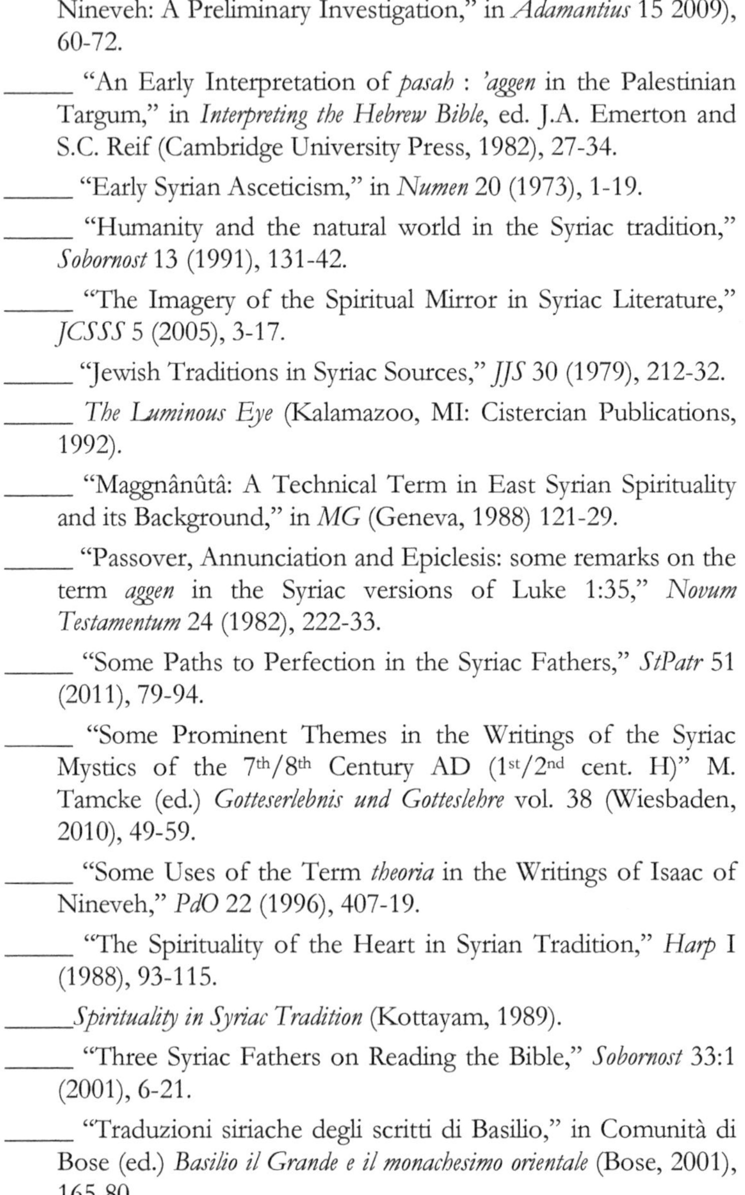

Nineveh: A Preliminary Investigation," in *Adamantius* 15 2009), 60-72.

_____ "An Early Interpretation of *pasah* : *'aggen* in the Palestinian Targum," in *Interpreting the Hebrew Bible*, ed. J.A. Emerton and S.C. Reif (Cambridge University Press, 1982), 27-34.

_____ "Early Syrian Asceticism," in *Numen* 20 (1973), 1-19.

_____ "Humanity and the natural world in the Syriac tradition," *Sobornost* 13 (1991), 131-42.

_____ "The Imagery of the Spiritual Mirror in Syriac Literature," *JCSSS* 5 (2005), 3-17.

_____ "Jewish Traditions in Syriac Sources," *JJS* 30 (1979), 212-32.

_____ *The Luminous Eye* (Kalamazoo, MI: Cistercian Publications, 1992).

_____ "Maggnânûtâ: A Technical Term in East Syrian Spirituality and its Background," in *MG* (Geneva, 1988) 121-29.

_____ "Passover, Annunciation and Epiclesis: some remarks on the term *aggen* in the Syriac versions of Luke 1:35," *Novum Testamentum* 24 (1982), 222-33.

_____ "Some Paths to Perfection in the Syriac Fathers," *StPatr* 51 (2011), 79-94.

_____ "Some Prominent Themes in the Writings of the Syriac Mystics of the 7th/8th Century AD (1st/2nd cent. H)" M. Tamcke (ed.) *Gotteserlebnis und Gotteslehre* vol. 38 (Wiesbaden, 2010), 49-59.

_____ "Some Uses of the Term *theoria* in the Writings of Isaac of Nineveh," *PdO* 22 (1996), 407-19.

_____ "The Spirituality of the Heart in Syrian Tradition," *Harp* I (1988), 93-115.

_____ *Spirituality in Syriac Tradition* (Kottayam, 1989).

_____ "Three Syriac Fathers on Reading the Bible," *Sobornost* 33:1 (2001), 6-21.

_____ "Traduzioni siriache degli scritti di Basilio," in Comunità di Bose (ed.) *Basilio il Grande e il monachesimo orientale* (Bose, 2001), 165-80.

_____ "World and Sacrament in the Writings of the Syrian Fathers," *Sobornost* 6:10 (1974) 685-96; repr. in *Studies in Syriac*

Spirituality (Kottayam,1988), 1-12.

T. Buchan, "Paradise as the Landscape of Salvation in Ephrem the Syrian," in *Partakers of the Divine Nature,* ed. M.J. Christensen and J.A.Wittung (Madison NJ: Fairleigh Dickenson University Press, 2007), 146-59.

G. Bunge, "Le 'lieu de la limpidité': a propos d'un apophthegme énigmatique: Budge II, 494," *Irénikon* 55 (1982), 7-18.

A. Casiday, "Universal Restoration in Evagrius Ponticus' 'Great Letter'," *StPatr* 47 (2010), 223-28.

D. Cerbelaud, "Aspects de la Shekinah chez les auteurs chretiens syriens," *LM* 123 (2010), 91-125.

S. Chialà, *Dall' ascesi eremitica alla misericordia infinita. Ricerche su Isacco di Ninive e la sua fortuna.* (Florence, 2002).

______ "Evagrio il Pontico negli scritti di Isacco di Ninive," *Adamantius* 15 (2009), 73-84.

______ "L'importance du corps dans la prière, selon l'enseignement d'Isaac de Ninive," *CDP* 119 (2010), 30-39.

_____ "Une nouvelle collection d'écrits d'Isaac de Ninive," *POC* 46 (2004), 290-304. (Part III)

_____ "L'umiltà nel pensiero di Isacco di Ninive: via di umanizzazione e di divinizzazione," in E. Vergani and S. Chialà (eds.), *Le ricchezze spirituali delle Chiese sire* (Milan, 2003), 105-20.

R.H. Connolly, "The Early Syriac Creed," *Zeitschrift fur die Neutestamentliche Wissenschaft und die Kunde des Urchristentums* 7 (1906), 202-23.

S. Daccache, "Figures Remarquables dans la Mystique Syriaque du VII-VIII Siècle," *POC* 60 (2010), 245-56.

J. Frishman, "Type and Reality in the Exegetical Homilies of Mar Narsai," *StPatr* 20 (1989), 169-75.

P. Gehin, "La dette d'Isaac de Ninive envers Evagre le Pontique," *CPE* 119 (2010), 40-52.

A. Golitzin, "The Image and Glory of God in Jacob of Serug's Homily On that Chariot that Ezekiel the Prophet Saw," *SVTQ* 43:3-4 (2003), 323-64.

______"The Place of the Presence of God: Aphrahat of Persia's

Portrait of the Holy Man," http://www.marquette.edu/maqom/aimilianus

S.Griffith, "Asceticism in the Church of Syria: the Hermeneutics of Early Syrian Monasticism," *Asceticism* ed. V. Wimbush & R. Valantasis (New York: Oxford University Press, 1995), 220-45.

P. Hagman, *The Asceticism of Isaac of Nineveh* (Oxford: University Press, 2010).

_____"St. Isaac of Nineveh and the Messalians," in M. Tamcke (ed.), *Mystik – Metapher – Bild. Beiträage des VII. Makarios-Symposiums* (Göttingen 2007), 55-66.

A. de Halleux, "La Christologie de Jean le Solitaire," *LM* 94 (1981), 5-36.

______"Le milieu historique de Jean le Solitaire," III *SympSyr*, ed. R.Lavenant OCA 221 (Rome, 1983), 299-305.

M. Hansbury, " 'Insight without Sight': Wonder as an Aspect of Revelation in the Discourses of Isaac the Syrian," *JCSSS* 8 (2008), 60-73.

______ "Love as an Exegetical Principle in Jacob of Serug," *Harp* XXVII (2012), 353-68.

P. Harb, "Doctrine spirituelle de Jean le Solitaire," *PdO* 2 (1971), 225-60.

I. Hausherr, *Études de spiritualité orientale,* OCA 183 (Rome, 1969).

_____"Par delà l'oraison pure, grace à une coquille: à propos d'un texte d'Évagre," *Revue d'Ascéetique et Mystique 13* (1932), 184-8.

_____" Un précurseur de la théorie scotiste sur la fin de l'incarnation," *Recherches de Sciences Religieuses* 22 (1932), 316-20.

H. Hunt, " 'Praying the Body': Isaac of Nineveh and John of Apamea on Anthropological Integrity," *Harp* XI-XII (1998-99), 153-58.

N. Kavvadas, "On the Relations between the Eschatological Doctrine of Isaac of Nineveh and Theodore of Mopsuestia," *StPatr* XLV (2010), 245-50.

______ "Theodore of Mopsuestia as a Source of Isaac of Nineveh's Pneumatology," *PdO* 35 (2010), 393-405.

E. Khalifé-Hachem, "L'Âme et les Passions des Hommes d'après un texte d'Isaac de Ninive," *PdO* 12 (1984), 201-18.

______ "La Prière Pure selon Isaac de Ninive," *MKS*, ed. F. Graffin (Louvain, 1969), 157-73.

J-M. Lera, "Theodore of Mopsuestia," *DSpir* XV (1991), 385-400.

A. Louf, "L'homme dans l'histoire du salut selon Isaac le Syrien," *CPE* 88 (2002), 49-54.

_____ "Pourquoi Dieu se manifesta, selon Isaac le Syrien," *CPE* 80 (2000), 37-56.

_____ "*Temha*-stupore e *tahra*-meraviglia negli scritti di Isacco il Siro," *La grande stagione della mistica Siro-orientale (VI-VIII secolo)*, ed. E. Vergani and S. Chialà (Milan: Biblioteca Ambrosiana, 2009), 93-119.

S. Maroki o.p., JEAN LE SOLITAIRE (D'APAMÉE) (5th Cent.): Quattre lettres inédites, Textes syriaques et traduction française," *PdO* 35 (2010), 477-506.

G. Nedungatt, "The Covenanters of the Early Syriac Speaking Church," *OCP* 39 (1973), 191-215; 419-44.

M. Nin, "La sintesi monastica di Giovanni il Solitario," *Le Chiese sire tra IV e VI secolo. Dibattito dottrinale e ricerca spirituale*, ed. E. Vergani and S. Chialo (Milan: Centro Ambrosiano, 2005), 95-117.

G. Panicker, "Prayer with Tears: A Great Feast of Repentance," *Harp* (1991), 111-33.

C. Pasquet, "Le Notre Père, une règle de vie pour le chrétien? L'enseignement de Théodore de Mopsueste," *CPE* 116 (2009), 50-61.

N. Russell, *The Doctrine of Deification in the Greek Patristic Tradition* (Oxford: University Press, 2004).

N. Sed, "La Shekhinta et ses amis 'araméens'," in *Mélanges A. Guillaumont. Contributions à l'étude des christianismes orientaux*, Geneva 1988 (CO 20), 233-42.

S. Seppälä, "In Speechless ecstasy: expression and interpretation of mystical experience in classical Syriac and Sufi literature," *Studia Orientalia* 98 (2007).

_____ "The Idea of Knowledge in East Syrian Mysticism," *Studia Orientale* 101 (2007), 265-77.

A. Shemunkasho, *Healing in the Theology of St. Ephrem* (Piscataway,

NJ: Gorgias Press, 2002).

C. Stewart, "Imageless Prayer in Evagrius Ponticus," *JECS* 9 (2001), 173-204.

E. Urbach, *The Sages* (Jerusalem: Magnes Press, 1979).

E. Vergani, "Isaia 6 nella letteratura siriaca. Due autori del V secolo: Balai e Giovanni il Solitario," *ASR* 7 (2002), 169-92.

S. Vethanath, "St. Ephrem's Understanding of Church as New Paradise and *Locus* of Divinization," *ChrOr* XXIX/1 (2008), 12-22.

TWO DISCOURSES OF THE *FIFTH PART* OF ISAAC THE SYRIAN'S WRITINGS

MARY T. HANSBURY

INTRODUCTION

Born in Beth Qaṭraye in the seventh century, Isaac the Syrian has left a large collection of writings:

First part

P. Bedjan (ed.) *The Ascetical Homilies of Mar Isaac of Nineveh* (Piscataway NJ: Gorgias Press, 2007).

A.J. Wensinck (tr.) *Mystic Treatises of Isaac of Nineveh* (Amsterdam, 1923; repr. Wiesbaden, 1969).

Second part

S. Brock (ed.) *Isaac of Nineveh 'The Second Part' Chapters IV – XVI*, CSCO SS 224–25 (Louvain: 1995).

P. Bettiolo (ed.) *Discorsi spirituali e altri opuscoli* (Magnano, IT: Edizioni Qiqajon, 1985, repr.1990.

Third part

S. Chialà (ed.) *Isacco di Ninive Terza Collezione*, CSCO SS 246–47 (Louvain: 2011).

And now there is the *Fifth Part*.[1] How the tradition attests to it has been amply demonstrated by Sabino Chialà.[2]

Available manuscripts of the *Fifth Part* have been found:

- Sharfet: Rahmani 80
- Baghdad: Dawra sir. 694
- Dawra sir. 938
- Vatican: sir. 592

Manuscripts where the *Fifth Part* is either cited or mentioned:

- Seert, Episcopio caldeo 109
- Mosul, Patriarcato caldeo 100
- Alqosh, Nostra Signora delle Sementi

And there are two lost manuscripts:

- Mosul, Patriarcato caldeo 97
- Diyarbakir, Episcopio caldeo 25

Until more of the *Fifth Part* is found, it cannot be ruled out that Isaac intended to amplify his thoughts on a final recapitulation. And that the "theological character" of what is included here: infinite mercy for creation and the design of universal salvation are of Isaac. The style is very different from Isaac I, II and III but I would tend to agree that it is by Isaac.

According to Chialà in one of his articles, Isaac is a "witness to God's mercy."[3] And mercy appears prominently in Isaac's schema of the mystic way: in repentance, in purity and in perfection.[4] This is not a linear development. Even at the state of perfection, one may return to repentance or to purity.

---

[1] For the critical edition, see Sabino Chialà, "Due discorsi ritrovati della *Quinta parte* di Isacco di Ninive?," *Orientalia Christiana Periodica* 79 (2013), 61–112.

[2] See also Chialà's article: "Two Discourses."

[3] "Witness to God's Mercy," unpublished article of Sabino Chialà (available online).

[4] See the discussion of this by Wensinck in his Mystic Treatises, xxiv.

> "And what is the sum of purity?"
>
> "A heart full of mercy unto the whole created nature..."
>
> "And what is a merciful heart?"
>
> "It is the heart's burning for the sake of the entire creation, for men, for birds, for animals, for demons and for every created thing; and at the recollection and the sight of them the eyes of the merciful man pour forth abundant tears. From the strong and vehement mercy that grips his heart and from his great compassion, his heart is humbled and he cannot bear to hear or to see any injury or slight sorrow in creation. For this reason he offers up prayers with tears continually even for irrational beasts, for the enemies of truth and for those who harm him, that they be protected and receive mercy. And in like manner he even prays for the family of reptiles, because of the great compassion that burns without measure in his heart in the likeness of God."[5]

At the conclusion of his article, Chialà suggests that it is out of Isaac's own experience of mercy, as described above, that he developed his theories of Apocatastasis and how they do not contain anything contrary to the Gospel. And that Isaac was informed and motivated more by his own insight and experience than by the controversy surrounding the issue.

"Apocatastasis is the teaching that everyone will, in the end, be saved: an ultimate reconciliation of good and evil; all creatures endowed with reason, angels and humans, will eventually come to a harmony in God's kingdom (Acts 3.21; 1 Timothy 2.4)."[6] It had appeared in Origen, Gregory of Nyssa and Maximus the Confessor.[7] But also in Theodore of Mopsuestia[8] and Diodorus whom Isaac quotes directly in Isaac II. XXXIX.

---

[5] Miller, *Ascetical Homilies*, Homily 71.

[6] See Apocatastasis in OrthodoxWiki, a definition used here for its precision and brevity.

[7] Chialà comments briefly on each of these authors and their possible influence on Isaac. See *Dall' Ascesi*, 269–76.

First from Isaac:

> I am of the opinion that He is going to manifest some wonderful outcome, a matter of immense and ineffable compassion on the part of the glorious Creator, with respect to the ordering of this difficult matter of (Gehenna's) torment: out of it the wealth of His love and power and wisdom will become known all the more – and so will the insistent might of the waves of His goodness. (Isaac II. XXXIX.6)[9]

Then from Theodore:

> In the world to come, those who have chosen here what is good, will receive the felicity of good things along with praise; whereas the wicked, who all their life have turned aside to evil deeds, once they have been set in order in their minds by punishments and fear of them, choose the good, having come to learn how much they have sinned, and that they have persevered in doing evil things and not good; by means of all of this they receive a knowledge of religion's excellent teaching, and are educated so as to hold on to it with a good will, (and so eventually) they are held worthy of the divine munificence. For (Christ) would never have said "Until you pay the last farthing" unless it had been possible for us to be freed from our sins once we had recompensed for them through punishments. Nor would He have said "He will be beaten with many stripes" if it were not (the case) that the punishments, measured out in correspondence to the sins, were finally going to have an end. (Isaac II XXXIX.8)[10]

---

[8] Kavvadas says that in his opinion: "…Isaac not only studied Theodore's tract (*Contra defensores peccati originalis*), but he was deeply influenced by this reading while developing his own eschatological doctrine." See Kavvadas, "Eschatological Doctrine," 248–49.

[9] For an analysis of the eschatological themes in Isaac II XXXIX–XI, see Alfyev, *Spiritual World*, 269–97.

[10] This passage is found in Solomon of Bosra (thirteenth century), *Book of the Bee*, ch. 60. According to Brock, Solomon quotes from Isaac. See Isaac II XXXIX.8, note 8.

Finally from Diodore of Tarsus:

> If the reward for labors is so great, how much greater is the time of immortality than the time of contests, that is, than this world; whereas the punishments are (far) less than the magnitude and number of sins. The resurrection from the dead should not be considered as belonging only to the good, but it also takes place for the wicked (as well). For God's goodness is greatly to be held in honor: it chastises sparingly. Isaac II XXXIX.11.[11]

I conclude with a ninth century witness to Isaac's tradition: Ibn as-Salt. He has written three letters which include extracts from the writings of Isaac.[12] What drew him to Isaac was apparently his teaching on mercy. To paraphrase:

> He preached insistently the love of mercy, which is the foundation of adoration, and humility which is the rampart of virtues… (13)

> Having recognized that the precepts of this Saint are in conformity with those of Jesus and his Apostles, I adhered to his doctrine. (14)

Of interest also is how Ibn as-Salt raises the question of Isaac's orthodoxy. Daniel Bar Tubanita, bishop of Tahal (seventh century), had written a work which is now lost: *Solutions to the questions on the fifth theological volume of Mar Isaac of Nineveh,* in which he refutes Isaac because of issues of Apocatastasis. Ibn as-Salt, in his third letter, asks of a visiting Church official if he prefers the teaching of Isaac or the refutation of Daniel. The response:

> Mar Isaac speaks the language of heaven and Daniel that of earth. Isaac's teaching is only suitable to advanced monks and

---

[11] From Diodore's Discourse V on Providence; this passage is also quoted by Solomon of Bosra, *Book of the Bee*, ch.60. Solomon may have quoted this from a source other than Isaac, see Isaac II XXXIX.13, note 1.

[12] See Sbath, *Traités religieux.*

to those living in solitude in their cells and who are dedicated to prayer. (75)

Since the work of Daniel is lost, it is helpful to read further comments of Ibn as-Salt regarding questions raised about Isaac's writings: that the actions of creatures do not cause a change in God; that he is merciful and that His immutable clemency is above punishment; that in the other world the mercy of God embraces all human beings.[13] The infinite mercy of God and Isaac's eschatology are outlined here.[14] This is what was so unacceptable to Daniel and even to a modern interpreter of Isaac.[15]

Actually now there is another witness available to the *Fifth Part* of Isaac: Shebadnaya, a fifteenth century priest from Northern Iraq. In his "Poem on God's Government from 'In the beginning' until Eternity," he has ten citations concerning ideas and opinions of Isaac's *Fifth Part.* Of particular interest: "Thus wrote Mar Isaac in that *Fifth Part* of his: The suffering which sinners undergo from the torments in Gehenna has a likeness to the suffering of the Son, that which he endures for our sins." This may suggest a redemptive quality, in addition to the punitive aspect of suffering in Gehenna, towards a final redemption.[16]

As startling as this may seem, it is best understood in the context of God's love for mankind. One of the most moving statements about this may be found in Isaac's Discourses (Bettiolo):

---

[13] See the six questions and answers in the 1st letter (16–20) in Sbath, 77–78. See also Chialà, *Dall'Ascesi*, 62–63.

[14] In these questions and answers, Chialà notes the theology of Theodore of Mopsuestia concerning God's immutability: that human sin cannot change God's project, see Dall' Ascesi, 63. For other comments of Chialà concerning Theodore's influence on Isaac, see his *Dall'Ascesi*, 92–101.

[15] Bedjan finds God's mercy and compassion for sinners and demons, as expressed in Isaac, to be unacceptable. See Bedjan, *Ascetical Homilies*, xi–xiii.

[16] For the quote and the context, see T. Carlson, "The Future of the Past," 185.

> The aim of the death of Our Lord was not to redeem us from our sins, nor for any other reason, but exclusively that the world might become aware of the love of God for creation. If all this had been aimed solely at the remission of sins, it would have been enough to redeem us in some other way.[17]

CONCLUSION

As to the actual translation, I am grateful to S. Chialà for the numbered paragraph divisions which he has devised that are not in the manuscripts. Also given the difficulties in translation, particularly of section II, I have often needed to consult with his translation. In addition to being difficult, the *Fifth Part* has a very different style which anyone who has read Isaac's other works will notice immediately. Basically, section I is a collection of Biblical passages in support of what will be affirmed in section II. Most of the quotations are from the Old Testament with few explanations given.[18] But the author concludes section I with an insightful paragraph:

> In fact, He is not the one who puts in motion actions of correction or of punishment, nor does He work in those who do the actions but He consents, only allowing that they occur where He wills that they occur. He does not even make good and bad actions happen by means of those with inclinations such as these. Nor does He set in motion the manner of the chastising and distressing action. (34)[19]

Chialà sums up the very difficult section II: "…nothing of what happens can be said to be outside God's plan, outside his economy (*mdabbrânûtâ*). God, then, takes care of creation, as the author

---

[17] Discourse 4.78, translation as found in Ramelli, *Apokatastasis*, 761; see also the context, 758–66.

[18] As noted by Chialà, Isaac uses predominately the Peshitta; citations from it are italicized throughout the translation.

[19] Perhaps realizing the possible difficulty of this passage, elsewhere Isaac assures that he speaks "according to what I have understood from both the divine vision of the Scriptures and from true mouths, and a little from experience itself…" See Miller, *Ascetical Homilies*, Homily 14.

hastens to affirm at the end of the second discourse."[20] And since Apocatastasis is never mentioned explicitly in this translation, Chialà attempts to link it to what is said in these two sections how: "...God will find a way to reintegrate every fragment of creation into his design of salvation, hence the sufferings of sinners in hell do not have a definitive character, but only cathartic."[21] Chialà thus sees a tie between the statement that "nothing happens without God willing it and the idea of a final recapitulation in which God finds a way to bring back to himself every fragment of creation, without violating its liberty..."[22] And though this may not seem obvious, Chialâ reminds that sections I and II of the *Fifth Part* are only part of a larger document that when found may contain more explicit statements to substantiate this.

BIBLIOGRAPHY

H. Alfeyev, *The Spiritual World of Isaac the Syrian* (Kalamazoo MI: Cistercian Publications, 2000).

W. Braude (tr.), *The Midrash on Psalms*, 2 vols. (New Haven: Yale Univ. Press, 1959).

T. Carlson, "The Future of the Past: The Reception of Syriac Qaṭraye Authors in Late Medieval Iraq," in Kozah, M., Abu-Husayn, A., Al-Murikhi, S. S., Al Thani, H., (eds.), *The Syriac Writers of Qatar in the Seventh Century* (Piscataway: Gorgias Press, 2014), 169–193.

S. Chialà, *Dall'ascesi eremitica alla misericordia infinita. Ricerche su Isacco di Ninive e la sua fortuna* (Florence, 2002).

——— "Two Discourses of the "Fifth Part" of Isaac the Syrian's Writngs: Prolegomena for Apokatastasis?," in Kozah, M., Abu-Husayn, A., Al-Murikhi, S. S., Al Thani, H., (eds.), *The Syriac Writers of Qatar in the Seventh Century* (Piscataway: Gorgias Press, 2014), 123–131.

——— "Witness to God's Mercy: Conference of Br. Sabino Chialà on Isaac of Nineveh," delivered at a colloquium in Ghent in 2006; posted on the internet 14 June 2008.

---

[20] Chialà, "Two Discourses," 7.

[21] Ibid., 7.

[22] Ibid., 8.

R.H. Connolly, "The Early Syriac Creed," *Zetschrift fur die Neutestamentliche Wissenschaft und die Kunde des Urchristentums* 7 (1906), 202– 23.
M. Hansbury (tr.), *Isaac the Syrian, Third Part* (in this Anthology).
N. Kavvadas, "On the Relations between the Escahatological Doctrine of Isaac of Nineveh and Theodore of Mopsuetia," *Studia Patristica* 45 (2010), 245–50.
R. Lavenant (tr.), *Jean d'Apamée, Dialogues et Traités*, Sources Chrétiennes 311 (Paris: Éditions du Cerf, 1984)
A. Louf (tr.), *Isaac le Syrien Oeuvres Spirituelles – III* (Éditions de Bellefontaine, 2009).
D. Miller (tr.), *The Ascetical Homilies of Saint Isaac the Syrian* (Boston: Holy Transfiguration Monastery, 1984; repr. 2011).
I. Ramelli, *The Christian doctrine of Apokatastasis*: A Critical Assessment from the New Testament to Eriugena (Leiden; Boston: Brill, 2013).
P. Sbath (ed.), *Traités religieux philosophiques et moraux, extraits des oeurvres d'Isaac de Ninive (VII siècle) par Ibn as-Salt (IX siècle)*, (Cairo, 1934).
Solomon of Akhlat, *The Book of the Bee*, ed. by E.A.W. Budge (Piscataway: Gorgias Press, 2006).

TRANSLATION

From the *Fifth Part* of Mar Isaac, bishop of Nineveh

I

Examples of confirmation from the Scriptures, against those who say that the world proceeds by chance, without a guide.

1. That a country or a city, or human beings individually even the whole universe, be guarded by God or with His gesture be handed over to misfortune, we learn this from divine Scriptures.

2. We learn this first of all from what is said: *On your walls, O Jerusalem, I have placed watchmen by night and by day, continuously.*[23] And this, Zion has said: "*The Lord has forsaken me and the Lord has forgotten*

[23] Isaiah 62.6.

me." <Can> a woman forget her newborn babe and not have compassion on the child of her womb? Even if these forget I will not forget you. Behold, on the palms of my hands I have graven you and your walls are continually before me.[24]

3. And again <God says>: *I will deliver this city into the hand of the king of Babylonia.*[25] And: *I will deliver you into the hand of those whom you have feared.*[26] And this: *Behold I make you a stranger, you and all your friends. They will fall by the sword of their enemies <while you look on>. I will deliver all of Judah into the hand of the king of Babylonia and he will kill them with the sword. I will deliver all of the fortresses of this city and all the fruit of its labor and all its magnificence; and all the treasures of the king of Judah I will deliver into the hand of their enemies; and they will lead them away captive and they will plunder them.*[27]

4. You see that it is God who delivers humans, each one into the hands of his neighbor, with their riches and their land; and then one is subject to his neighbor. Are you still in doubt? <God> says: *Raise the javelin which is in your hand against Ai, because I have delivered <the city> into your hands.* [28] And to Baruch, <Jeremiah> said: *I make evil to come upon all flesh, says the Lord, but for you I will preserve your life in all the places where you will go.*[29]

5. And it is said: *Saul was seeking David everyday but God did not give him into his hands.* And it is said: *David inquired of God and said: "Shall I go up against the Philistines? Will you give them into my hands?"*[30] And the Lord said to him: *Go up because I will give all of them into your hands.*[31] And in Zechariah <God> said: *Behold I will deliver all men, each into*

---

[24] Ibid., 49.14–16.

[25] Jeremiah 34.2.

[26] Ezekiel 23.28; Jeremiah 22.25.

[27] Jeremiah 20.4–5.

[28] Joshua 8.18.

[29] Jeremiah 45.5.

[30] 1 Samuel 23.14.

[31] 2 Samuel 5.19

the hands of his neighbor and into the hands of the king. They will divide the land and I will not rescue it from their hands.[32]

6. And <God said>: *It is I who incite men, each one against his neighbor.*[33] And again <God said>: *Do not fear him (Og the king of Basan) because I have given him into your hands, he and all his people, and all of his land.*[34] And again it says: *Do not harass the Moabites or contend with them in battle because I will not give you any of their land as a possession.*[35] And again: *See that I have delivered into your hands Sihon king of Heshbon, the Amorite, and his land: begin his destruction and contend with him in battle.*[36]

7. And again David said to Abiathar the priest: *Remain with me and do not fear because the one who seeks my life also seeks your life <but> with me there is a guard.*[37] He did not say "guards" but "guard", *that is to say an angel.* And, *Let <this> Benjamite curse, because it is the Lord himself who said to him: "Curse David!"*[38]

8. This is the passage where God says, *My Spirit remains in your midst: Do not fear!*[39] And He says: *Behold I will put a spirit upon him and he will hear a rumor and return to his land; and I will make him fall by the sword in his land.*[40] And concerning Egypt it is said: *The Lord has mingled within her an erring spirit and has made Egypt err in all their deeds.*[41] And <the Lord said to Joshua>: *See that I have delivered Jericho into your hands, and his king and all his army.*[42] And <the passage>: *The Lord thwarted them before the sons of Israel and they struck them with a great blow.*[43]

---

[32] Cf. Zechariah 11.6.
[33] Isaiah 19.2.
[34] Deuteronomy 3.3.
[35] Ibid., 2.9.
[36] Ibid., 2.24; 31.
[37] 1 Samuel 22.23.
[38] 2 Samuel 16.10–11.
[39] Haggai 2.5.
[40] 2 Kings 19.7.
[41] Isaiah 19.14.
[42] Joshua 6.2.
[43] Ibid., 10.10.

9. And <this passage>: *Do not fear them because tomorrow at this time I will cause that all of them be slain before the sons of Israel.*[44] And to Ahab, a prophet said: "*Thus says the Lord, Have you seen all this army? I will deliver it into your hands.*"[45] He would not have said that he would hand them over if they were not guarded by His providence.[46] Nor would He have said "I hand over" and "I do not hand over," if it were possible that someone rule over his neighbor unless God hand him over.

10. And according to what is said in the book of Numbers, *The sons of Israel made a vow to the Lord and said: If indeed you will give this people into our hands, we will utterly destroy their cities. The Lord listened to the voice of Israel and gave the Canaanites into their hands and they destroyed them.*[47] Now is it because they were preserved by God that it is said that the handing over was His work? Or is this referred to in Scripture with a word of irony?

11. And <this passage>: *The anger of the Lord was kindled against Israel. He delivered them into the hand of spoilers and they plundered them. And he delivered them into the hand of their enemies round about them and they were no longer able to rise up before their enemies. Wherever they went the hand of the Lord was against them for evil.*[48] And <where Debra> says: *The glory will not be yours, Barak, in the way you are going, for the Lord will deliver Sisera into the hand of a woman.*[49]

12. And < where the Lord said to Gideon>: *I will be with you and you will lay waste the Midianites as a man.*[50] And where he said: *This people is too numerous that I deliver the Midianites into your hands.*[51] And <the passage>: *The Lord set the sword of each one against his neighbor in*

---

[44] Ibid., 11.6

[45] 1 Kings 20.13.

[46] Providence (*bṭîlûtâ*).

[47] Numbers 21.2–3.

[48] Numbers 21.2–3.

[49] Judges 4.9.

[50] Ibid., 6.16.

[51] Ibid., Judges 7.2.

all the encampment. And <again>: *All slept because a deep sleep from the Lord fell on them, on those of the house of Saul.*[52]

13. And <it says>: *The Lord commanded to defeat the good counsel of Ahithophel, <so as> to bring evil upon Absalom.*[53] And of Rehoboam is said: *He did not listen to the counsel of the people because the stirring of strife was from the Lord.*[54] And the <passage>: *The Lord has put a spirit of lies in the mouth of all these your prophets and the Lord has spoken evil in your regard.*[55] And <the passage>: *Do not fear them, because those who are with us are more numerous than those who are with them.*[56]

14. And <the passage where God says>: *Behold I have created the smith who blows air on the fire and produces an instrument for his work; and I have created the ravager to destroy. No weapon that is fashioned against you shall be successful; and every tongue that shall rise against you in judgment, you shall vanquish.*[57] And again: *Behold, I am bringing upon you a nation from afar, says the Lord. A nation whose language you do not know nor can you understand what they say. They shall eat up your harvest and your bread; they shall eat up your sons and your daughters; they shall eat up your flocks and your herds; they shall eat up your vines and your fig trees; your fortified cities which you rely on, they shall destroy with the sword.*[58]

15. And to show again that situations, of both good and of evil are from Him, in Isaiah is found also this other <passage>, *The Lord has sworn by his right hand and his mighty arm: I will no longer give your inhabitants*[59] *in food to your enemies, and foreigners shall not drink the wine for which you have labored. But those who have gathered it shall eat it and*

---

[52] 1 Samuel 26.12.

[53] 2 Samuel 17.14.

[54] 1 Kings 12.15.

[55] Ibid., 22.23.

[56] 2 Kings 6.16.

[57] Isaiah 54.16–17.

[58] Jeremiah 5.15–17.

[59] While the four manuscripts have this reading, both the Peshitta and the Hebrew texts say "your grain."

praise the Lord, and those who have gathered it will drink it in the courts of my sanctuary.[60]

16. And again in Jeremiah it says: *Behold I will send and take the tribes of the kingdoms of the north, says the Lord, and Nebuchadnezzar my servant, and I will bring them against this land and its inhabitants to destroy them.*[61] And again it says: *I will give them into the hand of the army of the king of Babylon who are rising against them.*[62] *And again: Behold, I will command, says the Lord, and cause them to return to this city, they shall fight against it and take it and burn it with fire*, etc.[63]

17. And hear what is more wonderful and grievous! To explain that it is not possible that all these things happen without His approval and without the working of His sign, <God> says: *I will do with you something which I have never done, nor will I do again anything similar: in your midst fathers shall eat their sons and sons shall eat their fathers; and I will scatter to all the winds whoever remains in your midst.*[64]

18. And again: *Everyone shall eat the flesh of his neighbor in the siege and in the distress which I will bring on them.*[65] And again, wanting to show – when it says that the evils will end and deliverance will come – that it is He who provokes the distress and by Him that it ceases, *Thus says the Lord, your Lord: Behold, I have taken from your hands the cup of terror, and no more shall you drink from the cup of wrath. I will put it in the hand of those who afflict you.*[66]

19. And again <God says>: *I will judge those who judge you and save your children; I will make your oppressors eat their own flesh and become drunk on their blood as with wine; and all flesh will know that I am the Lord.*[67] You see, then, that all these kinds of good and evil come to us from the Lord.

---

[60] Isaiah 62.8–9.
[61] Jeremiah 25.9.
[62] Ibid., 34.21.
[63] Ibid., 34.22.
[64] Ezekiel 5.9–10.
[65] Jeremiah 19.9.
[66] Isaiah 51.22–23.
[67] Ibid., 49.25–26.

20. And where it says: *From my hands this will happen to you so that you will lie down in distress.*[68] And again: *I will send famine upon you and cruel beasts and they will destroy you. Pestilence and blood will pass in your midst, and I will bring the sword upon you.*[69] And it says: *Because you are afraid of the sword, I will bring the sword upon you, says the Lord of lords, and I will give you into the hands of foreigners.*[70] And the verse: *I will give their women to others and their property as plunder.*[71] And the verse: *Whoever is found will be pierced and whoever is taken will fall by the sword; and their children will be destroyed before their eyes, their houses will be plundered and their women dishonored.*[72] And: *Will there be an evil in the city which the Lord has not done?*[73]

21. And this <passage> in which Amos <said> to Amasia, *Thus says the Lord: Your wife shall be a harlot in your city, your sons and your daughters will fall by the sword, your land will be parceled out by a measuring-line, you will die in a polluted land and Israel will be deported in exile from its land." Thus the Lord has shown me.*[74] And the <passage> of Zechariah: *Behold the day of the Lord is coming and in your midst your spoil will be divided. I will gather all the nations to Jerusalem for the battle, the city shall be taken, the houses will be plundered and the women will be abused.*[75]

22. And again it says: *Women in Zion bore disgrace and virgins in the towns of Judea.*[76] And it says: *Who has ever spoken and this happened unless the Lord had commanded it? From the mouth of the Most High proceed good things and evil things.*[77] And the <passage where God says>: *I will lead your women before your eyes and give <them> to your neighbor, and he will lie*

---

[68] Ibid., 50.11.

[69] Ezekiel 5.17.

[70] Ezekiel 11.8–9.

[71] Jeremiah 8.10.

[72] Isaiah 13.15–16.

[73] Amos 3.6.

[74] Amos 7.17–8.1.

[75] Zechariah 14.1–2.

[76] Lamentation 5.11.

[77] Ibid., 3.37–38.

with them.[78] And it says: *I gave you the daughters of your masters and these women of your master, I have made lie down at your bosom.*[79]

23. And this: *I brought plunderers against the mother and against her children at midday, and I have made confusion and fear to fall upon them suddenly.*[80] And to Ebed-Melech the Ethiopian, <God by means of Jeremiah > said: *I send words for evil and not for good upon this city; in that day they will come to pass before you. But in that day I will save you, says the Lord, and you will not be delivered into the hands of those you fear. I will save you and you will not fall by the sword, because you trusted in me, says the Lord.*[81]

24. And again: *Behold I send ferocious serpents against you, which <cannot be charmed>, and they will bite you, says the Lord.*[82] And the <passage>: *From before me messengers will go out in haste to destroy Ethiopia which dwells in tranquility; and in their midst there will be confusion <as> in the day of Egypt; and behold it has come.*[83] And the <passage> which says: *I, the Lord, delivered the sons of Israel into captivity among the nations; and I have gathered them back into their land and have not left anyone there.*[84]

25. And this: *He will command his angels concerning you to guard you in all your ways; they will carry you in their arms that your foot not stumble.*[85] And this <passage>: *If he falls he will not be hurt, because the Lord holds him by the hand.*[86] And the <passage>: *He caused them to be pitied by all who carried them captive.*[87] And again: *And he gave them into the hand of the Gentiles and their adversaries had dominion over them.*[88] And: *In his anger he brought evil to come <upon them>.*[89]

---

[78] 2 Samuel 12.11.
[79] Ibid., 12.8.
[80] Jeremiah 15.8.
[81] Ibid., 39.16–18.
[82] Ibid., 8.17.
[83] Ezekiel 30.9.
[84] Ibid., 39.28.
[85] Psalm 91.11–12.
[86] Ibid., 37.24.
[87] Psalm 106.46.
[88] Ibid., 106.41.
[89] Cf. Jeremiah 49.37.

26. And <Jesus said>: *Two sparrows are sold for a penny yet not one of them will fall to the ground without your Father's <will>.*[90] And <also in the Gospel> it says: Herod *sent to cut off the head of John in prison.*[91] And the angel made Peter come out by the iron gates, while he was tied with two chains and slept between two soldiers; and <the text> says: *The chains fell from his hands and the iron door opened by itself.*[92]

27. And: *Even the hairs of your head are numbered* for him.[93] And it is said: Herod *killed James the brother of John with a sword.*[94] And, *The Lord said to Paul in a vision: "Do not fear, but speak and do not be silent, because I am with you and no one can hurt you."*[95]

28. And <Jesus said to Pilate>: *You would have no power over me if it had not been given to you from above.*[96] And it says: *Truly in this city were gathered together against your holy Son, Jesus whom you have anointed, Herod and Pilate, together with the Gentiles and the peoples of Israel, to do whatever your hand and your will had foreordained would happen.*[97] And <the Psalmist> says: *The Lord brings the counsel*[98] *of the Gentiles to nought and the Lord causes the projects of the peoples to cease; but the intelligence*[99] *of the Lord subsists forever and the intention of his heart for generations.*[100]

29. Complete liberty, in humans, consists and may be known in these two things: in the counsel which <comes> from the mouth, that is to say a sound of a voice[101] expressing the hidden will in the

---

[90] Matthew 10.29.

[91] Ibid., 14.10.

[92] Acts 12.6–10.

[93] Luke 12.7.

[94] Acts 12.2.

[95] Ibid., 18.9–10.

[96] John 19.11.

[97] Acts 4.27–28.

[98] Counsel (*malkâ*).

[99] Intelligence (*tarʿîteh*).

[100] Psalm 33.10–11.

[101] Sound of a voice: *ba(r)t qâlâ* (*bat kol*), "daughter of a voice," sound or resonance as found in Syriac and in some Midrash and Talmud

soul; and in the purpose of the intelligence which is the foundation of the faculty of speech and the essential element of liberty. Now, <Scripture> says that *the Lord brings to nought* the authority of both of these realities among people, because *the intelligence of the Lord stands <forever>*.[102] How is it then, some say that God does not hinder the deeds of rational beings, while many times bringing to nought their power, so as to establish the <works> of his providence.[103]

30. And again where Solomon says: *Many are the thoughts in one's heart but it is the intelligence of* the *Lord that confirms them.*[104] And again another sage says: *The Lord hardened the heart of Pharaoh, that his works be seen on earth.*[105] And in Isaiah: *Shall perhaps the axe vaunt itself over the one who hews with it? Or shall the saw exalt itself over the one who saws with it? Or shall a rod prevail over him who lifts it up?*[106]

31. Now there is an enlightened word, which shows how rational beings are placed before the will of God as instruments in the hand of the Artificer for the acts of the Economy of God,[107] that He accomplishes by means of them. As it were, it is the same God who with His hands holds the hand of the one who acts, at the time of correction which is in His hands; and He lifts up or brings down that <hand>, according to His will, because it is not possible that <rational beings> do anything outside of what is granted by His will. And thus, it is possible that one exercise some power upon oneself or one's possessions, or upon all which is one's own; each one upon his neighbor and upon his companion, according to how much power is given to him.

---

passages; an echo of a heavenly voice which revealed God's will, choice or judgment to mankind.

[102] Psalm 33.10–11.

[103] Providence (*mparnsânûtâ*).

[104] Proverbs 19.21.

[105] Exodus 9.12 *passim*.

[106] Isaiah 10.15.

[107] Economy of God (*mdabbrânûtâ d-alâhâ*).

32. And of Job it is said, *The Lord said to Satan: "Behold, I deliver <him> into your hands." Satan went out from the presence of the Lord and struck Job with a malignant ulcer, from the sole of his foot to his brain.*[108] And where it says: *The Lord gave and the Lord has taken; may the name of the Lord be blessed.*[109] And: *We have received good things of God, shall we not receive his evil things?*[110] It says both of these are of a just God.

33. And <God says>: *I cause to die and I make alive; I wound and I heal; and there is nothing that escapes from my hands.*[111] Understand this: *There is nothing that escapes my hands!* Which means there is nothing in all the entire world, mainly death, life, sickness and healing. And the demons said to our Lord: *If you grant it, we will enter these swine. And <Jesus> said to them: Go!*[112] And there are many other examples similar to these.

34. At this point, do you confess that in all of this there is an action of care or of betrayal by God, that without His permission nothing happens and there is nothing that may distress or satisfy on account of man or by man; or do you still believe that the happenings and stirrings of creation are by chance; <either way> it would not be right to let others say that God wills or lets go. In fact, He is not the one who puts in motion actions of correction or of punishment, nor does He work in those who do the actions but He consents, only allowing that they occur where He wills that they occur. He does not even make good and bad actions happen by means of those with inclinations or thoughts such as these. Nor does He set in motion the manner of the chastising and distressing action.

But how little knowledge there is of this and <far> from the truth![113]

---

[108] Job 2.6–7.

[109] Ibid., 1.21.

[110] Ibid., 2.10.

[111] Deuteronomy 32.39.

[112] Matthew 8.31–32.

[113] This seems to reflect a humble awareness on the part of the author concerning how precarious these assertions may be. Chialà notes a

II

Other examples with another intention

1. We will show now that the divine Scriptures do not even lack examples which clearly indicate how the impulse of the will, and the thoughts relative to the things which then happen – under the forms of a corrective action or favorable events – and also the total number of such actions, occur <on their own>.[114] But since, according to the divine dispensation and by divine Economy, <on their own> the thought and the will develop within <specific> beings, then what happens – which brings rest, or adversity, or affliction – happens by means of them.

2. Not that this is from them. But they are impelled by God to bring about what will annoy a person, or be good, or destroy, or save, or afflict, as the prophet says clearly: *The Lord has stirred up the spirit of the king of the Medes because his purpose concerning Babylon is to destroy it.*[115] And <Isaiah> says: *Behold, I am stirring up the Medes against you who have no regard for silver and do not delight in gold.*[116]

3. And it says: *The Lord will whistle for the flies of the rivers of Egypt, and for the bees which are in the land of Assyria. And they will all come and settle in the valley of Jathoth and in the hollows of the rock and in all the caves.*[117] And again it says: *The Lord will bring up the waters of the rivers against you, many and strong, even the king of Assyria and all his army. He will rise over all their brooks and walk upon all their fortified walls.*[118]

---

certain resemblance with the authentic Discourses of Isaac (Bettiolo, Discorsi): I, 51; II, 102.

[114] The translation "on their own" (Syr. *mene*), suggested by Chialà, is to resolve the contrast implied here between human initiative and God's action.

[115] Jeremiah 51.11.

[116] Isaiah 13.17.

[117] Ibid., 7.18–19.

[118] Ibid., 8.7.

4. And the <passage>: *The Lord will strengthen the oppressors of Rezin against him and stir up his enemies.*[119] And <where God> says: *It is I who have spoken and I have called, I have brought him and made his way prosperous.* And <the passage>: *I will raise up evil against you, from your house;*[120] He did not say "will rise against you," but "I will raise up against you."

5. And the <passage>: *I will provoke Egyptians against Egyptians, and brother will fight against his brother, a man against his neighbor, city against city and kingdom against kingdom.*[121] And the <passage>: *I am summoning the sword against all the inhabitants of the earth, says the Lord of hosts.*[122] And the <passage>: *Behold, I will rouse against you all your lovers whom your soul rejected, and I will bring them against you.*[123] And the <passage>: *Against Tyre I will bring Nebuchadnezzar, king of Babylonia.*[124]

6. And this: *Behold, I will bring strangers against you, the most powerful among the nations; they will draw their swords against the beauty of your wisdom, they will defile your glory and cast you down to destruction.*[125] And to Egypt He said: *Behold I will throw my net over you with a host of many peoples, and they will haul you up in their nets. I will cast you upon the ground and all the bright lights of heaven I will make dark over you.*[126]

7. And this: *I will embitter the heart of numerous peoples, when I bring about your ruin among the nations and in cities which you do not know.*[127] And the <passage>: *You betrayed the Israelites to the sword at the time of their distresses and at the time of their extreme iniquity.*[128] And the <passage>: *Behold I am sending many hunters, says the Lord, and they will*

---

119 Isaiah 9.11.
120 2 Samuel 12.11.
121 Isaiah 19.2.
122 Jeremiah 25.29.
123 Ezekiel 23.22.
124 Ibid., 26.7.
125 Ibid., 28.7–8.
126 Ibid., 32.3–4, 8.
127 Ibid., 32.9.
128 Ibid., 35.5.

hunt them on every mountain and on every hill, and out of the holes in the rocks. For my eyes are on all their ways, and they are not concealed *from me.*[129]

8. Moreover, since this occurs also because of these advantages and it is according to His will that the projects are set in motion, at His time, by means of those who are placed as intermediaries for their realization, <God> says: *Behold, I will lift up my hand to the nations, and raise a sign to the peoples; they shall bring your sons in their hands, and your daughters they shall carry on their shoulders. Kings shall be your foster-fathers and their princesses, your wet-nurses. With their faces to the ground they shall bow down to you, and wipe the dust of your feet.*[130]

9. And <where> it says: *The sons of Judah and the sons of Jerusalem whom you sold to the sons of the Greeks, removing them far from their border, behold, I will stir them up from the place where you have sold them, while I will bring your retribution on your heads. I will give your sons and your daughters into the hands of the sons of Judah and they will sell them to Saba, a distant people, because the Lord has spoken.*[131] And the <passage> which says: *The Lord was with Joseph and he showed him kindness and gave him favor in the eyes of the head of the prison.*[132]

10. And the <passage>: *The Lord gave the people favor in the eyes of the Egyptians <concerning> what they had asked for, and they despoiled the Egyptians.*[133] And the <passage>: *I will send my strength before you, and will lay waste all the peoples against whom you shall come, and I will make all your enemies turn their backs before you.*[134] And <where> it says: *For it was from the Lord that the heart of these people be strengthened and that they go out to battle against Israel in order that* he might deliver them into the hand of Joshua *to destroy them and they be without recourse;*[135] and <there

---

[129] Jeremiah 16.16–17.
[130] Isaiah 49.22–23.
[131] Joel 4.6–8.
[132] Genesis 39.21.
[133] Exodus 12.36.
[134] Exodus 23.27.
[135] Joshua 11.10.

are> other passages on which I will not linger longer because in the divine Scriptures there are endless <examples> like these.

11. And thus it happens for those who are without words or reason and make use of things.[136] <God> says: *Surely, I will begin to strike you and destroy you because of your sins*; in that <He> usually ordains these occasions of His Economy, for the most part, for the purpose of making to suffer. And it says <again>: *You will eat but you will not be satisfied, <you will be afflicted with> dysentery; you will seize but not save, and what you do save, I will deliver to the sword; you will sow and not harvest; you will tread olives but not anoint with oil; and you will crush grapes and not drink the wine.*[137]

12. And this: *You sow much and you reap little; you eat but never have enough; you drink but you never have your fill; you dress but do not feel warm; and whoever among you earns wages, earns them in a purse with holes in it.*[138] And again <it says>: *You expected much and there is little; you bring it home and I blow it away.*[139] And again this: *I will open for you the windows of heaven and will pour out blessings on you until you say: "Enough"!; and I will rebuke the devourer so that it will not destroy the fruits of the land, and not ravage for you even one vine in the land, says the Lord of hosts.*[140]

13. And again this: *The Lord prepared a great fish and it swallowed Jonah.*[141] And: *The Lord commanded the fish and it vomited Jonah upon dry land.*[142] And: *The Lord ordered that a young gourd plant grow and it sprouted and went up on Jonah's head. But the Lord God, as dawn arose, appointed a worm and it nibbled on the gourd and cut it off; then the Lord God ordered a parching wind and it dried up the gourd.*[143]

---

[136] Here Isaac refers to examples where divine intervention makes use of animals or inanimate objects.

[137] Micah 6.13–15.

[138] Haggai 1.6.

[139] Ibid., 1.9.

[140] Malachi 3.10–11.

[141] Jonah 2.1.

[142] Ibid., 2.11.

[143] Ibid., 4.6–8.

14. And again <this passage>: *I have commanded the ravens to feed you.*[144] And it <also> says: *I have commanded a widow to feed you.*[145] And this: *The Lord visited Anna and she conceived and gave birth to three sons and two daughters.*[146] And the <passage>: *The Lord commanded to bring to naught the good counsel of Ahithophel.*[147]

15. And in a thousand places, so to say, <it> is written in the Scriptures that the Lord commanded this or that, as the above <passages> indicate, making it sufficiently clear. And behold, these are shown to declare clearly the fact that the Lord has commanded such and such and also that these happen without delay. This is true as it is also true that he has said to me,[148] "How did He command?" He said to me: "Did He indeed command all these things by means of the sound of the voice?[149] Or is what God willed only the will and the impulse corresponding to these and <that> is set in motion in those <who have acted>?"

16. If in fact this occurred by a sound of the voice, with the fish or with the worm or with the young gourd plant or with the scorching wind or with the ravens, how did God speak and command voiceless creatures not even endowed with senses, by means of a sound of a voice? Or rather, where it is written that <He> spoke with the widow or that <He> commanded her, by a sound of a voice, to feed the prophet – which clearly refers to the action which <God> fulfilled providentially by means of her – Scripture also calls a "command" the will that <God> put in her to fulfill the action.

17. Or rather: how is it that <God> truly ordered Anna to conceive and give birth to sons and daughters, in that this was not of her will but of divine action? Or again: perhaps it is with a sound

---

[144] 1 Kings 17.4.

[145] Ibid., 17.9.

[146] 1 Samuel 2.21.

[147] 2 Samuel 17.14.

[148] Chialà resolves a difficult passage by suggesting that here Isaac refers and responds to someone specific who opposed his thinking.

[149] Sound of a voice (*ba(r)t qâlâ*), see note 79.

of the voice that <God> commanded Absalom and the people that were with him to not accept the counsel of Ahithophel, given that Scripture says that the Lord ordered to bring to nought <the counsel>; or according to what seemed to God, was the thought and the will to nullify the thing put in motion in them?

18. You see that by means of rational creatures and voiceless ones, God moves and works so that what He wills be accomplished without delay. It is, however, according to His will that the impulses of rational and voiceless creatures be transformed and confirmed for those things that God had willed that they might be. How then is it possible that it not be God who does or moves, according to His will, those things which actually happen in the manner of corrections or favorable things, by means of an action? On the contrary, it is surely He who truly wills and truly allows that they happen.

19. Not that, in such a way, also the preparation and impulse of the things which happen proceed – as if indeed only God can desire and permit, simply and without distinction – nor that from His interventions come <their> sequence and their quantity. But the "why," the "when" and the "how" are given to chance.[150] He in fact did not establish by Himself the limit[151] in which these things <will happen>, rather this has been given by Him to the will and the thought of those who bring it about.

20. If this happens by means of rational beings or irrational ones, and as to how one will be punished and why, and who will be punished is not determined; not even concerning glad events. Chance also serves the divine will about these things. Therefore to examine this word to see "how" < it occurs comes> from a supposition full of absurdity concerning the wonderful Wise One of the universe.[152]

---

[150] Chance (*suqbâlâ*).

[151] Limit (*tḥômâ*).

[152] This is a form of Lord of all (*mârê-kul*) or Lord of the universe. It is considered to be a trace of the early Syriac Creed. See Connolly, "Early Syriac Creed." It appears in Acts of Thomas, Aphrahat, Ephrem, *Book of*

21. What then? All the things which are, how they are and when they are, God wills according to what has been said? Or is it <only> those favorable events or those actions for correction that God wills, as He wills, when He wills, and by means of whom He wills? In the first case, then, God is guided in what and how He wills following the actions which are done; and not that the actions are stirred according to the will of God. Even if in the second case, it is clear that these actions, in their variety, are administered by the will of God, concerning time, limit and number.

22. What more? Already knowing ahead of time the things which are, God consented that they occur? Or, He had willed beforehand that these occur and the actions conformed to His will, one by one, according to all their impulses and their plans? In the first case, all which are provided for us are not even actions of wisdom, by the fact that His will is guided by chance; and He wills all that happens and when it happens – this then is not of wisdom. Wisdom, however, in all that it does keeps its own precept[153] and is not guided by chance in the doing of its actions. Every action is determined according to its will: this is said <to be> the beginning of wisdom.

23. In this other case, then, all things move in the limit defined by God, and in their timing they begin according to His will and are guided by His will; and all the <realities> which God ordains by means of rational beings or irrational ones keep to the precept of His wisdom. In fact <Scripture> says: *All which the Lord wills he does.*[154] But also this is still said in human terms. The Lord does not do everything He wills. All which He willed, not only recently as they come into existence, but eternally He willed the things which

---

Steps. It also may be found in the Jewish liturgy and in rabbinic literature as *ribbon shel ʿolam.* In *Midrash on Psalms*, practically every Psalm's commentary includes the invocation, see Braude. And in the Jewish prayer book, in the morning service, "King of the universe" (*melekh ha ʿolam*) occurs 27 times.

[153] Precept (*ṯḥômâ*).

[154] Psalm 135.6; cf. 115.3.

He willed – such that there is nothing that He willed only recently – nor does <He> desist from anything of all which He willed.

24. Therefore all which the Lord had willed exists. The will of the Lord is at work. However, instead <of speaking> of will, in the Scriptures all these realities whose names correspond to the variety of necessities are laid down. There is a <place> where it says that the "Lord commanded," another "the Lord said," another "acted," another "will do," or again "the sentence of the Lord," or "word of the Lord," and the rest of all these things.

25. Instead of saying that <God> had always willed and that things happened in their time, Scripture says all these things <noted above>. For God to do anything at all, willing alone is sufficient. For creatures, however, their will alone is not sufficient for the completion of their actions; but with the will they have need of assistance, a movement with regard to the actions – a going towards and a substantive motion regarding these matters. Then comes the perfection of the deed which they willed. I speak of spiritual realities – even if a small action – but still we humans struggle with corporal <realities>.

26. As to God, however, it is not possible that for the fulfillment of His will a natural impulse be joined, or someone's personal manner for the doing <of it> and so the action be completed. This, in fact, is of composed[155] and created beings or of those who need to make use of the word. Whereas God, whose will alone sufficed for Him to bring forth these primary elements, in the beginning, in silence, from nothing in existence – is said <of Him>: "You willed, and all exists before You."[156]

---

[155] Composed: though here a different Syriac word is used this may very well refer to the concept of composite <*mrâkâbtâ*> which concerns the discussion of human nature created with a composite structure having elements for its subsistence and being subject to growth in simplicity. Only in the world to come after the resurrection will humans have the complete simplicity of the angelic life. John the Solitary discusses this in detail, see Lavenant *Dialogues V*.

[156] Cf. Judith 9.5; Psalm 33.9.

27. Such is His will: the fulfillment of every action of rational beings and the transformation of their thoughts, even concerning the course of creation. And what He willed that it be, He does not do, but it is! As if He wanted to say, that if there is a flood, and the natural elements immediately be obedient to His will: at the time in which this appeared, the elements received a transformation beyond what is usual and inundated creation, as it is written.[157] And for God it sufficed only that He will it.

28. He willed again, and the tongues at the tower of Babel were confused. But suddenly they received the knowledge of tongues[158] <of which they had no experience> according as it is written. And again suddenly they received knowledge of tongues, translated outside of nature.[159] He willed again, and a fire descended on the Sodomites, and it enkindled against them, suddenly as it is written.[160] He willed again, and the heart of Pharaoh and of the Egyptians was hardened, in order that <God> might do signs in their midst, as it is written.[161] He willed and the sea was divided, and Israel crossed the dry land but <the sea> covered the Egyptians, as it is written.[162] He willed again, and the earth was split apart and swallowed <those> of the house of Dathan and Abiram, as it is written.[163]

29. He willed and suddenly the fire of their censors burned two hundred and fifty men, as it is written.[164] He willed again, and a fire came out from within the sanctuary and devoured the two sons of Aaron, as it is written.[165] He willed and the manna descended,

---

[157] Cf. Genesis 7.17–20.

[158] The apparatus notes an omission here for which Chialà supplies: <of which they had no experience>.

[159] Cf. Genesis 11.1–9. Chialà suggests this may refer to the "one language" and the subsequent confused language.

[160] Ibid., 19.23–25.

[161] Cf. Exodus 7–14.

[162] Ibid., 14.15–31.

[163] Cf. Numbers 16.31–32.

[164] Ibid., 16.35.

[165] Cf. Leviticus 10.1–2.

marvelous nourishment, and it nourished the people without effort, as it is written.[166] He willed and their clothes grew with their stature and lasted for forty years. He willed again, and water came out from the dry rock, against nature, and it flowed on the dry land, as it is written.[167]

30. Again He willed, and serpents broke out among them, and they killed many.[168] He willed, and they received the power of healing by means of a serpent made of inanimate material, and the sight of it gave healing to the body and to the mind.[169] He willed again, and they were handed over to the Canaanites who slew many of them, showing their weakness.[170] He willed again, and suddenly Israel's side was strengthened, while the side of the adversary became weak and was conquered, and they learned by this that all is from Him and everything is towards Him.[171]

31. He willed, and the fear of them fell on famous heroes, and these were shaken by the sound of them and they knelt before them.[172] He willed again, and the peoples gathered and captured them; but again He placed in them a thought according to His will, and their captors sent them back with honor. <God> said: *I have delivered into captivity the sons of Israel among the nations and then I gathered them into their land and let none of them remain there.*[173]

32. And there are many other <examples> such as these. Not one of these things happened according to human thought, alas these actions were impelled and completed corresponding to the precept[174] of the divine will. <Either> the will of God adapts to the origin of the actions, or the origin of the actions is by the will

---

[166] Cf. Exodus 16; Numbers 11.4–9; Deuteronomy 8.3, 16.
[167] Cf. Exodus 17.1–7; Numbers 20.1–11; Deuteronomy 8.15.
[168] Cf. Numbers 21.6.
[169] Cf. Numbers 21.9.
[170] Cf. Numbers 14.44–45.
[171] Exodus 17.11.
[172] Cf. Joshua 10.1–2.
[173] Ezekiel 39.28.
[174] Precept (*ṭḥômâ*).

of God. If it is the first case, therefore that which is ready to happen, God willed it, but nothing that God willed is a preparation for actions in a planification of <concrete> actions. But if this last possibility would be unseemly to be thought of regarding God, therefore it is known that the other <option> is true, that it is divine precept[175] guiding the impulse of the actions in those doing them.

33. It is said: *I command says the Lord, and they will return and fight against you.*[176] And there where <it says>: *You have feared this or that, and I will make this or that to come upon you.*[177] And the <passage>: *Do not fear them because I am with you and no one is able to do you harm.*[178] And the <passage>: *I begin to place the fear of you and the terror of you on all the peoples who are under heaven*;[179] but for the rest I will not add anymore <now>.

34. Who then is childish of heart and lacking in knowledge about all of this, so as to say that the distress or the benefits come to humans apart from God? Or which of even only one of the motions of creation is lacking in <divine> support? Not that I have said these things of myself, what a childish thought! I think, however, that not even one who is very insolent is willing to oppose or remain doubtful about this, like a child.

35. And this from well-known testimony, learned by experience and by inquiry, showing clearly how all these various realities are verified by God: that by God our being is <either> preserved or handed over to all evils. <Only> then may something which afflicts dare to strike a person. However one cannot even say that being consigned <to evil> is from God, but above all may the care that <comes> from Him be acknowledged. These things will be sufficient for the useful persuasion of those who ask.

---

[175] Divine precept (*ṭhômâ alâhâyâ*).

[176] Jeremiah 34.22.

[177] Cf. Deuteronomy 28.60; Ezekiel 11.8.

[178] Acts 18.9–10.

[179] Deuteronomy 2.25.

THE *FOURTH PART* OF ISAAC QAṬRAYA'S ASCETICAL HOMILIES IN GARSHUNI

MARIO KOZAH
AMERICAN UNIVERSITY OF BEIRUT

Isaac Qaṭraya, also known as Isaac of Nineveh, Isaac the Syrian or Isaac Syrus is perhaps, alongside Ephrem of Nisibis and Jacob of Serugh, the most well-known and influential author in Syriac literature. Isaac's work not only circulated among the various Syriac communities of the Middle East but was also translated into a variety of languages from the Middle Ages onwards. As a result, his writings have exerted a profound influence on the entire Christian world in both the East and the West. Despite his importance, however, biographical and bibliographical information about him is scant.

The origins of Isaac Qaṭraya are mentioned in a notice to be found in the *Book of Chastity* (ܟܬܒܐ ܕܢܟܦܘܬܐ) or *History of the founders of monasteries in the realms of the Persians and the Arabs*[1] by the ninth-century East Syriac author Īshōʿdnaḥ (ܝܫܘܥܕܢܚ) (fl. c. 860) who states in a short notice about Isaac that: "His origin, then, was from Beth Qaṭraye".[2] Furthermore, two thirteenth-century manuscripts of Isaac's works describe him as "the holy Mar Isaac Qaṭraya,

[1] ܫܪ̈ܒܐ ܕܡܫܡ̈ܗܐ ܕܟܠܗܘܢ ܐܒܗ̈ܬܐ ܐܝܠܝܢ ܕܒܢܘ ܥܘܡܪ̈ܐ ܒܡܠܟܘܬܐ ܕܦܪ̈ܣܝܐ ܘܕܛܝ̈ܝܐ : J.B. Chabot, "Le livre de la chasteté composé par Jésusdenah, évéque de Baçrah", in *Mélanges d'archéologie et d'histoire*. Ecole française de Rome, T. XVIe, Rome, 1896.

[2] ܓܢܣܗ ܕܝܢ ܡܢ ܒܝܬ ܩܛܪ̈ܝܐ ܐܝܬܘܗܝ (Ibid., p. 64).

bishop of the town of Niniveh".[3] One of these manuscripts, Mardin 46, was used by P. Bedjan for his edition of Isaac's works.[4] A more detailed fifteenth-century notice however from a Syriac Orthodox biographical notice and to be found published in the *Studia Syriaca* of I.E. Rahmani provides us with interesting biographical details such as the fact that Isaac was born in the region of Beth Qaṭraye and having been educated there in the writings of the Church Fathers became a monk and teacher himself in Beth Qaṭraye. These details reveal that this region was an important centre of education and learning. The final resting place of Isaac Qaṭraya was the Monastery of Rabban Shabūr[5] where he spent his last days in prayer, study and composition.[6]

---

[3] The two manuscripts are Mardin 46 and Seert 76.

[4] P. Bedjan (ed.), *Mar Isaacus Ninivita. De Perfectione Religiosa.* Paris/Leipzig, 1909; repr. Piscataway NJ, 2007.

[5] The location of this monastery is identified by A. Scher as being in the environs of the town of "Šouštar" (or Tustar). See A. Scher, "Notice sur la vie et les oeuvres de Dadishoᶜ Qaṭraya", *Journal Asiatique*, 10:7, 1906, p. 109, n. 1. J-M. Fiey, suggests that if the monastery was founded to the south of the town of "Tuster" in the direction of the village of Dūlāb, the birthplace of Rabban Shabūr himself, then it might be identified with "Dayr Ḥamīm" mentioned in the Muslim sources. See J-M. Fiey, "L'Elam, première des metropoles ecclésiastiques syriennes orientales", *Melto* 5, 1969, p. 247, n. 126. For a more recent article on the Monastery of Rabban Shabūr but which does not make any advance on Fiey's conclusions concerning its location see F. Jullien, "Le couvent de Rabban Shapour et le renouveau monastique en Perse", in M. Vannier, *Connaissance des Pères de l'Eglise, N° 119, septembre 20 : Isaac de Ninive.* Nouvelle Cité, 2010.

[6] "Afterwards he grew old and advanced in years (ܥܠܠ ܒܫܢܝܐ) and departed to our Lord. He was buried in the Monastery of Mar Shabūr (ܐܬܬܩܒܪ ܒܕܝܪܐ ܕܡܪܝ ܫܒܘܪ)". See I.E. Rahmani, *Studia Syriaca*, I. Charfet, 1904, p. ܠܣ. "When he became very advanced in age, he departed from temporal life (ܚܝܐ ܙܒܢܝܐ) and his body was buried in the Monastery of Shabūr (ܐܬܬܩܒܪ ܦܓܪܗ ܒܕܝܪܐ ܕܫܒܘܪ)". See J.B. Chabot, "Le livre de la chasteté composé par Jésusdenah, évéque de Baçrah", p. 64.

The works of Isaac in Syriac survive today in three confirmed "parts" (ܦܘܠܓ̈ܘܬܐ). "The First Part" edited by P. Bedjan was translated into English by A.J. Wensinck in 1923.[7] "The Second Part" was almost entirely edited and translated by S. Brock.[8] "The Third Part" which was recently discovered in Tehran has been edited by S. Chiala and was published[9] while translations in French and Italian have now also been published by A. Louf and S. Chiala.[10] A full English translation by Mary Hansbury is available in this anthology.

However, the question as to how many "parts" Isaac wrote remains unresolved and even the earliest sources that refer to him provide contradictory information. In the *Book of Chastity* Īshōʿdnaḥ states:

> He wrote books (ܟܬ̈ܒܐ) on the divine way of life (ܕܘܒܪܐ ܐܠܗܝܐ) of the solitaries (ܝܚܝ̈ܕܝܐ). He wrote three works (ܬܠܬܐ ܡܐܡܪ̈ܐ) which were disapproved of (ܠܐ ܐܬܩܒܠܘ) by many people.[11]

If the three works (ܬܠܬܐ ܡܐܡܪ̈ܐ) referred to by Īshōʿdnaḥ, or "propositions" as Chabot gives in his translation, can be considered an allusion to three "parts" (ܦܘܠܓ̈ܘܬܐ) in the form that Isaac's works survive today then we must look no further. However, the Syriac Orthodox biographical notice published by Rahmani states the following:

> He wrote five volumes (ܚܡܫܐ ܦܘܢܩ̈ܝܬܐ) which are known to this day [consisting of] sweet teaching (ܡܠܦܢܘܬܐ). This is

---

[7] A.J. Wensinck, *Mystic Treatises by Isaac of Nineveh*. Amsterdam, 1923; repr. Wiesbaden, 1969.

[8] S.P. Brock, *Isaac of Nineveh (Isaac the Syrian): 'The Second Part', Chapters IV–XLI, CSCO*: Scr. Syr. 224 (text) and 225 (tr.). Louvain, 1995.

[9] S. Chialà, *Isacco di Ninive. Terza Collezione, CSCO* 637/8, Syr. 246/7. Louvain, 2011.

[10] A. Louf, *Isaac le Syrien, Oeuvres spirituelles – III, d'après un manuscrit récemment découvert. Spiritualité orientale* 88, 2009. S. Chialà, *Isacco di Ninive. Discorsi ascetici, terza collezione*. Communità di Bose, 2004.

[11] J.B. Chabot, "Le livre de la chasteté composé par Jésusdenah, évéque de Baçrah", p. 64.

> attested by Mar Dāzedeq (ܡܪܝ ܕܐܙܕܩ) in the letter which he wrote to his pupil Būshīr (ܒܘܫܝܪ), to the monastery of Mar Shabūr (ܡܪܝ ܫܒܘܪ), saying thus: I thank our Lord for your diligence which has sent me the teaching of Mar Isaac of Niniveh.[12]

Could it be that these "volumes" are the equivalent to the "parts" as they survive today? In which case two further "parts" remain potentially undiscovered or unidentified. There are, in fact, reports of a number of manuscripts of a "Fifth Part". All of these manuscripts are reported to exist in various libraries in the Middle East apart from one incomplete manuscript in the Vatican. This "Fifth Part", now edited and published by S. Chialà[13] and translated into English in this anthology by Mary Hansbury, is, according to him, fairly short and having now analysed the text does seem to resemble Isaac's writings.[14] The existence of a "Fifth Part" would suggest that there was once a "Fourth Part" as well. However, no traces of it have so far been discovered in Syriac manuscripts.

To complicate matters further, there exist a number of Garshuni manuscripts which are translations of the writings of Isaac divided into four "parts" (ܓܙܘ). The oldest of these manuscripts are a couple which date back to the thirteenth and fourteenth centuries and are to be found in the Charfet collection.[15] Another very old Garshuni manuscript is to be found in the St Mary Al Sourian Monastery in Egypt.[16] Later manuscripts which contain or refer to four parts include a sixteenth century

---

[12] I.E. Rahmani, *Studia Syriaca*, I. Charfet, 1904, p. ܠܒ.

[13] S. Chialà, *Dall'ascesi eremitica alla misericordia infinita. Ricerche su Isacco di Ninive e la sua fortuna. Biblioteca della Rivista di Storia e Letteratura Religiosa, Studi 14*. Florence, 2002, p. 71–72.

[14] For a discussion of the "Fifth Part" see S. Chiala's article: "Two discourses of the 'Fifth Part' of Isaac the Syrian's Writings: Prolegomena for Apokatastasis?" in Kozah, M., Abu-Husayn, A., Al-Murikhi, S. S., Al Thani, H., (eds.), *The Syriac Writers of Qatar in the Seventh Century*. Piscataway, NJ: Gorgias Press, 2014.

[15] Charfet ar. 7/2 and Charfet ar. 7/3. I would like to thank Grigory Kessel for alerting me to the existence of these manuscripts.

[16] MS 153.

manuscript in the Vatican Library,[17] one in the Bodleian Library,[18] and a seventeenth century manuscript in the Cambridge University Library.[19] Finally, an eighteenth century manuscript with a *Fourth Part* is to be found in the Kaslik collection.[20] Although some variation is encountered in the content of the Garshuni *Fourth Part* (ܐܠܓܙܘ ܐܠܪܐܒܥ) as it has been preserved in a number of the above-mentioned manuscripts, the majority of them, it would seem from a preliminary survey, include much of the same material under fairly congruent headings:

The *Fourth Part* by the Saint Mar Isaac.[21]
[The First Sermon:][22] On the *Kephalaia Gnostica*.[23]
On the Changing Types of Cogitation.[24]
Profitable Counsels in the Course of Recognizing the Truth.[25]

---

[17] Vat. sir. 198. A partial copy of this MS is found in Borg. ar. 133 although it does not include the *Fourth Part* despite the fact that it is found listed in the contents page.

[18] Bodleian Syr. 150.

[19] Cambridge D.d.15.2. Another MS which may contain fragments of a *Fourth Part* is Cambridge 3279.

[20] Kaslik, OLM 1580. This appears to be a copy of Vat. sir. 198.

[21] ܐܠܓܙܘ ܐܠܪܐܒܥ ܠܠܩܕܝܣ ܡܐܪ ܐܣܚܩ. (Vat. sir. 198, f. 239ᵛ).
ܐܠܓܙܘ ܐܠܪܐܒܥ ܦܝ ܪܘܘܣ ܐܠܡܥܪܦܗ̈ ܠܠܩܕܝܣ ܡܐܪ ܐܣܚܩ.. (OLM 1580, f. 197ʳ; Charf. Arm. 7/2, f. 207ʳ; Charf. Rah. 261, f. 166ʳ): "The *Fourth Part* on the Kephalaia Gnostica by the Saint Mar Isaac".

[22] ܐܠܐܘܠ ܡܐܠ (OLM 1580, f. 197ʳ; Charf. Arm. 7/2, f. 207ʳ; Charf. Rah. 261, f. 166ʳ).

[23] ܦܝ ܪܘܘܣ ܐܠܡܥܪܦܗ (Vat. sir. 198, f. 239ᵛ).

[24] ܦܝ ܬܓܝܝܪ ܐܢܘܐܥ ܐܠܐܦܟܐܪ (Vat. sir. 198, f. 244ᵛ; OLM 1580, f. 199ʳ; Charf. Arm. 7/2, f. 211ᵛ; Charf. Rah. 261, f. 168ᵛ).

[25] ܡܫܘܪܐܬ ܢܐܦܥܗ ܦܝ ܣܝܪܗ̈ ܡܥܪܦܗ̈ ܐܠܚܩ (Vat. sir. 198, f. 245ᵛ; OLM 1580, f. 200ʳ).
ܘܐܝܨܐ ܠܠܩܕܝܣ ܡܫܘܪܗ ܢܐܦܥܗ ܦܝ ܣܝܪܗ̈ ܡܥܪܦܗ̈ ܐܠܚܩ ܝܥܡܠܘܢ ܒܐܠܨܡܬ (Charf. Arm. 7/2, f. 213ʳ; Charf. Rah. 261, f. 169ʳ): "Also by the Saint a Profitable Counsel in the Course of Recognizing the Truth which Are [sic.] Undertaken in Silence".

On the Saddening Darkness which Occurs during Stillness to those Contemplatives who Strive after Cognition.[26]
An Answer to a Question which Mar Isaac was Asked.[27]
Also the *Kephalaia Gnostica* by the Saint Mar Isaac.[28]
The Second Treatise on the *Kephalaia Gnostica* by Mar Isaac.[29]

In two of the earliest and most complete of the manuscripts that include a Garshuni *Fourth Part*, Charfet Arm. 2/7 and Charfet Rah. 261, the *Fourth Part* does not end here but concludes with six long *mayāmir* (sing. *maymar*) or sermons of the *Kephalaia Gnostica.*

The headings are as follows:

The first *maymar* of the *Kephalaia Gnostica* by the Saint Mar Isaac.[30]
The second *maymar* of the *Kephalaia Gnostica* by the Saint Mar Isaac.[31]

---

[26] ܥܠܝ ܐܠܛܠܐܡ ܐܠܡܚܙܢ ܐܠܚܐܕܬ ܦܝ ܐܠܗܕܘ ܥܠܝ ܐܠܕܝܢ ܝܬܥܒܘܢ ܐܠܡܥܪܦܗ̈ ܡܬܐܘܪܝܢ (Vat. sir. 198, f. 255v; OLM 1580, f. 205r).
ܘܐܝܨܐ ܠܠܩܕܝܣ ܥܠܝ ܐܠܛܠܐܡ ܐܠܡܚܙܢ ܐܠܚܐܕܬ ܦܝ ܐܠܗܕܘ ܥܠܝ ܐܠܕܝܢ ܝܬܥܒܘܢ ܐܠܡܥܪܦܗ [ܡܬܐܘܪܝܢ] ܡܘܨܚ ܗܕܐ ܐܠܦܨܠ ܥܠܝ ܐܠܗܕܘ ܘܡܐ ܝܥܪܨ ܦܝܗ (Charf. Arm. 7/2, f. 222v; Charf. Rah. 261, f. 174v): "And also by the Saint On the Saddening Darkness which Occurs during Stillness to those Contemplatives who Strive after Cognition. This Chapter Explains Silence and What it is Exposed in it".

[27] ܓܘܐܒ ܡܣܐܠܗ ܣܐܠ ܐܠܩܕܝܣ ܡܐܪ ܐܣܚܩ (OLM 1580, f. 206r).

[28] ܘܐܝܨܐ ܪܐܘܣ ܐܠܡܥܪܦܗ̈ ܠܠܩܕܝܣ ܡܐܪ ܐܣܚܩ (OLM 1580, f. 207r; Charf. Arm. 7/2, f. 224r; Charf. Rah. 261, f. 175v). A different heading is given for this section in Vat. sir. 198, f. 257r: ܘܐܝܨܐ ܠܠܩܕܝܣ ܡܐܪ ܐܣܚܩ ܐܩܘܐܠ "Sayings (apophthegmata) also by the Saint Mar Isaac".

[29] "The first treatise on the *Kephalaia Gnostica* is completed. The second treatise on the *Kephalaia Gnostica* by Mar Isaac". ܟܡܠܬ ܐܠܡܩܐܠܗ̈ ܐܠܐܘܠܗ̈ ܦܝ ܪܐܘܣ ܐܠܡܥܪܦܗ̈. ܐܠܡܩܐܠܗ̈ ܐܠܬܐܢܝܗ̈ ܦܝ ܪܐܘܣ ܐܠܡܥܪܦܗ̈ ܠܡܐܪ ܐܣܚܩ ܀ (OLM 1580, f. 210r). "The first treatise from the *Kephalaia Gnostica* is completed. And also from the *Kephalaia Gnostica* by the Saint Mar Isaac". ܟܡܠܬ ܐܠܡܩܐܠܗ̈ ܐܠܐܘܠܗ ܡܢ ܪܐܘܣ ܐܠܡܥܪܦܗ ܘܐܝܨܐ ܡܢ ܪܐܘܣ ܐܠܡܥܪܦܗ ܠܠܩܕܝܣ ܡܐܪ ܐܣܚܩ (Charf. Arm. 7/2, f. 228v; Charf. Rah. 261, f. 178v).

[30] Charfet Arm. 7/2, f. 241v; Charfet Rah. 261, f. 185v.

[31] Charfet Arm. 7/2, f. 249v; Charfet Rah. 261, f. 190v.

The third *maymar* of the *Kephalaia Gnostica* by the Saint Mar Isaac.[32]
The fourth *maymar* of the *Kephalaia Gnostica* by the Saint Mar Isaac.[33]
The fifth *maymar* of the *Kephalaia Gnostica* by the Saint Mar Isaac.[34]
The sixth *maymar* of the *Kephalaia Gnostica* by the Saint Mar Isaac.[35]

Thus far, scholars who have studied the Garshuni corpus have only managed to find an approximate correlation with the extant Syriac texts. It is hoped that a full edition and translation of the Syriac *Kephalaia Gnostica* from the "Second Part",[36] the Syriac "Third Part", the Garshuni "Fourth Part", and the Syriac "Fifth Part" will help with the identification of any of this material in the extant Syriac texts and by doing so identify any new material that is extant only in the Garshuni corpus. As a result significant progress would have been achieved in making the writings of Isaac Qaṭraya more accessible for advanced study and the deeper appreciation that they deserve.

A NOTE ON THE MANUSCRIPTS

This full critical edition of the Garshuni *Fourth Part* is based on Charfet Arm. 2/7 and uses, in addition, Charfet Rah. 261, Vat. sir. 198, Kaslik OLM 1580, and an online edition of Deir al-Suriyān 153.[37]

---

[32] Charfet Arm. 7/2, f. 257r; Charfet Rah. 261, f. 195r.

[33] Charfet Arm. 7/2, f. 265r; Charfet Rah. 261, f. 200r.

[34] Charfet Arm. 7/2, f. 271r; Charfet Rah. 261, f. 205r: "The fifth *maymar* of the *Kephalaia Gnostica* also by him".

[35] Charfet Arm. 7/2, f. 277v; Charfet Rah. 261, f. 211r.

[36] The Syriac *Kephalaia Gnostica* are to be found in chapter three of the Syriac "Second Part".

[37] ميامر مار اسحق السرياني أسقف نينوى المتوحد ببرية شيهيت المقدسة الجزء الرابع. من كتاب مار اسحق السرياني، المخطوط رقم 153 نسكيات بمكتبة دير السيدة العذراء مريم (السريان). اعده للنشر القمص تادرس السرياني. http://www.st-mary-alsourian.com/Library/Books/part4as.pdf

TEXT

1. Charfet Armalet 7/2 = A.
2. Charfet Rahmani 261 = R.
3. Vatican Syriac 198 = V.
4. Kaslīk OLM 1580 = K.
5. Deir al-Suriyān 153 = S.

الجزو الرابع في رووس المعرفة للقديس مار اسحق.. الاول قال
(A207r/R166r/V238v/K197r)

(1) اول مبادي سيرة تدبير المتوحدين هو التجرد بالسكون وعدم الارتباط بانسان، او بامر ما، والعمل الذي فيه هو الصبر على ما يعرض، والاتضاع[38] والصلاة. والاثمار التي[39] من هولاء الدخول الى الرجا والتنعم بالفرح بالله. والمخرج الصالح بهولاء هو تناول مفاتيح اسرار الروح (V239r) الممجده. وحد[40] الطريق هو مذاقه الحب، والداله من هاهنا الى ذاك الذي قد انحب.

(2) والذي مبادى الطريق ليس له، اعني التجرد والسكون، ظاهر ايضا ان ولا تواضع ولا صلاة له. والذي هو بطال من هولاء، بالضروره انه مشتبك[41] بالخطيه.[42] والذي هو خاطي ليس فقط بالملكوت ليس له مكان بل وبالجحيم قد اقتنا موضع معروف.

(3) اذا اردت ان تعرف[43] رجل الله استدل عليه من دوام سكوته،[44] ومن بكاه ومن انقباض نفسه الى ذاته.

(4) (A207v) وان اردت ان تعرف الرجل السايب القلب، استدل عليه من كثرة كلامه،[45] ومن تخبيط احواسه ومن مقاومته بكل شي يقول، ويريد ان

---

[38] واتضاع : A.
[39] الذي من : K.
[40] وحدا : S.
[41] متشبك : R.
[42] من الخطيه : K.
[43] تعرف : ساقطة V.
[44] سكونه وسكوته : K, V.
[45] كلامه الكثير : K, V.

يغلب، لان الذي قد ذاق[46] الحق ولا ايضا على الحق يقاوم ويحارن،[47] لان الذي يظن انه يغير لاجل الحق بحرانه مع الناس، هذا الى الان ما قد عرف الحق كيف هو، لانه لو اختبره بتحقيق ما كان يحارن[48] بالغيره لاجله. لان موهبة الله ومعرفته ليس هي سبب السجس والصراخ، بل مملوه سلام[49] وهدو،[50] لان حيث يحل الروح وايضا الحب والاتضاع[51] يوجد، هذه هي علامة وجود الروح، انه بهذه يكمل الذي قد حل فيه.

(5) لا يعتجب[52] احد بهذه انه ليس بسهولة يوجد جمع العقل، حتى ولا ذلك الجزوى[53] الذي في وقت الخدمه والصلاه، لانه ليس من اعمال الجسد فقط يكون، وليس لاناس مبتديين، (K197v) ولا كيف اتفق، وبوقت قليل يوجد متسهل. بل بسكون[54] كثير وبعمل القلب يعطا[55] لاناس بالكليه قد تركوا العالم،[56] وبالكمال (V239v) قد ماتوا من نظر الناس ومن اسماعهم،[57] فان كان احد كمثل بذوق ما يعد نفسه هكذا ومن اجل محبة الله يتهاون بالجسد وبالعالم، اوله يوهل لذلك الجزوى، وبعد هذا[58] كمثل الزرع ينشوا[59] به هذا الامر، ويبلغ بنعمة المسيح[60] لتلك الموهبه التي[61] ليس لها قياس. فتجذبنا يا احباي شهوة هذه الموهبه ونقطع[62] منا امور هذا العالم وننبذه، ونسرع سيرنا في[63] تبع المسيح[64] الى ان نحس بمعونة المسيح (R166v) قليل من كثير بحركات الاتضاع،

---

46 خاف : S.

47 ويحرن : S.

48 يحارب : A.

49 سلامة : A.

50 وهدوا : K, V, R.

51 واتضاع : A.

52 يتعجب : S / يعجب : A.

53 الجزوي : S.

54 سكون : S.

55 يعطى : K, S.

56 قد تركوا العالم بالكلية : S.

57 سماعهم : A.

58 بذوق ما ... كمثل : ساقطة R.

59 ينشو : A.

60 ܡܫܝܚܐ : K.

61 الذي : A.

62 نقطع : K, V.

63 سيرتنا الى : A.

64 ܡܫܝܚܐ : K.

(A208r) لا بالمذاقه ولا بمعونة[65] التي من اعمالك تحس، ولا ضميرك ينقبض من الطياشه ولا بتثبيت تصبر على العوارض الحادثه عليك والمصادفه[66] اياك بغير اضطراب ولا سجس.

(6) واذا ما برحمة الله بدوا[67] يتحركوا فيك متاسساً افكار التواضع من قبل كل شي[68] الضجر يوخذ[69] منك، ويعطا لك اعتراف وشكرا[70] دايم حتى اذا كنت جايع او شبعان او عطشان او محتاج او مريض او مضنوك من انسان دايما تعترف وتشكر، ولا يهدا لسانك من الشكر ساعة واحده، وتجد على الدوام انت ذاتك مذنب لكل احد في كل حين[71] وفي كل شي[72] ولم يظهر لك ان احد من الناس قد اسا اليك ابدا، بل بجميع الشرور التي حدثت عليك تجد ذاتك انت السبب لحدوثها ولكل ضنك وحزن. وباقتصار اقول لك الحق ما دمت ما وجدت التواضع اكثر من كل[73] الاشيا[74] تتجرب بالضجر، والضجر يولد لك الملامات على الدوام، وتنظر[75] كثرة الناس قد اسوا[76] اليك (V240r) واما اذا كنت تنظر في الصلاه حسناً حسب موجبها، ترا[77] انك مدبراً وغير[78] جيدا،[79] واذا كنت[80] بضد هذا تجد كل شيء بضد الواجب.

(7) لا تحب الراحات ليلا تكون ينبوع الافكار، وليس اقول مينا الرذايل، لا تصدق يا اخي ان من دون العمل ينعتق الانسان من الالام، او يشرق[81] له نور داخله لتنعمه.

---

[65] بالمعونه : K, V.
[66] المصادفه : A.
[67] بدو : K, V, R.
[68] كلشيً : V / كل شي : K / كلشي : R.
[69] يؤخذ : S.
[70] وشكر : V, S, K.
[71] كلحين : V.
[72] كلشي : V.
[73] منكل : V.
[74] الاشياء : V, S.
[75] تنظر : R.
[76] اسوا (اساءوا) : S / اسو : R.
[77] ترى : K, S.
[78] غير : A.
[79] جيد : S.
[80] سائراً : زائدة S.
[81] ويشرق : K, V.

(8) ننظر[82] جميع مواهب الروح انما عطيوا لاناس عمالين من الله، وليس احد[83] ابدا[84] نال من الله مواهب ولا استضا عقله واخذ قلبه دالة ليطلب منه، ولا اختلج فيه حركة شي من هولاء.

(9) (A208v) بالاعمال[85] اتعروا الانسان[86] العتيق ابابنا القديسين، واستحقوا تجديد النفس، ولا تظن ان التورع من المواكيل هو العمل فقط، او القيام في[87] الخدمه والصوم وحدهم يوصلون الانسان الى[88] النقاوه، بل الصبر[89] على البعد من مفاوضة الناس، والجثو[90] دايما قدام الصليب، اذ يقرن اوليك مع هولاء حسب المقدره والتواضع الكثير القلبي، وبقية مفاوضة[91] تدبير[92] سيرة المعرفه المسطور[93] في كتب اناس نيرين عارفين (K198r) وضعت للتربيه[94] بالالهيات المرسومه في هذه رووس[95] المعرفه قليل من كثير تجد.

(10) الذي ما يقبل انحلال الاعضا والملل والضجر في وقت الخدمه، ويفرح بحمل صعوبتهم والاختناق والظلام المحزن، وباقيه احزان القلايه كمثل عمل[96] تام قدام الله، بل يريد الانفراج والراحه منهم بالكليه، من غير ان[97] يشا الى يد شيطان الزنا يسلم. وعوض ذبيحه جسده الذكيه التي[98] بهولاء[99] يقرب[100] قدام الله كل يوم،[101] يذبح للشيطان ذبيحة (V240v) دنسه من اعضاه.

---

[82] تنظر : R.

[83] احدا : A.

[84] بدون اعمال : زائدة S.

[85] ابائنا القديسين بالاعمال : S.

[86] من : زائدة S.

[87] القيام في القيام في : R.

[88] الى : ساقطة R.

[89] بالصبر : S.

[90] والجثوا : V, S / وجثوا : K.

[91] ومفاوضة : R.

[92] تدبير : ساقطة A.

[93] المسطورة : S.

[94] التربيه : R.

[95] روس : K.

[96] عملاً : A.

[97] من ان غير : R.

[98] الذي : K.

[99] بهولا : K, R.

[100] كل يوم : زائدة K, V.

[101] كليوم : V, R.

(11) صدقني يا اخي ان الضجر (R167r) والملل، وثقل الاعضا والسجس وتكدر الضمير، وبقية المحزنات الحادثه على النساك بالجلوس الفريدي هن عمل الله تام.[102] ولا تظن ان الاستضا بالخدمه ونقاوة الضمير والتنعم وسرور القلب، والعزا الذي من الدموع الحلوه والهذيذ النقي مع الله، فقط هن عمل[103] الاهي.

(12) بالحق وحسب[104] رايي اقول حتى فكر التجديف والمجد الفارغ، وحركات الزنا السمجه التي[105] بتغصب يحدثون على المتوحد (A209r) بسكون القلايه، وتالمه لاجلهم ولو ان[106] يوجد مغلوب في وقت ما قدامهم، هو المتوحد ويصبر وما يخرج من قلايته حتى[107] وهذه ذبيحة نقيه تحسب وعمل الهي،[108] ما خلا العظمه فقط.

(13) لانه اتجلد بجهاد الرب على اليمينيات والشماليات العارضه عليه، اذ لم يكون حدوثهم بسبب انحلاله وتهاونه بل بنوع القتال تواتروا عليه فقط، ان لم يغلب[109] ويخرج من مصاف المعركه الذي هو الجلوس الفريدي بتجلد. ليس شي محبوب عند الله ومكروم[110] بعين الملايكه ويضعف الشيطان،[111] ومخوف على الجان،[112] ويهزم الخطيه، ويفيض المعرفه، ويجذب الرحمه، ويستاصل الخطايا، ويقني[113] الاتضاع، ويحكم القلب، ويجلب العزاوات، ويتحد به العقل، كمثل انه[114] على الدوام يوجد المتوحد جاثي[115] على الارض بالصلاه. هذه[116] هي[117] مينا التوبه التي[118] اليه اتصوب[119] جميع افكار الندم، مع الدموع وهي

---

102 التام : S.

103 عملا : A.

104 حسب : K, V.

105 الذي : A.

106 انه : K.

107 لحتى : S / وحتى : K.

108 الاهي : V.

109 ينغلب : K, V.

110 ومكرم : A.

111 الشياطين : S.

112 الجن : R.

113 وينقي : R.

114 الله : زائدة S.

115 على ركبتيه : زائدة K, V.

116 وهذه : K.

117 في : S.

(V241r) كنز الغفران وغسل القلب، ومنهج[120] الذكاوه،[121] وطرق الاستعلانات، وسلم[122] الذهن، هذه تجعل العقل شبه الله، ومختلج بحركاته بالمزمعات، هذه ديون[123] اهمال طويل بوقت قليل توفي، وافرازات اعمال مختلفه بانواع كثيره داخل من حدودها تحبس، لان ليس شي اعظم من مداومة المزامير بزيا[124] عفيف،[125] وان كان يغفل عنهم قليل لاجل انه قد ابتلع بشهوة هذه، ليس يحسب كمتهاون، بل كمثل من قد ارتفع الى درجة افضل، وعمل[126] اعظم منهم، (A209v) ومدنى الى الله، ومتداخل اكثر واستحق موهبه.

(14) ليس الى ان تطهر من (K198v) طياشه[127] الافكار وحينيذ تشتهي ان تصلي، بل لكي[128] من مداومة الصلاه وكثرة العمل فيها تنمحق الطياشه من الضمير، فان كنت الى ان تنظر الضمير كامل ومرتفع عن كل تذكار عالمي، عند ذلك[129] تبدى بالصلاه الى الابد ما تصلي.

(15) كما انه[130] لا يمكن ان[131] تنقا[132] نظرة القايم على جانب الدخان، الا ان ابتعد واتخلا[133] من هناك. هكذا لا يمكن ان يقتنى[134] نقاوة القلب وسكون من الافكار من دون الوحده المبتعده من دخان هذا العالم، الذي يبخر قدام الاحواس، ويغشى عيني[135] النفس.

---

118 الذي : K.
119 تصوب : A.
120 ومنهم : K, V.
121 الزكاوة : S.
122 وتسلم : K, V.
123 لديون : S.
124 بزي : K, V.
125 عفيفا : S.
126 وعملاً : A.
127 الطياشة : A.
128 لكن : R.
129 ذالك : R.
130 ان : A.
131 ان : ساقطة R.
132 تنقى : S.
133 اتخلى : S.
134 يقتنا : V, R.
135 على : K, V.

(16) لا يظهر احد[136] معرفة خرفه ويحارن بمقاومه على[137] هذا، لانه اذا كنا سكان في (R167v) العمر والانس افكار الانس تحدث لنا، واذا كنا في القفر افكار القفر تحدث لنا، واذا[138] كنا مع كثيرين افكار كثيرين تعرض[139] لنا،[140] واذا اتفردنا[141] من كل[142] احدا[143] وكنا بحركاتنا موتا للعالم،[144] ضميرا[145] متوحش[146] نقتني. ما هي افكار القفر (V241v) الا حركات تخرج من قلب مايت، لانه لا يمكن اذا كنا بحركاتنا[147] موتى[148] للعالم ان لا نتحرك بالله، اضروره ان[149] سكون الحركات العالميه تعطي فسحه للتحرك بالله، وبضنك[150] الجسد ضمير متوحد[151] نقتني.

(17) ليس ينبغي لنا ان نتضجر[152] بتطويل الخدمه، وامتداد[153] الصلاه والتلاوة الكثيره فيهن،[154] لان من العمل بتلاوة الكلام والصبر بالثبات فيهن، يتولد لنا دوامهن الذي[155] قلت. ينبغي (A210r) ان نعلم ان ليس موضع الثمره التي توجد تحسب[156] هولاء، بل موضع الاصول التي[157] من دونهن[158] ليس تظهر

---

136 من : زائدة A.

137 معى : K, V.

138 وان : S / واذ : R.

139 يعرضوا : R / تحدث : K, V.

140 علينا : S, R,.

141 انفردنا : S / تفردنا : K.

142 منكل : V.

143 احد : R, K, V, S.

144 وكنا بحركاتنا موتا للعالم : ساقطة V, S, R, K.

145 ضمير : V, S, R, K.

146 متوحد : K, S وفي حاشية V.

147 بحركات الجسد : S.

148 موتا : V, R.

149 بالضرورة لان : S.

150 بضنك : R / ويضنك : V, K.

151 ضميرا واحد : A.

152 نضجر : A.

153 امداد : K.

154 فيهم : K.

155 الذين : K, V.

156 نحسب : R / بحسب : K, V.

157 الذي : K.

158 دونهم : R.

الثمره، ولا تقع بيدينا ونعلم كما ان الثمره نحن مضطرين اليها كل يوم[159] وفي كل وقت، لكي نغتذى[160] بها ونتنعم،[161] هكذا وهولاء التي هن الاصول، ان رذلناهم نبرد كمثل انه[162] لا حاجة لهم، وبهذا نخيب ايضا ومن الثمره التي بوساطتهن[163] من عادتها تظهر فينا في وقت وقت، لانه ليس نتشاغل[164] من المداومه بهن كلما نحن لابسين هذا الجسد، ولا يظن احدا[165] من الناس ان لهن حد في هذا الوقت الحاضر.

(18) الذي هو كامل بالقامه ومقتني تشوق[166] الى الله من بعد خروجه من العالم، ليس يليق به ان يمكث في المجمع وقت[167] كثير بالدخول والخروج مع كثيرين بل من بعد وقت قليل اذا اتعلم تقلب الاخوه وترتيبهم، ونوع الاسكيم وزيه واتضاعه يفرز نفسه ليكون متفردا[168] في قلايه، ليلا يقتني مع كثيرين اعتياد وتنقلب بساطة بدوته[169] الى المكر (V242r) من مفاوضة الاخوه المنحلين التي في المجمع. لاني نظرت كثيرين عند خروجهم من العالم لما جاو[170] الى مجمع الاخوه،[171] كانوا[172] ودعا انقيا، ومن بعد ان مكثوا زمان كثير في المجمع، صاروا مكرين[173] وقحا ولم يعودوا يجدوا تلك الوداعة الاوله، فلهذا ينبغي ان يفرز نفسه الى مفاوضة شيخ فاضل، مشهود له بحسن السيره ومعرفة السكون، ومعه فقط يتفاوض ويتسارر ويتعلم سيرة السكون، ومع انسان اخر لا تكون له مفاوضه، (A210v) من ذلك[174] الوقت لكي في وقت قليل يوهل لمذاقة المعرفه.

---

159 كليوم : V.

160 نتغذى : S / تغتذي : V / تغذى : K.

161 وتتنعم : K, V.

162 ان : A.

163 بواسطتهن : S / بوساطتهم : A.

164 نتساعى : S / نتساغا : K, V, R.

165 احد : K, S.

166 بشوق : A.

167 وقتا : K.

168 متفرد : K, V, R.

169 بداوته : S.

170 جاو : R.

171 اخوه : K, V.

172 وكانوا : R.

173 ماكرين : S.

174 ذالك : R.

(19) (K199r) ليس بالعلم الكثير[175] وكتب مختلفه تقتنا[176] النقاوه، او توجد بل بالاعتنا بالصلاه، ماذا تنفع معرفة كتب كثير[177] وتفسير معانيهن،[178] واي حاجه بهن[179] لجمع الضمير ونقاوة الصلاه.

(20) بالحقيقه كل متوحد[180] من بعد ان يترك العالم ان عاد قرا[181] بشي من الكتب (R168r) ما خلا كتب سيرة الرهبنه، ان كان عالم حكيم او امي، فهذا فقد ضيع[182] اوله طرق الرهبنه، وقد مال ضميره[183] ليطلب[184] انشراح باوليك. ولو ان يصعدوك الى السماء الكتب البرانيه، ليس تنفعك[185] القراه بهن،[186] لانهم يعلموك طرق اخرى[187] غريبه. يكفوك كتب الحديثه، والذي[188] على سيرة الوحده الى كمال المعرفه وحسن الضمير، ومن بعد ان تبلغ الى النقاوه، قليل او كثير، ان قريت في اوليك ليس تتاذا، هوذا قد شاهدتك الحق بهولاء.

(21) ان[189] تطلب عزا حقيقي بالصلاه اهتم بنقا نيتك، وان تطلب تقويم النيه وتعديلها اهتم بالصلاه، لان الاهتمام بكل واحده من هذين[190] يصنع طهارة رفيقتها، (V242v) اصلاح النيه يصنع طهارة الصلاه، ونقا الصلاه يجلب دالة النيه.

(22) الذكاوه مع الخلطه ليس تنحفظ،[191] ولا تذكار الله مع الهم بافعال وخلطة الامور، كثيرين بشهوة البر يلقون انفسهم باضطراب هذه الامور فيخيبوا من

---

175 بعلم كثير : K, A.
176 تقتني : K, S.
177 كثيرة : S.
178 معانيهم : R / معانيها : K,V.
179 بهم : K.
180 متوحدا : K, S, R.
181 قرى : K.
182 طيع : A.
183 طميره : A.
184 بان يطلب : A.
185 تنفعل : R.
186 بهم : K.
187 اخره : K, V, R.
188 الذي : A.
189 وان : K, V.
190 هاذين : R.
191 تحفظ : R.

جزوا[192] هذا البر الاعظم، لانهم يظنون ان جميع افرازات البر، وكل وصايا سيدنا تلزم لكل واحد[193] من الناس، وينبغي[194] لكل احد حفظ[195] جميعهم، وما يعرفون (A211r) ان[196] وصايا سيدنا وضعهم لساير الرتب لكل رتبه[197] ما يليق بها، وليس يوافقوا جميعهم لرتبة واحده، حسب ما[198] افرزهم العظيم في القديسين فيلون. لانه افرز وصايا عظام تليق بالكاملين، كمثل قوله اترك كل شي[199] واتبعني، ولا تهتم بالغد وصلوا في كل حين،[200] ولا تملوا، وبقية ما يشبه هولاء، التي[201] ما يقدرون يحفظوهم[202] الضعفا في الايمان والمبتديين المفتقرين الى البقل[203] لكي يتطلبوا[204] به او لرضاع[205] اللبن لينشوا به، كمثل الامراة[206] الحكيمه التي تقدم لاولادها ماكول يليق برتبة قامة كل واحد، لان الحدث بالايمان والمبتدي هو كالطفل، والكامل في السيره كالرجل التام، وضع له وصايا عظام حسب التطوييات التي[207] اعطاها،[208] فلهذا قلنا ان[209] ليس يليق حفظهن[210] لانسان واحد.

(23) كيف يشبه قوله طوبا للباكيين[211] لانهم يتعزون،[212] لقوله[213] طوبا[214] لصانعي السلامه لانهم بني الله يدعون، كيف يقدر الذي هو[215] جالس في النوح

---

192 جزو : A.

193 واحدا : A.

194 ينبغي : R.

195 يحفظ : K.

196 ان : ساقطة R.

197 لساير الرتب، لكل رتبه : زائدة K, V.

198 حسبما : K.

199 كلشي : V.

200 كلحين : V.

201 الذي : K.

202 يحفظوها : A.

203 الماكول : R.

204 ينطبوا : R, V / يتطلبوا، وتفسيرها في الحاشية "يغتذوا" :A. / يتطيبوا :S / ينطقوا : K.

205 والرضاع : S.

206 الامرااة : K.

207 الذي : K.

208 اعطا : K, V, R.

209 ان : ساقطة K, V.

210 حفظهم : K, V.

211 الباكيين : R.

212 سيتعزون : K, V.

ويبكي ليل ونهار، ليبدل نفسه ويدور العالم لكي يصلح[216] (V243r) المتغاضبين[217] ويصنع السلام[218] بين كثيرين.

(24) او كيف تشبه[219] اسهروا وصلوا في كل حين،[220] (K199v) وقوله[221] ادخل الى خزانتك واغلق بابك وصلي لابيك بالخفي،[222] لقوله كنت مريض[223] وافتقدتموني، وغريب[224] واويتموني، ومسجون[225] وزرتموني،[226] الذي قد اومر ان يسهر ويصلي بخزانته، كيف يقدر ان يفتقد المرضى[227] ويدور على السجون، (A211v) ويحمل الاهتمام بالغربا، بل قول ادخل الى خزانتك واسهر وصلي بالخفي[228] لله، تليق (R168v) للتي[229] طوبا[230] للنواحين،[231] لكي بالحزن والسكون[232] تنقا الصلاه، وبالصلاه[233] يقبل عزا الباكيين،[234] الذي لا يمكن ولا يكمل الا بالنوح.

(25) الذي هو وحده منقبض مع ذاته حتى وفي[235] العالم، هذه هي سنة البكا ان باشيا[236] اخر ما يهتم في ايام بكاه الا بالنوح فقط، وهو عادم اهتمام كل شي[237]

---

213 لقولة : R.

214 طوبى :K.

215 هو : ساقطة K, V.

216 يصالح : S.

217 المتغايظين : K, V.

218 السلامه : A.

219 يشبه قوله : A.

220 كلحين : V.

221 وقولة : R.

222 بالخفاء : S.

223 مريضا : S.

224 وغريبا : S.

225 ومسجونا : S.

226 ومسجون وزرتموني وغريبا واويتموني. : K.

227 المرضا : K, V, R.

228 بالخفاء : S.

229 يليق للذي : A.

230 طوبى : S.

231 للنايحين : K, V, S.

232 ولسكون : R.

233 بالصلاه : K, V.

234 الباكين : S.

235 في : K, R.

اخر، لان النوح هو حزن واحد فريد قد[238] ضبطنا صور[239] واس في القلب، ولا يمكن ان يقبل اقنوع[240] لنوحه، الا من داخل يجد العزا على الشي الذي من اجله ينوح. لان ثم موجود من دون البكا الظاهر، بكا خفي ملقي في القلب، الذي هو[241] حامل في قلبه حزن دايم من اجل خطاياه، او قد انفرش على قلبه كابه بتذكار تواضع سيدنا، او محزون لاجل اناس خطاه، مكتيب مقطب حزين لاجل الامور السماييه بانتظارهم دايما،[242] ليس يتعزا[243] بشي من امور هذا العالم ولا يتسلا،[244] الا ان وجد شهوته التي من اجلها ينوح. هذا هو النوح الدايم التي[245] من دون[246] الدموع الظاهره[247] بالجسد، هذا دايما يبكي بخفاياه، والذي قد اقتنى[248] واحده من هولاء داخل منه له طوبا[249] النواحين[250] لانهم يتعزون، ولو ان (V243v) يبطى عزاك ايها النايح بافراز، لا تحزن لان من قبل ان تنتقل من الجسد، يظهر لك سعادتك[251] وعند ذلك[252] ينقلك من الجسد.

(26) **في تغيير[253] انواع الافكار.** الفكر الذي على الدوام يفحص (A212r) ضعف وعجز قريبه ويقوم اخرين بالحب، ليس يدرك النقاوه. الفكر الذي على الدوام يبكت رذايل ذاته ويطلب في نفسه[254] صالحات قريبه ساكن بسلام[255]

---

236 بشيا : R / بشيئا : S / بشي : K,V.

237 كلشيا : R / كلشي : V.

238 قد : ساقطة K, V.

239 ضبط ناصور : K, V.

240 قنوع : S.

241 هو : ساقطة R.

242 دايم : K, V.

243 يتعزى : S.

244 يتسلى : S.

245 الذي : K.

246 دون : ساقطة K.

247 الظاهر : K.

248 اقتنا : V, R.

249 طوبى : K, S.

250 للنائحين : S / للنواحين : K.

251 بسعادتك : K,V.

252 ذالك : R.

253 تغير : R.

254 نفسه : ساقطة K, V.

255 في سلام : K.

الضمير. الفكر الذي دايما يتنبا بالمزمعات وضميره مايل لمرضاة[256] الناس، ويتغير مع الضماير لكي يظن به انه بار وحكيم، ومحب كثيرين هو عبد[257] غاش لمحبة المدحه والكرامه، هذا ليس يوهل لحرية الفكر ونظر ضميره، ولو ان يتعب كثير[258] ليس يقوم لغرض الحق.

(27) الفكر الذي على الدوام ينلام[259] من نيته[260] ويندم ويقبل ويغصب ذاته ويعدل زلاته، يوهل للحريه ويعتق[261] من الطياشه.

(28) والفكر الذي دايما ينلام[262] من نيته ويسوف ويدوسها بلا تقويم، وان كان عنايه الله في[263] وقت وقت[264] تنبهه[265] للتوبه،[266] وفي وقت تودبه، وفي وقت تقمعه، وفي وقت تكرمه، وفي وقت ترذله، وتحزنه بالعوارض والامراض والخسارات، وتجذبه[267] بالرحمه للتقويم[268] فيتم[269] هو باطل متهاون مزدرى[270] ويستحقر[271] بهولاء الانفعالات وعن نخز[272] النيه يتغافل، ترتفع منه النعمة بغته، ويقع بيد العداله (K200r) لتقويمه، ولم يفلت حتى يوفي الفلس الاخير، اعني الذنوب التي[273] صنع ولم يذكر الاخره.

(29) الفكر الذي من الظنون[274] وتردد الافكار، ومن الاخبار (R169r) والحكايات،[275] ان هكذا هو فلان، (V244r) وهكذا ايضا[276] قال فلان، ويحب

---

256 لمرضات : K, V.

257 عبدا : K, V.

258 كثيرا : S.

259 يتلام : S.

260 حثه : K.

261 وينعتق : K, V.

262 يتلام : S.

263 في : ساقطة K.

264 وقت : ساقطة S.

265 تنبه : A, R.

266 الى التوبة : S.

267 وتغصبه : K, V, S.

268 بالتقويم : A.

269 فيقيم : S.

270 مزدراى : V.

271 ويستحق : K.

272 نقا : R.

273 الذي : A.

274 الضنون : A.

اسماعات[277] غريبه، ومتلهف الى الاخبار التي[278] من بعيد، ويعثر بهولاء، (A212v) وما يقمع هو ذاته، بل بالضد يخسر ليس ينعتق من الغيره والسجس وتكدر الضمير، ولا يوهل للطهاره ونياح الافكار، لاجل ان محب[279] المفاوضات والطياشه ليس له طب الا قمع التغصب[280] والقسر.

(30) الفكر الذي ليس من الطبع بل من الاعمال الاختياريه[281] يغصب هو ذاته، ليلا بخاصيات المفروزه بكل واحد واحد، قلبه قد قرب من مينا[282] السلامه ان حرس[283] مع[284] هولاء[285] ان يقتني الامور الواجبه الاخر.

(31) الضمير الذي على الدوام يتحيل ليوضع على ذاته نواقص[286] قريبه، كمثل ان هو الذي[287] قد اخطا ويبرر قريبه، ويشجب نفسه، هذا هو ابن السلام.

(32) الضمير الذي دايما يتحيل لكي يُقال[288] عنه من وجه كثيرين ويظن به انه ما فيه عيب، ولا يقطع اسباب الخساره بل انما قصده فقط ليخفي[289] الزلات التي صنع بالغش والمكر، هذا هو عبد غاش قد رهن[290] نفسه للمديح[291] البشري، يمقت[292] من النعمه ويظهر[293] مكره.

---

[275] والحكيات : K.

[276] ايضا : ساقطة A.

[277] سماعات : V, K, S.

[278] الذي : A.

[279] محبة : R.

[280] القمع بالتغصب : S.

[281] لاختياريه : V / لاختياره : K.

[282] مينة : K.

[283] حرص : K, V.

[284] من : A.

[285] هولا : K, R.

[286] نقايص : K.

[287] الذي : ساقطة A.

[288] يقل : V.

[289] ان يخفي : A.

[290] دهن : K, V.

[291] المديح : R / للمذبح : K, V.

[292] يمقد : R / بمقت : K, V.

[293] ويظهره : A.

(33) الضمير الذي قد ابتلع بمحبة صورة الله، ليس يهتم[294] لذاته اكثر من لقريبه[295] بكل شي، ويجعل نفسه بطال بقياس اخرين، هذا هو مكمل الوصايا.

(34) الضمير الذي يبكت ذاته ويعترف[296] انه غير مستحق، النعمه تفعل فيه.

(35) الضمير الذي موجود داخل منه عزا خفي، هذا في زمان الضوايق والتجارب ينتظر المزمعات.

(36) الضمير الضجور المتكدر[297] المتسجس، فرحه حزن، وعزاه ندامة.[298]

(37) (V244v) الضمير المكر[299] الذي يخفي غش قلبه، وبمرضات[300] الناس ياكل مخ[301] اعضام[302] اصدقاه، (A213r) وفي الاخر يثلبهم.

(38) الضمير الشيطاني الذي ربوة صلاح بخلة[303] واحدة[304] ينسا،[305] لان كل فكر يوعد[306] بالغلبه والمدحه بتواثبا[307] بغير صلاه وفحص، اعلم انه يسبب لك خزي واهانه.

(39) وايضا للقديس مار اسحق[308] مشورة[309] نافعه في سيرة معرفة الحق ينعملون بالسكون.

(40) الانسان الذي يغصب ذاته دايما ليتدبر بمقتضى حكم النيه، ليس يخطى بلا توبه.

(41) الذي دايما يهدس ضميره بالصالحات،[310] ليس ينظر[311] نواقص قريبه.

---

294 يهم : K, V, R.

295 قريبه : K, V.

296 وعرف : K.

297 المتكرر : R.

298 يذمه : S.

299 الماكر : S.

300 وبمراضاة : S, R, V / وبمراضات : K.

301 مح : S.

302 اعظام : K, V.

303 تجعله : K, V / بكلمة : R.

304 واحد : K, V, R.

305 ينسى : S.

306 يوعده : S / يوعدنا : K, V.

307 بتوابثا : R / بتواثب انه : S.

308 مار اسحق : ساقطة A, R, S, V.

309 مشورات : K, V.

(42) الذي يعود لسانه[312] ليقول[313] الصالحات على الاخيار والاشرار سريع[314] يملك السلام في قلبه.

(43) الذي فرش مراحمه بلا فرز على الصالحين والشريرين بالشفقه قد اتشبه بالله.

(44) الذي يبغض[315] صورة الله لا يستطاع ان ينحب من الله.

(45) الذي دايما يغلب خلق مشيته، هو مجاهد نشيط، والنعمه تفعل[316] فيه بزياده.

(46) الذي يغصب ذاته دايما ويقلب ضعف[317] خاصيات عوايده للحسنات، قد (R169v) ربط ذاته (K200v) باعمال الحفظ، واكليل متضاعف محفوظ له.

(47) الانسان الذي كم من مره ينلام من نيته وما يقوم نوع عوايده، ترتفع منه النعمه ويترك في يدي[318] التجارب ويتبهدل.

(48) الذي يجلب هواه الى ناحية اليمين، ويغلبه طباعه ليس غلاب[319] ينغلب.

(49) الذي من قبل ان يتالم القلب ويتضع، ويقوم النيه، يطلب منهم صلاح،[320] ليس هو مفروز من الذي يطلب عنب (V245r) من الشوك، وتين من القرطب.

(50) الذي استحق لموهبة معرفة[321] الافراز وحس[322] ان السما والارض وجميع ما فيهم (A213v) وملكوت الله وملايكته المختارين بتمثال تصوره

[310] في الصالحات : K.
[311] ينضر : A.
[312] يعود ذاته "لسانه" : S / لسانه عوده : K, V.
[313] يقول : A.
[314] سريعا : S.
[315] يغضب : A.
[316] تعسل "تفعل" : S.
[317] صعب : A.
[318] يدي : ساقطة A, R, S.
[319] انغلاب : S.
[320] خلاص : R.
[321] معرفة : ساقطة A, V, K.
[322] معرفة : زائدة A.

مربوطين، وبدا ليتجدد[323] بسر[324] معرفة الحق، وان غصب هو ذاته في السكون بحفظ واجباته، ينعتق من الطياشه ويوهل للانفعال[325] بالروح.

(51) الذي يد الكل عليه، ويده على الكل، ليس يتفرغ ليستريح بالسكون.

(52) لا يمكن ان يكون مع واحد بتكوينه مع كثيرين.

(53) والذي من اجل ان يكون له حسنا ينقلب مع الضماير بمراياة[326] الحب ويتكلم حسب شهوتهم، هو فاسق.

(54) الذي يشغل[327] ضميره باشيا[328] كثيره، ما يمكنه ان يتفاوض مع الواحد.

(55) المتوحد الذي قد حس بالراحه الذي من حقرية الذات، اخير من الذي وجد تكريم من[329] تاج المملكه.

(56) المتوحد الذي قد انضرب بالم حب[330] المديح والكرامه من الناس، ليس لجرحه شفا، واذا كان باعمال سيرته يقوم كثيرين، في عالم[331] المزمع تكون تدابير سيرته له مبكتين بعذاب الجحيم.

(57) الذي هو[332] حريص لينيح كثيرين ليس يمكنه ليكون عادم من الكل بالسكون، لاجل ان الذي يريد ان يكون يحب السجس، ليحب[333] السكون، ما يستطيع ان يرضي كثيرين وليداوم السكون.

(58) المتوحد الذي ما يحتمل لاجل السكون التعير[334] والخسارات، والتذمر والاستهزا، والمحقره[335] والضيم، مع جميع التجارب، لا (V245v) يمكنه ان

---

[323] يتجدد : K, V.

[324] كسر : R.

[325] بالانفعال : A.

[326] بمرايات : S, R.

[327] يشتغل : S.

[328] باشياء : V.

[329] من : ساقطة K, V.

[330] بحب الم : K.

[331] العالم : A.

[332] هو : ساقطة R.

[333] ويحب : S.

[334] التعيير : K, V, S.

[335] والمحقرا : R.

يتخلص من الشكوك والمغايضات[336] المصادفه له، ولا يقدر ان يهدا في السكون.

(59) الذي في كل وقت طرق سيرته منحله، ضميره بعيد من الله.

(60) والذي[337] قلبه ليس هو منسحق ومحزون بالله، ليس ينعتق من الطياشه.

(61) الذي (A214r) ما ينشق قلبه بالتحسر والتنهد، هو فارغ من صلاة الدموع.

(62) الذي هو عادم من القراه، هو ساير في التيه، لانه اذا اخطا ما يحس.

(63) الذي يمزج قراته بالتدابير والصلاة والحفظ والهذيذ بالفضايل، ينعتق من الطياشة.

(64) الذي اذا ما ضل وزل عن الحق واتهاون[338] وانحل واخطا، يعرف سبب مرضه، بالسهوله يشفا (R170r) بالتوبه.

(65) والذي على الدوام يقرع ولو انه ما يستجاب سريع، لاجل تحكيمه، ينعاق وينفتح[339] له.

(66) والذي سريع[340] دايما[341] يتسول، وبوقاحه ياخذ لاجل الاضطراب وعدم (K201r) التاديب، كم من وقت يضيع ما ياخذ.

(67) الذي يصوم فمه من الغذا، وليس يصوم من الخلق والحقد، ولسانه من[342] الاباطيل، صومه هو باطل، لان صوم اللسان اخير من صوم الفم، وصوم القلب والافكار اخير من الاثنين.

(68) قوت الجسد[343] المواكيل، وغذا[344] النفس الكلام والحكايات، وكما ان شره كثرة الماكول هو رغبة النفس،[345] هكذا السكوت هو ثمرة الحكمة المزمعة.

---

336 المفاوضات : S.

337 الذي : A.

338 او تهاون : A.

339 ويفتح : S.

340 سريع : ساقطة S.

341 دايم : K, V.

342 ما : R.

343 الجسم : K.

344 عزاء : S.

345 الجسد : S.

(69) الذي يزيل من ضميره هفوات قريبه، يزرع السلام في قلبه، وموضع[346] ليس فيه طعن القريب[347] ولا تحريك (V246r) يوجد الغضب يعني ولا زجر ولا تخريج[348] النفس.

(70) المتوحد الذي من بعد اعمال نشيطه اوهل لطفولية المعرفه، وتخلف عقله من تركيب الكلام، وانتهض فيه صمت السر الجديد، هذا قد استحق بالحقيقة ان يرتل مع الملايكه خفيا.

(71) (A214v) البحر الهادي السكين ليس لحسنه حد، وبحر الضمير الهادي السليم ليس لشرفه حد.

(72) الانقطاع من الكل هو بداية الانبساطه، وحد الانبساطة، هو بداية النقاوه، وحد النقاوه هو[349] بداية الحرية، وحد الداله بالصلاه هو مبدا الاتحاد بالمسيح.

(73) المتوحد الذي ما يزجر الفكر او الذكر الذي[350] يصعد على قلبه ويسكته، بل يقبله بامان ويتفاوض معه بفرح، ويتجاوب معه، ويخرج في طلبه، هذا[351] سوق عظيم وتجارات كثيره داخله فيه، ويبيعون ويشترون في وقت سم الموت،[352] وفي وقت دوا الحياة، ان لم ينهرهم بل يتفاوض مقابل الافكار النابعه، اخرته هي هلاك من الحق العتيد.

(74) المتوحد الذي يفطن للكلمه هي تركيب النفس، المتولده من تردد الافكار الداخله التي تكدر النقاوة، وعند ذلك[353] تتركب وتتميز وترسل الى عند مرسلها[354] وهو[355] يعد ذاته لسكون[356] الضمير الذي منه يولد الصمت البسيط، يسد[357] مسمعه من صوت الكلام وتردد الافكار ليلا يكون منه[358] تجارة

---

[346] وموضعا : K, V.

[347] للقريب : A.

[348] تحريك : A.

[349] وهو : R.

[350] للذي : K.

[351] هو : زائدة K, V.

[352] موت : R.

[353] ذالك : R.

[354] مرسله : R.

[355] ولو : A.

[356] بسكون : S.

[357] وسد : K, V.

[358] منه : ساقطة A.

المغايضات[359] والشكوك التي منهم تتولد[360] الحقد[361] والخلق[362] والحنق[363] والكابه[364] التي هي مخنقة[365] النفس، حتى وفي السكون (V246v) ايضا يفر من ينبوع التذكارات والافكار، ويستعين بصمت الضمير البسيط الذي هو صلب العقل، والاتحاد مع يسوع الذي هو السر الجديد، وثمرة الحكمه العتيده، ان كان[366] كل شجره انما تعرف من ثمارها[367]حسب الكلمة السيديه.[368] وهكذا كل[369] حكمه او كلام، (A215r) من الاعمال التي[370] بهن[371] تتفلح[372] التدابير، وتنعرف، وكما انه ان لم يلبس الانسان ثياب مستعاره لتغطي (R170v) جسمه تظهر فضيحته وتبان العيوب التي في جسده، ويتبهدل من ناظريه، فهكذا[373] ان لم تلبس النفس زي لكلامها[374] تظهر فضيحة[375] النفس[376] وتتبهدل.

(75) الذي وجد علم بلا تاديب ليس هو[377] مفروز من الذي بغته وجد ذخيره ليس هي له، ومع الذخيره اهلك حياته.

(76) الساذج الحكيم بالله، اخير من الفهيم الغاش بضميره.[378]

---

359 المفايضات : S.

360 يتولد : S.

361 والحقد : K, V.

362 والحاق : S / والقلق : R.

363 والخنق : R.

364 والكابه : K, V.

365 منقت : R / محنكة : S.

366 انكان : K.

367 ثماره : R / ثمرتها : A / ثمرها : K.

368 اي: الربانية.

369 وكل : R, S.

370 الذي : K.

371 بهم : K.

372 يتفلح : A.

373 هكذا : K.

374 كلامها : S.

375 فضيحتها : A.

376 النفس : ساقطة A.

377 هو : ساقطة A.

378 بضمير : R / في ضميره : K, V.

(77) فاعل[379] (K201v) الافعال عند[380] ذلك[381] ينبغي ان يتكلم اذا ما حصل من صمته موديه لكثيرين، والعارف[382] عند ذلك[383] ينبغي ان يتكلم متى ان كلامه يبني كثيرين، وينفع.

(78) الذي ياكل شبعه وينام شبعه هو ينبوع الالام، لاجل ان اتون البطن اذا ما اتوقد بزياده بمواكيل غليظه دسمه بالاكثر يتسع ويتلهف،[384] ويطلب.[385]

(79) الذي قمع واستعبد بطنه ولسانه اخير من الذي استعبد الاسد. الذي قمع الكلمه في قلبه اخير من الذي طمر وزنه[386] في الارض.

(80) الذي يفشي السر هو ابن جهنم، سر قلبه ما حفظ[387] كيف يحفظ وديعة (V247r) الروح.

(81) الانسان العادم من الصلاح ودايما[388] يجادل على الفضايل، ليس مفروز من الاعما العادم من النور، ويجادل على حسن الفصوص الكريمه والالوان الكثيره.

(82) الذي ما يفرح بالضوايق المصادفه اياه بسياسه،[389] يضل من مراحم عدالة الله.

(83) (A215v) الذي يماحك قبالة[390] التاديب يبعد منه المراحم الابويه.

(84) الذي يتذمر ويضطرب[391] مقابل التجارب تتضاعف عليه.

(85) الذي ما يتودب[392] هاهنا وينمقت بالتجارب، بلا رحمه يتعذب هناك.

---

379 العمال : S.

380 منذ : K, V.

381 ذالك : R.

382 عند...والعارف : ساقطة S.

383 ذالك : R.

384 وتلهف : S / ويتلف : A.

385 ويطلق : K, V.

386 زنة : V.

387 يحفظ : K.

388 وديما : R.

389 "ببشاشة" : S.

390 قبال : K, V.

391 ويتضطرب : A.

392 يتوب : S / يتادب : A.

(86) والذي بالشكر[393] وبفرح يصبر على التجارب فقد وجد اثمار الروح داخل منه.

(87) الذي قد[394] وجد عزا الروح داخله وداله في وقت الصلاه قد انعتق من السبي.

(88) الذي حتى واذا ما[395] كان خارج يهدس ضميره بكلام الله، بعمل متضاعف قد ربط نفسه، والنعمة تفعل فيه.

(89) الذي عود نفسه لكي يكون محترس داخل وخارج جهادا[396] عظيم[397] له، فان اتجلد[398] بالسكون ياتي الى قدام.

(90) الذي يغطس داخله[399] في السكون ودايما[400] يتحيل ليكون بمفاوضة[401] انسانه الجواني ينعتق من الطياشه.

(91) الذي هو في[402] داخل السكون يشت[403] ضميره برا منه وهو يرعا[404] في صلاح وشر اخرين، باطل هو عمله في السكون.

(92) الذي يبتعد زمان كثير من مفاوضة الكلام ونظر الوجوه، تنقلع[405] منه التذكارات القديمه.

(93) المتوحد المرتبط بواحد او بكثيرين لا بد له ان يتحرك معهم ويحزن ويفرح[406] كمثل اغصان الشجر التي تحرك (V247v) بعضها بعض وليس ياتي الى قدامه[407] بالله.

---

393 بشكر : K.

394 قد : ساقطة A, S.

395 ما : ساقطة A.

396 اجهادا : R / اجتهاد : K, V.

397 عظيماً : S.

398 تجلد : S.

399 ذاته : A.

400 وديماً : R.

401 مفاوضة : R.

402 في : ساقطة A, S.

403 ويشت : V / ويشتت : K / يشتت : S.

404 يرعى : K, S.

405 ينقلع : A.

406 معهم : زائدة K.

407 قدام : A.

(94) العادم من الصدقه[408] المفرزه هو عادم ايضا من الضنك. والذي يفيض حبه[409] ويرحم رحمة الاهيه[410] على الكل بلا فرز[411] قلبه[412] هو ينبوع الافراح.[413]

(95) ان تشا ان تكون محب بلا فرز لصورة الله لا تفتش دواخله.[414]

(96) الشجرة الكثيرة (R171r) الاثمار تنحني اغصانها من اثمارها، وليس تتحرك لكل ريح.[415]

(97) الشجره العادمه من الاثمار، (A216r) تتشامخ اغصانها ومن كل[416] ريح تتحرك، فهكذا هو ايضا المتوحد[417] الذي خطب نفسه باختياره للمسيح،[418] ليحفظ حريته متفردا بلا دنس، وفي السكون[419] يتوسوس ضميره، ويفتش ويدين ويخاصم[420] مع (K202r) قريبه، بالفسق عمال مع خطيبه المسيح بتذكاره.

(98) المتوحد الغاش بضميره وذو امرين يشتم ابن الله.

(99) المتوحد الذي خرج في طلب اهتمام المبصورات قد نسى ميعاده الاول.

(100) المتوحد الذي في وسط كثيرين يعمل بالوحده هذا هو مجاهد نشيط، وهو محتاج للمعرفة المقدسه المطيبة بحقرية الذات، وطول الروح والاتضاع، والانحطاط ليحمل نفسه ويصبر على ما ياتي عليه، لان ليس في كل شي يكمل احتياج[421] حقوقه، بل بشي[422] قليل يوجد باحتمال التغصب.

---

408 الاصدقا : K, V, R, S.

409 ورحمته : زائدة A.

410 الهية : A, S.

411 لصورة الله : زائدة S.

412 قلبه : ساقطة A.

413 الافراز : R.

414 داخله : K, V.

415 ريح : ساقطة K, V.

416 منكل : V.

417 المتوحد. المتوحد الذي... : K, V, R, S.

418 ܠܡܫܝܚܐ : K.

419 السكوت : A.

420 ويتخاصم : A.

421 الاحتياج : A.

422 في شى : A, S.

(101) المتنسك الذي يتغصب ويصبر مده بالسكونِ والوحده، بالاختفا[423] عن الوجوه، تبطل العوايد والتدابير الاوله والتحيل التي هن[424] رباطات النفس، (V248r) التي[425] بهن يموت ويعيش الانسان.

(102) الذي من قبل ان يتعرا[426] انسانه العتيق يتحيل ينهض[427] انسانه الجواني، باطل هو عمله وهو يفهم كلامي بالفعل.

(103) الذي من قبل ان يعدل خاصيات عوايده وانواع تقالييه، ويرتب احواسه، يبدى[428] ان يزين دواخله بالمحاسن الروحانيه، هذا جميع ايام حياته ما ينعتق من وثب الاضطراب.

(104) الذي هو قاسي قلبه ويقيم كلمته، ان قوم غرضه ويحفظ الحقد على الالام، يصير ناسك وعمال في[429] السيره، ولبساطة (A216v) الامانه ونقاوة النفس بعد جهد يوهل.

(105) المتوحد المتضع النفس الطفل القلب وبسيط ولم[430] يقيم كثير كلمته، ولو يظن[431] عنه انه ابله، ان اتقدم لتدبير العمل بسهوله يبلغ الذكاوه[432] والنقاوه، لان مساعدة[433] الطبع لاي ناحية مال نصف العمل، قالوا الابا يصنع، ان كان تسير معه النوح[434] والتغصب.

(106) الذي كل فكر[435] يصعد على قلبه[436] بغته يفعله بلا صلاه ولا مشوره ولا اختبار وفحص النيه، ليس هو مفروز من البهيمه، وفي الاخير[437] يندم.

---

[423] باختفا : A.
[424] هي : S / هي هن : K, V.
[425] الذي : K.
[426] يتعرى : K, S.
[427] لينهض : S.
[428] يبدا : A.
[429] في : ساقطة R.
[430] لم : K, V.
[431] ظن : A.
[432] للذكاوة : K, V, S.
[433] يساعد : K.
[434] والبكا : زائدة K, V.
[435] فكرا : A.
[436] اي: يخطر على باله.
[437] الاخر : S.

(107) الضمير النقي البسيط هو مسكن التقانه.[438] والضمير الغاش القاسي هو مسكن الالام.

(108) الطيب الذي يصعد من اللبان تفوح[439] رايحته حسب الماده التي[440] منها اتركب هو الطيب، وسلامه وفرح القلب يعطوا حلاوة في النفس حسب الماده التي منها[441] اتركب[442] هو السلام.

(109) المتوحد الذي بتربية منازل السيره من بدايه اولف بيت[443] الى كمال (V248v) القامة التامة الشين والثاو،[444] بطقس[445] الترتيب، ما يصعد (R171v) بالتدبير بل بمفرزات[446] الحيل يصيد انواع الكمال، هذا بغتة يسقط ومع سالبين بيت القدس يندان.

(110) المتوحد الذي تعرا الالام بالفضايل واوهل[447] ليفعل[448] العجايب، وما قد كمل بالحب الخالص والرحمه التي بلا فرز، هذا الى الان هو ناقص.

(111) المتوحد المحزون بحب المسيح[449] وقلبه منسحق بالشفقة على الصالحين والاشرار ببساطه، هذا قد لبس المسيح[450] خفي (K202v) واستضا عقله بالروح، وحس بالتجديد الذي مزمع طبعنا ان يقبله.

(112) ان كنت تجعل جسدك ذبيحة بالاعمال، (A217r) ونفسك تنقا[451] وتصنع العجايب، ولم تقتني داله في وقت الصلاه تعطي اقنوع[452] النيه،[453] ان قد اقتنت[454] تجديد بروح يسوع، لا تضل ليس ترث من هاهنا ميراث القديسين.

---

438 التقانة (التقوى) : S / النقاوة : A.

439 يفوح : R, S.

440 الذي : K, A.

441 منه : R.

442 تتركب : K.

443 الف با: K, V, R, S.

444 الواو والياء : S / الشين والتا : K, V, R.

445 بطكس : R.

446 بمفزات : K, V, S / بفراز : R.

447 او اهل : S.

448 ان يفعل : A.

449 ܠܡܫܝܚܐ : K.

450 ܠܡܫܝܚܐ : K.

451 تتنقى : S.

452 قنوع : A.

453 للنيه : A, S, V.

(113) الانسان الذي على الدوام يهدي نفسه ويتحيل بكل سبب، ان يقلع من قلبه الحسد والشر، ويزرع في نفسه الحب الصادق لكل احد، هذا فقد[455] عد[456] داخل منه[457] محل الثالوث المقدس، ومزمع ان يحصد من ارض قلبه اثمار الروح الذي هن الرجا والفرح والعزا الخفي.

(114) الذي يصالح ذاته، اخير[458] من الذي يصالح شعوباً[459] متقسمه، وهو مغضب متقسم[460] على ذاته.

(115) المتوحد الموجود داخل منه عزا[461] بلا سبب، هذا قد وجد يسوع متهلل[462] بالروح ومعترف لابيه الذي اظهر مجده (V249r) للاطفال بالمسيح.[463]

(116) الذي قد حس ان انسانه[464] الداخل[465] قد انتهض وانبسط لسانه بالشكر، وبدا يشخص بالصلاه الخفيه والسبح الملايكي، يجب ان يميت اعضاه[466] الارضيه، ويتجرد من التحيل ويداوم[467] متفردا[468] لمفاوضته،[469] ليلا يتضيق[470] وينضنك[471] ويطفا[472] او ينتقل، وهناك يكون البكا وصرير الاسنان بالندم.

---

[454] اقتنيت : K, V, S.

[455] قد : A.

[456] اعد : A, S.

[457] في داخله : A.

[458] خير : K.

[459] شعوب : R, S / قلوب : K.

[460] مغضوب منقسم : S.

[461] عزاء : V.

[462] متهلّ : K, V.

[463] ܒܡܫܝܚܐ : K.

[464] بانسانه : A.

[465] الداخلي : S / الجواني : K, V.

[466] اعطاه : A.

[467] ويدوم : A.

[468] متفرد : R.

[469] للمفاوضته : R.

[470] يتضايق : S / يتديق : A, R.

[471] وينطنك : A.

[472] ويطغا : K, V.

(117) كما[473] ان الابله[474] الذي يعرف الكتابه، نظرة اخرى[475] لازقه[476] لمعرفته، هكذا والذي تفعل فيه النعمه نظرة اخرى[477] وقوه لازقه[478] لكل شي[479] يصنع.

(118) كما انه ما يتعلمن الصنايع من حكمة الكلام، هكذا ليس تتعلمن الفضايل التي للسيرة[480] الصوم[481] والسهر والنسك والصلوات،[482] من قراءة (A217v) الكتب، وحدت[483] الحركات ودقة الفهم، من دون تجربه طويله بذواتنا نحتمل فلاحة الاعمال.[484]

(119) ابله يصنع صناعة بالتجربه في ذاته،[485] اخير من عارف يتعلم سيرة الروح من اسطر الكتب، وتسليم من اخرين، من غير تجربة محكمه بذاته.

(120) الذي قد فهم ان كل شي[486] يزدرع[487] او ينصب اولا في السفل تثبت عروقه، وبعد ذلك[488] ينموا[489] الى فوق، هو ايضا اولا يفلح ويتدرب ويقوم ويقع في السفل، وعند[490] ذلك[491] ينموا[492] بالروح الى[493] فوق.

---

473 وكما : A.

474 اي: الغشيم.

475 اخرى (أخرة) : S / اخره : K, V, R.

476 لاصقة : S.

477 اخرة : K, V, R, S.

478 لاصقة : S.

479 شيا : R.

480 السيره : R.

481 كالصوم : A.

482 والصلاوات : K.

483 وحدة : K, V, S.

484 لاعمال : R.

485 فيذاته : K.

486 كلشياً : R.

487 يزردع : V / يزرع : K.

488 ذالك : R.

489 ينمو : K, S.

490 ومنذ : K, V.

491 ذالك : R.

492 ينمو : A / ينمي : K.

493 الذي : K.

(121) الناسك الذي يعمل بالتوبه ويفلح بالنسك بكل الاعمال (R172r) وانواع الفضايل، ويتكل على بره وليس على النعمه، ليس[494] مفروز من الذي يجمع حجاره لتجرته.[495]

(122) ثم[496] من[497] صومه ابعده[498] من الحق واخر نسكه، واخر تجرده،[499] واخر (V249v) سهره، واخر عمله، واخر صدوقيته، واخر احتماله، واخر كمال اعماله الالهيه، وكم نريد ان نقول، لان ربنا جزم[500] ان من دوني ما تقدرون[501] ان تعملوا شي،[502] اعني بالهدوا[503] وتواضع القلب التي[504] بهن[505] انا غلبت العالم.

(123) اعمال الفضيله الممتزجين بالهدو[506] والتواضع، والخوف، والحيا، والصبر، والحفظ، ان وافقوا لغرض المتعلق على الصليب، ويعطي الحياه للعالم، هن[507] درج لمصاعد السيره، (K203r) وسيره الحريه من بعد هولاء،[508] هن عربون ملكوت السماء.[509]

(124) الذي قد وجد داخل[510] منه ذخيره فليحترص[511] من نار الحسد، ولا يظهر السر ويحرق اغمار[512] قلب رفيقه، ويندان من الحق، وليحذر ايضا بالاكثر، من الذين (A218r) هم[513] غايرين بالحسد.[514]

---

494 هو : زائدة K, V.

495 لتعزيته : S / لتعرته : A.

496 ام : K.

497 كان : زائدة S.

498 ابعد : S.

499 اتجرده : R.

500 زم : R.

501 لا تقدروا : A.

502 شياء : A, S.

503 بالهدو : K.

504 الذي : A.

505 الذي بهم : K.

506 بالهدوا : R.

507 هم : K.

508 هولا : K, R.

509 السموات : A / السما : K, R.

510 داخلا : A.

511 فليحترس : S.

512 ا_ مار : R / اجمار : K.

(125) الذي يصدق ان من الشرارة[515] الصغيرة تشتعل النار فليحذر ليلا يجمع داخل[516] منه نار الحسد والشر، لان حيث تجد ماده تلتهب وتفسد بغته العرم[517] والاجداس،[518] وافراح ارض قلبه،[519] ودخانه يعمي اعين كثيرين.

(126) كما انه لا يمكن ان يدفن نار بالتبن، وما يصير فساد، هكذا لا يستطاع ان يحفظ داخل نار الحقد والحسد والشر، او يتنازل مع الم الزنا، او[520] يتنازل بالم حلاوة المجد والكرامه، ولا يقبل منهم موذيه.

(127) المتوحد الذي جرب بذاته انه بكم انواع متواتره واعمال مديده بالصلوات،[521] اتفلح[522] القلب والعقل، حتى اتقووا[523] وغلبوا الاحواس، وقطفوا من الانسان[524] الحافظ العقب[525] دايما (V250r) ويتميز ويوزن ربح الناحيتين، الاول والاخر، ليلا غلبته تكون[526] له انغلاب، وربحه خساره.

(128) هنيذ الضمير ينفع اذا ما اترتبت[527] الاحواس[528] واهتدوا واتفقوا بالسلامه والود الافكار والعقل والضمير.

(129) الذي هدا ذاته[529] بالسلامه،[530] ووفق المتقسمين الذي داخل[531] منه، و زرع السلام بينهم، هذا هو الاه[532] وجميع الخلايق تتفق معه.

---

[513] هم : ساقطة K, V.

[514] بالجسد : R.

[515] شرارة : R.

[516] داخلا : A.

[517] العزم : K, V / العدم : R.

[518] الاكداس : S / والاحواس : K, V. الاجداس : في الحاشية V.

[519] تقلبه : K.

[520] و: K.

[521] بالصلاوات : K.

[522] اي: تنجّح.

[523] تقووا : K.

[524] لسان : K.

[525] العقب (العقل) : S / القلب : K.

[526] تكون غلبته : K.

[527] ترتبت : K.

[528] الحواس : A.

[529] هدى نفسه : S.

[530] والود الافكار...بالسلامة : A.

[531] داخلا : A.

[532] هوالاه (هؤلاء) : S.

(130) الذي يريد ان يهدي وحشة الحسودين، ويسالم بنقاوه حبه الالهي، فليخطف ضميره وافكاره لسلاما طفوليا بسذاجه، ويقابلهم اوله بالمديح والعطايا، ويلاقيهم بالتبجيل[533] والكرامة السليمه، بانحطاط ويخجل وجوههم بتقديم المايده، حسب ما تامر الكتب، والابا، ليلا من اجلهم نضيع[534] سلامة (A218v) قلوبنا.[535]

(131) الذي[536] ما توافقك مصادقته،[537] احذر ان[538] لا تجعله لك عدوا، بل حبه كشرع الناموس الروحاني، وانت مبتعد منه جزويا، وملاقاتك (R172v) له تكون بوداد مسالم معه، ليلا يتكدر ضميرك وتضيع سلامة قلبك، كل شي[539] اصنع وبكلشي اتحيل ان لا تضيع سلام[540] قلبك، وتتجرد من الله.

(132) واذا قيل عنك بردي وانحصر ضميرك ولو[541] ان تطوي يومين يومين بالمسح والتوبة وكل انواع الصلاه والدموع، ليس تنعتق من ضنك الضمير ولا يعطيك ربنا راحة، الا ان من كل قلبك بالحقيقه تضمر[542] انك مسي،[543] ان اخطيت او لم تخطي، بقنوع قلبك[544] انك بالحق[545] اسيت.[546]

(133) المتوحد الذي (V250v) بحكم النيه يتدبر ويسرع في تبع سلامه قلبه، بالحق ان اخطا[547] او لم يخطي يجلب الملامه على ذاته هذا ينيحه ربنا.

(134) مضادد كثير شرع الروحاني الحري[548] الذي به يتدبرون الذين بحكم النيه يسيرون، لاجل سلام[549] قلبهم الى شرع النفساني العادلي.

---

[533] اي: عظّم.

[534] نطيع : A.

[535] قلبنا : K, V, S.

[536] التي : K.

[537] بمصادفته : K, V.

[538] ان : ساقطة A.

[539] كلشي : R / وللاشيا : K, V.

[540] سلامة : A.

[541] لو : K, V.

[542] تظهر :S / تطمر : A / تفتكر : K, V.

[543] مسيح : R / موسي : A.

[544] قلبي : R, S / قلب : K, V.

[545] بالحقيقة : K.

[546] اسأت : S / اذنبت : K.

[547] اخطى : K.

[548] الجري : S.

[549] سلامه : K, V.

(135) الوحيد[550] الذي بحكم النيه يتدبر وجرب ان معاشرة الناس، الملوك والحقيرين الابرار والخطاه، من (K203v) دون الشهوه والغضبيه ومراياه[551] الحب، لا يمكن ان يعيش، وحس بالخساره التي[552] من هذه الاشيا، يفر هو على الدوام للسكون،[553] وكعاجز يستعين بالصمت، ليلا يضيع سلامة قلبه.

(136) الذي يخسر بعواجز الاخوه ليس لضربته شفا، والذي ينظر الخشبه التي[554] في عينه، ليس يتفرغ لينظر[555] الحسكه التي في عين[556] اخيه.

(137) الذي قد ارتسم بلا نسيان في قلبه صورة (A219r) الفريسي والعشار ليس يفتخر باعماله بانه نشيط.

(138) الذي راحته هي ضنك وتعب لاخرين هو ضد الله.

(139) الذي ما توافق بواطنه لظواهره ويسرع لكي يحس بميراث القديسين، هو مضل نفسه.

(140) الذي يعتني لكي يقوم في ذاته النواقص[557] التي تظهر له في اخرين الذي هو ساكن بينهم، مراةً[558] روحانيه قد وجد داخل منه.[559]

(141) المتوحد المرتخي المتهاون هو الذي يدعوا الالام لتفز[560] عليه.

(142) النشيط بالاعمال والافعال ترعب منه الشياطين، (V251r) وبغشهم يوقدوه بالحراره الى فوق.

(143) العارف المتدبر بافرازات المعرفه اوجاع عظيمه يصنع للشياطين، ويرصدون عقبه[561] ليلا[562] ونهارا[563] لكي يصطادونه.

---

[550] الوحيد (المتوحد) : S / المتوحد : K, V.

[551] ومرايه : R.

[552] الذي : K.

[553] السكون : R.

[554] الذي : A.

[555] ينظر: K, S.

[556] عين : ساقطة R.

[557] النقايص : K.

[558] مراااه : K.

[559] منة: K.

[560] بمعنى "لتفوز" . للهجوم : S / لتقر: A.

[561] عقله : K.

[562] وليل : K, V.

(144) المتوحد الذي يدوس نيته بالنور، هو عتيد ان يجلد منها مرارة[564] التبكيت وظلمة الندم.

(145) كما ان بجلوس الطير على البيض يسخنوا ويصنعوا[565] فراريج السلام، وهكذا ايضا هو المتوحد ما دام في سكون القلايه، هو كمثل البيضه والنعمه تحل عليه وتحوم كمثل الام، ويسخن بالحب الالهي، ويحتر بالروح ويورق في قلبه ثمرة[566] الروح، واما الذي يبعد نفسه بارادته من تحت النعمة التي هي ام العامه،[567] ويطيش ويتشتت بالدوران (R173r) يبرد ويرذل.

(146) النياحة المقدسة التي تكون للنفس من النعمه بعد اعمال التوبه، ليس لحلاوتها قياس ولا في[568] لسان كفوا[569] ان ينعت نوع مذاقتها.

(147) كما ان الاشجار الذين ينثروا[570] ورقهم وييبسون[571] في الشتا، في زمان نيسان ليس من ناحية اخره،[572] [573] بل من داخل حقريتهن[574] يخرج[575] مجد (A219v) وبها[576] كرامتهن[577] باوراق وازهار واثمار. وهكذا والقديسين[578] الذين[579] بارادتهم اماتوا اعضاهم الارضيه، بالضوايق والاحزان والشقا واعمال النسك، من بعد حفظهم[580] الوصايا غلبوا[581] الالام واتطهروا[582] ليس

---

563 ونهار : K.

564 بمرارة : S.

565 ويفرخوا : S.

566 ثمره : K.

567 العظمة : K, V.

568 شي : K.

569 كفئا : S.

570 ينثرون : A.

571 ييبسون : A, S.

572 اخرى : A, S.

573 يختسون : زائدة K, V.

574 حقريتهم: K, S, R.

575 يكون : K.

576 بهاء : S.

577 كرامتهم : K.

578 هكذا ايضا هم القديسين : K / وهكذا والقديسين : A, S, V / وهكذا القديسين : R.

579 الذي : A, R, S.

580 حفظهن : V, R.

581 جاهدوا : K, V.

582 وتطهروا : S.

خارج منهم، بل من داخل حقريتهم وتواضع صبرهم، بالتجارب تحيا النفس، وتتجدد[583] بسر القيامة وتلبس (V251v) حلة المجد، ويشرق العقل كمثلما[584] في الحياة[585] الجديده، لان قيامة[586] الصديقين المعقوله هاهنا هي سر وتمثال تلك التي للعامه.

(148) المتوحد الذي مشوات[587] اعمال سيرته ملتحمه مع مشوات اعمال ضميره، هو ابن ابا الروح، وعاجلا ينعتق من طياشة[588] الضمير.

(149) كما ان الاطبا ليس يامرون الذي هو في مرض اليرقان ان ياكل شهد العسل، بل ضد هذا يسقوه مرارة الافسنتين ليتغصص به،[589] فكذلك[590] الابا الروحانيين ليس يامرون الذي (K204r) الان ما قد[591] انعتق من الالام، ان يذوق بارادته[592] شي من شهد سلامة[593] القلب، ونياح[594] وفرح الروح الا بما هو ضد ذلك،[595] مرارة الاعمال وشقا النسك وضوايق وتجارب مختلفه، بالوحده والعوز والاستيحاش، لكي من وسط الشقوات توجد المراحم الالهيه،[596] والذي قد انعتقوا وصحوا ايضا نقول انهم محتاجين تغصيص الادويه[597] المطيبه،[598] بالازدرا والتجارب والضوايق، كمثل بولس الالهي الذي من اجل كثرة الاستعلانات اسلم الى شماته، ليكون يمقته ليلا يتعظم، لان هو جنسنا جميعه خاطي وميال،[599] وكل وقت هو مفتقر الى التوبه.

---

[583] ويتجدد : K.
[584] كمثل ما : K, V.
[585] الحياه : K.
[586] قيامه : K.
[587] مشى او تصرف، وفي حاشية A : "اعني خطوات".
[588] طياشه : K.
[589] بها : S.
[590] فكذالك : R / وهكذا : A.
[591] قد : ساقطة A, S.
[592] برادته : R.
[593] السلامة سلامة : S.
[594] ونياح : ساقطة R.
[595] ذالك : R.
[596] الالاهيه : R.
[597] ادويه : K.
[598] المضيقه : K.
[599] ميال : R.

(150) الناسك الذي من اجل[600] سيرته الالهيه يسكر بالظنون،[601] (A220r) وينتفخ ان كان[602] تتخلا عنه النعمه قليل،[603] ويسلم[604] ليس بيد الشياطين وحدهم، بل بضعف[605] جسده ومن[606] اضطرار الامراض[607] والاوجاع المختلفه، (V252r) يعتني بخدمة بطنه دايما، وينمقت من عبودية نتنها، لان ليس قتال اصعب منها واردا ولا اشنع، وعند ذلك[608] هو من ذاته يتعرف[609] موهبة الله ومراحمه وعنايته، على طبيعتنا الحقيره، لان بالحقيقه نجسه هي الصلاه التي تخرج من شبع البطن، حتى وعلى صاحبها.

(151) الفضايل[610] المجتمعه بالمجد الباطل في الاخر يبيدوا[611] بمحبة المديح.

(152) المتوحد الذي يشتهي ان يعلم ويقوم كثيرين، هو مسروق لمحبه المديح بوجه الفضيله ولم يحس، لان (R173v) حكمة الكلام ليس في كل وقت تنجح ولا مع كل احد، اما سيرة تدبير الفضيله والنسك في كل حين،[612] وفي كل مكان حتى وعند الزواني[613] يمدحونها.[614]

(153) الكلام المقفى المسقول على السيره والحكمه على معرفة الحق حتى وعند الانفس[615] الطمثه يوجدون، واما تدبير سيرة الحق ليس هن كلام مسقول مزين، بل طهاره ونقاوة النفس، لانه[616] كتب ان قلة الخبره بالكلام ليس تخسر في طريق الكمال.

---

600 منجل : A.

601 بالضنون : A.

602 كان : ساقطة K.

603 قليلا : S.

604 يسلم : A.

605 يضعف : A, K.

606 من : K.

607 الامرار : R.

608 ذالك : R.

609 يعرف : K, V.

610 والفضايل : K, V.

611 يبيدها : K.

612 وقت : K, V.

613 والعشارين : زائدة K.

614 يمدحوها : K.

615 انفس : K.

616 لان : A.

(154) كثرة المياه من الصفا يخرجون ليسقوا[617] فردوس الافراح، وكثرة العلوم على سيرة الحق من قلب[618] النفسانيين ينبع، ليسقي نفوس البسيطين الذي[619] من جهة سيدنا، العمالين في سيرة الروح.

(155) المتوحد الذي يحب السكون[620] واذا[621] انمقت من الذين[622] ينجحون[623] في السيره التي هي خارج من السكون، فاذا اتوجع من كلامهم ولم يحني عنقه لخدوعهم[624] بفرح، (A220v) وبالصلاه عليهم،[625] (V252v) بل يريد ان يتكرم ويمتدح معهم،[626] ويوري[627] انه يحب ان يحس باهلية[628] القديسين، انما هو ماسك زي السكون فقط، بخيالات الفنطسه، يتخيل من السماع على عزا القديسين الخفي.

(156) من تدبير سيرة الغلوة الاوله، التي[629] لبساطة الايمان[630] الذين يشعلون النفس بالدموع، ويسحقون القلب بالخوف من عذاب الجحيم، ومن المواعيد التي[631] يجذبون[632] النفس للتنعم بملكوت السماء،[633] جميع الناس يدخلون لملكوت السماء.[634] واما الذين من تدبير الحريه الذين يفحصون الحق (K204v) ويفتشون عن السيره بعد جهد، تجد قليلين يوهلون لعلو شرف السيرة.

---

617 ليسقون : K.

618 قلبه : R.

619 التي : R, S.

620 السكوت : K.

621 اذا : K.

622 الذي : K.

623 ينجحوا : R, S.

624 لخضوعهم : K.

625 عليهن : K, V.

626 منهم : A, S.

627 ويروي : S.

628 باهله : K.

629 الذي : K.

630 للبساطة الايمان : R / للبساطة والايمان : K, V.

631 الذي : K, A.

632 تجذب : S.

633 السموات : S / السما : K, R.

634 السموات : S / السما: K, R.

(157) الامانة تعطي اقنوع للضمير[635] بالاتكال[636] على الله وتلقي الخوف[637] الى خارج.

(158) ليس هو عذاب الجحيم الا النفس المضنوكه ومتضيقه بالكابة،[638] ومن عدم امانتها والثقه[639] بالله هي عادمه من العزا الخفي، وملكوت السما[640] هي ضمير يفرح برجا المواعيد.

(159) ان كان الذين يسكرون بالخمر، ويتلطفون بالادويه يخرجون عن[641] حدود المعرفة النفسانيه، فمعروف ايضا ان الذين يسكرون بالحب الالهي ويتلطفون[642] بعمل السيرة الروحانيه،[643] يوثبوا بفرح رجاهم على حدود النقاوة، ويحسون بالاسرار التي فوق الطبع.

(160) ان كان طبع الحب حلو[644] وحار طبيعيا،[645] من الضرورة اذا[646] ما فاض الحب الالهي في وقت الصلاه على انفس القديسين، يحتر القلب وتنبع النفس بالفرح، وتوهل (V253r) النظرة[647] العجيبه.

(161) ليس كل[648] احد يوتمن ذخيرة الروح ولا كل احد يحفظ وديعة[649] النعمة.

(162) المتوحد (A221r) الذي اكثر من مقدار (R174r) سيرة رتبته يتشوق لعظايم الله، ان كان هو غير مدرب ومحترس كم من وقت تصادفه عظايم

---

635 الضمير : R.

636 والاتكال : K.

637 الخوف : ساقطة K, V.

638 بالكابه : V / بالاكابه : A.

639 والثقا : A.

640 السماء : A, S, V.

641 من : K.

642 ويتلطفوا : K.

643 الروحانيين : V.

644 حلوا : R, V.

645 طبيعي : K.

646 عند اذا : K.

647 للنظرة : A, S, V.

648 كل : ساقطة V.

649 وديعة ... ولم يحفظ : ساقطة K, V.

الشيطان، واما الذي قد اهل[650] لموهبة الروح ولم يحفظ الوديعة بواجبات الحب والتواضع الالهي، في كمال سيره يسلم للمعذبين[651] ويستهزون[652] به.

(163) ان كان[653] الواحد بالتوحيد اتحد لله الكلمه، معروف ان ذكر[654] واحد او فكر[655] واحد متفرد يتحد ليسوع بالسر.

(164) ليس كلمن يحفظ الوصايا ينعتق من الالام، لان كثيرين[656] يحفظون[657] الوصايا وليس يحسوا[658] بالالام القاتله لهم، لان كل[659] الفضايل من الصبر والتغصب يتولدون، وبالاكثر السكون[660] والحفظ، لان نقاوة النفس[661] ونور الضمير من تدبير سيرة الحريه يتولدون.[662]

(165) المحب السكون والحفظ جميع مفاوضات[663] الوجوه لهم هو مخسر.

(166) الصلاة التي تتقدم لله من القديسين لاجل الخطاه، تشبه الدواء[664] الذي يتقدم من الطبيب للمرضى،[665] لان حسب قوة الضعيف يقدر الدوا ان يعين، فان كان القوات[666] الطبيعيه اتخلفوا عن[667] العقل،[668] ادوية الاطبا ليس تنفع شي عنده، فان كان موجود في النفس الايمان وغرض مخافة الله، وايضا ادوية الصلاه يقدروا[669] ان يعينوا، فلهذا الامرين يحتاج اليهم غرض[670] مخافة الله

---

650 اوهل : R.
651 المعذبين : R.
652 ويشهرون : S.
653 انكان : K.
654 ذكرا : A.
655 فكرا : A.
656 كثيرون : S.
657 يتظاهرون بحفظ : S / يرفضون : K.
658 يحسون : K.
659 مع : K.
660 والسكون : R.
661 النفس : R.
662 وبالاكثر...يتولدون : ساقطة K, V.
663 مفاوضاة : R / مفاوضته : K, V.
664 الدوا : K, V, R.
665 لاجل المرضى : K.
666 القواة : A.
667 من : K.
668 الفعل : S, R / اضنّها الفعل : في الحاشية A.
669 يقدرون : K.

لتحيا[671] بالافعال،[672] وليلتجا[673] بالمعونه التي من الادويه، لان صلوات القديسين يشبهون السلاح،[674] لان القوي اذا لبس الغلبه تتجر فيه،[675] والمحلول[676] يموت ويزدرا بالسلاح، فلهذا لا نلوم صلوات القديسين، (A221v) اذ[677] لم ناخذ سوالنا،[678] بل نقوم تدبيرنا لان تدبير[679] الحريه ليس هن انحلال بطريقهم، او انحلال[680] سيره وتسيب لسان، بل تدبير الحريه هن[681] طفولية معرفة الصيادين، الذين (V253v) بسذاجة قلوبهم يسبحون الله الذي انتخبهم من العالم، لكي بحقرية كرازتنا[682] يختزوا[683] حكما العالم بحسن تدبيرهم.

(167) المتوحد الذي دايما يكافي صلاح عوض الشرور، حسب وصية مخلصنا، قلبه هو ينبوع السلام ويثبت غير متسجس.

(168) الكلمة اللينة تحطم الاعضا،[684] وشرارة الغضبيه والبغض ان نفخت فيها[685] اثارت الحنق، وان تلاقيها بسلام وحب تطفيها، وحريتك مسلطة[686] على الامرين، ومن داخلك يخرجون الاثنين، اعني كلام الطيب والسلامه، وكلام الشماخه[687] والغضب.

---

670 يحتاج غرض : K.

671 لتحيي : R.

672 لتحيي الافعال : K, V.

673 ولتلتجا : A.

674 للسلاح : R.

675 اذا لبس سلاح الغلبة تظهر غلبته : S.

676 والمنحل : A.

677 ان : K / اذا : S.

678 سالنا : A.

679 تدبير : ساقطة K.

680 انحلان : K.

681 هم : K.

682 كرازتهم : S.

683 يخزوا : A.

684 الاعظا : A.

685 فيه : K.

686 بسلطة : K.

687 الشماته : K.

(169) القلب المتوقد بالغضب[688] هو فارغ (K205r) من العزا الخفي، وعادم ايضا من المعزيين التي[689] من برا، لان العزا الجواني هو الذي يقبل العزا البراني، ويهتم به ويتنيح فيه، فان كان ليس فينا من داخل عزا خفي، ليس موضع للعزا[690] الذي[691] من خارج ليستريح بنا، وعلى هذا النوع ايضا والصلاح الجواني، هو الذي يقبل الصلاح الذي من خارج، والشرور للشرور، والافراح الى الافراح،[692] والاحزان (R174v) الى الاحزان، لان كل جنس يقبل ابنا[693] جنسه وينيحه ويتنيح منه،[694] ان كان الشي الذي نقبله[695] بالاحواس ليس داخلنا ابن جنسه، لكي ينيحه، فالحال يمضي كالخاطر، فلهذا ممدوحه[696] جدا جود النفس اكثر من جميع الفضايل.

(170) فان قلب الانسان مثله سيدنا بالارض، والكلمه زرع في الارض، افهم كم من (A222r) غيارات تقبل[697] الارض من تغير العمل والزبل والسقي، من (V254r) الارض البايره الغير مفلوحه، ولا مزبله وعادمة من السقي، افهم ايضا غيارات الزروع الجيده والرديه التي[698] منك تزدرع فيها، وقايس الاراضي مع القلوب، وغيار الزرع لغيار الكلام، وافطن لخفايا ارض قلبك، وغيار انواع كلامك، من شبه تغير الاراضي وتغير الزروع التي من خارج.

(171) ان كان المعرفه اتمثلت بالماء[699] كقول الكتب،[700] افهم كم غيار تقتني الافرازات بقياس، بعضهم[701] بعض، وهكذا ايضا[702] وتغير انواع المعرفه وتغير الثاوريات،[703] افهم ان المعرفه مقتنيه معقول داخل انفس الناس.

---

[688] من الغضب : K.

[689] الذي : K / الذين : S.

[690] للعزاء : S / العزا : R.

[691] الذي : ساقطة K, V.

[692] للافراح : K.

[693] ابناء : A, S.

[694] معه : R.

[695] يقبله : K.

[696] ممدوح : K.

[697] يقبل : A.

[698] الذي : K.

[699] بالما : K, V, R.

[700] الكتاب : K, V.

[701] بعضهن : A, S.

[702] ايضا : ساقطة S.

[703] التاوريات : K, R.

(172) الذي يصمد[704] مايده جسدانيه لكثيرين بكل انواع المواكيل يزينها، حلو[705] ومر، ومالح وساذج، حريف وحامض، لكي كل واحد[706] حسب مزاجه وشهوته[707] يغتذي، هكذا والكتب الالهيه التي[708] هن[709] مايدة النفس، زينها الروح[710] بجميع تغير المذاقات لكي من كل كتاب تغتذي كل نفس، حسب مقدار منزلتها وقوتها،[711] وتغير شهواتها به تغتذي، فلهذا لا نلوم الكتب الالهيه الموضوعه بالروح، اذ فيهن[712] مضادده وتغير لمنفعة كل العامه.

(173) كما ان الاجسام تقبل الغذا من[713] خبز ساذج، وثم من[714] لحم وخمر، وثم من تغير فواكه وبقول، هكذا والنفس بتغير التدابير[715] يغتذوا، ويتعزوا بسير[716] مغيره، واحد بخدمة زايده، واخر بصلوات، واخر بقراه وتصور وفهم وهذيذ، واخر بمحبة العلوم، ووجدان امور[717] جديده، واخر بصوم ونسك، واخر بتجرد وسياحه، واخر بثبات (A222v) وسكون،[718] واخر (V254v) بتواضع وصبر وطاعه، واخر بسكون كامل، واخر ينيح كثيرين بعمله، وهو ايضا وقت يتنيح بهذا التدبير، الذي بذاك، وهولا[719] الكل دبرهم الخالق لمنفعة كل العامه.

---

704 يعد : S.

705 حلوا : R.

706 واحدا : A.

707 وشهته : R.

708 الذي : K.

709 من : R.

710 الرب : K.

711 قوتها ومنزلتها : K.

712 فيهم : K, V.

713 من : ساقطة K, V.

714 من : ساقطة S.

715 التدبير : A.

716 بسيرة : K, S.

717 اموراً : R, S.

718 واخر بثبات وسكون : ساقطة S.

719 وهولاء : A, S.

(174) وايضا للقديس على الظلام المحزن الحادث في السكون على الذين بتدبير[720] المعرفة يتدبرون[721] يوضح هذا الفصل على السكون وما[722] يعرض فيه.

(175) في وقت الظلام اكثر من كل شي[723] ضرب (K205v) المطانيات يوافقون وينفع، واعلم ان عدم عملك المطانيات وان لا تتجلد فيهم[724] هو قتال من الشيطان، فينبغي لك ان تجاهد قباله بهذه، لان[725] هو يعرف[726] المعونة التي تحصل من ضرب المطانيات، ولاجل ذلك[727] بكل قوته يجاهد ويحرص[728] ان لا يخليك تعملهن، واذا ما دنيت ان (R175r) تخر على وجهك يسجسك، ولو انك غلبته وضربت[729] مطانيات يغصبك، ان لا تثبت فيهن،[730] ولو ان تكون بارده ومظلمه حركاتك، اثبت في ضرب المطانيات، ولو ان قلبنا مايت في هذه الاوقات، وليس لنا صلاه ولا نعرف ماذا نقول، حتى ولا الفاظ الطلبه ياتونا ولا تضرع،[731] ومع هذا نوجد[732] ملقيين على وجوهنا دايما، ولو انه نكون في السكون، اذا ما احتجنا[733] الى[734] معونة الله في شي[735] ما، ولا تاتينا بالواجب ما ناخذ، بانه[736] لم ندنى الى الله بالصلاه بحرص، وحراره ليل[737] ونهار[738] ونصرخ اليه بوجع، بل ننتظر ان هو من ذاته يعطينا، اما هو[739] يتفرس لنا

---

[720] بتدابير : K.

[721] يتدبرون : ساقطة R.

[722] وعلى ما : زائدة K.

[723] كلشي : V.

[724] فيهن : K.

[725] ولان : K, V.

[726] عرف : K.

[727] ذالك : R.

[728] يحرس : A, R.

[729] وضرب : A.

[730] فيهم : K.

[731] اتضرع : R, S.

[732] توجد : S.

[733] احتجبنا : R / احتاجنا : K.

[734] الى : ساقطة A.

[735] شيا : A, R.

[736] وانه : K.

[737] ليلا : A.

[738] ليلا ونهارا : S.

[739] انه : K.

بسبب[740] لكي نتقدم اليه، فلهذا يتركنا (V255r) نتضيق، واما عن تاخيره في خلاصنا،[741] هو لكي نثابر قرع[742] بابه لمنفعتنا بالطلبه، واما (A223r) نحن عندما تاتينا[743] اسباب المنفعة نتغافل ونتخلف، ونتقاعد[744] عن المسالة،[745] ونعطي انفسنا[746] للملل[747] والضجر واكثر من الما[748] نبرد، في كل شر من التجارب التي[749] تاتي علينا، ان كان[750] من داخل او من خارج هوذا[751] طرق الصلاه قدامك، خر على وجهك ليلا ونهار،[752] واتضرع الى الله بحزن قلب،[753] والرب هو رحوم وصالح، وليس يتوخر[754] من ان يعطي عزا[755] وراحه اذا نظر انك تساله بحزن القلب، ان[756] لم تكن[757] مسالتك[758] خارج عن الطريق، في كل[759] ايام حياتك هكذا تكون، تعمل، تاخذ[760] وتضيع، وايضا تسال بحزن ويعطيك، وايضا يروح[761] منك، وتصادف شيا[762] ما في وقت، وتظن ان هذا

---

740 بسبب : ساقطة K.

741 صلاحنا : R.

742 نقرع : S / ونقرع : A.

743 تاينيا : A.

744 ونتباعد : K.

745 المسلة (المسألة) : S / المسله : R.

746 نفسنا : K.

747 الملل : A, R.

748 الماء : A, S.

749 للتي : K.

750 انكان : K.

751 هو ذا : R.

752 ونهارا : K, A, S.

753 القلب : K.

754 يتاخر : S.

755 عزاء : S.

756 اذ : K.

757 تكون : K, V.

758 مسلتك : R / مسالك : A.

759 كل : ساقطة K, V.

760 وتاخذ : K, V.

761 تروح : A.

762 شى : A.

هو حد القصد، وتطلبه في ساعة اخره[763] فما تجده، افهم ان هكذا هو ترتيب هذه الطريق[764] لا تضجر.

(176) **ايضاح الكلام** ليس ان الله سيد الكل بمسالتنا[765] ياخذ زياده على بحر مراحمه، التي ليس لها قرار، نفاق واثم هو ان نعتقد هذا الامر، بل ان بطلبتنا[766] متواترا[767] وحزن ضميرنا[768] نستضي[769] نحن ونقتني عزا، في الامور الضروريه من مفاوضة متواتره.[770]

(177) في وقت ذلك[771] الظلام المضغط الذي يقع على النفس، نتحذر[772] من قطع الرجا، اسمعني يا اخي كمثل التي تريد تطلق، احترس[773] ان لا تخرج من قلايتك، وكمن هو ملقى في عذاب وعقوبات شديده، لان العدو[774] اكثر من جميع (V255v) الاشيا يتحيل ان يخرجك من قلايتك، لاجل قلة[775] صبرك في وقت المعركة، وقصده بهذا الاغتصاب[776] كله لكي يخرجك، ليلا اذا ثبت[777] تدنى من ضرب المطانيات،[778] (A223v) لانه عظيم يخاف اكثر من كل شي[779] من هذا العمل.

(178) كمثل انه ما يتفق القش[780] والنار في موضع واحد، هكذا ولا العدل والرحمه في نفس واحده.[781] ان افضل مواهب الله عند العبد معرفة الحق

---

763 اخره : ساقطة S / اخرى : A.

764 الطرق : K.

765 بمسلتنا : A, R.

766 طلبتنا : A.

767 متواتره : A.

768 طميرنا : A.

769 نصتضا : K.

770 متواترا : S / متواتر : K / متاوتر : R.

771 ذالك : R.

772 نتحضر : K.

773 احترص : K, V.

774 العدوا : R.

775 قلت : K.

776 الاغصاب : S.

777 ثبتت : A.

778 المطانوات : K.

779 كلشي : V.

780 القرش : R.

781 **..ايضاح الحق** : زائدة K.

بماهيته، والمعرفة هي التي[782] يعرف بها الانسان الباري تبارك وتعالى، وما فوق الطبيعة، هذه المعرفة (K206r) يكسبها الانسان بالتعليم ويطلبها بالصلاة[783] والخشوع، وتعطا[784] له بنعمة روح القدس ويوصله[785] الى معدن النور، وتحصل للانسان بالتواضع والعقل المجرد من الهم، (R175v) ومتى اصاب الانسان لهذه طريق[786] الحق،[787] احس في نفسه[788] بحياه قد اتجددت له، لان الحق يشرق في قلب من قد عرفه، فاذا اردت ان تظفر بالمعرفة الصحيحة، فاحفظ نفسك من الشبه، لان الله قرن المعرفه بالامانه فحيث كانت احدتهما[789] فالاخره[790] توجد معها، لان بالامانه[791] يعطا[792] للانسان جميع سواله.[793]

(179) احرس قلبك من الافكار الردية فانه معدن الخير والشر والموت والحياه. يحتاج الانسان الى هذه الاربعه، وهي معرفة الله، والايمان به، والخوف منه، والرضا بتدبيره.

(180) ينبغي لمن اتشبه[794] بالملايكه، وانفرد عن الاشخاص البشريه، ان يرفض الشهوات الجسدانيه (V256r) لتحصل له تجارته الروحانيه.

(181) قرابين الابرار مقبوله بالدموع والخشوع، فاذا دعوا اجيبوا، واذا سالوا لم يمنعوا.

(182) الراهب هو من خرج من سلطان بطنه، وسلم من لحظات[795] عينيه، وخطرات[796] فكره، وزلات[797] لسانه، فان كان الفاضل[798] في العشره (A224r) فان العباده في الوحده.

[782] الذي : V, R.
[783] في الصلاة : K.
[784] تعطى : K, S.
[785] وتوصله : K, A, S.
[786] الطريق : V.
[787] الحق : ساقطة V.
[788] بنفسه : K.
[789] احدتها (كان احدهما) : S.
[790] فالاخرى : K, S.
[791] بامانه : K.
[792] يعطى : K, S.
[793] ساله : A.
[794] تشبه : K.
[795] لحضات : A.

(183) علامة قبول الصلاه فرح القلب بالتسبيح لله، وانحدار الدموع في وقت التضرع من غير اعتماد البكا.

(184) راس الرهبنه طهارة الجسد والاحواس[799] من الخطية، وعمارة القلب من التواضع والرحمة، وذكر الموت في الليل والنهار.

(185) اصعب الجهاد الصبر على الوحده،[800] والرضا بما يدبره الله.

(186) **جواب مسله سيل القديس مار اسحق.**[801] مسالتك ايها الحبيب ليس تليق لكل احد. بل الذين لهم سر الروح قلب قد هدى بالسلامه والنعمة وذاق الحق خفيا. وبالميتوته من الكل ويسعى تبع النقاوة لان السلامة موضع الله دعيت. المتوحد الذي يريد ان يكون قلبه مسكن لله ينبغي له ان بالاعمال النشيطة يفلحه ويهديه من جميع الحركات المسجسة التي للخلق. والمغايظات والملاقات النفافعه والمخسرة. وبالاكثر القريب. لان بواسطته يسجس الشيطان ويكدر نقاوة النفس ويتحيل ان لا يهدس الضمير مع احد داخله بالخليه. لا بذكر الاصدقا ولا الاقربا. بل يمسك حبه بمواددة ويهدي قلبه بلافراز واحد من الاخر. لان هذا العالم هو مسجس ومتكدر وينفعل فيه صلاح وشرور. وما يمكن ان نتخلص في العالم من الشرور ونعمل الفضيلة الطبيعيه بالبر كنوح وابراهيم وايوب. يستطاع. واماان نقتني في العالم ان نكون مسكن لله. بالطهارة والقداسه. ذواتنا ما نستطيع وان كان افراد قليلين بمعونة الله بنوع السياسة. ولهذا هربوا الابا القديسين من العمر الى القفر. لانهم كانوا مجمع متفق اخوة واحدة كما كتب بالبركسيس ان الشي الذي كانوا يقتنوه. كان للجو. وكل الاخوة كانوا نفس واحده وراى واحد بسلام ومواددة. بلا انقسام قلب وكانوا بملاقات (K206v) بعضهم بعض يصعدون الى السما بوفق ضمايرهم. واما في زماننا هذا كمل علينا المكتوب ان اثنين ينقسمون على ثلثة. وثلثه على اثنين ويكونوا الناس محبين ذواتهم محبين للشهوات اكثر من حب الله مفتخرين متكبرين واشر من هذا. فالذي يفهم في ذلك الزمان يسكت ويهرب من القلق الى السكون. لانها ايام رديه. وليس اثنين فقط متقسمين على بعضهم في جيلنا هذا بل هو الواحد متقسم على ذاته ومتكدر من كثرة المغايظة التي تلاقيه كل يوم. لانه يهدس قلبه جواه. ولو انه في السكون يهدم ويبني على الدوام بلا قيام

---

796 وخطراة : R.

797 والات : K.

798 الفضل : V.

799 والحواس : A.

800 الام حده : K.

801 هذه الفقرة موجودة فقط في K.

حسب المصادفات التي للضرورية المتواترة عليه. وايضا في الايام الاخيرة لما كثرة المجامع بزيادة الاخوة وبدا الانحلال يتواتر. وبردة الحرارة. الابا الذين وجدوا في تلك الاجيال هولا الذين خلصوا انفسهم بالاعمال النشيطة بالحبس والسكون في القلاية في مجمع كثيرين. وعندما حسوا ان بدت تظهر فيه اثمار الروح التجوا بالسكون الدايم واما هربوا من القلق والتكدر ليلا يطيعون سلام قلوبهم بكثرة التشويش الحاصل من الملاقات الضرورية الذين هم سكان بينهم. وحسبما اظن انه كمثل ما بدت الوحدة المباركة في المبدا انه كانوا يجلسوا الاخوة المتوحدين في مكان مكان[802] متفردين ويعملون الفضايل بالسلامه في الوسط. عندما اتسعت المجماع والاديرة ونموا جدا جدا. هكذا مزمع ان يجري في المنتها كما يتلوح لنا من رمز كلام سيدنا والابا. لانه عسر على الكاملين السكن مع كثيرين. لاجل اختلاف سير الاخوة بانه يضطرب الضمير للمتحفظ المصلوب الى الواحد عندما يريد ان يسير في جميع السبل واعمال الفضيلة. وتتخبط معرفة الاخ المفرز في وسط طرق الاخوة. لان ليس فيه كفو الطبع الضعيف الذي قد شقى في برية التوبة كل مدة الزمان ويتضيق ويتكدر في وسط كثرة السبل. والاخرة لاجل الاخوة المنحلين لان بوساطتهم يصنع الشيطان قتال مع النشاطا الذين يكملون الفضيلة كما قال اوغريس ان الشيوخ العمالين في المجمع يثيرون عليهم الشياطين الاخوة المنحلين. ولهذه الاسباب هربوا الابا من المجامع كمثل ما هرب شيشوي وسكن في مغارة انطونيوس لانه قال في الاول كنت مستريح مع سبعة اخوة والان ما اقدر اسكن مع كثيرين لانه يتكدر قلبي ويتخبط بغير ارادتي واخرين كانوا يبتعدون من المجامع. بالجسد وحاجتهم تكون من المجمع باتفاق مع الاخوة. والاب امون قال للاب بيمين لما اضطرب من اجل اخوة. انت الان حي يا بيمين موت من كل احد واضمر ان لك سنة في القبر لعلك تهدا. وايضا الابا الذين كانوا يرسلوا من الله لبنيان النفوس اوله في القفر والوحدة كانو يكملون وبعد ذلك (K207r) يرسلون لخلاص اخرين. ومنهم من سكن في المغاير والنواويس واجبال وجزاير نجوا حياتهم من القلق. الى الصلاة الطاهرة العل انه يقدر يبلغ الذي هو ساكن بين كثيرين. واما الصلاه الروحانية وليكون قلبه قدس للرب. ان لم يتجرد الانسان ليس من المفاوضة البشرية فقط. بل ومن تذكار عالمي. لكي يتجرد قلبه بالروح ويتفاوض عقله خفيا مع الروحانيين ومع ارواح الصديقين الذين كملوا ما يوهل كما كتب القديس يوحنا التبايسي ان الذي يبتعد لحرية السكون ينجا من امور كثيرة يضنكوه من خارج. وينعتق قلبه من مغايضات غير مرتبة تصدف سمعه كل يوم بملاقات ضروريه. وينجو من

---

[802] هكذا في النص.

المثلبة والدينونة والخلق والحيل المفضحة للانسان ومنجسين ذكاوته ومكدرين نقاوة نفسه. كما قال مقاريوس انه اذا غضبنا على الاخوة ينقلع تذكار الله من قلوبنا ويظلم العقل ويتكدر. واذا غضبنا على الشياطين بلا ضرر يثبت العقل. وكانوا الابا يطلبون من اجل الشياطين والنار والوحوش وينتفعون لعزا سذاجتهم. واما على الاخوة المنحلين. وعلى تغير تذاكير الاخوة العمالين. او على الملاقات النافعة والمخسرة الحاصلة في وسط كثيرين. لا القديسين كانوا يصلون لكي يتاذوا ولا الله كان يغضب. ولكن الفضايل الكبار والاعمال الصعبة التي يعملها المتوحد في المجمع في وسط كثيرين يكونوا جدا ناقصين بعينه بقياس عمل اخرين. لان ليس في واحد كفو ان يكمل جميع اعمال التوبة والمناسك المفترزة التي تصنعها كل واحد واحد من الاخوة وليوضعهم في ذاته على الدوام بانه ما اخذ قوة لتكميل الجميع. بل جزو من النعمة كمثل اللسان من الجسم. واحد من المتوحدين سال لشيخ انه قد اصطلحوا معي النار والوحوش. فاراد الشيخ العارف ان يكسر افتخاره. قايلا ان ردت ان تعرف كمالك امضي اخضع نفسك في المجمع لانه ليس لك سلطان هناك علا كوز ماء.

(187) **وايضا رووس[803] المعرفة للقديس مار اسحق.[804]**

(188) الله هو بالحقيقه اب الناطقين الذي اولد[805] بالنعمة، ليكونوا وارثين مجده في عالم الجديد[806] المزمع لتنعيمهم.

(189) الحق هو مخفي في ذاته من جميع ما خلق، والى هاهنا[807] منه بمدة كثيره[808] يسكنون الناطقين الذين خلقوا من اجله، وفي الوقت الذي ينبغي يظهر لهم كمثلما[809] يليق بالحق، واما حده هو مخفي بازليته.

(190) اربع غيارات فاضله تحدث لنا، اعني[810] على الطبع الناطق نجد افرازهم. الغيار الاول، بالذي يرجع من رداوة السيرة. الغيار الثاني الذي من ظلالة العقل يرجع الى الحس[811] بالحق بالكاينات الثانية. الغيار (V256v)

---

[803] روس : A.

[804] وايضا للقديس مار اسحق : V.

[805] اوعد : K.

[806] الجديده : A.

[807] هنا : K.

[808] كثيرين : K.

[809] كمثل ما : K.

[810] اعني : ساقطة K.

[811] الحسس : K, A, R.

الثالث بالذي من الدرجات المتقدمين بالمعرفة الروحانية، الى حركة طبيعة خلقته. الغيار الرابع بحركة حياة[812] الابد، كتاورية[813] الانجيلية.

(191) الذين[814] (K207v) اتقدموا بالكرامة سبقوا[815] بالتغير،[816] والذين سبقوا بالتغير صاروا مرشدين للتغير، عظيم هو ظلم الذين بدوا من الذين قبلوا.[817]

(192) دعوة الازمان مع حركة الاجسام تسير، وحيث ليس اجسام ولا ايضا غيار، وحيث ليس غيار ولا زمان ايضا، (A224v) ولا متجسمين، وحيث ليس متجسمين[818] ولا فوقانيين وسفلانيين باقنوم واحد في كل واحد واحد[819] من الاقانيم مساواه وحسب[820] مساواة[821] الاقانيم بالجواهر[822] الغير متحده،[823] (R176r) وان كان[824] ليس مساواة[825] افرازات هناك، ولا ايضا الوان،[826] وعلى هذا المعنا[827] تسير كل تاوريه[828] هذا الفصل.

(193) الذين يقولون ان نظرة سيدنا تكون في هذا العالم بنوع اخر خارج عن نظر التاوريا،[829] هم ارفاق[830] الذين يعتقدون ان في عالم الجديد هو شيا[831] محسوس التنعم[832] بملكوته، واستعمالا[833] عنصريا[834] وغلظ اقانيم، وهاذين[835]

---

812 حيات : K, V.

813 كالتاؤرية : S / كتااوريه : A.

814 الذي : R.

815 سبقونا : V.

816 بالتغيير : A.

817 قبلو : K.

818 وحيث ليس متجسمين : ساقطة K.

819 واحدا واحدا : A.

820 وحيث : S / حسب : A.

821 وحسب مساواة : ساقطة K.

822 بالجوهر : K.

823 متجده : R.

824 وانكان : K.

825 مساوات : K.

826 الاوان : K.

827 المعنى : K.

828 ثاءورية :S / تااوريه : A.

829 الثاءوريا : S / التااوريه : A.

830 رفقاء : S.

831 شيئا : S / شي : K.

832 للتنعم : K.

833 واستعمال : K, V.

الاثنين زاغوا عن الحق، لان بشبهه تكون اخوته ايضا، ان كان[836] يمينيه[837] او الشماليه[838] خلاف من درجات وافرازات بسكون، لان بشبهه يرتفعون من الاشكال الارضيه الى شكل ممجود[839] جدا، ولا ينظلم الجسد بل يتكرم بالغيار الذي قبل شيا[840] يفوق[841] شكله الاول. اوغريس شاهدا[842] امين بهذا، انه قال ان كان[843] الجسد (V257r) البشري هو جزوا[844] من هذا العالم فيزول شكل هذا العالم، فمعلوم بهذا ان شكل الجسد ايضا يزول.

(194) المتوحد الذي يزدرع في قلبه زرع روحاني، ويوتمن كنز ولم يجعل ذاته اخرس اطروش،[845] وغير عارف من جميع المفاوضات البشريه والافعال العالميه والاهتمام بالاشيا المربيه،[846] هو يضيع الوديعه[847] الطبيعيه[848] التي عنده.[849]

(195) الذي على الدوام يلوم نفسه ويشجبها[850] تحت كل انسان، ترعب منه الشياطين، وشيطان الغضب والحسد والحزن ليس يقربوا اليه، وتمتلي نفسه (A225r) امن[851] وسلام وحب وفرح، ويصير محبوب على الله والملايكه والناس، واما الذي يزكي ذاته ويلوم قريبه ويدينه بقلبه، شيطان الغضب يسلمه لشيطان الحزن، وشيطن الحسد[852] لشيطان الخلق،[853] وفي كل وقت يكون متكدر[854] متسجس، مغضب على الذين ما يمدحوه.[855]

---

834 عنصري : K.

835 وهذين : A, S.

836 انكان : K.

837 اليمينية : K.

838 شماليه : A, R.

839 ممجدا : A.

840 شيئا : S / شي : K.

841 ان يفوق : K.

842 شاهد : K.

843 انكان : K.

844 جزءا : S / جزو : K.

845 اطرش : A.

846 المرئية : S / المرية : K, V.

847 الوداعة : K.

848 الطبيعيه : زائدة V.

849 التي عنده : ساقطة V.

850 يسجبها : K.

851 امنا : A / امان : K.

852 الجسد : R / الحقد : K.

(196) بمقدار ما يتهاون الانسان بهذا العالم ويهتم بعمل مخافة الله، هكذا تدنى اليه العناية الالهيه، ويحس بمظافرتها ومعونتها خفيا، وتعطا[856] له حركات نقيه ليتنعم بها، ولو ان يكون بغير ارادته عادم من خيرات هذا العالم، بمقدار ما كان خالي منهن،[857] تلزق به الرحمة الالهيه.

(197) المجد للذي[858] باليمين والشمال يوضع لنا اسباب الخلاص.

(198) اذ لم ترجح فيك محبة المسيح،[859] لكي بجميع الضوايق الحادثة عليك تكون بلا حزن، من اجل فرحك[860] به، اعلم (V257v) ان العالم فيك حي اكثر من المسيح.[861]

(199) السهر في التاوريا[862] مع تدبير المعرفه، للذي[863] قد كمل الاعمال الجسدانيه ودنا من الشيخوخه وانحطاط الجسد،[864] يقدم الى التدبير الروحاني بالانقطاع فقط من البشر، ويقظة[865] وحرص العقل، وعلى الدوام تكمل عليه قولة[866] ان الليل يضي كالنهار، فينبغي ان يستيقظ (K208r) قليل قبال[867] تجارب التجديف، في هذا الباب،[868] فان كان الاتضاع عنده[869] موجود بسهوله ينعتق بوساطة نور الايمان الذي يشرق له بالنعمه، فان كان يميل الى التشتت والمحادثات، يظلم في التاوريا[870] ويضل[871] عقله ويمتحن بالتجديف، لانه اذا ما

---

853 القلق : R / الحنق : S.

854 متقدر : R.

855 يمدحونه : S.

856 وتعطي : K, S.

857 منهم : K, V.

858 الذي : R.

859 ܠܡܫܝܚܐ : K.

860 برحك : R.

861 ܠܡܫܝܚܐ : K.

862 الثاءوريا : S / التاوريا : A / التاوريه : K.

863 الذي : R.

864 وانحط الجسد : K.

865 ويقضة : A.

866 قولت : K.

867 قبالة : A.

868 التدبير : K.

869 عنده : ساقطة V.

870 الثاءوريا : S / التاوريا : A.

871 ويطل : A.

دنا من هذا التدبير ليس توديه (R176v) الراحه كمثلما[872] يضره الحديث وتشتت[873] الاحواس وطموحها.

(200) الاستضا[874] بالتاوريا[875] مع الهدو،[876] (A225v) يسير دايما وعدم الرسوم الظاهرة، لكي يكون في العقل كفوا[877] ليقوم دايما ويتامل اي تاوريا[878] تظهر له، والذي يقاومنا على هذا ليس فقط يضل الاخرين،[879] بل هو ذاته قد زاغ عن الطريق وما يحس ويسير في تبع الفي[880] بتخيل عقله.

(201) اذا ما كان زمان القتال وظلام، ولو ان نكون[881] في الطياشه نثبت في الصلاه وعمل[882] المطانيات على الارض، اذ[883] لم يكون[884] القتال متواترا[885] وظلام محزن، بل انما هو طياشة العاده بطموح افكار الهمج، نزيد جزوا[886] القراه[887] اكثر من الثبات في الصلاه، ونمزج الاثنين مع بعضهم بعض، (V258r) وناخذ من الكتاب دوا[888] نقدمه[889] للصلاه.

(202) ليل ونهار[890] لا تبطل هذه الصلاه من قلبك قايلا، يا رب نجيني[891] من ظلام النفس، وهذا هو حد كل صلاة المفرزه.[892]

---

872 كمثل ما : K, V.

873 ويشتت : R.

874 الاستطا : A.

875 بالتاءوريا : S / بالتااوريا : A / بالتاوريه : K.

876 الهدوا : R.

877 كفو : K.

878 تاءوريا : S / تااوريا : A.

879 لاخرين : A, R / اخرين : K.

880 الغي : S / للفي : K.

881 يكون : K.

882 وعلى : R.

883 اذا : S / واذا : A.

884 يكن : A.

885 متواتر : K.

886 جزء : S / جزو : K, A.

887 القراءة : S / القراية : K.

888 دواء : S / دوى : A.

889 تقدمه : A, S.

890 ليلا ونهارا : A, S.

891 نجني : V.

892 المفروزة :S / المعرفة : K.

(203) النفس المظلمة هي الجحيم الثاني، العقل النير هو شريك السارافيم،[893] طوبا[894] لمن انفتح قلبه وحس بالشي الذي هو الله مزمع ان يفعله مع جنس الناطقين.

(204) يا للعجب كيف تصبر الطبايع المعقوله لهذه البهجه، لانهم يعرفوا على تحقيق لاي رجا قد دعينا نحن وهم.

(205) التدبير الروحاني هو عمل بغير احواس، عقل مشترك مع الله باستعلان اسراره، كما قالت الابا، وكنوه عقل عاري، وفي وقت يدعوه نظره تفوق الاجسام، لان هو في ذاته ينظر نور بها[895] نفسه، وفي وقت الصلاه مناظر[896] سماويه ينظر[897] في ذاته، اعني يرا[898] مجد الله في نفسه، الذي[899] هو نظر اسراره. نظرة مجد الله هي ان يتحرك فيه فهم على عظمة طبيعته، يعني ويرفعه[900] من هذا العالم بحسه[901] وفي هذا الموضع يتحقق بالرجا المزمع، وهذا هو قنوع العقل، الذي (A226r) قاله بولس،[902] هكذا هو الصلاح موضوع في طبع النفس كالنار الموضوعه في طبع الحجر والحديد،[903] وهي مفتقره لمن[904] يحركها التي هي[905] نعمة الله، وحرص الانسان واجتهاده، التي[906] بهن يرتبط[907] بلا تغير، هاهنا بانقباض حريا[908] غير مرتبطه الاضطرار.[909]

---

893 السرافيم : R.

894 طوبى : K, S.

895 ينظر بهاء نور : S.

896 مناظراً : A.

897 وينظر : R.

898 يرى : K, S.

899 الذ : R.

900 يرفع : V / يرفعه : K.

901 بجسده : R.

902 بولوس : V / بولص : K.

903 والحديده : A.

904 لم : V.

905 هي : ساقطة V.

906 الذي : K.

907 يرتبض : A.

908 حرية : A.

909 الاضرار : V.

(206) الى ان نخاف ونمتنع من الشرور ما تتحرك محبة الصلاح في الانسان (V258v) بحلاوه وحراره، كما ان معقول الاب هو[910] في الملايكه المقدسين،[911] منظور، هكذا[912] ومعقول[913] المسيح[914] هي[915] في البشر، الذي يتنعم بالسكن[916] الهادي بتاورية[917] خاصيات المسيح[918] يتنعم،[919] عربون الملكوت العتيده من هاهنا اخذ له ميراث.[920]

(207) الراحات[921] تعمي الانسان، ان لا ينظر في الامور الالهيه بالدهش، بل بطلب فارغ يتفرس فيهن.

(208) يقفوا[922] الجلوس (K208v) المتفرد دهش[923] العقل وعدم التشتت، والاعمال بالضروره تحرك الدهش بوساطه[924] الحكمه التي تولد في القلب حركات حاره[925] مدهشه.

(209) كل شي[926] الذي هو شرب الماء للنصبات، (R177r) هكذا هو الصمت الدايم لتربية النفس، والمعرفه وكلام[927] الحكمه كمثل التعري[928] للعضو الذي يستحيا منه.

(210) ربنا المسيح[929] هو بكر وهو واحد،[930] ولم ينقام[931] هذين[932] الامرين في طبيعة واحدة، بكر لاخوة[933] كثيرين يكون، واحد وحيد[934] من غير ان يولد قبله

---

910 هو : ساقطة A.

911 القديسين : R.

912 وهكذا : K.

913 هكذا ايضا ومعقول : V.

914 ܕܡܫܝܚܐ : K.

915 هو : V.

916 بالساكن : K.

917 بتاءورية : S / تااورية : A.

918 ܕܡܫܝܚܐ : K.

919 الذي بالسكن الهادئ بتاءورية خاصيات المسيح يتنعم : S.

920 ميزان : R.

921 الرحات : R.

922 يقفو : K.

923 الدهش : K.

924 بواسطة : K.

925 حاررة : K.

926 كالشيء : S / كالشي : K.

927 والكلام : K.

928 التعرا : A, R.

وبعده، فصحت[935] هذين[936] الامرين باله وانسان[937] متحد لوجه[938] واحد، وليس تتخبط خاصية الطبع لاجل الاتحاد.[939]

(211) السحابة المعقوله هي[940] العقل المبتلع بالدهش بفهم[941] روحاني، بغته يقع في النفس ويقيم[942] العقل بلا حركه، وتنحجب[943] عنه جميع المنظورات بلا معرفه، ولا حسس بغرض هدسهن،[944] (A226v) ويثبت العقل هادي كالسحابه المحتوطه بالامور، وتحجز النظرة المتجسمه.

(212) الشهيد[945] بالحياه هو التايب[946] الحقيقي، لان (V259r) الدموع تغلب الدم بالفعل، الذي قد اقتنوا،[947] والتوبه[948] للشهاده، اما اوليك يتقدموا بالاكاليل[949] على هولاء،[950] لان التايبين في قيامه[951] العامه ياخذوا الاكاليل،[952] واما الشهدا من قبل العامه يورا انه متضاعف بالاكاليل[953] التايب الحقيقي.

---

929 يسوع : S / يسوع المسيح : R.

930 وحيد : K.

931 ينقم : K.

932 هاذين : K.

933 الاخوة : K.

934 واحيد : R / وحيد وحيد : K.

935 فصحة : R.

936 هاذين : K.

937 باله متانس : S / بالاه متانس : V / بيلاه وانسان : K.

938 للوجه : K.

939 الايتحاد : R.

940 هو : K.

941 كفهم : R.

942 وتقيم : V.

943 ونحجب : K.

944 هادسهن : K.

945 الشاهد : K.

946 الثابت : V.

947 اقتنو : K.

948 والتاوبه : V / التوبة : S.

949 بالاكليل : A.

950 هولاي : K / هولا : R.

951 القيامة : A.

952 الاكالين : R.

953 بالاكليل : K, V.

(213) عوض[954] التزمير يكون الكلام الهادي مع الله بتضرعا[955] سكينا،[956] وغير متسجس، ولا نكثر[957] العدد كالجهال وبافكارنا نطيش في الزبايل، ونخرج من هناك[958] ونحن فارغين[959] من جميع الخيرات، التي من عاده العقل المفرز[960] ان ينالها في مثل هذه الاوقات.

(214) كما انه ما يستطاع ان يقبل السامع الكلام من دون تركيب[961] الصوت، وهكذا لا يمكن ان يتفاوض العقل مع الالام داخله من دون الهيولاه.[962]

(215) كما انه ما[963] يستطاع ان يظهر طبع الشياطين[964] للعين، ان لم ياخذ اشكال الاحواس التي نحن لابسينها، هكذا لا يمكن ان يحرك افكاره داخل القلب[965] ويلفت العقل نحوهم،[966] من دون خيالات الامور.

(216) قصد تاورية[967] العالم الجديد تظهر بعقل الملايكه القديسين بنعمة الخالق، لان هذا هو غرضه منذ المبدا[968] لكي لمساواة[969] واحدة يكمل كل خليقة الناطقين، ولا يكون فرق بين اوليك لهولاء[970] لا بالتضاعف ولا بالانبساطه، ولا ينظلم الجسد الطبيعي ولا يعودوا ياتوا للفحص عند ذلك.[971]

(217) كثيرين اذا ما ضربوا مطانيه[972] ولهم صلاة طاهره[973] محزنه، يقطعوا حركتهم ويبطلوا المطانيات (V259v/A227r) المملوه صلاة نافعه، لظنهم

---

954 غرض : K, S.

955 بتضرع : K, V.

956 سكين : K.

957 متكثر : K.

958 هاهنا : A.

959 فارغون : V.

960 المفرا : K.

961 ترتيب : K.

962 الهيولات : S / الهيولا : K.

963 لا : V.

964 الناطقين : V.

965 قلبه : A.

966 نحوهن : V.

967 تاءورية : S / تاأوريا : A.

968 البدء (المبدأ) :S / البداء : A.

969 لمساوات : K.

970 لهولاي : K / لهولا : R.

971 ذالك : R.

972 مطانوة : K.

انهم قد بطلوا من[974] المزامير ومن غرض القراه ومن الثبات الكثير في هذا العمل العظيم، وما يفهموا منافعها ولا يعرفوا هولاء[975] الفضلا، ان استعمالنا المزامير والقراءة والتلاوه والهذيذ بهم، انما هو لكي يطهر الضمير من الطياشه وبنقاوه[976] يتحرك بالصلاة، التي هي المفاوضه مع الله، (R177v) الذي كل شي نعمل[977] انما هو لاجلها.[978]

(218) الامانة هي حركه مملوه اقنوع[979] من نعمة الله تزهر[980] في العقل، (K209r) على الشي الذي لا يمكن الاسطر ان يرسم[981] بهن[982] بل العقل المومن هو[983] الذي[984] له سلطان ان يعرف الشي الذي يستعلن للاصحا، واما المريض الذي غذاه البقل، ليس يعطا له غذا الاصحا.

(219) تاورية[985] متضاعفه تظهر لنا بالافهام على الطبايع المعقوله، وشي[986] اخر هي التاوريا[987] [988]التي ترمز بتصرفهم والعطايا الطبيعيه، التي[989] نالوها من الخالق.

(220) احدتهم تدل على سر خليقة قيامة العامه، باي طقس[990] عتيد ان يصير الشي السري الذي للقيامه،[991] وباي لمح،[992] والاخر يرمز على ذاك التصرف

---

[973] طاهره : ساقطة K.

[974] من : ساقطة R.

[975] هولاي : K / هولا : R.

[976] بنقاوه...لاجلها : ساقطة V.

[977] يعمل : A.

[978] من اجلها : K.

[979] قنوع : K, S.

[980] تظهر : K.

[981] ترسم : A / يرتم : V.

[982] بهم : R.

[983] هو : ساقطة K.

[984] للذين : R.

[985] ثاؤريا : S / تااورية : A /تورية : K.

[986] وشيا : A.

[987] الثاؤريا : S / التااوريه : A / التورية : K.

[988] الذي ندركها المكتومة بسر وقت خلقتهم وشي اخر هي التاورية : زائدة K.

[989] الذي : K.

[990] طكس : R.

[991] القيامه : R.

[992] لحم : R.

الجديد، الذي[993] به تكون الناطقين بتلك الحياه كمثلما[994] يليق بعظم انعام[995] الخالق، ويوهلهم في ذلك[996] بلد الروحانيه،[997] لكي من واحده واحده من هذين التاوريات[998] تظهر لنا اسرار العالم العتيد، متواريا، واي شيا[999] هن حاملات هولاء[1000] الجواهر السعيده،[1001] التي بهن اشا[1002] الخالق ان يعرف وسبق رمز من مبدا هذا العالم الشي الثابت المحق عنده، ان يفعله مع الخليقه في المنتها[1003] (V260r) وعلى فضل[1004] التكوين (A227v) الثاني التي هي عتيده ان تقبل، وباي نوع يكون دخوله وتصرفه[1005] في تلك التقانة.

(221) محب الاعمال ليس هو الذي ما يحب راحة[1006] الجسد، بل الذي ما يحب مفاوضة[1007] الجسد.[1008]

(222) اذا ما ضعفت الالام التي في النفس بوساطة السكون وصمتوا،[1009] وايضا الشهوات[1010] الجسد بسهوله تقهر[1011] الانسان.

(223) الذي يعمل باستقامه يجب ان يكون له هذا الغرض في اعماله، لكي يجعل عقله غير مغلوب من الالام، ويقيمه صحيح بلا تحريك.[1012]

---

993 التي : K.
994 كمثل ما : K, V.
995 انعام : ساقطة R.
996 ذالك : R.
997 الروحاني : R.
998 الثاؤريات : S / التاأوريات : A.
999 اشيا : R, V / شيء : S / شي : K.
1000 هولاي : K / هولا : R.
1001 السيده : R.
1002 أشأ (شاء) : S / شا : K.
1003 المنتهى : R, S, V.
1004 فضل : ساقطة K.
1005 وتصفه : R.
1006 الراحة : R.
1007 مفاوظة : A.
1008 الجسده : A.
1009 وصمتت : K.
1010 لشهوات : A.
1011 تنقهر : K.
1012 تحرك : K.

(224) غرض المعرفه ان تدنى العقل لموهبة نظرة[1013] الالهيه[1014] التي هي كمال التاوريا.[1015]

(225) حسس النعمه المعقول بعمل التوبه المعقول يوجد، وعمل التوبه المعقول هو بكا الانسان الجواني، الملقي في القلب على الزلل، في حب الاب وليس من رعب الدينونه، ويتفاوض به بالهذيذ الدايم بالله بتضرعا[1016] خفي بالعقل، الحامل حزنا[1017] كذبيحة ترضي الله في كل وقت.

(226) حاسية العقل المعقوله السابقه في عمل السكون هو التنعم بالرجا المفرح، بمذاقة القلب التي من داخل العقل تنبع، على الحب الذي انغاض،[1018] وهذه هي معنا[1019] قوله طوبا[1020] للحزانه[1021] لانهم[1022] يتعزون.

(227) اذا ما بلغ الانسان في طريق الفضيله لفرح الرجا بعمله، عند ذلك[1023] يتخلف عنه الشقا ويخف عليه ثقل العمل ومن[1024] هاهنا يترك[1025] عنه عمل المخافة ويبدا[1026] بعمل الحب، وينبذ[1027] عنه الرعب وخوف الطريق، ويثق[1028] قلبه ويبتهج ضميره، ولا (R178r) ينظر هذا العالم بالكليه، لانه دايما يتحرك في نفسه (V260v) الرجا في المزمعات، ويملوه (A228r) في كل وقت بهجه، وينحجب هذا العالم من قدام[1029] عينيه، ولا يعرف سببه فقط، بل ان[1030]

[1013] الموهبة النظرة : K.

[1014] الهيه : A.

[1015] الثاؤريا : S / التاوريه : A / التوريه : K.

[1016] بتضرع : K.

[1017] حزن : K.

[1018] انفاض : S.

[1019] معنى : K, S.

[1020] طوبى : K, S.

[1021] للحزانى : S / للحزانا : K, V.

[1022] فانهم : K.

[1023] ذالك : R.

[1024] من : A.

[1025] ينزل : S.

[1026] ويبدى : K, R, V.

[1027] ويبيد : A.

[1028] وينق : A.

[1029] بين : A.

[1030] ان : ساقطة A.

نفسه تفرح وقت وقت كمن هو قايم في عالم العتيد، هولاء[1031] (K209v) وما يشبههم ينظر ذاته في السكون[1032] دايما، وهذه[1033] تكون حسب قولهم في الوقت التي[1034] تبدى النفس في الانعزال من الشركه مع الخطيه، ويبدى[1035] القلب بوساطة السكون الدايم ان ينقا[1036] من افرازات التذكارات، المفرزة الصور، التي هي منبهه[1037] اعضا الانسان العتيق في القلب.

(228) اذا ما بدت بالانسان[1038] حركة الرجا بضميره والبهجه التي من هاهنا بلا سبب، التي في كل وقت تنموا[1039] في قلبه من هاهنا ما يعرف تعب ولا ثقل ضجر، ولا رعب من الموت، لاني بالحقيقه اعرف اخ بلغ لهذا الفرح جميعه، حتى لما كان يريد يمجد[1040] الله ويشكره في ذاك الفرح، ينكسر[1041] لسانه وما ينبسط ليبارك به الله، وكالطفل كان يلغلغ ويتكلم مع الله[1042] كطفل صغير[1043] مع ابيه. هكذا يسكر الفرح الانسان،[1044] وفي هذه قالوا انه يصفا القلب ويكون دخوله الى الاستعلانات، وهذه هي المذاقة الاولى[1045] التي بها يدخلوا[1046] قوم للمينا الالهي، وهذا هو كمال التوبه، وهذا هو العزا الذي وعدنا به بالانجيل، ولكن[1047] في وقت وقت ما ينال منه لكي يتضع،[1048] وتتواثب عليه شكوك[1049] واسجاس[1050] وظلام، ويعود ايضا يفرح ويتنعم، هذه (V261r) تحدث يا

1031 هولا : R / هولاي : K.

1032 في السكون ينظر في ذاته : K.

1033 وهذا : R.

1034 الذي : K, A.

1035 ويبداء : A.

1036 ينقى : K, S.

1037 منبهت : V, R.

1038 في الانسان : K / العتيق...الانسان : ساقطة V.

1039 تنمو : K.

1040 ان يمجد : K.

1041 ينعقد : S.

1042 الله : ساقطة V.

1043 زغير : K.

1044 للانسان : K, A.

1045 الاوله : A, R, V.

1046 يدخلون : A.

1047 ولكي : R.

1048 يتضيع : R.

1049 اشكوك : V, R.

1050 وسجس : V.

اخوتي[1051] من السكون الدايم والبعد الزايد من خلطة الناس، ويتفاوض بهولا[1052] وما يشبههم. يا الله اهلني لتلك[1053] المذاقه المتنعمه التي داخل من التوبة الحقيقيه موضوعة،[1054] التي منها يغتذوا[1055] كل يوم التايبون، (A228v) المحقون، اوليك الذين ما يرذلون البكا، بل يدعوه عمل الاطفال، واما هم يغتذون[1056] الشهد.

(229) من دون النظرة الروحانيه البكا مكروم عند الابا، كمثلما[1057] قيل على[1058] القديس ارسانيوس، ان جفون[1059] عينيه انتثروا من دوام البكا، وذلك[1060] الجبار الطوباني بولس،[1061] انا الروح التام، مده ثلاث[1062] سنين لم تهدا عينيه من البكا، الى ان يبلغ الانسان الى مذاقة الايمان في طريق سيرته بعجز وضعف يقوم قبال كل الالام، ويثقل[1063] عليه جميع اعمال السيره.

(230) الميتوتة الروحانيه هي التي[1064] بنظر الامور الغير منطوق بها، الالهيات بالانفعال يتفاوض العقل وتتسكت[1065] منه كل الافكار[1066] الارضانيه،[1067] بشبه التصرف العتيد، ويحصل بدهش بافهام الامور التي ليس هم[1068] من عالم الموتا، ويقبل بالعربون لتلك الملكوت، باحواس الروح بصعوده لتلك المنازل التي بلا جسد ولا دم، وهذه هي معنا[1069] قوله تاتي

1051 اخوه : A.
1052 بهولاء : V / بهولاي : K.
1053 للتلك : R.
1054 موجودة : A, S, V.
1055 تغتذي : K.
1056 يغتذوا : S.
1057 كمثل ما : K, V.
1058 عن : A.
1059 اجفون : R, S.
1060 وذالك : R.
1061 بولص : K.
1062 ثلاثة : A, R, V.
1063 وتثقل : A.
1064 بها يتنقى العقل بالانشغال : زائدة S.
1065 وتسكت : K, V.
1066 افكار : R.
1067 الارضية : K.
1068 هن : K.
1069 معنا (معنى) : S / معنى : K.

(R178v) ملكوتك، قبل الوقت اومرنا من سيدنا ان نطلبها بالصلاه،[1070] وان نهدس فيها كل وقت ونتشوق اليها بلا فتور.

(231) (V261v) ايها السر الخفي الذي ظهر[1071] بجسدنا الذي كان قد بلى، اظهر في سر تجديد القديسين الذي بالعربون[1072] يقبلوه[1073] هاهنا، لتحقيق الخيرات العتيده، يا الذي بتعري[1074] جسده فضح الاراخنه والسلاطين، والبس[1075] طبيعتنا لباس عدم الفساد، انت (K210r) يا رب عريني من الانسان الفاسد بسر التجديد، وحرك في اعضاي حركات[1076] الانسان الجديد، الذي البستني بالمعموديه بالسر، وفي العالم[1077] المزمع يعطا بالفعل، لتنعيم جميع محبي محبتك، الذي تعبوا لاجلك هاهنا.[1078]

(232) [كمل بعون الله كتاب القديس مار اسحق، والناسك المسكين احقر الناس وارذلهم العادم الفضايل الممتلي من كل الرذايل الذي بالاسم والشكل راهب وبعيد عن عمل الرهبان المحقين يسال من جهت محبة السيد المسيح لكلمن يقف على هذا الكتاب ان يقول بكل قلبه، يا ربي يسوع المسيح اغفر خطايا عبدك موسى وسامحه باثامه في اليوم المرهوب. ومن صلى وقال شيا الرب يعوضه اضعاف ذلك ثلاثين وستين ومايه في ملكوت السماء، بصلات القديس العظيم مار اسحق، انعم يا رب على الناسك الذي كتب هذه الستة كراريس والقاري والسامع بمغفرة الخطايا امين. ܗܘ. ܗܟܢ ܫܠܡ ܟܬܒܐ ܥܡܗ
ܐܝܬ ܠܡܒܝܢܐ ܕܐܫܟܚܬ ܒܠܝܠܝܐ ܐܝܟ ܡܬܝ ܡܠܝܢ ܡܬܒܠܝܢ ܚܫܐ ܚܕܐ ܒܟܠ
ܚܝܐ ܕܗܘ ܕܥܒܕ ܠܡܫܬܐܠ ܡܢ ܡܪܝܐ.][1079]

(233) كملت المقالة الاوله في رووس المعرفة (A229r) وايضا من رووس المعرفه للقديس مار اسحق.[1080]

[1070] في الصلاة : K.

[1071] كان ظهر : K.

[1072] بالرعبون : K.

[1073] يقبلون : K.

[1074] بتعرا : A, R.

[1075] ولبس : R.

[1076] حركة : A.

[1077] عالم : K.

[1078] امين : زائدة A.

[1079] نهاية V.

[1080] K: **المقالة الثانية في رووس المعرفة لمار اسحق..**

(234) القول على اتحاد المومنين بالاب والابن، الذي بنوع الصلاه في وقت الالام قيلت من الابن الى الاب، بسبوق اظهار السر في العالم الجديد تكمل[1081] بالفعل، اذا ما انتهت امور هذا العالم وبلغ مبدا تلك التقانه، عندما يرتفع سيدنا مع جوقات القوات السماييه[1082] المبجله[1083] لعظمته، من[1084] بعد ان يدين الارض دينونة ممتزجه بالرحمة،[1085] وترتفع معهم جميع المستحقين من هذا البلد الوسطاني، لذاك البلد الابدي، حيث هو[1086] الاب والابن، بغير حد وقياس، والوسيط[1087] يسوع المسيح[1088] سيدنا،[1089] الذي به نعاين بغير ادراك نظر[1090] الثالوث المقدس، كمثل بالمراه،[1091] وبه نقبل التنعم[1092] الذي[1093] يخرج من ينبوع الحياه، عند ذلك[1094] بوساطته يدنوا[1095] من الله الاب كل الناطقين الاولين والاخرين،[1096] وينالوا[1097] ذلك[1098] الفرح الذي لا يفترق منهم[1099] الى الابد، قالوا[1100] الابا ان في تلك الساعه التي فيها تنخطف القديسين من الغمز[1101] الالهي،[1102] ليرتفعون[1103] لسعادة[1104] ملاقات[1105] سيدنا الذي[1106] تجذبهم قوته،

1081 يكمل : A.

1082 السماويه : K.

1083 المجد وعز : R.

1084 ومن : A.

1085 بالحمه : R.

1086 هو : ساقطة A.

1087 والوسط : A.

1088 ܡܫܝܚܐ : K.

1089 سيدنا : ساقطة K.

1090 منظر : K.

1091 بالمراة : K.

1092 التنعيم : R.

1093 الذي به : K.

1094 ذالك : R.

1095 يدنو : K.

1096 الاوليين والاخريين : A.

1097 وينالو : K.

1098 ذالك : R.

1099 منه : A.

1100 قالو : K.

1101 الغمر : S.

1102 الايلاهي : K.

1103 ليرتفقوا : A.

1104 لساعدة : K.

كحجر المغناطيس[1107] التي[1108] تجذب قطع[1109] الحديد اليها، عند ذلك[1110] ينضمون[1111] لكنيسة واحده جميع رتب[1112] السماييين،[1113] وجوقات اولاد ادم، عند[1114] ذلك[1115] يكمل غرض راي الخالق الذي اليه كان منتظر من حيث انشا العالم، لما خلق الخليقه بالنعمه لهذا المخرج صوبها جميع جري العالم بافرازاته، وخدمته للناطقين بتغيراته[1116] كمثل السيد في دور الملكوت، يتنعمون بالعالم الذي لا انقضا له، (A229v) ولا غيار لتنعيم[1117] حياته.

(235) الذبيحه بالهيولى هي ذبيحة جسدانيه تشترك معها النفس بارادتها الفاضله.

(236) الذبيحه التي بلا هيولى هي ذبيحة نفسانيه، يشترك معها الجسد بالخضوع[1118] العفيف.

(237) الذبيحة التي[1119] بلا رسم[1120] هي[1121] سجود العقل،[1122] الذي يشخص بالكلمة الغير (R179r) هيولانيه[1123] بالروح وبجميع حركاته يطاطى راسه[1124] قدام العظمة.

1105 ملاقاة : A, S.

1106 التي : A.

1107 المغنيطس : A.

1108 الذي : A.

1109 فلاق : K.

1110 ذالك : R.

1111 ينظمون : A.

1112 الرتب : A.

1113 السمايين : R / السمائيين : S / السماويين : K.

1114 وعند : K.

1115 ذالك : R.

1116 بتغييراته : A, S.

1117 التنعيم : R.

1118 بالخدوع : A, R.

1119 تكون : زائدة K.

1120 رسوم : K.

1121 هو : R.

1122 الروح : K.

1123 هيوليه : K.

1124 يطاطى راسه : ساقطة K.

(238) فاضله[1125] هي المعرفه التي بلا هيولى بالصلاه، من الصلاه التي بلا رسوم.

(239) المعرفه بالصلاه التي بلا هيولى هي حسس روحاني بالصلاه، كلمه الهيولى التي بلا رسوم بالتضرع هي الصلاه الطاهره.

(240) ثم كلمه هيوليه بلا رسوم هيولى بالصلاه، وثم كلمه بلا هيولى ولا رسوم بالصلاه، والواحده منهن يشارك فعل الروح القدس، والاخره الارادة الصالحه النشيطه والنعمه، ومعونة النعمه خفيا وغير معروف وبغير حسس معرفه، وايضا بالهذيذ الفاضل حركات قنوميه فيه، ليس بالالام فقط، وهذه انما تكون بالانقيا والفضلا[1126] وليس بالصلاه.

(241) كل رسوم قنوميه بالصلاه هي نقص العقل في وقت الصلاه، وان كان حدوثهم انما يكون من العجز او من البلاده ليس عليه لوم، وان كان فيهم شي قد توخر من موافقة العقل لهم، وما جاهد قبالهم، يجعلوا المتوحد تحت اللوم قدام الله، فان كانوا الميه او تصويرهم بغير الم خارج عن الهذيذ الفاضل يكونوا في العقل.

(242) استعمال التقويم الثاني، الذي لكل مساواه يحد حركة[1127] هذا القيام الكثير الافرازات، بدا عند منتها[1128] ذلك[1129] الذي اتقدم بمعرفته في الضمير. الزارع[1130] عند رمي الزرع، (A230r) حرك[1131] الكلمه بالعنايه، اذ لكل عنايه مقابل الاستعمال، انتظر المخرج ذاك الذي سبق وحرك الفعل.

(243) صوت الاول تاورية[1132] ازلية اللاهوت، وصوت الاخير بسر الافرازات اقانيمها، زارعة هي المنادى الاول بالنور الاول هو النور المحسوس، وهو ايضا[1133] ارشد النيرين الى النور.

(244) انظر كيف بنقاوته المستويه من الاول لتمجيد[1134] كثرة النور، الاقراص[1135] المتقدمين[1136] حرك بحسنه، وهو ايضا بتقسيم اجزاه للاخوه

1125 فاضله هي ...او ظلام النظر : ساقطة K.

1126 والفضله : R.

1127 حرك : R.

1128 منتهى : R, S.

1129 ذالك : R.

1130 الزارع : R.

1131 حرك : ساقطة R.

1132 تاورية : A / تاؤرية : S.

1133 ايضا : ساقطة S.

التانيين بانواره من اظلم من النور، وتمجيد التاورية[1137] الاوله[1138] جذب اليه بحدها، وايضا[1139] تسر[1140] وترجع اليه ذاك الذي الجميع من معرفته صاروا الناطقين الكبار، التاورية[1141] الوحديه بوساطة الاجسام قبلوا التعليم،[1142] والتانيين هي الوحديه وحيديا صارت لهم معلم بشبه الاجسام التي هم لابسين، المجد لعظمة حبك الذي لا قياس له، المجد لعجب نعمتك التي[1143] لا شبه لها، المجد لعدم ادراك تنازلك الذي اقام الروحانيين بالتعجب الذي ليس له تفسير، وفي الاخر به بحقيقة اجسامهم رفعتهم للتاورية[1144] فكرها ازليا على تقانتهم.

(245) كل وقت يذوق العقل من افرازات التاورية[1145] الاوله الروحانيه الوحيديه، هكذا تنشا به الداله الى السبب الذي[1146] من التاوريه[1147] توخذ، واليها يتلف[1148] كل عقل حسب مقدار الافرازات التي بها (R179v) يستنير، يعطا[1149] موهبه حسبها وداله[1150] حسب كمية النور، ولكن ليس صغر النور وكبره ترفع[1151] او[1152] تقايس بعقل قابلهم، فلهذا[1153] في الافرازات يدنى الى حد الدهش، وثم منهم وبهم بقياس، ومن هاهنا يعرف الفيض، (A230v) او قياس النور في القابل الذي هو العقل، ونقاوة النظر او ظلام[1154] النظر.

1134 لتمجيده : S.

1135 للاقراص : S, R.

1136 من : زائدة S.

1137 التاورية : A / الثاؤرية : S.

1138 الاولى : S.

1139 وايضا : ساقطة R.

1140 تصر (تسر) : S.

1141 التاورية : A / الثاؤرية : S.

1142 للتعليم : R.

1143 الذي : R.

1144 لتاورية : A / لتاؤرية : S.

1145 التاورية : A / التاؤرية : S.

1146 التي : S, R.

1147 التاورية : A / التاؤرية : S.

1148 تتلف : R / تتخلف : S.

1149 يعطى : S.

1150 داله : R.

1151 ترفع : ساقطة R.

1152 اذ : S.

1153 ولهذا : R.

1154 الظلام : R.

(246) (K210v) ليس لكل ظلام وصعوبة جهاد، يقفوا[1155] في اثرهم موهبة، بل من كل بد لكل موهبة يتقدمها هولاء،[1156] اما (K211r) من قبل الوقت، او من قبل يوم، او من قبل شهر، او من قبل سنه، حسب مقدار العطية، لانه لا يمكن ان ياتي للصلاح[1157] ان لم يتقدم السجس والتكدر[1158] وظلام عظيم وتجربه، فلهذا كل وقت[1159] يوهل العقل لقبول موهبة نياح ما، جهاد عظيم وشر كثير موضوع قدامه، وبخروجه[1160] من هناك يلاقيه النور، وبمقدار الضغط يكون النور، ان كان الضغط شديد كذلك[1161] تكون عظيمه الموهبه، لانه تعاين[1162] جميع القديسين هكذا يجرا[1163] لهم، وبالاكثر في مبدا الدخول لتجربه عظيمه يدخلون، اذا ما اوهلوا ان يدنوا من النعمة الالهية محسوسا.[1164]

(247) اما الجهاد[1165] مع الشياطين يدخل، واما التجارب[1166] بالخفي، لكن طوبا[1167] لمن لا يميل الى الانحلال ويسيب[1168] نفسه الى المحادثات والنياحات، ويهرب من السكون ويستعين بالراحه،[1169] في هذه الاوقات المختبره.

(248) حرارة القلب في وقت الصلاة عندما تنحل الاعضا، وتنقبض الاحواس ويضعف اللسان،[1170] ويتخلف عن الحركه مع العقل، في ضرب[1171] المطانيات على مكانه مدة طويله، حسينا ان هذا يحدث من القراه[1172] بمعرفة التي بها يعرف ضويا[1173] الحق بثبت،[1174] عندما يدنى الانسان للصلاه تذكار القراه

1155 يقفو : A.

1156 هولا : R / هولاي : K.

1157 الصلاح : K.

1158 والتذكر : R.

1159 ان : زائدة K.

1160 وفي خروجه : K.

1161 كذالك : R.

1162 لاننا نعاين : S / لانه نعاين : K.

1163 يجري : S.

1164 محسوس : K.

1165 الجهد : R / للجهاد : K.

1166 للتجارب : K.

1167 طوبى : K, S.

1168 ويسحب : K.

1169 في الراحة : K.

1170 الانسان : K.

1171 ظرب : A, S.

1172 القراءة : S.

1173 ساطعاً : S / ضاوي : K.

يلهب المصلي بافهام الكلام الصحيح، الذي قيل عن الله، ومن قبل وقت كان (A231r) يتلوا[1175] بهم.

(249) الى ان يوهل الانسان لاستعلان[1176] الاسرار الالهيه الذي بالطهارة التامه يعرف العقل[1177] بفعل روح[1178] القدس، بهذا الغرض يتذوق[1179] التنعم المعقول، الذين في طريق المعرفه يسيرون ان كان بهذيذ المزامير، وان[1180] كان بمفاوضة[1181] القراه، وان كان بالصلاة، وان كان بهذيذ العقل الى الفعل يستحقون بالعقل، بهذا الدهش الجزوي وسرور القلب يتنعمون بالفرح بالله، بفهم الشي الذي يقبلون متوارياً[1182] في وقت وقت، اوليك الذين من اجل معرفة الله يعدون انفسهم ولم تصغر روحهم، ويتركون السكون.

(250) المجد للذي صار لنا وسيط لمثل هذه الخيرات، وبه استحقينا ان نقبل ونعرف ونحس بالايمان[1183] الشي[1184] الذي لم تنظره عين ولم تسمعه[1185] اذن ولم تستطيع الاحواس النفسانيه ان يضمروا[1186] بشي من هذه الخيرات، ذاك[1187] الذي بالجسد الذي اخذ[1188] منا الذي هو صورة حقيقي (R180r) الغير[1189] منظور، المتحد به الطبع الالهي، الذي لاجل رجا الناطقين اخذه منا، الاشيا المكتومه عنده منذ الابتدا،[1190] والان اخرجها للظهور، وبه عرفنا بشي[1191]

1174 كثبت : R / بثبات : S / بثابت : K.

1175 يتلو : A.

1176 الاستعلان : K.

1177 الع..ل : R.

1178 الروح : K.

1179 يتضوق : K.

1180 ان : K.

1181 بمافاوضة : R.

1182 متوارياً يقبلون : S, R / متواري يقبلون : K.

1183 بايمان : A.

1184 للشي : K.

1185 تسمع به : A.

1186 يطمروا : A.

1187 ذلك : S / لذاك : A.

1188 اخذه : K.

1189 للغير : K.

1190 الابدا : R.

1191 بشي : ساقطة K.

منهم لكي نتحقق على باقية الاشيا الحادثه في التجديد الذي[1192] نقبل زعم تلك التقانة.

(251) الوحده تشركنا مع العقل الالهي، ولنقاوة الضمير في اسرع وقت تدنينا، بغير تعويق.

(252) في وقت نظرة النور والسفر في الجو استعمل الحيل[1193] الظاهره باجتهاد، يعني ضرب المطانيات وطول التضرع وباقية ما (K211v) يشبه،[1194] يبدا بغته ويصعد الشمس منذ[1195] الراس، من غير انتظار ويطلق شعاعاته في وقت الى وسط الرقيع.

(253) البريه القفره[1196] (A231v) لاجل الهدو[1197] الذي فيها تقني[1198] لنا ميتوتة القلب،[1199] وتخدع[1200] العقل وتخلطه بالله، لاجل الشخوص والنظر الدايم اليه، اضروره[1201] ليلا[1202] ونهارا.[1203]

(254) التواضع هو حد انجماع العقل وكل وقت[1204] يكون النور مشتت من اعضا التواضع، قد انفسخ شي، وان كنت تقول ثم[1205] من هو منقبض داخله ويهدس في الشر،[1206] اوريني[1207] واحد من الم[1208] الشرور من دون تصور[1209] الامور ينقام بالعقل، فان كان العقل متصور باشكال الهيولى، ليس هناك

1192 به : زائدة K.

1193 الحال : K.

1194 شبه : K.

1195 من (عند) : S.

1196 القفرا : A.

1197 الهدوا : R.

1198 تقتنى : A.

1199 قلب : K.

1200 تخضع : K, S.

1201 ضروره : K, S.

1202 ليل : K.

1203 ونهار : K, R.

1204 ان : زائدة K.

1205 ثمة : S.

1206 الشرور : K.

1207 فانا اقول اوريني : S.

1208 الام : K.

1209 اتصور : R.

انجماع، لان الانجماع الحقيقي يعرف من اذا كان العقل منعتق من تصور اشكال الالام.

(255) سكون[1210] العقل هو قيام الحق في النفس، لان الحق انما يعرف بغير تصور اشكال الحق هو نقاوه الهذيذ الالهي المتقوم بالذهن.

(256) كل موضع[1211] تحصل فيه كون مفتردا[1212] بضميرك متوحدا[1213] غريبا[1214] بالقلب غير مختلط، ان كان جميع مصادفات النظر والسمع ينتهوا[1215] لتربية الافكار داخلا،[1216] اي منفعه للذين[1217] يسرعون[1218] باجتهاد للملاقاه[1219] ويماروا[1220] ان يسكتوا الافكار.

(257) لا تقايس كل السيره[1221] والاعمال العجيبه التي بها، مع ان يكون الانسان غير معروف ولا محسوب ويهرب من الكل لان الانفراد[1222] ينشا[1223] من ان يكون غير معروف ولا محسوب.[1224]

(258) ثق ان كل شي هو حامل غرض التاوريه[1225] الطبيعيه الثانيه يبطل[1226] في العالم الجديد مع جميع زيها[1227] لان شكل هذا العالم يزول مع جميع تراتيبه،[1228] معلوم من هذا ان التاوريه[1229] عليه مع النظر ايضا يبطل.

1210 اسكون : R.

1211 ان : زائدة K.

1212 متفرد : K.

1213 متوحد : K.

1214 غريب : K.

1215 ينهوا : S / ينتهو : K.

1216 داخل : K.

1217 من عمل الذين : K.

1218 يصرعون : K.

1219 للملاقات : K.

1220 ويمارون : A.

1221 للسيرة : K.

1222 الانفرار : R.

1223 ينشي : K.

1224 ويهرب...ولا محسوب : ساقطة A.

1225 الثاؤرية : S / التااوريه : A.

1226 سيبطل : S / تبطل : A.

1227 زينتها : A.

1228 ترتيبه : K.

1229 الثاؤرية : S / التااوريه : A.

(259) ان كان ليس[1230] شي من الذين يحركون التاوريا[1231] على الجسمانيات، ولا على الاحواس ولا على الذي يحلوا[1232] (A232r) عليهم يحتاج عند ذلك[1233] العقل قبل استيصال هولاء[1234] للبدو اللحمي،[1235] معروف ايضا ان ذكرهم اعني الشي الذي تسقط[1236] عليهم الاحواس بالكمال ينقطع من الطبع، وباي تقويم يقتنوا عند ذلك[1237] في كل لمح.[1238]

(260) القداسه هي ان الانسان في الصلاه[1239] بقوة فعل الروح القدس يتقدس.

(261) الى ان يتقدس قلبنا بروح الرب ما نقدر نفرز ضويا[1240] الحركات التي من افعال الشيطان،[1241] ومن الملايكه ومن الطبع، ومن تحريك روح القدس.

(262) الى ان تتقدس كلمتنا بقوة الروح ليس تكون مخوفه على الشياطين، ولا تخدع[1242] لها الطبايع الناطقه (R180v) او الصامته.

(263) الى ان نطهر من انفعال[1243] الخطيه، ما تحل[1244] في نفسنا[1245] انفعال روح[1246] القدس، ولا نستطيع ان نكون اواني لحلول السيد.

(264) بكر جميع الخلايق[1247] المنظورين والغير منظورين، لان هو اوله اتلد[1248] لحياة العالم[1249] الجديد، بقيامته من الاموات بالحق[1250] هو لنا بكر، بان

1230 ليس : ساقطة A.

1231 التاورية : K / الثاؤريا : S / التااوريه : A.

1232 يحل : S / يخلوا : R.

1233 ذالك : R.

1234 هولا : R / هؤلاء : S / هولاي بالكمال : K.

1235 البدوا اللمحي : R / لبدو لمح : K.

1236 يسقط : A.

1237 ذالك : R.

1238 لحم : R.

1239 بالصلاه : K.

1240 ضوئيا : S.

1241 الشيطان (الشياطين) : S / الشياطين : K, R.

1242 (تخضع) : S / تخضع : K.

1243 افعال : K.

1244 يحل : A.

1245 نفوسنا : K.

1246 الروح : K.

1247 الناطقة : زائدة K.

1248 ولد : S.

1249 الحياة للعالم : K.

ليس احد[1251] قبله اتلد[1252] لهناك،[1253] وحسنا[1254] دعي بكر ليس لنا فقط،[1255] بل وللطبايع[1256] الغير متجسمه، لان خلقتهم[1257] ايضا تنتظر لهذه الولادة.

(265) ينبغي ان تسجد الخليقه جميعها[1258] لصورة الملك، (K212r) حتى الان ما نظرنا واحد من البشر قد سجدت له الملايكه، الذي الخليقه جميعها تنتظر اليه وله تسجد المنظوره والغير منظوره، لانه دعي باسم الله يليق به هذا التسمي، والصوره الذي به مزمع ان يتقدم الكل الى الله، وبجسده الطاهر ننظر[1259] الخفي الغير مدروك.

(266) اما بالخليقه[1260] ليس بالملايكه المقدسين واحد اكبر من الاخر، بطبع خلقته، ومن بعد ما خلقهم (A232v) قسم[1261] لهم الرب درجات وكرامات[1262] كما شاء،[1263] واما بالمعرفه وحرارة الحب فيهم اوليين، واوساط، ومتوخرين، وليس في[1264] الرتب الحطيطه ما يتقدم بالاستعلان وبالمعرفه[1265] لمن هو اعلا[1266] منه رتبه، ولا في الذي اعلا[1267] من يتوخر بالتعقل لمن يتلوه طقس[1268] ودرجه.

[1250] بحق : K.

[1251] احدا : A.

[1252] ولد : S.

[1253] لهناك : ساقطة K.

[1254] وحسن : K.

[1255] فقط لنا : K.

[1256] ولطبايع : R.

[1257] خليقتهم : K.

[1258] جميعا : A.

[1259] ينظر : K.

[1260] الخليقة : S / بالخلقة : K.

[1261] وسم : A.

[1262] وكراما : K.

[1263] اشا : R / اشاء : S.

[1264] في : ساقطة R.

[1265] والمعرفة : S.

[1266] اعلى : K.

[1267] اعلى : K.

[1268] طكس : R.

(267) اذا ما قبل العقل حسس حسن[1269] طبيعته، عند ذلك[1270] بتربية الملايكه ينشو،[1271] ومن هاهنا يوهل للشركه[1272] مع الملايكه باستعلان عقله، لانه قام بترتيب طبع خلقته الاوله، تلك التي[1273] فيها امكان لقبول[1274] التاوريا.[1275]

(268) حلاوة الاوله التي للاستعلان المعقول العقلي هي تاورية[1276] عناية الله، التي بالافعال المحسوسه[1277] قوتها الفاعله للعقل تظهر بالحس.

(269) والحلاوة[1278] الثانيه عنايته بالكاينات، والحلاوة الثالثه تاورية[1279] خلقته، الحلاوة الرابعه تاورية[1280] حكمته بهم، وقوة فكرته الغير مدروكه بالغيارات الغير متشابهه لاحكامه، بالنظرة الاوله[1281] يتهاون[1282] من التحيل البشري، وهذه هي امانة الكاينات الاوله،[1283] بالنظره الثانيه بثقه وثكلان على الخالق يتثبت ويتحقق، بالنظرة الثالثه بالحب يبتلع[1284] كالطفل الذي قد[1285] حس بوالده،[1286] بالطقس[1287] الرابع بسحابة[1288] حكمة الباري المملوه افرازات ينحجب، بالاختلاج الخامس على[1289] عدم الادراك العسر التفسير[1290] بالذهول يتواسط.

1269 حسن : ساقطة K.
1270 ذالك : R.
1271 ينشوا : R.
1272 الشركة : K.
1273 التي : ساقطة R.
1274 للقبول : K.
1275 التاؤرية : S / للتاوريا : K / التااوريه : A.
1276 تاؤرية : S / تورية : K / تااورية : A.
1277 المحسوس : K.
1278 الحلاوة : A.
1279 ثاؤرية : S / تورية : K / تااورية : A.
1280 ثاؤرية : S / توريه : K / تااورية : A.
1281 الاولى : S.
1282 يهمل : K.
1283 الاولى : S.
1284 يبتلغ : S.
1285 قد : ساقطة A.
1286 بالوالدة : S.
1287 بالطكس : R.
1288 بحسابة : K.
1289 علا : K.
1290 للتفسير : A.

(270) الى ان يمتزج قوة الروح بهذيذ العقل، ما يختلط بحركاته بالدهش في الله، الى ان يصفا العقل ما يشترك لفعل الروح.

(271) اذا ما بدت الحركات تصفا[1291] عند ذلك[1292] يتضع القلب، (A233r) ويبقا[1293] كمثل في عمق ما[1294] حال، ومن هذا التواضع يدنوا للنقاوة.

(272) حب الوحده ولو انك عاجز عن[1295] جميع حقوقها، (R181r) صلاة واحده[1296] يقدمها الانسان لله وهو وحده، اخير منماية صلاة[1297] يخدمها مع الناس.

(273) بالحقيقه عمل ماية يوم بالسجس والخلطه يصوم ويصلي المتوحد ما توازن[1298] مع نوم ليلة واحده وهو وحده.

(274) صلي في وحدتك دايما قايلا، يا الله اجعلني مستحق لحزن النوح في قلبي،[1299] يا رب اقطع مفاوضة العالم من قلبي، هذه[1300] الصلاه تدخلك باسرار الله، ان[1301] تهتم بتكميل حقوق تفسيرها بعملك.

(275) العمل الذي بين الناس فيه افتخار، والضعف بالسكون فيه انسحاق القلب، من دون السكون ما يتواضع القلب، (K212v) ومن دون اتضاع[1302] القلب ما يتوقد القلب من الحركات المتواتره، ومع هولاء[1303] جميع اعمال المتوحد هم تراب ورماد.

(276) كما ان[1304] النور الغير ناطق لفرز الاجسام اوتمن وخلق، هكذا ايضا بالنور الحي للافرازات[1305] الروحانيه نعاين. ان كان العنصر النير

1291 تتصفا : S.
1292 ذالك : R.
1293 ويبقى : K, S.
1294 ماء : A.
1295 من : K.
1296 صلوة واحد : K.
1297 صلا : K.
1298 توازى : S / يوازن : A.
1299 قلب : K.
1300 وهذه : R.
1301 كنت : زائدة K.
1302 تواضع : K.
1303 هولا : R / ومن دون : S / هولاي : K.
1304 ان : ساقطة K.

لاستعلان[1306] الاجسام وفرز الاحواس الجسمانيات،[1307] لانه ثم وقت لا يكونوا الذين تفرزهم[1308] الاحواس، فمعلوم ان الشي الذي من اجل هذا لا حاجة الى الاستعمال به.

(277) نقي ضميرك من الافكار الجسدانيه، لكي تذوق التنعم الذي ما يقع تحت تركيب[1309] اللسان.

(278) رجا الاشيا المزمعه ينسي تذكار الاشيا الارضيه، من الضمير، ارفع ضميرك دايما واشخص في تلك المنازل، التي[1310] انت مزمع ان تنالها اخيرا.

(279) قطع الرجا يخرج (A233v) الانسان من نقا الافكار ويطمر[1311] قلبه في الارض، الضبط بالرجا[1312] يطهر القلب، وعلى الدوام يسكره لينتقل بشهوته من الارضيات،[1313] وفي المنازل السمايية[1314] يطيش بحركاته، لان بسهوله ينقا القلب بالامل.

(280) مذاقة الملكوت هي حركة الفرح،[1315] الذي فوق القوة يمتد في النفس على المزمعات، والجسد ينحل من قدامه جميع[1316] اعضاه لانه ينقهر من الصبر على تلك العظمه،[1317] حتى الشريانات والاعضام[1318] تتحلا[1319] بذلك[1320] السرور الخارج عن طقس[1321] الطبيعه.

1305 الافرازات : K.
1306 الاستعمال : K.
1307 الجسمانية : S / الجسمانياة : R.
1308 يفرزهم : A.
1309 ترتيب : K.
1310 الذي : S, R.
1311 ويضمر : K.
1312 بالرجاء : S.
1313 الارضانيات : R, S.
1314 السمائية : S / السماويه : K.
1315 القلب الفرح : S.
1316 بجميع : K.
1317 العصمه : A.
1318 والعضام : A.
1319 تتلذذ : S.
1320 بذالك : R.
1321 طكس : R.

(281) بقطع اياس الانسان من حياة الجسد يصادف قنيان النفس، الذين من فوق احواس الجسد يوجد.[1322]

(282) اذا الضمير كان مثبت[1323] برجاه ولو ان الجسد ينحط بالضعف، ما تنغلب النفس، ولا تنقص من غناها.

(283) البكا الدايم هو اذا ما العقل ضعف والجسد انحط، واتخلف عن السير، احذر[1324] ليلا يعطلك ضعف الجسد من حياة الوحده، ويبطل نجاحك متضاعف بانحطاط الجسد من الحياه[1325] الهاديه[1326] مع الله.

(284) احذر[1327] ليلا تحصل في مرضين مولدين الموت للغير[1328] مايت، الذين هم بطالة الجسد وانحلال النفس، بوساطة الاحواس،[1329] لان مرض الجسد مع الحرص ما يودي شي.[1330]

(285) ان كان النور الناطق بسهوله يمتد الى النور الاول، بلا تعويق، وهذا هو ايضا بالناطقين الاوليين التي[1331] الكلمه المخلصه شبهت[1332] بهم، فمعلوم (R181v) ان السر يكون في العالم الغير متجسد،[1333] وبه ايضا يقبلون ميراث النور، وليس بما دون الناطق ومتغلط[1334] كمثلما يخرفوا[1335] عديمي[1336] المعرفه، قصير هو (A234r) مدة حياتنا يا اخوتي وصنعتنا طويلة، والخيرات التي وعدنا بها ما ينطق بهم.

[1322] توجد : A.

[1323] متثبت : K.

[1324] احظر : K.

[1325] الحياة الحياة : K.

[1326] الهاديه : ساقطة K.

[1327] احظر : K.

[1328] الغير : R.

[1329] لاحواس : R.

[1330] شيا : R / يؤذي شيئا : S.

[1331] الذي : A.

[1332] شهت : R / تشبهت : A.

[1333] متغير : K.

[1334] المتلفظ : S.

[1335] يجزفوا : R.

[1336] عادمي : A.

(286) لذيذه هي اسباب الالام يا اخوتي، ولكن ليس هي كاثمار البر، مريره هي ومحزنه[1337] اسباب البر يا احباي،[1338] ولكن ليس كمنتها[1339] الخطية.

(287) لذيذه هي اسباب الخطيه ولكن[1340] مر جدا خروج كمالهن، مريره هي الاسباب المربيه الفضيله،[1341] ولكن[1342] حلوا[1343] جدا الاثمار الذي[1344] منهم يشرقوا، ولا حلاوة الاوليات اعني الخطية، ولا مرارة الثانيات اعني الفضايل، يدوموا كثير،[1345] بل انما يثبت عند الضابطين لهم المخرج الذي يكون منهن.[1346]

(288) ما اعجب الفكر على (K213r) تقانتك ايها الانسان، واعجب منه سر قيامتك، ومحزن جدا الفحص عن انحلال تركيبك، بل هو[1347] عظيم[1348] جدا شرف قيامتك، نفسي حزينه الى الموت، لكن اتسلا واتشجع بالايمان من اجل ذاك الذي سبق ومات[1349] وقام، واعطا بقيامته عزا الرجا لجنس[1350] البشر.

(289) خمسة هم[1351] قوات النفسانية القانيه اياهم النفس الناطقه بالجوهر المتحد، اعني بقولي عن الشهوة الطبيعيه التي للنفس، والقوة الغضبيه المساعده لشهواتها،[1352] لان الغضبيه بالطبع قد وضعت ان تتحرك بعد الشهوه، وحركة الحيوه[1353] التي بلا فتور تختلج في النفس، والنطق البسيط، والنطق المركب.

1337 محزنة : R.

1338 اخوتي : S / يا اخوتي : A.

1339 كنهاية : S.

1340 لكن : K.

1341 الفضايل : A, R.

1342 لكن : K.

1343 حلو : K.

1344 التي : R, S.

1345 كثيرا : S.

1346 منهم : R, K.

1347 هو : ساقطة A.

1348 بل عظيم جدا هو : S / بل عظيم هو جدا : R.

1349 مات : K.

1350 للجنس : R.

1351 هي : K.

1352 لشهوتها : K.

1353 الحياة : K, S.

(290) من هذه الخمس قوات النفسانيه مع فرقتها من الجسد، اثنين[1354] يبطلون بالكمال، الذين هم القوة الغضبيه، والنطق المركب، لان واحد من هولاء[1355] ما يصلح للتدبير[1356] المزمع، لان ليس هناك شي ينادي[1357] به الصوت،[1358] (A234v) ولا مضادد[1359] للصلاح[1360] لكي يستعمل[1361] الغيره قباله، واثنين اخر ايضا[1362] يحفظون بلا حركه، الى الوقت الذي[1363] يكون بعد القيامه، لاجل استعمالهم في العالم الجديد، لان بهن تكون السيرة السماييه[1364] احدهن هو الناطق البسيط، الذي هو العقل العارف، لان به[1365] تتحرك بالتاوريا[1366] على تلك الازليه التي[1367] هي هي[1368] حد[1369] كل ملكوت السماء،[1370] لانه ينظم داخل من الدهش بها عقل جميع الناطقين الاوليين والاخريين،[1371] وايضا شهوتها الطبيعيه لان بها تتحرك بحلاوة عظم محبة الخالق الذي به مزمع ان يكمل جميع طبع البشر، عند ذلك[1372] والملايكه جميع والشياطين،[1373] اما الملايكه هم فيه من الان بالكمال، واما البشر في وقت وقت، واما الشياطين عادمين منه بالكليه، وهم مزمعين ان يكملوا[1374] به في الاخر من اجل نعمة الذي خلقهم،[1375]

1354 الجسدانيين : S.
1355 هولا : R / هولاي : S.
1356 لتدبير : K.
1357 ينادي : ساقطة S.
1358 للصوت : R.
1359 مضاد : S.
1360 الصلاح : K.
1361 نستعمل : A.
1362 ايضا : ساقطة S.
1363 التي : R.
1364 السماوية : K.
1365 بهن : S.
1366 بالتاورية : K / الثاؤريا : S / بالتااوريا : A.
1367 الذي : K.
1368 هي : ساقطة K, S.
1369 غاية : S.
1370 السما : K, R.
1371 والاخرين : R / الاولين والاخرين : S.
1372 ذالك : R.
1373 والشياطين : ساقطة S.
1374 يكملو : K.
1375 واما الشياطين...خلقهم : ساقطة S.

فيتبقا للنفس شيا[1376] واحد[1377] من قواتها[1378] وهو يثبت معها عند (R182r) فرقتها[1379] من الجسد الى ان تعود تلبسه[1380] بغمز الخالق القويه، وهي حركة حيوتها[1381] الطبيعيه هذه فقط تتم فيها واياها تصحب الى ذاك العالم.

(291) النفس الذي[1382] مع الجسد وبه اخطت او تبررت، ليس بالعدل والواجب ان وحدها من دونه تنال افراح او احزان.

(292) اتفاضلوا بلا حد بالمعرفه الطبايع المعقوله بما فهموه[1383] من تدبير تجسد[1384] سيدنا المسيح، اشيا التي ما كانوا يعرفوها اول،[1385] اوليك التي[1386] من اجل عتق وتكميل هم ونحن جا،[1387] لان من بعد مجي المسيح[1388] اقتنوا هذه المعرفة الفاضله على حكمة الله الطبايع المعقوله، لنظرهم باي سياسة فاضله صنع اليهم، لكي يجمع الكل الى واحد، (A235r) بتدبير المسيح[1389] الشي الذي اذا نلناه كلنا، مزمعين ان نصير واحد، الذين من هاهنا نجتهد بمخافة الله ونحن عتيدين ان اتجلدنا[1390] فيها، بخيرات كثيره نتصرف مع القوات الغير منظوره، ومع المسيح[1391] سيدنا، وهناك نصير جميعنا[1392] بيعة واحدة لربنا.

(293) ثم[1393] فكر ملايكي (K213v) وتاوريا[1394] ملايكيه، اما الفكر الملايكي على الفضيله ندم حار يقع فينا او تعجب على طبايع الامور،[1395] كمثلما قال

1376 شي : K.

1377 واحدا : S.

1378 قوتها : S / قوايها : K, R.

1379 فرقها : R.

1380 تلبس : K.

1381 حيويتها : S / حياتها : K.

1382 التي : K, S.

1383 يفهموه : S.

1384 اتجسد : S.

1385 اول (اولا) : S / اولا : A.

1386 الذي : A.

1387 جا : ساقطة S.

1388 ܡܫܝܚܐ : K.

1389 ܡܫܝܚܐ : K.

1390 اتخلدنا : R.

1391 ܡܫܝܚܐ : K.

1392 جميعا : A.

1393 ثمة : S.

اوغريس[1396] في تاورية[1397] الذهب. واما التاورية[1398] الملايكيه على اسرارهم تقع نظرتها في انفسنا،[1399] تلك الاوله[1400] تحصل لكل الاخوة[1401] الفضلا المتقنين، واما هذه الثانيه انما تكون لاناس قديسين فقط.

(294) بثلثة[1402] معارف يقالوا من فوق الطهارة جميع حركات العقل محدوده بحركتهم الروحانيه، بالواحده يتدرب وبالاخره[1403] يكمل، وبالثالثه يتكلل، التنتين[1404] هم مجرا[1405] الطبيعى،[1406] والاخره[1407] فوق الطبع، الاوله تدعا[1408] معرفة الطبيعيه الثانية، والتي بعدها معرفة الطبيعية[1409] الاوله،[1410] والتي بها يتكلل هي معرفة الثالوث المسجود له، سر[1411] الروح، بتثبت[1412] وتحقيق.

(295) منتها[1413] التوبه هو مبدا الطهاره، وكمال الطهاره هو مبدا النقاوه، الطريق الى الطهاره هم[1414] عمل الفضيله، واما النقاوه تكون من فعل الاستعلانات.

(296) الطهاره هي التعري[1415] من الالام، والنقاوه هي التعري[1416] من الظنون واختلاف الضماير[1417] الى تحقيق معرفة الاسرار.

[1394] وتورية : K / وثاؤريا : S / وتاوريا : A.

[1395] الامور : ساقطة K.

[1396] مار اوجريس : R / ايوغريس : A.

[1397] تورية : K / ثاؤريا : S / تاورية : A.

[1398] التوريه : K / الثاؤريا : S / التاورية : A.

[1399] النفس : A.

[1400] هي : زائدة K.

[1401] الاوخوه : A.

[1402] بثلاثة : S, R / بثلاث : K.

[1403] وبالاخرى : K, S.

[1404] التنين (الاثنين) : S.

[1405] مجرى : K, S.

[1406] الطبيعه : R / الطبيعي : S.

[1407] والاخرى : K.

[1408] تدعى : K, S.

[1409] الطبيعة : A.

[1410] الاولى : S.

[1411] سرر : K.

[1412] يتثبت : S / بثبت : R / هو بثابت : K.

[1413] منتهى : R, S.

[1414] هي : A.

[1415] التعرا : R.

(297) جميع الذي بهن[1418] يتدرب العقل والى كمال حركاته يرتفع، ومتى يصادف استعلان حد كل الاسرار الذين بعد ما قد[1419] اتوا للتكوين، هكذا بلا تذكار يبتلعون عند الوسطاني،[1420] هذا الترتيب يضبط بلا حد، (A235v) التصرف الذي هو مزمع.

(298) الحسس[1421] الروحاني الذي[1422] لتاورية[1423] الاجسام والغير اجسام، هو طبيعي للعقل الناطق حسب قول الابا، واذا ما هدس في الثانيات[1424] بتكميل حركاته الطبيعيه يقوم، واذا ما كان بالاوله[1425] هو بالترتيب (R182v) الطبيعي الذي بعد التمام،[1426] لان الشي الذي ينعرف[1427] بوساطة الثانيين[1428] هو موهبه اعلا[1429] من الطبيعه يقال.

(299) العقل المتوحد يتولد من تفرد[1430] الجسم،[1431] وحسب اختلاط الجسد هكذا يختلط الضمير.

(300) كما انه ما ينغسل التوب من الوسخ الا ان انقصر وانمرس بالصابون،[1432] هكذا ايضا ما ينقا القلب من الالام ان لم ينسحق الجسد بالشقوات والتوحد.

(301) ثم[1433] عمل يدلك[1434] على سبل قاطعه ومن انواعه[1435] وزيه يعلمك التواضع ويوهلك لمعرفة ما، ويحببك فيها ويجعلك[1436] قريب، وثم[1437] اخر

1416 التعرا : R, K.

1417 الطماير : A.

1418 بهم : A, S.

1419 قد : ساقطة A.

1420 الوسطانيه : A.

1421 الحسس (الاحساس) : S.

1422 التي : K.

1423 لتاؤرية : S / للتاورية : K / لتااورية : A.

1424 التاوريات : R.

1425 بالاولى : S.

1426 التمام التمام : K.

1427 يتعرف : S.

1428 الاثنين : K.

1429 اعلى : K.

1430 بتفرد : A.

1431 الجسد : K.

1432 وبالصابون : K.

1433 ثمة : S.

يطوفك على جانب الطريق بنشاط، ويوضع قدامك سفر[1438] طويل واذ يكون المدخل قدامك يمنعك من ان تنظره[1439] ويجعل سيرك دورة كثيره، والاثنين يوصلون الى رب[1440] واحد من وجه العمل بهم، لان ليس كل احد[1441] ينظر الذي غير محدود، وهو قريب، فالذي يقرا يفهم معنا[1442] الفصل.

(302) طهارة الصلاه هي[1443] تسكيت[1444] مفاوضة الافكار الجسدانيه، وتحريك ما يخص النفس.

(303) هكذا ايضا نقاوه القلب هو حسن الضمير الذي بلا اجهاد،[1445] الذي قد اقتنا[1446] اختلاج دايم من غير الاراده[1447] على الخفيات، ويرسم في العقل نقص تذكارات امور الجسد.

(304) شي اخر هي معرفة الحروب، واخر هي[1448] معرفة التاديب (K214r) وسبل[1449] حركات معرفة الحروب مفتقره الى التجربه، (A236r) هذه التي كم من وقت ذو العقل والحكمه بتاديب رياضتهم يتحيروا فيها، واما السذج والاميين[1450] بالمعرفه يقتنوها من العمل.

(305) كما انه لا يستطاع ان[1451] تتعلم[1452] صناعة[1453] رمي النشاب في وسط الجموع والاسواق، بل في موضع قفر خالي، يصلح لسوق الخيل ورمي

[1434] يدل : A.

[1435] اعماله : A.

[1436] يجعلك : R.

[1437] وثمة : S.

[1438] سفرا طويلا : S / سفرا : R.

[1439] تنظر : K.

[1440] الرب : K.

[1441] احدا : A.

[1442] معنى : S.

[1443] هو : K.

[1444] تسكين : R.

[1445] اجتهاد : S.

[1446] اقتنى : S.

[1447] اراده : A.

[1448] هو : K.

[1449] وكل : K / وشكل : S / وسل : R.

[1450] والامين : S.

[1451] ان : ساقطة K.

[1452] يتعلم : K.

النشاب لكيلا[1454] يتعطلوا من الجري قبال الاماج الموضوع،[1455] هكذا ايضا ما[1456] يقدر انسان ان يتعلم صناعة القتال الروحاني، والجري الدايم قبال الاماج الالهي حسنا،[1457] وليعرف[1458] صنعة الافكار وحكمة النوتية الروحانيه، في هذا البحر المخوف، وليتحنك بحيل وصنايع كثيره، ان لم يثبت في السكون الدايم، والفرغة من[1459] كل شي ينضبط فيه،[1460] ويبطل به العقل ويتخلف عن الصلاه والتضرع الدايم،[1461] والذي ما يصنع هذا[1462] يسقط.

(306) اذا ما تحرك العقل في الامور من نعمة الله لاجل حلاوة تلك المعرفه يتخلف عن الهذيذ[1463] والتذكار[1464] وقتا[1465] كثير،[1466] وهو ساكت متعجب، وليس اعني عن ذلك[1467] الانقباض الكلي الذي بالتاورية[1468] الالهيه، تتغير[1469] حركات العقل للدهش[1470] ويبقا[1471] بلا حركه يوم ويومين، او اكثر او بشي من التاوريات[1472] الاخر ليس هو هذا التخلف الكلي بالفكر وخروج الطبع من المعرفه الى عدم المعرفه تلك التي اعلا (R183r) من كل معرفه، حسب قول الابا، بل انما هو سكر وحرارة قلب وسلامه وفرح، يكون دهش كلي بالصلاه وعدم حسس تام بهذه[1473] الامور الحاضره، ولا بشي من المعارف وحلاوة[1474]

[1453] صناعة : ساقطة K.

[1454] لكي لا : K.

[1455] الموضوعه : A.

[1456] لا : A.

[1457] حسن : K.

[1458] واليعرف : K.

[1459] في : A.

[1460] فيه : ساقطة K.

[1461] والفرغة...والتضرع الدايم : ساقطة S.

[1462] هذه : K.

[1463] الحديث : K.

[1464] التذكارات : A, S.

[1465] وقت : K.

[1466] كثيرا : S.

[1467] ذالك : R.

[1468] بالثاؤرية : S / بالتاورية : A.

[1469] يتغير : A.

[1470] الدهش : R.

[1471] ويبقى : S.

[1472] الثاؤريات : S / التاوريات : A.

[1473] بهاذه : K.

[1474] حلاوات : K.

الروح ما[1475] خلا من واحده فقط، واما نوع الدهش الاخر، ولو ان يحصل للانسان[1476] دهش ويذوق حنك عقله التنعم (A236v) الروحاني، ولكن ليس خاليا[1477] من معرفة الامور التي هاهنا، بل انما تنقبض[1478] الاحواس داخله ويصمتوا من الهذيذ العاده، ومحفوظ عنده معرفة شي من هاهنا، ويعرف ويسمع ويحس، ولكن هو منقبض من الطياشه ولا يميل الى هذيذ[1479] ما، بل يكون بلذة ذاك التميز الروحاني الذي[1480] وقع فيه، ويدهش ويقوم بالصمت او ينحني على الارض من اضطرار تلك الحلاوة التي لا ينطق بها، ولاجل ان الجسد[1481] ما يصبر على حمله[1482] لان احواسه تنقبض وتتخلف[1483] اعضاه من[1484] غير الاراده يقع على وجهه، وبضميره هو مرتفع عن[1485] هذه الارضيات، وكمثل[1486] انه في التدبير المزمع قد بلغت سفينته، وحسس ما متواريا[1487] بلا هذيذ بالاشيا، التي هاهنا يكون عنده، لانه ينجذب من لذة ذاك التميز[1488] الروحاني الحاصل،[1489] يعرفون الشي الذي اقول من قد قبلوا[1490] تجربة هولاء[1491] بانفسهم، ان هذا[1492] هو هكذا معناها، واما ان يكون بلا فكر ولا معرفه ولا حسس للطبع[1493] مدة ايام، كما كتب عن الابا، بالحسس بالله فقط يكون، واما بالباقيه ولو ان يكون العقل هادى عنده حس بالاشيا الحاضره،[1494]

1475 من : R.

1476 الانسان : K.

1477 خالي : K.

1478 تنقبط : A.

1479 هذيذا : A.

1480 قد : زائدة K.

1481 الجسم (الجسد) : S.

1482 تلك : زائدة S.

1483 ويتخلف : A.

1484 ومن : A.

1485 على : R.

1486 كمثل : A.

1487 متواري : K.

1488 التمييز : A.

1489 معه : زائدة S.

1490 قبلو : K.

1491 هولا : R / هولاي : K.

1492 هذه : K.

1493 الطبع : K, R.

1494 الظاهره الحاضره : A.

واما الذي بالله (K214v) اذا حدث العقل[1495] استعلان ليس يبقا[1496] فيه حسس.[1497]

(307) حسب[1498] ما تقل[1499] افكار العالم من الضمير، هكذا ينفتح قدامك باب الى الفرح بسيدنا، ولا يمكن ان يحس عقلك بهذا الفرح الا بعد انقباض دايم بالصلاه، كل الابا القديسين لنقص[1500] المجاهده مع الافكار التي هي القيامه من السقوط في الطياشه،[1501] وجعلوا[1502] سكنهم (A237r) في المواضع التي تسبب نقص[1503] الافكار، ولا كثرتهم، ولا[1504] قدروا بغرض الجهاد ان يجدوا الانقباض[1505] بالعقل[1506] في الصلاه بشجاعتهم، الا[1507] ان الافكار من قلتهم اهتدوا ووجدوا[1508] هناك فصحه،[1509] واعلم ان هذه لا تمكن مع دوام[1510] الملاقات[1511] بالبشر والبشريات، وان كنت[1512] تقول ان[1513] ليس لي[1514] مقدره على الحبس دايما الذي بلا انقطاع، ولا البعد[1515] الكلي من العالم بالسكن المفترد،[1516] فان كان يا اخي هذا حالك، لا تطلب الشي الذي ما يحظى[1517]

1495 حدث للعقل : S / حصل للعقل : A.

1496 يبقى : S.

1497 حسس (احساس) : S.

1498 وحسبما : K / وحسب : R.

1499 يقل : A.

1500 الناقص : K.

1501 والطياشة : S.

1502 وجعله : R / (قد) جعلوا : S.

1503 نقصة : K.

1504 وما : K.

1505 لانقباض : K.

1506 العقل : ساقطة S / العقل : K, R.

1507 الى : K.

1508 وجدوا : K.

1509 فسحه : R / فسحة : S.

1510 دوام : ساقطة K.

1511 الملاقاة : S.

1512 دوم : زائدة K.

1513 ان : ساقطة K.

1514 فيك : K.

1515 للبعد : K.

1516 المتفرد : S.

1517 يحظا : R / يحضا : A.

بوجوده[1518] الا المتصرفين بما يفوق العالم، الذي هو[1519] السكون من تواتر الافكار، وهو سبب الفرح الحاصل من الانقباض في الصلاه بفكر[1520] واحد (R183v) متشوق بالله، ومن هاهنا يوهل لنقاوة القلب، وبالدوام ينتقل من[1521] العالم خارج عن الاراده بقيام العقل دايما بالله، بحسب موضع[1522] تصرفك تنقص وتكثر الافكار،[1523] او لكثرة الجهاد يدنى الانسان.

(308) من[1524] بعد موضع السكن كم من وقت يحس المتوحد بحركه تفوق الجسد، ولو انه قليل الاعمال، وهذه لاجل كثر الميتوته من الناس، لانه بمقدار ما يبعد الانسان من سكن العالم ويتداخل في قفر البريه، هكذا يحس القلب بالبعد من الطبع، وحسب ذلك[1525] يقبل سكون[1526] من الافكار، وليس نتعب[1527] في الجهاد كثير معهم، لان نظر القفر بالطبع تميت[1528] الحركات العالميه وتجمعه من تواتر الافكار.

(309) كما انه لا يستطاع ان تصفا[1529] نظرة من هو[1530] قايم على جانب الدخان، الا ان (A237v) فر وبعد[1531] من هناك، هكذا لا يمكن ان يقتنا[1532] طهارة القلب وسكون من الافكار من دون الوحده المبتعده من دخان هذا العالم، الذي يبخر قدام الاحواس، ويعمي عيني النفس.

(310) لا ينبغي لاحد[1533] ان يخرف بمعرفة باطله ويقاومنا في هذه، انه اذا كنا قرب سكن[1534] الناس، افكار السكن[1535] تحدث لنا، واذا كنا في القفر افكار القفر

1518 بوجودها : K.
1519 هو : ساقطة R.
1520 بفكرا : A.
1521 عن : A.
1522 مواضع : K.
1523 والطهارة : K.
1524 ومن : A.
1525 ذالك : R.
1526 اسكون : R, S.
1527 يتعب : A.
1528 القلب من : زائدة K.
1529 تصفى : K, S.
1530 هو : ساقطة R.
1531 فروا وبعدوا : S.
1532 يقتني : K, S.
1533 لاحدا : A.
1534 سكان : K.

تحدث لنا، واذا خالطنا كثيرين افكار كثيرين يحدثوا[1536] لنا، واذا اتفردنا[1537] عن الكل ضمير[1538] متفرد نقتني، ايش هم افكار القفر، الا حركات تخرج من قلب مايت، لا يمكن اذا كنا موتا من[1539] العالم بحركاتنا، ان[1540] لا نتحرك بالله. من الضروره ان سكون حركات[1541] العالميه يعطي[1542] فسحة (K215r) وموضع الى التحرك بالله، وايضا من شقوات واتعاب الجسد نقتني ضمير[1543] متفرد.

(311) بمواضع القفر اضنك الجسد بالضوايق والاعمال، ليلا في الخلطة[1544] ولو ان يسقط الجسد ويتريض لاجل المفاوضه يميل الى الرخاوه والانحلال، ويمتلي الام واما في وحدة القفر تثبت[1545] طهارته فيه، وبهذا يمكنا ان نخيب من اعمالنا الاوله، ونتجرد منها، وبوساطة الاعمال ونقص الافكار الحادث[1546] من سكن القفر سريع[1547] ندخل[1548] بحرية[1549] النفس التي تفوق العالم، وفي كل[1550] وقت اشارات[1551] الاهيه[1552] بتجديد العقل في انفسنا[1553] ناخذ، ولموهبة[1554] الله بسهوله نقبل.

[1535] الناس : R.
[1536] يحدث : K.
[1537] تفردنا : K.
[1538] ضميرا : A.
[1539] عن : K.
[1540] ان : ساقطة K.
[1541] الحركات : A.
[1542] تعطي : A.
[1543] ضميرا : A.
[1544] بالخلطة : K.
[1545] يثبت : A.
[1546] الحادثه : A.
[1547] صريع : K.
[1548] تدخل : S.
[1549] الحرية : R / لحرية : K, S.
[1550] كل : ساقطة A.
[1551] اشاراة : K.
[1552] الهية : K, S.
[1553] نفوسنا : K.
[1554] لموهبة : R.

(312) ان كان[1555] تنظر يا اخي ان من[1556] اجل التعبد وشقا السكون والوحده...[1557]

[هذا ما وجدناه من اقوال وتعاليم الاب القديس مار اسحق يرحمنا الله ببركة صلواته المستجابة امين واطلب من القاري محبة في سيدنا يسوع المسيح الذي صلب لاجل خلاصنا يذكرني في عقيب صلواته والرب يعطيه الفهم والعمل بما في هذا الكتاب المرشد للسايل.

وقف موبد برسم راهبات دير مار سيسين اللبنانيات][1558]

...تصغر نفسك، بانها تحزن لاجل انها تنظر هذه الحياه قد (A238r) اضمحلت والجسد قد اتخلف وضنى، وتنظر فكرك قد ضعف وقزح[1559] لهذا الامر، اوضع قبال هذا[1560] فكرا[1561] عادل وضمير مخافة الله وعزي نفسك بهذا الشي الذي هو حق، ان اوفق حياة قصيره بالبر حسب ارادة الله، ولا عمرا[1562] طويل بما يغضبه (R184r) واذكر حياة القديسين القدما الذي ما حسبوا انفسهم بالقياس الى ارادة الله، وبمثل هذه الحياه صبروا جميع ايام حياتهم،[1563] ان كان[1564] في المسكونه او في القفر، الى حيث انتقالهم وتركهم هذا جسد الاتضاع، وبعد جهد[1565] كثير قدروا ان يكملوا طريق مخافة الله بسبب عطلة الجسد، وفي وقت انتقالهم من هذا العالم فرحوا جدا عظيم، لاجل انهم استطاعوا بضوايق قليله حاضره اتخلصوا من الشرور التي تحارب لكي تفسد النفس، ووجدوا في وقت انقالهم[1566] في اهلية الله وما يخصه.

(313) الطهاره هي بلد هدو[1567] الطبع الذي قد[1568] غلق[1569] بوجهه[1570] باب الالام، الذي اذا فتح الانسان هذا الباب ما امكنه ان يدخل الى بلد الطبع الهادي،

1555 انكان : K.

1556 من : ساقطة R.

1557 نهاية K.

1558 خاتمة K.

1559 قد ضعف (فزع) : S.

1560 هذه : R, S.

1561 فكر : R, S.

1562 عمر : R, S.

1563 ايامهم : R, S.

1564 كانوا : R.

1565 جهدا : A.

1566 انتقالهم : R, S.

1567 هدوء : S / هدوا : R.

لانه اذا اوهل للدخول[1571] حسب ضنى[1572] يقبل حسس[1573] تجديده، بوساطة الاشاير النقيه المتحركه في عقله.

(314) مع تخلف[1574] الانسان من ترتيب مصاف الجهاد، بدخوله الى الطقس[1575] الذي بعده باتساع خصب العقل يبدى، الذي هو طقس[1576] تدبير الانسان الجواني، اذا انقبض الانسان بمعونة الله من الهم الذي من[1577] خارج، ومن الهذيذ بكثيرين ويصير انسان واحد، من هاهنا يبدى ان ينظر (A238v) في ذاته امورا[1578] جديده واشاير وعلايم محسوس ومخفي، ومن هاهنا يوهل لذاك التجديد[1579] الذي في قيامة الكل ويذوقه[1580] بالغمز، بان دفعات كثيره وفي وسط اوقات النهار يحس في نفسه ان قد انقبض العقل الى ذاته من غير ان يعتني به، بصمت لا يفسر،[1581] فالذي يقرا ليفهم وهذا يحدث في الخدمه وقت في القراه، وايضا الذين قد اهلوا للذكاوه[1582] مفروزه[1583] هي حركه احلامهم في النوم، من الذين هم متالمين بالعقل ان كانوا الان يجاهدوا بالقتال، مقابل هولاء.[1584]

(315) ان كنت تريد العزا الحقيقي بالصلاه اهتم بتقويم نيتك، وان تطلب تقويم النيه اهتم بالصلاه، لان الاهتمام باحدتهن[1585] يصنع طهاره في رفيقتها، تقويم النيه يصنع نقاوة الصلاه، ونقاوة الصلاه يمنح دالة النيه، لان الطهاره ما تنحفظ مع الاشتباك والخلطه ولا الذكر يثبت مع الاهتمام بالافعال والخلطه

1568 قد : ساقطة A.

1569 اغلق : S.

1570 بوجه : S.

1571 الدخول : R.

1572 ظني : S.

1573 حسن : S.

1574 اتخلف : R.

1575 الطكس : R.

1576 طكس : R.

1577 هو : A.

1578 امور : R.

1579 التجديد : ساقطة S.

1580 بالفم : زائدة S.

1581 يتفسر : R, S.

1582 الذكاوه : R.

1583 مفرزوه : A.

1584 هولا : R.

1585 باحدتهنا : S / باحدتهم : R.

بامورا[1586] كثيره، الذين بشهوة البر البراني يلقوا نفوسهم[1587] الى[1588] الاضطرابات[1589] والسجس يخيبوا من جزو[1590] البر الاعظم ويتعطلوا.

(316) اول بدو[1591] تدبير الوحده هو التجرد والسكون، وعدم الارتباط بانسان، او بامر او بفعل ما، والعمل في السكون هو الصبر على ما يعرض والتواضع والصلاه، والاثمار المتولده من هولاء،[1592] هو الدخول الى[1593] الرجا[1594] والتنعم بالفرح بالله، والمخرج الصالح الذي من هولاء،[1595] هو (R184v) تناول مفاتيح اسرار الروح الممجده، وحد الطريق هو مذاقة الحب والداله من هاهنا مع ذلك[1596] الذي قد انحب، والذي ما اقتنا[1597] مبادى الطريق، الذين هم التجرد والسكون، (A239r) ظاهر انه ليس له لا[1598] صلاه ولا تواضع، والذي هو بطال من هذين من الضروره انه مشتبك بالخطايا، والذي هو خاطى ليس فقط ماله موضع في الملكوت بل وفي الجحيم قد اقتنا[1599] مكان معروف.

(317) اذا اردت ان تعرف رجل الله تعرفه من دوام صمته، ومن بكاه ومن انقباضه مع نفسه، وهكذا ايضا الجاهل وعادم العقل، تعرفه من كثرة الكلام ومن تخبيط الاحواس وقيام الهوا.[1600]

(318) لا تحسب انه بطاله الثبات الكثير في الصلاه قدام الله، لان ليس مزمور اعظم منها، ولا في الاعمال شي افضل منها،[1601] ولا شي من الفضايل التي يفعلها الانسان تساويها،[1602] ومذا اقول الفضايل، حتى ومن عمل الفضايل هو

1586 بامور : S.

1587 انفسهم : R, S.

1588 في : R, S.

1589 اضطرابات : R.

1590 حزوا : R, S.

1591 بدو (بدء) : S / بدوا : R.

1592 هولا : R.

1593 الى : ساقطة R, S.

1594 للرجاء : S.

1595 هولا : R.

1596 ذالك : R.

1597 اقتنى : S.

1598 لا : ساقطة A.

1599 اقتنى : S.

1600 الهوى : S.

1601 ولا في الاعمال شي افضل منها : ساقطة A.

1602 تفعلها الناس يساويها : R, S.

مايت لاجل دوامه مع الله، هي دلايل الميتوته من العالم، وجميع الخيرات الحاضره والمزمعه[1603] بها توجد، لا يكون في عينك[1604] قليل هذا ان كنت تستطيع ان تصنعه بلا فتور، اذ تجحد كل شي حتى بنفسك، وله فقط تداوم ما ينعت طوباك بلسان ارضي، ان ابذلت[1605] ذاتك لهذا، لان الشي الذي[1606] تحظا[1607] به وتلاقيه هو امر[1608] عجيب، لان من هاهنا تقتني الخروج الكامل من العالم بالحق ومن كل التدابير الفاسده، وهو حد كل الاعمال وحابس جميع الوصايا، وكمال ساير الفضايل.

(319) اذا ما نظر العدو[1609] المتوحد قد اعطا نفسه واستعد للجهاد[1610] قباله وجسر عليه، في كل امر[1611] يتحيل بكثرة[1612] دهاه لكي بجميع الاسباب يربط عقله بالعلمانيين، ومن هاهنا بغير تعويق كل وقت يريد بسهوله يخدعه ويرميه في ثلثة[1613] الام كبار، في الم الزنا، والحسد، والغضب، لان اذا سبق المتوحد انفا، واتقيدت (A239v) يديه ورجليه باشباكه، معهم على الدوام يسقطه ويصعب عليه ويثقل[1614] جدا الاهتمام بالصلاه والتدبير بالسيره والطهاره.

(320) محب الاعمال ليس هو الذي ما يحب نياحات الجسد، بل الذي ما يحب المفاوضات الجسدانيه.

(321) حسس النعمه المعقول في عمل التوبه المعقول يوجد.

(322) تاه عن كثيرين هذا[1615] وما يعرفوا وما[1616] يفهموا، ان نحن المتوحدين ليس من اجل ان نعمل الفضايل نحبس انفسنا[1617] داخل الباب، بل وان نكون

1603 والمعرفه : R.

1604 عينيك : S.

1605 بذلت : R.

1606 الى : R.

1607 تحظى : S.

1608 امرا : A.

1609 العدوا : R.

1610 الجهاد : R.

1611 امرا : A.

1612 كثرة : S.

1613 ثلاثة : R, S.

1614 ويتقل : S / وينتقل : R.

1615 هذه : R, S.

1616 ولا : R, S.

1617 انفسنا : ساقطة R.

ايضا موتا[1618] من الفضايل، لان الفضيله المنعمله بالسكن مع كثيرين، الاحيا يعملوها، فان كنا نحن نطلب من السكون عمل الفضايل، التي تفعلها اخوتنا المتقنين[1619] في المجمع، ما لنا بالهرب والحبس في قبر القلايه، بل انما نحن ننتظر ان نقتني (R185r) من عمل السكون الشي الذي اذا تعلقنا بجفون اعيننا[1620] ما نقدر نجده بالسكن مع كثيرين.

(323) لو كان قصدنا عمل الفضيله ايش المانع من عملها مع السكن مع كثيرين، واعني بهذا عن الصوم وخدمة الاوقات والصدقه، وما تبقا[1621] مما يشبه هولاء،[1622] بل وبالاكثر[1623] ينشط سكن المجمع على عمل هولاء،[1624] وما نعرف فضيله خارج عن هولاء،[1625] واما التنعم الروحاني الذي بالعمل الخفي المكتوم يوجد ليس ينعد مع الفضيله لانه سيد الفضايل، اما الفضيله هي كل عمل طاهر بالاحواس الجسديه[1626] يكمل من اجل الله، ولكن نعمل هذه الفضايل اولا[1627] في المجمع، وبعد ان نتخرج ونتدرب ندخل للسكون،[1628] ونتامل ان نقتني فيه شي هو معروف ان صوت الطير يكدره. اترك خروج ودخول كثيرين، ومناظرا[1629] دايمه، (A240r) وهوذا ننظر كثيرين، من الابا الروحانيين، ما كان لهم قوه في جسدهم التي بها تنعمل الفضايل، وما راوا[1630] ان يتركوا السكون، بل كانوا مرميين داخل والباب مسدود في وجوههم، وكانوا هاديين فقط، لعل[1631] كان ينبغي لهم ان يتركوا[1632] السكون لاجل ان[1633] ليس لهم اعمال،[1634] لكن ما كانت تتركهم حلاوة الوحده ان يعطوا انفسهم لنظر

1618 موتى : S.
1619 المتقننين : S.
1620 اعينا :R.
1621 تبقى : S.
1622 هولا : R.
1623 بالاكثر : A.
1624 هولا : R.
1625 هولا : R.
1626 باحواس الجسد : R, S.
1627 اولى (اوله) : S / اوله : R.
1628 السكون : R.
1629 ومناظر : S.
1630 راو : R.
1631 العل : S.
1632 يتركون : R.
1633 ان : ساقطة R.
1634 عمل : A.

المجامع على الدوام، كان حلو[1635] عندهم صلاة واحده بالسكون في قلبهم، وهم ملقيين بحزن حلوا واتضاع يقدموها لله، اخير من ربوات[1636] صلوات واعمال يقدموها لله خارج عن قلاليهم، وافضل من نظر ومفاوضة فضلا العالم، وحضور الاعياد.

(324) حد الفضيله هو المفاوضه الوحديه والهذيذ الهادي العقلي بالله، لان المتوحد ليس له عيد على[1637] الارض، عيد المتوحد هو حزن نوحه وعوض الاعمال التي يفتخروا بها اخرين بالنزهه[1638] مع بعضهم، هذا شقاه في السكون هو عزاه، لعلك يا اخي عدم الانس والمفاوضه والنوح وحزن القلب[1639] والتمرغ قدام الله كل وقت، ما تعده عمل، بل الصوم فقط، وكثرة التلاوه تحسبها عمل، اعلم ان عمل القلب والتجلد في الوحده[1640] هو العمل الفاضل. صدق انه سعيد وموهل لله الذي ياكل كل يوم وينام[1641] وهو مداوم السكون، وصعوبة الوحده جميع ايامه، ولو انه دفعة واحده في النهار يتنهد على نفسه، وهو محزون ملقي قدام الله، اتميز ان كثيرين او لعلهم جميع النصارى[1642] يحملون اعمال الجسد بحلاوه، وشجاعه، وكل الفضايل المذكوره بفرح (A240v) يعملون وعلى السكون ما يجسرون. ولا[1643] تحزن ايها الاخ الضعيف الجسد الساكن[1644] في الهدو،[1645] لاجل ان ليس لك اعمال جسدانيه لان نصيبك اعظم من اوليك،[1646] الذين يعملون كل الفضايل الكبار وهم خارج عن السكون، عظيمه هي الموهبه التي حظيت بها التي هي التجلد ومحبة السكون، افضل من كل اعمال (R185v) الجسد، وسبب اني طولت هذا الفصل اكثر من البقيه، لانه[1647] انظر ليس خسارة قليل حصل لكثيرين من هذا الامر، اذ يصلحون لتدبير السكون لاجل استضاهم وتواضعهم وحرارتهم

[1635] حلوا : R, S.

[1636] ربوات (ربوة) : S / ربوة : R.

[1637] في : R, S.

[1638] بالنزها : R.

[1639] العقل : R, S.

[1640] الوحد : R.

[1641] ينام : R.

[1642] النصارا : R.

[1643] لا : R, S.

[1644] السكن : R.

[1645] الهدوء : S / الهدوا : R.

[1646] هولايك : R.

[1647] لاني : S.

الكثيره، وازدراهم بالعالم، وبسبب ان ليس لهم قوة جسد في الاعمال اعني ما يقدروا[1648] يصومون ويسهرون، ويعملون بالجسم مثل كثيرين يقطعون رجاهم من السكون، وكثير من الحكما المفتخرين بالجسد يعطلوهم بكلامهم الخرف[1649] من هذا العمل بالحبس والانقباض مع انفسهم، الذي هو عظيم عجيب جدا الذي ما حظي به الا افراد[1650] قليل، فقط بنوع الموهبة والانعام من الله، لكي بضعف اعضاهم يصبرون[1651] على صعوبة الوحده والعمل وحزن القلب، الذي الشجعان والجبابره تنفر وترعب منه، بالحقيقه عمل ماية[1652] راهب بالعشره والسجس، يصومون ويخدمون[1653] ما يوازن عمل راهب واحد بالسكون، ولو انه ضعيف عاجز ما خلا فقط انه عادم من العشره ومفاوضة الناس، ومحبوس داخل الباب بلا انقطاع، وليس احد يدخل اليه ويخرج وليس اعني بقولي هذا عن الذين يمسكون (A241r) السكون بالجسد ولهم من يدخل اليهم ويخرج بسهوله، بل اعنيت بالذين من يوم الاحد الى يوم الاحد يسدون ابوابهم، وليس لهم عشره ومفاوضه مع احدا،[1654] ويحبسون سوابيع محدوده بالكمال، او جميع السنه ما خلا من تناول الاسرار الالهيه، ولا يلاقون احد[1655] ولا يحضرون الاعياد والكنايس، حيث[1656] الجماعات. ان[1657] ثم[1658] متوحد فيه كفو[1659] لهذه نعمة السكون،[1660] وحظي بهذه الموهبه من الله، وواحد[1661] من[1662] الاساقفه او رووسا[1663] اديرة الاخوه، اما من اجل غيره وحسد او عمل جسداني، او نياح، يمنعه من هذه الموهبه عليه دينونه قدام الله، ومزمع ان يعطي جواب قدام منبر المسيح.

1648 يقدرون : R, S.

1649 الخرق : R.

1650 الافراد : R.

1651 يصبروا : R, S.

1652 مائة : S / مايت : R.

1653 يصوموا ويخدموا : R, S.

1654 احد : R, S.

1655 احدا : R, S.

1656 وحيث : S.

1657 ان (كان) : S.

1658 ثمة : S.

1659 كفؤا : S.

1660 ولا يحضرون...نعمة السكون : ساقطة R.

1661 واحد : R, S.

1662 من : ساقطة S.

1663 رؤساء : S.

(325) وان كان يا اخوه[1664] جيلنا هذا الردي ما يساعد على موضع موافق انفسنا[1665] للسكون الحقيقي، كمثل الاجيال المتقدمه، كل موضع نحصل فيه ننقبض مع انفسنا ولو انه يوم واحد، اما في دير واما في طريق او تحت صخره، ولا ننتظر الترتيب والاستعداد، كل وقت يقع بيدينا السكون نضبطه حسنا يوم او يومين، لان الحكما هكذا يقتنوا[1666] انفسهم في هذه مدة حياتهم القصيره، ليلا يدركنا الموت بغته وما نبلغ مقصودنا، ولا ندرك املنا.

(326) ولربنا المجد دايما وعلينا رحمته الى الابد امين.[1667]

(I) (A241v) **الميمر الاول من رووس المعرفه للقديس مار اسحق يفيد[1668] العقل الذي قد بلغ لمينا[1669] السلامه وعلى الدوام يهدس باسرار العالم الجديد ويتفاوض خفيا بالالهيات وبمصعد القلب يرسم التصور في الاسرار التي تحدث على المتوحدين المحقين في زمان الجهاد ويرشد القارى من تصور الى تصور ويوصل الى اسرار (R186r) المعرفة المقدسه.**

(I .1) **الميمر الاول قال** امانة المسيح هي نور معقول، وحياة تعليم يسوع هي معرفة الحق، التي بوساطة كلمة النور يطفح[1670] على المومنين، ويعطيهم نور وحياة حقيقيه، نفخه[1671] في وجوه[1672] تلاميذه وقال اقبلوا روح القدس، هي مواهب وداله منحها لهم.

(I .2) قيامة يسوع هي تمثال قيامة العامه، بارقليط روح العزا الذي قبلوه الرسل في العليه واقتناهم[1673] تجديد، هو سر التجديد المعقول الذي تقبله القديسين هاهنا، والعزا في[1674] انسانهم الجواني.

1664 اخوتي : R, S.

1665 انفسنا : ساقطة R, S.

1666 يقتنون : R, S.

1667 ولربنا المجد دايم امين امين امين : R / بركة الثالوث المقدس الاب والابن والروح القدس الاله الواحد تشملنا ولالهنا المجد دائما ابديا امين : S.

1668 تفيد : R, S.

1669 لبلد : R, S.

1670 يطمح :R.

1671 نفخ : S.

1672 وجه : R, S.

1673 واقناهم : R, S.

1674 في : ساقطة R.

(I .3) الايمان الحقاني هو راس النفس، وراس الحق هو راس التدابير المتقنه، هذا الذي لحرية الارادة يجذب ويخدع.

(I .4) نور المعقول وحياة الناطقين هو معرفة الحق، والذي[1675] بالايمان والرجا يخرج في طلبه بالصلاه يجد داخل منه كنز[1676] الحياه، والذي يبعد عنه في الظلام يسير.

(I .5) الذي له العزا الجواني يطرد منه المفاوضة البرانيه، ليلا يضيع العزا الداخل، لان الذي وجد الحق داخل منه، ليس يعمل بالحيل.

(I .6) الذي له نور معقول (A242r) ليس هو محتاج الى[1677] النور[1678] المحسوس، لان نور العقل هو معرفة الحق، الذي به تفرز النفس الحق من التشبه، والذي وجد هذا قد اقتنى[1679] ذخيرة الحياه.

(I .7) الذي له غنا[1680] هو ناقص عن[1681] غنا[1682] المملكه، لان هو مع غناه يخاف[1683] الملك، وهو تحت الخوف من الجوانيين والبرانيين، واما الذي قد ابهج[1684] له الملك وسكب عليه موهبه،[1685] وجعله ابن سره ومداخل في المملكه، ولو انه حقير ومسكين، هو متفاضل على جميع ارفاقه، لان ذخيرة المملكه ليس تقع تحت خوف السالبين،[1686] ما دام ليس يصير سبب الخطا بارادته.

(I .8) الذي قد وجد الكنز داخل منه ليس يطلب صدقه من البرانيين، ولا يسفسر مع[1687] انسان، بل يحترس بماله وهو مسالم مع كل احدا،[1688] ليلا يضيع وديعة الحب ويتسجس.

1675 والذين : R.

1676 كثر : R.

1677 الى : ساقطة R.

1678 محتاج للنور : S.

1679 اقتنا : R.

1680 غنى : S.

1681 من : S.

1682 غنى : S.

1683 يخاف : ساقطة R, S.

1684 اربح : S.

1685 مواهبه : R, S.

1686 السالكين : R.

1687 ولا يخدم عند : S.

1688 احد : R, S.

(I .9) ان كان معرفة الخير والشر داخل القلب تتولد كما قال السيد، ما دام قلبنا مضبوط من[1689] شيطان الغضب والحسد او محبة المجد الباطل، ويهدس مع الناس، اضروره[1690] فالاولاد[1691] المتولدين منه لابايهم[1692] يشبهون في معرفة الغضب، وما تبقا،[1693] وهكذا ايضا افعالهن، وعلى هذا[1694] المعنا[1695] ايضا افهم في سلامة القلب الذين هم ضد هولاء.[1696]

(I .10) الملايكه بالنار والهوى، والشياطين بالظلمه واللجج،[1697] والناس بالهوى والماء بحريه ارادتهم.

(I .11) ان كان المعرفه التي على اسرار الثالوث المقدس هي اقدم من كل المعارف، وتحوي كل المعارف، وفي الكل تفعل، فهي افضل من الكل، فمعلوم ان الذي هو عادم من هذه هو بعيد من الحق.

(I .12) (A242v) معرفه الانواع والحيل، هي معرفة الصبيان،[1698] التي بتاديب الغضب (R186v) والقصر توصلنا الى معرفة الحق.

(I .13) معرفة الحق هي نور حرية الاثنين التي بوساطة تدابير الحريه، الاختياريه تكلل العمالين بها.

(I .14) وان كان المعرفه هي سابقة التدابير، ولكن بكور التدابير تتفلح، لحسنه هي المعرفه وتشرق وتجلب الاثمار الصالحه.

(I .15) ان كان السكون يولد السكون، والمعرفه للمعرفه، والتدبير للتدبير، كقول الابا، معروف ايضا ان الصبر الارادي، من الصبر على الاعمال الغضبيه الاقتصاريه يتولد.

[1689] مع : A.
[1690] لضرورة : S.
[1691] بالاولاد : A.
[1692] لابيهم : R.
[1693] تبقى : S.
[1694] هذه : A.
[1695] المعنى : S.
[1696] هولا : R.
[1697] وللجج : R.
[1698] الصبا : S / الصبان : R.

(I .16) الصبر اذا ما كمل وهدى بوساطة التدابير التعبه التي للحق، يولد اتساع النفس، والاتضاع، والهدو،[1699] والجود، والمسالمه، والحب، مع بقية الاثمار الروحانيه التي كتبها بولس.

(I .17) حسن الفضايل ليس من فرز اسمايهم[1700] يمتدح، بل من افراز غرض وقصد فاعليهم.

(I .18) الفضايل ليس باقنومهم فيهم صلاح وشرور، بل بالقوه والفعل بارادة[1701] نوع غرض فاعلهم يختبرون.

(I .19) ان كان قوة الفضايل نقتنيها باقنومنا،[1702] ولكن تكميل افعالهن وافراز الخير والشر[1703] بميالة حرية الاراده تاتي[1704] للظهور.

(I .20) والفضايل التي تنعمل بالجسد ظاهره،[1705] يدهشون من ينظرهم ويقدمون للتوبه، كمثل المنظور الى الاعين البرانيه ينير وبنوره يخلصون كثيرين من الظلمه.

(I .21) والفضايل التي تنعمل خفي[1706] داخل النفس معقول بهذيذ العقل، ينيرون عيني النفس ويمنحوهم نظر وحسن الاهي، فوق الطبع بلذة ليس لها تفسير.

(I .22) تنعم الملكوت وعذاب (A243r) الجحيم ليس اقنوم الفضايل يقني للناطقين، بل فرز غرض ونوع ارادت[1707] فاعلهن.[1708]

(I .23) مراحم عناية الله بنا بمجاذبات تنعم الملكوت، وخوف عذاب الجحيم، يصطادنا[1709] للحياة الجديده بالله.

1699 والهدوء : S / والهدوا : R.

1700 اساميهم : R, S.

1701 وبإرادة : S / وباراده : R.

1702 باقنومها : R.

1703 والشرور : R, S.

1704 ياتي : S.

1705 ظاهر : R, S.

1706 خفيا : S.

1707 ارادة : R, S.

1708 فاعلهم : R.

1709 تصطادنا : R, S.

(I .24) الشهوه اذا ما تسلطت[1710] بالنفس، واستعبدتها ان كان اليمين او الشمال، تخرجها من حرية نطقيتها، وتنجذب غصب لتكمل الشي التي[1711] تامرها الشهوه، ولم تنقلع من النفس.

(I .25) الا بمحبة شهوة اخرى،[1712] تضاددها،[1713] لان الشهوه بشهوه ايضا تبطل، ومحبه بمحبه، وعاده بعاده، ومفاوضه بمفاوضه، يتغيرون[1714] هولاء[1715] وينقلعون بذكر الله والصلاه والدموع.

(I .26) الغضبيه ليس لها ان تقاتل لاجل ذاتها، بل كمثل الكلب ينبح[1716] لاجل صاحبه، لان هكذا والغضبيه تنبح باخرين لاجل الشهوه، او لاجل اي الم كان، واوله تسجس وتكدر لبيت[1717] صاحبها، وبعد ذلك[1718] توذي[1719] اخرين.

(I .27) ما دام الاتضاع في النفس هي هاديه مسالمه وموجود فيها ذكر حب المسيح، وكم احتمل لاجل الخطاه والمنافقين والضعفا، ليس موضع للسجس[1720] ان يدخل على (R187r) النفس الشقيه، لكي يفتح باب للالام ليدخلوا[1721] يتسلطوا عليها، ويكدروها وينجسوها بالامور السمجه الغير واجبه.

(I .28) افراز التدابير الكثيره المختلفه من افرازات الاغراض تتولد، وافرازات الاغراض من ميالة حرية الاراده.

(I .29) كما ان جميع فضايل سيرة التوبه والنسك، الذي اقتنينا بتعب اعمال متواتره، ان كنا نتهاون بعملهن يضيعون قليل بقليل،[1722] واما الفضايل المخصوصه بالسكون، (A243v) ليس اقنوم الفضايل فقط تهلك،[1723] بل

1710 اتسلطت : S / اتسلطة : R.

1711 الذي : R, S.

1712 اخره : R.

1713 تضادها : S.

1714 يتغيروا : R, S.

1715 هولا : R.

1716 تنجح : S / تنبح : R.

1717 البيت : R.

1718 ذالك : R.

1719 تؤذي : S.

1720 السجس : R.

1721 يدخلوا : R.

1722 قليل قليل : R.

1723 يهلك : R.

وتذكار اقتناهم يضيع وينتسى[1724] كما كتب الاب مرقس، الاشيا التي اتهاونا بالكمال من عمل تدبيرهم، وايضا ذكر عملهن قليل بقليل[1725] ينتسى.

(I .30) واذا[1726] ما طهر العقل وقام بنور طبيعته، ليس بتنقله من موضع الى موضع يقبل الاتحاد بالمسيح، بل به وفيه بافراز الانفعال يرتفع من تصور، الى تصور ومن معرفه، الى معرفه حتى يتوج بنور طبيعة خلقته.

(I .31) اذا ما اتهاون العقل عن العمل الخفي، وباراده[1727] يطيش في طلب اباطيل هذا العالم، وينسبي بالضلاله ويظلم من الحق، ليس انتقال تنتقل منه ذخيرة الحياه، بل يخيب هو منها وتبطل عنه باهمال الالام.

(I .32) اذا[1728] كمل الانسان بتربية معرفة الحق، يتغير ويتجدد بالروح ويتعرا الالام العتيقه، وينهض الانسان الجديد الروحاني، ويشرق فيه نور العالم الجديد.

(I .33) بتربية معرفة الحق تبطل معرفة الطغيان، وبالهذيذ الدايم في الخيرات العتيده يضمحل ويذوب[1729] هذيذ هذا العالم، ومفاوضته الباطله، ويبقا[1730] الانسان متوج بطبيعة خلقته.

(I .34) مذبح قدس الاقداس القلبي، اذا ما اتقدس بترفرف الروح عند ذلك[1731] ترتفع عليه ذبيحة روحانيه، الافكار البكوريه،[1732] التي تنذبح من العقل مقربها بالصلاة الطاهره، التي ليس توجد في[1733] حيوان الشرور، ولا توجد وتنقسم[1734] من تثنية[1735] القلب.

1724 تضيع وتنسى : S / تضيع وتنتسى : R.

1725 قليل قليل : R.

1726 اذا : R, S.

1727 وبارادته : R, S.

1728 ما : زائدة R, S

1729 ويزول ويذوب : S / ويدوم : R.

1730 ويبقى : S.

1731 ذالك : R.

1732 البتولية : S.

1733 توخذ من : R, S.

1734 وتتقسم : R, S.

1735 ثنية : A.

(I .35) مذبح القلب الجواني الذي ما طهر وما[1736] كمل، بنور عدم الالام، ولا افرز واتقدس بحلول الروح، ولو ان يقدس عليه رييس الكهنه بالصلوات، (A244r) المتواتره هو قربان ساذج، وليس ذبيحة مقبوله، كما ان[1737] المذبح[1738] البراني الذي[1739] للاسرار ان لم يفرز ويتقدس بالتكريز،[1740] ان[1741] تصعد عليه القرابين، ليس يدعا[1742] قربان ذبيحة محييه[1743] جسد ربنا ودمه.

(I .36) ذبيحة الصلاه الروحانيه، اذا ما اتقدمت على المذبح الجواني المفروز المقدس بالروح، العقل المكهن يقبل الحسس ان قبلت ذبايحه الكامله ام لا، كمثلما يحس الرامي بالقوس (R187v) النشابة الصايبه ام لا.[1744]

(I .37) اذا ما اشرق في وقت القربان نور النعمه على نور عدم الالام، عند ذلك[1745] النفس تنظر هي ذاتها بشبه[1746] لون صافيلا،[1747] او لون السماء، الذي نظروا بني اسراييل تحت ارجل الله، الذي يسموه الابا موضع الله الداخل منا، وحسن اقنومنا[1748] وتقانة الذهن وميراث القديسين، بنور النور.

(I .38) هذه هي العلامة انه قد افرز واتقدس المذبح الجواني، قدس الاقداس الذبيحة الروحانيه، بالكمال انجاس الشرور لم تصعد عليه، مثل مذبح البراني المسكوب على ارض القلب البخور المختار، الذي هو الحب، والسلامه، الصلاح، الورد، المسك، مع رايحة واحده طيبه لذيذه، الذي هو الفرح الروحاني، الذي ليس له سبب اوحد.

(I .39) اذا ما استحق الذهن قليل او كثير بتقانته[1749] الاوله، تبطل عند ذلك[1750] التخيلات[1751] وتتخلف الافكار مع اختلاج حركات الداخله، وفي وقت الصلاه

1736 ولا : R, S.

1737 ان : ساقطة R.

1738 مذبح : R, S.

1739 التي : R.

1740 بالتكرير : R.

1741 لم : زائدة R.

1742 يدعى : S.

1743 المحييه : R, S.

1744 ام لا : ساقطة S.

1745 ذالك : R.

1746 تشبه : R, S.

1747 لون صافيا :S / لون المها الغير صافيلا : A.

1748 اقنوما : S.

1749 بتقانة : R, S.

يتكلل العقل باكليل متضاعف النور والمجد، كمقدار[1752] هدو[1753] تقانته، في ذلك[1754] بلد السلامه، ويرجع الى موضعه.

(I .40) تقانة (A244v) العقل تنقام من الطهاره والنقاوه وعفة النفس الهاديه، ومن تواضع القلب، والحب الغزير، ومن النعمه التي تقدس وتهدي طاهري القلب.

(I .41) العقل الذي تاسس فيه الحب الالهي واستحق بالنعمه لمعرفة الحق، ليس يهدا من الهذيذ الروحاني بالاسرار بالله، وفي وقت يهدس بعناية الله اللازقه لموجودات الكل، وفي وقت يتفرس بسياسة[1755] مراحمه التي في كل الاجيال، وفي وقت ينظر في حكمة خلقته المملوه افرازات، ويرجع ايضا الى تضاعف تقانة نفسه، ويعتجب باتحاد النفس بالجسد والاسرار المخفيه فيه وعلى التاوريات[1756] والافهام التي تظهر فيه، فوق الطبع، وكيف هو هكذا شريف ممجود،[1757] مهان مرذول، متعالي عن الفساد، نجس مسجون بالفساد[1758] للمياله.[1759]

(I .42) النفس التي باجنحة الفضايل ترتقي الى ارتفاع تدبير العقل، لتعبر الى بلد السلامه والهدو[1760] تجوز في بلادا[1761] صعبه، وتجارب عسره مختلفه، وضوايق مره شديده، وتكون قد عدت[1762] ذاتها لمقاسات هولاء،[1763] لان لا بد منهم لاجل حسد الشياطين، وتجارب الجسد.

1750 ذالك : R.

1751 التحيلات : R.

1752 بمقدار : R.

1753 هدوء : S / هدوا : R.

1754 ذالك : R.

1755 بسياتة : A.

1756 التاؤريات : S / التاوريات : A.

1757 محمود : S.

1758 بالافساد : R, S.

1759 المياله : R.

1760 والهدوء : S / والهدوا : R.

1761 بلاد : R, S.

1762 اعدت : S.

1763 هولا : R.

(I .43) والحركات الصعبه التي من الطبع، والقريب، وهي مفتقره الى النعمه، والى صيانة التحفظ، والى افرازات[1764] المعرفه، والى الصبر كمثل الادامس، ليلا تنسحب من وثبات[1765] المحيره والالام المضطربه، وحيل الشياطين الدغله والتجارب الصعبه الحادثه من الجسد والقريب.

(I .44) اذا رتب العقل الاحواس ويخرج[1766] (R188r) في طلب الافكار والكلام والافعال، ووفق انقسامهم واصطلح، (A245r) الثالوث الذي فينا واهتدت الحركات الجوانيه، عن طلب وهذيذ وتصور تاورية[1767] الاجسام والغير اجسام، وقام فيما يخصه، عند ذلك[1768] يلبس الكاهن الجواني حلة الكهنوت ويوضع في راسه اكليل القدس المشرق بالمجد والنور، الذي لا شبيه له ويقرب ذبايح[1769] بخور ذكي.[1770]

(I .45) الصلاه الطاهره وانقباض الضمير الصغير والنور الذي من افهام الكتب، وعزا النفس التي من القرااه والصلوات، وما تبقا من تدريب النفس واستضا العقل، وحدة الحركات، يستطيعوا يدركوا بمعونه الله الذين يغلوا[1771] بالتدابير، ويتفاوضوا بهذيذ الكتب، ويحرسوا باعمال التوبه بنشاط.

(I .46) واما مفاوضة الصلاه الروحانيه، الذهنيه، ونظرة الضمير، وعقل مشترك مع الله باستعلان اسراره، وحسس بالحياة الجديده والفرح بالله، التي بلا عله ولا سبب، هولاء[1772] وما يشبههم[1773] من دون عدم التالم الهادي الذي يفوق الطبع، وفعل النعمه لا يمكن ان يحصلوا.

(I .47) بمقدار ما هو مرتفع درجه البنين عن رتبة العبيد، هكذا هو متعالي[1774] تدابير الحريه من التدابير[1775] الغصبيه.

1764 افرازت : A.

1765 الوثبات : S.

1766 وخرج : R, S.

1767 تاورية : A / ثاوْرية : S.

1768 ذالك : R.

1769 ذبائحه : S / ذبايحه : R.

1770 زكي : S.

1771 يغسلوا : S.

1772 هولا : R.

1773 يشبهم : R.

1774 هي متعالية : R, S.

1775 تدابير : R.

(I .48) الصلاه الروحانيه من حرية النفس تتولد، والحريه تكون من قلب قد انعتق من الالام واصطلح مع الكل، وافاض حبه بمواددده على الصالحين والاشرار بغير فرز كمثل الله.

(I .49) كما ان الذي هو واقف في موضع عالى يقبل الهوى وينشرح ويتقوا[1776] اكثر من الذي هو واقف في السفل والظلمه وكمرة الجو[1777] (A245v) هكذا ايضا الذي على رجا مواعيد الروح يعمل، بالايمان الحقيقي، يقبل عزا وفرح وتسليه اكثر من الذي بالندامه والحزن ومرارة[1778] القلب، يعمل بتغصب القصر،[1779] بلا تميز[1780] مينا الرجا.[1781]

(I .50) ما دام غيرة النفس تهدس وتنبح، لاجل البر باخرين ليس فينا حرية[1782] المسيح.

(I .51) اذا ما غطس الذهن من كل شي، وتداخل وقام بحرية طبيعته، يشرق فيه نور عدم الالام، واذا ما تعرا[1783] الكل واختفا[1784] عن كل شي، يلبس شمس البر.

(I .52) حب يسوع اذا ما التهب ووقد في قلوب القديسين، سماء جديده يرسم في نفوسهم.

(I .53) نور يسوع هو نور معقول، طوبا[1785] للنفس التي[1786] استحقت نظرته.

(I .54) من قبل ظهور مخلصنا معرفة الكاينات كانت ترشد الابرار والصديقين[1787] الى الحق، واما باب القديسين هو يسوع عند ابيه، وطوبا[1788] للذي[1789] دخل فيه.

[1776] ويتقوى : S.
[1777] الجوا : R.
[1778] وحرارة : S.
[1779] القصد : S.
[1780] تمييز : S.
[1781] الرج : R.
[1782] حركة : R.
[1783] تعرى : S.
[1784] واختفى : S.
[1785] وطوبا : R / وطوبى : S.
[1786] الذي : R.
[1787] القديسين : R.
[1788] وطوبى : S.

(I .55) صلاة القديسين هي كمال الوصايا في ذواتهم، بالعمل، (R188v) وغلبتهم هي استيصال[1790] الالام، واكليل روسهم[1791] هو نور عدم الالام، الذي يظهر في انسانهم الجواني.

(I .56) النفس التي بلا مياله تصرخ بحزن القلب وانسحاق واوجاع الى الله، ليس يغفل عن اجابتها.

(I .57) عمل القديسين بني النور هو عمل ميخاييل وجبراييل، ومن مايدة واحده يغتذون.

(I .58) صلاة القديسين بني النور ليس تنقطع، لان قد اتقدس هيكل انفسهم، وانمسح الكاهن الجواني وضع مايده روحانيه وقام الكاهن ليقرب ذبيحة محيية، لاجل شعب المسيح.

(I .59) النفس التي باعمال[1792] مختلفه دخلت لميراث (A246r) القديسين واحصيت بكهنوت السماء، واتكت على مايدة الاسرار، فينبغي ان تحترس بذهنها، ليلا عندما تكون متكيه على مايدة حضن المسيح، لتقبل الاسرار الممجده التي للملكوت، يفسق ذهنها ويطيش بشوارع الاسواق، ليهدس مع الالام، وللكهنه[1793] ما تظهر سر الحياة الجديده، وينمحي اسمها من سفر الحياه، وعوض ميراث القديسين ترث[1794] مخنقة[1795] الندم والظلمه، وتخيب من النظرة الروحانيه، التي هي عربون ميراث القديسين.

(I .60) نطقية الانسان جعلت مسكن للاهوت[1796] المسجود له، وبحرية ارادته يمضي، اما للنعيم[1797] واما لعذاب الجحيم.

(I .61) هيكل الله ليس يقع تحت عبودية الموت البسيط، وبميالة حريته يختار له الموت المعقول، او حياة جديده تفوق الطبع، بالنعمه، معونة نعمة المسيح يلزق لعمل البر، وليس الخطيه.

1789 الذي : R.

1790 اصتيصال : R.

1791 رؤوسهم : S.

1792 متواترة : زائدة S.

1793 والكهنة : R, S.

1794 يرث : R, S.

1795 محنقة : R.

1796 اللاهوت : R, S.

1797 النعيم : R.

(I .62) اما ان يكون الانسان او لم يكن، ليس هي له،[1798] واما ان يكون بارا،[1799] وخاطي[1800] هي لنا، والمعونه للمسيح،[1801] مساعدة نعمه[1802] تلزق بعمل، وليس بعمل الخطيه.

(I .63) مسكن الله بلا عوز خلق، وهيكل الله وقدس الاقداس الداخل، وملكوت الله جميعهم هم داخلنا، فالنفس مفتقره الى اعمال التوبه، والتعليم والكتب،[1803] ولحفظ الوصايا، والصلوات الدايمه، لكي بحريتها تقتني من الذخيره التي جواها حياة جديده، معقوله تفوق الطبيعه، او موت معقول خارج عن الطبع، بتغافل ارادتها.

(I .64) جعل[1804] الله نطقية الانسان، باختيار الاراده، ان يعد لذاته في كمال (A246v) سعيه، ان شا[1805] اكليل البر والفضايل بمعونة الله، وان اختار الخزي والعذاب بالمياله الى تلذذ دغدغة الالام.

(I .65) وان كان هم صعبات الضوايق، التي لاجل التوبه بسبب تواتر[1806] الاحزان المختلفه الحادثه على النفس الشقيه، ولكن عظيم هو وممجد[1807] العزا الخفي، الذي يظهر في القلب لتعزية (R189r) ضعفنا.

(I .66) والذي يبدى بالتوبه يطلب باي نوع من النسك وكسر القلب[1808] وانسحاقه بالتوبه ليكمل[1809] في ذاته بالفعل، وباي نوع اعانه الله ونجح فيه، وبغير شبع يعمل هذا النوع باقنوم ذاته.

(I .67) محزني[1810] القلب[1811] وذوي النفس المريره، المضنوكين[1812] والمتضيقين، والموجوعين، ان كان بغته ما يدركهم العزا بمراحم الله خفيا، لم كان[1813] يحيا كل ذي جسد.

[1798] واما له : زائدة R.

[1799] بار : R.

[1800] او خاطئا : S / او خاطي : R.

[1801] ومعونة المسيح : S.

[1802] النعمة : S.

[1803] ولتعليم الكتب : S / والتعليم الكتب : R.

[1804] جل : R.

[1805] اشا : R.

[1806] اتواتر : R.

[1807] وممجود (ممجد) : S / وممجود : R.

[1808] في : زائدة R.

[1809] ليكمله : R, S.

[1810] محزوني : R, S.

(I .68) هنيذ تذكار الانسان اذا[1814] كان يهدس بمفاوضة العالم الجديد، ينموا ويبهج بالله وتمتلي نفسه رجا وعزا وفرح، واذا ما هدس في امور العالم وتركيب حيلة الموذيات، يمتلى كاابه وحزن وندم.

(I .69) للعالم[1815] المزمع صوب ارادة الباري، ولكن لاجل منفعة الكل سبق اتقن هذا، واعطا[1816] لاولاده حرية الاراده، لكي باختيار ارادتهم يعدون لانفسهم اي ناحية ارادوا، اما ناحية عذاب،[1817] او مكان نعيم.

(I .70) ها هنا وضع جهاد ومصاف والمحاربين،[1818] وجعل لهم ايضا معرفة الغلبه والانغلاب[1819] في طبع خلقتنا، واظهر شرف الغلبه وعار الانغلاب بوصاياه المحييه، وضع في طبيعتنا قوة (A247r) الغلبه مقابل العدو،[1820] ومجاذبات الخير، مع حرية الاراده.

(I .71) الذين ما يعطون[1821] لذواتهم راحه في هذا العالم، لاجل الحرب الموضوع قبالهم، في عالم الجديد يستريحون[1822] من ثقل اعمالهم بالروحانيه التي يقتنوا بنعمة المسيح، تنعم[1823] لا يزول عندما يرتفع الفساد والمياله، ويكون الله كل في كل،[1824] وبضد هولاء[1825] يلبسون الخطاه، الخجل ويبيدون[1826] مع الشياطين المرده، الذين اتنيحوا[1827] معهم[1828] هاهنا.

1811 القلوب : R, S.
1812 والمضنوكة : S / والمضنوكين : R.
1813 يكن : S.
1814 ما : زائدة R, S.
1815 العالم : R.
1816 واعطى : S.
1817 العذاب : S.
1818 ومحاربين : R, S.
1819 وعار الانغلاب : S.
1820 العدوا : R.
1821 يعطوا : R, S.
1822 يستربحون : R.
1823 اتنعم : R.
1824 الكل في الكل : S / كل في الكل : R.
1825 هولا : R.
1826 وينبذون : R, S.
1827 اتنحوا : R.
1828 معهن : R, S.

(I .72) الله خالق الطبايع هو غير محدود في ازليته، ومخفي من الكل، المعرفه على لاهوته وضعها في كل الطبايع، كمثل الكتابه على الطبايع امام الامور،[1829] للخلايق[1830] من خارج، وعلى قلوب البشر، من داخل مرسوم، لكي بنور الافهام وافراز المعرفه يكون يقرا فيهم العقل، ويتميز بنور نطقيته، بذاك الذي هو مخفي ومكتوم، وهو يفعل في الكل.

(I .73) التهاون والضلاله هم اسباب[1831] الخطايا.[1832]

(I .74) الازدرا بالقريب ومقته، هم سبب عدم المعرفه وقلت[1833] الايمان والتجديف.

(I .75) المعرفة الساذجه[1834] المبتعده من التدابير المتقنه، واعمال التوبه، وهي مرتبطه مع حدة الحركات، وادراك[1835] الافهام، تولد الاستزرا[1836] والتنفخ والافتخار.

(I .76) ملح تدابير المتقنه واعمال التوبه والنسك، هو الصبر والمخافه، والحيا، التي يتولد منهن، طول الروح واتساع النفس، والاتضاع الحقاني.

(I .77) الشياطين المرده ولو انهم اعدا خليقة الله، ولكن من دون ان نكون (A247v) نحن بارادتنا سبب للتخليه، ويجدون فينا ماده لشرورهم (R189v) فما يقدرون[1837] يوذونا.

(I .78) صنارة النفس هي محبة ذاك الشي التي ارتبطت النفس بشهوته، ومجتذبه لكل ناحيه غضب لذاك الشي الذي[1838] تحبه، ولم تنظر معه شي اخر، الا الذي تريده وتحبه، ان كان صالح او ردي.

(I .79) لم تقتني الام المربيه رحمه وحب مع ولدها، كمثلما[1839] تقتني عناية الله اللازقه لضعفنا من المبدا، رحمه وتحنن وتربى وتحرس لطفوليتنا من كل

[1829] الطبايع والامور : R, S.

[1830] الخلايق : R.

[1831] اسبب : R.

[1832] الخطية : S.

[1833] وقلة : R, S.

[1834] السرجه : R.

[1835] بداية فقرة جديدة : A.

[1836] الازدراء : S.

[1837] ان : زائدة R, S.

[1838] التي : R.

الاذيات، ان كنا نثبت بطفوليتنا ولا نميل بحرية ارادتنا، بالكمال الى لذة الشهوات ودغدغة الالام.

(I .80) عناية الله من بدو[1840] خلقة العالم[1841] هي لازقه لكل طبع،[1842] لثبات ازليته وليس لتقويم ميالته، لانه مكتوب عناية الله بنا هي سايره تبع حرية الاراده، ودينونته العادله[1843] بعد تدبير حرية الاراده تنقام.

(I .81) ازلية الطبايع عناية الله هي، فان كان ترتفع هذه من الوسط، يتلاشا[1844] امر الخليقه للعدم ليس[1845] للميالة،[1846] السماء والارض مملوه مني قال الرب.

(I .82) كما ان النفس هي مخفيه في الجسد وتحركه، وعندما تنتقل منه يصير جثه ويفسد، هكذا عناية الله لازقه بالخليقه، وبها تحيا وتثبت وتتحرك وتوجد، ان[1847] كان تنقبض منها يوول امر الخليقه الى العدم، وليس تفسد كمثل الجثه.

(I .83) ان كان ترتفع عناية الله عن[1848] ابليس وشياطينه المرده، تنتهي حيرتهم وارادتهم[1849] الى (A248r) العدم وتتلاشا، لان عناية الله تقمعهم ولا تتركهم يكملوا بالفعل شرور خلقهم وارادتهم الرديه.

(I .84) ملايكة النور الموضوعين لخدمة حياتنا، لم يسمح لهم ان تساعدوا[1850] بالغصب لميالة حريتنا، ولا ان يظهروا بالفعل رحمة جود ارادتهم الينا.

(I .85) الملاك المداوم عندنا[1851] ليس بشي اخر يتكدر ويغضب، اكثر من الذي من غير ضروره نبعد انفسنا من خدمة الاسرار المقدسه، وتناول القربان

[1839] كمثل ما :R.

[1840] بدوا : R.

[1841] الخليقة (خلقة العالم) : S.

[1842] خلق : زائدة R, S.

[1843] من : زائدة R, S.

[1844] يتلاشى : S.

[1845] وليس : R, S.

[1846] الميالة : R.

[1847] وان : R, S.

[1848] عن : ساقطة R.

[1849] تنتهي ازليتهم : R, S.

[1850] يساعدوا : R, S.

[1851] (لنا) عندنا : S.

المحبيه، لان[1852] في الساعه التي يقدم الكاهن فيها ذبيحة جسد المسيح ودمه المحيي،[1853] يحل الروح[1854] القدس ويمنح الغفران للخليقه،[1855] والشاروبيم والسارافيم[1856] والملايكه يقفوا بدهش عظيم وبخوف وفرح، ويفرحون[1857] بالاسرار المقدسه بعجب لا ينطق به، ويبتهج الملاك المداوم عندنا لانه هو ايضا يشترك بتلك النظره المخوفه، فلهذا ما يرا[1858] ان يخيب من تلك المفاوضة[1859] الكامله، لان الروحانيين روحانيا يفرحون بالاسرار الروحانيه[1860] المحبيه، ويتنعمون بها كمثل ان القديسين بعين الروح يفرحون، اذ[1861] ينظرون في الاسرار المتقربه.

(I .86) ان كان فينا واحد[1862] قد منعه قانونا[1863] محدود[1864] وضرورة[1865] ما غصبيه، او بسبب نافع نفساني، يمتنع من التناول، ينبغي له ان[1866] في ذلك[1867] الوقت[1868] المرعب من الملايكه،[1869] ان يكون في مفاوضة الصلوات المتواتره بغير انقطاع، ليلا يتوبخ من نيته، (R190r) انه قد اقصر[1870] عن الحق، (A248v) حسب ما تصل مقدرته اليه.

(I .87) بتجديد العامه ليس يستحي الانسان ويتبكت من الجموع العلويه والسفليه، كمثلما[1871] يتبكت من نيته ويستحي من ملاك العنايه الذي معه.

1852 بداية فقرة جديدة : S.

1853 المحي : R.

1854 روح : R, S.

1855 الخليقه : R.

1856 والساروفيم : R, S.

1857 ويفرحوا : R, S.

1858 يرى : S.

1859 المحبية : زائدة S.

1860 الروحانيه : ساقطة R, S.

1861 اذ : ساقطة R.

1862 احد : S / احدا : R.

1863 قانون : R, S.

1864 محدودا : S.

1865 او ضرورة : R.

1866 ان : ساقطة S.

1867 ذالك : R.

1868 الوقت : ساقطة R.

1869 الملاكه : R.

1870 قصر : S.

1871 كمثل ما : R.

(I .88) متضاعف يفرحون الملايكه والصديقين، اذا ما بلغت سفينتهم للمينا وتحزن الشياطين.

(I .89) يحزنوا[1872] الملايكه للناس[1873] الخاطيين عندما تفارق انفسهم اجسادهم بلا توبه، وتفرح الشياطين الذين صاروا لهم مخطيين[1874] وخداعين الى الم الخطيه.

(I .90) الانسان الذي قد جعل لفمه حد ان من دون نطقية العقل، لا يدخل ويخرج فيه شيا،[1875] وقمع داخل منه وحشية[1876] جميع حصون الالام المرذوله.

(I .91) النفس الذي[1877] انعتقت من المجاذبات[1878] والخباطات واتسييت[1879] في تبع افهام كثيره، وتصور عقلها في وقت يهدس، بتماجيد الله وباسرار معرفة الحق، ونمتلى فرح، وتعود ترجع ايضا لما يخصها، ومع سكون[1880] عقلها تبطل ايضا من[1881] فرح قلبها.

(I .92) كما ان الهذيذ بالمنظورات هو طياشه بالقياس الى الهذيذ بالمعقولات، وهكذا ايضا الهذيذ[1882] بالمعقولات هو طياشه بالقياس الى الهذيذ باسرار معرفه الثالوث المقدس.

(I .93) الهذيذ المعقول بكلام الله ووصاياه[1883] وبحكمته وشرف خلقته العالم الجديد، هو احلا من العسل والشهد، وهو تحت الحدود، والهذيذ باسرار معرفة الثالوث المقدس المرتسم جميعه بجميعه بالقلب[1884] والنفس والعقل، ويصطبغون بالنور والحق والحياه، ويمتلوا فرح، (A249r) لا حدا له.[1885]

[1872] وحزنوا : R.
[1873] ملايكة الناس : R, S.
[1874] محرضين : S / مرضين : R.
[1875] شي : R, S.
[1876] وحسيته : S.
[1877] التي : R, S.
[1878] المحادثات (المحاربات) : S.
[1879] واتسييت : S / واتسببت : R.
[1880] اسكون : R.
[1881] في : R, S.
[1882] والهذيذ : R, S.
[1883] وبوصاياه : R, S.
[1884] القلب : R / جميعه يجعل القلب : S.
[1885] فرحا لا حد له : S / لاحد : R.

(I .94) الذهن المشتاق بان يحس باستعلانات اسرار الله، لم يقتني مع الله شيا ولا يقبل ان يدخل جواه فكر[1886] غريب[1887] لا صالح ولا ردى.

(I .95) الهادس بامور كثيره هو غذا[1888] النفس ان كان صالح او ردى، او مخلوط من هولاء وهولاء.[1889]

(I .96) بعد جهد تثبت النفس عند هذيذ واحد وهذه هي التي كملت بالله، او[1890] كملت بالشيطان، والوسطانيه[1891] بالمضاددات[1892] يطيشون. الاولانيين يرتفعون من معرفه الى معرفه ومن فهم الى فهم، ومن تصور الى تصور، حتى يبلغوا الى الحق، والاخرانيين ينتقلون من عدم معرفه الى عدم معرفه، وينحدرون[1893] الى ضلاله الشيطان الكامله.

(I .97) والهذيذ المختلط هو عذاب للنفس،[1894] وبعد جهد تشفا ضربتها، لان الذي هو نفساني بمعرفته يطيش ذهنه بمعرفة الصالحات والشرور الجميع.

(I .98) الهذيذ بالواحد هو الانحلال من الكل، والارتباط بالواحد، هو الابتلاع بمحبته والمفاوضه معه.

(I .99) اذا ما انحلت النفس من الكل وارتبطت بالواحد، وابتهجت بحبه وشغبت[1895] بشهوته، ليس لها عزا من ناحية اخرى،[1896] فانها[1897] لا[1898] تنظر معه شيا[1899] لا روحانيين ولا جسدانيين، وتفهم ان السما والارض مملوه

1886 فكرا : R, S.
1887 غريبا : S.
1888 غذاء : S.
1889 هولا وهولا : R.
1890 كملت بالله، او : ساقطة R.
1891 والوسطانيين : R, S.
1892 بالمضادات : S.
1893 وينحرون : R.
1894 النفس : R.
1895 وشغفت : S / وشغبة : R.
1896 اخره : R.
1897 بداية فقرة جديدة : S / انها : S / بانها : R.
1898 ما : R, S.
1899 شي : R, S.

منه،[1900] وبه نحن احيا ومتحركين وموجودين، وما (R190v) تستطيع ان تهدا من التهاب محبته، ولتعرفه كمثل ما تنعرف.[1901]

(I .100) لان طبيعته هي ارفع من نظرة ومعرفة الروحانيين.

(I .101) ابن الله لكي ينيح بولس (A249v) عندما كان ملتهب[1902] بحبه، بالنظره العجيبه التي تفوق الطبع بالمراه فوق الطبع، نيحه من تعبه كما يعرف هو، ورجع الى بلد غربته.

كمل الميمر الاول.[1903]

(II) الميمر الثاني من رووس المعرفه للقديس مار اسحق.[1904]

(II.1) حقانية المسيح اقنا العالم[1905] نور وحياه، كلمة يسوع هي اعلا[1906] من جميع المعارف، وبوصاياه المقدسه ظهرت معرفة الحق، بقلب المومنين.

(II.2) الباب الذي به تدخل القديسين لمعرفه الحق، هو تعليم الكتب المقدسه، لانه بنور نطقية النفس تحسس[1907] الاسرار المخفيه في الكتب بالافهام[1908] الغويصه، يعرفون عناية الله وسياسته وحكمة خلقته، وشرف العالم الجديد.

(II.3) وكلما تزيد وتتلطف بالتدابير يتزايدون بالاكثر[1909] بالعلم والافهام، وتجس السماء والارض وجميع ما فيهم مقابل غرض ضميرهم، واكثرهم يصطادوا كالحجل في قفص،[1910] وبعضهم كالسحب[1911] يحيوا انفس كثيرين

[1900] معه : R.

[1901] كما ينعرف : S.

[1902] يلتهب : R, S.

[1903] كمل الميمر الاول : ساقطة S.

[1904] للقديس مار اسحق : ساقطة S.

[1905] مخلص العالم : S.

[1906] احلى : S.

[1907] تجسس : R.

[1908] وبالافهام : R, S.

[1909] بالكثره : R, S.

[1910] العالم : زائدة R, S.

[1911] كالسح : R.

بكلامهم، ومنهم من ينهمك بالخلق والحسد وبقيه الالام، واخرين يكونون[1912] كالسرج[1913] على منارة البيعه، وبعد جهد تجد[1914] فيهم قليلين يحبوا مسكنة صليب يسوع، ويهملوا غنا[1915] العلم الذي جمعوا ويختاروا بساطة الصيادين، وسذاجتهم، وبوداعة قلوبهم يكونون[1916] اكاليل بتاج المسيح.

(II.4) يا ما اصعب جدا تحصيل العلم وتحصيل غناه،[1917] واصعب باضعاف كثيره تبديده.

(II.5) الويل لمن لا يقتني باعمال نشيطه[1918] غنا[1919] التعليم، لانه اعما[1920] من تميز النور الذي للحق. الويل[1921] ثم الويل للذي جمع وفرق، (A250r) لانه لم يتفرغ من امور كثيره، ليكون واحد[1922] مع يسوع، بسر محبة[1923] بسيط.

(II.6) اه من غنا[1924] النفس التي كلما[1925] تسعد وتزيد معرفتها بتعليم الكتب، بالاكثر تشبك ذاتها بالحيل الغويصه المتالمه، اللطيفه الدقيقه ومرادات الضلاله، ولم تشا ان تدنى لحلاوة المسيح،[1926] وتنازله مع الضعفا والخطاه.

(II.7) النفساني هو ديان وقاضي الابرار والخطاه، الاحيا والاموات، ومنصوب في قلبه شجرة معرفة الخير والشر، الذي اومر مبدا جبلتنا ان لا يذوقها ليلا يموت، ومنها تغتذي معرفته كل وقت.

(II.8) عقل النفساني[1927] في كل حين يطير على شجرة الحياة، ويحل عليها وقت وقت، وينشرح باوراقها كمثلما[1928] تفعل الشياطين، واما ان ياكل من لذة اثمارها ما[1929] يقدر حسب قول السيد.

[1912] يكونوا : R, S.
[1913] كالسراج : S.
[1914] نجد : S.
[1915] عنا : S.
[1916] يكونوا : R, S.
[1917] عناه : S.
[1918] بالاعمال النشيطه : R, S.
[1919] غنى : S.
[1920] اعمى : S.
[1921] والويل : R, S.
[1922] واحدا : S.
[1923] محبته : R, S.
[1924] غنى : S.
[1925] كل ما : R.
[1926] يسوع : R, S.

(II.9) ليس لنا ان ناكل من شجرة الخير والشر، وان ناكل من شجرة الحياه بالسوا، لان ذاك يولد تكدر[1930] الخلق[1931] ويثير الحسد، وهذا يجلب الهدو[1932] ويولد طيب الحب ويسكب على العقل نور.

(II.10) لان هي (R191r) النفس بالطبع ما فيها كفو[1933] للناحيتين، ان تهدس بهن جميع، ولا يمكنها ان تنعتق من احدهن، لان متا[1934] يوضع عليها هذيذين او ثلثه[1935] تنقسم هي لكثيرين، وتتميز في الواحد بالغش، وتتكلم بالاخر بالحيل، وتفعل في الاخر بالضلاله،[1936] واذا ما هي النفس انقسمت[1937] على ذاتها لا بد لها ان تخرب حسب كلمة السيد.

(II.11) العقل الذي يسعد روحاني بكل معرفه وتعليم، وفهم وتصور وكرامه، ويلقي الى وراه جميعهم، ويصلح الثالوث الذي فيه، (A250v) من اجل يسوع، ويغلي بحبه ويلتهب بمحبته، ويرتبط بالهذيذ ومفاوضة الصلاه بالهدو،[1938] ولا ينظر معه شي اخر، ولا يبطل فيه وقيد حبه ومحبته، الى ان يتحد معه ويرتسم في قلبه بلا انقطاع،[1939] كمثل صورة الملك المرتسمه في الدينار، هذا هو بالحقيقه مسكين بالروح، الذي قد ورث داخله ملكوت الله.

(II.12) المجاذبات التي تخوف، ورعب العذاب والحرارة الطبيعيه المولودين[1940] الحرارة المخبله، ووحشية الالام ومعرفة الحيل، واعمال انواع هولاء[1941] وما يشبههم، ينفعون الى حيث البلوغ لمعرفة الحق.

[1927] نفساني : S.

[1928] كمثل ما : R.

[1929] من : R.

[1930] تذكر : R.

[1931] الحق : R.

[1932] الهدوء : S / الهدوا : R.

[1933] كفوءا : S / كفوا : R.

[1934] متى : R, S.

[1935] ثلاثه : R, S.

[1936] بالظلاله : A / بالاضلاله : R.

[1937] اتقسمت : R.

[1938] بالهدوء : A / وبالهدوا : R.

[1939] انتقال : R, S.

[1940] المولدين : R, S.

[1941] هولا : R.

(II.13) واما معرفة الحق من نور عدم الالام تتولد، ومن هناك ملكوت الله ينادي بها بالسر، كمثل بالمراه بحرية النفس ومعرفة الذهن وسلام القلب، ونياح الضمير، وهدو[1942] الافكار والفرح بالله، المبتعد من كل خباط، لان هولاء[1943] يولدون من تدبير العقل اللابس المسيح.

(II.14) ازلية اكليل عقل القديسين هو قرص لون صافيلا،[1944] بشرفه، واشراق نور طهارته هو نور مجد روح القدس.

(II.15) مبدا تدبير الانسان[1945] الجديد بهذه الحياه الحاضره، هي طهارة النفس من الالام، وعندما[1946] تتعرا[1947] من جميع حركات الجسد المتكدره، وتسالم ذاتها، وتقلب الغضبيه والشهوه والافكار من غير الطبع للطبيعيه.[1948]

(II.16) مينا تدابير المتقنه التي للانسان[1949] الجديد، حسب الاستطاعه بهذه الحياة الحاضره، هي النقاوه، وهدو[1950] النفس عندما تقوم في طبيعة[1951] خلقتها الاوله.[1952]

(II.17) النقاوه هي مينا القديسين الذين شقوا وتعبوا هاهنا بالالام، وبمعونة الله (A251r) نجوا حياتهم الى البلد الخالي من عثرات الشرور والحسد[1953] والخلق، والمغايضات[1954] ومرارة النفس، لبلد السلام وامن وفرح.[1955]

(II.18) اذا ما انقلعت من النفس زروع الشرور التي زرعها الشيطان، وتنبت وتنموا الزروع الطبيعيه التي هي طبع خلقتها[1956] المحجوبين بشرور الالام،

1942 وهدوء : S / وهدوا : R.

1943 هولا : R.

1944 صافيا : S.

1945 انسان : R, S.

1946 وعند ما : R.

1947 تتعرى : S.

1948 للطبيعة : S / الطبيعيه : R.

1949 للانساً : R.

1950 وهدوء : S / وهدوا : R.

1951 طبعة : R.

1952 الاولى : S.

1953 والجسد : R.

1954 والمفاوضات : S.

1955 والامن والفرح : S.

1956 خلقتنا : R, S.

ويقوم الطبع بمجد ذاته ونور عدم التالم، يشرق للصديقين والفرح للانقيا قلوبهم.

(II.19) النقاوه ليس تسما فضيله، لانها ليست طريق به تتفلح الفضايل للسيره، بل هي نياح القديسين، البلد الصافي الخالي (R191v) من شرور الالام وهو مملوا سلامه، وفرح،[1957] وفيه تستريح المتعوبين، ويتنعموا باستعلان اسرار الله، ويوهلون بعقولهم لمعرفة سر العالم الجديد الروحاني.

(II.20) نياح القديسين الكامل هي ارض الميعاد اورشليم السماييه، تلك التي ما يدخلون اليها ما داموا لابسين هذا توب الجسد، بل يوهلون لنظره مجده كمثل بالمراه في[1958] بلد النقاوه، كمثل العظيم موسى، ويستريحون من شقاهم في بلد السلامه، كمقدار ما يوهلوا لتعرا[1959] الجسد وما يخصه، لانهم يتنعمون بالنظرة المدهشه.

(II.21) ليس لنا ان نبلغ للمينا[1960] الهادي بالوثبات، ولا ان نعبر للبلد[1961] النقي بلا صبر على الضوايق، والتجارب المختلفه، ولا ان ندخل لبلد السلامه من غير مقاسات شر الشياطين، والجهادات والحروب الصعبه، الى الدم، ولا ان نحس بالحق من دون النعمه، وهداية الاب الروحاني.

(II.22) بعد جهد الشيوخ الاعفا[1962] الذي من الشبوبيه[1963] (A251v) الى الشيخوخه اضنكوا انفسهم بالنسك في كرم الرب، بالتدابير الحسنه، يوهلون[1964] جزويا لواحده من مواهب بلد السلامه، واما الصبيان بحرارة الوثبات الطبيعيه والغلوة المسجسه، يترووا[1965] بما ليس هو لهم، ويتخلوا[1966] بحدة حركات الابا المخفيه في كتبهم، او يقبلون بالتعليم وتسليم من اخرين بغير[1967] واجب، تمقتهم

[1957] فرح : R.

[1958] من : R, S.

[1959] لتعري : S.

[1960] المينا : R.

[1961] البلد : R.

[1962] الاعضاء : S.

[1963] الصبوبيه : R, S.

[1964] يوهلوا : R, S.

[1965] يتراءون : S.

[1966] ويتخيلوا : R, S.

[1967] وبغير : R.

النعمه وتحكمهم، ان يصبروا ويطيلوا ارواحهم ولا يقروا[1968] على العظايم، بل يعملون[1969] في الكرم بهدو،[1970] الى زمان النياحة الحقيقيه.

(II.23) واذا ما اتجاسروا بزياده تتخلا عنهم النعمه قليل، ويقعون في ربوات[1971] تجارب، وينمقتون بالام الجسد الاشيا التي كانت مزدريه في اعينهم، ويتعبون بظلمات النفسانيه[1972] وتستهزى بهم الشياطين، ويعرض[1973] لهم زلات متواتره وحيره وضجر[1974] وصغر نفس التجنن.

(II.24) يا ما اصعب واقسا[1975] الضوايق والتجارب والفخوخ، الموضوعه في هذه الطريق[1976] الدقيقه التي لسيدنا، قدام الذين بالمفرات[1977] الطبيعيه والحرارة المخبله وحدة[1978] الحركات، والتسليم من اخرين، يريدوا ان يدخلوا الى منزل الحياه، لياكلوا من شهد الروح.

(II.25) بعد جهد النساك المحقين الذين اضنكوا انفسهم بالنسك، وانحلت[1979] عنهم الوثبات الطبيعيه والحرارة الاوله، ويسيروا بهدو[1980] وسلامه[1981] في الطريق[1982] بلا الام، يستحقون مواهب الروح، لان امور سيدنا من ذات انفسهم ياتون، ان كان الموضع طاهر وغير دنس من الالام والشرور، لان ملكوت السماء ما تاتي بالرصد.

(II.26) النفس التي احنت[1983] ذاتها للمسيح، وذهنها (R192r) حس باسرار الملكوت، (A252r) واتكا على المايدة الروحانيه، وبمفاوضة الصلاة الخفيه

1968 يفزوا : S.

1969 يعملوا : R, S.

1970 بهدوء : S / بهدوا : R.

1971 ربوة : R, S.

1972 نفسانية : S.

1973 وتعرض : R, S.

1974 وضجر : ساقطة R.

1975 واقسى : S.

1976 الطرق : R, S.

1977 بالمفزات : S.

1978 وحدت : R.

1979 واتخلفت : R, S.

1980 بهدوء : S / بهدوا : R.

1981 بهدوء السلامة : S / بهدوا السلامه : R.

1982 الطرق : R, S.

1983 احبت : R, S.

ذاق عظايم اسرار الله، وصار ناظر تمجيداته المتعاليه[1984] عن الطبع، ونست ذاتها، وبدا ضميرها يطيش في افهام الخلايق ويغوص في المنظورات، ويقايض مايده بموايد ومفاوضه بمفاوضات، اولا[1985] تيقظه[1986] النعمه بنخز النيه، وبعد ذلك[1987] تخوفه بتخايل النوم، وتغضبه[1988] بالمناظر العجيبه، وتمقته بالموذيات الخفيه والظاهره، والامر لها ان تختار لذاتها الحياه الجديده والموت المعقول.

(II.27) الباب الذي به يدخلون الذين يريدون[1989] بوثبات[1990] الغلوه،[1991] الموهلين للطهاره، هو الالتهاب[1992] بفعل شهوة الزنا من غير الم القتال، من فيه كفوا[1993] ان يفهم فليفهم، مع ربوات تجارب ومصاعد، وانغلاب وفساد الدم المصادفه اياه.

(II.28) باب الحق الذي به تدخل الشيوخ العمالين الى ارض الميعاد، هو غطسهم[1994] بنهر الاردن بمجاري الدموع السايله من عيونهم من غير غصيبه، ولا اراده، بل من الفرح الذي فوق الطبع، ومع هذا مفتقر لمعونة النعمه وهداية الاب الروحاني.

(II.29) ليس ينبغي ان ياتي لقطع الرجا المتوحد الذي اوهل لعدم الالام، وحس بما يفوق الطبع باسرار عظايم الله، عندما يغلب من الالام الطبيعيه، بل يشفي جرحه بالتوبه، لان الالام الطبيعيه[1995] يثبتون مع الطبع، وتنضغط القديسين بالضوايق وهم مفتقرين للتوبه الى اخر نسمتهم.

1984 المعاليه : R.

1985 اوله : R, S.

1986 تيقضه : A.

1987 ذالك : R.

1988 وتغضيه : R.

1989 ان : زائدة R, S.

1990 وثبات : R.

1991 يبلغوا الغير : زائدة S.

1992 للالتهاب : S / اللالتهاب : R.

1993 كفوءا : S.

1994 غطهم : R.

1995 الالام الطبيعه : R, S.

(II.30) ما دام الالم يثبت في القلب وتتنازل معه النفس بمحبه، الى الان ما وجد فيها روح الله راحه، بل يقرع ولا يعبر، وان كان يضابر[1996] ويثبت (A252v) هي دلايل محبته.

(II.31) الذي قد ولد روحاني[1997] من العماد المقدس واتلمذ[1998] للتدبير الملايكي،[1999] ينبغي له ان يعمل ويجاهد مقابل الالام ويسال نعمة الله، ان يولد الطهاره ويوهل الى ما هو فوق الطبع، لسر استعلان الروح، لكي من هاهنا يقبل باستعلان سريا عربون مجد كنز البنوه، التي بالفعل هو عتيد ان يقبل في تجديد العامه.

(II.32) يسكن المتوحد بربنا، وربنا بالمتوحد، عندما يبلغ قلبه الى منزل الذكاوه ويعاين في ذاته نور عدم الالام.

(II.33) ينسكب في وقت نور استعلان المسيح على نور العقل، ويصمت بالدهش ويرجع الى بلده.

(II.34) العقل الذي أُهل[2000] لاستعلان الروح واتحد مع سيدنا بالسر، لا ينبغي ان يدخل الى حجلته تذكارا وفكر غريب، وينجس مسكن الروح القدس.

(II.35) ناخذ روح القدس من العماد كالعربون لتبطيل الخطيه، وقوه لنقاتل قبال الالام والشيطان[2001] واذا ما بوساطة اعمال السكون والجهاد، مقابل الالام نوهل لذكاوة القلب، هو ايضا الروح يزيد لنا (R192v) قوه منه، لكي نستطيع[2002] ان نكون فوق الطبع، وان نقبل مجد ربنا باستعلان نور مجده الغير منطوق به.

(II.36) هذه[2003] قوة روح القدس، كملت الابرار والصديقين، في اجيالهم، وتكمل ايضا القديسين، فوق الطبع بالنعمه من اتحاد يسوع المتحد بالله الكلمه فوق الطبيعه.

1996 يثابر : S / يضاكر : R.

1997 روحانيا : R, S.

1998 واتعمد : R.

1999 الملايكيه : R.

2000 استؤهل : S / اوهل : R.

2001 والشياطين : R.

2002 نسيطيع : A.

2003 هي : زائدة S.

(II.37) هذا هو روح القدس الذي دعى من ربنا روح البارقليط، ومن رسوله سمي مكمل القديسين، ومن الابا اتكنا[2004] روح الاستعلانات.

(II.38) غيارات كثيره تقبل النفس كما قالوا الابا، الى ان تكمل بنور طبيعتها، وتوهل ان تقبل نور (A253r) استعلان ربنا عليها، ظلام واشراق، قتام ونور، حق وطغيان.

(II.39) وكمثلما[2005] ان كثيرين هم غيارات منازل ومقادير ذكاوة مراة[2006] قلوب القديسين، وهكذا ايضا هن كثيرين غيارات استعلانات ربنا للقديسين.

(II.40) وان كان بانواع مختلفه وغزيره يستضا عقل القديسين، بتاوريات[2007] مختلفه بكلام الروح وبايمان المواعيد، وبهذيذ مجد العالم الجديد، وصلاة[2008] جمع الضمير الخفيه، مع ما تبقا ولجميعهم ينيح المسيح بالسر، ولكن بنور عدم الالام يفعل بزياده استعلانه الممجوده،[2009] عندما يتعزا[2010] الضمير من كل شي بنور طبيعته، ويبتلع بمحبته ويصير[2011] معه واحد.

(II.41) قالوا الابا الذين اوهلوا لنور الضمير،[2012] في[2013] وقت مفاوضة الصلاه والهذيذ يشرق بالليل وبالنهار[2014] حسب ارادته، على قدر[2015] بهجة وقيام[2016] فضا جو رقيع القلب.

(II.42) الشمس الذي يشرق ويغيب متواترا، هو علامة ودلايل عدم التالم والتهاون.

(II.43) اكليل عقل القديسين هو اشراق القرص الطاهر في رقيع[2017] القلب.

2004 اتكنا كني : S / اتكا : R.

2005 وكمثل ما : R.

2006 مرات : R, S.

2007 بتااوريات : A.

2008 وبصلاه : R, S.

2009 استعلاناته الممجدة : S.

2010 يتعرى : S / يتعرا : R.

2011 ونصير : R, S.

2012 الطمير : A.

2013 ان في : R, S.

2014 والنهار : S / بالنهار : R.

2015 قد : R.

2016 وقتام : R, S.

2017 ارقيع : R.

(II.44) اذا ما بهج[2018] جو القلب وان كان ليس قمر معقول، العزا موجود من اشراق نور الكواكب، واما بقيام[2019] كابة القلب ليس فيها عزا بل ظلمه والنفس مملوه ندم.

(II.45) الشمس الذي يظهر في رقيع[2020] القلب، سحابة[2021] الحسد والخلق[2022] والشر تحجب شعاعاته جزويا، وغمامة الغضب والتسخط بالكليه تستاصله.

(II.46) سلام القلب ونياح الضمير وهدو[2023] الافكار والفرح بالله، انما يولدون[2024] من بعضهن[2025] بعض، واذا كان الامر هكذا، ما يوهل الانسان لجميعهن بالسويه، (A253v) بهذه الحياة الحاضره الا جزوى وعند الانتقال.

(II.47) الضمير الوحيد الذي قد مات من العالم، ومعرفته، وعلى الدوام يهدس بتمجيدات العالم الجديد، ظهيرته بهجه جدا.

(II.48) افعال استعلانات المسيح كثيره ومختلفه وتفوق الكلام، وليس تقع تحت القياس والحد.

(II.49) ما دامت النفس تفعل قواتها الاثنين[2026] الشمال واليمين،[2027] ما[2028] يظهر لها عزا[2029] طبيعتها، وان جسرت والقت في ذاتها شعاعات مجدها، تنتهر.[2030]

(II.50) اذا ما صنع المتوحد (R193r) الجهاد وكمل الاعمال الجسدانيه والنفسانيه، واوفا ديون الالام واوهل للذكاوه، يستحق عقله الى ما هو فوق الطبيعه، يبلغ للتدبير الروحاني، الذي من غير اعمال الجسد واتعاب الضمير

2018 يهيج : S.

2019 بقتام : R, S.

2020 ارقيع : R, S.

2021 اسحابة : R.

2022 والحلق : S.

2023 وهدوء : S / وهدوا : R.

2024 يتولدون : R, S.

2025 بعضهم : R.

2026 الاثنتين : S / الا : R.

2027 الشمال واليمين : ساقطة S / واليمين : ساقطة R.

2028 الكمال ما : S.

2029 عري : R, S.

2030 تنبهر : R, S.

ينقام، لانه حركه روحانيه من النعمه تختلج،[2031] ويناغي خفي[2032] في مخازن القلب، ويحرك حركات النفس للصلاه الروحانيه.

(II.51) نظرة[2033] الضمير ونمو القلب وعقل منقبض مهتدي، هو سوق[2034] روحاني للنفس،[2035] وبيت محل روح القدس.

(II.52) اذا ما اهتدوا حركات النفس بالسلامه، يتقدس المذبح الجواني، ويلغلغ ويمجد الكهنوي[2036] بلسان الملايكه وبحاسية[2037] الذهن.

(II.53) لم تهدا حركات النفس ولا ياكلوا من شجرة الحياه، ما دامت شجره معرفة الخير والشر ما انقلعت من القلب، حسب قول السيد.

(II.54) شجرة معرفة الخير والشر هي حاجز من الالام، وابوابها[2038] الظلمه ظلام النفس.

(II.55) الضمير المستضي ويتعالى[2039] بحدت[2040] الحركات بتاورية[2041] الكاينات، بعد جهد يهدا، والذي يلتهب بالحراره ويشره يهلك ذاته.

(II.56) الضمير المتعالي بالاعمال الصعبه، (A254r) والجهادات العسره بجهد عظيم يتضع من قبل ان ينمقت من النعمه، والذي يفتخر بالعصمه والقوه هو مسكن الالام.

(II.57) الضمير المستضي بتصديق المواعيد يحيا، والذي يهذ في شرف العالم الجديد ينعتق من الطياشه، والذكي السكران بالحب يعاين المسيح.

(II.58) الضمير الذي بتكميل الاعمال الصالحه يرضي الله باتضاع ينير تدبيره، وانسانه الجواني بالنعمه كالشمس.

[2031] يختلج : R, S.

[2032] خفيا : S.

[2033] بداية فقرة جديدة : A, R.

[2034] قوس : R.

[2035] النفس : R.

[2036] العقل الكهنوتي : S / العقل الكهنوي : R.

[2037] بحاسية : R, S.

[2038] وابوابه : R.

[2039] ويتعالا : R, S.

[2040] بحدة : R, S.

[2041] بتاؤرية : S / بتااورية : A.

(II.59) ان لم يغلب تواضع النفس بالحزن والدموع بافراز للتقلبات[2042] الهاديه، النطقيه الناميه من فرح القلب، ويذهلون الانسان الجواني ويمقتون نيته بالزلات، التي سبقوا منه[2043] بميالة الطبيعه، وينمقت من النعمه مربيته وينلام من نيته، كم من وقت يزل ويخطى وما يحس، وان لم[2044] يوضع ضميره ويحطه من انتفاخ العظمه والظنون بالندم على اوليك[2045] الذنوب، والا يهلك الانسان الشقي.

(II.60) الفضايل التي تعملها القديسين يخفيهم المسيح من تذكار الضمير، ليلا بسببهم تهلك انفسهم، كما كتب ان لم يلقي الطحان الغما[2046] على عيني البهيمه، كان ترجع وتاكل اجرتها.

(II.61) صنع[2047] الله اذا دنت من المفرز ان كان بتاديب وان كان بسلامه يعطى[2048] للفهم[2049] تذكار،[2050] بالتاديب تقوم زلته، وبالسلامه تناوله حرصا.

(II.62) احد الاخوه في مبدا دخول القلايه اراد ان بالكليه يغلب[2051] الطياشه، من قبل ان يقوم حواسه[2052] البرانيه ويرتب حركاته الجوانيه، طلب ان يزمر ويصلي بلا طياشه، بنياح قبال وجهه بخاطره فقط، وفي بعض من الايام وهو يظابر[2053] انضبط بغته (R193v) بتلذذ حركة الشهوه، وانضنك قلبه واعطاه بالحلاوه (A254v) حتى قرب الموت كمثل ما[2054] خبر هو في[2055] وقت ما، وسمع صوت يناديه من غير ان ينظر احد، لا تتذمر بل قاسي جيدا، فان عدت تضابر[2056] بمقاومه وتطلب بغير واجب هذا قتال الشهوه يلاقيك.

[2042] التقلبات : R.
[2043] مينه : R.
[2044] والم : R.
[2045] اولايك : R.
[2046] الغمى : R, S.
[2047] اصبع : S / صبع : R.
[2048] تعطى : R, S.
[2049] للفهيم : R.
[2050] تذكارا : R, S.
[2051] يغلب : ساقطة R.
[2052] احواسه : R, S.
[2053] يثابر : S / يظاكر : R.
[2054] كمثلما : S.
[2055] في : ساقطة R, S
[2056] تثابر : S / تظاكر : R.

(II.63) شيخ اخر عانه الله على[2057] امور كثيره،[2058] وكان مضنوك بالامراض وفي[2059] ليلة الاحد[2060] تهاون[2061] وزل بارادته، ولم يتجلد وكان ملقى على فراشه وينضغط بطياشة افكار[2062] نجسه مده، فاتاه صوت بلا نظر وهو ماسك اصبعه[2063] اليمين، ويعصرها، وكتب له ماية وعشرين يوم في السنه انت محتاج للتوبه، كما اخبرنا هو، وخاف[2064] قايلا بالحقيقه الاراده ضعفت وليس الطبيعه، وانا خايف لاجل هذا.

(II.64) شاب اخر حد[2065] الحركات كما قد دخل القلايه مستجد،[2066] وكان يغلي بتدبير العقل ويتشوق لعدم التالم، وللعظايم،[2067] اخبرنا قايلا عندما كنت[2068] التهب بالصلوات والدموع النهار والليل وانا جاثي في الخدمه، بغته التهب قلبي وحمى جسمي بلذة حلاوة دغدغات الشهوه، حتى اني وقعت على الارض واردت ان اكدمها باسناني، وبقيت بلا عقل ولا حاسيه، وعندما رجع ذهني الى قمت فحسيت[2069] بالكليه ليس ذكر الم[2070] الزنا بل ضده، وهكذا احترق قلبي بمحبة المسيح حتى ان عندما اذكر لحبه، ولهذا تدبير القديسين، او اقرا او اصلي، يتقد في قلبي نار ويحترق جسمي بلذة الدغدغات، ويحدث لي وجع راس متواترا، حتى انه[2071] ان لم كنت احفظ نفسي كنت اسقط.

(II.65) يعقوب اسرايل[2072] ولو انه كان[2073] يحب راحيل، ولكنه[2074] صبر وعمل لاجلها سبع سنين متشوقا، وما عطيت له من قبل ليا، واتجلد ايضا

2057 في : R, S.

2058 كثير : R.

2059 في : R, S.

2060 الاحد : ساقطة R.

2061 اتهاون : R, S.

2062 افكار : R, S.

2063 صبعه : R, S.

2064 وضاف : S.

2065 حد (حاد) : S.

2066 مستحد : R.

2067 والعظايم : R, S.

2068 كتب : R.

2069 ان : زائدة R, S.

2070 لالم : R, S.

2071 انه : ساقطة S.

2072 ايسراييل : R.

2073 اذ كان : S / كان : ساقطة R.

2074 فقد : S.

وعمل (A255r) سبع سنين اخر، وعندما اخذها لم تلد اولاد حتى كملت ليا جميع اولادها، هكذا هو المتوحد وان كان يشتاق لتدبير العقل ولفضايل[2075] القديسين المرتفعه،[2076] لم يوهل لهم ان لم يصنع الجهاد اوله ويشقي[2077] احواسه البرانيه، ويكمل الاعمال الجسدانيه والنفسانيه، ويوفي دين الالام ويحفظ الوصايا.

(II.66) كما ان الصيادين يغيروا[2078] اللقط للطير[2079] والاسماك والوحوش،[2080] حسب ماكول كل واحد في الاوقات، هكذا والشياطين ايضا ياخذون منا ماده ويغيرون المجاذبات ويدغدغون بالالام، ناحية تميل الاراده للصلاح[2081] ام للشر.[2082]

(II.67) وان كان جميع الشياطين متلهفين لهلاكنا، ولكن اخرين هم الذين يقاتلون[2083] مع التدبير الجسداني، واخرين هم الذين يقاتلون[2084] مع تدبير[2085] العقل، واخرين هم الذين يرصدون[2086] القلب، ويخدعون[2087] بتنكر للذين[2088] يشتاقون للكمال.[2089] الشياطين المقاتله مع المبتديين يسموا مرده، وبغير ماده وبحده[2090] يقاتلوا، (R194r) والذين يقاتلوا مع النفسانيين، هم لطيفين وكثيرين الماده ومتحيلين بانواع كثيره، والذين يقاتلون[2091] مع الكاملين هم مهتديين،[2092] ومتجلدين، ومرصدين الاوقات ومساعدين على السيره، وما يحاربوا بحده بل

[2075] والفضايل : R.
[2076] المتفعه : R.
[2077] ويشفي : R, S.
[2078] يغيرون : R, S.
[2079] للطيور : R, S.
[2080] وللوحوش : R.
[2081] الصلاح : R, S.
[2082] الشر : R, S.
[2083] يقاتلوا : R, S.
[2084] يقاتلوا : R, S.
[2085] تدبير : ساقطة R.
[2086] يرصدوا : R, S.
[2087] ويخدعوا : R, S.
[2088] الذين : R, S.
[2089] بداية فقرة جديدة : R, S/ الكمال : R.
[2090] ويحده : R.
[2091] يقاتلوا : R, S.
[2092] هادئين : S.

بهدو،[2093] واما بطول المده اربعين وستين سنه، كما كتب في سير[2094] الشيوخ، والذين بالتغاير يقاتلون[2095] هم اشرار وقحين، منافقين غير رحومين ويدعوا خطافين.

(II.68) المتوحد الذي طرقه سايبه ومنحل في تدبيره، يزل من امواج والى[2096] امواج، من غير ان يدرا[2097] ويحس، والمتوحد زلله هي تحذير[2098] وطب للالام نفسه، لانه[2099] عندما يتالم يندم ويقوم.[2100]

(II.69) لا تطلب سلامه (A255v) من القلب ما دامت الاحواس تطيش، والنيه تنخز[2101] وتطعن من اختلاجات المجد الفارغ، ينمون من القلب افهام خفاياك ان كنت حكيم، ومن احلامك ايضا.

(II.70) طهاره النفس ببر الجسد تقتنا، وحقانية النفس بعدالة الجسد والصوم والصلوات،[2102] والسهر بالرجا والرحمه بالحب، ومن حفظ هولاء[2103] وموافقتهم، يتولد انعام التدبير الروحاني، فوق الطبيعه ويتقدس المتوحد بالروح، ويصير لله مسكن بالنور.

(II.71) القلب الذي قبل رسوم[2104] الحق، وبالهذيذ الدايم الروحاني اصطبغ بالفضايل الرييسيه، السلام والحب الروحاني، وجذور نظره الداخل انحل من الكل، وارتبط بالحب الالهي، ويفيض حياة جديده.[2105]

(II.72) الحق والنور والحياه المعقوله، في بعضهم بعض يسكنوا[2106] جوانا،[2107] وببعضهم بعض ينعرفون، ويظهرون ويقتنوا[2108] النفس.

[2093] يهدوا : R.

[2094] سيرة : R, S.

[2095] يقاتلوا : R, S.

[2096] الى : R, S.

[2097] يشعر : S.

[2098] تحزير : S.

[2099] ولانه : R.

[2100] ويتقوم : R, S.

[2101] تنخر : S.

[2102] بالصلوات : R, S.

[2103] هولا : R.

[2104] ارسوم : R.

[2105] الجديده : R, S.

[2106] يسكنون : R, S.

[2107] خوانا : R.

(II.73) وان كان الحق هو متعالي عن الخليقه، ولكن فيها هو ساكن، واذ طبيعته غير مايله يسكن في المايلين، بغير ميلان.

(II.74) حياة القديسين الذين صاروا مسكن لله، هي مرتفعه عن الرعب، وليس يقعون تحت الموت المعقول.

(II.75) حي ليس ذاك الذي لم يمت،[2109] بل الذي الموتا يحيي.

(II.76) مجد القديسين ليس هو طبيعي، وفرحهم ليس هو اختياري، واكليل عقلهم هي موهبة الله.

(II.77) ممجود جدا هو نور الشمس، وليس كمثل نور القديسين.

(II.78) هو بهي جدا الرقيع بنور الكواكب وليس كمثل رقيع[2110] قلب القديسين.

(II.79) بهجه جدا الارض في نيسان، واكثر منها ارض قلب القديسين.

(II.80) نجم الصلاه الذي يظهر في القلب، هو سلام الله المتعالي من كل عقل.

(II.81) النفس التي بلغت للسلامه، بوداعة[2111] قلبها تمجد الله، ويكونوا العقل (A256r) والضمير والافكار مهتديين، ويختلجون بفرح ما له سبب.

(II.82) فرح النفس من سلام القلب يتولد، وسكون[2112] الضمير هي علامة عدم التالم، وهدو[2113] الافكار من نور عدم الالام يولد.

(II.83) الطياشه تسما[2114] رديه عندما يطيش الذهن المجسم بامور المجسمة العالميه.

(II.84) والطياشة (R194v) الجيده هي اذا ما طاش العقل بهذيذ معرفته المخصبه،[2115] النفسانيه، بانتقال من تدبير الى تدبير، ومن تاوريا الى تاوريه[2116] ومن فهم الى فهم.

2108 ويقيتوا : R, S.

2109 يموت : R, S.

2110 ارقيع : R, S.

2111 بوادعة : R.

2112 واسكون : R, S.

2113 وهدوء : S / وهدوا : R.

2114 تسمى : S.

2115 المـ..ـصبه : R.

(II.85) جمع الذهن وسكون[2117] الضمير، يقال اذا ما هدت افكار حركات[2118] النفس من هذيذ الروحاني، على عناية وسياسة حكمة الله،[2119] التي في هذا الجميع، وتدهش النفس بسبح[2120] الله المرسوم داخل القلب.

(II.86) كثيره هي سلامة القلب ونياح الضمير، وبسهوله يكملون بالفهم وعجبا[2121] عظيم، اذا ما كان واحد من اعضا الجسد الغلاض[2122] متالم، فجميع الجسد متشوش، وهكذا هي ايضا النفس الناطقه اذا كان واحد من قواتها متقسم بالمياله، ليس تقول[2123] ان ثم هناك[2124] سلامه.

(II.87) ما دام الضمير متقسم[2125] على[2126] ذاته بخدوع[2127] واحد من الافكار، والكلام[2128] والافعال، تتكدر النفس وتتسجس الى ان يغلب الضمير بنعم او بلا.

(II.88) حركات النفس لاحواس[2129] الجسد تدبر، وحركات النفس الاراده[2130] تدبر، فان كانت الاراده منعتقه من الالام، بحسب ارادة الله يدبر، وان كان فيه الالام الى ذاك الالم[2131] بزياده يميل الذي هو غالب فيه، كمثل ان الجسد ينحرف مزاجه بحسب الكيموس الغالب مزاجه في الجسد.

(II.89) فكر الكابه كمثل بالكمين يرصد في وسط افكار الفرح، وعندما تتلهف النفس بالشهوه تقع في الكابه، (A256v) وتتعذب[2132] بجحيم الحزن،

2116 تاؤريا الى تاؤريا : S / تاوريا الى تاوريه : A.

2117 واسكون : R, S.

2118 وحركات : R, S.

2119 لله : R.

2120 كسبح : R.

2121 وعجب : R, S.

2122 (الغلاظ) : S.

2123 نقول : R, S.

2124 هاك : R.

2125 منقسم : S.

2126 في : R, S.

2127 بخداع : S.

2128 والكلام : ساقطة R.

2129 لاحواس (لحواس) : S.

2130 والارادة لحركات النفس : S.

2131 الى ذاك الالم : ساقطة S.

2132 وتتعدل : R.

لان[2133] عندما تنغلب الالام من النفس يسلموها للكابه، لكي تسحقها بوجه الفضيله.

(II.90) قيود النفس التي ما تتركها تتقدم على الرجا، هي الكابه، لانه عندما تعما[2134] النفس بالكابه تخيب من معرفة اسرار الله.

(II.91) ليس تقوا الكابه على النفس الا عندما تنغلب من الشهوه، او من بعض واحد من الالام.

(II.92) دلايل كثرة الالام وتمكنهم[2135] بالنفس وبمعرفة[2136] العالميات هي الكابه.

(II.93) المتوحد المكتيب في زمن[2137] الشيوخه،[2138] هو شاهد على نفسه انه ما عمل بالفضيله ايام مبداه، والالام ربطوه بحبال الكابه واسلموه لجلد عذاب الندم والحزن.

(II.94) النفس[2139] التي سبيت بالكابه ليس فقط هي عادمه من الصلاة الطاهره، بل ومن اشراق الشمس وحياتها هي[2140] مظلمه.

(II.95) ان كان طريق سيدنا بالنعمه اتدربت[2141] وليس بالعداله، ما ثم[2142] كابه في طريق سيدنا.

(II.96) الحزن الذي من اجل الله يملا[2143] القلب فرح، ويحلى[2144] كل مرارة تدنوا من النفس، وتهديها من سجس التكدر والغيره، وتعطيها وجه وداله بالرجا على الله.

2133 بداية فقرة جديدة : R, S.

2134 تعمى : S.

2135 وتمكينهم : R, S.

2136 وبالمعرفه : R, S.

2137 زمان : S / زما : R.

2138 الشيخوخه : R, S.

2139 والنفس : R.

2140 كلها : S.

2141 تدبرت : S.

2142 ثم (ثمة) : S.

2143 يملى : R, S.

2144 وتحلى : R, S.

(II.97) ليس طب للكاابه[2145] كمثل محقرة الذات والازدرا بنفسه، وانه لا يحسب نفسه شي ولا يطلب مديح.

(II.98) ليس في الكاابه سلامه، بل تكون النفس مملوه عذاب وندم وظلمه وقلبا مر. (R195r)

(II.99) سلام النفس الدايم يتولد من بساطة الضمير، ووداعته، او من كمال الذهن والافراز والتميز المرتب على الدوام، ويحفظون الضمير والافكار ان لا يتحركوا[2146] بالخباط والغيره.

(II.100) سلام النفس يشبه الماء[2147] الصافي المجموع الذي ليس فيه[2148] دبيب من داخل، ولا تكدر من خارج، يحركون ويخبطون، (A257r) نقاوتها[2149] لان صفواتها هي كمثل المراه للعيون، بصقالة[2150] المراة النفسانيه، ان لم تتكدر والافكار من داخل، ولا تتكدر بوساطة السماع النظر[2151] وبقيه ما تدخله الاحواس من خارج، لان اذا ما كانت مراة النفس صافيه، تنظر وتتعجب النفس[2152] بحسن طبيعتها.

(II.101) لذيذه جدا هي تصور تاورية[2153] عناية الله وسياسته،[2154] وعندما يجوز الذهن على المتجسمين[2155] والغير متجسمين، وعلى افعال القوات الروحانيه المخفيه الفاعله في هذا الكل، وترفع النفس وتجعلها بغير اهتمام.

(II.102) تاورية[2156] النفس اذا ما جازت على الطبايع وامور الخليقه، ترتفع وتنحط معهن بالانتقال من هذا الى هذا، والطياشه الى نظرة الحق.

(II.103) بتاوريا[2157] الثالوث المقدس ليس مصاعد وحدورات[2158] ولا طياشة انتقال، بل نظرة متساويه تربط بالدهش بها، لجميع الذين استحقوا نظرتها.

[2145] الكاابه : R.
[2146] يتحركون : R, S.
[2147] الما : R.
[2148] فيه : ساقطة R.
[2149] بداية فقرة جديدة : S.
[2150] بسقاله : R.
[2151] والنظر : R, S.
[2152] النفس : ساقطة R.
[2153] ثاؤرية : S / تاورية : ساقطة A.
[2154] بداية فقرة جديدة : S.
[2155] المجسمين : R, S.
[2156] ثاؤرية : S / تااورية : A.

(III) الميمر الثالث في رووس المعرفه للقديس مار اسحق.[2159]

(III.1) ايمان مواعيد المسيح اقنا[2160] لطبيعة[2161] البشر الرجا والثقه.

(III.2) بمحبة حقانية تعليم يسوع بطلت جميع علوم معرفة الطغيان.

(III.3) اذا ما ثبتت[2162] رجا الانسان بامانة المسيح وملكت المواعيد داخل في النفس، عند ذلك[2163] تلتهب النفس بالحب الالهي وتنفتح في الحال الابواب الداخله، القلبيه، ويشرق بغته النور والفرح والعزا.

(III.4) بقدر ما يلتهب الانسان بحب المسيح ويتامل رجاه ويتلهف لمواعيده، ويهدس بهن، هكذا يبتلع بالسيره ويستضي ضميره بالروح.

(III.5) المتوحد المتيقظ[2164] الحريص بتدبير السيره، ونفسه متواضعه وبسيط بضميره،[2165] (A257v) فان كان يغلو[2166] بحب المسيح، ويحفظ حقوق سكون القلايه، ويحترس بماله، وفيه افراز، بالسنه الاوله[2167] من جلوسه، في القلايه كمثل العربون تذوقه[2168] سر[2169] روح التوبه، لعزا ضعفه باقتصار حد كل التدبير.

(III.6) ان كان ما يطيش وينجذب في امور[2170] كثيره، وينعتق من المجاذبات وخباط[2171] هموم المربيات،[2172] ويقتني احتقار لذاته[2173] ويحب الثبات في

[2157] بثاؤرية : S / بتااوريا : A.

[2158] واحدودات (حدود) : S / واحدورات : R.

[2159] ايسحاق : R.

[2160] اقنى : S.

[2161] الطبيعة : R.

[2162] ثبت : S / تثبت : R.

[2163] ذالك : R.

[2164] المتيقظ : R, S / المتيقض : A.

[2165] بطيره : A.

[2166] يغلوا : R, S.

[2167] الاولى : S.

[2168] تدوق (تذوقه) : S.

[2169] سر : ساقطة S.

[2170] امور : R, S.

[2171] واخباط : R, S.

الهدو،[2174] ويسرع في تبع سلامة القلب، ويحترس بعمله ويحفظ حقوق سكون القلايه، ويخر كل يوم[2175] قدام النعمه، تكمل هي النعمه قليل بالفعل جميع ما دوقته (R195v) سريا بالسنة الاوله، حسب ترتيبه وعمله[2176] بالسيره.

(III.7) اذ[2177] كان الله ساكن في كلا[2178] بالكل بالتمام، ولكن كل واحد كمقدار[2179] امانته بالمسيح يقدر ينظر افعاله.

(III.8) بيت قدس الاقداس الجواني الذي للقلب هو مسكن المسيح من العماد، ولم ينفتح الا بكلية الرجا به، ولم يدخل داخل من حجاب بابه شي من اختلاجات حركات النفس ابدا، بل هو العقل العاري المتكمل بنور طبيعته،[2180] وقد لبس الايمان والرجا[2181] والحب الحقيقي.

(III.9) من حين خالف ادم الوصيه والى[2182] حين جا المسيح، ليس من فتح هذا الباب الجواني القلبي، بل ربنا المسيح بكمال طاعته لابيه فتحه بالروح وسكن فيه.

(III.10) كلمن قد اعتمد بالروح عندما يتعرا[2183] الانسان الالام[2184] العتيق مع[2185] جميع تقلبات الجسد وشهواته، ويلبس المسيح بالكليه بحفظ وصاياه، بنور الايمان والرجا به، يوهل عقله ان يدخل وينظر وجه المسيح بوجه مكشوف، وداله.

(III.11) المتوحد الذي تتلهف نفسه ان (A258r) تحس[2186] باسرار الله الخفيه، ان كان ما يشبع[2187] نفسه من شهوات ارادته ما ينظر مجد الله هاهنا.

2172 المريات : R, S.

2173 الذات : R, S.

2174 الهدوء : S / الهدوا : R.

2175 وقت : R, S.

2176 تربية عمله : R, S.

2177 اذا : S.

2178 ساكن كل : R, S.

2179 بمقدار : R, S.

2180 طبعته : R.

2181 ولرجا : R.

2182 الى : R, S.

2183 يتعرى : S.

2184 الالمي : S.

2185 من : S.

2186 يحس : R, S.

(III.12) ايها التايب الحقاني لا تترك مبد[2188] ووسط درجات التوبه، وتضبط بغته درجه الكمال وتقول ان الله رحوم، وان شاء[2189] يعطيني مراحمه انعام، كما اعطا لكثيرين مواهب نعمته في كل الاجيال، ليس بمعرفه تضمر[2190] بهولاء،[2191] لان العجايب والقوات ليس من اجل المومنين يعطوا، بل لاجل الغير مومنين.[2192]

(III.13) فضيحة عظيمه وحزن النفس في العالم الجديد، عندما تتعرا[2193] من البر الظنون،[2194] وتلبس الخجل وخزية الندم، تجاه جميع الملايكه والبشر.

(III.14) البر المضنون[2195] هاهنا بالعالم المزمع خجل وخزي وظلام يعد للنفس بالجحيم.

(III.15) الشياطين هم راصدين ارادتنا ليلا[2196] ونهار، لينظروا لاي[2197] ناحيه يميل ضميرنا، وبحسب[2198] ميالة الاراده والضمير يصلحون مجاذبات بكل نوع، ويخدعون النفس وما يعرفوا،[2199] ان تنجح[2200] ضرباتهم ام لا، لانه ليس فيهم قوه ان بالغضب يخطفون حريتنا، لان مشيتنا[2201] هي حره، ان تريد الشمال او ناحية اليمين تميل.

(III.16) الانسان بطبيعته هو تام كمثلما[2202] ناسوت المسيح، ويهوذا الدافع، وبحرية ارادته يميل اما ان يرث مجد ربنا المسيح،[2203] او هلاك يهوذا الاسخريوطي.

2187 تشبع : R, S.
2188 مبدا : R, S.
2189 اشاء : S / اشا : R.
2190 تضمر (تذمر) : S.
2191 بهولا : R / هؤلاء : S.
2192 المؤمنين : S.
2193 تتعرى : S.
2194 المضنون (المظنون) : S / المظنون : R.
2195 المضنون (المظنون) : S.
2196 ليل : R, S.
2197 لكي اي : R, S.
2198 وحسب : R, S.
2199 يعرفون : R, S.
2200 تنجح : ساقطة R.
2201 مشيئتنا : S.
2202 كمثل ما : R.
2203 يسوع المسيح : S.

(III.17) نفس الانسان هي مناسبه ملايكة النور، والشياطين الانجاس، وبارادتها ترث اما نور الملايكه القديسين، او ظلام الشياطين المنافقين.

(III.18) اذا ما العقل يفتقد، يفتقد[2204] افكار الشهوه او لواحد من الالام، الذين[2205] قد هدوا وسكتوا، ان كان يثبت في مفاوضتهم (R196r) ويتنازل[2206] معهم بالام، يحركون (A258v) الفعل ويغرقوه بالذكر، وينجسوا العقل الطاهر.

(III.19) ليس التاورية[2207] العاليه نور الافهام والمعرفة الدقيقه، وفضايل السهر والصوم والتورع والنسك، تعد الاكاليل للقديسين، بل الغرض والقصد الذي لاجله تنعمل الفضايل، مقابل الالام.

(III.20) مقبول عند الله سقوط[2208] باتضاع وندامه، اكثر من القيام بافتخار.[2209]

(III.21) نور الضمير الذي تقول عنه الابا هو نور التواضع والهدو،[2210] والذي[2211] اوراه ربنا بذاته.

(III.22) ليس لنا ان نتعلم علوم الحق من دون قراة الكتب المقدسه، والهذيذ بالفضايل، واعمال التوبه، والسهر، والصلوات، والدموع.

(III.23) قراه الكتب هي ماده لتعليم معرفة الحق، اعمال التوبه، والنسك، والبقيه هم ابواب بوساطتهم يقبل الضمير نور عدم الالام، والهذيذ بالفضايل الرييسيه هم رسوم روحانيه، يرسم[2212] فيهم مراة القلب.

(III.24) كما ان نور الضمير هو اشرف من نور الشمس، للذي[2213] قد استحق هكذا، وايضا النمو[2214] الذي ينبت من[2215] القلب الطاهر الغني بالله، هو افضل من الماده التي تقبل من اخرين، من غير العمل في ذاتنا.

2204 يفتقد : ساقطة S.

2205 الذي : R.

2206 يتنازل : R.

2207 الثاؤرية : S / التاورية : A.

2208 اسقوط : R.

2209 بالافتخار : R, S.

2210 والهدوء : S / والهدوا : R.

2211 الذي : R, S.

2212 يرتسم : R, S.

2213 الذي : R.

(III.25) وان كان العقل من قوة الكتب المقدسه يتيقظ[2216] ان يقبل ثانيا زروع التعليم الروحاني،[2217] ولكن ميقظين الزروع الصالحه التي لطبيعتنا[2218] في[2219] خلقتنا.

(III.26) بلا منفعه هي النطقيه اذا ارتفعت عنها الحريه، وهكذا ايضا والحريه اذا ارتفعت عنها النطقيه.

(III.27) النطقيه الحقانيه هي التي تقانتها مسلطه على حرية الاراده، وتتمدح[2220] افعال حريتها من النية الصالحه الذاتيه، ومن اخرين.

(III.28) الينبوع الذي يسعد من جري السيول، عندما تبطل (A259r) السيول ينشف النبع، والقلب الذي يستغني من التصور الذي[2221] من غير الهذيذ الدايم العقلي، واعمال القلب مع سكون اللسان تبطل فرحته.

(III.29) سعيده هي الارض التي ينبع منها الذهب والفضه والفصوص الكريمه، واسعد منها القلب الغني بالحب والهدو[2222] والسلامه والفرح.

(III.30) غنا[2223] النفس المباركه هو نبات صالح ينمو[2224] من القلب بالنعمه.

(III.31) كل غنا[2225] ان يكون من برا وهو محدود من القلب هو تحت الخوف والخطر، وكل فرح[2226] يكون من برا النفس هي التخيلات، وكل ذكرا[2227] يكون خارج عن عالم الجديد هو ظلالة[2228] الاحلام.

2214 النموا : R.

2215 في : R.

2216 يتيقض : A.

2217 الروحانيه : R, S.

2218 لطبيعة : R, S.

2219 في : ساقطة R, S.

2220 وتتمرح : R.

2221 التي : R.

2222 والهدوء : S / والهدوا : R.

2223 عنى : S.

2224 ينموا : R.

2225 غنى : S.

2226 فرط : R.

2227 ذكر : R, S.

2228 ظلالة (ضلالة) : S.

(III.32) طوبا[2229] للنفس الساكنه بالكليه، وقد ذاقت في داخلها شهد نمو[2230] نبات القلب.

(III.33) طوبا ثم طوبا[2231] للعقل الذي تجر[2232] بتصورات اخرين، واستغنا غنا[2233] روحاني في ذاته، وصار غني بما له وباخرين، وهو هذا الكاتب الذي قال عنه سيدنا انه قد اتلمذ لملكوت السماء.

(III.34) (R196v) ينبوع نور القلب الذي سالم كل انسان واصطلح مع الكل، ومع ذاته.

(III.35) الشمس[2234] الجديد المشرق في قلب النفس، التي ما فيها شر، وتفرح جميع الناس بالسويه.

(III.36) ليس احدا[2235] حي فيه كفوا ان يعيش بالبطاله، ان لم تنربط[2236] بشي، لان بحسب الامر الالهي ان بعرق جبينك تاكل خبزك.

(III.37) المتوحد الذي يحفظ عقله، ويظن به من كثيرين انه بطال من كل عمل، ليس[2237] احدا[2238] اتعب منه ولا عمال مثله.

(III.38) بسكون العقل فقط يبطل كل عمل، لان العقل ابتلع فوق الطبع بالحب الالهي، وصار اله[2239] في وسط الناس بخفيه[2240] عقله.

(III.39) (A259v) مبدا الهذيذ هو ان يغصب الانسان ذاته قصر،[2241] ان يعدم من كل مفاوضة بشريه، ويداوم قراة الكتب والتزمير، لان من هولا يتولد داخل العقل نمو[2242] الهذيذ الروحاني، ومن مداومة الهذيذ يكون جمع العقل.

[2229] طوبى : S.

[2230] نموا : R.

[2231] طوبى ثم طوبى : S.

[2232] تاجر : S.

[2233] واستغنى غنى : S.

[2234] شمس : R, S.

[2235] احد : S.

[2236] يرتبط : S.

[2237] وليس : R, S.

[2238] احد : S.

[2239] الاه (اله) : S / الاه : R.

[2240] بصفاء : S.

[2241] قصرا : S.

[2242] نموا : R.

(III.40) مبدا نمو[2243] الهذيذ بالعقل، هي ان يجلس الانسان في الاوقات[2244] في موضع مظلم، ويهذ في قلبه الصلوات والتسابيح، التي[2245] يعرفهن، ويرتب تلاوه من عنده حسب قوته، وهو مهتدي وعقله مجموع بالهذيذ، ولا يقطع هذا الهذيذ، لا ليلا[2246] ولا نهار، ولا ان خرج لعمل[2247] او ينام.

(III.41) فان كان هو مفرز ويحفظ حقوق القلايه ويحترس بما يخصه، حتى لا يسقط جسده، ويحترس بلا فتور على الدوام بتيقظ،[2248] ليلا يضحك به من طغيان الشيطان،[2249] ويطيل روحه داخل السكون مده، ويسال نعمة الله بحزن ودموع بقلب منسحق، يوهل لنبات القلب الروحاني.

(III.42) خبر اخ ان من كثرة الحراره التي في قلبي، نمت بعد مزامير الليل، وانا جالس، وعندما اتيقظت[2250] خدمت مزامير بكره بهذيذ قلبي جميعهم، بلا نقص والتلاوه ايضا وبقية الصلاه.

(III.43) ليس ينكتبوا[2251] كلام الروح على دفتر القلب بقلم اللسان الا بهذيذ العقل.

(III.44) ليس يوهل المتوحد لنور الضمير ما دام يجري تبع امور يجدها ليشبع بها جوعه الى ان يشبع من الكل، ويقبض[2252] ذاته من الكل، ويصير واحد.

(III.45) ما يستطيع الضمير يقبض ذاته من الكل، الا بهذيذ العقل المخفي من[2253] الكل.

(III.46) كل غنا[2254] وكل سلام ونياح وفرح يكون من برا القلب محدود، هو ظلاله[2255] وتخيل السلام.[2256]

2243 نموا : R.

2244 الاقوات : R.

2245 الذي : R, S.

2246 ليل : R, S.

2247 ما : زائدة R.

2248 بتيقض : A.

2249 الشياطين : R, S.

2250 اتيقضت : A.

2251 ينكتبون : R, S.

2252 ويمسك : S.

2253 في : R.

2254 غنى : S.

(III.47) لم يقتني المتوحد (A260r) حرية النفس واتساع القلب، من دون الانفراد عن خلطة الناس، ولا القلب يوهل للنمو[2257] الروحاني الذي من النعمه، ما دام العقل ما يبطل ينبوعه من نبات كل معرفه.[2258]

(III.48) لا يمكن ان يسكن[2259] مع (R197r) القريب بالسلامه من غير مراياة الحب، ولا يمكن ان يسكن[2260] المعرفة النفسانيه مع نمو[2261] الروح.

(III.49) اذا ما اسلم المتوحد بكل كليته نفسه لله بمفاوضة الصلاه والهذيذ الخفي، وجمع الضمير وحفظ القلب من الطياشه، ولم تبعد[2262] الشياطين اللطيفه من عنده بل يرصدوه من غير ان يقاتلوا معه، ويزرعوا فيه حراره بزياده، ويتحيلوا عليه بخداغ بطلب سيرة عاليه، لعلهم يستطيعوا[2263] ان يرموه اذا ما طمع بالسير الى قدام، كمثلما كتبوا الابا.

(III.50) المتوحد الذي بالكمال اسلم نفسه للمسيح هو مفتقر الى احتراس عظيم خارج وداخل، والى محقرة الذات، والى معونة[2264] النعمه، والى هداية اب روحاني، الذي جرب الامور في ذاته وشقى في برية التوبه، وصبر على الضوايق وحس بكمينات الشياطين، وحيلهم وسقط في الالام وقام بنعمة الله، وعبر الاردن.

(III.51) عسر جدا الم الرغبه ومحبة الذهب والقنيان، ومع هذا ما يساوي رغبت[2265] النفس في العلوم لتجد امورا جديده وتفهم اشيا كثيره.

(III.52) لذيذ جدا اقتنا الذهب وليس كمثل اقتنا الحكمه، حلو[2266] هو الشهد في الفم، وليس كمثل العلم للنفس،[2267] ردية هي الشهوة الكلبيه برغبتها، وليس كمثل القلب الذي يحب ان يفيض امورا جديده.

[2255] ظلالة (ضلالة) : S.

[2256] الاحلام : S.

[2257] للنموا : R.

[2258] معارف : R, S.

[2259] نسكن : R, S.

[2260] تسكن : R, S.

[2261] نموا : R.

[2262] تبتعد : R, S.

[2263] يستطبوا : R.

[2264] معرفة : R.

[2265] رغبة : R, S.

[2266] حلوا : R, S.

[2267] النفس : R.

(III.53) اه من النفس (A260v) التي تبذل برغبتها الم الذهب والمقتنا[2268] بالم الحكمه والعلم بالتحيل والصنايع، لان الرب عارف بما في القلوب، ويكافي كل واحد حسب غرضه وعمله.

(III.54) غنا[2269] الجسد سهل تبديده[2270] اكثر من جمعه، وغنا النفس سهل جمعه بحرارة حدة الحركات من ان يخفيه، واما الاتحاد بالمسيح واحد هو المطلوب وغيرها لا وهي[2271] الحب التام الى القريب، لان به يكمل حب الله.

(III.55) ما دام يتقسم ضميرك بتاوريا[2272] ما من[2273] بعد وجودها، النفس والجسد[2274] موتا، فان كنت عايز، اكثر الدموع والصلوات واجمع ضميرك من الكل الى واحد.

(III.56) حياة الصلب مخفيه من الميتوته من الكل، ولا يمكن الصعود لصلب الاراده ما دامت مرتبطه بشي،[2275] اطرد وانفي[2276] من قلبك الاهتمام بمعرفة الخير والشر، لكي يدخل ويسكن فيك المسيح شجرة الحياه، وتحس بالامور الشريفه التي فوق الطبع واسرار العالم الجديد.

(III.57) المتوحد الذي لا[2277] يشخص في قلبه عندما يصلي ويزمر، انما يصارع الريح، ولا يستضي بالصلاه.

(III.58) المتوحد الذي يشخص[2278] عيني عقله في قلبه عندما يصلي، سريع (R197v) يوهل للرحمه.

(III.59) المتوحد الذي يقرن لسانه مع ضميره، بالروح يزمر.

(III.60) وان كان بقمع احواس الجسد يتضع وينير القلب، ولكن اثمار القلب اشرف من اثمار اللسان، لان من فضلات القلب تنطق الشفتين.

2268 المقتنيات : S.

2269 غنى : S.

2270 تبتيده : R.

2271 وهو وهي : A.

2272 بتاورية : A.

2273 من : ساقطة R, S.

2274 الجد : R.

2275 بداية فقرة جديدة : S.

2276 وانف : S.

2277 ما : R, S.

2278 تشخص : R, S.

(III.61) خطر هو على المتوحد الكثير الاوراق ان كان الاثمار قليل، ولو ان الورق في العين حسن ولكن ما ينعصرون في قدح الملك، مكتوب ان الورق هو للطب[2279] (A261r) والشفا[2280] للاحواس،[2281] والاثمار هم غدا النفس.

(III.62) لم ينعتق المتوحد من الطياشه الا بمداومة مفاوضة الصلاه، ولم يوهل لمفاوضة الصلاه، الا بجمع العقل، ولا ينجمع العقل من الطياشه الا بهذيذ تدبير الضمير، وليس تتولد التدابير الروحانيه بالنفس الا من القرااة الدايمه والثبات في السكون، وتذكار الفضايل.

(III.63) لم يقبل القلب الرزع الروحاني ان لم تنمحي[2282] من القلب جميع الصور، الخلق،[2283] والغضبيه، والحسد، والشر، وتصطبغ[2284] النفس بالفضايل الرييسيه، السلام، والحب، والفرح،[2285] والعزا بروح القدس.

(III.64) اربع غيارات الارض[2286] اظهر سيدنا في بشارته، ان في قلب كل واحد واحد[2287] منا، ولكن ينبغي ان كل واحد يفهم نوع ارض قلبه، لكي من هاهنا يعرف الناطق المفرز نوع عمل ارض قلبه، وزرع يوافق تربية ارض قلبه، ليلا يزرع[2288] بتغير شي عوض شي، ويصير تعبنا باطل.

(III.65) وحتى اذا ما ازدرع الزرع الروحاني بالقلب، فهو مفتقر لسقي كلام روح القدس، واعمال وسياج الحفظ، والتنظيف من الم الزوان،[2289] والى مدة ايام يتربا[2290] الزرع ويطول.

(III.66) ويصنع[2291] اثمار الروح، ليلا عوض السلام والنور، ينبت علقم وصبر ظلام النفس.

2279 طب : S / الطب : R.

2280 وشفاء : S.

2281 الاحواس : R, S.

2282 تمتحي (تنمحي) : S / تمتحي : R.

2283 القلق : R.

2284 وتسطبغ : R.

2285 الفرح : R.

2286 للارض : S.

2287 واحد : ساقطة S.

2288 نزرع : R.

2289 الزيوان : R, S.

2290 تتربا : R, S.

2291 بداية فقرة جديدة : A.

(III.67) من الذي ما هو مشابهك بغرض ضميرك اتجنب منه بسلام ومعرفه، ولا تعاشره لان الماء الذي من العلو[2292] بسهوله ينزلون الى اسفل، واما من اسفل بعد جهد يصعدون، لانك عندما ترفعه الى فوق ينحدر بالنزول الى اسفل.

(III.68) ليس الم بسهوله يهدم بنيان برج الفضايل،[2293] (A261v) التي للسلامه كمثلما تكون جالس، وتتفكر في اخيك لكي تعرف ان كان تدبيره حسن ام لا.

(III.69) حياة المتوحد[2294] المعقوله الحقانيه مخفيه بحفظ القلب، فالذي ما يحفظ قلبه بكل احتراس لا يمكنه ان يصير بار بالفعل، ولا يقدر ان يتضيق ويحتمل التجارب التي تحدث عليه بغير تذمر.

(III.70) اما ان يكون واحد صديق ويحصا[2295] مع جملة القديسين سهل ويمكن،[2296] من غير تصفيه واختبار في كور التجارب، من اجل مراحم سيدنا المسيح المسجود له، الذي صار وسيط[2297] (R198r) بين الله للخليقه ليدعو[2298] الخطاه للتوبه.

(III.71) بعد جهد يوجد صديق[2299] قد اختبرت صدوقيته بكور التجارب المختلفه والضوايق الصعبه، والمرض والعوز مع المحقرات والعار[2300] والازدرا من الاصدقا والمعارف، وحمل جميعهم بغير تذمر كالابا القدما.

(III.72) لان الشعب الاسرايبلي دفعة واحده سميوا بالله، من اجل الابا ابراهيم[2301] واسحق ويعقوب ويوسف وموسى، وبقية الابا الذي[2302] صفيوا واختبروا واتنقوا بالتجارب، والضغطات واخذوا رسم الختان والسنن والاحكام

2292 العلوا : R.

2293 الرييسيه : زائدة R, S.

2294 المتوحدين : R, S.

2295 وييصي : R / ويحصى : A.

2296 يمكل : R.

2297 وسيطا : S.

2298 ليدعوا : R, S.

2299 ضيق : R.

2300 مع المحقرات والعار : ساقطة A.

2301 ابرهيم : R.

2302 الذين : S.

والشهادات، وعندما زاغوا بني اسراييل من الله، ولم يحفظوا[2303] السنن والاحكام الموضوعه لهم، وجا عليهم التاديب بقصاص يستحقوه، صرخوا الى الله قايلين لم نطلبك ولا نريد السنن والاحكام التي وضعت[2304] لنا، اتركنا نتدبر كالشعوب الغريبه الذي ما دعي اسمك عليهم.

(III.73) اجاب الرب الرحوم ليس اترككم تتدبرون مثل الشعوب الغريبه، التي بلا اله، من اجل ابايكم الذين صبروا لتجاربي،[2305] (A262r) واختبر حبهم الصادق معي، واعطيتهم عهد ليكونوا اولادهم لي شعبا وانا اكون لهم اله، ولا يمكن ان اكون اله للذين لم يحفظوا[2306] سنني، واحكامي ووصاياي.[2307]

(III.74) كل واحد واحد منا الذين بحرية ارادتنا في ذاتنا،[2308] قبلنا رسم مفروز وعاهدنا الله عهدا، ان نحفظ بر المسيح بحفظ وصاياه[2309] المقدسه، وافترزنا من العالم باسكيم البر الطاهر، ينبغي ان[2310] ندين كل يوم نياتنا، ان كان يوافق تدبيرنا كل وقت للعهد الذي عاهدناه، منذ المبدا، وان لا، من غير ارادتنا كالاولاد الاحبا نودب[2311] بالرحمه، بكور التجارب والضوايق والامراض، والعوز والعار، والازدرا من القريبين والبعدين،[2312] لكيلا نبقا غربا من ميراث المسيح، الذي اليه دعينا انفسنا، ونتجلد ونحتمل بشكر وفرح، ولا[2313] نتذمر كالجهال، الذين ليس لهم اله، بل نفرح برجانا.

(III.75) نتذكر يا احباي بربنا ذلك[2314] المكتوب ان بضوايق كثيره ينبغي لنا ان ندخل ملكوت[2315] الله، والاخره ان من يحبه الرب يودبه، كمثل الاب الذي يودب بنيه، وايضا ان اسلمت نفسك لله اصبر على جميع التجارب، وما تبقا، ونصبر بفرح بارادتنا،[2316] لانه ليس لنا مفاص[2317] من التجارب، لم يشا الله ان

2303 يحفظون : R, S.

2304 اوضعت : R, S.

2305 تجاربي : R, S.

2306 يحفظون : R, S.

2307 ووصاي : R.

2308 ذواتنا : R, S.

2309 وصياه : R.

2310 ان : ساقطة R.

2311 نتودب : R, S.

2312 البعيدين : R, S.

2313 ولا : ساقطة R.

2314 ذالك : R.

2315 لملكوت : R, S.

2316 وبغير ارادتنا : زائدة R, S.

الذي قد دعي اسمه عليهم ان يكونوا بني الهلاك، بل يقاصصنا بكل نوع ويدخلنا لميراثه المقدس، ليلا نتخلف خارج عن الباب.

(III.76) الله خالق طبيعتنا منذ المبداء،[2318] اقرن الشفا لميالة طبعنا، معرفة الخير والشر مع حرية الاراده، وزاد على يد موسى ناموس سنة العدل، (A262v) لكي كل واحد عوض ميالته يقدم مفرزا اعتراف ذبيحة الغفران في الهيكل الذي بيروشليم، المسيح ربنا خالق طبيعتنا الذي له السلطان (R198v) على كل شي كالسيد[2319] على بيته، عوض العداله اجاد بالنعمه مجانا،[2320] قايلا كل احدا[2321] في كل موضع بنفسه داخل وخارج.

(III.77) التوبه هي مراحم المسيح ربنا، لازق[2322] بالكل ومشجع طبعنا قايلا،[2323] ان كنت زليت واخطيت اعترف بذنبك وتوب وانا معك اساعد ضعفك.

(III.78) ذبيحة التوبه بربنا هي القلب الذي[2324] اتضع وانسحق وانكسر بدموع الصلاه قدام الله، ويطلب المغفره لضعف ميالته، وعجز قريبه وذاته هو.

(III.79) نعمه المسيح ربنا بالتوبه حاله وتسال الناس اطلبوا بالصلاه وخذوا، ليلا يكون علينا لوم من العداله.[2325]

(III.80) النفس التي تفرز بالعدل الصالحين من الاشرار، والصديقين من الخطاه، ولها هي ايضا تفرزها معرفتها من الله، من غير ان تحس.

(III.81) المتوحد الذي بالعداله يدبر حياته ويوزن صلاحه قبال شروره، ويدعا لابس المسيح، وينتظر لمكافات[2326] اعماله الصالحه، الى الان ما قد حس بضعفه، ولا ايضا بنعمة المسيح الفايضه على الخطاه والصديقين مجان.[2327]

2317 مناص : S.

2318 مبدا : R.

2319 كل سيد : R.

2320 مجان : R.

2321 احد : R, S.

2322 لازقة : S.

2323 قالا : A.

2324 قد : زائدة R, S.

2325 العدالة (العادلة) : S / العادله : R.

2326 لمكافأة : S.

2327 مجانا : S.

(III.82) الناموس القديم جميعه يعلم العدل، وصيه المسيح هي ضد العدل، نعمه ورااقه[2328] ورحمه مجان،[2329] اعترف بما اخذت وامن انك تاخذ، بما انت اليه محتاج، واسال واطلب بالصلاه تاخذ.

(III.83) الف وسبعماية سنه واكثر خدم ناموس العداله، ولا صديق واحد ما اذنب للناموس وقدم قربان (A263r) عوض ذنبه وجد فيهم نعمه، المسيح ربنا في وقت قليل عتق الوف وربوات مالها عدد، بالتوبه مجان عتق من الخطيه وجمعهم الى اهرا الملكوت.

(III.84) نطقية النفس من حين خرجت من بلد بساطتها ووداعة الطبيعه، قامت في مفرق الطرق بالشكوك، بدم ذاتها على حد حرف سيف معرفة النفسانيه، اذ تجد بها دغدغة الالام والشياطين بقوه هاهنا، وتجد بها ايضا مجاذبات تنعم الملكوت ومجد القديسين الى هاهنا، والنعمه ترصد وحاملة اكليل العدل، وسايره تبع حرية الاراده بلا تغصب، والنيه تونب وتبكت وتدين وتهدد غصب، وتوري الاثمار[2330] التي من الناحيتين، والحريه لها ان تميل اما لليمين او للشمال.

(III.85) الخير والشر يلاقي القديسين في طريق تدبير الفضيله، وليس يسموا برا[2331] او خطيه اذا ما نشطنا في[2332] الحق.

(III.86) الخطايا من الالام تتولد، والالام من عدم الايمان، وعدم الايمان من عدم المعرفه.

(III.87) من حركات شهوة النفس تتولد حرارة الغلوه، ومن الحركات الغضبيه تتحرك النشاط[2333] الطبيعيه في الانسان، ان لم يحتر ويلتهب بمحبة ذاك الشي الذي يحبه ويقتنيه.

(III.88) النفس عندما تشتعل بشهوة الشي الذي تحبه، عند ذلك[2334] تتحرك الغضبيه بالنشاط الطبيعي، ليساعد الشهوه لتكمل[2335] ارادتها، وتبدى تحتر (R199r) من داخل وتنبح مقابل الذين (A263v) يقاوموا لمضادد الشهوه.

[2328] ورافه : R, S.

[2329] مجانا : S.

[2330] الثمار (الاثمار) : S.

[2331] بر : R.

[2332] في : R, S.

[2333] (اعني الوثبات) : زائدة S / اعني الوثبات : زائدة R.

[2334] ذالك : R.

(III.89) الالام بحلاوه يصنعون[2336] لذة الدغدغات، ان كان اليمين او الشمال الذين من الشهوه يتولدون، كمثل محبة المديح والكرامه، والشره والشر والزنا وما تبقا، والم الغضبيه الخارجه عن الطبع هم الخلق الردي والغيض، والكابه والحسد والشر.

(III.90) الرجل الشهواني ان[2337] كان ما هو رزين وهادي، لكن[2338] يفيض[2339] منه حلاوة الحب والرحمه، والرجل الغضوب وان كان متاسس ومتفهم ولكن عكر الدم الاسود يفعل فيه الظلام، ونفسه مريره ومملوه كابه وغيض، وكمثل الاكل والشرب يزيد عليهم، ومتغير اللون، وسيي المنظر والحلم.[2340]

(III.91) والشهوه الطبيعيه اذا ما اشتاقت بالطبع تكون للالهيات، والغضبية الطبيعيه تنبح بالطبع في الالام والشرور، والشهوة الغير طبيعيه تشتاق الى الالام السمجه والشرور، والغضبية الغير طبيعيه ايضا، تنبح في الفضايل وتضادد الصلاح.

(III.92) الفضايل الطبيعه،[2341] اعني البر والصدوقيه، وحفظ الوصايا، مع[2342] الغلبه للالام، تستطيع النفس ان تقتنيهم ما داموا قوتيها الاثنين اعني الشهوه والغضبيه بالطبع يتحركوا،[2343] ويفعلون مقابل الالام والشرور، وان تحس بالاسرار المكتومه الالهيه المقدسه فوق الطبع بمعرفة الحق والعالم الجديد ما تستطيع، الا ان قوتيها الشهوه والغضبيه يقمعون وحشية الالام وهم ايضا يضعفوا ويهتدوا،[2344] ويستيقظ[2345] العقل (A264r) والذهن والافراز والتمييز،[2346] ويتجددوا بالسلامه القلب والافكار والضمير، من مقاومتهم وغيرتهم مقابل الالام والشر.

2335 لتكميل : R, S.

2336 يصنون : A.

2337 وان : R, S.

2338 ولكن : R, S.

2339 تفيض : R, S.

2340 وغير حليم : S.

2341 الطبيعيه : R, S.

2342 من : R.

2343 يتحركون : R, S.

2344 بداية فقرة جديدة : S / ويهدءوا : S.

2345 ويستيقض : A.

2346 والتميز : R.

(III.93) الام الجسد من بذخ[2347] البطن يتولدون، والام النفس من[2348] قلة التاديب ومن عدم معرفة العقل، ومن قلة الامانه تتشجع الالام ويتكملون بالاراده اذا قبلتهم، ويتحركون للفعل[2349] بالتذكار والاحواس.

(III.94) الام الجسد هم الشره الزنا نياح الجسد، وما تبقا، الام النفس الشهوه الغضبيه والافكار، الجسد الضجر والافتخار، والشر وما تبقا، ومن الشهوه ياخذون ماده لفعلهم، وان كان ليس شهوه لم تفعل الغضبيه، وان لم تتحرك الغضبيه ويملك الخطباط[2350] ما تفعل الالام.

(III.95) كل الم يقاتل معنا اذا ما بلطافه نفتش على سببه، نرا[2351] ان من الشهوه ياخذ المبتدا، ان كان ليس احواس من خارج وتذكار من داخل تبطل،[2352] الالام وتبقا بلا فعل، فان كان الاراده شجيعه قويه باليمينيات، ولو ان يتقحمون[2353] الالام ليس يقبلهم العقل، بل يقمعهم ويخدعهم بطول روح وصبر،[2354] او يزجرهم وينهرهم بلا تكدر، واما يهديهم بحيل المعرفه.

(III.96) ميالة الناطقين وعدم ميالتهم، الى الم الخطيه، مخفيه بمعرفة الخير والشر، وتطهر (R199v) بحرية الاراده بفعل حفظ الوصايا، مولده ومربية الالام والشرور، البر والطهاره هي معرفة الخير والشر، يظهر حسنها وسماجتها بشجاعة الاراده ورخاوتها.

(III.97) اذا[2355] اصطبغت النفس بالصلاح بالكليه انقلعت معرفة الشر[2356] من القلب، واذا ما اصطبغت هي (A264v) بعمق الشرور بالكليه، انقلعت معرفة الخير من القلب،[2357] واذا ما كانوا الاثنين يفعلوا في النفس بالسويه، في وقت معرفة الخير تنجح، وفي وقت معرفة الشر ليس سلامه موجوده، وتشبه النفس

[2347] بد : R.

[2348] ومن : R.

[2349] الفعل : R.

[2350] الخباط : R, S.

[2351] نرى : S / نراء : A.

[2352] تتعطل : R, S.

[2353] يقتحموا : S / يتقحموا : R.

[2354] وبالصبر : R, S.

[2355] اذا ما : S / واذا ما : R.

[2356] الخير : R.

[2357] واذا ما اصطبغت هي بعمق الشرور... من القلب : ساقطة R, S.

الذي بيد واحده يبني وبيد[2358] اخرى[2359] يهدم، الى ان تحل الرحمه، وانما يعرض هذا الامر من رخاوة الاراده.

(III.98) صنارة النفس الى الخير والشر هي الشهوه، لان اذا ما اجتذبت النفس بالشهوه الصالحه التي للالهييات،[2360] لم تقبل الاسهام الموقوده التي للالام والشرور، واذا ما اجتذبت[2361] بالالام تجسر على الفضايل العاليه كمثل المرذولات.

(III.99) وان كان الناس على الدوام يشربوا الخمر ولكن بالعارض يسكروا، وان كان على الدوام تستعمل النفس واحد واحد من الالام، كمثل الة[2362] العالم تميل وتسكر فيهم.

(III.100) بغيارات كثيره يسكرون بالمشارب، وبغيارات كثيره تسكر النفس بالالام، اذا[2363] ما سكرت ليس هو لها ان تغلب، بل هي مفتقره للمعونه ظاهرا[2364] وخفي.

(III.101) المتوحد الذي احب اختياره لعدم التالم، وقطع في ضميره[2365] بغضه الى الالام وبدا يجاهد مع الشرور والالام، فيعد نفسه بارادته للصبر على الضوايق وتجارب مختلفه وعوز، وربوات شرور، ليلا عندما يصادفوه التجارب والاحزان، بغير ارادته يتكدر ويتذمر، وباضطرار الغضبيه[2366] يقبلهم، ويصير الم خلقه ماده لالم الكابه والحزن والضجر، ويبقا[2367] عقله بطال، لانه قد[2368] كتب ان كنت تعمل صلاح انتظر الشرور تاتيك،[2369] والتجارب، (A265r) لان العالم المتالم الميال، ما يهدا الى ان ينتقم من الذين يحبون عدم التالم، ويريدوا ان يسيروا بغير مياله في العالم المتالم الميال،

2358 وبيدا : A.

2359 اخره : R, S.

2360 للالهيات : R, S.

2361 اجتذب : R.

2362 بالة : R, S.

2363 واذا : R, S.

2364 ظاهر : R, S.

2365 طميره : A.

2366 الغضبية (الغصبية) : S.

2367 ويبقى : S.

2368 قد : ساقطة S.

2369 تاتينك : S.

وليس يجلب لهم كرامه ونياح، بل ضد هولاء[2370] يضنك ويحزن ويشبعهم ازدرا، ومقت وتعير[2371] من[2372] كل نوع، وسبب حسب ما يقدر ويسمح له.

(III.102) الراهب الذي يريد ان يكون غير متالم، قد نافق على العالم المتالم،[2373] لانه يريد ان يضادد[2374] الالام الذين هم الة العالم،[2375] فوق الطبع هو عدم الالام والمياله، الذي اقتنوا القديسين ببغضهم الى الالام، ومن دون معونة[2376] ومراحم ربنا يسوع المسيح، وعونه خفي وظاهر ما يطهرون.[2377]

(III.103) الانحلال والداله هم الة الشيطان، لان بهن يحرك الالام ويطمر الفخوخ ويصطاد بهن الناس الى الخطيه،[2378] الخوف والحيا والسكون والتحفظ هم الة الملايكه، بالقديسين،[2379] التي بهم يحركون (R200r) الفضايل ويجذبون[2380] لمعرفة الحقايق.

كمل الميمر الثالث.

(IV) الميمر الرابع في رووس المعرفه للقديس مار اسحق.[2381]

(IV.1) راس النفس هو الايمان الصحيح، مع معرفة الحق، ومبدا التدابير المتقنه هو القصد المستقيم مع صلب الاراده مقابل الالام، بوساطة عمل الوصايا.

(IV.2) مبدا التدابير المتقنه، هي الميتوته من كل مفاوضة الوجوه بشهوة الامور الالهيه، لان منها يتولد الحب والحراره لتدبير الحق.

2370 هولا : R.

2371 وتعيير : S.

2372 في : R, S.

2373 لانه قد نافق على العالم المتالم : زائدة A, R.

2374 يضاد : S.

2375 المتالم : زائدة S.

2376 معرفة : R.

2377 يتطهرون : R, S.

2378 للخطية : R, S.

2379 المقدسين : S / القديسين : R.

2380 ويجذبونا : R, S.

2381 ايسحق : R.

(IV.3) حرارة النفس تتولد من القراة الدايمه في سيرة التدبير، المقرون مع الاعمال والصلوات المتواتره.

(IV.4) مبدا الصلوات الحاره تكون[2382] غلوة (A265v) الاجتهاد وهولاء[2383] الصلوات المتواتره، بالسكون مع القراه الدايمه بافراز يوصلون الى هذيذ العقل.

(IV.5) ومن الهذيذ الروحاني الذي للعقل يتلد فينا جمع الفكر، ومن انقياض[2384] الضمير، يتولد الانعتاق من الطياشه، ومن حصول هولاء[2385] يتولد فينا صلاة مفاوضة العقل الخفيه.

(IV.6) اذا[2386] بتغصب وقسرا[2387] دايما تنحفظ[2388] حقوق السكون، وتتربا بالنعمه وهداية الاب الروحاني، في مده من الزمان تنمحي من القلب الصور والرسوم، والتذكارات الغريبه التي هي[2389] خارجه عن تدبير السكون، وتصطبغ النفس بالفضايل الرييسيه، السلامه والحب والهدو[2390] والبشاشه والفرح الروحاني، هن هذه الفضايل يصبغون النفس بالصلاة الروحانيه، ومن هولاء[2391] نوهل بالرحمه للصلاة الخفيه مع الله، بحسس سري بالذهن.

(IV.7) ومن هاهنا ببساطة ايمان[2392] النفس وكلية الرجا تعيش ويعطا لنا بالنعمه فوق الطبع عربون الحريه، ودالة ثقة البنين، بشهاده النيه لصلاة الحب الالهي.

(IV.8) صلاة الحب الالهي هي سكون الضمير المثاله،[2393] الذي قد ارتسم بالله ويختلج ويلغلغ خفيا بحسس الذهن.

2382 من : زائدة R, S.

2383 وهولا : R.

2384 انقباض : R, S.

2385 هولا : R.

2386 واذا : R, S.

2387 وقسر : R, S.

2388 نتحفظ : R.

2389 هي : ساقطة R, S.

2390 والهدوء : S / والهدوا : R.

2391 هولا : R.

2392 ايام : R.

2393 المتالم : S.

(IV.9) وان كان درجة الحب الالهي ارفع من الصلاه، ولكن من دون الصلاه[2394] والدموع المحزنه الدايمه مع السهر والنسك ما يقتنا الحب.

(IV.10) الحب الالهي الذي بالاعمال الدايمه والصلوات والدموع والميتوته من الكل، يرتسم في القلب الطاهر، مثل صورة الملك المرسومه في الدينار، وكما انه لا يمكن ان تنظر[2395] في الدينار من دون ايقونة الملك،[2396] وهكذا (A266r) ايضا لا يمكن الذي قد ارتسم وابتلع بالحب الالهي، ليشخص نظر ذهنه في قلبه وقت الصلاه ان لا يحس ذهنه بسر الحياة الجديده، وينسا ذاته ويصمت بالدهش.

(IV.11) لا تضل[2397] ايها الانسان الحقير ولا تعتجب وتنتفخ بالظنون، ليس هذه لك ولطبعك الميال ولا لارادتك الصالحه وافراز اعمال نسكك،[2398] بل انعام النعمه التي تريد لكي بمذاقتك[2399] الحياه الموضوعه، بالصنارة الروحانيه تصيدك للحياة الجديده المعقوله، (R200v) ان تشا نفسك او لم تشا، وفي الوقت الذي تتصفا فيه وتختبر بكور التجارب والاحزان والتضجر، قوم انت في ذاتك وابعدهم عنك، ومن دون الصلاه والصبر لا يمكن.

(IV.12) افهم ايضا هذه الاخرى[2400] حتى وان العشارين والزناه لم تهدا النعمه من ان تدعيهم، وتيقض[2401] وتجذبهم للتوبه، وتضوقهم[2402] ماكول الحياه بصنارة روحانيه الجاذبة الحياه، وهي لهم، ونحن[2403] ايضا ان ننطاع[2404] للحق والحياة الجديده المعقوله، او لظلالة[2405] الالام والخطيه.

(IV.13) من فيه كفوا ان ينعت افعال النعمه التي بمجاذبات الروح، بعربون كنز البنوه الذي[2406] داخلنا قبلناه بالعماد المقدس، تذوق[2407] طفوليتنا خفيا[2408] في

[2394] والتضرع : زائدة R, S.
[2395] ننظر : R, S.
[2396] غير ممكن : زائدة S.
[2397] تطل : A.
[2398] نسكك : ساقطة R.
[2399] مبذاقتك : R.
[2400] الاخره : R, S.
[2401] وتيقض (تيقظ) : S.
[2402] وتضوقهم (تذوقهم) : S.
[2403] وتحن : R.
[2404] نخضع : S.
[2405] لظلالة (لضلالة) : S.
[2406] التي : R, S.

وقت وقت بحاسية الذهن، وبحلاوة مجاذبات الروح تجذب بساطة نقاوتنا الى اعمال التوبه، ومعرفة الحق بمصاعد الروح في القلب.

(IV.14) من يجسر ان ينعت نبات السلامه الذي[2409] بغته ينمو[2410] من القلب وينسكب[2411] على القلب وينفرش[2412] على الاعضا، وتهتدي الحركات والحواس من غير العاده، (A266v) وتنذهل الافكار وتبقا[2413] بلا فعل.

(IV.15) من يهدس على نمو[2414] الفرح الروحاني المختلج من القلب، ورقس حركات النفس ببهجة وبشاشه من غير العاده.

(IV.16) من هو الذي ذاق حلاوة الحب الالهي الذي يختلج في القلب ويحلى حنك النفس،[2415] وتنسا[2416] ذاتها من قوة التهاب المحبة الالهيه.

(IV.17) من فيه كفو[2417] ان يعد نمو[2418] الافهام والهذيذات الروحانيه، التي تصعد بالنعمه بمصاعد القلب، وتجسس بنور الضمير القوات الروحانيه، المحتوطه[2419] الفاعله خفيا بطبايع الخليقه، ويجوزون[2420] بتصور على عناية الله وسياسته، بهذا الجميع وتبقا[2421] هي النفس بدهش عميق في اسرار الله الخفيه، التي لا ينطق بها.

(IV.18) من هو الذي يقدر يخبر على مصاعد الروح الكاينه في القلب، عندما يسكر الذهن بسيرة السكون، من وثبات الحراره.

2407 نذوق : R.

2408 خفيتنا : R.

2409 التي : R, S.

2410 تنموا : R, S.

2411 وتنسكب : R, S.

2412 وتنغرس : S / وتنفرش : R.

2413 وتبقى : S.

2414 نموا : R.

2415 وتسكر هي النفس : زائدة R, S.

2416 وتنسى : S.

2417 كفوءا : S / كفوا : R.

2418 نموا : R.

2419 المحطوطه : R.

2420 ويحوزون : S.

2421 وتبقى : S.

(IV.19) او من يقدر يقول على نور التاوريا[2422] المشرق في القلب من قراءة الكتب، والهذيذ بالصلوات المتواتره المحدثه.[2423]

(IV.20) من هو الذي حس بالنعمه بالحزن الحد،[2424] الذي بغته ينمو[2425] من القلب ويصعد للراس، ويدمع العينين ويجري[2426] الدموع المفرحه وتسري السخونه[2427] باللذه في جميع الاعضا، من الحلاوة المختلجه في القلب، وتضمحل الالام وتصمت الحركات، والافكار بالدهش.

(IV.21) وان كان في جميع افعال الروح يشبه الشيطان ضلالته، كما كتب، ولكن بالاكثر في هذه يشبه، لانه يحسس الكلا[2428] والاعضا السفلانيه، ويدغدغ ويصعد الى فوق، يسكب سخونة[2429] لذة (A267r) الدغدغات الشهوانيه (R201r) في جميع الاعضا، ويبقا[2430] الانسان بغير حاسيه.

(IV.22) اي ضمير فيه كفوا[2431] ان يدرك شرف نور الفهم والعقل الذي ينبسط كالشمس الجديد[2432] في رقيع[2433] القلب، ويفرز[2434] ويوري النفس الحق من تشبه الطغيان.

(IV.23) من يهدس على نمو[2435] الروح داخل القلب الذي من غير الاراده يفرح ويسبح بلغلغت[2436] الروحانيين،[2437] بحسس الذهن بفعل[2438] النعمه.

2422 الثاؤريا : S / التااوريا : A.
2423 المحتده : R, S.
2424 الحاد : S.
2425 ينموا : R, S.
2426 وتجري : R, S.
2427 السخونا : R.
2428 الكلي : R, S.
2429 السخونة (سخونة) : S / اسخونة : R.
2430 ويبقى : S.
2431 كفوءا : S.
2432 الديد : R.
2433 ارقيع : R, S.
2434 ويفوز : S.
2435 نموا : R.
2436 بلغلغة : R, S.
2437 الروحانيه : R.
2438 تفعل : R.

(IV.24) اي ذهن فيه كفوا[2439] بقوة نفسه في وقت الصلاه ليقبل نور النعمه على نور عدم الالام، باستعلان الروح فوق الطبيعه بالرحمه.

(IV.25) من هو الذي افتقدته النعمه في وقت التزمير والصلاه وانقلب بغته خلاف ما كان اوله، وسكت اللسان واتخلفت حركات النفس وهدوا[2440] بذهول بفعل النعمه.

(IV.26) من هو المتوحد الذي عرف تلك الرايحه[2441] اللذيذه التي تفوح بغته وتجدد ضميره وتستاصل الالام والحروب وتيقظ النفس لتسبيح[2442] جديد، ويفهم تلك الرايحة النجسه الرديه التي تفوح بغته وتحرك[2443] الافكار النجسه وتلهب الالام.

(IV.27) هو المشم[2444] واحد[2445] من الخمسة احواس يقبل حسس فعل الروح ويفرز مع الذهن الافعال، ان كان يمينيه او شماليه.

(IV.28) وان كان هم الشياطين يشبهون ضلالتهم[2446] بفعل النعمه في الابتدا للسذج،[2447] بل العارفين[2448] في طريق سيدنا الذين اتجربوا بهولاء[2449] وسقطوا وقاموا بالنعمه، يفهمون حيلهم المكره، لان فعل النعمه بالاكثر من القلب يبدا ويصعد الى فوق وينشف الراس، والمخ ويضنك العظام، واما فعل الشيطان بالاكثر من الكلا[2450] والاعضا[2451] السفليه التي هي الات الشهوه، والافكار تبتدى[2452] وتصعد للقلب والراس وتهلك الانسان.

[2439] كفوءا : S.

[2440] واهتدوا : R, S.

[2441] الراحة : R.

[2442] لتسبح : S / للتسبيح : R.

[2443] ويحرك : R.

[2444] المشمر : R.

[2445] واحده : R, S.

[2446] طلالتهم : A.

[2447] للسجد : R.

[2448] عارفين : R.

[2449] بهولا : R.

[2450] الكلي : R, S.

[2451] واعضا : R, S.

[2452] تبدى : R, S.

(IV.29) وثم[2453] وقت ايضا النعمه[2454] من القراه تبتدى ووقت من الهذيذ بالفضايل، وثم[2455] وقت من الصلوات المحترزه، ولكن بالاكثر من الاشتياق والامل والهدس بالفضايل السيرة المتعاليه والمسطوره للروحانيين[2456] تبتدى، وتصور[2457] في ضميره الاشيا العاليه الكاينه للقديسين، وكمثل انه يشخص فيهم ويتشوق للتشوق[2458] بتدبيرهم، وكل شي[2459] هو مثل هولاء[2460] بالاكثر من القلب يبدى.[2461]

(IV.30) واما الامور الضديه انما ترصد الشياطين الاوقات وياخذون منا ماده وفصحه،[2462] وعندما يحسوا ان اعضا النفس قد احترروا بهذيذ الفضايل والاشتياق بالالهيات، والتهبوا بالتضرع والصلوات الحاره من ساعتهم يحركوا بحيلهم الاعضا السفليه بشهوة لذيذه، وتسري تلك اللذه الى فوق (A267v) وعندما تحما[2463] احواس الجسد تبقا[2464] الاعضاء بلا فعل، هذا[2465] الامر بعد جهد تفرزه الكاملين.

(IV.31) صدقني يا اخي القاري ان هو العدو[2466] يفعل هذين الامرين في الانسان على الدوام، ولو كان يترك بالكمال[2467] ان يعمل[2468] بالكليه في الانسان ويقلب فعله بالصلاح للشر، ما كان (R201v) مفروز من فعل ملاك النور كما قال بولس، لكن عليه اضطرار من الله ليغير قتاله وفعايله، وكم من وقت عندما تبدى النعمه تعمل في القلب،[2469] يبتدوا ايضا الشياطين يحركوا فعايلهم بتحيل

2453 وثمة : S.

2454 للنعمة : S.

2455 وثمة : S.

2456 الروحانيين : R.

2457 ويصور : R, S.

2458 للتشبه : S.

2459 شيا : R.

2460 هولا : R.

2461 يبدا : R, S.

2462 وفسحه : R, S.

2463 تحمى : S.

2464 تبقى : S.

2465 وهذا : R, S.

2466 العدوا : R.

2467 من الله : R, S.

2468 يفعل : R.

2469 القل : R.

في اعضا الشهوه، وفي هذا النوع المشم يقبل الحسس بالرايحة اللذيذه والرايحة[2470] النجسه، وتمتلى النفس سلامه واضطراب، حب وتكدر،[2471] ويتقسم فيها النور ويتخيل[2472] الذهن وما يستطيع يفرز الحق من التشبه والطغيان،[2473] وتتخلف الاعضا عن الفعل وهذا النوع هو اصعب من جميع الاشيا.

(IV.32) لان بالاكثر هو الشيطان ايضا الالام[2474] النجسه[2475] يغيرها عندما يحرك في المشم، وبرداوة صناعته كم من وقت يشبه الرايحه النجسه الرديه بالرايحة اللذيذه الطيبه، لكي يضل[2476] السذج، وعندما يتصور هذا الشبه بالضمير ويغرق النفس الشقيه باللذة السمجه.

(IV.33) ليس لهن[2477] حد غيارات انواع المشم الذي[2478] تعرض من فعايل الشياطين كمثل انه ايضا ليس لهن حد غيارات انواع فعايل[2479] الصلاح والشرور، ولكن كل واحد يعرف على قدر[2480] ما جرب او تسلم من اخرين.

(IV.34) الذين يتشوقون بعمل[2481] الكمال بالاكثر بقتال الشهوه يسمح ان يتجربوا بقوه، لكي يختبر حبهم للحق ان كان صادق، وينمقتون من نياتهم دايما ويتدبرون[2482] بدوام عمل الاتضاع والصبر، ليلا يتعظم قلبهم بالظن وينتفخون ويسقطون بعظمة الشيطان.

(IV.35) فان كنت تسال انه كيف يستطاع ان النعمه والشيطان يفعلون في نفس واحده[2483] بسويه، ولا يضمحل الشيطان من قدام النعمه، وانا ايضا اسالك

2470 او الرايحة : R.
2471 واتكدر : R, S.
2472 ويتخبل : S / ويتكبل : R.
2473 الطغيان : R.
2474 الام : R, S.
2475 النجس : R, S.
2476 يطل : A.
2477 لهم : R.
2478 التي : R, S.
2479 فضايل : R.
2480 ما قد : S / قد : R.
2481 لعمل : R, S.
2482 ويتدربون : R, S.
2483 يفعلون : زائدة R, S.

كيف يمكن البر والخطيه ينعملون في ضمير[2484] واحد وارادة واحده، ولا[2485] تستاصل الخطيه من بر الصدوقيه، لان هكذا هي احكام ربنا انه تركهم يتدربون ويتخرجون المختارين والقديسين، وينمقتون بتجارب كثيره مختلفه، لكي يحسون بالنعمه يحافظهم[2486] ومعتقهم برحمته الغزيره.

(IV.36) اما الشيطان بكثرة دهاه ما يفتر من ان يشبه طغيانه بفعايل الروح، ويتحيل ان يعطي ضلالته[2487] للسذج[2488] او المختارين[2489] كشبه الحق، كما كتب بولس ان كان[2490] الشيطان يتشبه بملاك النور وايضا خدامه، والاب مرقس كتب ان ثم[2491] فعل (A268r) للنعمه[2492] غير معروف للاطفال والمبتديين.

(IV.37) واما نحن ينبغي لنا ان[2493] نخر قدام نعمة الله ونسال سيدنا بحزن الصلوات وبدموع، ليخلصنا من هلاك الضلالة[2494] الشيطانيه ويسترنا تحت كنف نعمته، وحقيقة مراحمه، ونصعد له ولابيه ولروح القدس[2495] تسبيح دايم بتضرع، ليحفظ سيرة تدبيرنا بسبله الروحانيه بخفي وظاهر بغير موديه، ساير ايام حياتنا.

(IV.38) هولا واكثر منهم ما لم يدرك ولا يوصف (R202r) تذوق نعمة الروح[2496] القدس للذين يداومون السكون بقصد مستقيم، كل مدة حياتهم بلا مفرات، تفعل وتجذب بانواع مختلفه وغزيره لتعزية الساذجين، وتجذبهم للحياة الجديده بالله.

2484 ضمير : R, S.

2485 وما : R, S.

2486 حافظتهم : R, S.

2487 طلالته : A.

2488 السذج : R.

2489 للمختارين : R.

2490 كان : ساقطة S.

2491 ثمة : S.

2492 النعمه : R.

2493 ان : ساقطة R.

2494 الطلالة : A.

2495 وروح قدسه : R, S.

2496 روح : R.

(IV.39) هكذا ايضا والشياطين[2497] تجذب وتوسوس وتخدع وتفعل بطغيانهم[2498] بلا فتور، بوجه البر لعل يستطيعو[2499] ان يضلوا[2500] المختارين.

(IV.40) هذه هي اثمار اسكون[2501] القلايه، وهذه هي التي كتبوا الابا ان يحل عليك قوه سلامة السكون.

(IV.41) لو كان عقل السذج والورق فيه كفوا لقبول الحق، امور كثيره عجيبه كانت تحصل للابا الروحانيين وكانوا يكتبوها، الاشيا الموجهه اليهم من نمو[2502] القلب بتحريك الروح بفعل النعمه، عند الذين قد نقى قلبهم من الالام ومن الشرور وصاروا لله مسكن.[2503]

(IV.42) تقتنى[2504] وتنموا زيارات الروح[2505] في[2506] المبدا بقلب المتوحد الجالس في الهدو[2507] تحت ظلال[2508] الرب، فالاول يكون من استعداد نيته عندما يغصب هو ذاته، ويقصرها على التدبير بالسكون، ويدعوا ويسال مراحم النعمه ان تاتي اليه وتساعده بالخفي والظاهر، ويحترس[2509] بعمله ويحتفظ من جميع مفاوضات الوجوه، وكل هذيذ غريب خارج عن تدبير السكون، ويصلب ضميره ليلا[2510] ونهار[2511] متشوقا بتامل رجاه ليقبل العزا خفي[2512] من المسيح، ويحرس على القراة المفرزه بالجلوس الفريدي في كوخ ضيق مظلم، ويجمع[2513] ويقبضه[2514] اليه من كل تذكار وهذيذ[2515] يكون خارج

2497 والشيطان : R, S.

2498 يجذب ويوسوس ويخدع ويفعل بطغيانه : R, S.

2499 لعله يستطيع : R, S.

2500 يضل : R, S.

2501 سكون : S.

2502 نموا : R.

2503 مسكنا : S.

2504 تقتنا : R, S.

2505 القدس : زائدة S.

2506 في : ساقطة R.

2507 الهدوا : R.

2508 ظل ظلال : S.

2509 ويحتر : R.

2510 ليل : R.

2511 ونهارا : S.

2512 خفيا : S.

2513 عقله : زائدة S.

2514 ويقبض : S.

عن السكون، بالصلب الفكري متشوقا للعزا الخفي من المسيح، ويترجا وينتظر في[2516] كل وقت وساعه لمراحم النعمه بالصلوات الحاره متواترا، الناميه[2517] بفرح من حرارة القلب بلا انقطاع.

(IV.43) المتوحد الذي يشتهي ويتشوق لمقتنا الفضايل الرييسيه داخل منه واثمار الروح التي كتبها الطوباني بولس، الاشيا التي وجدتها القديسين جواهم في كل الاجيال، بالصبر الدايم والضوايق الصعبه والتجارب المضغطه التي قاسوها في السكون، بقصد مستقيم وحب غزير روحاني لجميع الناس، (A268v) وبعد هولاء[2518] وجدوا جواهم من بعد الهذيذ الكثير بالصلاح والحب والرحمه، وانقلع ذكر الشر من قلوبهم ولم عادوا عرفوا شر كما كان داوود.

(IV.44) المتوحد الذي هدا[2519] ذاته وسالم نفسه مع الكل واتفق[2520] الثالوث الذي فيه، هو مفتقر لجلوس الحريه بسلام السكون، والانتظار والتامل[2521] كل ساعه لعزا[2522] الروح، ومحتاج ايضا لمحقرة الذات والانحطاط، لان هذين يعتقون الانسان من الغيره والخباط، ومفتقر الى انقباض الضمير وجمع الافكار من الطياشه، والاحتراس الكثير من فعايل الضلالة[2523] الشيطانيه، وهو محتاج ايضا لهداية[2524] اب روحاني (R202v) يرشده وقد مارس الامور بنفسه ووقع[2525] وقام.

(IV.45) حركة الغضب والاضطراب والخلق والحسد[2526] ينموا بالنفس من القلب الشرير، الذي بسهوله يقبل الافكار الشريره ان كان من الذكر او من الاحواس، ويهدس بالشر على قريبه او على كلمن كان، ولم يزجر افكاره

[2515] وهذيذا : R.

[2516] في : ساقطة R, S.

[2517] الى امكنه : R.

[2518] هولا : R.

[2519] هدى : S.

[2520] اتفق : R.

[2521] والتمل : R.

[2522] بعزاء : S.

[2523] الطلالة : A.

[2524] اهداية : R.

[2525] وقع : R, S.

[2526] والشر : R, S.

ويقلبها لهذيذا[2527] صالح جيد حتى ومن غير ضرورة[2528] اغتصابيه يقبل ضميره هذيذا[2529] ردي.

(IV.46) الموضع الذي فيه حركة الغضب والخباط والخلق[2530] والحسد والشر، لم يثبت[2531] ولا تنقام فيه الفضايل والصالحات الكاينه بمصاعد القلب، ولو انهم يوجدوا ينحجبوا بظلمة الغضب والغيره والتكدر.

(IV.47) اعرف انسان قديس عندما كان يلاقي احدا[2532] مغلوب[2533] من شيطان الغضب او من[2534] النجاسه، بالمشم كان يفرزه.

(IV.48) واخر انسان شيخ اتغافل بارادته من تناول الاسرار المقدسه فنظر[2535] في حلمه انهم يوزعون الاسرار على كل الشعب، وهو لم يعطوه شيا،[2536] ولما جاهد لكي يتناول اخذ خبز ساذج.[2537]

(IV.49) اخبرنا موسى تلميذ القديس يوحنا الشيخ المتاوي، ان في بعض[2538] الايام نظرت اخ نايم بشقيف جبل واتكلمت معه كثير فلم يجيبني، ولما اعلمت الشيخ امرني ان اودي له قليل خبزا[2539] وماء وحذرني ان لا اكلمه، ومن بعد ستة ايام في اليوم السابع جا الى عند الشيخ واظهر له افكاره، واوعظه الشيخ ونيحه ومن بعد ان اطلقه سالت الشيخ عن احواله، قال لي ان[2540] من يد السراق[2541] الداخل منه وجد قليل راحه ونسى الخبز والماء[2542] وهرب للسكون لكي يستريح قليل.

2527 لهذيذ : R, S.
2528 اضروره : R.
2529 هذيذ : R, S.
2530 والقلق : R / والحلق : S.
2531 تثبت : R, S.
2532 احد : R, S.
2533 مغلوبا : S.
2534 الم : زائدة R, S.
2535 ونظر : R, S.
2536 شي : R, S.
2537 خبزا ساذجا : S.
2538 من : زائدة R.
2539 خبز : R, S.
2540 لي ان : ساقطة S / ان : ساقطة R.
2541 السراس : R.
2542 والما : R.

(IV.50) مضينا انا وواحد من الاخوه الى جبل متى الى عند شيخ،[2543] وعندما قبلنا وسالنا عن الاخوه وعلى جبرابيل رييس الدير، عرفناه ان انسان بدوي انغاض[2544] عليه ويطلب ان يقتله[2545] بالغش اعني[2546] لرييس[2547] الدير، فنهرنا الشيخ وحرك ذاته ودخل الى قلايته الجوانيه، ومكث زمان، وعندما خرج وقف بعيدا[2548] عنا فما قدرنا ان ننظر في وجهه، لانه كان يقيد كمثل[2549] النار، فكلمنا ببشاشه (A269r) وقال البدوي هو احمر الذقن، فقلنا[2550] نعم، فقال قد مات، ولما رجعنا وجدناه[2551] قد مات بغته.

(IV.51) معرفة الحق من غير التدابير المتقنه ليس توجد، والتدابير المتقنه من دون معرفة الحق والاعمال لم يوجدوا.

(IV.52) ايمان الحق[2552] من دون طهاره التدابير المتقنه ليس يقتنا، ونظر النفس السري مفتقر الى الايمان الحقاني ومحتاج الى التدابير المتقنه، والذكاوه وعدم التالم.

(IV.53) تاوريا[2553] الطبايع الروحانيه واحده هي بالمعرفه، وبالحراره ترتفع[2554] وتنحط للناس مع الحراره ايضا بتاورية[2555] المعرفه يفرزون، ولهذا يفرزون ايضا بتدابيرهم.

(IV.54) بشهوة العين خرج ادم من ميراثه، (R203r) وبشهوه الحب لصليب يسوع يرجعون الناس لميراثهم الروحاني.

(IV.55) كما ان العين مختلف تنظر والاذن بتغير تسمع، ويذوق[2556] ايضا الحنك، والذهن ايضا هكذا يغير البلاد والمعرفه اذ يجوز بتصوره من مكان

[2543] شييخ : A.

[2544] انغاض (انغاظ) : S.

[2545] يقتل : S.

[2546] اعني : ساقطة R, S.

[2547] رئيس : S.

[2548] بعيد : R, S.

[2549] مثل : S.

[2550] قلنا : R, S.

[2551] وجدنا : R.

[2552] المحق : R, S.

[2553] ثاؤريا : S / تاوريا : A.

[2554] وترتفع : R.

[2555] بثاؤرية : S / بتاورية : A.

[2556] وبذوق : R.

الى مكان ومن حال الى حال، اذ مقرون معه الذكر وهدس الافكار والفهم ليصطاد الصيد، لان بحرية ارادته يخرج من بلد السلامه ويدخل الى بلد الغيره والغضب وكل موضع يدخله يتغير ومعهم ينقلب[2557] ويتفاوض كمثل في السوق حسبما[2558] يعرض.

(IV.56) لان نطقية النفس محبة الزيادات هي بالطبع وتلتهب بالشهوه وتزدري بما قد اقتنت وتعلمت، وتسرع العظايم[2559] لتدركهم ولو ان عسر وجودهن.

(IV.57) كما ان الذي يغطس بالماء ان كان ما هو معتاد يتضيق ويصعد ليتنفس[2560] جوا ذاته،[2561] هكذا هو ايضا العقل الذكي عندما بالنعمه يغطس من العالم ويصير في الطبع بالاسرار المعقوله التي للروح، ان لم يكون قد اتدرب، يتضييق[2562] وينتفخ ويدهش ويصمت ويرجع يتنفس في بلد غربته.

(IV.58) عندما تملك[2563] بغته على جميع حركاتك[2564] سلامه وهدوا من غير العاده، وتبتهج نفسك بالفرح ويتخلف عنك كل هذيذ وفكر، اعلم ان في تلك الساعه قد اهلت[2565] لفعل النعمه.

(IV.59) واذا من غير سبب يشتد عليك الضجر وضيق العضن،[2566] وتتكدر نفسك وتختنق وتتعذب بحزن الضمير، اعلم انك انت صرت السبب، ولمنفعتك سلمتك[2567] النعمه للمعاقبين لتتحكم بالطريق[2568] الملايكيه[2569] ان هكذا تقتنى،[2570] فان كان تتجلد بغير تذمر وبشكر تقبل وبفرح داخلك، اترجا بالامل لفعل النعمه.

2557 يتقلب : S.

2558 حسب ما : S / وحسب ما : R.

2559 للعظائم : S.

2560 ليتفس : A.

2561 جو ذاته : S / جوذاته : R.

2562 يتضيق / R, S.

2563 يملك : R, S.

2564 واعضائك : زائدة S / واعضايك : زائدة R.

2565 أؤهلت : S / اوهلت : R.

2566 العضن : ساقطة S.

2567 اسلمتك : R, S.

2568 بطريق : R, S.

2569 الملوكية : S / الملايكه : R.

2570 تقتنا : R, S.

(IV.60) الضمير المتفرد الذي باعمال دم نفسه هدا ذاته وسالم كل احد، وقبض نفسه عن الكل بالسلامه وانتقل عن الجميع بتجديد عقله، وصار واحدا[2571] بخفاياه من الكل لكيما يتحد مع الواحد فوق الطبيعه بالسر، عندما يوجد داخل منه ضميرا[2572] غريب، (A269v) او فكر وهذيذ ملتوي برداوه قد قبله بالاحواس، او بالتذكار يمنعه من المفاوضه مع الواحد، ويتعطل من الاتحاد مع الواحد بالروح بما يفوق الطبع.

(IV.61) ليس فيه كفوا ضمير المتوحد ان يتفاوض بالصلاه مع الواحد بالسر ما دام جوا منه ضميرا[2573] اخر، وفكر[2574] وهذيذ غريب، حتى يخرجه من ميراث القديسين ويصير بالبساطه واحد مع[2575] الواحد.

(IV.62) لا يمكن التفاوض فوق الطبع بسر الصلاه مع الخالق ومع خليقته جميع، بل اذا ما اراد العقل[2576] يدخل بالسر الى عند الواحد يتعوق من الغربا الذي عنده، وان اتجاسر يقال له بمحبه كمثل العظيم موسى، انزع[2577] عنك جميع من معك وتعال الى منفرد،[2578] السر هو خفي باستار[2579] وينطق[2580] بالروح (R203v) وبما هو فوق من الطبع يندآق بفعل النعمه، السر لي والسر لاهل بيتي.

(IV.63) كم من وقت يتعب الضمير في طلب تاوريا[2581] وما يجدها، وفي حال ما يقوم في الصلاه[2582] يتحرك فيه ذكر وجدانها، فان وجدها ضيع اثمار الصلاه، وان كان ما استضا بها يندم ويتكدر ويخيب من مفاوضة الصلاه، معروف الان ان في وقت الصلاه الروحانيه ليس اثنين بل واحد، ضميرا[2583]

[2571] واحد : R.
[2572] ضمير : R, S.
[2573] ضمير : R, S.
[2574] او فكر : R, S.
[2575] عند : R, S.
[2576] ان : زائدة R, S.
[2577] اترك : R, S.
[2578] منفردا : S / متفرد : R.
[2579] وبالتسارر : R, S.
[2580] ينطق : R, S.
[2581] ثاؤريا : S / تاوريا : A.
[2582] للصلاة : R, S.
[2583] ضمير : R, S.

وحيد[2584] بسيط مسالم هادي، يقبل سر النعمه بالرحمه، فان كان معه شي غريب لم[2585] يستحق كمثل الاول.

(IV.64) كمثلما[2586] كتب القديس باسيليوس بالسر الى اغريغوريوس اخيه، المجمع الذي به تعمل نفس المتوحد الفضايل هو الفم واللسان، وقلايته التي فيها يقدس ويرتل خفيا[2587] بلسان الروحانيين تسبيح ملايكي بلا فتور القلب والعقل ومن غير اتفاقهم مع بعضهم بعض باطل هو كل العمل النفساني.

(IV.65) ما دمنا في المجمع البراني نعود لسان عقلنا بالهذيذ الروحاني لكي ينبسط لسان العقل ليمجد بشبه الروحانيين، ولا نوجد بطالين عندما نهدس بتخريف[2588] ضميرنا، لان روح القدس بالاكثر تفعل فينا وتصلي عوضنا[2589] بسكون الضمير والافكار بسرا[2590] لا ينعت، كما كتب الرسول الطوباني.

(IV.66) تدابير الضمير هم مهديين وثبات حرارة الاعمال الجسدانيه.

(IV.67) يسهل مقتنا البساطه اتضاع[2591] الاحواس، مع الازدرا، بوساطة نار حرارة الاعمال الجسدانيه، من مقتنى[2592] تدبير الضمير بوساطة الهدو[2593] والذهول والصبر لانه عسر جدا.

(IV.68) ليس يتضيق من الافكار الجوانيه الذي له عزا من الاحواس البرانيه، لانه تتشتت الافكار الداخله بالملاقاة[2594] النافعه والمخسره، الدافعه لها من موج الى موج ولم تختنق النفس من الافكار.

(IV.69) الذي له عزا خفي من هذيذ تقلب الافكار[2595] الجوانيه ويحسس بتاوريه،[2596] يصور[2597] عقله السماء والارض، (A270r) وجميع ما فيهن لكي

[2584] واحد : S.

[2585] لن : S.

[2586] كمثل ما : R.

[2587] خفية : S / خفيان : R.

[2588] بتخريف : ساقطة R.

[2589] عوضا : S.

[2590] بسر : R, S.

[2591] اتصال : R.

[2592] مقتنا : R.

[2593] الهدوء : S / الهدوا : R.

[2594] بالملاقة : R.

[2595] الافكر : R.

[2596] بتاؤرية : S / بتااوريه : A.

يزيد على علم معرفته علم وجود معرفة جديده تفيض عليه من كل نواحيه، ليس هو مفتقر للعزا[2598] الذي من الاحواس البرانيه، الان الاثنين هم انقص من الحق وغريبين من الوحده، ايش المنفعه[2599] تقتني[2600] من السلام البراني، الا ان يملوا قلبنا تردد شلش الافكار.

(IV.70) نمو صلاة الروحانيين[2601] التي للعقل الكاينه[2602] بالنعمه هذه علامتها، انه بكل نسمه يتحرك في القلب ذكر بحلاوة العقل ويلغلغ بلسان الروحانيين ويقدس بالتجديد، بهدو[2603] الافكار والضمير فوق الطبيعه.

(IV.71) واحد من احاد[2604] من المتوحدين قبل هذه الموهبه جزويا واخر نوع جزويا من جزوا.

(IV.72) الى ان تسكر هي النفس ويستهزا بها من اخرين وتنداس وتنحقر من (R204r) الناظرين ليس بقليل، ولم تغلب من[2605] قلبها ولم تبالي لم يتجدد الضمير[2606] الجسدي ولا تضعف الالام، ولا تنقطع من القلب تذكارات الشرور الاولانيه من[2607] تقلب الافكار بالضنون، ولا تتاسس[2608] وترتبط هي النفس بكلية[2609] الرجا بالله، لان ما دام قيام اوليك ليس حريه ولا عدم الام.

(IV.73) اشتهيت ان القا متوحد هادي نقيا حبه منبسط مع كل احد، وثم قيام ثابت لضميره وهو وحيد في كل وقت وبكل صدفه تلاقيه يثبت عدم تالمه بغير مياله، فما وجدت، فان كان ما تضعف الالام من داخل ولا[2610] تتالم الاحواس

2597 تصور : S / صور : R.

2598 العزا : R.

2599 منفعه : R, S.

2600 نقتني : R.

2601 الروحانيه : R, S.

2602 الكايبة : R.

2603 بهدوء : S / بهدوا : R.

2604 الاخوه : R.

2605 على : R, S.

2606 ضمير : R.

2607 مع : R, S.

2608 تتسس : R.

2609 بكليته : S.

2610 والا : R, S.

من خارج، لان بهن يقبل الضمير تغير المياله عندما يصادف الملاقاة[2611] العارضه، والذكر والعقل الى الان ليس ماتوا ولا قاموا واتحدوا بالروح.

(IV.74) المتوحد الذي في زمان الطاعه وعمل المجمع يختار لنفسه راحه حرية البنين،[2612] في زمان راحته[2613] الحقيقيه بالعدل يبكي ويجوع وينضنك بالندم.[2614]

(IV.75) المتوحد الذي في زمان جمع اغمار الفرح يملك عليه الندم والحزن، هو شاهد على نفسه ان في زمان الزرع وخدوع[2615] طاعة المجمع ما صبر على صعوبه البرد والجليد، ليشق بالمحراث الروحاني خطوط عميقه في ارض قلبه ليحفظ فيهن بدار[2616] خبز الحياه، وهو الان في ايام الحصاد ينضنك بالجوع.

(IV.76) صعبه هي جدا اعمال الضمير من الاعمال[2617] الجسدانيه، وان لم يقرنهم مع بعضهم بعض هو اصعب تعب، واما اقران عمل هولاء[2618] مع عمل[2619] الضمير نور وحياه وتجديد يقني للمتوحد.[2620]

(IV.77) الذي ما يعترف بقيامة الجسد ما يعترف بالاعمال الجسدانيه، والذي ما يعترف بالتجديد المزمع للنفس ان تقبله،[2621] ما يعترف بتدبير العقل، والذي ما يعترف بالتجديد المزمع ان[2622] يقبلوه (A270v) الاثنين يعمل بالسوى[2623] بتربية المنزلتين.

(IV.78) كثيرين عملوا[2624] اعمال كثيره بغير قصد مستقيم، واما الاثمار الحقيقيه انما تخرج من القصد وليس من الاعمال.

2611 الملاقات : R, S.

2612 الابنين : R.

2613 الراحة : S / راحة : R.

2614 بالندامه : R, S.

2615 وخضوع : S.

2616 بذار : S.

2617 اعمال : R.

2618 هولا : R.

2619 عمل : ساقطة R.

2620 المتوحد : R, S.

2621 نقبله : R.

2622 ان : ساقطة R.

2623 بالسوا : R, S.

2624 يعملون : R, S.

(IV.79) جميع عمل المتوحد ان لم يكون مصلوب لقصد مستقيم بحفظ الوصايا هو عمل بطال وكل عمال غالب ما قد غلب المه بشهادة النيه، غلبته هي انغلاب ورذل[2625] لنفسه.

(IV.80) ليس للمتوحد غلبه ونجاح الا ان قهر الامه،[2626] وليس للمتوحد قهريه الا ان انغلب من الالام المقاتله معه.

(IV.81) المتوحد الذي يغلب قريبه بتحيل الطغيان قد خاب من صدق تحقيق نيته.

(IV.82) ثياب العرس[2627] الروحاني الذي اعد المسيح للقديسين بني النور هو عدم التالم.

(IV.83) الثياب الوسخه التي يمنعوا المتوحد من الدخول لعرس القديسين هي الالام.

(IV.84) اما ان لا نتوسخ بالالام ليس هي لنا، واما ان نغسل وننظف[2628] بصابون[2629] الاعمال والنسك ودوى[2630] (R204v) التوبه، الذي[2631] انعم على بيعته بالرحمه لكي نغسل من ذواتنا وسخ الالام هي لحرية ارادتنا.

(IV.85) لا يمكن ان نغلب الالام ونتخلص منهم بقوة انفسنا بل بمراحم ربنا يسوع المسيح المسجود، الذي صار لنا منظرا[2632] صالح بالاعمال النشيطه، ولنطلب الرحمه والعون بالصلوات[2633] والدموع الغزيره.

(IV.86) اعمال التوبه وصلوات الدموع باتضاع وانسحاق قلب ليس يقلعون الالام من النفس فقط، بل ومن الموتى[2634] يقيموها.

(IV.87) حفظ الاحواس تقطع الخطايا وحفظ القلب يقطع[2635] الالام، الذين[2636] هم ابا ومولدين الخطايا.

2625 وذل : R.

2626 الالامه : A.

2627 العرس : ساقطة R.

2628 وننضف : S.

2629 يصانون : R.

2630 ودواء : A / ودوا : R.

2631 التي : R, S.

2632 منظر : R, S.

2633 الصلوات : R.

2634 الموتا : R, S.

(IV.88) المتوحد الذي يجاهد مقابل الالام بحفظ الوصايا ليقلعهم من القلب لم تهدا النعمه ان[2637] تساعده خفيا.

(IV.89) اذا ما بدت الالام تضمحل وتضعف بقوة المسيح تنير النفس ويتشجع[2638] الضمير بالاعمال على الالام، كمثل الضعيف الذي انضنك بالامراض مدة زمان وبدا الطبع يتقوا على الالام[2639] المرض، ان حفظ حقوق السكون وحراسة القلب يغلب الالام ويوهل لعدم[2640] التالم.

(IV.90) جناحات النفس هي عدم الالام واوساخ النفس التي[2641] يمنعوها من الله هم الالام.

(IV.91) ليس للمتوحد بر وخطيه وتنعم الملكوت وعذاب الجحيم، الا نور عدم الالام، والظلام بالالام.

(IV.92) النفس التي بنعمة الله بالاعمال الجسدانيه والنفسانيه جاهدت قبال الالام والخطيه والشيطان، ونجحت بالمعونة الالهيه، عندما تنتقل[2642] من الجسد تتنيح في المنازل التي بلغتها[2643] اليهم، لواحظ عدم الالام، الذي[2644] اقتنت الى يوم تجديد الكل، وما دامت متقلبه بالجسد تسري معرفتها على بلاد السلامه، (A271r) وبيوت النور الموضع الذي ترفعها اليها جناحات عدم الالام.

(IV.93) الشياطين يحركون[2645] الالام في النفس لكيما بلذة دغدغة الالام يغرقون النفس الشقيه بتجاوز الوصيه والامور الواجبه، حتى تكون مغلوبه من الالام من قبل انتقالها من الجسد، يلاقوها في الجو ويخطفوها الى بلد الظلمه الميراث الذي لهم.

2635 تقطع : R, S.

2636 التي : R, S.

2637 من ان : R, S.

2638 ويتشجل : R.

2639 الام : S.

2640 بعدم : R.

2641 الذين : R, S.

2642 تنتقل : A.

2643 بلغته : R.

2644 التي : R, S.

2645 يحركوا : S.

(IV.94) وحسب قول الابا ان النفس اما هاهنا او[2646] وقت خروجها من الجسد تقبل حسس بلد ميراثها.

(IV.95) اكثر الابا يقولون ان نفوس الصديقين يسبحون الرب[2647] في الموضع الذي يكونوا[2648] فيه، واخرين يقولون انه[2649] كمثل بنوم [2650] لذيذ يستريحون في مظلاتهم،[2651] بلا انفعال يختلجون.

(IV.96) انفس القديسين بالمسيح الذين استحقوا بتجديد ضماير هن[2652] ان[2653] يقبلوا هاهنا في وقت وقت استعلان روح القدس، فوق طبيعة الجسد بحسسا غير منطوق به، يقبل ذهنهن[2654] عربون بمقدار حسهن[2655] باى نوع يمجدون، او يختلجون ويستريحون (R205r) في منازلهم الى تجديد الكل.[2656]

(IV.97) وان كان من باكر الى العشا بحرص يجتهد ويعمل الانسان[2657] الفضايل،[2658] ولكن في وقت رقاده[2659] في النوم بالاكثر يجتهد ان يلقي البخور المختار الذي هو الهذيذ الصالح على مبخرة قلبه، ليبخر طول الليل، لكيما ينعتق من الاحلام السمجه والمناظر الليليه.

(IV.98) الصديقين[2660] الذين من الشبوبيه الى الشيخوخه يعملون بسيرة تدبير الفضيله،[2661] ولكن عندما يغرقون بنعاس نوم الموت بالاكثر يعملون، لان[2662]

2646 في : زائدة R, S.

2647 للرب : R.

2648 يكونون : R, S.

2649 انهم : R, S.

2650 بنور : R.

2651 مظلاتهن : R, S.

2652 ضمائرهم : S.

2653 ان : ساقطة R.

2654 ذهنهم : R.

2655 حسسهن : S / حسسهم : R.

2656 الكل : ساقطة R.

2657 الانسان : ساقطة R.

2658 الا فضايل : R.

2659 ارقاده : R, S.

2660 الصديقون : S.

2661 الفضايل : R, S.

2662 بداية فقرة جديدة : S / لانه : R, S.

يبخر في انفسهم بخور الفضايل والحب الالهي، الى حيث ينتبهون في تجديد العامه.[2663]

(IV.99) افكر كمثل انه ارسل من الملك[2664] كتاب الى اخوين،[2665] ان احدهم في الغد يوضع على راسه اكليل رياسة الكهنوت، والاخر في الغد يقبل خروج قضية الموت، واثنينهم غرقوا[2666] في النوم الليلي، فمعلوم ان كل واحدا[2667] واحد[2668] منهم بحسب ما تشهد له نيته وهذيذه بفرح او بحزن، يهدس بخيالات الاحلام.[2669]

(V) الميمر الخامس في رووس المعرفه للقديس مار اسحق.[2670]

(V.1) الله كل شي يريد يدرك والعارف الحقاني كل شي يدركه يختاره.

(V.2) ليس كل شي يريده ضميرنا في طبيعتنا قوه ان تعرفه،[2671] بل كل شي في طبيعتنا كفوا لتجده وايضا ضميرنا يدركه.

(V.3) الكنز الغير مسلوب المقنى[2672] الحياه هو مقدار الانسان وليعرف ذاته ومنزلته ويتميز في اخرته.

(V.4) النفس التي تحزن بالعوارض التي يصادفها به الطبع، هي عادمه من العزا[2673] الجواني. (A271v)

(V.5) المتوحد الذي كمل بالمعرفة الجوانيه، قد ارتفعت نفسه من الذين يفرحون ويحزنون من برا.

2663 العالم : R.

2664 الملك : ساقطة R.

2665 اخرين : A.

2666 عرفوا : R.

2667 واحد : R, S.

2668 واحد : ساقطة S.

2669 كمل الميمر الرابع : زائدة R.

2670 له ايضا : R / للقديس مار اسحق : ساقطة S.

2671 نعرفه : R.

2672 المقتنى : S.

2673 عزا : R.

(V.6) المتوحد الذي تدرب بالصبر واقتنا اتساع النفس ليحمل الصعوبات المصادفه اياه بغير تكدر، عوض العزا الذي من الاثمار الداخله يوهل عقله ليقبل اسرار روح القدس.

(V.7) كتاب الطبيعي القلبي الذي هو طاهر ونقي طبيعيا، معونة كثيره يعطي للكاتب البراني، لكي بتاديب[2674] التعليم ينكتب عليه تدبير معرفة الحق.

(V.8) فرق كثير[2675] بين[2676] الكتاب الطبيعي النقي[2677] قتاله[2678] من الالام وقصده غير ملتوي من المتالم، كمثل الفرز الذي بين الورق المعمول المسقول والراحه التي تحصل به، من الورق[2679] الردي الغير معمول الكتاب[2680] البراني.

(V.9) ليس ينسقل وينقا الرق الذي تنكتب عليه الكتب المقدسه من دون الكلس المحرق المنظف،[2681] ولا يقبل الكتابه ورسوم الصور والاحرف الا ان انجرد منه الشعر، وكل شي[2682] يوسخ بالكلس الحد الذي به ينعمل وينقا ويصلح للكتابه.

(V.10) لم ينعمل كتاب القلبي وينقا من الالام وينكتب عليه الابشلش[2683] وثب الغلوه وقصر الذات وغصبية[2684] تدبير الاعمال المولمه المحزنه ولا يصنع الاثمار التي كتبهم الطوباني بولس ولا يقبل الرسوم الالهيه، الا ان رجع وهدى (R205v) بالحب المضبوط الروحاني ويستريح بالحريه من شلش الحركات المحزنه، التي تزعج من خارج وداخل ويهدا من كل انفعال.

(V.11) الموضع الذي تشخص[2685] اليه عروق ناظر العقل الجواني الى هناك يمضي الذهن، وفيه يطيش ويتنيح ويرتبط الضمير الهادس فيه بمحبه.

2674 بتأدب : S.

2675 كثيرين : R.

2676 بين : ساقطة R.

2677 النقي : ساقطة R.

2678 صقاله : S.

2679 الرق : R.

2680 للكتاب : S.

2681 المنضف : S.

2682 شيئا : S / شيا : R.

2683 الابشلش (الابصلمص اي المزامير) : S / الا بشلش : R.

2684 وغصيبة : R.

2685 يشخص : R, S.

(V.12) الانحلال من الكل هو الارتباط بالواحد، ولا يمكن الارتباط بالواحد الا ان انحل الضمير من الكل.

(V.13) ان كان ما فيك قوه ان تعتق ضميرك من طياشة الافكار لكي يكون لك ضمير مصلوب الى الواحد بمحبه، كون مفسر الكتب المقدسه واهدس بهن[2686] وفسر بضميرك المزامير التسابيح والصلوات، والكتب بقصد مخافة الله روحانيا حسب قوتك، وبالهذيذ بهولاء[2687] ينعتق ضميرك من طياشة تقلب[2688] الافكار بالاباطيل، وتوهل لجمع العقل، لانه عظيم جدا سكون[2689] الضمير القريب لله.

(V.14) ان كان سكه[2690] تنقلع بسكه[2691] وعاده بعاده،[2692] معلوم ايضا ان فكر[2693] ينقلع بفكر، وينقطع بسكين تدبير السيره الذين هم الاتضاع والصبر والنسك والسهر والميتوته من العالم، ومداومة الصلوات التي تقويها[2694] وتثبتها، قراأة الكتب على الدوام والهذيذ بالفضايل.

(V.15) يا الذي يهرب من الشلش البراني الى السكون،[2695] (A272r) احترس من شلش قلب[2696] الافكار الذي[2697] داخل منك، لانه اصعب جدا واشر واقسا شلش تقلب الافكار الجوانيه المختلجه قبال الضماير النابعه في القلب، من الشلش البراني المصادف[2698] الاحواس ويكدر القلب.

(V.16) اذا ما انحل الضمير من التحفظ وزاغ عن الحق، واندفق تبع الخراق[2699] المتولده من تقلب الافكار بالمضاددات، النابعه قبال ذاك الذي

2686 بهم : S / به : R.
2687 بهولا : R.
2688 اتقلب : R, S.
2689 اسكون : R.
2690 سلة : S.
2691 بسلة : S.
2692 بعاده : ساقطة R.
2693 فكرا : S.
2694 تقويه : R.
2695 للسكون : R, S.
2696 تقلب : R, S.
2697 التي : R, S.
2698 المصادفة : S.
2699 الخرافة : R, S.

حركه الفعل اكثر من جريان البحر ترتفع وتتعالى[2700] امواج جري بحر الضمير، بمراددات الضلاله[2701] المظنون[2702] بهن محقين ومثبتين[2703] ولايقين وواجبين،[2704] بعدالة قصد مخافة الله بوجه الفضيله، قبال ذاك الذي سبب التحرك بحر[2705] الضمير ويزكي نفسه في ضميره بالعدل، ويشجب رفيقه ويدينه ويزجره، ليس ينبغي لنا ان نخدع بهولاء[2706] بل نضاددهم ونزجرهم منذ المبدا، ولنقمع وحشيتهم الفاعله بوجه فضيلة البر، من قبل ان يخرجونا من بلد السلامه وهدو[2707] الحب.

(V.17) ما يمكن ان نحفظ الوصايا السيديه بتدبير عدالة الناموس، لان هناك يقول العين عوض العين، والسن عوض السن والبقيه، ونعمة المسيح تامر قايله اغلبوا الشرور بالخير، يعني من يضربك على خدك اليمين رد[2708] له الاخر، ومن ياخذ ثوبك اترك له رداك.

(V.18) ليس في الضمير كفو[2709] ان يصبر على مضاددة العدالة والنعمه جميع، لان تلك غضب وغيره تحرك، وهذه تلقي على الضمير سلامه (R206r) وحب ورحمه.

(V.19) ليس يليق لضمير المتوحد الذي يسير تبع سلامة القلب،[2710] ان يلوم او يشجب انسان لا بالوجه ولا بالقلب، لان بولس الطوباني قال لم تكونوا تحت العداله بل تحت النعمه.

(V.20) المتوحد الذي يقطع راس مبدا نبات[2711] الافكار هو مجاهد نشيط، ويوهل بسهوله للذكاوه وينعتق من الطياشه.

[2700] وتتعالا : R, S.

[2701] الطلاله : A.

[2702] المصنون : A.

[2703] ومتكبتين : R.

[2704] واجبين : R, S.

[2705] لبحر : S.

[2706] بهولا : R.

[2707] وهدوء : S / وهدوا : R.

[2708] ارد : R, S.

[2709] كفوا : R, S.

[2710] قلبه : R, S.

[2711] انبات : R.

(V.21) المتوحد الذي يتنازل مع الافكار ويتفاوض معهن هو عمال بالفسق خفيا داخل ضميره، ويعطي ماده للالام ان تتواثب عليه في الاخير.

(V.22) المتوحد الذي قد انسحق قلبه بالنسك وعلى الدوام يشخص نظر عقله بالمسيح ويتامل بالرجا كل ساعه لمعونة النعمه، وحريص بمفاوضة الصلاه ويحترص بما يخصه ليس يطيش ضميره بالاباطيل، ولا تجرحه[2712] اسهام الشرير ليحركوا فيه الالام.

(V.23) القصد المستقيم بتدبير الضمير هو ان يشجب[2713] الانسان بمحبة التعليم، بقراءة الكتب ويستضي بهذيذ افهامهم، ويذوق حلاوة الاسرار الروحانيه المخفيه في الكتب،[2714] وهذا ليس له مانع ان تسكر هي النفس بالحب الالهي بتدبير سيرة النسك القاطعة الالام ولا يغلب من لذتهم.[2715]

(V.24) (A272v) المتوحد الذي قصده مستقيم وضميره مصلوب الى هذيذا[2716] واحد وقد قطع من ذاته كل هم وفكر لا يوافق ذلك[2717] الهذيذ الواحد، وبلا فتور يهدس[2718] ويتفاوض ويتدرب ويعمل فيه مده زمانه[2719] هكذا يقبل في قلبه من النعمه والعاده كمثل الصورة المرتسمه في الدينار حتى وفي النوم ايضا به يهدس ضميره ويتفاوض بغير ارادته.

(V.25) الضمير المتقسم[2720] على ذاته فيعمل بقصد تدبير ما ويهدس فيه ويتفاوض، وفي وقت يقصد تدبير اخر غير ذلك،[2721] هذا ما ينجح لا بهذا ولا بذاك راسا.

(V.26) اذا ما عبر الذهن بتصور تاورية[2722] المعرفه على بلاد النفس المعقولين، ليغتذي او يلتجي او ينشرح فيهم او لياخذ[2723] منهم[2724] ماده،

[2712] يجرحه : R, S.

[2713] يشغف : S.

[2714] ويستضي بهذيذ...في الكتب : ساقطة R.

[2715] لذتها : S.

[2716] هذيذ : R, S.

[2717] ذالك : R.

[2718] يهدي : R.

[2719] زمانيه : R, S.

[2720] المنقسم : S.

[2721] ذاك : R.

[2722] ثاؤرية : S / تااورية : A.

[2723] لياخر : R.

[2724] منهن : R, S.

يغير[2725] زيه ولسان لغته للموضع الذي يدخل اليه، ومعهن ومثلهن[2726] يتفاوض وعند ذلك[2727] يفيد ويستفيد منهم، وبنوع واحد يثبت وقت الصلاه وهذا جميعه بكليته يوهل للاسرار المقدسه التي للثالوث المقدس.[2728]

(V.27) بنوعين تنعمل تدابير السكون، وكل واحد واحد منهم بانواع مختلفه ينفلح،[2729] لان ثم[2730] سكون[2731] حرية البنين وثم[2732] سكون[2733] عبودية التغصب، واعني بالتغصب عن انواع السكون المرتبطه بحدود القوانين.[2734]

(V.28) السكون المتضيق لكيما تنعتق الاحواس والضمير من الخباط والشلش[2735] البراني، ويهتدوا[2736] بالسكون الجواني وينعتقون من الملاقات والصدف النافعه والمخسره[2737] والغيظ والخلق، ويوهلون للذكاوه.

(V.29) بهذا السكون المتضيق من الانقباض الدايم الجواني يتولد الخوف والحيا[2738] (R206v) وانسحاق[2739] القلب، ومن تغير ضوايق الاعمال الغصيبيه[2740] يتولد التواضع والحفظ والصبر الغصبي، وترتيب الاحواس.

(V.30) من الصلوات الغصيبيه[2741] المتقدمه بحزن وخضوع[2742] وانسحاق قلب، تتولد صلاة النعمه الاراديه المتصليه[2743] بنياح وراحه، ومن صلاة المفاوضه التي تكون بتصور العقل بهذيذ الكتب والطبايع وافهام الكلام على

[2725] بغير : R, S.
[2726] ومثلهم : R.
[2727] ذالك : R.
[2728] الممجد : S / الممجود : R.
[2729] بداية فقرة جديدة : S / يتفلح : R, S.
[2730] ثمة : S.
[2731] اسكون : R.
[2732] وثمة : S.
[2733] اسكون : R.
[2734] التي للسكون : زائدة S.
[2735] وشلش : R, S.
[2736] ويهدوا : R.
[2737] والمخسه : R.
[2738] والحياة : R, S.
[2739] وانسحق : R.
[2740] الغضبية : S / الغصبيه : R.
[2741] الغصبيه : R, S.
[2742] وخدوع : R.
[2743] المصلاة : S / المتصلبه : R.

اللاهوت، يتولد صلاة الهذيذ، ومن صلاة الهذيذ المتقويه من قراة الكتب يكون جمع العقل، ويتكون الانقباض.

(V.31) ومن الصلوات المتواتره والهذيذ الدايم بالله المتكون من جمع العقل وانقباضه، يتولد داخل القلب نور الضمير ليفرز بافهام المعرفه الحق من تشبه الطغيان، ومنذ ذاك بالنعمه فوق الطبيعه يوهل للصلاه الروحانيه التي للذهن ويكمل بالحب.

(V.32) سكون[2744] الحريه هو سكون[2745] الضمير الهادي المختلج بالله داخل وخارج، وهو زهره السكون الغضبي وهذه دلايله، (A273r) حرية الافكار سلامة[2746] القلب دايما نياح الضمير عدم الخوف من جميع طبايع الخليقه، المتجسده[2747] والغير متجسده،[2748] والبعد[2749] من جميع مفاوضات الوجوه، محبة قفر البريه، لكيلا تتعبد حرية ضميره وافكاره بغصبية[2750] خوف المرايا الشرفه[2751] والدنيين المكرمين والحقيرين، ولا يتقسم على ذاته ويتوبخ من نيته، بميتوتة الضمير من الالام وارتفاعه من العالم واتحاد الذهن بالله ويصير هو في الله والله فيه.

(V.33) ليس ولا تمرمر يكدرون نقاوة نفسه لان ضميره يبقا[2752] بلا هم لا جيد ولا ردي كالمتوحش، ليس حفظ من غيرة[2753] اعدا ولا عذاب الاحواس والحركات وليس ماده للريا والاخذ بالوجوه، ليس خوف للسقوط، ليس ماده للالام[2754] ليتحركوا[2755] للفعل،[2756] سبى العقل واتبلع[2757] بمحبة ذاك الذي احبه، وصلا وطلب ووجد وامتحا من ذكره السماء والارض وصار متوحش للمفاوضة البشريه، ونسى قصد هذا العالم وعزاواته.

2744 اسكون : R, S.
2745 اسكون : R, S.
2746 حلامة : R.
2747 المتجسمه : R, S.
2748 متجسمه : R, S.
2749 البعد : R, S.
2750 بغصبية : S.
2751 الشرفاء : S / الشرفا : R.
2752 يبقى : S.
2753 غير : R, S.
2754 للألم : S.
2755 ليتحركون : R, S.
2756 بالفعل : S.
2757 وابتلع : R, S.

(V.34) يفكر ان ليس خليقة اخرى[2758] الا هو مسكن الله لم يسمع ان يعيش مع الناس، لانهم ما يعرفون لغاة[2759] لسان بعضهم بعض، لانه قد اوهل للغة الملايكيه[2760] وبها يرتل بخفية عقله.

(V.35) كما انه ما يستطيعون[2761] الخوف المتولد من الغصبيه[2762] والحريه المتولده من النقاوه ان يسكنوا جميع هكذا ما يستطاع[2763] ان يسكنوا جميع، تدبير التغصب مع تدبير النقاوه،[2764] لان ذاك يولد تكدر[2765] وكاابه وهذا سلامه وفرح.

(V.36) وان كان اثمار التي تولدها تدابير[2766] الغصبيه[2767] وتدابير الحريه هم اضداد بعضهم بعض الواحد يولد نور والاخر ظلام النفس، واما التي تقبل[2768] كل تدبير حسب غرض وقصد فاعله، من داخل وليس بغرض براني.

(V.37) كثيرين (R207r) يستعدون بكل نوع من الاستعداد يصلح لوقيد سراج انفسهم مع[2769] زيت الرحمه، وقليلين هم الذين يوهلون للنور حسبما[2770] تعرف سياسة مراحم الله، لمنفعة ذات ذاك الانسان او لفايدة العامه، وكل واحد بمقدار ما فيه كفوا ليحتمل.

(V.38) المجازاة الكامله العتيده مقابل وقيد المصباح من النعمه هي، واما اعداد سراج فضايل[2771] ذاتنا مع الزيت بغير عوز هي لنا، واما وقيده من هاهنا ليس هي لنا بل للرب السراج.

2758 اخرة : S / اخره : R.

2759 لغات : R, S.

2760 الملائكة : S / الملايكه : R.

2761 يستطيع : S.

2762 العضبية : S / الغضبية : R.

2763 يستطيع : S.

2764 ان يسكنوا... مع تدبير النقاوه : ساقطة R.

2765 اتكدر : R.

2766 تذكير : S.

2767 الغصبية : S / الغصبيه : R.

2768 الله تقبل : R / الله يقبل : S.

2769 من : R.

2770 حسب ما : R, S.

2771 فضايل : ساقطة R.

(V.39) العالم الجديد هو نور معقول وكل انسان حسب الماده التي اعد من هاهنا، للنور المعقول الذي[2772] هناك، من وقته يشعل سراج نفسه ويشرق بمقدار سير تدبيره.

(V.40) كل واحد منا نور وظلام عالم الجديد داخل منه هو حامل وموجود فيه، ومن داخلنا يشرق نور الفرح، وظلام الكابه والندامه، (A273v) وليس من ناحية اخره ياتيه ذلك[2773] او يقبله.

(V.41) وان كان صعب جدا وعسر هو اقتنا تدبير الحريه، وشديد ومر جدا الجهاد الذي قباله ومخاطرة صعبه في جمع الغنا الروحاني.

(V.42) مع هذا هو اسهل جمعه وتحصيله،[2774] من الاحتراس في صيانته وحفظه، لانه اذا نام قليل وتغافل طلب الشي فما وجده.[2775]

(V.43) سهل هو المشي على حرف السيف من القيام بلا مياله على حد السيف، مدة السيف مدة زمان فمن اجل هذا اللذين[2776] اهلوا[2777] للكمال بين الناس على تحقيق ينيحهم المسيح برحمته حسب تاملهم كالقول، اريد ان انتقل لكي اكون مع المسيح.

(V.44) ثم[2778] اخوه طوبانيين من قبل ان تسقط اجسادهم بسيرة الاعمال الجسدانيه والنفسانيه ويتضعون بالنسك ويقعون ويقومون في الالام، ويدخلون بنار التجارب، ويحتملون في انفسهم البرد والحر وشدة الظهيره التي لصعوبة الاعمال بترتيب السيره وحدود قوانين الابا، ويطيبون في مذاقتهم يوثبون[2779] على ازيد من مقدارهم بحدة الحركات، وياخذوا لهم مادة التحجج[2780] من الكتب المقدسه وقول الابا الروحانيين، في تدبير العقل، ويتخيلوا بفنطسة اذهانهم تدبير الحريه ويحتروا بالهمج ويسكروا والى الان الامهم[2781] بالحيا ما قد

[2772] التي : R.
[2773] ذالك : R.
[2774] وحصيله : S.
[2775] يجده : R, S.
[2776] الذين : R, S.
[2777] اؤهلوا : S / اوهلوا : R.
[2778] ثمة : S.
[2779] يوتون : S / يرتبون : R / يوثبون : A.
[2780] للتحجج : R.
[2781] الافهم : R.

ماتت، والاحواس الحركات[2782] والعوايد المتقدمه والخاصيات ثابته كمثل الاول، وعندما تبطل عنهم الحراره ويستفيقوا من السكر اذا تيقظوا توجد انفسهم فارغه متجرده، من جميع تدبير سيرة الرهبنه الحقيقيه، وقد انتشف من روسهم بتخيل مصاعد[2783] خرافة[2784] المتقدمه.[2785]

(V.45) القديس اغريغوريوس[2786] اب جميع العارفين لاجل كثرة حرصه واجتهاده باعمال واتعاب مختلفه ونسك خمسة عشر سنه، نقى قلبه بالمعونة الالهيه، واتت عليه تجارب كثيره مختلفه ووثبت عليه ضغطات وضوايق وعذاب وجلد من المضاددين[2787] حتى كادت نفسه تخرج (R207v) من الجسد كما يخبر كتاب سيرته، حتى اتحنن عليه المسيح ونيحه بالسلامه.

(V.46) عسره هي جدا ورديه السقطه من تدبير السيره ومفتقره للتوبه على مقدار السقوط، من علو الفضيله، ولكن اشر من هذه وهي مملوه خطر من يسقط من علو التدبير الروحاني، التي للحريه، ولو ان تشفى[2788] ضربته بدواء[2789] التوبه،[2790] بعد جهد قليل من ينجا من الخطر.

(V.47) سلابين لطيفه[2791] وجلودين يرصدوا[2792] اثر الذي يشتاق للكمال، وما يشفقوا[2793] على بطالة مدة سنين كثيره وتعب كما كتب عنهم.

(V.48) محبوب (A274r) عندهم صيد جبار واحد كم من وقت قد قطع شباكهم وكسر فخوخهم وعصى على لذة ودغدغه المجاذبات واقتنا في ذاته كنز الحياه، اخير من ربوات[2794] تعالب كثيره صغار[2795] الذي بلا تعب وعنا هم يسقطوا انفسهم ويعثرون لهلاك ذواتهم من غير اعتنا الصيادين.

2782 والحركات : R, S.

2783 المصاعب : S.

2784 خرافة : ساقطة S / رافة : R.

2785 جزافا : زائدة S.

2786 اغريس : S / مار اوجريس : R.

2787 المضادين : S.

2788 تشفا : R, S.

2789 بدوا : R, S.

2790 للتوبة : S.

2791 الشياطين : زائدة S.

2792 يرصدون : R, S.

2793 يشفقون : R, S.

2794 ربوة : R, S.

2795 صغيرة : S.

(V.49) الصيادين الماهرين اذا ما وقع في مصايدهم سبع جبار ضاري[2796] كم مره قطع حبال فخوخهم،[2797] يخفون انفسهم ويكمنون له من كل ناحيه، ويحزقون اوتار مصايدهم عليه الى ان يعثر هو من نفسه ويشتبك وتضعف قوته، عند ذلك[2798] يوثبون[2799] عليه ويقلعون اضفاره[2800] ويكسرون انيابه، وياخذون منه سلاحه حتى تضمحل قوته ويتركوه مرمي في وسط الناس، ليلعبون به الصبيان.

(V.50) على هذه الصفه هو المتوحد الشجيع النفس الذي[2801] بمعونه الله كم من وقت كسر فخوخ الشياطين، وقطع حبال مصايدهم وارعب صفوف عساكرهم، ومرمر حياتهم بقوة النعمه، اذا ما نام بالغفله والاهمال قليل، او اتعظم[2802] بالافتخار وانتفخ بالظنون[2803] وادعا بالعظايم، وتكبر[2804] على الضعفا[2805] كمثل غالب قد قهر الالام والخطيه[2806] والشياطين، بانه خدع نفسه مدة زمان باعمال النسك واستحق الرحمه، وجا الوقت الذي به يستريح ويتمجد من ناظريه، معما اتبقا،[2807] ولم يعطي غلبته للرب، بل لنشاط ارادته الجيده، ترتخي عنه العنايه وتسمح النعمه ان يقع في شباك[2808] الشياطين الذين يصرون اسنانهم عليه وينقهرون منه.

(V.51) الشياطين المنافقين هم متلهفين لهلاكنا، وعندما يقع بغته متوحد شجيع[2809] القلب في فخوخهم[2810] ما يصدقون، بل يخفون انفسهم ويرمون عليه تخيلات[2811] ويمتحنوه ان كان يتنازل بافكار الالام الذي اولا[2812] ما كان يقبلهم،

2796 ضاري : ساقطة R.

2797 افخوخهم : R.

2798 وعند ذالك : R.

2799 يثبون : S.

2800 اضافره : S.

2801 التي : R, S.

2802 واتعظم : S.

2803 بالضنون : A.

2804 واتكبر : R.

2805 الضعفه : R.

2806 الخطيه : R.

2807 تبقى : S.

2808 اشباك : R, S.

2809 سجيع : R.

2810 افخوخهم : R.

2811 اتخيلات : S / اتحيلات : R.

ويسرقوه بالكسل والاهمال والتضجر ويوسوسون له بشره البطن، والزنا ونياح الجسد، الاشيا التي كان يزدري بها، فاذا نظروا قد ارتخا ضميره ومال لقبول الالام المرذوله بسهوله، واشتبك بالالام بالكليه واعتاد بالنياحات، ولم يحس بالتخليه[2813] ولا يقض قلبه للتوبه، بل بالضد يفتخر عند (R208r) السقوط ويتخرف[2814] بفنطسة القيام، وانه مثبت[2815] بالنهوض،[2816] عند ذلك[2817] يجددون حيلهم ويوسوسون بكمال الابا القديسين، الذين كملوا واهلوا[2818] للاستعلانات وعملوا العجايب، لكي بالتمام يسقط من النعمه ويترك بيديهم ويستهزون[2819] به.

(V.52) (A274v) ما دام المتوحد واقف في الجهاد بنشاط وحرص لا هو ينغلب كيف اتفق ولا هم الشياطين يقاتلون بقوه بل يرصدون الاوقات الموافقه للصيد، وعندما يكمل الجهاد وبطل الحرب ووثق المجاهد بغلبته والقا عنه سلاحه، كمثل غالب، وعند[2820] ذلك[2821] الشياطين كمثل مقهورين قد انغلبوا من نشاطه ووقعوا الى اسفل، بحيل المديح يخدعوه بالافكار لكي بسهوله يصطادوه.[2822]

(V.53) المتوحد الذي قد اوهل للرحمه اعني الكمال، ينبغي له في كل حين ان لا يرمي سلاحه عنه الذين هم التواضع الهدو[2823] الانحطاط، حمل ضعف القريب، الصبر الاحتمال طول الروح، الازدرا بالذات وان[2824] لا يحب ان يغلب التي هي اصل كل الشرور،[2825] محبة الذات ام جميع الالام، وبصيانة

[2812] اوله : R, S.

[2813] بالت ليه : R.

[2814] وينحرف : S.

[2815] متثبت : R, S.

[2816] بالنهوط : A.

[2817] ذالك : R.

[2818] واوهلوا : R.

[2819] ويستهزئون : S.

[2820] عند : R, S.

[2821] ذالك : R.

[2822] يصطاده : R.

[2823] الهدوء : S / الهدوا : R.

[2824] ان : ساقطة R.

[2825] شرور : R.

ذهن يفتش دايما ضميره وافكاره وارادته، وينظر الى[2826] ايما من الالام يميلون وايما هو من الالام يتحيلوا ليسلبوا[2827] النفس خفيا بوجه الفضيله ويعتقها منهم.

(V.54) الامور الكريمه التي[2828] دعي اسم الملك عليهم[2829] والى الان ما عبروا لكنز الملك، يكونوا مكرمين على خدام الملك افضل من الذين عبروا بمجد وكرامه لخزانة[2830] الملوكيه وانفسد جمال حسنهن داخل الخزانه، والقيوا الى خارج واتبهدلوا وصاروا موطا[2831] للناس، وانتزعت العنايه عنهن.

(V.55) تايب يعمل على الرجاء بكرمة المسيح ولو انه عاجز حسب قوته، اخير من صديق بار قد اتفاضل بجميع محاسن الفضايل وقد اوهل بالرحمه لسر استعلان معرفة الحق، وفي الاخر فسد داخل بلاط المسيح وعدم من عناية الملايكه بتخلية النعمه.

(V.56) تدابير حرية النفس ان لم يكون الانسان محترس فيهم بصيانه، وبشهادة النيه عندما يظن ان قد بطل عنه القتال خفيا وظاهر،[2832] وسكنت الرواميز الالاميه[2833] عن النفس، ووثق[2834] انه قد بلغ الى مينا السلامه، ان اتهاون[2835] بارادته بغته من غير ان يدري[2836] ويظن، تتحرك[2837] الامواج الخفيه داخل بحر ضميره ويهدمون[2838] سفينة[2839] النفس، ان لم يستيقظ الذهن الرييس وباتضاع القلب وبانسحاق[2840] يصرخ بحزن الى المسيح محيي كل الخلايق بمراحمه.

[2826] الى : ساقطة S.

[2827] ان يسلبوا : R, S.

[2828] قد : زائدة R, S.

[2829] عليه : R.

[2830] الملك : زائدة S.

[2831] موطئا : S.

[2832] وظاهرا : S.

[2833] اللالاميه : R.

[2834] ووقت : R.

[2835] تهاون : S.

[2836] يدرا : R.

[2837] يتحرك : R.

[2838] ويعدمون : S.

[2839] اسفينة : R.

[2840] وانسحاق : R, S.

(V.57) تدابير الحريه بدم[2841] النفس يقتنون، وان لم ينحفظوا بمراحم ربنا يسوع المسيح، وتكون النيه مصلوبه مقابل الاراده والضمير والافكار ليلا[2842] ونهار[2843] ليلا يخرجون برا عن حدود الحريه بمراياه.

(V.58) لان تدابير (R208v) حرية النفس هم مرتفعه عن تحيل غش المراياه المولدة النجاسه في النفس النقيه.

(V.59) تدابير الحريه عندما ينظر[2844] الحق ينادي على الحق، وعندما ينظر الضلاله[2845] يشهر[2846](A275r) ببساطه وعندما ينظر ويسمع يقبل بلا حريان، ويتكلم بلا ريا[2847] واخذ بالوجوه، ولا يعتني لا بالكرامه ولا بالاهانه، بغلبه وانغلاب احلام هذا الزمان، ولو دعوه الناس ابله مرذول بلا فحص، وبعد جهد يقدر ان يعيش في وسط كثيرين.

(V.60) نقاوة القلب الحقيقيه هو الحب الكامل التام بغير فرز لجميع طبع البشريه بالسوا وهذه من غير حفظ الوصايا والغلبه على الالام ونور عدم التالم والنعمه لا يستطاع ان تكون.

(V.61) ولا يمكن اقتنا هولاء[2848] باتفاق وشبكه مع كثيرين، كلما الاحواس قايمه منتبهه، لان الذي قد نقى قلبه قد اقتنا بساطة الامانه والمعرفه ولم ينظر شر انسان، وعندما يسمع ان فلان جيد وفلان ردي يصدق ببساطه بلا فحص، كمثل الطفل، فان كان يفتش[2849] بمعرفه ليس هناك طهاره ولا نقاوه، وان ينظرهم بعد هذا بسويه يعسر على القلب ويغتصب لان القلب اتنجس بغير ارادته ولو لم يشأ.

(V.62) في عدم الخباط والشلش بسهوله يقتني الانسان طهارة القلب وبساطة الامانه، ويوهل للنقاوه ان حفظ حقوق السكون واحترس بواجبات السيره، ويهدس دايما في مخافة الله.

2841 ندم : R.

2842 ليل :R.

2843 ونهارا : S.

2844 تنظر : S.

2845 الطلاله : A.

2846 يشهد : R, S.

2847 رياء : S.

2848 هولا : R.

2849 نفتش : R.

(V.63) هناك يكون الانسان معقولا،[2850] المكان الذي ضميره وافكاره به يهدس وينجذب بصنارة[2851] المحبه وعشق تدبير السيره[2852] الذي قد احب، واما الذي يسكن في المجمع كمثل الذي هو في السوق، ولو ان يغمض احواسه لا يمنكه ان يفلت من الملاقاة[2853] النافعه والمخسره، التي تصادفه من الضروره.

(V.64) ان كان بين الحجر[2854] لرفيقه[2855] تعبر السكه، بالضروره وبين النظر والسمع والكلام والافعال، تغبر[2856] العوايد والخاصيات الذي هو ساكن معهم بتحرك[2857] الضمير، وينتقل مما[2858] يخصه من غير ان يشا، ويقبل رسوم[2859] هيولاينه حسب العلل والعوارض التي تتفق، واذا ما طار الذهن بجناحات الروح على بلاد الداخله التي للسلامه، وبيوت النور[2860] كمثل الاول، تتعطل نظرته من ظلام الهيولى الذي[2861] قبل، ويخيب من النظره الروحانيه، وعندما ينتبه ويغصب ذاته ويلقى منه الاشيا الاوله، يرجع ايضا يقبل رسوم[2862] اخر.

(V.65) ان كان ليس للنفس ان تركب اشكال ومناظر وخيالات النظر، ولا ان تحرك تذكار او هذيذ وفكر ان لم تقبل[2863] عليهم معرفه مع الجسد بالخمسة احواس، فطبيعتنا[2864] (R209r) لها شي ارفع من طبيعة الجسد، معروف الان ان في وقت الصلاه فوق من تركيبها مع الجسد تقبل، (A275v) معرفتها بالنعمه حسس جديد لا شبه له ما لم تنظر عين ولا تسمع به اذن وما تبقى،[2865] واما الذي مع تركيب[2866] الجسد لا يمكن ان ينعتهم احدا.[2867]

2850 معقول : R, S.
2851 بسنارة : S.
2852 السير : R.
2853 الملاقات : R.
2854 الحجرين : S.
2855 لرفيقه : ساقطة S.
2856 وتغير : R, S.
2857 يتحرك : R, S.
2858 من ما : R, S.
2859 ارسوم : R, S.
2860 النور : ساقطة R.
2861 الى : R.
2862 ارسوم : R, S.
2863 يقبل : R.
2864 فطبيعتها : R, S.
2865 تبقا (الخ) : S / تبقا : R.
2866 ترتيب : R.
2867 احد : R, S.

(V.66) ما هو الشي الذي به يحس[2868] بالحق ما نعرف قد سكن واهتدا وقبل حسس حياة الجديده من غير انفعال.

(V.67) السارافيم تقدس[2869] الاقداس يقدسون[2870] سرا بغير حركات، والملايكه[2871] بالهيكل يعملون جميع.

(V.68) البر هو ثمرة الافعال الصالحه التي تنعمل.

(V.69) قبل ظهور[2872] اشراق شمس البر الاعظم القداسه[2873] هي ثمرة روح القدس الذي يقدس النفس بكمال جري جهادها ويتوجها باكليل المجد المزمع، ويمنحها نظرا روحانيا فوق الطبيعه.

(V.70) اذا ما بالاتعاب الاراديه المفرزه بني بيعتك الداخل تظن انه قد اتزين، واتكمل[2874] هيكل نفسك الجواني بمحاسن الفضايل، وتريد تعرف ان كان قد[2875] فاضت الرحمه وانفتح الباب الجواني الذي[2876] لقدس الاقداس، واتقدس المذبح[2877] الجواني الذي[2878] للغفران، وحلت النعمه، واوذن للكاهن الجواني ليدخل[2879] يقدس سريا ويوضع بخور الصلاه دايما، هولاء[2880] وما يشبههم[2881] تفهمهم[2882] من غيار انواع البخور الذكي، السلامه والحب والفرح الروحاني، الذي على الدوام يفوح داخل منك، بوساطة الذكر والهذيذ الدايم المطبوع فيه هم[2883] حب الله، وفرح وعزا خفيا يختلج بنفسك اذا لم تكون[2884] انت لهم سبب.

2868 نحس : R, S.

2869 بقدس : S.

2870 يقسون : A.

2871 الملايكه : R, S.

2872 اظهور : R, S.

2873 بداية فقرة جديدة : S.

2874 وانكمل : S.

2875 قد : ساقطة R.

2876 التي : R.

2877 مذبح : R, S.

2878 التي : S / الذي : ساقطة R.

2879 ليتكل : R.

2880 هولا : R.

2881 يشبهم : R.

2882 نفهمهم : S.

2883 هم : ساقطة S.

2884 يكون : S.

(V.71) تصور الورق وكلام العلوم واستضا ادراك العقل وضماير مختلفه وافكارا[2885] لطيفه، وافهام غويصه وتاوريات[2886] وافراز تصور التاوريات[2887] المختلفه، هم امور الزياده في المعرفه التي بهن تفحص النفس وتدرك عناية سياسة الله، وبحكمة خلقته فوق وتحت وتدابيره في كل الاجيال، والعوالم بجميع تغيراتهم.

(V.72) من العمل القلبي الدايم وتدرب العقل وتخرجه بالهذيذ بمثل هولاء[2888] يتصور ويرتسم قوة حقيقتهم جسمانيا منظور، على الواح مذبح القلب الذكي،[2889] لكي[2890] من هاهنا ينعتق الذهن الكاهن من الطياشه والتفتيش والبحث على وجود هولاء[2891] جميعهم، ويصير ناظر قوة الحق وليس حسس بالافهام والتاوريات[2892] من هذا الى هذا من الاجسام الى الغير متجسمين الروحانيين والجسدانيين، بل يهدا ويسكن[2893] ويستريح من الكل[2894] الى عند سر النعمه الموجود داخل منه.

(V.73) ليس هو موافق ان يفتقر قلبنا ويحتاج الى الاسطر، لولا ضيعت حريتنا عزا فهم[2895] الحق، لان ينبغي ان تكون تدابيرنا نقيه ان الشي المكتوب على قلبنا بروح الله وتشهد لنا نيتنا، كقول الكتاب لا (R209v) نخيب من حقانية فهمه.

(V.74) (A276r) لو دام طبعنا مقتنى قلبا[2896] طاهر، لم كان يضطر الله ان برسم الاسطر يتكلم معنا، ولكن كمثلما[2897] اتكلم مع نوح وابراهيم وايوب وموسى، من غير وساطة كتاب.

[2885] وافكار : R, S.
[2886] ثاؤريات : S / وتااوريات : A.
[2887] الثاؤريات : S / التاريات : R.
[2888] هولا : R.
[2889] الذي : R.
[2890] لكن : S.
[2891] هولا : R.
[2892] والثاؤريات : S / والتااوريات : A.
[2893] ويستكن : R, S.
[2894] كل : R.
[2895] عرافهم : R.
[2896] قلب : R, S.
[2897] كمثل ما : R.

(V.75) ومن حيث[2898] تدهور[2899] وسقط طبعنا في عمق الشرور، واتكلم الله معنا بالاسطر على الواح حجريه علامة قساوة قلبنا.

(V.76) حتى ولا سيدنا المسيح لرسله[2900] القديسين بالاسطر اسلم سر تعليمه، بل عوض الاسطر ميعاد[2901] روح القدس اعطاهم، وقال هو يذكركم كل شي[2902] يليق ويوافق الحق،[2903] وايضا في النبي، هكذا كتب، اوضع ناموسي في عقولهم وعلى قلوبهم اكتبه، ويكونوا معلمي لله.

(V.77) حتى وايضا هذه ان من الاسطر تتقوم[2904] تدابيرنا هي سمجه عند النطقيه التي قبل طبعنا منذ المبدا.

(V.78) كم بالاكثر ننرذل[2905] من الله اذا ما رذلنا الكتاب الطبيعي القلبي، المسطور على يد موسى والانبيا ولنور بشارة الحياه انجيل مخلصنا ونجلب[2906] على ذواتنا قضية الموت اذ[2907] لم ننتفع لا من الكتاب الخفي، ولا من الكتاب الظاهر، ولا من بشارة وصايا سيدنا المحييه مخلصنا يسوع المسيح.

(V.79) حتى ولا الانسان الذي يعمل ويداوم بالصلاه والقراه والتصور والفهم، ينجح عند الحق ولا يستضا[2908] عقله بالروح، ان لم يوافق غرض ضميره لقوة ذاك الشي الذي قد كتب بالروح على كتاب قلبه.

(V.80) حاجز الالام المحجوب على قلبنا لم يتركنا ان ننظر في الحق الذي بالروح كتب على قلبنا، بل اذا ما صلينا وقرينا وزمرنا يجوز عايم[2909] على

2898 حيثا : R.
2899 اتدهور : S / دهور : R.
2900 برسله : A.
2901 ميلاد : R.
2902 شيئا : S / شيا : R.
2903 بداية فقرة جديدة : R, S.
2904 يتقوم : R, S.
2905 نرذل : S.
2906 ويجلب : R.
2907 اذا : S / ان : R.
2908 ويستضاء : S / ويستضا : R / ولا يستطا : A.
2909 عايم (ظاهر) : S.

قلبنا، ولم نحس[2910] بالحق الجواني، فان كنا نرفع حاجز الالام يحفظ الوصايا تنظر[2911] عيون[2912] الروح الحق المرتسم على[2913] قلبنا.

(V.81) ما دام حريتنا تندان من نيتنا على الشرور الخارجه عن الواجب التي نفعل، او افكارنا تنقسم على كلامنا، وكلامنا على افعالنا، والثالوث الذي فينا ما اصطلح، لا نسرع على ان نصالح لاخرين، لا الله، ولا البشر، ولا نظن ان بخور صلواتنا تصعد الى الله وتنقبل.

(V.82) فان كان الثالوث الذي فينا اتفق بالحب والفرح، وحريتنا وقت النور ما تتبكت من نيتنا، وبغير فتور تقدم نفسنا صلاه وشكر لله وهي هاديه،[2914] وجميع الخليقه تصطلح معنا بالحب والمحبه.

(V.83) فان كان النور[2915] الذي[2916] فينا ظلام فظلامنا كم يريد يكون، اعني ان كان سلام قلبنا متكدر بالخلق والغيض والحسد، وهو متقسم على ذاته من داخل، فكدرنا كم باحرى[2917] يكون.

(V.84) عندما تكون منغاض[2918] مر نكد،[2919] انظر[2920] بلطافه في العدوين الصعبه المتحركه فيك من الجوانيين (R210r) ومن البرانيين جميع، من الجوانيين الالام المره والخلق[2921] والحقد والغضب والحسد والشر، الواثبين على فضايل[2922] تقانة نفسك المفسدين لهم، ويخيبوك (A276v) من حلاوة الحب الالهي، ومن البرانيين الناس الاشرار الذين يخجلوك ويعيرون بك اصدقايك، وعندما تكون حلو[2923] بشوش[2924] طيب[2925] انظر داخل منك، كيف

2910 يحس : R, S.

2911 ننظر : R, S.

2912 بعين : R, S.

2913 في : R, S.

2914 هادئة : S / هديه : R.

2915 النور : ساقطة R.

2916 هو : زائدة R, S.

2917 بالحري : S / بالخزي : R.

2918 منغاض (منغاظ) : S.

2919 متكدر : S.

2920 انظر : ساقطة R.

2921 والحلق : S.

2922 الفضائل : S / الفضايل : R.

2923 حلوا : S / خلوا : R.

2924 بشوشاً : S.

بني بيتك يفرحون ويفرحوك، اعني السلام والهدو[2926] والحب[2927] والود[2928] نور[2929] المعرفه الرجا على الله.

(V.85) ما دام كل يوم يصطبغون الضمير والافكار بالوان واشكال، ناطقين بعضهن[2930] بعض بالملاقات النافعه والمخسره، او[2931] يسمح مع هذا لطيبة قلبه، ومع الاخر لغرض ارادته، ومع هذا لنياح شهوته ومع ذاك لنياح[2932] غضبه وقساوه خلقه، متى يثبت[2933] الذهن فيما يخصه ويهدي ذاته، وما ينقسم لاشيا كثيره ويصير واحد[2934] عند الواحد، ويصعد اثمار روحانيه لنياح ارادة الله.

(V.86) كما ان الوجوه مفترزه كذلك[2935] الاراده والضماير ايضا[2936] والاغرظ والعوايد، والخاصيات وكل موضع يلاقي الضماير بغيار الضماير، وبتغير المشيات والاغراض والعوايد، ان كان يريد ان يجاور[2937] قريبه بسلامه معه ومثله ينبغي ان يكون، بمراياة الحب والريا وهذه هي الطريق[2938] المثبتة[2939] سلامة[2940] القلب، فلهذا اعظم من جميع الفضايل السكون يكون متفاضل عندنا، لانه ينيحنا من ساير الشرور، فلنهرب للسكون[2941] يا اخوتي لنخلص من نخز[2942] النيه ونوهل لتجديد الضمير.[2943]

2925 طيبا : R, S.

2926 الهدوء : S / الهدوا : R.

2927 الحب : R.

2928 الود : S / الو : R.

2929 نور : ساقطة R.

2930 بعضهم : R.

2931 اذ : R, S.

2932 النياح : R, S.

2933 متيثبت : R.

2934 الواحد : R.

2935 كذالك : R.

2936 وايضا : S / ايضا : ساقطة R.

2937 يجاوز : R.

2938 الطريقة : S.

2939 المثبكته : R.

2940 بسلامة : R.

2941 للسكوت : R.

2942 ن : R.

2943 الضمائر : S.

(V.87) الاسرار المقدسه تظهر خفيا للنفس التي قد[2944] اتجددت بالروح، وهن مرتفعه عن الاشكال المنظوره، لانه فعل الروح القدس كمثلما[2945] هو للروحانيين.

(V.88) كما ان الصوت الفضاح يتركب بالكلمه للنفس، ويتصور بالدوا على اللوح، ويظهر لاعين الجسد، هكذا والعقل الحي بوساطة النعمه يصور ويرسم معقولا لكلام الصلاه الروحانيه البسيط، بقلم الهذيذ الروحاني على لوح كتاب القلب، ليقرا فيهن وقت يطيش الضمير او[2946] يرقد الكينار، او يضعف او يظهر نوع[2947] عدم الالام ويشرق عليه شعاع شمس البر الاعظم.

(V.89) ارض القلب المفلوحه المزبله بمخافة[2948] الله، المحروثه اول وثاني بهذيذ الكلام الالهي، العطشانه ومتلهفه[2949] لشرب كلمة الحياه، عندما يزدرع بها العلم الروحاني ويسقيها كلمة النور، تختلج بغته بالايمان مقابل كلمة الحياه[2950] المثمره للواحد[2951] ثلثين[2952] وستين[2953] ومايه.

(V.90) ارض القلب القاسيه ولو ان تفلحها وتزبلها لم تنتبه قبال البدار،[2954] وسقي كلمة الحياه ويعوم[2955] عليها كلام النور والحياه، كمثل الماء على الصفا وتبقا بلا اثمار، بسبب الصفا الصمه[2956] المتسع والحلاوه كالقول السيدي.

(V.91) ليكون الانسان عارف الحق هو جزو[2957] (R210v) من الحق وليعمل بسيرة تدبير الحق هو فلاح[2958] (A277r) الفضايل وجزوا من الحق،

2944 قد : ساقطة R, S.

2945 كمثل ما : R.

2946 واو : R.

2947 نور : S / تور : R.

2948 بخوف : S.

2949 متلهفة : S / المتلهفه : R.

2950 عندما يزدرع بها...كلمة الحياة : ساقطة R.

2951 الواحد : S.

2952 بثلاثين : R, S.

2953 وبستين : R.

2954 بذار : S.

2955 ويقوم : S.

2956 الصمي (الصماء) : S / الصمي : R.

2957 جزوا : R, S.

2958 فلاح : ساقطة R.

واما ان يكون ناظر مجد الحق ومسارر بحسس الحياة الجديده هو الكمال هاهنا واما ان يقنيه[2959] بالتمام بلا مياله، هو التمام[2960] المزمع.

(V.92) لا تتحير ايها القارئ[2961] ولا تصعد الافكار على قلبك من اجل ان جميعهن روح واحده تدبر لكل واحدا واحدا[2962] حسبما[2963] يليق لحياته بالله، وفيه كفوا ليحمل.

(V.93) الذي من بعد اعمال التوبه والنسك والدربه بالكتب والهذيذ الدايم بالتااوريه[2964] الروحانيه، مع بقية الفضايل واوهل لنور الضمير، فينبغي ان يحترس متغصبا بغرض هذيذه وتااوريه[2965] معرفته كمثل براس ايمانه، ليلا بنور ضميره وبعمق فهمه عوض هذيذ واحد بعد معرفة الحق ببساطة حب المسيح يتغير ضميره ويسرع مبتلع بمحبة التعليم، وتاديبات اليونانيين بلا قصد الاول، وبحدة حركاته يقع في لجج الكتب وتفاسير وعلوم، وينجذب[2966] بكثرت[2967] العلوم والتااوريات[2968] المختلفه المفننه[2969] وبنور ضميره يصير مبدع امورا جديده، ومفيض اشيا مدهشه او يصادفه شكوك وحسد، ويقع من علو[2970] تدبير سيرته الممجده، وعوض ما اراد ان يكون ناظر لمجد الحق وحساس بسر الحياة الجديده، يتغرب من دعوته ووحديته.

(V.94) الظلام بالنور ينفسد، والنور بكثرة الظلام ينحجب، هكذا والمعرفة البسيطه التي للحق بكثرة معارف الحيل تظلم وتتقتم.

(V.95) عندما تعرف الحق بنور ضميرك احذر من التخيلات التي بعد كثرة معارف مختلفه، الذين[2971] يخيبوك من بساطة الحب والايمان، والصق[2972]

[2959] نقتنيه : S / يقتنيه : R.
[2960] الكمال : R, S.
[2961] القارى : R.
[2962] واحد واحد : R, S.
[2963] حسب ما : R, S.
[2964] بالتاؤرية : S / بالتاوريه : R.
[2965] وبتاؤرية : S / بتاورية : R.
[2966] ويتجذب : S.
[2967] بكثرة : R, S.
[2968] والثاؤريات : S / والتاوريات : R.
[2969] المتفننة : S.
[2970] علوا : R.
[2971] الذي : R.
[2972] والزق : R, S.

ببساطة الحق بانسانك الجوني بايمان[2973] بغير شك، بحب يغلي من كل قلبك، ومن كل[2974] ضميرك ومن كل قوتك كما كتب، وبذلك[2975] الهذيذ الواحد اهدس بتامل عقلك كمثل[2976] العطشان المتلهف للماء[2977] البارد، وحب المسيح وحده وليس لمواهبه والخيرات التي منه تعطا لك.

(V.96) العروسه ليس المواهب والخيرات التي تعطا[2978] لها من الختن تشتاق وتتامل،[2979] بل لذات الختن تطلب، ولو ان يعطا لها تاج المملكه عوض الختن الذي خطبها لا[2980] تقبل ولا تريد.

(V.97) نقتني المسيح حياتنا بانساننا الجواني الخفي، بحب يغلي بحفظ وصاياه، واذا ما اقتنيناه[2981] واتحدنا معه بالسر كل شي[2982] هو له لنا يكون، ان كان الحاضرات وان كان العتيدات. سماجة هي ان نحب[2983] عظايم الله ومواهبه اكثر من الله.

(V.98) نقتني الله عندما نرفض كل شي حتى وملكوت السماء،[2984] من اجل محبته، كمثل الرسول الطوباني، ويكون هذيذنا ورجانا وتاملنا معلق بيسوع المسيح، بقلب حار يغلو[2985] بالرب وسيط خيراتنا، (R211r) (A277v) بمفاوضة الصلاه خفيا وظاهرا، وعند ذلك[2986] حسب اشتياقنا يظهر لنا وينحينا[2987] كمثلما يعرف هو.

[2973] بالايمان : R, S.

[2974] كل : ساقطة A.

[2975] وبذالك : R.

[2976] مثل : S.

[2977] للما : R.

[2978] يعطا : R, S.

[2979] وتتمل : R.

[2980] ما : R, S.

[2981] اقتنياه : R.

[2982] شيا : R.

[2983] يحب : R.

[2984] السما : R.

[2985] يغلوا : R, S.

[2986] ذاك : R, S.

[2987] ينيحنا : S.

(V.99) المتوحد الذي طهر نفسه وزينها بحسن الفضايل كمثل العروس المزينه، وقبل المسيح في داخله وسلم له اختياره وجميع ارادته وكل شي[2988] له، ولم يعتني بشي[2989] اخر لا بجيد ولا بردي، بجميع ما يصادفه، هذا في كل وقت يغتذي بقوت الملايكه من مايدة[2990] المسيح، وطوبا للنفس التي[2991] استحقت هذا.

(V.100) متعالي هو كثير جدا ومتفاضل محب الملك وصاحب سره، ومجالسه على مايدته اكثر من جميع الشجعان والجبابره الذين يصنعون القتال، وينتصرون في الحروب المسميين بالشجاعه الكثيرين الاموال.

(V.101) هكذا يتاسس ويثبت فينا حب المسيح كمثل الصوره في الدينار، وذلك[2992] يكون بهذيذ الضمير دايما لان باي ناحيه يهدس فيها العقل يجلو[2993] النفس ويحدها وتسبا[2994] به الافكار والذهن، وتطلب ذاك الشي المتولد من ذاك الهذيذ والواحد.

(V.102) ينموا بغته من القلب حزن واحد حار نوراني ويسحق القلب، وينظفه ويشقه ويلهمه بتلهف فرح روحاني وتصعد بخار حدته للراس والعينين والمنخرين، كمثل شلهبة نار[2995] وتهطل دموع الفرح كمثل المياه الحاره،[2996] ولا يقدر يضبطهن بربوه حيل كثيره وينيح النفس من كل تذكار الالام، ويهديها من كل اضطراب وخباط.

(V.103) نوع واحد نوراني من النعمه ينموا بغته من القلب من غير ان نحس، ويسقي النفس ويرويها بالفرح ويغرق[2997] الزيوان بالمجاري السايله من العيون، هو اخير من ربوات[2998] صلوات ومطانيات نصنعهم وما نحن حاضرين بذهننا موضع نصلي، بل يعوموا على القلب والضمير كمثل السقيط

[2988] شيا : R.

[2989] بشيا : R.

[2990] مائدة : S / مادة : R.

[2991] الذي : R.

[2992] وذالك : R.

[2993] يجلوا : R, S.

[2994] تسبى : S.

[2995] النار : R, S.

[2996] الحاده : R.

[2997] ويفرق : S.

[2998] ربوة : R, S.

الغير تام، فاحذر ها[2999] هنا من ضلالة الشياطين لانهم يشبهون طغيانهم بمثل الحق، وايضا لا تدفع منك نعمة الله، لان ضلالة الشياطين[3000] مع الانفعال بالقلب، وايضا الاعضاء السفلانيه التي للشهوه[3001] يحركون ويدغدغون بلذة التنازل.[3002]

(VI) الميمر السادس في رووس المعرفه للقديس مار اسحق.

(VI.1) كمال الحق ينقام من تدابير الفضيله، الذين بالقصد المستقيم ينعملون ومن معرفة الحياة الروحانيه الخفيه، الفاعله في الطبايع، ومن الايمان البسيط المتشوق لمعرفة الحق.

(VI.2) عدم الالام يكمل في النفس بتدابير الفضايل المتقنه، وحفظ الوصايا، والوصايا مع المعونة الالهيه بالغصب الكثير القصري (R211v) ينحفظون، عندما يسيل دم النفس كمثل عرق الجسد.

(VI.3) معرفة الحق تقتنا في الذهن بالصلاه والهدو[3003] والاتضاع وطول الروح والصبر على جميع ما يعرض.

(VI.4) (A278r) الحب الروحاني الذي يغلي ويتسع بحراره في النفس، بالرحمه والبشاشه والحلاوه والشفقه بلا فرز الجيد من الردي، اعني الصالحين من الاشرار بالسويه.

(VI.5) الرجا يثبت ويتاسس في الانسان، بالتشوق والتامل للصالحات[3004] المنتظره.

(VI.6) الايمان يشرق وينير في النفس برجا مواعيد الروح المزمعه[3005] ان تظهر فينا.

2999 ها : ساقطة S.

3000 لانهم يشبهون...ضلالة الشياطين : ساقطة A.

3001 الشهوه : R, S.

3002 كمل الميمر الخامس : زائدة R.

3003 والهدوء : S / والهدوا : R.

3004 الصالحات : R.

3005 المزمع : S.

(VI.7) ليس يتحد الانسان بالكليه ويحس بجو[3006] الحريه[3007] الا ان بليوا واتخلفوا جميع الحركات واحواس الطبع القديم بحيل الاعمال وتدبير السيره، وينتبه ويقوم الانسان الجديد المعتمد الذي لبسناه من المعموديه، متردي[3008] بالسلامه والهدو[3009] والذهول والحب الروحاني وما تبقى.[3010]

(VI.8) سلامة[3011] النفس الجديد مع الهدو[3012] والذهول والحب الذي من النعمه، ان[3013] كان من الاعمال الاراديه يقتنوا[3014] بل[3015] اذا كملوا بروح القدس، ليس هم للطبع ولا للاختيار[3016] ايضا وليس تقع حقيقتهم تحت الطبيعه والاراده، ولا ينطق من دون النعمه.

(VI.9) طوبا[3017] للذي قد[3018] استحق عندما يزمر ويصلي تشخص عيني عقله بنور عدم الالام، وينظر بالعقل في كلام الصلاه معقول، المكتوب بقلم[3019] الروح على مراة قلبه، ومنهم يصعد التمجيد[3020] للذي[3021] اعطاه موهبة نظر النفس.

(VI.10) الذي اصلح ذاته ولم ينقسم على نفسه ليكون اثنين او كثيرين، بل هو واحد عند الواحد في كل حين وكل وقت، وبكل مكان، هذا بالحقيقه اصلح الثالوث[3022] الذي فيه وله زمان يهدس بهولاء.[3023]

3006 بجوا : S / بجو : ساقطة R.
3007 الحركه : R.
3008 متردي (مرتدي) : S.
3009 والهدوء : S / والهدوا : R.
3010 تبقا : R, S.
3011 سلام : R, S.
3012 الهدوء : S / الهدوا : R.
3013 وان : R.
3014 يقتنون : R, S.
3015 بل : ساقطة R.
3016 الاختيار : R, S.
3017 طوبى : S.
3018 قد : ساقطة R, S.
3019 بعلم : R.
3020 للتمجيد : R.
3021 الذي : R.
3022 لثالوث : R.
3023 بهولا : R.

(VI.11) حرية الحقيقيه هي بنت[3024] نور[3025] عدم الالام والسكينه[3026] والهدو[3027] وسلامة العقل، وافكار الحريه[3028] هم بنات الهدو[3029] العظيم الغير متحرك ولا متزعزع ببحر الضمير.

(VI.12) هدو[3030] البحر يكون عندما تهدا الارياح محركة الامواج، وهدو[3031] الضمير نحس[3032] به اذا ما سكن هذيذ التذكارات من طلب جميع الافهام.

(VI.13) ليس تهدا السفينه وتستكن في البحر من الحركات المخبطه ولو ان يهدا البحر ويسكن، الا اذا ما بلغت المركب الميناء الهادي والسلامه، وانزلوا القلع[3033] من مهب جميع النواحي وارموا المرسى في السفل.

(VI.14) هكذا لم تهدا وتستكن سفينة النفس من تحريك الامواج المضطربه بكثرة الضماير والافهام، وتستطيع تنظر ذاتها ما دام مصلوب العقل والضمير والفكر بشبه القلع[3034] مقابل الالام، بحفظ الوصايا ويسرعوا (R212r) في تبع تااورية[3035] الكتب،[3036] ليجمع ذخيره ليلاقي الحروب المصادفه من الالام والخطايا والشيطان، وليهدم الافكار النابعه، وليجمع الذهن من الطياشه، (A278v) وليقبل جميع ما ياتي عليه بلا اضطراب، يفرز[3037] فهمهم بافرازات معرفة الحق.

(VI.15) الى ان توفي النفس دين هولاء[3038] بالكليه ويكمل الذهن بما يخصه وتغطس الاحواس البرانيه مع الحركات الجوانيه من جريهم تبع كل ضماير

3024 بن... : R.

3025 نور : ساقطة A.

3026 السكينة : R, S.

3027 والهدوء : S / والهدوا : R.

3028 الهدوا : R.

3029 الهدوء : S / الهدوا : R.

3030 هدوء : S / هدوا : R.

3031 وهدوء : S / وهدوا : R.

3032 يحس : R, S.

3033 الولج : R.

3034 الول... : R.

3035 ثاؤريا : S / تاوريا : R.

3036 والطبائع / والطبايع : زائدة R, S.

3037 وليفرز : R, S.

3038 هولا : R.

وافهام، وتذكارات، تنشوا وتستريح النفس في المينا الهادي، الذي هو الابتلاع بالحب الالاهي،[3039] لم تستطيع ان تنظر ذاتها.

(VI.16) ليس يهدوا[3040] هولاء[3041] ويسكنوا[3042] من التدريج والطلب ويكملوا[3043] بما يخصهم، الا ان امتلت[3044] دواخل النفس من كل ناحيه بنور عدم الالام، وملك السلام والحب والفرح والعزا بروح القدس.

(VI.17) اذا قامت هي النفس انقص قليل بحرية طبعها تنير سراج عدم تالمها بنور النعمه الجديد، وتنظر كنوز المعقولات التي جمعت، وتختبرهم بافراز الروح[3045] بشبه الشبكة التي وقعت في البحر ومن كل جنس جمعت،[3046] وفي الاخير جلسوا وانتخبوا، عند ذلك[3047] تتنيح وتتمجد[3048] بالنعمه التي حظيت[3049] بها.

(VI.18) كما انه ليس انسان ذو افراز باختياره يجلس بالسفينه ويطلق مركبه في البحر[3050] الاعظم المتسع، لكي يضنك كل ايام حياته بامواج البحر الصعبه بغير رجا المينا الهادى وتسير[3051] الراحه، هكذا ليس تايب مفرز يسيب سفينة[3052] نفسه في بحر التوبه العظيم، من دون الرجا العظيم بمينا النعمه الهادي وستر سلامة المراحم الالاهيه.[3053]

3039 الالهي : R, S.
3040 يهدون : R, S.
3041 هولا : R.
3042 ويستكينوا : S.
3043 ويكملون : R, S.
3044 امتلات : S.
3045 الروح : S / بالروح : R.
3046 وتختبرهم بافراز...جنس جمعت : ساقطة A.
3047 ذالك : R.
3048 نتنيح ونتمجد : S.
3049 حضيت : A.
3050 بحر : R, S.
3051 تستر : R, S.
3052 اسفينة : R.
3053 الالهيه : R, S.

(VI.19) والا كيف يقبل قوله الذين يزرعون بدموع النفس بفرح الروح يحصدون، هاهنا عربون كمثل بالمراه، وهناك وجه مقابل وجه، كمثلما[3054] تعرف وتدبر سياسة مراحم[3055] الله.

(VI.20) لا تضل[3056] ايها القارى المفرز ولا تهدا وتستكن ولا تبطل، بك[3057] حركات نفسك من الهذيذ المحق، والاعمال بافراز بالسكون،[3058] ولو ان تبلغ الى حد الحدود ليس لك طمع راحه هاهنا تامه بالكمال بتدبير الفضيله.

(VI.21) لم تصادفني حلاوه ولذه مثل[3059] هدو بحر الضمير من كل حركات الغلوات، وبهج جو[3060] رقيع القلب واهتدا واستكن واهتدت حركات النفس من كل فعل وانفعال، وسكنت[3061] الاراده والفهم والمعرفه[3062] والافكار من طلب[3063] كل جيد وردي، ودهشت[3064] النفس وغطست الحركات والاحواس بلذه، كمثل بالنوم[3065] الحلو.[3066]

(VI.22) ظلام هذه الموهبه وكل فعل الروح هي تسيب اللسان بدالة المفاوضات، والحريان[3067] والخلق والحيل (R212v) الموذيه الغاشه وقساوة القلب، ويظلمها بقتام[3068] تذكار مولد اضطراب ومحرك غضب وترادد[3069] وتهدد[3070] في القلب.

3054 كمثل ما : R.

3055 ومراحم : S / ومراحمة : R.

3056 تطل : A.

3057 بك : ساقطة R.

3058 السكون : S / وبالسكون : R.

3059 كمثل : R, S.

3060 جوا : R, S.

3061 وسكتت : R, S.

3062 والم...فه : R.

3063 طلبة : S / طلبت : R.

3064 ودهش : R.

3065 النوم : S / بالنور : R.

3066 الحلوا : R.

3067 والجريان : S.

3068 بقيام : R.

3069 ويزداد : S / ويرادد : R.

3070 ويهدر : S / ويهدد : R.

(VI.23) اواني الاله التي بها تنفلح[3071] الفضايل، (A279r) وتنحفظ[3072] الوصايا وتنغلب الالام في المبدا حتى تنفلح[3073] وتتدرب[3074] وتبلغ[3075] الى الذكاوه والنقاوه والحريه والحب الالهي هم التغصب[3076] وقصر الذات والخلق الغيور، وقساوة القلب والتخيلات، الحقد، والتمرمر، وقيام الهوى[3077] لتغلب.

(VI.24) معرفة الحيل بوساطة هولاء[3078] تعمل[3079] الفضايل وتنغلب والخطيه والشيطان، وما دامت هولاء[3080] اواني الاله ثابتين بالنفس ليس حريه حقانيه، بل هي النفس الى الان تحت عبودية الفضايل وفي طريق الفضايل، وليس بحرية طبيعتها.

(VI.25) حيث يكون الغصب الاضطراري ليس ثم[3081] حريه، وحيث تكون التخيلات،[3082] ليس ثم[3083] ذكاوه، وحيث لم تكون[3084] غيره ليس نقاوه، وحيث ثم[3085] معرفة الحيل، ليس موضع لمعرفة الحق وحيث[3086] توجد[3087] مراره ليس هدو[3088] واتضاع، وحيث يوجد محبة الغلبه، ليس حب وحيث ما ثم[3089] حب روحاني، ليس يوجد نور عدم التالم، وحيث ليس نور عدم الالام،[3090] لم يسكن هناك نور النعمه، وحيث توجد[3091] ملاقاة[3092] نافعه ومخسره، ليس ثم[3093]

3071 تتفلح : R, S.
3072 وتحفظ : R.
3073 نتفلح : S / نتملح : R.
3074 ونتدرب : R, S.
3075 ونبلغ : R, S.
3076 التصب : R.
3077 الهوا : R, S.
3078 هولا : R.
3079 ينعمل : S / تنعمل : R.
3080 هولا : R.
3081 ثمة : S.
3082 التحيلات : R.
3083 ثمة : S.
3084 يكون : R, S.
3085 ثمة : S.
3086 وبحيث : S.
3087 يوجد: R, S.
3088 هدوء : S / هدوا : R.
3089 ثمة : S.
3090 التألم (الالام) : S.
3091 يوجد : R.

سلامه، وحيث ما ثم[3094] حق قايم لذاته حريا بغير ريا[3095] واخذ بالوجوه، ليس نخز[3096] نيه، وحيث ليس نخز نيه، النفس محتاجه للتقويم ومعتازه وغير كامله.

(VI.26) القديس انبا اشعيا كتب على حرية النفس قايلا،[3097] ما دام تبكتك النيه من اجل شي خارج عن الطبع نفعله، نحن غربا من الحريه، لان حيث توجد[3098] تبكيت النيه ليس هناك حريه.

(VI.27) عند ذلك[3099] تكون[3100] بالحقيقه وقد دخلنا النياحة المقدسه كمسرة الله اذا ما صلينا وما نتبكت[3101] من نيتنا بالقسط، لا عن تذكار ولا عن فكر غريب، وتكون[3102] قد اهتدت وسكنت احواسنا مع حركاتنا، وبطلوا من المقاتله بالامور الشماليه بمراحم المسيح.

(VI.28) اذا ما وجد فينا جميع استعداد المسكن المعقول لقبول المسيح شمس البر جوانا، وبالصلاه ينحفظ[3103] المسكن كمسرته، تكون لنا الغلبه بالرب، وهو يحل في نفسك وهو يصلح فيك بيت مسكن محله وراحته بالنعمه.

(VI.29) فان كان ما هو يسبق ويصلح فيك موضع راحته بعد الذكاوه انعام، باطل هو جميع فلاحة عملنا، وليس فينا قوه لنرضيه كارادة روح القدس، ولا ان نحفظ المسكن بطهاره بلا شر.

(VI.30) ان كان سحابة السلامه ظللت على مسكن الحب، وثمرة الحياه الصالح حل داخل المسكن، وظهرت اشراقات جو الحريه الممجوده، وفاحت تلك الرايحة[3104] اللذيذه واتشجع القلب واتقوا وقبل العزا الروحاني، ولم يعود

[3092] ملاقات : R.

[3093] ثمة : S.

[3094] ثمة : S.

[3095] رياء : S.

[3096] نخز (نخس) : S.

[3097] قلايلا : R.

[3098] يوجد : R, S.

[3099] ذالك : R.

[3100] نكون احراراً : S / نكون : R.

[3101] يتبكت : R.

[3102] ويكون : R, S.

[3103] ينحط : R.

[3104] الراحة : R.

يحرقك (A279v) الشمس بحفظ النهار، (R213r) ولا القمر بضلالة[3105] عدم المعرفة النفسانيه[3106] هذه هي الحرية الحقانيه.

(VI.31) اسكولين[3107] مكتب جوا منا واحد لتدريب المعرفة النفسانيه التي هي معرفة الخير والشر، والتعليم الاخر التدريب بمعرفة الحق التي هي معرفة الحياه ونور النعمه، وتتفلح بمكتب اسكول الاختبار والتصفيه، معرفة العدل هي معرفة الخير والشر وهذه معرفة العدل تولد للانسان الغيره والخباط والخلق والحسد والغضب، ويحب ان يغلب وبقية الالام، واما مكتب النعمه ينعمل فيه الحب والسلام والهدو[3108] والتواضع والصبر مع بقية اثمار الروح التي كتبها بولس، لانه مكتوب ان من الثمره تعرف الشجره، فتميز الان ماذا يعلمك[3109] هذا[3110] مكتب الخير والشر، وافهم من اين هي ومن من. اذا[3111] ما دخلت النفس لمكتب معرفة الخير والشر الذي ينعمل فيها العدل ومملوه غيره واضطراب[3112] وغيظ[3113] وحسد وحزن وخلق، واذا ما دخلت النفس لمكتب النعمه الذي[3114] جميع اولادها يسعون تبع الحريه، والموضع الذي تفيض فيه النعمه بالرحمه والتحنن[3115] على الصالحين والاشرار بالسوى،[3116] ومملوه حب وسلام وفرح هدوا اتضاع، صبر حمل ضعف القريب وعجزه وبقية اثمار الروح.

(VI.32) ان كان غلبة[3117] النفس وانغلابها هو الهذيذ الباطل الذي يثير التكدر والغضب، والهذيذ باثمار الروح يولد حب وسلام وفرح، ومن هذين الهذيذين هي شجاعة الاراده ورخاوتها، مع الماده التي نستفيدها من اقربانا[3118]

3105 بطلالة : A / بظلاله (بضلالة) : S.

3106 النفسانيه : ساطقة R, S.

3107 اسكولين (مدرسة) : R.

3108 والهدوء : S / والهدوا : R.

3109 تعلمك : R, S.

3110 هذه : R, S.

3111 بداية فقرة جديدة : R, S.

3112 واطراب : R.

3113 وغيض : A.

3114 الذين : R, S.

3115 والتحننن : R.

3116 بالسواء : S / بالسوا : R.

3117 غلية : R.

3118 اقربائنا : S.

فحسنا[3119] كتب ان الموت والحياه من الرفيق، لانه يعطي ماده لعمل المكتب الاسكول[3120] الجواني.

(VI.33) اكثر الناس بمكتب العدل يكملون حياتهم وقد جعلوا قضاه وحكام لجميع افعال الناس، ويوزنون[3121] الاعمال الصالحه والرديه التي لاخرين بالعدل، ولم يحسون انه ثم[3122] مكتب فيه تعليم النعمه ورحمه وتحنن، اظهره[3123] سيدنا ببشارته، وقليلين بعد جهد يفلتون من مكتب العدل ويدخلون لمكتب النعمه والرحمه، وفي الحال يصادفوا[3124] الحب الفايض والسلام والرحمه على الصالحين والطالحين بالسويه، ويعجبوا بعظم[3125] مواهب الله.

(VI.34) نطقية[3126] البسيطه التي للنفس هي نور معقول الذي من الله عطى انعام لطبع الملايكه والانفس،[3127] نطقية[3128] المركبه هي رباط وتركيب صنعة الكلمه تتركب وتتسلط بتاديب التعليم والفهم، وتتزين بكور العقل، بسندال[3129] الذهن ومطرقة الفهم، (A280r) وكلبة الذكر ونار العمل، وحطب الافعال، وبالتدريج والتدريب والتخريج بمكتب النفس الخفي.

(VI.35) ينبوع الكلمه البسيط[3130] الجواني غير مركب هو مع الصوت، بل هو قوة معقوله مغروز[3131] بالنفس ويختلج (R213v) على الدوام كمثل هيولى بسيط غير معدل ولا مزين، تتركب وتتزين هي الكلمه بنور النطقيه وتخرج للفعل بوساطة الاصوات والاحواس.

(VI.36) كل صانع كان اذا ما اراد ان يصنع امرا من الامور اولا[3132] يرتسم في ذكره ماهية ذلك[3133] الشي وكيفيته وكميته، ويدخله[3134] لكور الادراك،

[3119] فحسن : S.

[3120] اسكول : R, S.

[3121] ويوزنوا : R, S.

[3122] ثمة : S.

[3123] اطهره : A.

[3124] يصارفه : R.

[3125] بعطم : A.

[3126] النطقية : S.

[3127] بداية فقرة جديدة : R, S.

[3128] النطقية : S.

[3129] بسندان : R, S.

[3130] البسيطه : R, S.

[3131] مفروز : S.

[3132] اوله : R, S.

ويمده بمطرقة الفهم، ويفحصه على سندال[3135] الذهن، وينظر فيه بنور النطقيه، ويميز ويفرز ان كان كافي لتركيبه ويقوم لذاته[3136] ام لا، وتميل الارده[3137] وتقبله النيه من داخل، وعند ذلك[3138] يخرج شبه الفعل كل هذا وما يحس الصانع بهذا المكتب الجواني، لانه محجوب عنه لاجل حاجز الالام، وعلى هذا المثال افهم عن الحق، وعن الضلاله[3139] وتشبه بالافكار والكلام، والاعمال المفلوحه منا.

(VI.37) شعاعات العقل بخيالات[3140] الكلمه ينطلقون الى خارج، وينظافون[3141] من الفرزين[3142] هم ظل وفي تصور الصلاح والشر، المصنوعين على مراة القلب وبالكلمه يرسمون لكل شي يقع عليهن،[3143] ويعرفون البرانيين الحسن والسماجه، وماهية الشي الموضوع على العقل والقلب.

(VI.38) ان كان الاحواس البرانيه هم كتاب الكتاب[3144] القلبي، النسخه التي منها يكتبون هي امواد من الامور العالميه ياخذون، وبالملاقاة[3145] النافعه والمخسره تسبب[3146] بالضروره حياة وموت الانسان من الملاقات[3147] النافعة والمخسره[3148] الذي[3149] هو ساكن معهم هي.[3150]

3133 ذالك : R.

3134 ويتكلها : R.

3135 سندان : R, S.

3136 أداته : S.

3137 الارادة : R, S.

3138 ذالك : R.

3139 الطلاله : A.

3140 بخيلات : R.

3141 ويذاق : S / وينضافون : R.

3142 المفرزين : R, S.

3143 عليهم : R.

3144 كتاب : S / الكتاب : ساقطة R.

3145 وبالملاقات : R.

3146 تسبب : زائدة S.

3147 الملاقاة : S.

3148 تسبب بالضروره...النافعة والمخسره : ساقطة A.

3149 التي : R, S.

3150 تسبب : زائدة S.

(VI.39) ان كان الاحواس البرانيه هم فلاحين يزرعون ارض القلب، معلوم ان من مادة البذار الذي يجدوه[3151] في اقربايهم يزرعون الارض، فان كان زيوان ام حنطه، وذاك الشي الذي يزرعه الانسان اياه يحصد.

(VI.40) فان كان الاحواس هم انهر يسقون ارض[3152] القلب، ضروره[3153] انه بحسب مادة الماء[3154] الذي من برا، يسكب في مجاري[3155] الاحواس يسقون القلب، ان كان كدرين او[3156] نقيين،[3157] ان[3158] حلوين او[3159] مرين، ولا يمكن العتق من العالم واموره وملاقاته الا بالموت، ان كان البسيط الضروري او المعقول الذي من حرية الاراده.

(VI.41) الذكر[3160] هو خزان[3161] دار القلب، يقبل من ذخاير[3162] الصلاح والشرور ويرجع يذكره[3163] بهم بالهذيذ.

(VI.42) الافكار الغير متميزه تنبع من الكلا[3164] كمثل بخارا[3165] ما،[3166] وتقبل الرسم والتصور من القلب كمثل رسمه في ذلك[3167] الوقت، ان كان لليمين او للشمال.

(VI.43) من بخار اليقظه تتولد الافكار، ومن بخار السقيط النوم[3168] تتولد الاحلام، (A280v) وكمثلما قد اومرنا بالنهار ان ننقي تدبيرنا ليكونوا نقيه

3151 يجده : R.

3152 ارض : ساقطة R.

3153 اضروره : R.

3154 الما : R.

3155 مجرى : R, S.

3156 ام : R.

3157 نقين : R.

3158 كان : زائدة R, S.

3159 ام : R.

3160 الكدر : R.

3161 ...زان : R.

3162 ذخايره : R, S.

3163 يذكره : ساقطة S.

3164 الكلى : R.

3165 بخار : R, S.

3166 ماء : S.

3167 ذالك : R.

3168 النور : R.

افكارنا، هكذا اومرنا ايضا بالليل ان نطهر اجسادنا وانفسنا بالصلاه، لكي ننعتق من الاحلام السمجه، لان الشياطين يحركون حيلهم ويرسموها.

(VI.44) الافراز الجيد بالقلب كلما يهدس ردي يكتبه على كتاب القلب، من نسخه الاحواس والتذكار، ويمحي (R214r) ويستاصلهم ان لا يخرجوا للفعل.

(VI.45) النية الصالحه في كل حين تحكم وتونب[3169] وتبكت النطقيه، ان لا تكتب شرور وتبكت الاحواس وتوعظهم[3170] ان لا يعطوا مادة رديه ويعينوا[3171] الافراز حتى اذا[3172] انكتب شي ردي يمحيه ولا يخرج للفعل، الضمير والتمييز[3173] والفهم[3174] هم المرتبين ومطكسين[3175] وسراج كل بيت القلب.

(VI.46) اللسان الكنعاني يسرق كنوز القلب ويفضح النفس ويفرقها،[3176] واما النعمه لكلمن يريد لنفسه عمل الصلاح تعينه وتعاضده،[3177] والذي يختار لذاته الشر يسقط من النعمه ويعاضده[3178] الشيطان ويعينه لهلاكه.

(VI.47) كل واحدا واحدا[3179] منا بمقدار ما يسد طيقان الاحواس ويحفظهن من الملاقات، ليلا تدخل المياه المكدره الى جواه ويحركون تذكارات غريبه وينجسون بيت القلب، هكذا يستنير في الصلاه.

(VI.48) اذا ما انقلعت الالام بحفظ الوصايا وانقشط[3180] ضباب ظلمة الطغيان بالاعمال، وما يبقى[3181] شي من ظل وفي الالام على النفس، وقام الطبع بمجد طبيعة خلقته بالنعمه ينظر هو ذاته بنور عدم الالام، ويفرز الحق من التشبه والظلاله، ويخرج للفعل والافكار[3182] والكلام والاعمال بلا بلبله ولا تخبيط.[3183]

[3169] وتؤنب : S.
[3170] وتوعضهم : A / وتوضعهم : R.
[3171] وليعينوا : R, S.
[3172] واذا : R, S.
[3173] والتميز : R.
[3174] والذهن : R, S.
[3175] ومطقسين : S / والمطكسين : R.
[3176] ويفقرها : R, S.
[3177] وتعضده : S.
[3178] ويعاضدته : R.
[3179] واحد واحد : R, S.
[3180] وانقشع : S.
[3181] يبقا : R.
[3182] الافكار : R, S.
[3183] تخبط : S.

(VI.49) متى لم يبقا[3184] في وجه العقل الام ورسوم هيوليه للعالم[3185] المحسوس، لا بالذكر ولا بالهذيذ ولا بالافكار عند ذلك[3186] يقدر الذهن ان ينعتق من الهم والاحزان والخلق والغيره، والمغايضات والتخيلات[3187] منجسين الانسان ومرذليه ويزرع داخل القلب السلام الروحاني، والفرح السيدي.

(VI.50) ان كان ليس في ملكوت الله خباط وتكدر وحزن وكاابه، ندم وتغصب خوف وعذاب، معروف ان الذهن قد مات معقول[3188] للخطيه،[3189] وقام بالروح للبر[3190] والصدوقيه، وانعتق من الندامه والحزن والخوف، وملك فيه السلام والحب والفرح بروح القدس.

(VI.51) احذر ليلا[3191] تطغا[3192] وتغير السلام بالسلام، والفرح بالفرح، والعزا بالعزا، معما[3193] تبقا[3194] كل سلامه وفرح يتولد من سبب ليس هم قايمين لذاتهم، لاجل ان لهم سبب من العالم، والعالم هو ميال، والموضع الذي (A281r) ليس فيه حريه حقيقيه منعتقه من ميالة الالام، ليس هناك سلام وفرح حقيقي.

(VI.52) الصبر والتجلد هن بنات التغصب، طول الروح واتساع النفس والتمهل هن بنات الحريه، فلهذا بالصلوات الدايمه والدموع المحزنه والتضرع والطلبه والتمرغ[3195] والمطانيات، وتلهف القلب المحزون بالله، واشتياق واتضاع بانسحاق الندم، نتامل ونترجا[3196] كل ساعه لفعل النعمه، ونجلس في

3184 يبقى : S.
3185 العالم : R.
3186 ذالك : R.
3187 والتحيلات : R, S.
3188 معقولا : R, S.
3189 الخطيه : R.
3190 البر : R.
3191 ان لا : R, S.
3192 تطغى : S.
3193 مع ما : S.
3194 تبقى : S.
3195 والدموع : R.
3196 ونترجى : S / ويترجا : R.

السكون تحت ستر ظلال العالي، لنوهل انعام لذلك[3197] السلام والعزا الذي لم تنظره عين ولم تسمع به اذن ولم يخطر على قلب بشر.[3198]

(VI.53) ما دام داخل فينا الم تكون النفس باختيارها مرتبطه[3199] (R214v) بحبه، ليس يفعل فينا الروح استعلانه الممجود،[3200] وان كان يفعل في وقت لمجاذبة السذج وعزاوهم يعمل.

(VI.54) شي اخر هو قوة الفضيله المعموله منا بتغصب وقصر كمثل العبيد، من اجل اضطرار الشريعه والناموس والقوانين المحدوده، وشي اخر هو قوة الفضيله المنعمله منا اختياريا بحرية ارادة البنين، من حرارة الحب بالسلام والفرح السيدي.

(VI.55) قوله[3201] اعبر عن الشر واتجاوزه هي الفضيله الغصبيه التي من تدبير الاضطرار القصري الشرعي، تولد البر، واما غصبية[3202] اصناع الصلاح هي فضيله التدبير الانجيلي التي[3203] بالاختيار تنعمل، بحرية البنين وتشركنا بروح القدس، وتقدس النفس وتملوها سلامه وعزا وفرح.

(VI.56) التدابير الفاضله التي بالغصيبه[3204] ينعملون من اجل ضرورة[3205] الناموس، وليس من اجل الرجا المزمع ليس فيهم فرح حقيقي ولا سلام وحب روحاني، يفرح في كل شي، ويصبر على كل شي بل هي[3206] برا[3207] اغتصابي من اجل الخوف والحكم والعذاب.

(VI.57) والتدابير الفاضله التي بالاختيار ينعملون بالحب الالهي ليس[3208] فيهم تغصب[3209] واضطرار، يطالب ويلوم ويهدد، بل هي النفس مرتبطه بالحب الالهي بالرجا العتيد، ومملوه[3210] فرح روح القدس.

3197 لذالك : R.

3198 انسان : R, S.

3199 مرتبة : S.

3200 استعلاته الممجوده : R.

3201 قولة : R.

3202 غصيبة : R.

3203 الذي : R, S.

3204 بالغصبية : S.

3205 الضروره : R.

3206 هو : S.

3207 بر : R, S.

3208 فليس : R, S.

3209 اتغصب : R.

(VI.58) لا تطغي[3211] المتوحد روح فرز الدعوات والاسامي واللفظ، ويخيب ضميره من حقانية فهمهم، ولا يقرا بهمج ولم يفرز نيرا اما ذاك يولد، حريان وتقسم الضمير، وهذا يولد بطاله وطغيان.

(VI.59) حياة المتوحد وامل رجاوه[3212] هو ان يتعرا[3213] العالم المنظور، ويمحي تذكار تصوره من قلبه ويصور العالم الجديد بعقله، ويرسم فيه ذكره والهذيذ به بلا فتور.

(VI.60) بهذا العالم المتغير، المملوا اضطراب وتحير[3214] ليس فيه حق، قايم لذاته بغير مياله، بل ونور عدم الالام الذي توهل[3215] له (A281v) القديسين انغام،[3216] هو اشراق نور العالم[3217] الجديد، الذي من اشتياق حبهم بالالهيات كمثل بالمراه يستحقوه، وايضا الحق الذي به يعمل[3218] الاعمال الحسنه هم شعاع الحق الذي داخل فينا.

(VI.61) عندما بالحقيقه بالاعمال من كل القلب وبالحق بديت في ذاتك ان تحفظ الوصايا،[3219] لتجاهد مقابل الالام ولتكون مكمل التواضع لاجل حب المسيح وسلامة القلب،[3220] عد نفسك ان تقبل جميع ما ياتي عليك من المضادد[3221] ومن الاصدقا والمحبين، ازدرا وتعير[3222] ومحقره وخساره وهزوا[3223] وامراض مختلفه، وانحلال الجسد وعدم وجود ما تحتاج[3224] اليه لاستعمال القوت الضروري، مع ربوات[3225] شرور، لانه قد كتب ان حب الله

3210 ومملوءة : S.

3211 يطغي : R, S.

3212 رجاؤه : S.

3213 يتعرى : S.

3214 وتحير : ساقطة R.

3215 تؤهل : S.

3216 انعام : R, S.

3217 عالم : R, S.

3218 تعمل : S / نعمل : R.

3219 بداية فقرة جديدة : R.

3220 قلبك : R, S.

3221 المضاد : S.

3222 وتعيير : S.

3223 وهزؤ : S.

3224 يحتاج : R, S.

3225 ربوة : R, S.

بالاشيا الضديه يختبر فان[3226] احتملت هولاء[3227] بغير تذمر بشكر، ثق وارفع راس[3228] نفسك[3229] واقبل داخل منك فعل النعمه[3230] (R215r) بالخفي، وعيش بالسر لله بعزا[3231] نفسك الخفي.

(VI.62) لم تنقلع الالام بشي من النفس كمثل بغلوة الحب الالهي، هذه الحراره هي جهاد النفس التي بحده تقاتل مقابل الالام.

(VI.63) ليس سلامه في المجاهده مع الالام بل عندما تحزن النفس على خيبوبتها من السلامه تحتد بالبغضه[3232] مقابل الالام الذين يخيبوها من السلامه، وتجاهد حتى الى الموت لكي اما تغلب او تنغلب، وتقهر الاعدا وتستريح بالسلامه او بحدة الغلوه بالجهاد مع الالام مكدرين السلام الجواني، لانه يفهم ويعرف ان كان يموت في هذه الحراره قبال الالام، ولاجل سلامة قلبه، في العالم الجديد ينعتق من الندامه ويوهل للسلامه[3233] والتنعم مع المسيح.

(VI.64) ما دام الالام يفعلون بوحشيه[3234] ليس موضع للذكاوه، وقد خُطفت[3235] بتغصب واستعبدت لذاك الالم[3236] الذي منه انغلبت، لان السلام يملك في النفس بعد الذكاوه والنقا[3237] من الالام، وينحفظ بمراحم ربنا يسوع المسيح، بالانفرار من جميع الملاقاة[3238] النافعه والمخسره.

(VI.65) الذي يسير في البحر مستجد وهي المركب كبجناحات تطير[3239] لكل ناحية تصوب، ويظن انه واقف على مكانه، هكذا والذي يزل من الحق اذ كل يوم ينحط[3240] الى اسفل بسيرة تدبيره بخيبوبته من النعمه، يظن انه الى قدام

3226 فاذا : S.
3227 هولا : R.
3228 رأسك : S.
3229 نفسك : ساقطة S.
3230 النعمى : R.
3231 بعزاء : S.
3232 باليقظة : S.
3233 السلامه : R.
3234 بوحشه : R, S.
3235 النفس : زائدة R, S.
3236 الاثم : S.
3237 والنقاء : S.
3238 الملاقات : R.
3239 يطير : R.
3240 يحط : R.

بقول[3241] ما امتد، بل اني من الموضع الذي انا فيه لم[3242] اتحرك، هذه تعرض لنا لانه ندين ضعف وعجز ارفاقنا، ونقبل عليهم المثلبه[3243] فيهم، ونبرر انفسنا بقياس اخرين.

(VI.66) الذي يريد ان يتشبه بالله بعظم معرفته، عوض سلامة قلبه ولاجلها يحمل عجز الكل كالله، بغير تبرم[3244] ويثبت مع الضعفا الذين احط منه، (A282r) ولا يتغير[3245] وينقلب من الصلاح الاول المرتسم فيه، وان اضطر في وقت ان يغير[3246] نوع زيه لاجل تقويمهم، يحرس ويحفظ ما يخصه بشبه[3247] الله، اذ هو يقدم لاخرين الشفا ليلا يحكم[3248] فيه هو نفسه جرح قساوه القلب، ويتمكن فيه[3249] الم الزهرده.[3250]

(VI.67) الالم هو مرض النفس والنفس التي ما انعتقت من الالام ليس ترث ملكوت الله التي داخل فيها.

(VI.68) لم تظهر الابا[3251] لاولادهم اسرار كنوز ذخايرهم ما دامت الاعدا مستترين في بيوتهم، ولا روح القدس[3252] يظهر سر ملكوت الله الداخله فينا ما دامت النفس باختيارها مرتبطه[3253] بالالام.

(VI.69) كل الم او فكر يدخل جوا فينا وينقبل ويثبت اعلم ان له جنس داخل فينا، وهو يغذيه ويهتم به، وان لم يكون له من جنسه بسهوله يضمحل ويستاصل، فان انقبل[3254] بلذة يتسع ويمسك[3255] ناصور[3256] في القلب، ان كان اليمين او الشمال، ولا يمضي وينطرد من دون التغصب والقصر والصلاه.

3241 يقول : R, S.

3242 ما : R, S.

3243 المتعبه : R.

3244 تكرم : R.

3245 يتعثر : S.

3246 تغير : R.

3247 بسه : R.

3248 تحكم : R.

3249 فيه : ساقطة R.

3250 الزهرة : S.

3251 الاباء : S.

3252 الاقدس : R.

3253 مرتبطا : R.

3254 اتقبل : S.

3255 ويسك : S / ويمسكنا : R.

(VI.70) الانسان الذي اوفا ديون الالام واتكمل[3257] بتفطن المعرفه، ليس عنده[3258] خوف عذاب (R215v) الجحيم، ولا حزن وكاابه ان يخيب من تنعم الملكوت، وقد ابتلع بدهشة عمق اسرار الله واتعجب ضميره من شرف ومجد العالم الجديد، بل يحزن على طغيان الناس المخيبين باراداتهم[3259] من مايدة اسرار الله، وهم الذين اعدموا ذواتهم من المايدة الروحانيه اسرار المسيح الخفيه، ويريد ان كان يمكن ان يندبح[3260] من اجلهم وهم يرجعون لميراثهم.

(VI.71) خيالات سكون[3261] القلايه العميقه المرتقيه بمصاعد الظنون هم قويين جدا، ومتفقين،[3262] واهلكوا كثيرين بتردد الافكار، وليس ينغلبون الا بصلاة التواضع وانسحاق القلب ومحقرة الذات، الذي يزدري هو بنفسه ويمقت ذاته، ويتعجب من طول اناة[3263] الحامل والصابر على زلات ضعفنا.

(VI.72) كل شي[3264] بغته تتكلم او تفعل بحدة وثب الخباط قصد شهوتك كملت.

(VI.73) كل فكرا[3265] بغته يصعد وتتعجب بحسنه وتدهش من تحريره وبالكرامه والمديح الذي يصادفك[3266] من بعد ان تتكلم او تفعل، وما يكون قد هديت حدته واختبرته ويحثك[3267] ضميرك ان سريع وعاجل افعله، اعلم انه فعل الشيطان، يضل ويزعج ويتحيل ان يكدر نقاوة نفسك.

(VI.74) كل فكر يوعدك بغلبه ومديح بحدة الوثب من غير تميز النية الحسنه، اعلم انه يجلب لك محقره ورذله.

3256 صور : R.
3257 واتتمل : R.
3258 عند : R.
3259 بارادتهم : R, S.
3260 يندبح : S.
3261 اسكون : R, S.
3262 ومتقفين : R.
3263 انات : R.
3264 شيا : R.
3265 فكر : S.
3266 يصدافك : R.
3267 ويحتك : S.

(VI.75) كثير جدا هي دقيقة المكتب اسكول الجواني من الاسكول البراني، وشرورا[3268] كثيره تنعمل بها من غير تميز[3269] وفحص نية الحقانيه بشبه الحق.

(VI.76) ويكونوا بالاكثر حدين الحركات (A282v) منحرفين متحيرين، وليس يزرن[3270] ضميرهم بسلام هادي متثبت بل اذا ما بنوا بالواحده هدموا بالاخره بلا قيام.

(VI.77) حد معرفة الحق هي واحده عندما بالتحرير يفهم الضمير المفرز، ان هذا هو الحق وتشهد له نيته بشبه بولس العظيم، انه الى الان ما قد عرف حقيقة الفعل كمثل ما[3271] ينبغي ان يعرف، ولعل بهذا[3272] يوجد السلام الهادي والفرح السيدي جوا فينا.

(VI.78) هوذا الحق قدام عينيك يا اخي، فتش وافهم ان كان عطي لك واعجب بكلما ينكتب ضويا[3273] وبما[3274] ينقال مستقيما ويتصدق به في هذا العالم، بحق مع هذا هو ناقص جدا عن حقيقة[3275] المزمع كمثل نقص وعوز الظل والفي عن الجسم.

(VI.79) كما انه كل فضيله في موضعها تشرق، هكذا وايضا الحب الالهي في بلد الروح يتذاق للقديسين[3276] بالسر.

(VI.80) كما ان الثوب النقي بعد جهد يثبت بياضه بين الصباغات، هكذا والذهن الطاهر ايضا بعد جهد ينحفظ بلا عيب في وسط كثيرين.

(VI.81) وان كان الذهن العاري اذا ما عبر على الصلاحات والشرور لم ينضنك، بل ما دام مع اللحم والدم مشتبك وبجزويا (R216r) يوثب على حدود السلامه، وعدم الالام، ويرجع الى موضعه.

[3268] وشرور : R, S.

[3269] تمييز : S.

[3270] يتحرزن : S / يترزن : R.

[3271] كمثلما : R, S.

[3272] بهذه : R.

[3273] ضوئيا : S.

[3274] وكما : R.

[3275] حقيقية : R.

[3276] القديسين : R.

(VI.82) كمال عدم الالام هو الانعتاق من المياله، لانه ما ينقام مع الخلطه باللحم والدم، الذي من مزاج تركيب العناصر المتغيره، ولكن ليس كلمن هو مع تركيب العناصر للمياله مربوط، من الضروره وايضا تحت العناصر منخدع.[3277]

(VI.83) العقل الذي بالتمام نقى واستنار وايضا في الافكار الجيده متواترا يقدر ان يقبل.

[(R216r): كمل ما وجد من تعليم القديس العظيم مار ايسحق ولربنا والاهنا ومخلصنا يسوع المسيح المجد والعظمه والسجود الى اخر الدهور امين. وكان الفراغ من هذا الكتاب في اول راس شهر ايار في جبل مار متى في سنة ܐܨܦ (1589AD) والناسك المسكين احقر الناس وارذلهم العادم الفضايل الممتلي من كل الرذايل الذي بالاسم والشكل راهب وبعيد عن عمل الرهبان. اسال من محبين السيد المسيح الذين يقفوا على هذا الكتاب ان يقولوا بكل قلوبهم يا ربنا يسوع المسيح اغفر خطايا عبدك يوسف وسامحه اثامه في اليوم المرهوب. ومن اصلح وقال شيا الرب يعوضه اضعاف ذالك بثلاثين وستين ومايه في ملكوت السما بصلاة القديس العظيم مار ايسحق. انعم يا رب على الناسك والقاري والسامع بمغفره الخطايا امين امين امين..]

(A282v) والمجد لله.

كمل ما وجد من تعليم القديس العظيم مار اسحق ولربنا يسوع المسيح المجد والعظمه الى الابد امين. والناسخ المسكين احقر الناس وارذلهم العادم الفضايل الممتلى من كل الرذايل الذي بالاسم والشكل راهب وبعيد عن عمل الرهبان المحقين بضرب[3278] المطانون ويسال من جهة محبة السيد المسيح لكلمن يقف على هذا الكتاب ان يقول بكل قلبه يا ربي يسوع المسيح اغفر خطايا عبدك غبريال وسامحه باثامه في اليوم المرهوب ومن اصلح وقال شي الرب يعوضه اضعاف ذلك ماية ضعف في ملكوت السماء بصلوات القديس العظيم مار اسحق وجميع الذين ارضوه باعمالهم الصالحة.. وقد قيل في نسخة الاصل ان الاب القس يعقوب نقلها من السرياني الى العربي على يابس السرياني لاجل ان الذين سقلوا الكلام العربي اضاعو[3279] فهمه الروحاني لانهم قصدوا فقه العربيه. نقل هذه الكتب على اليابس ليكون يفهمهم من انار الرب فهمه بعمل الرهبنه والتلميذ امتثل مرسوم ناسخ الاصل وكتب على مثاله فالقارى يحمل

[3277] منخضع : S.

[3278] بطرب : A.

[3279] اظاعو : A.

الفاظها[3280] روحانيا لا على سقل الكلام وتنميقه والرب الاله ينور علينا الجميع بنور معرفته الالهيه ويهدي لكل مشتاق الى هذه السيره الفاضله وذلك بتاريخ اول بابه سنه الف 995 للشهده الاطهار (1278AD) بها الرب بركه صلوا لهم لعر...

(A283r) ان هذا الكتاب المبارك الاربع كتب الذي لماري اسحق انا قرياقس اوهبت هذا الكتاب لابونا القسيس برصوم يكون يقرا فيه ويعزا فيه ولا لاجل سلطان من قبل الله ان ياخذه منه وهذا الكتاب انا وصيت على كتابته ويعفيه من عند صاحبه ابونا القس برصوم الرب يجعله من العاملين بما وضع فيه امين.

اثناسيوس.

اوقفا هذه الذخيره المباركه الذي من قول ابينا مري اسحاق اسقف مدينه نينوى الاولاد المباركين غريب واخيه يوسف على الرهبان المقيمين في دير القديس ماري موسى الحبشي الذي بارض قرى النبك ليكون للواقفين المذكورين الذكر الجميل ولواديه[3281] الرب ينقبل منهم ذلك ويغفر خطايهم وينيح انفس امواتهم وكل من اخرجه من الدير المذكور بسبب استحقاق لم طماع يكفر بحروم.

بسم الله الحي الازلي وبه نعين. طالع في هذا الكتاب الشريف والكنز المنيف الذي هو كلام كبير العشاق مري اسحاق المذنب العبد العاجز الحقير الراهب يوحنا الزبان ابن العزيز[3282] في تاريخ اول شهر اذار سنة الف وتسعمايه واربعه وسبعون (1663) حامدا لله على نعمايه امين.

(A283v) قد جدد وقفيت هذا الكتاب المبارك المدعو كتاب الجليل في القديسين ماري اسحق اب الرهبنه اسقف نينوي على دير القديس ماري موسي الحبشي من قرى النبك الشماس انطون ابن المرحوم شماس حنا ابن مقدسي الياس كجمون وقد جعله وقفا موبدا وحبسا مخلدا على الدير المذكور لانه قد كان حكموا اناس قليلين خوف الله واخرجوا هذا الكتاب عن الوقفيه وطمعوا عليه وهذا الاخ المبارك حين وقف عليه وراه مخروج عن الوقفيه فغار عليه غيرة روحيه ورده الى وقفيته الاصليه فجزاه الرب كل خيرا بشفاعة البتول وماري موسي صاحب المكان المعمور وكان ذلك في رياسة الاب المحترم البطريرك المعظم ماري اغناطيوس كيوركيس الرهاوي صاحب الكرسي الانطاكي ادار الله حياته سنة 2060 يونانيه 1749 مسيحيه.

3280 الفاضها : A.

3281 غير واضح في المخطوطة : A.

3282 غير واضح في المخطوطة : A.

وفي هذه السنه المرقومه صار فتوح بلاد الهند اي اقليم ميليبار على يد ماري باسيليوس المفريان شكر الله ومضى الى عندهم حتى يرشدهم الى معرفة الحق لانهم كانوا غنم بلا راعي الرب يردهم الى الايمان والاعمال ولله الكمال.

BIBLIOGRAPHY OF WORKS CITED

ANCIENT AUTHORS AND TRANSLATIONS

Abba Isaiah

R. Draguet, *Les Cinqs recensions de l'Asceticon syriaque d'Abba Isaïe*, *CSCO SS* 120–23 (Louvain, 1968); cited by Discourse and section number.

Acts of the Martyrs

P. Bedjan (ed.), *Acta Martyrum et Sanctorum* I–VII, (Paris – Leipzig, 1890–97).

Acts of Thomas

W. Wright, *The Apocryphal Acts of the Apostles*, Vol.1 *Syriac Texts* (London, 1871); cited by page.

Ammonius

M. Kmosko, *Ammonii Eremitae Epistolae* (PO 10, 6; 1914).

Aphrahat

A. Lehto (tr.), *The Demonstrations of Aphrahat the Persian Sage* (Piscataway: Gorgias Press, 2010).

K. Valavalonickal, *Aphrahat, Demonstrations*, I–II (Moran Etho 23–24; Kottayam, 2005).

Babai

Babai the Great, *Commentary on Evagrius' Centuries* in W. Frankenberg, *Evagrius Ponticus* (AKGWG, 1912), 8–471.

Basil

M. Forlin Patrucco (ed.), *Basilio di Cesarea. Le lettere I* (Turin, 1983).

Book of Steps

R. Kitchen and M. Parmentier, *The Book of Steps: The Syriac Liber*

Graduum (Kalamazoo: Cistercian Publications, 2004).
M. Kmosko, *Liber Graduum*, *Patrologia Syriaca* 3 (1926).

Dadisho Qaṭraya
R. Draguet, *Commentaire du livre d'Abba Isaie (logoi I–XV) par Dadisho Qatraya (VII e s.)*, *CSCO SS* 144–5 (Louvain, 1972); cited by Discourse and section number.

Ephrem
E. Beck, *CSCO SS*: *Hymns on Faith* 73–4; *Hymns against Heresies* 76–7; *Hymns on Paradise* 78–9; *Hymns on Nisibis* 92–3, 102–3; *Hymns on Unleavened Bread* 108–109.
S. Brock (tr.), *The Paradise Hymns* (New York: St. Vladimir's Seminary Press, 1990).
M. Hansbury (tr.), *The Hymns of St.Ephrem the Syrian* (Oxford: SLG Press, 2006).
L. Leloir (ed.), *Commentaire de l'Évangile Concordant, Texte syriaque*, Chester Beatty Monographs 8 (Dublin, 1963; French trans., *SC* 121 Paris 1966).
J.B. Morris (tr.), *Selected Works of St. Ephrem the Syrian* (Piscataway: Gorgias Press, 2008).
E. Mathews and J.P. Amar (tr.), *St. Ephrem the Syrian Selected Prose Works* (Washington: CUA Press, 1994): *The Homily of Our Lord.*
C. Mc Carthy, *St. Ephrem's Commentary on Tatian's Diatessaron* (*JSS* Supplement 2, 1993).

Evagrius
J-E. Bamberger (tr.), *Evagrius Ponticus The Pratikos Chapters on Prayer* ((Kalamazoo MI: Cistercian Publications, 1981).
A. M. Casiday (tr.) *Evagrius Ponticus, The Early Church Fathers* (London: Routledge, 2006): *The great letter* (Letter to Melania); *On Thoughts*; *Notes on Ecclesiastes.*
W. Frankenberg, *Evagrius Ponticus*, Berlin 1912.
P. Gehin (ed.), *Évagre le Pontique. Scholie aux Proverbes* SC 340 (Paris, 1987).
A. Guillaumont and C. Guillaumont, *Le Gnostique* SC 356, 1989.
A. Guillaumont (ed.), *Les six Centuries des "Kephalia Gnostica" d'Évagre le Pontique* (*PO* 28, I; 1958); cited by Century and number.
W. Harmless and R. Fitzgerald (tr.), "The Sapphire Light of the Mind: The Skemmata of Evagrius Ponticus," *TS* 62 (2001),

498–529.

J. Muyldermans (ed.), *Evagriana Syriaca* (Louvain, 1952). *Admonitio paraenetica*; *Paraenesis*; *La foi de Mar Évagre*; *Les justes et les parfaits*.

M. Parmentier, *Evagrius of Pontus* "Letter to Melania," Bijdragen 46 (1985) 2–38; repr. E. Ferguson, *Forms of Devotion* (New York: Garland, 1999).

G. Vitestam (ed.), *Seconde partie du traité qui passe sous le nom de "La grande lettre d'Évagre le Pontique a Melania l'ancienne" publiée et traduite d'après le manuscrit du British Museum Add. 17192*, Lund 1963.

Gregory of Cyprus

I. Hausherr (ed.), "Gregorii Monachi Cyprii De Theoria," *OCA* 110, 1937.

Hierotheos

F.S. Marsh, *The Book of the Holy Hierotheos* (London/Oxford, 1927).

Holy Women

S. Brock – S. Ashbrook Harvey (tr.), *Holy Women of the Syrian Orient* (Berkeley: Univ. of California Press, 1987).

Isho'dad of Merv

M. Gibson (ed.), *The Commentaries of Isho'dad of Merv on the New Testament*, The Acts & Epistles in Syriac and English Vol. IV (Cambridge: University Press, 1913).

Isaac the Syrian

P. Bedjan (ed.), *Mar Isaacus Ninivita, de Perfectione Religiosa* (Paris/Leipzig, 1909).

P. Bettiolo (tr.), *Isacco di Nineve. Discorsi Spirituali* (Magnano, IT: Edizioni Qiqajon, 1985; 2nd ed., 1990). (Kephalia gnostica/ *Keph.*)

S. Brock (ed.), *Isaac of Nineveh 'The Second Part' Chapters IV–XVI, CSCO SS* 224–25 (Louvain: 1995). (Part II)

S. Chialà (ed.), *Isacco di Ninive. Terza Collezione, CSCO SS* 246–47 (Louvain: 2011). (Part III)

M. Hansbury (tr.), *Isaac of Nineveh, On Ascetical Life* (New York: St. Vladimir's Seminary Press, 1989).

A. Louf, *Isaac le Syrien, Oeuvres Spirituelles – III*, Spiritualité Orientale 88 (Bellefontaine, 2009).

D. Miller (tr.) *The Ascetical Homilies of Saint Isaac the Syrian* (Boston, 1984).

A. J. Wensinck (tr.), *Mystic Treatises by Isaac of Nineveh* (Amsterdam, 1923; repr. Wiesbaden, 1969). (Part I)

Jacob of Serug

P. Bedjan (ed.), *Homiliae Selectae Mar-Jacobi Sarugensis* I–V (Paris/Leipzig, 1905–10).

H. Connolly (tr.), "A Homily of Mar Jacob of Serugh on the Memorial of the Departed and on the Eucharistic Loaf," Bedjan, *Homiliae Selectae*, V 615–27; trans. in *The Downside Review* 29 *NS* 10 (2010), 260–70.

A. Golitzin (tr.), *On that Chariot that Ezekiel the Prophet Saw* (forthcoming, Gorgias Press).

"A Homily on the Ten Virgins Described in our Saviour's Gospel," Bedjan, *Homiliae Selectae*, II 375–401; trans. in *The True Vine* 4 (1992), 39–62.

John of Dalyatha

R. Beulay, o.c.d. (ed.) *La Collection des Lettres de Jean de Dalyatha PO* 180 (Belgium: Brepols, 1978).

B. Colless (ed.), *The Mysticism of John Saba*. Syriac text and English trans. of the *Discourses*, reprint of Ph.D. thesis submitted in 1969 to the University of Melbourne.

M.Hansbury (tr.), *The Letters of John of Dalyatha* (Piscataway: Gorgias Press, 2008).

N. Khayyat (ed.), *Jean de Dalyatha, Les Homélies I–XV Sources Syriaques* (Lebanon: CERO/UPA, 2007).

John the Solitary

P. Bettiolo, "Sulla Preghiera: Filosseno o Giovanni?," *LM* 94 (1981), 74–89.

S.P. Brock (ed.), "John the Solitary, On Prayer," *JTS* ns 30 (1979), 84–101.

——— (ed.), "Letter to Hesychius" in *The Syriac Fathers on Prayer and the Spiritual Life* (Kalamazoo: Cistercian Publications, 1987), 78–100.

M. Hansbury (tr.), *John the Solitary on the Soul* (Piscataway: Gorgias Press, 2013).

R. Lavenant (tr.), *Jean d'Apamée, Dialogues et Traités, SC* 311 (Paris:

Éditions du Cerf, 1984).
S. Maroki (ed.), "Jean le Solitaire 'Quatre lettres inédites' Textes syriaques et traduction française," *PdO* 35 (2010), 477–506.
D. Miller (tr.), Mar John the Solitary, "An Epistle on Stillness" in *The Ascetical Homilies of Saint Isaac the Syrian* (Boston, 1984).
L. Rignell (ed.), *Briefe von Johannes dem Einsiedler* (Lund, 1941); cited by page.
——— (ed.), *Drei Traktate von Johannes dem Einsiedler* (Lund, 1960); cited by page.
W. Strothmann (ed.), *Johannes von Apamea Sechs Gesprache mit Thomasios, der Briefwechsel zwischen Thomasios und Johannes und drei an Thomasios gerichtete Abhandlungen. Patristiche Texte und Studien* 11 (Berlin: Walter de Gruyter, 1972).

Joseph Hazzaya

P. Harb, F.Graffin (ed.), *Joseph Hazzaya, Lettre sur les trois étapes de la vie monastique, PO* 45, 2 (Brepols, 1992).

Macarius

W. Strothmann, *Die syrische Uberlieferung der Schriften des Makarios,* Teil 1, Syrischer Text (GOFS 21, 1981).

Mark the Monk

T. Vivian and A. Casiday (tr.), *Counsels on the Spiritual Life* (Mark the Monk) 2 vols. (Crestwood, NY: St.Vladimir's Press, 2009): *On Baptism*; *Concerning Those Who Imagine That They Are Justified by Works*; *On the Spiritual Law*.

Narsai

J. Frishman (ed.), *The Ways and Means of the Divine Economy*. An Edition, Translation and Study of Six Biblical Homilies by Narsai (Diss. Leiden, 1992): V, *Homily on the Tabernacle*.

Nilus

P. Bettiolo (ed.), *Gli scritti siriaci di Nilo il Solitario* (Louvain-la-Neuve, 1983): *Discorso di ammonimento*; *Discorso sulle osservanze*; *Lettera per gli uomini virtuosi*; *Perle*; *Sulla virtù e sull'uscita da mondo*; *Sulla virtù e sulle passioni*.

Odes of Solomon

J.H. Charlesworth (tr.), *The Odes of Solomon* (California, 1977).

J.A. Emerton (tr.), *The Odes of Solomon* in *The Apocryphal Old Testament* ed. H.F.D. Sparks (Oxford, 1984).

Paradise of the Fathers

E.A.W. Budge (tr.), *Paradise of the Holy Fathers,* 2 vols. (London: 1907; repr. Blanco, Texas: New Sarov Press, 1994).

Philoxenus

E.A.W. Budge, *The Discourses of Philoxenus* I (London 1894); cited by page.

Pseudo-Dionysius

Colm Luibheid (tr.), *Pseudo-Dionysius, the Complete Works* (New York: Paulist Press, 1987).

Rabbinics

P. Alexander (tr.), *3 (Hebrew Apocalypse of) Enoch* in The Old Testament Pseudepigrapha ed. J.H. Charlesworth, 2 vols. (New York: Doubleday, 1983), vol.1.

W. Braude (tr.), *The Midrash on Psalms,* 2 vols. (New Haven: Yale Univ. Press, 1959).

S. Buber (ed.), *Midrasch Tehillim,* 2 vols. (Trier, 1892–93).

A. Cohen (ed.), *Minor Tractates of the Talmud,* 2 vols. (London: Soncino Press, 1965).

I. Epstein (ed.), *The Babylonian Talmud* (London: Soncino Press 1935–52).

Sahdona

A. de Halleux (ed.), *Martyrius (Sahdona). Oeurvres spirituelles, CSCO SS* 86–7, 90–91, 110–113 (Louvain, 1960–65); cited by text volume and page.

Sergius of Reshʿaina

P. Sherwood, "Mimro de Serge de Reshayna sur la vie spirituelle," *OS* 5 (1960), 433–59; 6 (1961), 95–115, 121–56; cited by section number.

Shemʾon d-Taybuteh

P. Bettiolo (tr.), *Simone di taibuteh. Violenza e Grazia. la coltura del cuore* (Rome, 1993).

A. Mingana, *Early Christian Mystics* (*WS VII*, 1934) 282–320; cited by page and column.

Shubhalmaran

D. Lane (tr.), *Šubḥalmaran The Book of Gifts*, *CSCO SS* 236–37 (Louvain, 2004).

Synodicon Orientale

J.B. Chabot (ed.), *Synodicon orientale ou recueil des synodes nestoriens* (Paris, 1902).

Theodore of Mopsuestia

R. Greer, *Theodore of Mopsuestia. Commentaries on the minor Epistles of Paul* (Atlanta, Ga: Society of Biblical Literature, 2010).

R. Hill (tr.), *Theodore of Mopsuestia: Commentary on the Twelve Prophets* (Washington: CUA Press, 2004).

F. McLeod (tr.) *Theodore of Mopsuestia, The Early Church Fathers* (London: Routledge, 2009).

J.-P. Migne, *Patrologia Graeca* (1856–66) Vol. 66.

A. Mingana, *Commentary of Theodore of Mopsuestia on the Nicene Creed WS* V (Cambridge, 1932); cited by page.

——— *Commentary of Theodore of Mopsuestia on the Lord's Prayer and on the Sacraments of Baptism and the Eucharist WS* VI (Cambridge, 1933); cited by page.

H.B. Swete, *Theodori Episcopi Mopsuesteni in Epistolas B. Pauli Commentarii* 2 vols. (Cambridge, 1880 and 1882).

R. Tonneau and R. Devreese, *Les Homélies Catéchétiques de Théodore de Mopsueste* (Rome, 1949).

J. Vadakkal (ed.), *The East Syrian Anaphora of Mar Theodore of Mopsuestia. Critical Edition, English Translation and Study,* (Kottayam: Vadavathoor, 1989).

J-M Vosté, *Theodori Mopsuesteni Commentarius in Evangelium Iohannis Apostoli, CSCO SS* 62–3 (Louvain, 1940); cited by page of text volume.

MODERN WORKS

L. Abramowski, "The Theolgy of Theodore of Mopsuestia," *Formula and Context: Studies in Early Christian Thought* (Variorum, 1992), 1–36.

H. Alfeyev, *The Spiritual World of Isaac the Syrian* (Kalamazoo: Cistercian Publications, 2000).

I. de Andia, "Hesychia et contemplation chez Isaac le Syrien," in *Collectanea Cisterciensia* 53 (1991), 20–48.

I.A. Barsoum, *The Scattered Pearls* A History of Syriac Literature and Sciences, 2nd rev. ed. tr. Matti Moosa (Piscataway: Gorgias Press, 2003).

A. Becker, "The Dynamic Reception of Theodore of Mopsuestia in the Sixth Century," in *Greek Literature in Late Antiquity*, ed. S.F. Johnson (Aldershot, Hampshire: Ashgate, 2006), 29–47.

——— *Fear of God and the Beginning of Wisdom* (Philadelphia PA: University of Penna. Press, 2006).

P. Bettiolo, " 'Avec la charité comme but': Dieu et création dans la méditation d'Isaac de Ninive," in *Irénikon* 3 (1990), 323–45.

——— "Esegesi e purezza di cuore. La testimonianza di Dadišo' Qatraya (VII sec.), nestoriano e solitario," *ASE* 3 (1986), 201–13.

——— "Lineamenti di Patrologia Siriaca" in *Complementi interdisciplinari di patrologia*, ed. A. Quacquarelli (Rome: Citta Nuova, 1989), 503–603.

——— "Povertà e conoscenza. Appunti sulle Centurie gnostiche della tradizione evagriana in Siria," *PdO* XV (1989), 107–25.

——— " ' Prigioneri dello Spirito'. Libertà creaturale ed *eschaton* in Isacco di Ninive e nelle sue fonti," *ASR* 4 (1999), 343–63.

R. Beulay, *L'Enseignement Spirituel de Jean de Dalyatha* (Paris: Beauchesne, 1990).

——— *La Lumière sans forme. Introduction a l'étude de la mystique chrétienne syro-orientale* (Belgium: Éditions de Chevetogne, 1987).

B. Bitton-Ashkelony, "The Limit of the Mind (ΝΟΥΣ): Pure prayer according to Evagrius Ponticus and Isaac of Nineveh," *ZAC* 15 (2011), 291–321.

G. G. Blum, *Mysticism in the Syriac Tradition* (Kerala: SEERI, vol.7).

T. Bou Mansour, "La distinction des écrits des Isaac d'Antioche," in *JECS* 57 (2005), 1–46.

——— *La pensée symbolique de saint Ephrem le Syrien* (Lebanon: Kaslik, 1988).

——— *La Théologie de Jacques de Saroug*, 2 vols. (Lebanon: Kaslik, 1993).

B. Bradley, "Jean le Solitaire," *DSpir* VIII (1974), 764–772.

S.P. Brock, "Dieu Amour et Amour de Dieu chez Jacques de Serug," Actes du Colloque VIII, *Patrimoine Syriaque* (Lebanon: CERO, 2003), 175–182.

——— "Discerning the Evagrian in the Writings of Isaac of Nineveh: A Preliminary Investigation," in *Adamantius* 15 2009), 60–72.

——— "An Early Interpretation of *pasah*: *ʾaggen* in the Palestinian Targum," in *Interpreting the Hebrew Bible*, ed. J.A. Emerton and S.C. Reif (Cambridge University Press, 1982), 27–34.

——— "Early Syrian Asceticism," in *Numen* 20 (1973), 1–19.

——— "Humanity and the natural world in the Syriac tradition," *Sobornost* 13 (1991), 131–42.

——— "The Imagery of the Spiritual Mirror in Syriac Literature," *JCSSS* 5 (2005), 3–17.

——— "Jewish Traditions in Syriac Sources," *JJS* 30 (1979), 212–32.

——— *The Luminous Eye* (Kalamazoo, MI: Cistercian Publications, 1992).

——— "Maggnânûtâ: A Technical Term in East Syrian Spirituality and its Background," in *MG* (Geneva, 1988) 121–29.

——— "Passover, Annunciation and Epiclesis: some remarks on the term *aggen* in the Syriac versions of Luke 1:35," *Novum Testamentum* 24 (1982), 222–33.

——— "Some Paths to Perfection in the Syriac Fathers," *StPatr* 51 (2011), 79–94.

——— "Some Prominent Themes in the Writings of the Syriac Mystics of the 7th/8th Century AD (1st/2nd cent. H)" M. Tamcke (ed.) *Gotteserlebnis und Gotteslehre* vol. 38 (Wiesbaden, 2010), 49–59.

——— "Some Uses of the Term *theoria* in the Writings of Isaac of Nineveh," *PdO* 22 (1996), 407–19.

——— "The Spirituality of the Heart in Syrian Tradition," *Harp* I (1988), 93–115.

——— *Spirituality in Syriac Tradition* (Kottayam, 1989).

——— "Three Syriac Fathers on Reading the Bible," *Sobornost* 33:1 (2001), 6–21.

——— "Traduzioni siriache degli scritti di Basilio," in Comunità di Bose (ed.) *Basilio il Grande e il monachesimo orientale* (Bose, 2001), 165–80.

——— "World and Sacrament in the Writings of the Syrian Fathers," *Sobornost* 6:10 (1974) 685– 96; repr. in *Studies in Syriac Spirituality* (Kottayam, 1988), 1–12.

T. Buchan, "Paradise as the Landscape of Salvation in Ephrem the Syrian," in *Partakers of the Divine Nature,* ed. M.J. Christensen and J.A.Wittung (Madison NJ: Fairleigh Dickenson University Press, 2007), 146–59.

G. Bunge, "Le 'lieu de la limpidité': a propos d'un apophthegme énigmatique: Budge II, 494," *Irénikon* 55 (1982), 7–18.

A. Casiday, "Universal Restoration in Evagrius Ponticus' 'Great Letter'," *StPatr* 47 (2010), 223–28.

D. Cerbelaud, "Aspects de la Shekinah chez les auteurs chretiens syriens," *LM* 123 (2010), 91–125.

S. Chialà, *Dall' ascesi eremitica alla misericordia infinita. Ricerche su Isacco di Ninive e la sua fortuna.* (Florence, 2002).

——— "Evagrio il Pontico negli scritti di Isacco di Ninive," *Adamantius* 15 (2009), 73–84.

——— "L'importance du corps dans la prière, selon l'enseignement d'Isaac de Ninive," *CDP* 119 (2010), 30–39.

——— "Une nouvelle collection d'écrits d'Isaac de Ninive," *POC* 46 (2004), 290–304. (Part III)

——— "L'umiltà nel pensiero di Isacco di Ninive: via di umanizzazione e di divinizzazione," in E. Vergani and S. Chialà (eds.), *Le ricchezze spirituali delle Chiese sire* (Milan, 2003), 105–20.

R.H. Connolly, "The Early Syriac Creed," *Zeitschrift fur die Neutestamentliche Wissenschaft und die Kunde des Urchristentums* 7 (1906), 202–23.

S. Daccache, "Figures Remarquables dans la Mystique Syriaque du VII–VIII Siècle," *POC* 60 (2010), 245–56.

J. Frishman, "Type and Reality in the Exegetical Homilies of Mar Narsai," *StPatr* 20 (1989), 169–75.

P. Gehin, "La dette d'Isaac de Ninive envers Evagre le Pontique," *CPE* 119 (2010), 40–52.

A. Golitzin, "The Image and Glory of God in Jacob of Serug's Homily On that Chariot that Ezekiel the Prophet Saw," *SVTQ* 43:3–4 (2003), 323–64.

——— "The Place of the Presence of God: Aphrahat of Persia's Portrait of the Holy Man," http://www.marquette.edu/maqom/aimilianus

S.Griffith, "Asceticism in the Church of Syria: the Hermeneutics of Early Syrian Monasticism," *Asceticism* ed. V. Wimbush & R. Valantasis (New York: Oxford University Press, 1995), 220–

45.

P. Hagman, *The Asceticism of Isaac of Nineveh* (Oxford: University Press, 2010).

——— "St. Isaac of Nineveh and the Messalians," in M. Tamcke (ed.), *Mystik – Metapher – Bild. Beiträage des VII. Makarios-Symposiums* (Göttingen 2007), 55–66.

A. de Halleux, "La Christologie de Jean le Solitaire," *LM* 94 (1981), 5–36.

——— "Le milieu historique de Jean le Solitaire," III *SympSyr*, ed. R. Lavenant *OCA* 221 (Rome, 1983), 299–305.

M. Hansbury, " 'Insight without Sight': Wonder as an Aspect of Revelation in the Discourses of Isaac the Syrian," *JCSSS* 8 (2008), 60–73.

——— "Love as an Exegetical Principle in Jacob of Serug," *Harp* XXVII (2012), 353–68.

P. Harb, "Doctrine spirituelle de Jean le Solitaire," *PdO* 2 (1971), 225–60.

I. Hausherr, *Études de spiritualité orientale*, OCA 183 (Rome, 1969).

——— "Par delà l'oraison pure, grace à une coquille: à propos d'un texte d'Évagre," *Revue d'Ascéetique et Mystique 13* (1932), 184–8.

——— "Un précurseur de la théorie scotiste sur la fin de l'incarnation," *Recherches de Sciences Religieuses* 22 (1932), 316–20.

H. Hunt, " 'Praying the Body': Isaac of Nineveh and John of Apamea on Anthropological Integrity," *Harp* XI–XII (1998–99), 153–58.

N. Kavvadas, "On the Relations between the Eschatological Doctrine of Isaac of Nineveh and Theodore of Mopsuestia," *StPatr* XLV (2010), 245–50.

——— "Theodore of Mopsuestia as a Source of Isaac of Nineveh's Pneumatology," *PdO* 35 (2010), 393–405.

E. Khalifé–Hachem, "L'Âme et les Passions des Hommes d'après un texte d'Isaac de Ninive," *PdO* 12 (1984), 201–18.

——— "La Prière Pure selon Isaac de Ninive," *MKS*, ed. F. Graffin (Louvain, 1969), 157–73.

J-M. Lera, "Theodore of Mopsuestia," *DSpir* XV (1991), 385–400.

A. Louf, "L'homme dans l'histoire du salut selon Isaac le Syrien," *CPE* 88 (2002), 49–54.

——— "Pourquoi Dieu se manifesta, selon Isaac le Syrien," *CPE* 80 (2000), 37–56.

——— "*Temha*-stupore e *tahra*-meraviglia negli scritti di Isacco il Siro," *La grande stagione della mistica Siro-orientale (VI–VIII secolo)*, ed. E. Vergani and S. Chialà (Milan: Biblioteca Ambrosiana, 2009), 93–119.

S. Maroki o.p., JEAN LE SOLITAIRE (D'APAMÉE) (5th Cent.): Quattre lettres inédites, Textes syriaques et traduction française," *PdO* 35 (2010), 477–506.

G. Nedungatt, "The Covenanters of the Early Syriac Speaking Church," *OCP* 39 (1973), 191–215; 419–44.

M. Nin, "La sintesi monastica di Giovanni il Solitario," *Le Chiese sire tra IV e VI secolo. Dibattito dottrinale e ricerca spirituale*, ed. E. Vergani and S. Chialo (Milan: Centro Ambrosiano, 2005), 95–117.

G. Panicker, "Prayer with Tears: A Great Feast of Repentance," *Harp* (1991), 111–33.

C. Pasquet, "Le Notre Père, une règle de vie pour le chrétien? L'enseignement de Théodore de Mopsueste," *CPE* 116 (2009), 50–61.

N. Russell, *The Doctrine of Deification in the Greek Patristic Tradition* (Oxford: University Press, 2004).

N. Sed, "La Shekhinta et ses amis 'araméens'," in *Mélanges A. Guillaumont. Contributions à l'étude des christianismes orientaux*, Geneva 1988 (*CO* 20), 233–42.

S. Seppälä, "In Speechless ecstasy: expression and interpretation of mystical experience in classical Syriac and Sufi literature," *Studia Orientalia* 98 (2007).

——— "The Idea of Knowledge in East Syrian Mysticism," *Studia Orientale* 101 (2007), 265–77.

A. Shemunkasho, *Healing in the Theology of St. Ephrem* (Piscataway, NJ: Gorgias Press, 2002).

C. Stewart, "Imageless Prayer in Evagrius Ponticus," *JECS* 9 (2001), 173–204.

E. Urbach, *The Sages* (Jerusalem: Magnes Press, 1979).

E. Vergani, "Isaia 6 nella letteratura siriaca. Due autori del V secolo: Balai e Giovanni il Solitario," *ASR* 7 (2002), 169–92.

S. Vethanath, "St. Ephrem's Understanding of Church as New Paradise and *Locus* of Divinization," *ChrOr* XXIX/1 (2008), 12–22.

INDEX

BIBLICAL REFERENCES

Genesis
1:1 158, 209
1:6–8 158
1:16 355
2:13 346
2:21 308
3 352
3:5 404
3:7–21 334
4:11 322
5:1 170
7:17–20 468
11:1–9 468
12:1 259
15:21 308
19:23–25 468
28:12 367
39:21 462

Exodus
3:1–2 370
3:2 349
7–14 468
9:12 458
12:36 462
13:21–22 371
14:15–31 468
16 469
17:11 168, 469
19:16 373
19:18 371
20:20–21 373
20:21 344–345, 371, 397
20:24 362
23:20–21 371
23:21 371
23:27 462
25:17 346
25:21–22 346
31:15 182
32:1–14 333
34:7 389

Leviticus
10:1–2 468
16:2 346
16:13–15 346
19:2 303
26:11–12 359

Numbers
11:4–9 469
14:44–45 469
16:1 65
16:31–32 468
16:32 65
16:35 468
21:2–3 452
21:6 469
21:9 469
21:21 68
26:9 65

Deuteronomy
2:9 451
2:24 451
2:25 470
2:26 68
2:31 451
3:3 451
5:22 372
8:3 469
8:16 469
9:6 65
27:26 329–330
28:60 470
32:39 459
34:1–4 380

Joshua
6:2 451
8:18 450
10:1–2 469
10:10 451
11:6 452
11:10 462

Judges
4:9 452
6:16 452
7:2 452
9:8 344
11:19 68

1 Samuel
2:21 464

22:23 451
23:14 450
26:12 453

2 Samuel
5:19 450
12:8 456
12:11 456, 461
12:13 333
16:10–11 451
17:14 453, 464
22:17–20 162

1 Kings
1:33 346
8:27 359
8:39 316
8:46 121
12:15 453
13:20–25 176
17:4 4, 464
17:9 464
20:13 452
21 334
22:23 453

2 Kings
6:16 453
19:7 451
19:34 288, 334
20:6 288, 334

1 Chronicles
28:2 344

2 Chronicles
5:13–14 359
5:14 344
7:1–2 344, 359

Job
1:21 459
2:6–7 459
2:10 459
33:30 340

Psalms
7:9 10
9:5 348, 382
14:3 329
33:9 467
33:10–11 457–458
37:24 456
42:2 162
42:7 162
50:23 368
51:5 349
66:12 162
71:15 347
74:16 380
78:4 408
78:22 403
82:1 27
84:3 347
85:3–7 348
85:10 405
89:2 162
91:11–12 456
93:5 269
101:2 162
103:1 347, 362
104:33 347
105:17 65
106:41 456
106:46 456
110:1 386
112:4 374
115:3 466
116:7, 347
119:47 184
119:64 184
135:6 466
138 354
140:5 238
141:1–2 217
141:2 168
141:8 168
142:4 355
143:2 343
143:6 168
145:1 362
145:17 331
146:1 347

Proverbs
1:7 91
14 234
17:28 4
19:21 458
22:9 121

Ecclesiastes
7:20 121

Isaiah
6:2 418
6:6–7 165
7:4 49
7:18–19 460
8:7 460
9:11 461
10:15 458
13:15–16 455
13:17 460
14:12–15 407
19:2 451, 461
19:14 451
37:35 288, 334
49:14–16 450
49:22–23 462
49:25–26 454
50:11 455
51:22–23 454
54:16–17 453
56:1 363
56:7 357
62:6 449
62:8–9 454

Jeremiah
5:15–17 453
8:10 455
8:17 456
15:8 456

16:16–17 462
17:10 10
19:9 454
20:4–5 450
22:25 450
25:9 454
25:29 461
34:2 450
34:21 454
34:22 454, 470
39:16–18 456
45:5 450
49:37 456
51:11 460

Lamentations
3:37–38 455
5:11 455

Ezekial
5:9–10 454
5:17 455
10:3–4 361
10:4 361
11:8–9 455
11:8 470
11:19 382
23:22 461
23:28 450
26:7 461
28:7–8 461
30:9 456
32:3–4 461
32:8 461
32:9 461
35:5 461
39:28 456, 469
40:1–2 360
40:4 360
43:1–2 361
43:1 360
43:2–4 361
43:5 360

Daniel
2:5 36
3:29 36
4:13 345
4:17 345

Joel
4:6–8 462

Amos
3:6 455
7:17–8:1 455

Jonah
2:1 463
2:11 463
4:6–8 463

Micah
6:13–15 463

Haggai
1:6 463
1:9 463
2:5 451

Zechariah
11:6 451
14:1–2 455

Malachi
3:10–11 463

Matthew
3:11 273
4:1–11 404
5:7 186
5:8 186
5:9 186
5:14 115
5:16 115
5:17–6:8 299
5:21–28 228
5:39 233
5:45 307, 310
5:48 170, 219
6:7 300
6:8 302
6:9 303
6:10 304
6:11 305
6:12 305
6:13 305
6:14 119
6:25–34 300
6:31 301
6:32 302
6:33 246, 302
8:31–32 459
10:29 457
10:37–38 8
10:37 204
10:38–39 226
10:38 179
11:29 175, 179
12:29 359
12:42–44 180
13:17 346, 363
13:43 265
13:44 376
13:52 398
14:10 457
14:24–31 381
18:2–5 244
18:20 265
19:21 179, 199, 204, 226
19:26 399
19:28 114, 290, 373, 388
20:1–16 230
20:26–27 56
21:9 114
22:1–14 382
22:21 55, 64
23:9 121
24:20 59
24:24 54
24:30 112, 385

24:31 112
24:46 200
25:1–13 378–379
25:6 110–111
25:29 170
25:31–34 158
26:14–15 176
26:38 273
26:39 379
26:41 115
27:32 116
27:45 118
27:51–52 118
28:2 117
28:19 122

Mark
8:34 204
9:26 358
10:21 204
10:35–40 227
12:14 55
12:41–49 229
13:26 385

Luke
1:26–38 229
2:25–32 347
2:36–38 229
3:39–43 335
6:29 233
6:37 119
7:36–50 229
7:39 175
7:41–42 334
7:47 175, 342
8:9–14 229
9:23 204
10:19 173, 223
10:24 346
10:26–28 181
10:38–42 206, 229
10:42 205, 387
11:22 55
11:23–25 180
12:7 457
14:26 204
14:27 226
15:10 344
15:11–32 335
15:17 356
15:31–32 205
16:8 203
16:9 204, 246
16:24 383
18:3 381
18:9–14 335
18:9–13 175
19:1–9 205
19:12–15 385
20:36 7
21:25 110
22:19 119
22:41–44 380
22:48 176
23:32–43 229
23:40–43 176
23:42 262
23:43 158, 209
24:50 168

John
1:14 287, 372
1:18 287
3:5 117
3:14 115
3:16 175, 287, 337
3:18 287
3:28 114
5:37 372
7:38 398
8 244
8:12 355
9 352
9:39 46
10:10 45
11:41 168
11:42 314
13:25 180
14:2 260
14:23 182
14:27 119
15:5 166, 216
17 204
17:1 168
17:3 45
17:5 315
17:11 115
19:11 457
20:12 117

Acts
1:24 316
2 372
2:1–2 380
2:23 345
2:38 316, 317
3:21 443
4:6 61
4:27–28 457
6:1 61
7:35–36 371
9:15 9
10:9 368–369
10:11 368
10:45 316, 317
12:2 457
12:6–10 457
12:7–8 55
15:8 316
17:29 385
18:9–10 457, 470
21:13 307

Romans
1:20 294
2:5 408
3:12 329
3:20 328
3:22 328
3:25 397

4:5 330
4:13 328
5:8 337
5:10 337, 405
5:17–19 322
5:20 335
6:3 397
7:14 381
7:22 375
7:23 380–381
8:1–12 319
8:15 303
8:17 307
8:28 405
8:32 348
8:35 308
9:27–29 386
11:33 273
12:1–2 204
12:1 341
12:2 388
12:5 323, 385
12:12 248
13:10 181
14:10 120
14:17 341
16:25–26 348
16:27 310

1 Corinthians
1:31 328
2:6 373
2:9 309, 321
2:10–11 373
2:15 377
3:16–17 361, 363
3:16 357
4:16 226
7:1 179, 226
7:7 179
9:19–23 249
10:27 250
11:1 179
11:17–34 392
11:27–29 391–392
11:33–34 393
12:12 323, 385
13:12 105, 297, 325, 373
13:13 250
13:8 174
14:1 319
14:12 319
15:28 342
15:50 340
15:52 111–112

2 Corinthians
1:21–22 353, 379, 385, 418
2:15 150
3:3 317
3:18 297, 303
4:6 349, 356
4:16 375
5:5 353, 379, 385, 418
5:7 325, 344
6:10 337
9:6–12 246
10:4–6 60
10:4 60
10:6 60
10:17 328
12:2–3 370, 415
12:2 158
12:4 208
12:9 350

Galatians
2 61
2:16 328, 330
3:10 329–330
3:27 397
4:4 356
4:24 303
5:16–17 319
6:14 307

Ephesians
1:2 63
1:13–14 353, 375, 379, 385, 418
1:17 291
1:21 422
1:22–23 323, 385
2:4 326, 338
2:6 388
2:9 328
2:13 303
3:10 338
3:20–21 63
4:13 272
4:23 388–389
5:30 323, 385
5:32 324
6:10–11 59
6:10 56, 408

Philippians
2:7 324
3:15 373
3:21 273
4:6–7 248
4:10 341
4:18 368, 407

Colossians
1:16 422
1:18 123, 323, 385
2:9 123
2:12 388
3:1–3 339
3:1 168, 218, 388
4:6 300

1 Thessalonians
4:15 111
5:23 248

2 Thessalonians
1:5 408
2:3 54–55

1 Timothy
1:1 363
2:4 396–397, 443
2:8 167, 217
3:1 162, 212
4:1 249
4:4–5 362
6:6–8 305
6:19 396

2 Timothy
3:7 397
3:16 91
4:8 350, 412

Titus
1:6 341
2:12 301, 348
3:3 405
3:5 318, 388
3:13 363

Hebrews
1 263
2:2–3 372
2:2 371–372
2:4 373
2:5 287, 314, 317, 331, 340, 372–372, 376, 397, 415
3 263
3:5 422
5:9 368
5:30 387
6:5 314, 317, 331, 340, 372–373, 376, 397, 415, 422
8:2 358
9:11–12 345
9:13–14 346
9:14 330
10:1–18 368
10:10 396
10:26 397
11:19 46
11:38 402, 407
12:22 348
13:15 368, 381

James
1:17 379
2:7 362
2.8 181
2:10 329–330
2:14–17 220
2:17 170
2:26 170
4:8 337

1 Peter
1:2 345
3:3–4 319, 340
4:8 389, 396

2 Peter
1:19 349, 356

1 John
1:1 324
2:1 396
2:13 310
2:15 181
3:2 313, 325
4:9 287
5:4 349

Revelation
21:5 349, 351

Apocrypha
Judith
9:5 467

2 Maccabees
9:18 408
12:43–45 390
14:35 344

3 Enoch
28:1–3 345

4 Esdras
6:32 289

Sirach
36:15 344

Odes of Solomon
33:12 290

ANCIENT SOURCES

Anaphora of Mar Theodore 393
Anonymous Commentary 89, 148
Apophthegmata Patrum 192
Ascetical Discourses 358
Book of Chastity 1, 472, 474
Book of Steps/Liber Graduum 194–196, 200, 288, 290, 301, 313, 358, 423, 465–466

Book of the Aims of the Psalms 89–95
Book of the Bee 110, 444–445
Book of the Mysteries 100
Book of the Paradise 247
Book of the Perfection of Disciplines 164
Book of the Three Monks 190–192
Book of the Way of Life 214
Chapters on Knowledge 253–254
Commentary (of Dadishoᶜ on *Paradise of the Fathers*) 155–157, 190, 197–200
Commentary on the Liturgical Offices (or *Interpretation of the Offices* of Abraham) 97–104
Commentary (of Gabriel) 98–99
Compendium 156–157
Concerning those Who Imagine that they Are Justified by Works 300, 306, 422
Description of the Offices 99–102
Discourses (of Philoxenos) 195–196
Ecclesiastical Hierarchy 100
Filekseyus 189–197, 220
Gnostic Chapters (*Kephalaia gnostica*) 253–254, 287, 289–291, 293, 297, 299–300, 303, 306, 308–309, 311–313, 315–320, 322–323, 325–326, 335, 340, 348, 352, 355, 360, 364, 366, 370, 374–375, 377, 388–389, 391, 395, 397, 403, 415, 417, 419, 422
History (of Mar Awgen) 1
History (of Mar Qardag) 1, 35
History (of Yawnan) 1–3
History of the founders of monasteries in the realms of the Persians and the Arabs 471
Homelies (of Theodore of Mopsuestia) 300–301, 303, 305, 359, 388
First Part (of Isaac of Nineveh) (Is.I) 281, 284, 287–294, 297, 299–300, 303, 305–306, 308, 311, 313, 315–318, 322–323, 325, 328, 333, 340–341, 344, 348, 351, 355, 357–358, 360, 363–366, 368–370, 374–375, 377, 381, 388–389, 391, 395, 397–398, 400–401, 403–404, 406, 413–417, 419–420, 422–423, 441, 473
Second Part (of Isaac of Nineveh) (Is.II) 281, 284, 287–291, 296–297, 299–301, 303, 305–306, 308, 312–313, 316–317, 320–322, 325, 328, 335, , 338, 340, 344, 346, 348–349, 352, 354, 357–358, 360, 365, 370, 374–375, 377, 387–391, 395, 397–398, 400, 404, 413–416, 419, 422–423, 441, 473,
Third Part (of Isaac of Nineveh) (Is.III) 281, 287, 296, 300, 302, 305, 311–312, 314, 317, 320, 331, 333, 338–339, 343, 352, 357, 359, 374, 376, 402, 419, 423, 474, 478
Fourth Part (of Isaac of Nineveh) 471, 474–477
Fifth Part (of Isaac of Nineveh) 441–442, 446–449, 474, 477
Lausiac History 160
Law Book 147
Letter 17 (of Īshōᶜyahb III) 45–47

Letter 18 (of Īshōʿyahb III) 47–57
Letter 19 (of Īshōʿyahb III) 57–59
Letter 20 (of Īshōʿyahb III) 59–63
Letter 21 (of Īshōʿyahb III) 64–69
Letter to Hesychius 309, 328, 352, 364, 375
Life of Ishoʿsabran 43
On the Spiritual Law 306
Paradise of the Desert Fathers (The Garden of the Monks) 166
Paradise of the Egyptian Fathers 155–157, 190–191, 197, 199, 206, 214
Parts (of Isaac of Nineveh) 253, 474–475
'Poem on God's Government from "In the beginning" until Eternity' 446
Questions and Answers from the Egyptian Monks 189–198
Solutions to the questions on the fifth theological volume of Mar Isaac of Nineveh 445–446
Soul (John the Solitary) 287–288, 293–294, 300, 308, 315–316, 325, 358, 360, 365–366, 369, 375, 377, 397, 416, 420, 422–423
Synodicon Orientale 148, 333

SUBJECTS

adultery 223, 228, 402
almsgiving, alms, charity 195, 203, 207, 217, 229, 246, 364, 390
anchorite 3–6, 16, 27, 40, 218
angels 7, 33, 60, 92–93, 107–109, 111–113, 117–118, 120, 159, 165, 168–169, 172, 174, 183, 202, 204, 207, 209–210, 214–215, 218, 222–224, 234, 238–239, 244, 258, 263–264, 271, 275–276, 309, 319, 324–325, 338–339, 343, 345, 347–348, 355, 358, 401, 406, 443, 451, 456–457, 467
as Watchers 345, 347
angelic revelations 264, 271, 276, 345, 348, 360, 370–373
animals 4, 111, 118, 194, 200, 219, 238, 297, 346, 402, 443, 463
lion/lion attacks 4, 15, 29, 32–34, 239
baptism 33, 45, 64, 113, 116–117, 167, 170, 216, 219, 282, 341, 352, 391, 397
bishop 1, 9, 13, 18, 30, 35, 40, 43–45, 47–51, 53–59, 63, 65–68, 100, 103, 147–149, 162–163, 179, 189, 198, 208, 212–213, 226, 237, 281, 363, 398, 402, 445, 449, 473
blasphemers 50–51, 107, 160, 210, 263, 390
Catholicos 43–44, 46, 99, 281
cave 13, 28, 30, 38, 169, 181, 402
cenobitic monks 9
conversion 205, 329–330, 334, 350, 354, 391
deacon 17, 53, 102, 106, 114, 116–118, 120, 165, 215
eunuch 242
exorcism 169, 171, 176
demons 17, 54, 60, 64, 66, 92, 111–112, 161, 166, 170,

173, 181, 215, 224, 231, 238, 241, 247, 249, 251, 264, 270, 335, 411, 443, 459
of anger 171, 174, 211, 216–217, 221, 225, 242, 276
of fornication 159–160, 169, 172, 178, 208–211, 218, 222, 225, 227, 235, 242, 276
of pride 167, 171, 176–178, 210, 225, 244, 263, 276, 355
possession of 216
temptation of 34, 204, 218–219, 223, 230, 245, 305, 307
torment of 23, 208, 222, 403, 446
Divine Economy 289, 308–309, 324, 338, 371, 393, 416, 460, 463
fasting 90, 94, 164, 167, 171, 173, 181, 185, 199, 201, 203, 208, 214, 216, 220–222, 242, 276, 364
genitals, mutilation of 208, 218, 242
Gospel 18, 45, 55, 64, 114–117, 170, 183, 219, 302, 381, 443, 457
reading of 8
healing 24, 33, 40, 48, 90, 94, 241, 267, 333, 338, 352, 414, 459, 469
heretics / apostasy 48, 57, 63, 101, 283, 390–391, 402
hermit 2, 9, 160, 165, 247
icon 3, 13, 117, 287
illness/sickness 8, 21, 24, 41, 48, 64, 186–187, 201–202, 217, 233, 241, 407, 459
Jew(s) 26–27, 61, 118, 228, 249, 372
Julianists 67
Magians 14, 29, 33, 35–36
Marcionites 67
martyrdom 61, 90, 95, 258, 403, 409, 411
medicine 8–10, 94, 167, 216
metropolitan 43–44, 59, 66–67, 99, 147–149, 156
Monasteries 3, 7, 9, 13–14, 16–17, 20–23, 26–32, 38–39, 42–43, 57, 102–103, 155, 166–167, 169, 176, 181–183, 185–187, 196–199, 207, 209–210, 213, 217–219, 223, 233, 235, 237, 239, 248, 250, 283, 472–473
in Egypt 2, 12, 160, 165, 214–215, 249, 475
in Gulf 1
in Mesopotamia 2
ruins of 18
offering 2, 6, 26, 38, 57, 106, 223, 346, 368, 389–390, 393–394, 411
old age (great age) 4, 22, 176, 187, 229, 234, 241
patriarch 5, 43, 67, 97–98, 102, 191, 200, 212, 248–249
poverty 8, 26, 151, 224, 245, 259, 308, 318, 327, 336
priest 3, 30, 61, 102–103, 107–108, 114, 116, 118–123, 147, 149, 165–167, 215, 271, 346, 390, 393–394, 446, 451
resurrection 48, 51, 90, 95, 110–112, 119, 121–123, 235, 260, 273, 282, 284, 287, 289, 295, 319, 340–341, 376–377, 388–389, 394, 397, 445, 467
saints 1, 3–7, 26, 59, 63, 164,

181, 222, 232, 269, 285, 288, 296–297, 313, 341, 349, 357, 360, 362–363, 372, 375, 379–380, 384, 406, 412, 423
and drinking 180, 227
and melancholy 230
and women 179, 226
chastity/celibacy of 180, 379
education of 4, 166
food/eating of 227
healing of 48, 241, 338
imitation of 227, 402
miracles of 3, 6–7, 48
parents of 7–9, 241
physical mortification of 208, 218, 296, 402
purity of 162, 167–168, 172, 179–180, 226–227, 338, 402, 413
reading books 110, 114–115, 119, 161, 166, 171, 211, 216, 220–221, 232, 242, 259, 265, 276–278, 282, 284, 302, 308, 319, 364–368, 421
selling possessions 171, 179, 184, 203
singing 11, 94, 110, 244–245, 347, 477
starvation of 171, 214, 220
virtue of 5, 166–167, 171, 175, 203, 226, 261, 271, 412, 445
Severians 67
Shekinah 359–361
torture 7, 358, 406, 410
translators 99, 147–149, 151, 190, 193, 251, 254
vegetarian 402

NAMES

Abba Abraham 216, 235
Abba Agathon 234
Abba Ammon (Amoun) 157, 161, 179, 187, 208, 226, 236–237
Abba Apellen 169
Abba Apollo 177–178, 218, 224–225
Abba Arsenius 183–184, 186, 202, 207
Abba Awr (Or) 232
Abba Barhabdbeshabba 35
Abba Bawmā 199, 201–202
Abba Bessarion 169, 219
Abba Elijah 159, 169, 209–210, 218
Abba Hor 179, 226
Abba Isaiah 155, 247, 358, 423
Abba Isidore 167, 179, 216, 226, 233
Abba Jacob 241
Abba John of Assiut 208
Abba Luke 230
Abba Macarius (Macarios) 158, 160, 164–165, 169, 179, 184, 193, 209, 214–215, 219, 226, 231, 233, 238, 313, 317, 319, 357, 375
Abba Moses the Black 166–167, 177, 183, 202, 215–216
Abba Poemen 235–236, 238, 242
Abba Sarmag (Sarmatus) 228, 230
Abba Serapion 179, 183, 400–401
Abba Sisoes 168, 176, 187, 218, 235
Abba Theodore 230, 232

Abba Yestir 201
ʿAbdishoʿ bar Brikā 89, 155–156
Abraham (leader of Masmahig) 58
Abraham Qaṭraya bar Lipah 97–103
Abuna Abba Sälama Matargwem 191, 200
Aḥūb Qaṭraya 89–95
Alʿazar (Lazarus) 239
Ammonias 208, 322, 339, 375
Anahid 409
Ananisho 190
Anastasios of Sinai 198
Anastasius Caesar 108
Anstasios 214
Aphnimaran 254
Aphrahat 287–288, 290, 344, 375, 414, 422
Arcadius 181, 228
Arius 243
Athanasius 5–6
Babai the Great 254, 348, 357
Babnuda *(see Paphnutius)*
Bamanuda 226
Barsanuphius 198
Basil 101, 109, 243, 245, 302, 363
Bastomag 43
Bessarion 219
Būshīr 474
Constantine 7, 101, 108, 239–240
Cyril 107
Dabra Natron 215
Dadishoʿ Qaṭraya 1, 11, 155–187, 191–192, 194, 196–200, 283, 340, 357, 360
Daniel bar Tubanita 445–446
Democles 211
Diodore of Tarsus 323, 335, 445
Dionysius bar Salibi 254
Ebediesu of Soba 99
Elisha 29
Eltawgalos 243
Enanisho 163
Ephrem 287–290, 294, 308–309, 320–322, 325, 340, 344, 352, 356, 374–375
Epiphanius 9
Eulogius 166
Eustathius 163
Filekseyus 189–198, 220
Gabriel Qaṭraya bar Lipah 98–99
George (Bishop of the Arabs) 100
Girlos 243
Gīwargīs I 98, 281
Gregory of Cyprus 308, 348
Gregory of Nyssa 243, 245, 306, 443
Hieronymus 180, 227
Hilarion 241
Iaunan 103
Ibn as-Salt 445–446
Ignatius of Antioch 283
Ioannis 9, 11–12
ʿIsa son of Isaiah 102
Isaac of Nineveh (the Syrian, Qaṭraya) 191, 253–254, 281–284, 289–290, 292–294, 296–297, 299–300, 308, 319–320, 326, 331, 335–336, 340–341, 357, 360, 363, 368, 374, 387, 389, 391, 398–399, 414, 416, 420, 422, 441–447, 449, 463–464, 472–478
Īshōʿdnaḥ 1, 7, 9, 472, 474
Išōʿyabhi I 100
Īshōʿyahb III 43–44, 97–98
Jacob of Serug 290, 294, 325, 344, 378, 390, 472
John bar Penkaye 254
John Chrysostom 245

John of Lycopolis (John of the Thebaid) 403
John Saba of Dalyatha 191, 254, 290, 293, 413, 420, 423
John the Solitary 282–283, 287–294, 296, 300, 302, 308–309, 315–316, 352, 358, 360, 364, 366, 369, 375, 377, 388, 397, 413, 416, 418, 420, 422–423
John, son of Zebedee 179, 226
Joseph Hazzaya 242, 254, 289, 319, 357, 413
Jovian 13, 35
Julian (emperor) 13
Khosro 24
King al-Nuʿmān III (Lakhmid king of Ḥīra) 147
King Theodosius the Younger (the Great) 107, 181, 227
Laban 179
Maḥya 410
Mar Abda 231
Mar Alonis 240–241
Mar Antony 157–158, 168, 179, 183, 202, 208–209, 226, 228, 230, 232–234, 236–241
Mar Awgen (Awkin, Awgin, Eugene) 1–2, 6, 8, 11–15, 17, 29–30, 35–36, 239–240
Mar Dāzedeq 474
Mar Elia VIII (Jean Maroghin) 102
Mar Evagrius 160, 171–172, 174, 180, 183, 208, 210, 222–224, 227, 234, 236, 249, 251, 253–254, 282–283, 290–291, 294, 296, 306–307, 320, 325, 348, 357, 414
Mar Giurgis 59
Mar Miles 13
Mar Moshe 26
Mar Papa 7, 29, 31, 35, 37–38
Mar Qardag 1–2, 35
Mar Thomas 2–4, 17, 28, 32, 38
Mar Yawnan 1–7, 9, 11–19, 21, 23–31, 33–37, 39–40
Mar Yohannan 35
Mark (the Less, disciple of Sylvanus) 166, 215
Mark (the mourner, Graeco–Egyptian) 165, 176, 214–215
Mark (the Syrian, also known as Malchus) 165, 215
Mark the Monk 300, 306, 422
Martha 194, 200, 205, 229, 409
Martinianus 401
Maximus the Confessor 443
Melchizedek 165, 215
Moses bar Kepha 100
Mushe of Telbarqe 36
ʿNānishoʿ 156, 163, 190
Narsai 100, 320, 346, 360
Nestorius 243
Nimparuk bar Dustar 68
Nuʿaym 20–22, 25, 29
Origen 443
Pachomius 2, 12, 173, 179, 223, 226, 233
Palladius 160, 164–165, 180–181, 211, 214, 227–228, 239, 251
Paphnutius 159, 179, 206–207, 210, 226, 231–232
Paul the Hermit 400
Paulinus, Bishop of Antioch 162–163
Peṭros bar Yawsep bar Yuḥanon bar Esṭefanos bar Abraham 44
Philon 2, 16–17, 27–30
Philoxenos 189–191, 195–196, 200, 289, 292, 308, 344

Pope Innocent XIII 44
Pope Pius XI 102
Pseudo-Dionysius 100, 306, 320, 348, 422
Rabban ʿAbdishoʿ 35
Rabban Šabūr (Shabūr) 155, 472–474
Sahdona 289, 312, 340, 344, 357–358, 360, 364, 408, 422
Sergius 348
Severus 243
Shabur (Shapur or Safor) 13–14, 35–37, 239
Shahdost 17, 31, 37
Shebadnaya 446
Shemʿon d-Taybuteh 254, 308, 340, 357
Shubḥalmaran 99, 289, 375
Simeon the Pharisee 229
Simeon the Stylite 183
Simon of Rev Ardashir (Mar Shemʿūn) 63, 147–149
Solomon of Bosra 110, 444–445
Soso of Araden 103
Sylvanus 166, 215, 233, 242
Tarbo 409, 411
Thekla 409
Theodore of Mopsuestia 100, 111, 122, 162, 164, 191, 212, 237, 282, 292–293, 300, 303, 305, 308, 311–312, 315, 323, 325, 341, 357, 359–360, 368, 388, 392–393, 397, 404, 415, 422, 173, 230, 232, 390
Theophilus 248
Thomas of Marga 99
Timothy I 98–100
Yawsep 14
Zadoy 2–4, 32
Zarqon 22–23

PLACES

Adiabene 43
Ahwaz (Khuzistan) 239
Alexandria 165–166, 215, 241, 248–249
Alqosh 44, 102–103
Anṣakiya 212
Antioch 162, 164, 214–215
Arbela 43–44
Babylon 31, 109, 360, 450, 454, 460–461
Bahnasa 179
Barnug 215
Behunos 226
Bet Gangi 44
Beth ʿAbe 43
Beth Aramaye 37
Beth Huzaye 14, 37, 51, 281
Beth Parsaye 12
Beth Qaṭraye 1–2, 32, 38, 43–44, 50–51, 59, 64, 66, 68, 97–98, 147–149, 157, 191, 281, 441, 472–473
Black Island 2–3, 17, 27
Cana 26
China 22
Cyprus 7–10
Dayrīn 53, 98
DBWKTY 18
Edessa 13, 164
Egypt 2, 8, 11, 109, 160, 165, 178, 214–215, 225, 233, 241, 248–249, 371, 400, 451, 456, 460–461
Euphrates 1, 4, 34
Fars 12, 25, 44, 48–51, 55, 66, 98
Hagar 53
Hatta 53, 68
Ḥīra 147
Izla 13

Jerusalem 13, 108, 113–114, 116, 164, 207, 214, 233, 333, 348, 359–360, 362, 449, 455, 462
Khosro 24
Kuplana 43
Mʿarre 13
Magra 239
Marden 239
Maron 20–21, 46
Mashmahig / Masmahig 53, 58
Mazun (Oman) 20, 44, 49
Mesene 59
Miles 13
Milon 22
Nineveh 43–44, 281, 398
Nisibin 239
Nisibis 13, 35, 43, 100, 472
Nuʿaym 20
Parnouj, monastery of 165
Persia 147, 239, 409
Piroz Shabur 1–2, 4, 14–16, 28–29, 31–33, 37, 39–40
Qardag 35
Rabban Šābūr, monastery of 155
Rab-kennārē, monastery of 155
Rome 7–8, 44, 239
Scetis Desert 160, 169
Seert 103
Seleuca-Ctesiphon 44, 98
Shahdost 17
Syria 166, 215, 240–241
Tahal 445
Talon 53
Tappa 16
Telkef 44
Thomas, monastery of 2–4, 17, 28, 32, 38

ܫܠܡ ܒܥܘܕܪܢ ܡܪܢ ܘܐܠܗܢ ܟܬܒܐ ܗܢܐ ܕܒܪܢܫ ܐܫܬܘܐ
ܥܠ ܒܝܕ ܡܫܡܫܢܐ ܫܠܝܚ ܒܡܕܝܢܬܐ
ܕܒܗ ܐܬܐ ܒܛܘܪ ܠܒܢܝ ܕܒܢܝ
ܠܡܠܟܐ ܡܫܝܚܐ ܡܬܪܝܐ ܦܪܘܩ
ܒܪ ܐܬܐ ܡܪܘܚܐ
ܘܠܐܠܗܐ ܫܘ
ܐܡܝܢ ❖